RECOLLECTIONS OF SEXUAL ABUSE

By the same author
Healing the Incest Wound: Adult Survivors in Therapy
Adult Survivors of Child Sexual Abuse: A Workshop Model

A NORTON PROFESSIONAL BOOK

RECOLLECTIONS OF SEXUAL ABUSE

Treatment Principles and Guidelines

Christine A. Courtois, Ph.D.

W. W. Norton & Company
New York • London

For information about permission to reproduce selections from this book, write to
Permissions, W.W. Norton & Company, Inc.
500 Fifth Avenue, New York, NY 10110

7/99

Library of Congress Cataloging-in-Publication Data

Courtois, Christine A.
Recollections of sexual abuse : treatment principles and
guidelines / Christine A. Courtois
p.   cm.
"A Norton professional book."
Includes bibliographical references and index.
ISBN 0-393-70281-2
1. Adult child sexual abuse victims.   2. Recovered memory.
3. False memory syndrome.   I. Title.
[DNLM: 1. Stress Disorders, Post-Traumatic—therapy.   2. Child
Abuse, Sexual—therapy.   3. Repression.   4. Memory.
5. Psychotherapy—methods.   6. Psychotherapy—standards.   WM170
C866r   1999]
RC569.5.A28C68   1999
616.85'8369—dc21
DNLM/DLC
for Library of Congress   98-42100CIP

W.W. Norton & Company, Inc., 500 Fifth Avenue, New York, N.Y. 10010
http://www.wwnorton.com

W.W. Norton & Company Ltd., 10 Coptic Street, London, WC1A 1PU

1 2 3 4 5 6 7 8 9 0

To Tom
who provides my personal home base
and who gives me the emotional support that keeps me going

To Joan A. Turkus, M.D.
mentor, friend
and an innovator
in developing inpatient treatment for abuse survivors

To survivors of abuse and trauma and those who assist them:
In hopes of finding middle ground so that the work of
healing can continue

CONTENTS

Acknowledgments   ix

Introduction   xiii

1. Establishing the Context: The Recovered Memory/False Memory Controversy in Sociohistorical Perspective   1

2. The Present Context: An Overview of the Recovered Memory/False Memory Controversy   31

3. Trauma and Memory   72

4. Child Sexual Abuse and Memory   117

5. Evolving Standards of Practice and the Standard of Care: Philosophy and Principles of Practice   147

6. The Evolving Consensus Model of Posttrauma Treatment: Sequenced, Titrated, Focused on Symptom Relief and Functioning   176

7. Clinical Guidelines and Risk Management for Assessment and Diagnosis   219

8. Clinical Guidelines and Risk Management for Working with Memory Issues   258

9. Countertransference Issues and a Treatment Decision Model: Application to Ten Clinical Memory Scenarios   296

Afterword   341

Appendices

    A. Professional Task Force Reports   353

    B. Summaries of Selected Reports of Professional Task Forces on Delayed/Recovered Memoris   355

    C. Model Forms: Policies and Procedures and Informed Consent   369

References   377

Index   413

ACKNOWLEDGMENTS

Any undertaking such as this would be impossible without personal and professional support. Many individuals, knowingly or unknowingly, have contributed to this book over the years. Because I am unable to thank them all by name, I offer a collective note of appreciation for their support, caring, and scholarship. I do, however, want to take this opportunity to thank some individuals personally for their efforts and contributions.

My parents, Norman and Irene Courtois, my husband Tom, and my extended family are unfailing in their support and encouragement. In particular, I want to thank Claire Riley, who for years told me to keep going on this project, and my godson Christopher Riley, who graciously excused my absence from his college graduation in order for me to keep on deadline. My three Rhode Island aunts, Marion Butler, Annette Dufort, and Beatrice Sirois, are quite special in their ability to provide personal sustenance—they have always been there for me. Dennis and Gail Sirois, their children, and the "Hawaii gang" have provided much needed respite and fun in paradise two years in a row and are effusive in their love and encouragement.

Lynne and Neil Hazard and Cherie and Jeb Brownstein and their respective families, Robbie Brockwehl, Waldi and John Crawford, Katie and Bill Holmes, Joan Turkus, and Evie Wadsworth make up my local family and are available when I most need them. Drs. Leslie Jadin and Cathi Sitzman, over many years of weekly lunches, have provided a touchstone of continuity and offered much professional and personal nurturance. Dr. Mary Ann Dutton has repeatedly demonstrated the ability to ask just the right question and offer personal support and professional acumen in just the right way. Dr. Jean Carter has gone out of her way to promote the impact of my work, for which I am grateful. Dr. Bill Pican has provided thoughtful critiques and commentary along the way.

One of my professional homes is The CENTER: Posttraumatic Disorders Program of the Psychiatric Institute of Washington, a program I cofounded and where I serve as clinical director. I wish to applaud the dedication of the members of The CENTER staff over the years and thank each and every one for their many contributions. In particular, I acknowledge Dr. Joan Turkus for her clinical wisdom, hard work, and leadership as medical director of The CENTER, and for her support of the extra time I needed away from the hospital to complete this manuscript. She is an exemplary colleague and has been a wonderful mentor. I also recognize Pam Oakley Whiting, Florence Hannigan, Laura Howard, and Mary Strigari for "going the extra mile" for me, often many times over.

My second professional home is my private practice. I thank Drs. Carole Giunta, Sylvia Marotta, Philip Silverman, Jeanne Duffin, and Sarah Baraboy Reed for years of professionalism and friendship. Yet another home base is the Division of Counseling Psychology (Division 17) of the American Psychological Association. Members of the division, especially the Section on Women, have long fostered my work and deserve my gratitude. I also acknowledge the confidence and encouragement that has been generated within my professional consultation and peer supervision groups in both my practice and various community mental health centers in the DC area, and in my professional training activities across the country. Thanks to all involved.

Over the years, I have developed many associations and friendships with colleagues across a spectrum of organizations and activities, many having to do with traumatization and its consequences. I thank Drs. Judie Alpert, Sandy Bloom, John Briere, Laura Brown, Eve Carlson, Rich Chefetz, James Chu, Constance Dalenberg, Bob Geffner, Liz Kuh, Laurie Pearlman, Ken Pope, Kay Saakvitne, and Mark Schwartz, along with Lori Galperin and David Calof for their collegiality and encouragement. I also thank the organizers of the NATO-sponsored conference, Recollections of Trauma, Drs. Steve Lindsay and Don Read for the invitation to participate, and all conference participants for contributing to a rich and stimulating learning experience.

To Mary Anne Reilley, I send a long overdue acknowledgment and appreciation for her early efforts researching and summarizing information for both this book and for the American Psychological Association Working Group on the Investigation of Memories of Childhood Abuse. I am also grateful to Paul Donnelly for his even-handed support of the efforts of the Working Group. Andrea Tisi long ago conducted the preliminary research for this book. I also owe her a debt of gratitude for being a superb researcher as well as a generous and understanding housesitter/petsitter. Mary K. Pedigo was instrumental in providing computer services—her equanimity helped me in times of computer angst. Tom Kocot made a major contribution to the editing and finalizing of the manuscript and did so with grace and good humor. Molly Bryan helped with her gentle touch and availability. Inès Barragon and her daughter, Inès, are long-term supporters who make my work focus possible.

My editor, Susan Barrows Munro, is to be credited for her patience in nurturing this effort along. It took longer than anticipated and Susan was supportive of the efforts and activities that distracted me from the book but ultimately contributed to an expanded knowledge base from which to produce it. I am enormously grateful for her editorial judgment, her knowledge of the behavioral sciences, and her sensitive touch.

Last but certainly not least, I thank the many individuals I have had the opportunity to work with as patients, in both inpatient and outpatient settings. Their struggles and courage are constant sources of inspiration and motivation. For many, the memory controversy has added an additional burden of disbelief and denial to what has always been there and has interfered with their recovery efforts. The intent of this book is to assure that clinical services continue to be available to all who have been traumatized, whether their memories are intact or not, and to support therapists in their efforts to provide assistance and relief.

INTRODUCTION

At the time of this writing, the heated and highly contentious controversy surrounding recollections of sexual abuse is entering its sixth
year. On one side of the issue are those professionals who believe that
traumatized individuals often have disturbances of memory and can
recover accurate memories of past abuse/trauma either within or outside
of psychotherapy after a period of time during which memories were forgotten. On the other side are those professionals who challenge this view
of recovered memory for past trauma and who hold that delayed memories are either false or illusory and largely the result of faulty and suggestive therapeutic practice. The controversy has generated considerable
public discourse and confusion and has had a pronounced impact on the
mental health professions and the practice of psychotherapy. The public's view of and confidence in psychotherapy have been negatively influenced, and many therapists now feel anxious and even endangered when
they treat patients for current or past child sexual abuse, whether recovered memories are involved or not.

The impact of the controversy has extended beyond the consulting
room to the courtroom. Lawsuits charging therapists with malpractice for
suggesting or implanting false memories of past abuse through the use of
flawed technique and inappropriate influence have been filed in increasing numbers, most often by disgruntled former patients but more recently by third parties as well. A false memory defense is now quite routine
in litigation involving allegations of contemporaneous as well as past
child sexual abuse. The controversy has further extended to the legislative arena. Bills have been introduced (but not passed as of this writing)
in several state legislatures that would place restrictions on clinical practice by setting conservative criteria regarding what constitutes a credible
memory of past abuse, acceptable conditions for the initial disclosure of
such information, and acceptable versus proscribed therapeutic tech-

niques. The impact of the controversy has already been enormous, and its effect can be expected to continue and possibly to accelerate.

The gist of the arguments that make up the controversy are as follows: Proponents of the false memory position charge that a substantial number of therapists, on the basis of mistaken notions about the workings of human memory, erroneous theory regarding repressed and recovered memory for trauma, and suggestive therapeutic technique, have caused gullible patients who have no previous recollection to recover false memories of abuse. Patients go on to develop "false memory syndrome," whereby they regress and become dependent on a therapeutic program that actively pursues missing memories of abuse, often of the most bizarre and improbable forms. A number of these patients, in turn, have gone on to accuse their parents (and others) of abuse based on these memories and many have cut off all contact with families and even initiated civil lawsuits, causing further harm and distress to innocent families and individuals.

Proponents of the traumatic stress position argue that recovered memories do not automatically equate with false memories and that documentation has been inadequate in substantiating the serious charges leveled by defenders of the false memory position and sensationalized in the media. They further hold that false memory critics and memory researchers have limited understanding of human traumatization and its effects (particularly incest/sexual abuse) on which to base their critique. Researchers have relied upon and prematurely generalized from the findings of memory studies conducted in the laboratory on nontraumatized subjects (mostly college students) and have not yet adequately studied trauma and traumatic memory in either the laboratory or the field. Disturbances of memory have long been identified as part of the immediate and/or long-term consequence of traumatization; therefore, it is not unusual for traumatized individuals to have variable recollections of past abuse and trauma, some of which might be expected to emerge during psychotherapy—not as false memory and not necessarily as the result of suggestive influence. Traumatic stress researchers also question the asymmetrical attention that has been placed on false memories: They have been emphasized in alleged victim/accusers yet virtually ignored in alleged perpetrators, even though research has consistently documented patterns of denial and disavowal (and therefore false memory) in perpetrators of documented abuse.

Advocates of the traumatic stress position agree with the false memory critics that false accusations of abuse are tragic and must be prevented whenever possible; yet they argue that the denial or disregard of the prevalence and damage associated with real abuse is equally, if not more, tragic. They point to the substantial body of research that documents the widespread prevalence of all forms of child abuse and family violence and their great potential for detrimental effects to the individual, the family, and society. These ought not be lost in the debate nor lost in an overemphasis on false accusations that occur on a significantly more limited basis.

The controversy has been so adversarial and vehement that it is quite routinely described as "the memory war" (Berliner, 1997) or as a civil war within psychology (McConkey, 1997). It was recently described as being analogous to a religious war in terms of the stridency with which positions are taken (Pezdek & Banks, 1996, p. xii). Although the controversy is presented as a scientific one, in fact the case is easily made that it is highly politicized and more political than scientific (Brown, Scheflin, & Hammond, 1998; Courtois, 1997a; Pezdek & Banks, 1996). A rational middle ground that is less divided and that attends to the complexity of the issues involved while incorporating the legitimate issues and critiques of each side has been lacking but is now beginning to emerge (Butler, 1996; Lindsay & Briere, 1997; Read & Lindsay, 1997). A number of cognitive memory and trauma researchers have recently found some common ground and are engaging in collaborative research and clinical efforts. A rational middle ground in clinical practice that incorporates information on memory processes is also emerging (Briere, 1997a; Chu, 1998; Courtois, 1997a, 1997b; Pope & Brown, 1996; Knapp & VandeCreek, 1997).

Collaboration leading to a reasoned middle ground that is responsive to all parties has a number of noteworthy benefits: (1) It insures that the relatively new field of traumatic stress studies continues to develop and cross-fertilizes with other fields of study. (2) It assures that efforts to provide treatment to those reporting recollections of abuse and trauma (whether continuous or with variable accessibility) proceed and become more articulated and sophisticated. Adults abused as children make up a high percentage of patients in mental health settings; they have historically been misdiagnosed and underserved, a situation that was changing as the controversy surfaced (and, in fact, is partly responsible for the emergence of the controversy). In order that treatment advances not be prematurely attenuated and that these individuals get needed treatment, it is critical that clinical development is not abandoned due to outside pressure. (3) It helps clinicians by providing rationale and guidance for their work with adults who report memories or suspicions of abuse as children. In the current contentious and litigious climate, many therapists are confused, scared, and in need of education and information.

The material in this book aims to fill this educational and informational need. It proposes guidelines and principles of treatment for individuals where memory of abuse is at issue. It attempts a balanced perspective on the complex issues at hand to assist clinicians in taking a therapeutic stance that neither inappropriately suggests nor suppresses reports or suspicions of abuse in a patient's background. This book does not provide an immutable "set in concrete" treatment model; rather, it suggests general principles and guidelines as the foundation of reasonable practice that is explorative and empowering to the patient rather than suggestive. The need for such a set of principles and guidelines was articulated by psychologists Follette and Naugle (1995) in a book on practice guidelines and standards of practice:

> Yet we know of no one text that clearly and fairly explicates the state of our scientific knowledge with regard to these issues. Despite the polarization of this debate, even the strongest proponents of "False Memory Syndrome" do not deny the tragic consequences of child sexual abuse. Similarly, reasonable scientist-practitioners in the area of child sexual abuse acknowledge the finding that memory is in fact imperfect and can be affected in a variety of ways. A book that explains what is currently known regarding this problem would be of great public benefit. The text would include matters such as what we know about rates of abuse and what we know about the hypothesized sequelae of that abuse, including data suggesting that some persons do not appear to show significant symptomatology in relation to this event. Current theories of memory would be discussed and a description of the potential for false memories would be presented. Psychological theories of the effects of abuse and their respective treatment approaches should be explicated, as well as data that either supports or refutes the theory. Suggestions about what to look for in a therapist would be provided, as well as warning about practices that at this point are considered questionable. Appropriate references should be provided for those individuals who wish to do additional reading. One challenge here is to present all of this information in a straightforward, non jargon laden manner. While this may seem to be a tall order, we believe that the public is eager for this type of information. (p. 29)

It is obvious that therapists are eager for this type of information as well. The principles and guidelines presented here are based on the currently available empirical and clinical findings regarding human memory processes for both emotional/traumatic and normal events and recovered and false memories (of abuse, of other types of trauma, and of other life events), much of it newly available in the last several years and expanding at a rapid rate; on empirical and clinical data on the treatment of posttraumatic conditions in general and child sexual abuse in particular, a database that has expanded dramatically in the past decade; on the legitimate critiques and concerns voiced by false memory critics, some of whom are cognitive scientists who specialize in the study of memory and suggestibility issues; and on recommendations made by a number of professional task forces and advisory committees charged with studying the issues involved in the controversy. These principles and guidelines are thus current with the available literature but will require revision and updating with the emergence of new findings and observations.

The intent of this book is (1) to provide explanatory material to the working clinician in a form that is accessible as well as practical; (2) to outline the middle ground and the evolving standard of clinical practice and standard of care that encourage the clinician in a stance of supportive neutrality towards the patient and his/her productions in therapy, a stance that neither suggests nor suppresses exploration of memories or suspicions of past abuse; and (3) to provide this material to improve clinical practice and care of patients (and by implication to attend to third-party issues) and as risk management for the clinician.

This book has four sections. The first, consisting of two chapters, provides an overview of the recovered/false memory controversy in socio-historical context. Chapter 1 reviews significant historical antecedents as well as contemporary events and issues related to the controversy's emergence. Chapter 2 goes on to outline the major issues of each side of the debate, the middle ground that has been achieved, and the findings and recommendations of professional task forces impaneled to study relevant issues in the debate. The second section of the book provides a review of trauma and memory in two chapters. Chapter 3 provides descriptions of trauma and the process of traumatization, reviews literature on the effects of traumatic stress including posttraumatic and dissociative reactions and their relation to memory, and presents theories of traumatic memory integrated with information on normal event memory. Chapter 4 reviews the characteristics and dynamics of incest/child sexual abuse that make it a unique stressor with high potential for traumatization and, in corollary fashion, that offer explanations for possible memory loss and delayed recall. The available and expanding research base on variable memory in the aftermath of sexual abuse is reviewed and discussed, especially in terms of its implications for clinical practice.

Section 3, made up of five chapters, is devoted to treatment issues and clinical practice. Chapter 5 presents the evolving standard of practice and the standard of care in working with recollections of sexual abuse, whether they were constantly available or recovered after having been forgotten. This chapter describes the meta-issues that form the backdrop of more specific treatment principles and guidelines presented in subsequent chapters. Chapter 6 describes the evolving consensus model of posttrauma treatment, a model not focused on memory recovery per se as either a strategy or goal, but instead organized around the patient's diagnosis and symptom picture and directed towards symptom stabilization and improved personal mental health and functioning. Traumatic memory is the specific focus of treatment only where warranted. Work with traumatic memory is generally directed towards the analysis of available memory in terms of its meaning to the individual rather than the retrieval of new memory content. This occurs in the interest of integration of various aspects of the memory and ultimately of personal resolution and the amelioration of posttraumatic symptoms. The model is carefully sequenced with treatment offered in phases and therapeutic tasks that are organized progressively and hierarchically. Three main phases of treatment are described in considerable detail, as each has its own primary emphasis and calls for different strategies and techniques.

Chapter 7 addresses issues of assessment and diagnosis. Assessment is discussed as both a baseline and a process: It provides data for making a diagnosis that, in turn, guides the treatment plan. Evaluation strategies are discussed for a variety of memory accessibility patterns and for situations of disclosure and non-disclosure. Available instruments and resources designed specifically for the assessment of posttraumatic symptoms are also presented. Chapter 8 offers clinical guidelines and risk management for work with memories of trauma and related issues, based upon recommendations of professional task forces and other authoritative writing on the topic. Particular attention is directed towards strategies that are recommended versus those considered risky and even countertherapeutic.

Chapter 9 addresses issues within the therapeutic relationship, specifically transference, countertransference, and vicarious traumatization, and choices of therapeutic strategy illustrated by ten clinical scenarios. It is now recognized that particular forms of transference and countertransference are likely to emerge in the treatment of traumatized/sexually abused individuals that simultaneous challenge and inform the clinician and that must be acknowledged and monitored. These issues are further affected and compounded by the controversy and by the additional risk and liability entailed in work with this population, especially when delayed/recovered memories are at issue. Ten clinical scenarios, each of a different memory presentation ranging from continuous memory of abuse disclosed at intake, to suspicions of abuse in the total absence of memory, to recantation of previous beliefs or memories, are presented. Each scenario is illustrated by a case example and includes a discussion of therapeutic strategies and the transference and countertransference reactions that are likely. The scenarios are provided as examples of the myriad ways memory issues might present clinically and the different challenges and degrees of risk that they present to the therapist.

The last section of the book consists of an afterword. It offers reflections on the controversy and its impact and the diverging viewpoints and emphases of the two sides. It discusses the dilemmas that arise in clinical practice in attempting to maintain a balanced approach and middle ground on the issues. It also touches on implications for research and forensic practice and the need for greater inclusion of issues of trauma and memory in professional curricula and training.

A number of appendices have been included to provide an easy reference for the reader. Appendix A contains a listing of the various professional task forces charged with studying issues involved in the controversy. Appendix B contains summations from the Australian Psychological Society, British Association of Counseling, New Zealand Psychological Society, The Royal Australian and New Zealand College of Psychiatrists, and the Royal College of Psychiatry—Great Britain. Appendix C contains model information for patients and informed consent forms.

It is the specific intent of this book to provide in an accessible format what Follette and Naugle identified as missing: a resource for professionals and the public alike on clinical approaches to the recollections of past abuse, whether they have been constantly or variably accessible and/or whether they have emerged or been recovered after a delay. We begin by placing the recovered/false memory controversy in a sociohistorical context as an aid to understanding the various issues at play.

RECOLLECTIONS OF SEXUAL ABUSE

Chapter 1

ESTABLISHING THE CONTEXT

The Recovered Memory/
False Memory Controversy
in Sociohistorical Perspective

A hundred-year history of debate and controversy surrounds the topic of adult recollection of child sexual abuse. It is once again a *fin de siè-cle* issue, having first emerged at the end of the last century and reemerged at the end of this one. The recent configuration is the result of a confluence of many issues and events in the present; yet it revisits and incorporates central issues from the past. It also involves the overarching issue of a society's ability to identify and sustain recognition of human trauma, especially interpersonal victimization and the sexual abuse of children, particularly when such abuse occurs within the family. The history of human trauma and its aftermath is one marked by discovery and acknowledgement offset by denial, recoil, and indifference (Herman, 1992b). Child sexual abuse is prototypic of this alternating acknowledgment and disavowal. These are essential aspects of the current debate.

The crux of the controversy revolves around three issues: (1) whether traumatic memories can be forgotten and remembered again; (2) the accuracy and credibility of recollections of childhood sexual abuse; and (3) the role of therapeutic influence on memories. Freud and his contemporaries were the first to identify the possible etiological role of childhood sexual abuse in adult distress. He later shifted his theory regarding the historical versus psychic reality of sexual abuse, a shift that has had enormous and far-reaching implications for psychiatry and Western culture throughout much of the twentieth century. The current controversy promises to have even more impact. It is already more visible and publicly accessible by virtue of the far-reaching influence of both the traditional media and the new information technology. Its repercussions (both positive and negative) have been tremendous and are expected to persist and even expand.

At the time of this writing, the debate continues to be quite contentious, although its tone is somewhat less strident and the media interest considerably less constant. Some notable developments have occurred in the past two years. Professional task forces impaneled to study the issues and make recommendations to clinicians, researchers, and forensic practitioners have issued reports calling attention to the need for more research and urging a move away from extreme and polarized positions to more dispassionate and rational ones. Several efforts at collaboration have been successful, as moderates on both sides of the debate have increased their communication and found some common ground, including opportunities for joint research and applied practice. Hopefully, these efforts herald ongoing collaborative inquiry and new discoveries.

Simultaneously, the false memory defense has been used very successfully in civil lawsuits that have been brought on the basis of recovered memories. Consequently, this avenue of legal redress has become much more problematic for any plaintiff seeking damages for past abuse on a delayed discovery basis (whether recovered memories are at issue or not) and, as a direct result, fewer and fewer such lawsuits are being filed. A simultaneous development has been the increase in legal action against therapists for misdiagnosis, malpractice, and alleged implanting of false memories of abuse (particularly where allegations of satanic ritual abuse or other organized abuse are involved). A number of these legal initiatives against therapists have been precedent-setting. Several high-profile malpractice suits have resulted in settlements or judgments amounting to millions of dollars (Belluck, 1997; Grinfeld, 1995), and one high-visibility case has expanded to the the filing of criminal charges at the federal level in the aftermath of the monetary settlement of civil charges (Grinfield, 1997). Recently, two appelate courts held that therapists owe a duty to third-party accused parents in malpractice suits (False Memory Syndrome Foundation Newsletter, May 1998). It is expected that legal efforts of this sort, aimed at stopping what its proponents believe to be significant therapeutic malpractice, will continue to intensify in the immediate future.

This chapter provides an overview of the recovered memory/false memory controversy in its sociohistorical context. It begins with a discussion of some of the past and more recent historical events and sociopolitical forces that have contributed to the controversy's emergence and force. The intent is to help the reader become familiar with these historical events and political, scientific, and psychological issues that have shaped the controversy and contributed to its complexity. This familiarity is especially important for the working clinician, because it provides a scientific and political background from which to understand the critique of therapeutic practice and abuse-related memory issues. It helps to establish a foundation for therapeutic decision-making and, in this way, also contributes to practical risk management.

THE CONTROVERSY IN
SOCIOHISTORICAL PERSPECTIVE

Freud, Janet, and the Study of Hysteria

In many ways, the current controversy returns to and reworks issues concerning adults' retrospective reports of childhood sexual abuse that emerged at the turn of the century. A brief review is in order. The modern study of traumatized individuals (and those thought to have been traumatized) began in the late 1800s. Hysteria, a commonly recognized but ill-defined condition that afflicted mainly women and was comprised of a constellation of psychological and somatic symptoms, came under clinical and scientific investigation by the eminent French neurologist Jean-Martin Charcot. Charcot's status lent the topic legitimacy and respectability; previously hysterics had been understood as malingerers who were accorded little, if any, credibility due to their symptoms and their suggestibility (Herman, 1992b). Charcot's predominant contribution to the understanding of this condition was to demonstrate that its symptoms were psychological as opposed to neurological because they could be induced and reversed through the use of hypnosis.

Charcot's followers set out to move beyond the study of hysterical symptoms to an understanding of their origin. By the 1890s, two clinical researchers, Pierre Janet in France and Sigmund Freud (with his collaborator Josef Breuer) in Vienna, independently arrived at a similar conclusion, that hysteria was a condition caused by psychological trauma (Herman, 1992b). Overwhelming traumatic events caused unbearable emotional reactions (or "vehement emotions," according to Janet) that were difficult for the traumatized individual to tolerate or process. In some cases, the individual entered an altered state of consciousness as a coping mechanism at the time of the event or later. This altered state interfered with normal cognitive and memory processing and induced symptoms of hysteria. Of special pertinence to the current controversy was the recognition by both Freud/Breuer and Janet that the somatic symptoms of hysteria were coded representations of events so traumatic that they could not be retained in conscious awareness (i.e., memory) and were retained in the altered state. Janet labeled the alteration of consciousness "dissociation" (or *"desagrégation"*). He wrote that a major consequence of this dissociation is that the split-off traumatic material remained active as "subconscious fixed ideas" or "automatisms" that under certain circumstances became activated and had a "behind the scenes" impact on a variety of conscious experiences and on memory processes and accessibility (amnesia or hypermnesia) (Janet, 1889). Breuer and Freud labeled the alteration of consciousness used to ward off the unassimilated material as "double consciousness" and wrote that "hysterics suffer from reminiscenses" or from the return to conscious awareness of anxiety-provoking ideas/memories or "exciting events" in symbolic and symptomatic form (Breuer & Freud, 1892/1959).

Although Freud's and Janet's work initially had much in common, including a belief that actual traumatic experiences were the cause of splits in consciousness and that recovery and integration of memory were necessary for resolution and symptom relief, their work was to diverge dramatically in subsequent years. In 1896, Freud published *The Aetiology of Hysteria*, his report of 18 cases in which he identified premature traumatic sexual experiences in early childhood, often within the family, as the root of hysteric reactions. He wrote: "I put forward the proposition, therefore, that at the bottom of every case of hysteria will be found one or more experiences of premature sexual experience, belonging to the first years of childhood" (Freud, 1896/1959, p. 198).

Freud's formulation, known as the seduction theory, was scandalous in its implications and not well received by his contemporaries. For what are likely a number of reasons, not the least of which were issues concerning his own father, the negative implications of being rejected by his peers and the disgraceful societal implications of acknowledging widespread prevalence of sexual abuse and incest, Freud dramatically changed his position on the traumatic origins of hysteria and replaced the seduction theory with the oedipal (or fantasy) theory (Masson, 1984; Rush, 1980). His psychoanalytic theory attended to issues of childhood sexuality but, when it came to adult-child sexual contact, favored the perspective of fantasy or wish on the part of the child versus actual sexual trauma. This revised formulation shifted from the psychological defense of double consciousness as a response to real events to the defense of repression as a response to internal conflict generated by forbidden wishes and impulses (Rush, 1980). It is the original formulation and Freud's subsequent shift to the oedipal fantasy theory that became a source of controversy, one that continues as the central focus of the contemporary debate.

Freud's theoretical alteration was challenged by the Hungarian psychoanalyst Sandor Ferenczi, one of his best students and a highly talented clinician in his own right. He believed his patients' stories of childhood sexual abuse and, in so doing, created a major schism in the psychoanalytic world (described in Masson, 1984). His paper, "Confusion of tongues between parents and the child" (Ferenczi, 1933/1988) described how the child exposed to ongoing sexual abuse within the family must psychologically accommodate or adapt by simultaneously knowing and not knowing (confusion of tongues) of its occurrence in order to remain attached to the abusive or neglectful caregiver(s). He articulated the multitude of ways that childhood sexual trauma affects the victim in later life, and also the numerous nonverbal forms that memories of abuse might take. Ferenczi's paper was suppressed following its initial reading at an international psychoanalytic congress in 1933 and not published until 1939. Today, it has reemerged as an important work that presaged many of the clinical issues and dilemmas currently in play (Gartner, 1997a).

Also in contrast to Freud, Janet continued his study of hysteria as a response to genuine traumatic events. His articulation of the role of dissociation as the primary defense mechanism used in response to traumatization was published in *The Mental State of Hystericals* (1894/1901), *L'Automatisme Psychologique* (1889), and *The Major Symptoms of Hysteria* (1907). Janet's theory emphasized hysteria as fundamentally a disorder of consciousness and constricted awareness. Kihlstrom (1994) recently offered the following useful description of hysteria: "Hysterical patients are unaware of events of which they should, under ordinary circumstances, clearly be cognizant; and they are influenced by ideas, memories, affects, and needs that are excluded from or denied introspective access" (p. 369). Janet's view of treatment was to help the patient to process the split-off traumatic memories and essentially to make them accessible to introspective access. He conceptualized a treatment process of three stages, the first involving the establishment of the therapeutic relationship and symptom stabilization; the second, the accessing and processing of traumatic memory and affect into consciousness (often with the use of hypnosis), with the goal of integrating previously split-off dimensions of the traumatic material; and the third involving identity and relationship development and improved functioning (van der Hart, Brown, & van der Kolk, 1989). The goal of treatment was to sufficiently process and integrate memory so that emotional content was resolved and symptoms ameliorated. This model is the early prototype of the contemporary sequenced or phase-oriented treatment model that, with a number or updates and modifications, is becoming the contemporary standard of treatment (Brown et al., 1998; Courtois, 1997c; van der Kolk, McFarlane, & van der Hart, 1996) (described in chapters 5 and 6).

Janet's ideas about dissociation held sway among many of his contemporaries but were eventually eclipsed by the ascendency of psychoanalytic theory, with its emphasis on repression and a different theory of unconscious mental life. Classical psychoanalytic theory has been the major influence for most of the twentieth century but has come under increased questioning and challenge in the last two decades, both in general (Crews, 1994; 1995) and within the field of psychoanalysis (Gartner, 1997a), and as pertains to sexual abuse and the shift from the seduction to the fantasy perspective (Masson, 1984; Rush, 1977, 1980). Ironically, during these same two decades, Janet's formulations have been revived, first among cognitive psychologists in the late 1970s, spurred by Hilgard's neodissociation theory of divided consciousness (Hilgard, 1977/1986), and later among clinical researchers investigating psychological dissociation, multiple personality disorder, and psychic trauma (Braun & Sachs, 1985; Kluft, 1985; Putnam, 1985a, 1985b, 1989a, 1989b; Putnam, Guroff, Silberman, Barban, & Post, 1986; Ross, 1989; Ross, Heber, Norton, & Anderson, 1989; Ross, Norton, & Wosney, 1989; van der Kolk, 1987; van der Kolk & van der Hart, 1995). The diagnosis of hysteria is no longer formally used, having been eliminated as a separate category and subsumed within the categories of dissociative, conversion, and somatoform disorders in the later editions of the *Diagnostic and Statistical Manual (DSM)* (American Psychiatric Association, 1980, 1987, 1994).

In many ways, Freud's change in perspective was calamitous both for individuals who had been sexually abused and for the study of sexual traumatization. It ushered in what Armstrong (1978) labeled "The Age of Denial." Many of Freud's followers literally interpreted his theoretical shift as a repudiation of the possibility of *any* genuine sexual abuse. As a result, for the better part of this century, reports of incest/sexual abuse by patients were routinely discounted, disbelieved, and/or prematurely foreclosed by therapists who viewed them instead as fantasy or as the child's wish for the opposite-sex parent. A book published in 1980 was instrumental in highlighting the significance of this stance and the resultant plight of sexually abused children and adults who sought treatment. In *The Best Kept Secret*, feminist author/social worker Florence Rush sharply critiqued the prevailing psychoanalytic perspective on sexual abuse and the role of the psychiatric community in treating current or past abuse (Rush, 1980). She documented the significant prevalence of abuse in the history of many psychiatric patients, lambasted Freud's shift away from the seduction (trauma) theory (labeling it the Freudian cover-up in her 1977 article), and challenged mental health professionals not to automatically dismiss their patients' accounts of abuse and instead to give them a fair hearing.

The study of sexual traumatization was prematurely foreclosed for many decades by the Freudian reversal. Early reports documenting pervasive child maltreatment in Europe (including child murder and torture) were published in the medical literature at the turn of the century. These led to early efforts at child welfare and protection, efforts that unfortunately dissipated after World War I, accompanied by a decline in public interest that lasted until the 1950s, when the topic began, however tentatively, to reemerge. Kinsey's landmark study of human sexual behavior provided the first empirical documentation of the prevalence of child sexual abuse (Kinsey, Pomeroy, Martin, & Gebhard, 1953); however, he and his colleagues downplayed their prevalence findings and minimized the potentially damaging consequences of sexual abuse in childhood.

Interestingly, although they countered the analytic perspective of the day, case reports and case series of all forms of child abuse, including incest and child sexual abuse, were published in the professional psychiatric and sociological literature throughout the first half of this century (Courtois, 1979). At the time, these cases were viewed as rare anomalies; they came to be viewed as more prevalent and less aberrant when systematic study and documentation began in the '60s and '70s, as the medical community again began to recognize physical abuse of children by caretakers. The early findings of the pre-1970s studies were nonetheless both valuable and problematic. In terms of their value, the studies provided preliminary information on the characteristics, dynamics, and aftereffects of child abuse, much of which has been substantiated by contemporary research using more rigorous methodology. The limitations of the studies, mainly in terms of sampling, resulted in inaccuracies and stereotypes regarding prevalence and demographics that persist to this day and are related to the current controversy. The original studies and case reports were of highly biased and nonrandom samples, of mostly lower-income and minority individuals whose abuse was serious enough to warrant police investigation and social service and/or criminal justice intervention, i.e., those who lacked the social and economic status to evade such intervention or to mount a legal defense. As a result, child abuse in general and incest/sexual abuse in particular came to be viewed as problems of the lower classes and minorities.

In contrast, more recently conducted randomized studies have documented that abuse occurs in all social classes and economic strata and across all ethnic groups and cultures; furthermore, it might actually occur more frequently in the middle, upper-middle, and upper classes than previously realized (Butler, 1978; Russell, 1983; Finkelhor, 1979). In part, this broadened recognition of the occurrence of abuse has also been a factor in the emergence of the current controversy. Individuals of affluence have more to lose in terms of status and money when abuse is alleged. They also have more resources with which to defend themselves than do the less well-off.

Contemporary Events and Initiatives

THE STUDY OF CHILD ABUSE AND DOMESTIC VIOLENCE. The contemporary study of incest and other forms of child sexual abuse began in earnest in the 1970s, leading Armstrong (1978) to label this time period "The Age of Validation." It followed the lead of two areas of study undertaken in the 1960s: (1) child physical abuse beginning with the identification and publicity surrounding the "battered child syndrome" and (2) violence against women generated by the resurgence of feminism. These two areas of investigation cross-referenced each other in significant ways.

The publication of an article entitled "The Battered Child Syndrome" by pediatrician Henry Kempe and his colleagues (Kempe, Silverman, Steele, Droegemueller, & Silver, 1962) was a watershed event. The article documented medical evidence of childhood physical abuse and took medical personnel to task for both their denial of what was often abundant physical evidence of serious and even life-threatening abuse caused by parents and other caretakers and their failure to protect child victims. It led to increased response and study by medical practitioners and the development of a medical profile of indicators of child physical abuse. It also led to increased recognition of child abuse as a serious social and public health issue.

A concurrent development was the emergence of the second wave of feminism in the form of the Women's Liberation Movement. Feminist study directed attention to patterns of gender socialization and stereotyping, beginning with the patriarchal structure of the nuclear family and its influence on childrearing patterns. It shattered the image of the benign and wholesome contemporary family by unearthing widespread and previously unacknowledged violence that occurred in the privacy of the family, used predominantly by men to achieve and maintain control over women and children, i.e., those with the least power within the family structure (American Psychological Association, 1996b; Walker, 1979). It also uncovered extensive and previously unrecognized/undisclosed sexual violence against women in the society at large, some perpetrated by strangers but the majority perpetrated by someone known to the victim, including family members. Physical and sexual violence against women both within the family and the broader society was documented as a grave problem with far-reaching personal and societal consequences (Brownmiller, 1975; Chapman & Gates, 1978; Rush, 1980; Russell, 1984; Walker, 1979).

Research was also undertaken at this time to document the prevalence, patterns of occurrence, and initial and long-term aftereffects of all forms of child maltreatment. For our purposes, we focus here on studies of incest/child sexual abuse. The aggregate data generated by a number of initial studies (Benward & Densen-Gerber, 1975; Burgess & Holmstrom, 1974; Burgess, Groth, Holmstrom, & Sgroi, 1978; Butler, 1978; Courtois, 1979; Donaldson & Gardner, 1985; Finkelhor, 1979; Forward & Buck, 1978; Gelinas, 1983; Herman, 1981; Herman & Hirschman, 1977; Lindberg & Distad, 1985; Meiselman, 1978; Mrazek & Kempe, 1981; Peters, 1976; Russell, 1983) identified child sexual abuse as more prevalent than previously recognized and as a serious interpersonal stressor with high potential to traumatize the victim both at the time of its occurrence and later. Incest was documented as having an even higher traumatic potential because the societal taboo against its occurrence and the related proscription of its disclosure left victims silenced and powerless in situations of victimization that were often chronic. Powerful family dynamics, relational betrayal, and role conflicts contributed to its traumagenic potential for developmentally and physically immature victims. Last but not least, its disclosure posed serious challenges to the family structure and functioning, and the child who disclosed was often blamed rather than helped (these issues are discussed in greater detail in chapter 4).

THE STUDY OF WAR TRAUMA AND THE DEVELOPMENT OF THE PTSD DIAGNOSIS. A related and simultaneous development was the study of war trauma. The study of the traumatic consequences of combat exposure was initiated during the two world wars but abandoned at the end of World War II and largely ignored during the Korean conflict. It resumed with a vengeance with the controversies surrounding the war in Viet Nam and the return of veterans traumatized by both the war and their homecoming into a hostile and unwelcoming society. The renewed attention to war trauma resulted in the development and inclusion of formalized diagnostic nomenclature and criteria for severe posttraumatic reactions, Posttraumatic Stress Disorder (PTSD), in the *Diagnostic and Statistical Manual, Third Edition* (*DSM*, American Psychiatric Association,

1980). This new diagnosis was very significant in that it challenged the traditional view of psychopathology as predominantly intrapsychic. Researchers and clinicians began to identify the previously unacknowledged etiological role of external trauma in the development of acute emotional distress and physical and mental illness, at both the time of exposure and later.

The diagnosis closely followed the model of war trauma originally articulated as a physioneurosis by Kardiner (1941) and later refined by Lindemann (1944) and Horowitz (1976/1986) in their studies of exposure to other types of traumatic stressors (e.g., disasters, bereavement, sexual assault). Diagnostic criteria included alternating patterns of reliving/reexperiencing and numbing/denial of the trauma, along with chronic physiological hyperarousal. A hallmark of the diagnosis was the difficulty that many traumatized individuals experienced in integrating the emotions associated with the overwhelming nature of the traumatization. Such disparate defensive operations as dissociation, somatization, and fixation on the trauma, including patterns of amnesia and hypermnesia, were identified and incorporated within the diagnosis from the start, an issue of major relevance to the current controversy.

Until the articulation and inclusion of the PTSD diagnosis in the DSM, specific traumas (i.e., rape, war and concentration camp experiences, accidents, child abuse, traumatic loss, natural disasters and accidents) were generally viewed as being outside of the range of normal human experience, described separately, and only rarely viewed as having anything in common. The codification of the PTSD diagnosis led to the realization of consistent patterns of response across different types of traumatization. This realization, in turn, suggested that the diagnosis was often an appropriate and overarching diagnosis and was applicable to other types of traumatization besides exposure to war. It also led to preliminary efforts to study the effects of traumatization (including effects of memory processes) more broadly across different types of traumatic events and in different populations such as children (Eth & Pynoos, 1985; Green, 1983; Terr, 1988; Yule & Williams, 1990). As different forms of overwhelming and traumatizing life events increasingly came under study, they were viewed, individually and collectively, from a posttraumatic perspective. Thus, the significance of the external traumatic stressor to the individual's current distress and symptomatology was acknowledged as never before and treatment methods that included an emphasis on the traumatization and its aftermath, among other issues, developed.

RESUMPTION OF THE STUDY OF DISSOCIATION. The study of psychological dissociation, mostly dormant since the turn of the century when

Janet's work lost influence, resumed during this same time period. It was partially influenced by the new investigations of child abuse, domestic violence, and war trauma, and followed the publication of an influential book on the unconscious by Ellenberger (1970). A specific category of dissociative disorders—with roots in the categories of hysterical neuroses (conversion and dissociative types) and hysterical personality (histrionic personality disorder but without the label hysteria)—was first included in the *DSM-III* in 1980, the same year the diagnosis of PTSD was introduced. The essential feature of this class of disorder was defined as "a disruption of the normally integrated functions of consciousness, *memory*, and identity." The dissociative disorders included psychogenic amnesia, psychogenic fugue, depersonalization, derealization, multiple personality disorder (MPD), and dissociative disorder not otherwise specified (DDNOS).

Studies of individuals with MPD and DDNOS found that they reported childhood physical, sexual, and emotional abuse in the 90 percent range and at an extreme level of severity and chronicity (Coons, Bowman, & Milstein, 1988; Kluft, 1985; Putnam et al., 1986; Putnam, 1989a; Ross, 1989; Ross, Miller, Bjornson, Reagor, Fraser, & Anderson, 1991). Research identified the use of dissociative defenses in response to childhood physical and sexual abuse (Chu & Dill, 1990), especially severe forms of abuse (Putnam, 1985a; Putnam et al., 1986; Ross, et al.,1989) and chronic incest beginning in early childhood (Pribor & Dinwiddie, 1992; Strick & Wilcoxon, 1991). Although much of this abuse was reported to have occurred within the family, some was reported outside in organized groups, often with the involvement of family members. Reports of pedophile organizations, child pornography and child prostitution rings, military mind control experiments, day care abuse, and organized sadistic abuse that occurred in satanic and other religiously-based cults (and crossover between some of these) first emerged during this time period, much of it related to the study of dissociation.

DEVELOPMENT OF PRELIMINARY OR "FIRST GENERATION" TREATMENT MODELS. The new research findings in these three domains, (1) incest/child sexual abuse and other forms of domestic violence; (2) war trauma and other forms of traumatic stress and their aftermath; and (3) psychological dissociation and its relation to trauma, led to the development of preliminary contemporary treatment models for traumatized individuals. These initial models, now identified as "first wave" or "first generation," were founded on some of the early approaches espoused by Freud, Ferenczi, and Janet and on some of the battlefield approaches devised during World Wars I and II. They provided the foundation for the more recently developed "second and third generation" approaches discussed throughout this book. The first articulation of general principles of contemporary treatment from a posttraumatic perspective was found in articles and books by Brown and Fromm (1986), Figley (1985, 1986), Horowitz (1976, 1986), McCann and Pearlman (1990a), Ochberg (1988), Parson, (1984), van der Kolk (1984, 1987), and Wilson (1989), works that stressed the role of exogenous trauma in the development of psychological distress. They emphasized the necessity of recognizing and treating the effects of psychic trauma and paid particular attention to the processing of emotions and cognitions associated with traumatization and its aftermath.

Preliminary treatment models for abused children and formerly abused adults developed concurrently. These models, also posttraumatic in orientation, emphasized the reality of abuse and identified it as an important antecedent to a host of debilitating symptoms and psychiatric diagnoses. Abuse-related issues were incorporated into the treatment, an approach that contrasted markedly with therapeutic orientations that tended to dismiss or minimize abuse reports (and those most criticized in the aforementioned book, *The Best Kept Secret*) (Briere, 1989; Burgess et al., 1978; Butler, 1978; Courtois, 1988; Courtois & Watts, 1982; Gil, 1988; Herman, 1981; Jehu, 1988; Meiselman, 1978; Sgroi, 1982).

Models for treatment of dissociative conditions, especially multiple personality disorder (now dissociative identity disorder), also developed during this time period (Braun, 1986; Kluft, 1982, 1984a, 1984b; Putnam, 1989a; Ross, 1989). These too stressed the role of past trauma in the development of the patient's dissociative symptoms and the necessity of addressing the trauma during treatment. Therapists treating individuals with MPD were often faced with patients reporting extreme forms of trauma, including organized and ritualized sadistic abuse, some of it satanic and some of it in other contexts such as child pornography and military experiments. These issues provoked intense debate as to their historic reality, debate that continues in the current controversy. Therapists were found along a continuum of belief, with some totally believing their patients' accounts of the most horrific and/or bizarre types of abuse and others disbelieving all of them.

Many of the treatments for dissociative disorders included the use of hypnosis (often, but not always, to work with traumatic memories and sometimes to assist in the retrieval/processing of traumatic memories on the part of one or more alter personalities in the case of multiple personality disorder). Hypnosis as a memory retrieval method has become a major issue in the current controversy. Hypnotic techniques are among those that are identified as the most likely to produce false and elaborated memories of events that did not occur; moreover, they are believed to confound the individual's confidence level in what has been produced under hypnosis and the ability to later distinguish belief and confidence from fact (Barnier & McConkey, 1992). These problems are the most pronounced when hypnosis is used repeatedly with individuals who are highly hypnotizable/suggestible (as seems to be the case with many dissociative patients).

Many similarities can be found across the various treatment models. These include their posttraumatic orientation and their adoption of either an abreaction strategy or a more cognitive approach emphasizing integration of split-off material to treat the abuse (van der Hart & Brown, 1992). Abreaction was a technique first described by Breuer and Freud for the treatment of repressed memories of trauma, later adapted for the treatment of posttraumatic stress disorder in war veterans. It involved the revivification/reexperiencing of the trauma with the goal of processing and working through blocked (repressed) emotions and cognitions. This technique was often used in combat conditions to rapidly restabilize soldiers in order to return them to battle. Its use with traumatic reactions of long duration, with other traumatized populations, and with child-onset trauma was not tested; nevertheless, variations of this technique were adopted for use in the retrospective treatment of adults reporting a history of childhood trauma, in the hope that they would have a beneficial therapeutic impact. Indeed, in some cases, their use led to dramatic reduction of symptoms and overall life improvement; in others they were not beneficial, seemed to cause significant regression and life destabilization, and were therefore contraindicated (Chu, 1998).

Another perspective found in most, if not all, of these post-abuse treatment models was the normalcy of memory disturbance in a substantial number of traumatized adults. This viewpoint was largely based on clinical findings with traumatized adults; it further derived from the criteria associated with the PTSD diagnosis (e.g., the numbing phase of the response involved inability to recall, and the reexperiencing phase, the recollection and revivification of the trauma) and was associated with criteria for the dissociative disorders, notably dissociative amnesia, which is characterized by "an inability to recall important personal information, usually of a traumatic or stressful nature, that is too extensive to be explained by ordinary forgetfulness" (American Psychiatric Association, 1994, p. 478).

DEVELOPMENT OF PROFESSIONAL ORGANIZATIONS. Two main professional organizations were established as a result of the emergence of these specialized fields of study. The International Society for the Study of Multiple Personality and Dissociation (now the International Society for the Study of Dissociation) was founded in 1984. A journal, *Dissociation* was launched not long after to disseminate findings regarding research and clinical strategies. In 1985, the Society for Traumatic Stress Studies (now the International Society) was founded. Its publication, the *Journal of Traumatic Stress,* provided another outlet for emerging research and clinical findings regarding traumatization and its aftermath. It is of note that the results of some of the early research investigations on trauma and dissociation (especially multiple personality disorder) were originally not accepted for publication by the more established and traditional psychiatric and psychological journals because they were "outlier" issues and/or the content was deemed too radical. This position shifted as issues of traumatization and victimization entered the public domain and began to receive more professional attention and interest.

PUBLICATION OF A LAY LITERATURE, THE DEVELOPMENT OF LAY THERAPIES, AND THEIR OVERLAP WITH THE ADULT CHILD AND RECOVERY MOVEMENTS.   Other noteworthy initiatives were the simultaneous and parallel publication of a lay literature and the development of lay therapies. Concerning the former, some of the original feminist and war trauma literature was produced not by professionals but by "grass roots" activists and paraprofessionals. During that time period in particular, professionals were often viewed as untrustworthy, and as implicated in the denial, misunderstanding (and often mistreatment) that had previously attended sexual assault and all forms of family violence as well as war trauma. Quite ironically however, the information conveyed in this lay literature often provided a foundation for and was integrated within the professional trauma literature as it began to develop.

As the "first generation" professional literature on abuse, trauma, and treatment was published, its perspectives were made accessible to the public in a profusion of self-help books including first-person accounts of abuse and recovery (Allen, 1980; Fraser, 1987) and crossover professional/trade books (Armstrong, 1978; Blume, 1990; Butler, 1978; Engel, 1989; Forward & Buck, 1978; Miller, 1981,1984; Poston & Lison, 1989). The best-known and best-selling of these was *The Courage to Heal* (Bass & Davis, 1988), along with the companion work *The Courage to Heal Workbook* (Davis, 1990), and Alice Miller's *Prisoners of Childhood* (1981). Interestingly, as the professional and self-help literatures cross-referenced and cross-fertilized each other, many of the self-help books were used as resources by professional and lay therapists in their work with clients reporting abuse (the implications of this are discussed further in chapters 5 & 6). *The Courage to Heal* by Ellen Bass and Laura Davis and *Secret Survivors* by e. sue Blume were particularly influential and related to the emergence of the controversy. Both works helped to popularize the notion that abuse memories could be repressed and recovered. On the basis of a "symptom picture," i.e., having several of the symptoms found by researchers to be correlated with a past history of abuse, individuals might begin to identify a possible unremembered (or repressed) abuse history. These books and ideas have drawn considerable criticism from proponents of the false memory position as being overly suggestive of abuse—*The Courage to Heal* in particular.[1]

All of these works were published as issues of parental alcoholism and chemical dependency came to public attention as never before, followed by the development and proliferation of structured treatment programs. The concept of the dysfunctional family (initially associated with the consequences of parental alcoholism/chemical dependency and later expanded to include codependency of the nonaddicted parent and the relevance of these problems to the abuse and neglect of children within the family) received widespread dissemination through a number of popular books (Beattie, 1989; Bradshaw, 1988; Mellody, 1989; Whitfield, 1987) in addition to those listed above. The influence of all of the self-help books increased exponentially when John Bradshaw developed his ideas into a PBS series that was broadcast repeatedly and viewed by millions.

These works popularized the concepts of the "adult child" raised in a dysfunctional (alcoholic and/or abusive) family, whose precious, hurt, or wounded "child within" or "inner child" needed attention and healing to regain personal authenticity. They countered the prevailing view of the American middle-class family as wholesome and healthy, stressing instead dysfunctional parenting and widespread abuse. They legitimized the role of the therapist as a substitute parent of sorts who could correct the injury and re-parent the wounded adult child. The notion of recovery was legitimized, whether through self-help groups (many modeled on the 12-step Alcoholics Anonymous and Al-Anon formats, which had already expanded to include issues of overeating and sex, love, and relationship addiction) or through inpatient and outpatient recovery programs (often of 28 days' duration and modeled on chemical dependency treatment programs). These works further popularized the idea that many difficulties and pathologies in adulthood could be traced to childhood maltreatment *even if unremembered*. The concept of the "inner child"

---

[1] Authors Bass and Davis, although not in agreement with much of the criticism, nevertheless published a third edition of their book in which they changed some of the language that the critics found particularly problematic and suggestive. In the new edition, they included a section entitled "Honoring the truth—A response to the backlash" (Bass & Davis, 1994).

who "remembered" what the adult did not or could not remember became confused with some of the terminology describing individuals with diagnosed dissociative disorders. In some quarters, recovered memory was taken as the norm and was always to be believed, no matter what the individual was reporting and no matter how fantastic or improbable the report.

A direct offshoot of all of these efforts was the proliferation of additional self-help services (again following the AA model), offered mainly by abuse and trauma survivors advanced enough in their own recovery to help others. Some of these services remained informal, but some became highly organized and structured. Programs and services to address issues of family dysfunction and abuse multiplied rapidly, some within the context of religiously-sponsored treatment programs. The number of self-identified abuse specialists (many with personal experience but little or no professional training, expertise, or supervision) expanded in kind. It is evident that these services benefited some participants who were able to "break the silence" associated with the abuse taboo in a supportive context; however, they were harmful to others whose already fragile defenses were overwhelmed and who were retraumatized instead of helped. Quite a few became regressed, increasingly symptomatic, and more dysfunctional, as their focus narrowed to abuse memories and narratives to the neglect of personal functioning and symptom improvement. The limitations of the self-help model became apparent with the identification of a subpopulation of previously abused (and nonabused) individuals with serious impairments who were in need of psychotherapy conducted by trained professionals (Chu, 1998).

For a period of time, this type of lay treatment approach was common. By and large, it most resembled what the critics have labeled "recovered memory therapy" and fostered the greatest therapeutic excesses and errors (although this should not be taken to mean that some percentage of professionally-trained therapists did not practice in similar ways and/or go astray in their work with adults reporting abuse). Critics such as Tavris (1993) and Haaken and Schlaps (1991) decried an oversimplistic focus and a misguided reification and reinforcement of victim status in the philosophical foundations of many of these approaches and programs, whether self-help or professional. (Tavris lumped them all together under the heading of the "incest-survivor machine.") Critics also charged that an unrelenting focus on memories of abuse created conditions conducive to the iatrogenic production of reports of additional and more serious forms of abuse, possibly the result of dependent/suggestible participants' attempts to please the therapist/caregiver or fit in with their peers. They believed that such a focus encouraged abdication of personal responsibility and a stance of entitlement in clients (i.e., the "abuse excuse"). These critiques highlighted some of the major weaknesses inherent in these programs, namely overemphasis on identifying and working through abuse and underemphasis on other issues, including improved mental health and personal functioning and symptom stabilization and reduction. They also highlighted the need for a high level of professional training and expertise to work with such difficult client issues and dynamics. Armstrong (1994) and Haaken and Schlaps (1991) decried another deficiency of the recovery movement: the pathologizing and medicalization of a social problem. They charged that the pathology/treatment focus ironically served to obscure the seriousness of the problem as a social issue and, in so doing, impeded more broad-based social policy and prevention efforts.

THE ROLE OF THE MEDIA.   The role of the media in promulgating these perspectives, issues, and services cannot be overstated. Beginning in the 1970s and continuing to the present, the media accorded unprecedented public exposure to issues of sexual assault and domestic violence (including wife battering, incest/child sexual abuse, and family dysfunction/parental alcoholism) and to personal recovery and self-help efforts. The result of this coverage was that the most private of family events went from being absolutely taboo and unspeakable to being discussed quite routinely in a number of media outlets. The early reports were generally quite restrained and cognizant of the sensitive nature of the material under discussion and the difficulties experienced by victims of abuse. They also emphasized abuse prevention. Over time, however, the media coverage changed and an underside surfaced. Later reports (many spurred by the increasingly tabloid format of daytime TV and the network rating wars) sensationalized and in some cases even glamourized the most bizarre forms of abuse (e.g., the most nonrepresentative forms of incest, satanic ritual abuse, alien abduction abuse, past life abuse), along with the most extreme and pathological of responses, often representing them as the norm. In the process, the "average" or more "mundane" forms of abuse and their aftereffects were trivialized and relegated to the background (Courtois, 1995b). As abuse became more exposed and normalized, its potential for damage was deemphasized. In many ways, the recovered/false memory controversy emerged, in part, in reaction to the overexposure through saturation coverage, misrepresentation, and sensationalization by the media of this most sensitive (and emotionally explosive) material, and the resultant impact that it had on public understanding, therapeutic services, and legal initiatives.

The coverage had a number of additional (and more positive) effects deserving of mention: (1) It acknowledged and validated experiences of abuse that heretofore had remained private and secret; (2) in some cases, it provided a trigger for the recognition/remembering/disclosure of previously unacknowledged, suppressed, repressed, and/or dissociated experiences of abuse (see discussion of research findings on the triggering role of the media in chapter 4); (3) it publicized the research findings on the major consequences of abuse; (4) it legitimized involvement in treatment for the aftereffects of abuse, whether through traditional psychotherapy or self-help recovery methods or both; and (5) in some circles, it spurred prevention and early intervention efforts.

AN INFLUX OF INDIVIDUALS SEEKING TREATMENT FOR REMEMBERED OR SUSPECTED PAST ABUSE.   Largely as a result of the media coverage but also as part of the social zeitgeist involving consciousness-raising, personal empowerment, self-help recovery efforts, and dysfunctional family/adult child perspectives, individuals in unprecedented numbers sought help for past abuse, whether remembered or suspected. While many sought out credentialed mental health professionals, a significant number became involved with self-help programs of the sort described above and worked with minimally trained and uncredentialed lay helpers and therapists.

Over time, it became evident that, for a number of reasons, a segment of this treatment population posed formidable challenges to all practitioners. Even professionally trained, licensed, and seasoned clinicians were hard pressed to provide adequate therapeutic assistance to the most symptomatic subpopulation. Most professional therapists had received little or no instruction in the treatment of interpersonal victimization and trauma in their training programs, an unfortunate long-term fallout of the psychoanalytic dismissal of abuse and other forms of trauma that continues to the present. This lack of inclusion is a glaring omission that has certainly contributed to the controversy and that has been repeatedly mentioned by professional task forces as being in need of immediate attention and correction (American Psychological Association, 1996a, 1996b). (This issue is further addressed in the chapters that make up Part III and in the afterword in Part IV). Therapists of all persuasions were hampered in their attempts to provide treatment by this lack of training. As a result, they tended to receive their training "on the job and in the trenches" and through their reading of the available literature and participation in continuing education courses on "first generation models"—a less than optimal scenario. This, too, has obviously contributed to difficulties that have given rise to the controversy.

During this time period, feminist clinicians Haaken and Schlaps (1991) wrote a significant critique of the emerging professional treatment model. They criticized the newly developing model as too narrowly focused on abuse issues, to the detriment of other etiological factors and therapeutic issues. They also discussed the reciprocal influence between the lay literature/self-help movement and professional practice as both beneficial and problematic. Their article presaged some of the concerns raised in the memory controversy and spurred some of the "course corrections" made by professional therapists as they became more experienced with the population and developed more sophisticated treatment models. Haaken and Schlaps wrote:

> . . . clinicians who develop specialized practices in the area of abuse often rely on the growing popular clinical literature on sexual abuse. This literature, often written for a lay audience, is replete with useful information about general patterns, symptoms, and feelings associated with abuse, as well as exercises aimed at changing feelings and cognitions. Typically, this information follows from a framework explaining how abuse happens and how it is not the victim's fault. This literature is widely used in treatment programs which include group and invididual therapy. The assumption is that information and knowledge offer power and with that comes curative results. This literature has included a very positive effort on the part of survivors to tell their stories and to educate themselves and the mental health community about sexual abuse. It also provides a powerful phenomenological vehicle for giving meaning to their own histories and experiences.
>
> On the other hand, these materials have been appropriated by mental health providers and implemented in ways that promote both overconfidence in a limited set of techniques and singleminded focus on sexual abuse in treatment. Clinicians who are not grounded in broad-based, theoretically guided training are often vulnerable to these new clinical trends and to formulaic specialization of clinical practice. Unifying the phenomena associated with incest and other forms of abuse does have an important political aim in raising public consciousness about sexual abuse and can have heuristic value in clinical situations. But if the therapist relies on this normative literature as a substitute for more complex clinical knowledge, it becomes an obstacle to therapeutic understanding. (p. 46)

Despite these problems and limitations, the posttraumatic approach of the "first generation" model was acknowledged as giving therapists an important new way to understand and treat patients with a reported abuse history. A number of survivor-patients clearly benefited from the new approach and were able to resolve longstanding abuse-related issues. On the other hand, some patients deteriorated as their symptoms increased and their functioning decreased. And some reported an ever intensifying spiral of abuse memories, including those involving extremely fantastic and sadistic abuses, some of which were improbable.

It now appears that at least three issues contributed to this situation. In some cases, as suggested by Haaken and Schlaps, many therapists (both lay and professional) and their patients adopted a too narrow, almost exclusive focus on abuse. They held the erroneous belief that treatment of current symptoms and difficulties *required the identification and abreaction of memories of the known or suspected abuse* that was believed to be etiologic of their distress. In the case of unremembered abuse, this often meant an overly strong focus on retrieving traumatic memories, at the expense of other therapeutic work. The second issue had to do with the wide variability in the patient population. With increased experience with this treatment, clinicians came to realize that the population of abuse survivors is anything but homogeneous. A subset of the group proved to be highly complex and difficult to treat due to comorbid conditions and diagnoses, chronic and intractable symptoms, intrapsychic deficits, emotional and relational instability, and many high-risk behaviors, including suicidality and self-injury (Chu, 1998). They most closely resembled patients who fit within the borderline personality disorder spectrum, a clinical observation given support by research that showed a substantial overlap between what Briere (1984) posited as a post-abuse syndrome and the criteria used in the diagnosis of borderline personality disorder (Herman, Perry, & van der Kolk, 1989; Kroll, 1993; Ogata, et al., 1990).

A number of writers, including Briere (1989), Chu (1988), Courtois (1988), Danieli (1984), Kluft (1989), and Putnam (1989a) identified a third issue, the transference and countertransference reactions and challenges in treating traumatized patients, challenges compounded in those with a borderline-type disorder and other comorbid conditions. Chu (1992) used the analogy of a therapeutic roller coaster to describe the intensity and difficulty of both the treatment and the management of transference and countertransference responses that are elicited. Obviously, this subset of abuse survivors needs the most highly trained and experienced clinicians who, although not immune to the treatment difficulties encountered with this population, would be expected to be able to identify and manage them more therapeutically (Chu, 1988, 1998).

DEVELOPMENT OF SECOND AND THIRD GENERATION TREATMENT MODELS. As research and clinical observation led to elaboration of the characteristics of abuse survivors and the complexities of their clinical presentation and needs, therapists began to develop what is now identified as a "second generation" treatment model (Alexander & Anderson, 1994; Blizard & Bruhn, 1994; Briere, 1991, 1992; Chu, 1992; Courtois, 1994; Davies & Frawley, 1994; Dolan, 1991; Herman, 1992b; Kepner, 1995; Kirschner, Kirschner, & Rappaport, 1993; Kluft, 1990; Kluft & Fine, 1993; Kroll, 1993; McCann & Pearlman, 1990a; Meiselman, 1990; Pearlman & Saakvitne, 1995; Salter, 1995; Waites, 1993; Wells, Glickhauf-Hughes, & Beaudoin, 1995; Wilson & Lindy, 1994) and, more recently, a "third generation" model (Alpert, 1995; Briere, 1996a, 1996b; Brown et al., 1998; Chu, 1998; Courtois, 1997a, 1997b; Gartner, 1997b; Ross, 1997; Roth & Batson, 1997; van der Kolk, McFarlane, & Weisaeth, 1996; Waites, 1997). These updated models retain much of the original posttraumatic and abuse-focused orientation but have broadened considerably. They now include more attention to memory issues, as well as attention to other formative life events, object relations, attachment style, and characterological issues that might reinforce or dilute reactions to abuse. Consequently, they broaden the choice of treatment approach and focus.

The sequence of treatment is also much more articulated. It generally consists of a comprehensive pretreatment assessment followed by three treatment phases. Emphasis is placed on the development of the patient's ego capacities, skills, functioning, and life stability in the first phase, before any direct work with abuse trauma is undertaken (usually in the second phase), and on pacing and titration of the overall treatment process. Furthermore, these models, especially those of the "third generation," focus more on the complexities of delayed memory issues, particularly the maintenance of therapeutic neutrality with regard to recovered rather than continuous memories and/or suspicions rather than actual knowledge of abuse. Finally, these models pay more attention to the complex transference, countertransference, and vicarious traumatization issues that typically emerge, and to the damage that might ensue when countertransference is acted out with the patient rather than understood and managed therapeutically (discussed more fully in chapter 9).

LEGISLATIVE INITIATIVES AND ALLEGATIONS OF PAST ABUSE IN THE FORENSIC SETTING: ENTER THE MEMORY EXPERTS. As all of these events and issues played out in the media, self-help, and clinical arenas, they began to materialize in the legal venue as well. In state legislatures across the United States, adult survivors and their supporters lobbied for an extension of the statutes of limitations to make it possible to file civil actions for damages due to past incest/sexual abuse. The rationale for the extension was derived from the new research on the long-term consequences of child abuse. Specifically, this concerned the inability of the plaintiff to bring suit in a timely manner (as specified by the existing statutes of limitation) due to emotional damage attributable to the abuse and/or the unavailability of memory for past abuse for a period of time due to amnesia and/or other emotional defenses. Virtually all states changed the statutes of limitations and delayed discovery requirements to allow more adult survivors the opportunity to bring civil actions against alleged perpetrators, often family members.

As such lawsuits were filed and began to make their way through the courts, clinical practitioners were often called as experts for the plaintiff to explain both the emotional damages resulting from abuse and, more importantly to the emergence of this controversy, the process by which memories could be recovered after a period of being unavailable. These clinicians (many of whom had no experience in forensic settings and who often did not know about or differentiate between the standard of evidence required in the courtroom versus that required in the consulting room) sometimes served as both the content expert and the treating therapist (and often, by extension, as plaintiff advocate)—an untenable situation due to the confounding of roles that were contradictory in purpose. Defense attorneys began to hire as their experts cognitive scientists (some of whom were trained as forensic psychologists) who challenged the theory behind the recovery of repressed memory as inconsistent with the available literature on the workings of human memory. The defense experts criticized as naive and in error therapists who testified that their patients' delayed memory productions were veridical representations of historical truth rather than narrative reconstructions replete with error and inaccuracy. They further suggested that clinicians' misunderstanding about these issues could result in confirmatory bias and suggestive therapeutic practices, leading to illusory memories of abuse that never occurred. Their testimony was often enough to cast doubt on the allegations of past abuse, especially in cases based solely on recovered memories or those where little evidence or corroboration was available to support a claim. Additionally, plaintiffs were challenged as to their credibility and in some cases were countersued by parents and other family members, who charged that both their allegations and the memories on which they were based were false.

Development of the Countermovement:
The Emergence of the Memory Controversy

In the early 1990s, a remarkable confluence of issues, events, and people led to the development of a countermovement and the emergence of the recovered/false memory controversy, leading Armstrong (1994) to label the decade the "Age of the Backlash." These issues and events took place against the framework of the broader sociohistorical context described above. Let us now review the most predominant of these recent issues and events.

CHARGES OF CONTEMPORANEOUS CHILD ABUSE IN THE FORENSIC SETTING: ENTER THE MEMORY EXPERTS.   One outcome of the increase in information about the prevalence of child physical and sexual abuse was the passage of the federal Child Abuse Prevention and Treatment Act (CAPTA) (the Mondale Act) in 1974 followed by the passage of similar legislation in virtually every state. This legislation mandated professionals to report suspected or disclosed abuse by caretakers and not only granted them immunity from prosecution for reporting but also threatened them with legal penalties for failure to report. Record numbers of abuse reports were made following the passage of these legislative initiatives (American Humane Association, 1988; Sedlak & Broadhurst, 1996). CAPTA also provided funding to states for the development of assessment and treatment programs for victims and improvement of the investigation and prosecution of offenders. Multidisciplinary teams were formed and given broad powers to investigate allegations of abuse; unfortunately however, assessment guidelines and standards were not available at the time. The lack of uniform standards and adequate training for conducting child interviews and the subjectivity and bias of interviewers quite frequently resulted in suggestive, leading, and sometimes coercive, rather than neutral, questioning. As the need for guidance and training in this endeavor became apparent, a modern literature on children as witnesses and their ability to testify began to emerge (Ceci & Bruck, 1993; Goodman & Bottoms, 1993; Perry & Wrightsman, 1991).

As criminal charges were filed based on abuse reports and investigations and cases made their way into the courtroom, these investigatory methods and the competency of children (especially preschoolers) to testify were challenged by defense attorneys. To buttress the defense, attorneys turned to cognitive scientists with expertise in child development, children's memory and suggestibility, and the credibility and reliability of children's testimony. These experts highlighted pertinent developmental issues in children's memory retention and suggestibility and the conditions conducive to their testimonial competence. In general, although reliable age differences in suggestibility in children have been found and children can be influenced in a variety of ways, even very young children are capable of recalling much that is forensically relevant and thus are able to credibly and reliably testify if sources of influence are limited (see Bruck, Ceci, & Hembrooke, 1998; Ceci, 1993; and Ceci & Bruck, 1993, for reviews of the literature; see Brown et al., 1998, for a somewhat different interpretation). Cognitive experts specifically pointed out problematic confounding of the roles of therapist and investigator in many cases and suggestive interview techniques employed in some of the investigations. Through their research, they demonstrated how certain pre- and post-event suggestions could sway and contaminate a child's memory. They critiqued some of the investigatory methods as creating the same type of suggestion and thus contributing to false beliefs and reports (and hence false accusations) of abuse (Ceci, 1993; Ceci & Bruck, 1993). They also made suggestions for better and more neutral ways to conduct investigatory interviews of young children so as not to influence the findings.

The testimony of the memory experts lent credence to the arguments of those fighting allegations of abuse and their supporters. In 1984, a group named VOCAL (Victims of Child Abuse Laws) had been organized by parents who claimed to be falsely accused of sexually abusing their children. The organization's aim was to expose and counteract the excesses and errors in child protection investigations that led to false accusations and legal charges and the resultant disruption of families. VOCAL was the forerunner of another organization, the False Memory Syndrome Foundation, established nearly a decade later. A crossover regarding memory issues in child criminal cases and adult civil cases became apparent in the decade between the establishment of the two organizations. In some cases, the same memory experts testified in adult and child cases and noted the similarity of some of the memory and suggestibility issues in both. Those studying investigatory and trial transcripts and those testifying as experts raised alarms about the issues with their colleagues and found an applied setting for the results of their laboratory studies on children's memory and suggestibility and for integrating them with the findings on adult suggestibility and recovered memory concerns (Ceci, 1993; Ceci & Bruck, 1995; Loftus, 1993).

THE FREYD FAMILY AND THE ESTABLISHMENT OF THE FALSE MEMORY SYNDROME FOUNDATION.   The spark that galvanized the emergence of the false memory movement was the allegation and denial of sexual abuse within one middle-class professional family. In brief, in late 1990, psychology professor Jennifer Freyd accused her father, Peter Freyd, a mathematics professor, of having sexually abused her and denied her parents access to her children. Peter and his wife Pamela were highly distressed by the allegations, which Peter denied. The couple began to research information on abuse allegations (a search that put them in touch with the evolving professional and lay literature on repressed/recovered memories of abuse in adults and the controversies developing about false accusations of contemporaneous child abuse) and consulted with colleagues and therapists. In 1991, Pamela Freyd, a professional educator, anonymously published "How Could This Happen?" (Freyd, 1991) in *Issues in Child Abuse Accusations*, a journal established by psychologists Ralph Underwager and Hollida Wakefield, cofounders and active members of VOCAL who often testified for the defense in cases involving allegations of child abuse. In this account of a mother's confusion, shame, and rage, and her dawning belief that her daughter's allegations were suggested by her psychotherapist on the basis of erroneous theorizing and technique, can be found the initial impetus for and reasoning behind the false memory perspective. The article hit a nerve. Couples whose stories resembled that of the Freyds and who alleged that they were being falsely accused of past abuse by adult children contacted them through the journal and through VOCAL to request help and support.

Although the accusations made by their daughter Jennifer were made in private, in 1992 the Freyds (with Ralph Underwager and others) organized a public response by establishing and incorporating the False Memory Syndrome Foundation. They solicited and attracted a Scientific and Professional Advisory Board of eminent professionals, who immediately lent credibility and influence to the organization and its message. On this board sat many cognitive scientists specializing in memory, some of them Jennifer Freyd's professional colleagues. (Incredibly, the Freyds even asked Jennifer to serve as an advisory board member, ostensibly to keep communication open between them. She refused their invitation.) A number of those who became board members or supporters had served as experts in the type of cases described above. Thus, many were already active in questioning the theory of repressed/recovered memory and the role of suggestive therapy in adult cases and suggestive interviewing in child cases. Their testimony and writing were put to use by attorneys representing accused families in both criminal and civil cases. This information was later used in third party lawsuits against therapists.

Jennifer, in contrast to her parents, chose to keep her abuse allegations private. She publicly discussed them only once, at a professional conference in Ann Arbor, Michigan, in August 1993, where she told her side of

the story (Freyd, 1993). She questioned why, as an established and credible adult as well as a respected scientist specializing in memory, her recollections and allegations should be given less credibility than her
father's denials, especially since he had acknowledged treatment for
alcoholism during the years she believes the abuse occurred. She also
countered her parents' belief that her memories had been unduly influenced by her therapist. At the time of her original allegation she had seen
her therapist for only a few sessions.

The Freyd family dispute has not progressed toward resolution; unfortunately for all concerned, it may never be resolved. Other family members have spoken out in support of Jennifer's contentions and charges
(Freyd, 1995) but the Freyds maintain their innocence. The family continues to represent the poles of the controversy, Pamela and Peter in
regarding Jennifer's memories as false, and Jennifer in regarding her parents' memories and denial as false. Jennifer has continued to research
memory, but the focus of her investigations has shifted. In 1996, she wrote
Betrayal Trauma: The Logic of Forgetting Sexual Abuse (Freyd, 1996), in
which she articulated a theory about the blockage of information when
retention would interfere with a child's ability to function within a dependent and essential relationship (discussed further in chapters 3 and 4).

The stated purpose of the False Memory Syndrome Foundation was
to challenge the recovered memory position with a false memory claim
and to research and publicize the occurrence and damaging consequences of so-called false memory syndrome to both primary and secondary victims, all with the intent of preventing new cases. The organization charged that, under the influence of ill-prepared and naive therapists and a "disastrous" course of suggestive psychotherapy that was
labeled by the foundation as "recovered memory therapy" (or RMT),
many adults developed a psychological syndrome that included recovery
of false memories of abuse. "False memory syndrome" (a term coined by
the organization) is defined as: "a condition in which a person's identity
and interpersonal relationships are centered around a memory of traumatic experience which is objectively false but in which the person
strongly believes. *Note that the syndrome is not characterized by false
memories as such* . . . . Rather, the syndrome may be diagnosed when
the memory is so deeply ingrained that it orients the individual's entire
personality and lifestyle, in turn disrupting all sorts of other adaptive
behaviors" (definition attributed to Dr. John F. Kihlstrom, False Memory
Foundation brochure, 1993, italics added).

From early on, the media shifted from a focus on abuse and its effects
to a focus on false memory concerns (Beckett, 1996). The media extensively disseminated the false memory position; however, it did so with-

out substantial investigation or challenge. Specifically, media reports failed to establish the origin of "false memory syndrome" or the data that supported the claims about its prevalence. Instead, the syndrome was taken at face value and as fact, as something that was causing immeasurable suffering and dividing thousands of families (Stanton, 1997). The innumerable newspaper and magazine articles (and, somewhat surprisingly, even articles in professional journals) were formulaic in their conceptualization of the problem, its scope, and the damage it was said to be causing. They were also formulaic in how the articles were written— almost as though they followed a script or talking points or, in some cases, had a ghostwriter. Concerning media coverage, one might say that false memory reports took off where delayed memory reports left off. As before, the media benefited from sensationalizing the issue. Within a year's time, the controversy over repressed/recovered memory and false accusations of abuse was well underway and a sea change took place in how recollections of abuse were understood and how anyone alleging abuse on the basis of delayed/recovered memories was treated.

The impact and influence of the Foundation and its message have been truly astounding. Brown et al. (1998) explained its influence as follows:

> How do we understand the sudden success of the FMSF? From a wider social perspective, the FMSF represents a backlash against increasing accusations about the dysfunctional nature of the American middle-class family, particularly against therapists who symbolize parent-blaming (Haaken, 1994). From the narrower perspective of childhood sexual abuse, the FMSF represents two extremes—the painful agony of those accused without due process, but also a potentially clever legal defense for justly accused perpetrators. The problem, of course, is in accurately knowing the proportions of alleged abusers that are genuinely or falsely accused.
>
> The reason the FMSF has gained such popularity so quickly is that it has served as a conduit for a number of very different interest groups: (1) falsely accused parents who are seeking due process, (2) genuine perpetrators who need support in "science" for their legal defense, (3) memory scientists in search of a new area of practical application beyond eyewitness research, (4) researchers on coercive persuasion and brainwashing who now have a wider arena than the cult phenomenon, (5) clinicians who are uncomfortable with the excesses in treatment inherent within the stereotype of self-help trauma treatment, (6) sociologists, anthropologists, and historians seeking to understand the transformation of contemporary American society, and (7) biological psychiatrists skeptical of therapy. (p. 16)

Although many would agree that an organization like the False Memory Syndrome Foundation would someday materialize in order to challenge and curb some of the excesses and missteps of the day (in therapy, media presentations of survivors, self-help programs, child abuse investigations, the overdiagnosis of multiple personality disorder, and charges of improbable forms of abuse), some of the remedies espoused by those associated with the Foundation have been criticized as extreme and excessive. From the time of its establishment, the Foundation placed the blame for the alleged false memory problem squarely on therapists, who were lumped together almost without distinction regardless of their training or methods of practice. Disgruntled parents who denied abuse and who blamed therapists for suggesting or implanting recovered memories were taken at their word without formal investigation or inquiry. Furthermore, they were encouraged to take action, ranging from corresponding with or requesting a meeting with their (adult) child's therapist to present their side of the story, bringing licensing board or ethics complaints against the therapist, secretly audiotaping or videotaping an intake interview or therapy sessions, picketing therapists' offices, to suing therapists for malpractice. Former patients who recanted their memories of abuse recovered during therapy were also believed without question and encouraged to take similar types of action. The Foundation appeared to operate on the belief that all denials/recantations were truthful and therefore to be believed, and that all abuse memories discussed or recovered during psychotherapy were false and therefore not to be believed. The actions that they recommended also challenged some of the most basic principles of psychotherapy, namely the duty owed by the therapist to the primary patient (versus third parties), therapist-patient privilege, and the confidentiality of psychotherapy (see Pope, 1996, for a detailed critique).

THERAPIST LAWSUITS AND ATTEMPTS TO LEGISLATE THE PRACTICE OF PSYCHOTHERAPY.   In fairly short order, therapists treating adult survivors found that they and their work were under scrutiny in some quarters and that they were increasingly regarded with suspicion, if not outright hostility. Quite soon after the false memory organization's founding and with the direct support of its proponents, the critique moved beyond the media into the courtroom and state legislatures. Aggrieved parents who claimed to have been falsely accused on the basis of therapeutic malpractice began to file third-party lawsuits against therapists. The first to be decided, the case of Ramona (*Ramona v. Isabella*, California Superior Court, Napa, C61898), has become a legal landmark (Ewing, 1994). In this case, a counselor and a psychiatrist were found guilty of malpractice for using sodium amytal to retrieve abuse memories, for giving their patient erroneous information about the veridicality of retrieved memory, and for making what were deemed suggestive comments about symptoms and their likely relation to child sexual abuse. Plaintiff Gary A. Ramona (the father of the patient) was awarded $500,000 in damages.

"False memory syndrome" has come to be used routinely by defense attorneys in cases involving allegations of abuse. This strategy is even being used when no memory loss is alleged, i.e., when the abuse is in the present or the immediate past and repressed or delayed memory is not an issue and/or when abuse has not been forgotten. It has nevertheless been a potent tool for the defense. In addition to litigation, aggrieved parents and patients have been encouraged to bring ethics charges and licensing challenges against treating therapists.

On the legislative front, a bill variously titled "The Mental Health Consumer Protection Act," "The Consumer Fraud Protection Act," or "The Truth and Responsibility in Mental Health Practices Act" (sponsored by five state chapters of Friends of FMS) (Barden, 1994) has been introduced into several state legislatures. Its stated aim is the protection of consumers from harmful and fraudulent therapy practices (of which "repressed memory therapy" is a prime example) by regulating the practice of psychotherapy. The necessity and utility of these bills have been challenged by professional organizations, notably the American Psychological Association, which responded with a white paper on the topic (American Psychological Association, 1996a; Hinnefeld & Newman, 1997). Thus far, none of these legislative initiatives has been passed, but they are expected to be introduced again in the future.

The controversy, including its rapid escalation, its high visibility, its inclusiveness in criticizing therapists who treat adults who report abuse (ascribing poor practice regardless of degree status, training, legitimacy, caution, the specifics of each case and the treatment used), and its ferocity and vehemence in suggesting redress via lawsuit and regulatory challenge, has caught many therapists by surprise. Some have reacted by refusing to treat anyone seeking therapy for suspicions of abuse and others by practicing overly defensive "lawsuit therapy" (Dobson, 1998). Others have been less surprised by the controversy but are confused. Does the controversy constitute a needed corrective to a perspective founded on erroneous assumptions and/or to practitioners using shoddy and fraudulent techniques or practicing in ways that outstrip their knowledge base? Or, does it constitute a backlash against new discoveries about abuse and new ways of working with abuse-related syndromes, including memories that are inaccessible for some period of time and that emerge after a delay? In the next chapter, we discuss the main points of the controversy made by those on both sides of the issue, followed by a discussion of scientific versus political issues that are involved.

SUMMARY

In an attempt to place the current controversy in sociohistorical context, this chapter has identified several historical antecedents to its emergence. It has also traced a number of recent events and issues, such as the recognition of child abuse as a prevalent and significant social problem, the role of trauma on the development of posttraumatic conditions and disturbances of memory in many traumatized individuals, the development of therapeutic approaches that have a posttraumatic orientation, the role of the media and the self-help/recovery movement in influencing large numbers of individuals to seek treatment for abuse related issues, and their respective contributions to the development of the false memory controversy. In the next chapter, the profile of the debate is further articulated.

Chapter 2

THE PRESENT CONTEXT

An Overview of the Recovered Memory/False Memory Controversy

The recovered memory/false memory controversy essentially revolves around three issues: (1) whether trauma can be forgotten and then remembered, (2) the accuracy and credibility of memories of childhood sexual abuse, and (3) the role of therapeutic influence on memories. Proponents on either side of the controversy, those favoring the recovered memory or traumatic stress perspective (hereafter referred to as the traumatic stress perspective) or those favoring the false memory perspective, have quite different viewpoints regarding these issues. Those at the extremes have viewpoints that are in some cases diametrically opposed. Quite recently, moderates have denounced the excesses of the extremes and have begun to search for common ground and areas of agreement. Happily, efforts of this sort have begun to succeed. They have been supported by the findings and recommendations of professional task forces convened to study issues involved in the controversy released within the last several years.

The conclusions of these working groups are remarkably similar. In combination, they caution that care must be taken to assure that the controversy neither obscures real childhood abuse as a grave social issue nor undermines response to victims of current and past abuse. They strongly suggest a more dispassionate approach and call both sides to task for making pronouncements and taking action based on anecdotes and impressions rather than on systematic empirical evidence and for closing doors to inquiry rather than opening them. As a corrective, they call for more restraint, tolerance, and sensitivity, for greater efforts at establishing points of commonality, and for a great deal more study on the part of all involved.

In this chapter, the main points made by those on both sides of the controversy are presented. The first section includes overviews of the traumatic stress and false memory perspectives, followed by a brief overview of the rebuttal/countercritique of the traumatic stress proponents. The middle section reviews factors that have led to the extremism and vehemence of the controversy since its inception. This is followed by an articulation of points of commonality and compatibility that have recently been found between the two perspectives and that allow a more rational and professional orientation towards these issues. The last section reviews findings and recommendations of various professional task forces.

POINT, COUNTERPOINT: AN OVERVIEW OF TRAUMATIC STRESS AND FALSE MEMORY PERSPECTIVES

The Traumatic Stress Perspective

Over the course of a century's worth of study (albeit intermittent study at times, as discussed in chapter 1), researchers and clinicians involved in traumatic stress studies have noted memory disturbance and pathologies of memory in response to psychic trauma. While some traumatized individuals retain full memory of the trauma (and, indeed, some are hypermnestic and suffer from the retention of highly detailed memory and a corresponding inability to forget or to not remember), some remain fully or partially amnestic in the immediate and/or long-term aftermath of trauma. These disturbances of consciousness and memory, first identified at the end of the last century with regard to the studies of hysterics and childhood trauma, were again identified in this century in traumatized soldiers suffering from combat fatigue. They have since been identified in victims of a wide range of traumata, including accidents, natural disasters, rape, physical abuse, kidnapping, torture, concentration camp experiences, etc. The vagaries of memory in traumatized individuals and in posttraumatic conditions were incorporated in the early descriptions of these conditions and ultimately in the diagnosis of Posttraumatic Stress Disorder and within the category of the dissociative disorders, both first published in the DSM-III (American Psychiatric Association, 1980).

Trauma refers to experiences or events that, by definition, are out of the ordinary in terms of their overwhelming nature. They are more than merely stressful—they are also shocking, terrifying, and devastating to the victim, resulting in profoundly upsetting feelings of terror, shame, helplessness, and powerlessness. While traumatization can take place through personal exposure and experience, it can occur through witnessing as well. Traumatic events and the repercussions that accompany them are highly variable, and all cannot be assumed to be the same. They interact with characteristics of the individual and the environment to determine reactions at the time of the event and in its immediate or long-term aftermath (See chapters 3 and 4 for additional discussion of traumatization and posttraumatic response). Dissociation is a psychological defense mechanism that may occur spontaneously at the time of trauma (peridissociation) and may be related to disruptions in memory encoding and later memory oscillations.

Trauma that occurs in childhood may cause reactions that resemble those found in adults, but significant differences may also be evident due to the child's physical and psychosexual immaturity and dependent status. The characteristics and dynamics (alone or in combination) of child sexual abuse are particularly traumagenic and have been found to reinforce patterns of nondisclosure, silence, forgetting, dissociation, repression, and denial. Additionally, repeated, chronic, and escalating abuse (especially incest and other forms of domestic violence over the course of childhood) requires extreme defensive operations on the part of the child, including a greater use of dissociation and other numbing strategies that may result in memory disturbance caused by encoding, storage, and retrieval difficulties.

Proponents of the traumatic stress perspective have underscored the role of dissociation in memory disturbance, based upon recently gathered research findings and clinical observations. Dissociation is understood as a primary mechanism for the inhibition of access to memory and is hypothesized to differ from the concept of repression. Although some writers have used the terms "repression" and "dissociation" interchangeably, they are, in fact, different by definition. Repression represents a hypothesized unconscious mechanism in psychodynamic personality formations that, in effect, causes the warding off of intolerable or conflictual material and affect from conscious awareness (Davies, 1997; Vaillant, 1990). Dissociation, in contrast, results in a compartmentalization of mental processes so that "for a period of time, certain information is not associated or integrated with other information as it normally and logically would be" (West, 1967), causing a "disconnection, independence or separation of one part of memory from other" (Yates & Nasby, 1993). In pathological dissociation, "specific memories are inaccessible because they are associated with a highly charged negatively toned affective component. *Dissociation is not forgetting.* In dissociation, *the item is encoded but cannot be retrieved"* (Yates & Nasby, p. 309, italics added).

Exposure to trauma has been shown to increase the prevalence of certain dissociative symptoms, which have, in turn, been theorized as related to the development of PTSD. These dissociative symptoms include detachment, alterations in perception, and alterations in memory. According to the literature, reports of peritraumatic dissociative detachment (e.g., "I felt as if I were watching myself from a distance"; "I felt numb, as if I were in no pain"; "I felt I wasn't myself anymore") have been reported by significant numbers (between one-quarter and one-half) of traumatized individuals (Spiegel, 1993). Recent research findings (Bremner et al., 1993; Marmar, Weiss et al., 1994; Spiegel, 1994b) suggest that dissociating or numbing at the moment of the trauma (that is, the involuntary separation of affect and cognition associated with the experience) is the most important long-term predictor of the later development of PTSD.

At present, trauma researchers are accumulating data derived from investigations and clinical observations that imply that memory for traumatic events may be encoded (as well as stored and retrieved) differently from memory for unremarkable events. This memory may then be reexperienced differently, in sensorimotor or somatosensory ways (e.g., visually, kinesthetically, behaviorally), rather than through conscious memory and verbalization. Encoding differences are hypothesized to be mediated by psychophysiologic and neurophysiologic changes and dysregulations that accompany traumatization. These findings have led trauma researchers to posit that traumatic event memory may be different from normal event memory. (See chapter 3 for a more in-depth presentation of these issues.)

Studies of childhood trauma and memory have become available in recent years. This research implies that children interpret and respond to trauma according to their developmental level, their degree of physical and emotional maturity, and numerous objective and subjective elements of the traumatization (Pynoos, Steinberg, & Goenjian, 1996; Pynoos, Steinberg, & Aronson, 1997; Perry, 1993a, 1993b; Terr, 1991). Another line of research, that on childhood dissociation, has also contributed to the traumatic stress perspective. Research findings suggest that, on average, children are more dissociative than adults and that dissociation declines with age. Children are hypothesized to have a higher propensity and capacity to dissociate during trauma than adults in similar circumstances (Putnam, 1997). In a number of studies, adults with documented dissociative disorders have reported a very high prevalence of the most severe and chronic forms of abuse in their backgrounds, often within the family or otherwise involving family members (Chu & Dill, 1990; Putnam, 1985; Ross, Miller et al., 1990). Researchers have speculated that repeated, inescapable, severe abuse calls for the most extreme defenses and is therefore most likely to result in the use of dissociative (among other extreme) defenses. As noted above, dissociation refers to a process whereby cognitive processes, including memory, are compartmentalized. For this reason, it is implicated in memory disturbance, including memory loss and its delayed return.

In the past decade or so, studies of memory disturbances in traumatized adults have increased, spurred initially by observations about delayed and recovered memories made in clinical practice and more recently by the controversy. (These studies are presented in detail in chapter 4, so their findings are only briefly summarized here.) Taken together, they provide empirically derived data that a proportion of traumatized individuals report amnesia or memory loss (ranging from brief to extensive) for various periods of time for traumatic experiences. Memories may return in delayed fashion after a period of absence, commonly in response to cues or triggers that are somehow reminiscent of the trauma. Although these cues often appear in the general environment (media reports, movies), they also occur in more idiosyncratic and personal circumstances (developing trust and intimacy in a relationship, sexual activity, somatosensory prompts specific to some aspect of the trauma). They appear in the clinical setting as well, often as a result of therapist inquiry about abuse/trauma and/or due to being in a context where disclosure and examination of very private and personal material are expected and supported.

These empirical findings have cross-referenced those that have emerged from clinical practice, leading to the belief that previously repressed/dissociated memories of childhood trauma (especially child sexual abuse) can emerge during the course of therapy and at other times as well. Clinicians have found that many adults enter therapy *after their memory has been triggered* in some way and usually *after* they have become symptomatic. In fact, some present for treatment with the complaint of intrusive memories and flashbacks that won't go away. A posttraumatic model of treatment has been developed that centers around the exploration of the significance of the traumatization to the individual. Among other therapeutic tasks, the patient is helped to discuss the experience and to work with available memory so that its meaning can be processed and integrated instead of remaining split off or held out of consciousness. During the course of this exploration, it is not unusual for additional memories or details to emerge. The model is predicated on the expectation that intrusive and numbing symptoms (i.e., the problematic emotions, memories, and cognitions associated with the traumatization) will become more benign and ultimately remit once the material has been adequately accessed and processed.

A range of therapeutic models and techniques, each with relative belief in the accuracy of the patient's memory productions and different approaches to memory retrieval and processing, has been developed. Brown et al. (1998) have helpfully categorized some of the recovered memory positions taken by various authors and their respective models of treatment into those that are moderate, extreme, and balanced. Concerning those that they define as moderate, they write:

> The *moderate trauma accuracy position* largely consists of scientists who have written extensively on the assessment and treatment of trauma. The assumptions of most of these writings are that (1) at least narrative memory for early trauma is sometimes unavailable to consciousness, (2) psychotherapy and hypnosis can facilitate memory processing and retrieval, and (3) under normal circumstances a generally accurate memory representation of at least the gist of the traumatic experience becomes available, but not necessarily an accurate representation in every respect. (authors' italics) (p. 38)

The literature they associate with this position (Gelinas, 1983; Courtois, 1988; Briere & Conte, 1993; Harvey & Herman, 1994; Herman, 1994; Terr, 1994; van der Kolk, McFarlane, & Weisaeth, 1996) has not been directed exclusively at abuse-related issues or memories and has paid attention to stabilization as well as functioning and stress management. These models have, however, recommended a variety of therapeutic approaches and strategies for identifying and working with traumatic material, including some that have been strongly criticized by false memory supporters. These include the adjunctive use of such techniques as reading, art therapy, writing/journaling exercises, and group therapy in addition to hypnosis and guided imagery (whose indiscriminate use for memory retrieval per se *has not* been generally recommended), all under the purview of the primary therapy. (As opposed to the position of the critics, sodium amytal interviews have been neither routinely suggested nor routinely utilized.)

By comparison, Brown et al. describe the more extreme position regarding trauma accuracy:

> The *extreme trauma accuracy position* is largely represented in the self-help books, *The Courage to Heal* (Bass & Davis, 1988) and in *Repressed*

Memories (Frederickson, 1992). Frederickson makes a distinction between two types of responses to childhood sexual abuse—posttraumatic stress disorder and repressed memory syndrome (p. 40). According to her, *repressed memory syndrome* is defined as "no memory for the abuse or remembers but significant amnesia" (p. 40). She believes that repressed memory syndrome is more specific to the long-term response to childhood sexual abuse than PTSD (p. 40). (authors' italics) (p. 39)

Along with others working from this position, Frederickson (1992) contends that memory retrieval is integrally related to an individual's ability to heal and proposes an active approach to the retrieval of repressed memories. Recommended strategies include the use of guided imagery, hypnosis, journaling, body therapy, art therapy, and emotional work to retrieve components of traumatic memory in enough detail that the abuse picture emerges and counters the patient's feelings of doubt and "having made the whole thing up." Working from this extreme memory accuracy position, practitioners are likely to be inclined to take the reality or veridicality of their client's memory productions at face value and as reported, to support rather than question reports of abuse where no memory was previously available, and to encourage a search for the missing memories.

It would appear that, prior to the controversy's emergence, the majority of therapeutic perspectives and interventions for the treatment of abuse fell somewhere between these moderate and extreme perspectives. By and large, therapists took the position of believing the reality of sexual abuse memories, often leaning in the direction of uncritical belief of their patients' productions as the needed revision of and antidote to the psychoanalytic perspective of disbelief that had been in place for so long. This updated therapeutic perspective emphasized the recovery and reliving of emotionally traumatic memory as curative and as enhancing the self through the integration of important material that had been previously denied and warded off. At times, on the basis of work with these recollections, therapists advocated that patients disclose or confront the alleged abuser and other family members (both within and outside of the treatment setting) and, in some cases, seek legal redress for emotional damages caused by the abuse. Occasionally (although this does not seem to have been the norm), therapists encouraged temporary or permanent cut-offs from family members, most often for safety or protection but sometimes for the patient to get enough distance/detachment to be able to separate from predominant family dynamics and problems. Some survivor/patients made the decision to separate from family members independently of their therapists (prior to, during the course of, or after treatment), believing that such a separation was in their own best interests and/or those of other family members.

The False Memory Perspective

The false memory position, simply put, is that therapists are overzealous in suggesting incest and other forms of abuse that never happened to individuals who previously had no memories or inkling of having been abused in childhood. Therapists suggest abuse on the basis of their belief that it is common for people (especially those seeking mental health assistance) to harbor repressed memories of sexual abuse from childhood. Many overinterpret and overrely on symptom checklists (often found in the lay literature) or particular presenting problems (eating disorders and depression, most commonly) to make their assessment and diagnosis of repressed or unremembered abuse. They then suggest abuse scenarios through the repeated use of a variety of "recovered memory therapy" (RMT) techniques and, in so doing, cause great secondary harm to innocent and falsely accused individuals and entire families. In therapy of this type, on the basis of suggestive practice, confirmatory bias, erroneous theory, and misconceptions regarding how memory and hypnosis work and "in the absence of attempts to disconfirm the therapist's own beliefs about the abuse or to seek independent corroboration" (Brown et al., 1998, p. 40) or to consider other possible reasons for a patient's symptoms or memory disturbance, therapists are responsible for the iatrogenic creation of illusory or false memories.

According to the critics, in RMT, therapists routinely use a wide range of questionable techniques to hunt for missing memories of abuse: direct suggestion, hypnosis and hypnotic age regression, sodium amytal interviews, guided imagery, journal-writing, dream interpretation, body work and body memory interpretation, recommendation of self-help books such as *The Courage to Heal* (Bass & Davis, 1988), and participation in groups that are themselves loaded with misinformation and that create conditions of social compliance. Therapists uncritically accept as accurate any mental products that are recovered through these means, thus giving rise and credence to false memories of abuse.

Individuals suffering from "false memory syndrome" get caught in a spiral of producing memories of more and more serious forms of abuse, often due to dependence upon and attempts to please the therapist. These abuses (including reports of satanic ritual, past life, and alien abduction abuse) are accepted uncritically and without challenge by the therapist, who may thus (unwittingly) reinforce their production. On the basis of these abuse memories and without corroborating evidence or meetings with accused family members to request corroboration or explanation, therapists working from this model routinely suggest that their patients cut themselves off from family or, even more seriously, encourage them to initiate lawsuits against family members. Actions of this type have the effect of making patients more dependent on their therapists and on their treatment; as a result, patients caught in the throes of dependence, compliance, and memory production regress in their ability to function and get significantly worse over the course of treatment. Therapists then derive economic benefit from their patients' extreme dependence and ongoing need for treatment. The following quote exemplifies some of the critics' contentions regarding the excesses of such therapy.

> Patients as well as their families can be scarred for life. They are led to believe that bringing suppressed memories to light will banish their symptoms. On the contrary, the symptoms usually get worse because of traumatic breaks with loved ones. Moreover, this treatment can also cause a patient to refuse needed therapy from psychiatrists who have not fallen prey to the FMS epidemic. Pamela Freyd has likened the traumatists to surgeons doing brain surgery with a knife and fork. Others see the epidemic as similar in many ways to the great witch-hunts of the past, when disturbed women were made to believe they were in Satan's grip. The Devil has been replaced by the evil parental sexual abuse. Thousands of victims are being induced by traumatists to recall childhood participation in satanic cults that murder babies, eat their flesh, and practice even more revolting rituals. Police have yet to uncover any compelling evidence that satanic cults exist. Yet under hypnosis and soporific drugs, memories of witnessing such rituals can become as vivid as memories of sexual abuse. (Gardner, 1993, pp. 271–272)

Proponents of the false memory position charge that little evidence exists for the repression and delayed recall/recovered memory of child sexual abuse, according to the available laws of human memory derived from 100 years of research. In support of this position, they routinely cite a review article by Holmes (1990) that asserts that the concept of repression is not supported by empirical evidence and is therefore not a likely explanation for memory loss. Memory critics also point out that—as opposed to the beliefs held by a "not insignificant number of therapists" that memory returns in original, unsullied form, like a camera image or a videotape—studies of memory show it to be inexact and reconstructive.

The encoding, storage, and retrieval of information are highly variable between individuals and circumstances and can be biased by a host of influences, including suggestion by therapists. Events that reoccur (such as chronic abuse) are expected to leave a *greater rather than lesser* memory trace and therefore are *more rather than less likely to be remembered*. The notion that memory for trauma differs from normal event memory (in ways that might not yet have been identified) is rejected. According to Ornstein, Ceci, & Loftus (1996a):

> Although everyone would agree that physical and psychological seque-lae to trauma can and do occur, there is no compelling biological or social evidence to support the view that once-viable memories of trau-matic experiences can be submerged and then recovered after intervals that extend many years. (p. 107)
>
> . . . What type of mechanism could account for such retroactive era-sure? How can traumatic experiences be accessible for long periods of time and then suddenly become inaccessible as a function of addition-al similar experiences? Doesn't such a conceptualization fly in the face of research showing that memory improves with repetition? Are these special memories that do not behave according to the principles discov-ered by researchers over the course of more than 100 years of the study of memory? Such forms of repression, if they could be supported by sci-entific data, would allow for the view that, when repressed, memories are preserved in their pristine state where they go "underground" and presumably not be subject to the usual processes of decay, alteration and interference that influence ordinary (i.e., non-repressed) memories. (p. 108)

False memory commentators also point out that therapists are often unaware of child development and maturation issues that have a bearing on memory. Due to their brain immaturity, children may be physiologi-cally incapable of encoding experiences in a way that later results in con-scious memory; furthermore, infantile or childhood amnesia is at play in early childhood (the exact age of the offset of childhood amnesia varies by study but is believed to occur between the ages of two and a half and three and a half, on average). Abuse that occurred when the child was preverbal may create later problems with retrieval, since retrieval using a similar coding mechanism may be necessary. Additionally, research find-ings indicate that children are more suggestible than adults. On average, older children remember more and better than younger children, and younger children are more responsive to suggestion and misleading infor-mation than are older children (Ceci & Bruck, 1993).

Cognitive scientists have found little or no empirical support for dissociation or repression as explanatory concepts for lost and recovered memories, a position that has led memory critics to believe that both have been overblown as explanatory concepts. Dissociation as a primary defensive operation in the face of overwhelming trauma, a concept so favored by the advocates of the traumatic stress viewpoint, is not compelling to the majority of false memory proponents and, as noted earlier, repression is dismissed since it lacks empirical substantiation (in accordance with the perspective espoused in the Holmes review). The suggestibility of dissociative patients and their high overlap with those who score high on hypnotizability and suggestibility scales has instead been flagged by the false memory camp. They believe that these are critical dimensions that are likely to contribute to confabulation and the production of false memories, dimensions that the critics believe therapists have been uninformed about or have willfully ignored.

In a related vein, false memory critics condemn what they view as naive overreliance on hypnosis for the retrieval of memory, especially with patients who are highly dissociative and/or suggestible. They contend that many therapists hold erroneous beliefs about repression, dissociation, and hypnosis that have led them to overuse hypnosis and to accept uncritically the veridicality of material produced when it is used. On the basis of their misinformation and naivete about hypnosis and suggestibility, therapists have assumed that the vivid imagery and intense emotionality that sometimes accompany hypnotic recall reflect (and in fact reinforce) the historical reality and reliability of the material. This is in direct contrast to experimental findings that hypnosis may have the effect of increasing a subject's confidence in memories produced under hypnosis, even for events that are demonstrably false, and that high emotionality and vivid imagery do not mean that the memory is veridical. Thus, although hypnosis may well assist in the retrieval of true memory, it may also result in the retrieval of false memory or memory for events that did not occur. Moreover, memory retrieved under the influence of hypnosis may be confounded in ways that are problematic and may cause subjects or patients to hold these memories with great confidence, regardless or their veracity (Yapko, 1994b).

As they did with the traumatic stress perspective, Brown et al. (1998) categorized the false memory perspective along a continuum. Describing the more moderate position represented by the writings of Haaken and Schlaps (1991), Gardner (1991, 1992), Frankel (1993), and Yapko (1994b), they wrote: "The *moderate false memory position* is represented by clinicians and memory scientists who have been concerned about overzealous therapeutic methods used with adults and investigative methods used in child sexual abuse allegations" (p. 39). Those taking this position have criticized therapist naivete and "incest resolution therapy" that is too narrowly focused and formulaic and that neglects other pertinent life issues and events or other therapeutic modalities (Haaken & Schlaps, 1991). They have challenged an overreliance on the idea of repressed memory versus other mechanisms of forgetting, the confounding of historical and narrative truth in some of the approaches to the treatment of dissociative disorders (MPD in particular) (Ganaway, 1989), and the lack of knowledge about issues of hypnosis and memory in a significant number of therapists (based upon survey findings from convenience samples of therapists) (Yapko, 1994a, 1994b). They have also criticized the overreliance upon a wide variety of techniques they view as suggestive, saving special criticism for the overacceptance or overinterpretation of memory material produced through these techniques, especially in individuals who previously had no memory or awareness of having been abused. According to Brown et al., the moderate position is in keeping with the original scientific position of the False Memory Syndrome Foundation.

By comparison, Brown et al. (1998) write the following about the extreme position, exemplified by the writings of Loftus (1993), Loftus and Ketcham (1994), Ofshe and Watters (1993, 1994), Spanos (1994), Underwager and Wakefield (1990), and Wakefield and Underwager (1992):

> The *extreme false memory position* is best reflected in the writings of Elizabeth Loftus. Based on two decades of laboratory research on eyewitness suggestibility (the misinformation effect), Loftus has attempted to demonstrate that misleading post-event information can significantly transform the original memory for an event. She has interpreted these research findings to mean that memories for nonexistent events can be "implanted" or "created" and that individuals can be made to accept and believe with a high degree of confidence false memories for events that never happened. While no research data on false memory creation in psychotherapy per se yet exist, Loftus has readily generalized her findings from eyewitness studies to psychotherapy. (p. 41)

The authors go on to describe how the original position associated with the False Memory Syndrome Foundation broadened considerably quite soon after its introduction to include many premises that could be considered part of the extreme position:

> The more controversial assumptions or claims made by at least some members of the FMSF's Scientific Advisory [sic] Board and/or by attorneys associated with the FMSF include: dissociated amnesia for child-

hood sexual abuse does not exist; recovered memories are necessarily inaccurate; recovered memories of childhood sexual abuse or ritual abuse are necessarily caused by therapeutic suggestion; psychotherapy is a form of coercive persuasion; dissociative identity disorder does not exist and is an iatrogenic product of psychotherapy; and professional trauma treatment is a form of memory recovery therapy. (p. 19)

Additionally, others extrapolated from Loftus's perspective to an even more extreme false memory perspective. Drawing from their own work on mind control/thought reform and cults, Ofshe and colleagues likened patients to victims (Ofshe & Singer, 1994; Ofshe & Watters, 1994). Their victimizers are their therapists who, through a combination of social influence, suggestion, and hypnosis, implant memories of past abuse, which they then reinforce through rehearsal and techniques of interpersonal influence. Ofshe and Watters went so far as to label "recovered memory therapy" as "quackery" and the "greatest psychiatric hoax of the Twentieth Century," its widespread use a form of brainwashing that is highly damaging to both patients and falsely accused innocent families.

Wherever they fall on the continuum, those on the false memory side of the argument are fairly unimpressed by the traumatic stress viewpoint regarding repressed/dissociated memory and the available data used to buttress it, *especially when memory for abuse has been totally absent before its recovery, whether within or outside of therapy.* As noted in chapter 1, the false memory perspective is now routinely used to defend against charges of contemporaneous abuse, especially when these allegations are made in the midst of a divorce and child custody dispute. This position is now being buttressed with the false memory perspective and research findings regarding the suggestibility of children.

The Traumatic Stress Rebuttal and Countercritique

Trauma therapists and researchers have responded in several ways. They have expressed concern about irresponsible and misguided therapeutic practices and about false memories and false accusations against innocent parties but have also challenged many of the charges as exaggerated and overgeneralized. They have further countered that therapists as a group have been unfairly scapegoated and painted as victimizers of their patients who routinely and exclusively use RMT techniques to surface absent memories. Additionally, psychotherapy has been misrepresented to the public through the confounding of self-help modalities and fringe-type therapies with professional treatment. Traumatic stress advocates have nevertheless reviewed the critiques and, in response to those evaluated as the most legitimate and reasonable, established guidelines for more neutral and nonsuggestive clinical practice.

The countercritics also have refuted the memory researchers' contention that recovered memories are not possible and that none has been corroborated. They have urged scientists to study the phenomenon of recovered memory rather than rejecting it out of hand. Arguing against the assertion that the defense mechanism of repression has no research substantiation, they have challenged memory researchers to look beyond repression to other defensive operations and psychic mechanisms (including motivated forgetting) that could lead to memory loss. Finally, they have challenged the ecological validity and generalizability of many laboratory studies of memory of normal events to traumatic circumstances. They strongly suggest that memory researchers include attention to real and personally experienced trauma in their investigations before assuming that the established parameters of memory for normal events always and automatically apply in cases of psychic trauma. They point to an emerging literature on clinical and field study observations documenting memory disturbances across a variety of traumatic circumstances, in support of the possibility that traumatic memory might differ from normal event memory.

THE CONTENTIOUSNESS OF THE DEBATE AND WORKING TOWARD MIDDLE GROUND AND PROFESSIONALISM

> The debate over memories of traumatic experience has itself become a traumatic experience for clinicians, patients, family members, and researchers. Increasingly, it has come to pit therapists, trauma survivors, and researchers on child abuse against families, sociologists, and researchers on memory. As is often the case in such situations, each side has come to take a rather one-dimensional view of the other. The "recovered memory" movement sees criticism as a shield behind which child abusers hide, whereas the "false memory" movement accuses psychotherapists of using their professional credentials as a hunting license, with family reputations being fair game.
>
> This issue is too important to be left to the domain of accusation. (Butler & Spiegel, 1997, p. II–13)

The descriptions given in the previous section concerning the main issues of the controversy do not do justice to the fierceness, intensity, and even the destructiveness with which some of the positions have been held. Extremists/activists on both sides of the issue have, at times, used vigilante and harassment tactics that have caused personal and professional damage, all in the interest of preventing damage as they understand it. Over the years, there have been reports of phone harassment; denunciations, ridiculing, and *ad hominen* attacks in the media, via e-mail, and on the internet; defamatory letters written to third parties; picketing of offices and homes; physical assaults, restraining orders, and jail sentences; threats of physical and sexual assault and even death threats; civil and criminal charges and proceedings for assault and for professional malpractice; threatened or actual complaints to state licensing and ethics boards; and derogatory and misleading characterizations of "one side" by the "other" (Calof, 1997; Lindsay, 1997; Lindsay & Briere, 1997; Pope, 1996). Obviously, such a heated environment impedes a stance of professionalism and presents major obstacles to collegiality and rationality in finding middle ground.

This debate has been framed and presented to the public as a scientific one, but it certainly has major political aspects as well (Brown et al., 1998; Courtois, 1997a); Pezdek and Banks (1996) introduced their book, *The Recovered Memory/False Memory Debate*, which presents a continuum of issues and perspectives in the controversy, with the difficulties they found in trying to maintain a median position:

> We tried to hew a middle course, looking for value on all sides, but the middle road here is more like a tightrope than a broad viaduct. To keep in the middle is to do battle with an unstable equilibrium. Look at one set of evidence, and the damage done by the false memories seems of overwhelming importance. Look at another set, and anger boils at the perpetrators who are able to humiliate and dismiss their victims with accusations of false memories. An additional lure pulling us away from the center is the chemistry of the debate on the issues and the temptation to use evidence to battle an opponent rather than to find the truth. (p. xii)

Factors Contributing to the Contentiousness of the Debate

It is helpful to understand some of the political and social factors (in addition to the sociohistorical events and issues discussed in chapter 1) that have led to such contentiousness. This will enable us to put the debate in some perspective and to avoid some of the most obvious pitfalls that have impeded collaborative understanding of the topic (Lindsay & Briere, 1997).

First, many terms and positions have been dichotomized into extreme positions that are overly simplistic and unhelpful. Some examples of this stance include: (a) seeing all members of one's "side" as good and those of the other as bad; (b) bifurcating memories into all-or-nothing polarities rather than placing them along a continuum; (c) viewing individuals with continuous memories as good or exemplary and those with memory gaps and recovered memories as deficient and flawed (i.e., "good" victims versus "bad" victims); (d) viewing recovered memories as always false or, alternately, as always veridical. Positions of this sort may make good "sound bites" to be picked up and publicized by the media or delivered in the courtroom without regard to the supporting data, but they do not present the entire picture and they certainly conceal the complexities of the issues (Lindsay & Briere, 1997).

As discussed previously, the topic of child sexual abuse (and particularly incest) is highly emotional and volatile. Many in the debate have personal involvement in it either as victims themselves, as victim advocates who have worked towards societal recognition and prevention of further abuse, as therapists who treat victims directly and experience their anguish, as those who assist falsely accused individuals and experienced their anguish, as those who have been falsely accused, and as abusers with a need for a potent defense. To some, the debate represents a true backlash against the societal uncovering of the prevalence of violence against women and children and serves to overshadow the real issue and its gravity while protecting those who have a vested interest in its continuance. To others, it is a corrective against legislative and therapeutic excesses that end up creating false accusations due to sloppy technique and overzealousness on the part of investigators and therapists.

Longstanding rifts between researchers and practitioners (especially in psychology where the schism between scientists and practitioners has had a long history) also contribute. Academically-oriented researchers are trained to approach problems in different ways and to use different methods of reasoning than are clinically-oriented practitioners. These differing epistemologies, world views, research methods, work settings, and applications have given rise to separate professional languages and divergent ways of thinking and understanding. It has also routinely led to dismissal or devaluation of each other's position. In many ways, the controversy reflects and builds upon some of the most obvious science-practice differences. This has led to the making of artificial distinctions between the two sides and alignment with one side *or* the other. It has been assumed, for example, that because experimentalists and academics tend to be more aligned with the false memory position, they are exclusively in the false memory camp. It has also been assumed that, because practitioners work predominantly in clinical versus research settings, that they, as a group, are ascientific or ignorant about research methods and findings and are exclusively in the traumatic stress position. In reality, as noted by Lindsay and Briere (1997), many professionals practice as both scientists and practitioners and are not exclusively aligned with one side or the other (e.g., some practitioners are among those who have questioned memory recovery techniques—Ganaway, 1989; Haaken & Schlaps, 1991; McHugh, 1992—and some academics have presented data that argue against or tone down some of the predominant memory critiques or that offer support for the recovered memory position—Freyd, 1997; Pezdek, 1994; Williams, 1994b). It is true, however, that these voices (often calling for moderation and thoughtfulness about the valid points of the other side) have been blunted in the raucousness of the debate as it has evolved.

Differences in terminology and the way key terms are understood and used has been another impediment to communication between the two camps. Recovered memories have been posited by some to be the result of a special form of repression, variously described as "robust" or "massive," while for others they have no such association to such a special mechanism. Similarly, recovered memories can be seen as impossible, because there is little or no empirical support for the concept of repression, yet repression is certainly not the only mechanism by which memory can be lost. On the other hand, repression should not be viewed as a mechanism that secures intact memories to be recovered in whole and in totally accurate detail in adulthood (Pezdek & Banks, 1996, p. xiii). "Amnesia" is another term that holds different connotations. For many proponents of the traumatic stress position, it connotes loss of memory (through a variety of mechanisms, including dissociation) for the experiencing of an event that happened. For memory scientists, its use is problematic for that very reason; its use presupposes that an event did happen and thus it is not appropriate terminology to describe an event that did not occur (Read, 1997).

Similarly, the scope of the problem and the relative emphasis placed on certain issues by each side have contributed to miscommunication and misunderstanding. Traumatic stress proponents, by and large, believe that most individuals retain all or part of their memory (or have partial or selective amnesia) for traumatic events. In contrast, some of the false memory proponents have made it sound as though the return of complete and pristine memory after its absence for years and with no prior inkling of past abuse is the norm. It is obvious that both of these circumstances exist and are documented, yet they do not occur with the same frequency. Commentators must make every attempt to be as specific as possible in their communications and to make clear what type of memory loss and its relative frequency they are discussing. They should also avoid grossly overgeneralizing their perspective beyond the available data.

Finding Common Ground

At the present time, to use several clichés, "the heat is beginning to be turned down" and attempts are being made to not "throw the baby out with the bathwater" (Whitfield, 1995), as the "dust settles" from the early and extremist positions in the debate and as "cooler heads" prevail. According to Butler (1996), "the black and white debate is shading into gray." Several events and efforts are making this possible. The irrational and extreme polarization of issues and the destructive potential (as well as the actual damage done to date) have been increasingly criticized and challenged by moderates and the leaders of professional associations (Fox, 1995). Many have been offended by both the rhetoric and the hubris of those at the furthest extremes and have called for restraint and toning down. The moderates have become more vocal over time and have worked to increase communication and to find points of commonality and agreement (Courtois, 1995c; Lindsay, 1997; Lindsay & Briere, 1997; Pezdek & Banks, 1996). The media coverage has changed as well. Butler, in her 1996 update to her earlier reports on the controversy, noted that "in the last four years, more than a dozen cases of well-corroborated recovered memory have surfaced and the popular press has begun to back off from the notion that all recovered memories are bogus." Press coverage has decreased and become less frenzied (with the exception of reports of some large settlements in therapist lawsuits), as the controversy has grown stale, become "old news" and therefore much less interesting as a source of ratings and income for the media. This media stand-down has resulted in less need to rigidly adhere to and defend positions and has thus allowed greater communication between less-guarded commentators on both sides.

Data have been collected in these intervening years that support both perspectives and that have also caused proponents of each position to pause and reflect. A more complex picture of traumatic and false memories has emerged. These provide corroboration for recovered memories as well as substantiation for false memories. Recovered memory does not automatically mean false memory, a denial or retraction does not automatically mean that abuse or trauma did not occur, and memories for traumatic events are not ever present and never lost. As a continuum of memory possibilities becomes more obvious, it is also apparent that much can be learned from studying those who have reported recovered memories and those who have reported false memories (in those cases where corroboration of the respective position is available). Moreover, it has become apparent that each case is idiosyncratic and requires assessment and determination according to its own merits.

Collaborative efforts have begun. An example of progress in this direction is the North American Treaty Organization (NATO) Advanced Studies Institute on "Recollections of Trauma" that took place in 1996. More than one hundred experts with diverse and varied professional backgrounds and interest in the topic met over the course of the 11-day institute to debate and discuss the issues. The conference participants were representative of the many researchers and clinicians who recognize the necessity of continuing to support and offer treatment for survivors of abuse and trauma. They were simultaneously interested in giving proper attention to excesses and iatrogenic influences in therapy practice that have created some of the difficulties while halting the overgeneralization of findings from laboratory to clinical and other real world settings (Lindsay & Briere, 1997). The proceedings of this conference have recently been published (Read & Lindsay, 1997). They provide a fascinating compendium of the complex issues and perspectives involved as well as a glimpse at collaborative possibilities.

Finally, a number of professional working groups have studied the issues and reported their findings. These panels of experts have also been important in calling for greater professionalism and moderation and in heightening the urgency for finding common ground. Their reports have helped to articulate the major scientific and practice issues in the debate, as well as future directions. These are presented in considerable detail in the next section.

Findings and Recommendations of Professional Association Task Forces and Working Groups

From early on, it was evident that the controversy over recovered memories had the potential to be extremely impactful, to threaten many of the traditional foundations of clinical practice, and to sully the public's view of and confidence in psychotherapy. Consequently, almost immediately, professional associations responded by impaneling groups of experts to study the issues and to make recommendations to their membership and to the public. In general, the professional reports share certain content similarity, but in some of the reports the positions taken are clearly shaped by the allegiance or bias of members to one side of the debate or the other. Despite some obvious shortcomings, these reports are helpful in determining preliminary points of agreement and in delineating important scientific and clinical issues. The issues covered and the recommendations made in the various reports were recently compared and contasted by Grunberg and Ney (1997). Their review is discussed in chapter 8.

Many of the major reports are reviewed here in chronological order by date of publication; the executive summaries of some additional reports are presented in Appendix B.

The American Psychiatric Association

"The Statement on Memories of Sexual Abuse" (American Psychiatric Association Board of Directors, 1993) was the first report to be published and a forerunner of the others. The statement is fairly evenhanded in its approach to both sides of the issue and begins as follows:

> This statement is in response to the growing concern regarding memories of sexual abuse. The rise in reports of documented cases of child sexual abuse has been accompanied by a rise in reports of sexual abuse that cannot be documented. Members of the public, as well as members of mental health and other professions, have debated the validity of some memories of sexual abuse, as well as some of the therapeutic techniques which have been used. The American Psychiatric Association has been concerned that the passionate debates about these issues have obscured the recognition of a body of scientific evidence that underlies widespread agreement among psychiatrists regarding psychiatric treatment in this area. We are especially concerned that the public confusion and dismay over this issue and the possibility of false accusations not discredit the reports of patients who have indeed been traumatized by actual previous abuse. *While much more needs to be known,* this statement summarizes information about this topic that is important for psychiatrists in their work with patients for whom sexual abuse is an issue. (italics added)

The Statement goes on to address issues of working neutrally with memory issues brought to treatment given that: "It is not known how to distinguish, with complete accuracy, memories based on true events from those derived from other sources. "The authors of the statement show sensitivity to abused patients and caution against automatically disbelieving reports of abuse, yet additionally caution against pressuring patients to believe in events that may not have occurred. Psychiatrists (and other mental health professionals) are reminded that a treatment plan that addresses all of the patient's clinical concerns (not just memory issues) should be drawn up, based upon the findings of a comprehensive assessment. Therapists are advised to caution patients and help them assess the impact of any extratherapeutic action and life decisions and to help those patients with unclear memories that do not clarify or resolve to adapt to the uncertainty. Finally, psychiatrists are urged not to abandon their commitment to the basic principles of ethical practice as delineated in *The Principles of Medical Ethics with Annotations Especially Applicable to Psychiatry,* especially as they concern "public statements about the veracity or other features of individual reports of sexual abuse" and "the impact of their conduct on the boundaries of the doctor/patient relationship."

The American Medical Association

In 1994, the American Medical Association Council on Scientific Affairs issued "Memories of Childhood Abuse," a fairly balanced report in response to Substitute Resolution 504, A-9e, which states, "The AMA considers the technique of 'memory enhancement' in the area of childhood sexual abuse to be fraught with problems of potential misapplication." After reviewing the issues and related AMA and American Psychiatric Association policy, the Scientific Affairs Council wrote:

> The resolution was adopted in response to concerns about the growing number of cases in which adults make accusations of having been abused as children based solely on memories developed in therapy. In many cases the accusations are made against the parents of the accuser, although others, such as members of the clergy, teachers and camp counselors, have been targets of allegations. Questions have been raised about the veracity of such reported memories, one's ability to recall such memories, the techniques used to recover these memories, and the role of the therapist in developing the memories.
>
> The general issues have come to be referred to under the umbrella term "repressed memories" or "recovered memories." Both terms refer to those memories reported as new recollections, with *no* previous memories of the event or circumstances surrounding the event, although some "fragments" of the event may have existed. Considerable controversy has arisen in the therapeutic community over the issue, and experts from varied professional backgrounds can be found on all sides of the issue. At one extreme are those who argue that such repressed memories do not occur, that they are false memories,

created memories, or implanted memories, while the other extreme strongly supports not only the concept of repressed memories but the possibility of recovering such memories in therapy. Other professionals believe that some memories may be false and others may be true.

The Council on Scientific Affairs issued the following conclusions and recommendations:

> The AMA has a long history of concern about the extent and effects of child abuse. Child abuse, particularly child sexual abuse, is underrecognized and all too often its existence is denied. Its effects can be profound and long-lasting. The Council on Scientific Affairs recommends that the following statements be adopted:
>
> 1. That the AMA recognize that few cases in which adults make accusations of childhood sexual abuse based on recovered memories can be proved or disproved and it is not yet known how to distinguish true memories from imagined events in these cases.
> 2. That the AMA encourage physicians to address the therapeutic needs of patients who report memories of childhood sexual abuse and that these needs exist quite apart from the truth or falsity of any claims.
> 3. That Policy 515.978 be amended to read as follows: The AMA considers "memory enhancement" in the area of childhood sexual abuse to produce results of uncertain authenticity, and therefore that efforts to enhance memories should be exercised with great care and only by properly trained professionals who are skilled in the application of the associated techniques and that all memories recovered with these techniques be considered seriously, although subject to external verification.
> 4. That the AMA encourage physicians treating possible adult victims of childhood abuse to subscribe to the *Principles of Medical Ethics* when treating their patients and that psychiatrists pay particular attention to the *Principles of Medical Ethics with Annotations Especially Applicable to Psychiatry.*
> 5. That Policy 80.996, which deals with the refreshing of recollections by hypnosis, be reaffirmed.

Although this document is fairly well-balanced, Brown et al. (1998) criticized the last statement reaffirming Policy 80.996 regarding hypnosis and memory inaccuracy as failing to take into account the current state of knowledge about hypnosis (see Brown et al., 1998, and Scheflin & Shapiro, 1989, for a discussion of the AMA policy on hypnosis).

The American Psychological Association

The American Psychological Association Working Group on the Investigation of Memories of Childhood Abuse[1] met over the course of two and a half years beginning in 1993 with the charge of reviewing the literature on memory, trauma, and child abuse and making recommendations regarding clinical and forensic practice and research. Its membership was made up of three clinicians associated with the traumatic stress perspective and three memory researchers, one of whom was the leading spokesperson for the FMSF Advisory Board and thus strongly identified with the false memory position. This composition made arriving at consensus difficult and resulted in the most split of the professional reports to be issued, and one that has not been particularly well publicized or well received; nevertheless, the perspectives of both sides are broadly represented in the 239-page final report (American Psychological Association, 1996b).

In 1994, the Working Group issued its first set of findings in the form of an interim report. Key points of agreement among members of the Working Group were listed as interim conclusions (American Psychological Association, 1994b). These were:

- Controversies regarding adult recollections should not be allowed to obscure the fact that child sexual abuse is a complex and pervasive problem in America, which has historically gone unacknowledged.
- Most people who were sexually abused as children remember all or part of what happened to them.
- However, it is possible for memories of abuse that have been forgotten for a long time to be remembered. The mechanism(s) by which such delayed recall occur(s) is/are not currently well understood.
- It is also possible to construct convincing pseudomemories for events that never occurred. The mechanism(s) by which these pseudomemories occur(s) is/are not currently well understood.
- There are gaps in our knowledge about the processes that lead to accurate and inaccurate recollections of childhood abuse.

The APA Board of Directors supplemented the interim report with the following points of guidance for the public and the profession:

---

[1] The author was one of the clinican members along with Judith L. Alpert, Ph.D. (cochair), and Laura S. Brown, Ph.D. Memory researcher members were Stephen J. Ceci, Ph.D., Elizabeth F. Loftus, Ph. D., and Peter A. Ornstein, Ph.D. (cochair).

- There is no single set of symptoms that automatically means that a person was a victim of childhood abuse.
- All therapists must approach questions of childhood abuse from a neutral position.
- The public should be wary of two kinds of therapists: those who offer instant childhood abuse diagnoses, and those who dismiss claims or reports of sexual abuse without exploration.
- When seeking psychotherapy, the public is advised to see a licensed practitioner with training and experience in the issues for which treatment is sought.

In the Final Report issued in 1996 (American Psychological Association, 1996b), members of the Working Group reiterated their common agreement on the key points of the Interim Report. Yet they also highlighted the significant differences in the perspectives of the researcher and clinician members. They wrote:

> As significant as these areas of agreement are, it is equally if not more important to acknowledge frankly that we differ markedly on a wide range of issues. At the core, the clinical and research subgroups have fundamentally differing views of the nature of memory. These contrasting conceptions of memory have led to debate concerning (a) the constructive nature of memory and the accuracy with which any events can be remembered over extended delays; (b) the tentative mechanisms that may underlie delayed remembering; (c) the presumed "special" status of memories of traumatic events; (d) the relevance of the basic memory and developmental literatures for understanding the recall of stressful events; (e) the rules of evidence by which we can test hypotheses about the consequences of trauma and the nature of remembering; (f) the frequency with which pseudomemories may be created by suggestion, both within and outside of therapy; and (g) the ease with which, in the absence of external corroborative evidence, "real" and pseudomemories may be distinguished. (p. 2)

The Working Group noted the very different training and epistemologies between those psychologists who study memory and those who study and treat trauma and called for steps to resolve these differences and develop consensual definitions about what is being studied and discussed. They then went on to make recommendations for clinical and forensic practice and for research and training. The clinical recommendations are presented below. Concerning practice:

The deliberations of the Working Group strongly underscore the importance of a careful and science-based preparation for practice in psychology. Many possible errors in working with adult survivors, or with clients who present as recovering memories of childhood abuse, could be avoided if the therapist were well-grounded in developmental psychology (particularly developmental psychopathology and cognitive development), cognitive psychology (especially the study of memory), and research on trauma (with emphasis on the range of responses to interpersonal violence). Both the scientist practitioner (Ph.D.) and the scholar-practitioner (Psy.D.) models of training embrace this necessity. Given the very high rates of histories of some kinds of interpersonal violence among the patient population (Jacobson & Richardson, 1987), all doctoral level training programs in professional psychology, including those whose primary focus is the training of clinical researchers, should insure that students are exposed to formal course work and supervised practica in which the role of interpersonal violence as a risk factor for psychopathology is central. (p. 4)

A second important implication of our findings for clinical practice is that care, caution, and consistency should be utilized in working with any client, and particularly one who experiences what is believed (by either client or therapist) to be a recovered memory of trauma.

. . . When clients report what they phenomenologically experience as memories of previously unrecollected trauma, therapists should take a number of steps to avoid imposing a particular version of reality on these experiences and to reduce risks of the creation of pseudomemories. If these materials are intrusive and create problems for the client's functioning, the first goal of treatment should be stabilization and containment following the recommendations of many experts in the field of trauma treatment. It is important to remember that the goal of therapy is not archeology; recollection of trauma is only helpful insofar as it is integrated into a therapy emphasizing improvement of functioning. Therapists should avoid endorsing such retrievals as either clearly truthful or clearly confabulated. Instead, the focus should be on aiding the client in developing his or her own sense of what is real and truthful. Clients can be encouraged to search for information that would add to their ability to find themselves credible . . . and to carefully weigh the evidence. Therapists should consider all alternative hypotheses, including: (a) that the retrieved material is a reasonably accurate memory of real events; (b) that it is a distorted memory of real events, with distortions due to developmental factors or source contaminations; (c) that it is a confabulation emerging from underlying psychopathology or difficulties with reality testing; (d) that it is a pseudomemory emerging from exposure to suggestions; or (e) that it is a form of self-suggestion emerging from the client's internal suggestive mechanism. (pp. 5–6)

The section concludes with the following:

> In short, a responsible path for therapists to pursue is one in which clients are empowered to be the authority about their own lives and reality, where the emphasis is on recovery and function, and where memories of trauma are viewed within the context of what one might tentatively assume to be a post-traumatic response. This approach, however, may mean that clients occasionally reach conclusions about what may have happened to them that we find difficult to accept. Nonetheless, respect for the dignity of adults who seek treatment must inevitably temper therapists' efforts at reality testing. Therapists need to eschew the roles of advocate, detective, or ultimate arbiter of reality, unless the veracity of the material being constructed/retrieved becomes important for either therapeutic or legal reasons. (p. 7)

The American Society of Clinical Hypnosis

In 1994, 11 members of the American Society for Clinical Hypnosis (ASCH) task force on memory and hypnosis released their report, "Clinical Hypnosis and Memory: Guidelines for Clinicians and Forensic Hypnosis," following a comprehensive review and critique of the relevant literature (Hammond et al., 1994). The report contained four sections: (1) current concepts about memory and factors influencing memory; (2) the current state of scientific research on hypnosis and memory; (3) ASCH recommendations for clinicians working with hypnosis and memory with patients who may have been abused; and (4) recommendations for the conduct of forensic hypnosis. This report has been viewed as balanced by some (Brown et al., 1998)[2] and has been criticized as unbalanced and much too lenient in its position vis-à-vis the utility of hypnosis for memory retrieval by others (Lynn, Myers, & Malinoski, 1997) and as leaning too far in the traumatic stress direction.

Some of the major findings resulting from the task force's comprehensive review and critique of the literature are the following, as reported by Hammond (1995):

---

[2] D. Corydon Hammond, Ph.D., coauthor of Brown, Scheflin, and Hammond (1998), was the primary author of the ASCH report and Alan Scheflin, J.D., L.L.M., M.A., was a member of the task force.

- Memory can be malleable and may be influenced by external, contemporary influences (emotional and traumatic memories, however, are very different from the normal memory processes usually studied in the laboratory by academic researchers).
- Traumatic amnesia exists and may occur in response to natural disasters, war-time situations, sexual or physical abuse, burns, or accidents. The legitimate questions is not whether amnesia—or repressed memory—exists, but rather how frequently it occurs.
- Forgotten memories may be recovered later in life.
- Hypnosis may facilitate the increased recall of memory, but the only way to know if a memory—whether it is recalled in therapy, through hypnosis, or is spontaneous—is accurate is through independent corroboration.
- Pseudomemories or false beliefs can occur and can be produced in or out of therapy and with or without hypnosis. Research clearly documents, however, that hypnosis and the use of hypnotic age-regression are not the factors responsible for the production of pseudomemories. False memories may be produced just as easily without hypnosis. The primary variables involved in such instances include hypnotizability level (this is not to be confused with the actual use of hypnosis; rather, it means that people with higher hypnotizability are more prone to produce distortions in hypnotic or nonhypnotic situations), social influence (e.g., leading questions and suggestions from peers, media, groups, or therapists), the patient's expectations and beliefs prior to treatment, and recall of an event that is unclear and nonverifiable, but is perceived by the person as likely to have occurred.
- False memories for entire events of a traumatic nature may be much more difficult to produce than are pseudomemories for details produced in laboratories. Even when hypnotic suggestions produce pseudomemory reports, most people, once they are interviewed by another experimenter away from the laboratory setting, can distinguish genuine from suggested memories. Thus, much of this research may be producing "reports" that represent response bias and demand characteristics rather than genuine distortions of memory. (p. 1)

Therapist guidelines for working with hypnosis and memory with patients who may have been abused direct that the practitioner be educated and qualified in the use of hypnosis, thoroughly evaluate the patient in general and in terms of hypnotic responsivity, educate the patient regarding hypnosis and memory (including issues of neutral expectations concerning the production of new or accurate memories and of inquiry during hypnosis) and gain informed consent, keep adequate documentation and records, be neutrally supportive of the patient, discourage confrontation or legal action on the basis of memories alone without corroboration, discourage involvement in activities that are potentially contaminating regarding abuse issues, avoid verifying as accurate the patient's memories, and be aware of "red flag" patients and issues. (see Table 8.4 on page 295 for a listing).

Recommendations were also made for the conduct of forensic hypnosis. Because these are less pertinent to the topic under discussion in this book, they are not reproduced. The interested reader is referred to section 4 of the task force report.

The British Psychological Society

The Report of the Working Party of the British Psychological Society was issued in 1995. The Working Party had been charged with "reporting on the scientific evidence relevant to the current debate concerning recovered memories of trauma and with commenting on the issues surrounding this topic" (British Psychological Society, 1995, p. 373). Its members reviewed the scientific literature, carried out a survey of relevant members of The British Psychological Society, scrutinized the records of the British False Memory Society, and issued a report that is fairly well-balanced but has been criticized by some as leaning too much in the recovered memory/traumatic stress direction. The reader will note, however, the congruence of some of the main points and recommendations of this report with those of the others reviewed above and below.

The Working Party listed the following conclusions in the executive summary section of its report:

> • Complete or partial memory loss is a frequently reported consequence of experiencing certain kinds of psychological traumas including childhood sexual abuse. These memories are sometimes fully or partially recovered after a gap of many years.
> • Memories may be recovered within or independent of therapy. Memory recovery is reported by highly experienced and well-qualified therapists who are well aware of the dangers of inappropriate suggestion and interpretation.
> • In general, the clarity and detail of event memories depends on a number of factors, including the age at which the event occurred. Although clear memories are likely to be broadly accurate, they may contain significant errors. It seems likely that recovered memories have the same properties.

- Sustained pressure or persuasion by an authority figure could lead to the retrieval or elaboration of "memories" of events that never actually happened. The possibility of therapists creating in their clients false memories of having been sexually abused in childhood warrants careful consideration, and guidelines for therapists are suggested here to minimize the risk of this happening. There is no reliable evidence at present that this is a widespread phenomenon in the United Kingdom.

- In a recent review of the literature on recovered memories, Lindsay and Read (1994) commented that "the ground for debate has shifted from the question of the possibility of therapy-induced false beliefs to the question of the prevalence of therapy-induced false beliefs." We agree with this comment but add to it that the ground for debate has also shifted from the question of the possibility of recovery of memory from total amnesia to the question of the prevalence of recovery of memory from total amnesia.

The following were the overall conclusions of the Working Party's report:

- Normal event memory is largely accurate but may contain distortions and elaborations.

- With certain exceptions, such as where there has been extensive rehearsal of an imagined event, the source of our memories is generally perceived accurately.

- Nothing can be recalled accurately from before the first birthday and little from before the second. Poor memory from before the fourth birthday is normal.

- Forgetting of certain kinds of trauma is often reported, although the nature of the mechanism or mechanisms involved remains unclear.

- Although there is a great deal of evidence for incorrect memories, there is currently much less evidence on the creation of false memories.

- Hypnosis makes memory more confident and less reliable. It can also be used to create amnesia for events.

- There are a number of significant differences between false confessions and false (recovered) memories which preclude generalizing from one to the other.

- There are high levels of belief in the essential accuracy of recovered memories of child sexual abuse among qualified psychologists. These beliefs appear to be fueled by the high levels of experience of recovered memories both for CSA and for non-CSA traumatic events. The nondoctrinaire nature of these beliefs is indicated by the high level of acceptance of the possibility of false memories.

- There is not a lot of evidence that accusers fit a single profile. From the British records, at least, there is no good evidence that accusers have invariably recovered memories from total amnesia. Further documentation of the phenomenon is needed by the False Memory societies in order to obtain a more reliable picture. It appears that only in a small minority of instances do the accusations concern abuse that ended before the age of 5.
- Guidelines can be laid down for good practice in therapy.

The Working Party further made a number of recommendations: that training courses include appropriate attention to the properties of human memory, that increased priority be given to research in the areas covered in the report, that the findings of the report be taken into consideration when psychotherapy services are reviewed as to the quality of services and training, that appropriate parts of the report be brought to the attention of the general public, and that chartered psychologists who practice therapy do so in accordance with their guidelines for therapists. These guidelines are as follows:

1. It may be necessary clinically for the therapists to be open to the emergence of memories of trauma that are not immediately available to the client's consciousness.
2. It is important for the therapist to be alert to the dangers of suggestion.
3. Although it is important always to take the client seriously, the therapist should avoid drawing premature conclusions about the truth of a recovered memory.
4. The therapist needs to tolerate uncertainty and ambiguity regarding the client's early experience.
5. Although it may be part of the therapists' work to help their clients to think about their early experiences, they should avoid imposing their own conclusions about what took place in childhood.
6. The therapist should be alert to a range of possibilities, for example, that a recovered memory may be literally true, metaphorically true, or may derive from fantasy or dream material.
7. If the role of the professional is to obtain evidence that is reliable in forensic terms, they need to restrict themselves to procedures that enhance reliability (e.g., use of the cognitive interview and avoidance of hypnosis or suggestion and leading questions).
8. CSA (child sexual abuse) should not be diagnosed on the basis of

presenting symptoms, such as an eating disorder, alone—there is a high probability of false positives, as there are other possible explanations for psychological problems.

The Canadian Psychiatric Association

In 1996, The Canadian Psychiatric Association issued "Adult Recovered Memories of Childhood Sexual Abuse," a paper prepared by its Education Council that ". . . does not refer to survivors of childhood abuse with continuous memories of their ill-treatment, nor does it deal with individuals who have recovered memories that have been corroborated. Serious concern exists about uncorroborated memories recovered in the course of therapy that is narrowly focussed on the enhancement of memory of what is hypothesized to be repressed sexual abuse. Differences of opinion have emerged about the frequency and the veracity of such recovered memories of sexual abuse, which have also been referred to as part of a 'false memory syndrome.'" (Canadian Psychiatric Association, 1996). The Council's report offered "brief advice to all members involved in circumstances where recovered memories of sexual abuse play a role" through these conclusions and recommendations:

- Sexual abuse at any age is deplorable and unacceptable and should always be given serious attention. All spontaneous reports should be treated with respect and concern and be carefully explored. Psychiatrists must continue to treat patients who report the recollection of childhood sexual abuse, accepting the current limitations of knowledge concerning memory, and maintain an empathic, nonjudgemental, neutral stance.
- Lasting serious effects of trauma at an early age very probably occur, but children who have been sexually abused in early childhood may be too young to accurately identify the event as abusive and to form a permanent explicit memory. Thus, without intervening cognitive rehearsal of memory, such experiences may not be reliably recalled in adult life.
- Reports of recovered memories of sexual abuse may be true, but great caution should be exercised before acceptance in the absence of solid corroboration. Psychiatrists should be aware that excessive emphasis on recovering memories may lead to misdirection of the treatment process and unduly delay appropriate therapeutic measures.
- Routine inquiry into past and present experience of all types of abuse should remain a regular part of psychiatric assessment. Psychiatrists should take particular care, however, to avoid inap-

propriate use of leading questions, hypnosis, narcoanalysis, or other memory enhancement techniques directed at the production of hypothesized hidden or lost material. This does not preclude traditional supportive psychotherapeutic techniques, based on strengthening coping mechanisms, cognitive psychotherapy, behavior therapy, or neutrally managed exploratory psychodynamic or psychoanalytic treatment.

- Since there are no well-defined symptoms or groups of symptoms that are specific to any type of abuse, symptoms that are said to be typical should not be used as evidence thereof.

- Reports of recovered memories that incriminate others should be handled with particular care. In clinical practice, an ethical psychiatrist should refrain from taking any side with respect to their use in accusations directed against the family or friends of the patient or against any third party. Confrontation with alleged perpetrators solely for the supposed curative effect of expressing anger should not be encouraged. There is no reliable evidence that such actions are therapeutic. On the contrary, this type of approach may alienate relatives and cause a breakdown of family support. Psychiatrists should continue to protect the best interests of their patients and of their supportive relationships.

- Further education and research in the specific areas of childhood sexual abuse and memory are strongly recommended. (p. 306)

Following the publication of this report, a number of Canadian psychiatrists responded in a letter to the members of the Education Council (Armstrong et al., 1996). In this letter, they expressed support for the timeliness and importance of the position statement but concern about a number of shortcomings they identified beginning with the membership of the Council, "most of whom seem to be operating outside of your areas of greatest interest and experience" and with terminology and interpretation, which they criticized as "following too closely the FMSF (False Memory Syndrome Foundation) agenda." They appended a suggested editing of the Position Statement that they believed maintained its original intent while avoiding the shortcomings identified in their letter and requested that the Council submit this version to the association Board of Directors for consideration.

We include some of their comments regarding identified shortcomings as illustration of the tensions and different professional positions in this debate:

1. The terminology "false memory syndrome" and "recovered memo-

ry therapy" were coined by the so-called "False Memory Syndrome Foundation" headquartered in Philadelphia, PA. The terminology has not independently occurred in the scientific literature. The FMSF is not a professional medical body, but a lay organization and legal defense lobby. It is professionally and scientifically inappropriate and misleading for the Canadian Psychiatric Association to incorporate nonprofessional, nonscientific nomenclature into an official Position Statement without accurately putting such nomenclature into its proper sociolegal context. The CPA ought not to act, nor seem to act, as a client organization of an American legal defense lobby.

2. The Position Statement follows too closely the FMSF agenda, which is narrowly preoccupied with the purported manufacture of false memories, and confrontation or legal pursuit of alleged perpetrators. The vast majority of cases that are of clinical relevance, however, are those where memories of childhood sexual abuse are first experienced in adulthood, but which involve no confrontation or legal pursuit of alleged perpetrators. The two issues are separate, and ought to be better teased out one from the other. In addition, the Position Statement contains valuable passages on memory in general and on diagnosis. The more rational agenda would be to deal first with memory in general, then with diagnosis, then with memory in therapy, and lastly with confrontation and accusation of alleged perpetrators.

3. The Position Statement neglects the following clinically significant groups of survivors of childhood sexual abuse: those who deny memories of ill-treatment, despite corroboration; those who experience memory of childhood sexual abuse *spontaneously* in adulthood; those with fluctuating awareness, who oscillate between clinical pictures of acute PTSD symptoms on the one hand, and amnesia with emotional blunting on the other. . . .

7. The Position Statement neglects the direct dangers to the patient of decompensation, suicidal gestures and rehospitalization that are often associated with planned or anticipatedconfrontation or accusation of alleged perpetrators. Clinically, such decompensation is more often encountered than disruption of family relationships, either because family relationships are already significantly disrupted, or because the decompensation prevents the confrontation from occurring.

8. The Position Statement is inconsistent on memory when it states: "When recovered memories are found to be false, family relationships are unnecessarily and often permanently disrupted." Just as

we ought not to conclude that so-called "recovered memories" are true, we ought not to conclude that recantations or legal decisions are true. Furthermore, even when so-called "recovered memories" are true, family relationships need not be disrupted, and may be improved, as may occur when the accused perpetrator confesses, corrects or embellishes an accusation and an estranged family relationship is mutually mourned and healed.

9. Hypnosis is mentioned twice, both times as a "memory recovery technique" (again borrowing from the FMSF) and lumped with narcoanalysis as well as with specific psychotherapeutic technical errors such as leading questions, pressure to recall and suggestion of abuse. . . . There are the following objections to this:

9a. hypnosis is generally disparaged in being linked with specific technical errors.

9b. it is unclear if the CPA is recommending that psychiatrists avoid *inappropriate* use of hypnosis, or rather recommending that it be avoided altogether.

9c. much psychiatric hypnosis has nothing to do with survivors of child sexual abuse, nor with enhancing memory. Even in patients who are, or who may be, survivors of child sexual abuse, much hypnosis still has little to do with enhancing memory, but rather with intrapsychic restructuring for the purpose of symptom control and the management of behavior, such as suicidality and self-mutilation, and the interruption of general decompensation that would otherwise require hospitalization. . . . The Position Statement should not, under any circumstances, condemn, nor seem to condemn, this useful medical modality. The Statement needs to accommodate the appropriate psychotherapeutic use of hypnosis, which according to the practice of many CPA members may constitute an essential therapeutic adjunct in the treatment of certain patients.

The National Association of Social Work

The National Council on the Practice of Clinical Social Work published "Evaluation and Treatment of Adults with the Possibility of Recovered Memories of Childhood Sexual Abuse" (National Association of Social Work, 1996). This balanced, albeit brief, report provided guidance for clinical social workers in the evaluation and treatment of their clients. The Council members wrote:

The validity of some recovered memories of sexual abuse has been the cause of passionate debate among mental health professionals, attorneys, and the public. In addition to the questions of validity of undocumented reports of sexual abuse and the therapeutic techniques used to elicit these techniques have been placed under scrutiny [*sic*]. Our concern is for the clients who believe they have been traumatized by childhood sexual abuse as well as the people who believe they have been falsely accused of being a sexual abuser. This statement addresses and reiterates the basic clinical and ethical principles and standards that NASW and the social work professional have followed, applied to the assessment and treatment of clients for whom the possibility of childhood sexual abuse may be present.

This report, like that of the American Psychiatric Association Statement, stressed the importance of a treatment plan based on a complete psychosocial and diagnostic assessment, of adequate documentation of the treatment, and of an adequate knowledge/competence base from which practitioners work on these issues. The authors further recommend that:

> Clinical social workers should explore with the client who reports recovering a memory of childhood abuse the meaning and implication of the memory for the client, rather than focusing solely on the content or veracity of the report. The client who reports recovering a memory of sexual abuse must be informed that it may be an accurate memory of an actual event, an altered or distorted memory of an actual event, or the recounting of an event that did not happen.

The following guidelines regarding the therapeutic relationship and the goals of treatment were issued:

- establish and maintain an appropriate therapeutic relationship with careful attention to boundary management
- recognize that the client may be influenced by the opinions, conjecture, or suggestions of the therapist
- not minimize the power and influence he or she has on a client's impressions and beliefs
- guard against engaging in self-disclosure and premature interpretations during the treatment process
- guard against using leading questions to recover memories
- be cognizant that disclosure of forgotten experience is a part of the process but not the goal of therapy
- respect the client's right to self-determination

The clinical social worker's role is to be empathetic, neutral, and non-judgmental. Awareness of one's own attitudes toward repressed memories is crucial. Attitudes of enthusiastic belief or disbelief can and will have an effect on the treatment process. The therapist's responsibility is to maintain the focus of treatment on symptom reduction or elimination and to enhance the ability of the client to function appropriately and comfortably in his or her daily life. (p. 2)

Finally, the group drew attention to the possible impact of a social worker's actions on a group not mentioned as directly in the other reports, namely third parties and the effect the treatment may have on others besides the client. Social workers need to be aware that a duty may be owed a family member who meets with the social worker and client to discuss the abuse. It is recommended that the purpose of the session be clarified and that all parties agree to participate with informed consent based on full notice obtained from all participating parties before such a meeting takes place.

The International Society for Traumatic Stress Studies

"Memories of childhood trauma" was issued in June of 1998 by the International Society for Traumatic Stress Studies.[3] The intent of the report was to comment on the current science base on the topics of trauma and memory. The report reviewed literature in five areas: (1) the prevalence and consequences of childhood trauma; (2) delayed recall of traumatic events after a period of forgetting; (3) human memory processes, traumatic memory, and delayed recall of traumatic events; (4) application of the current scientific knowledge base to clinical practice; and (5) application of the current scientific knowledge base to forensic practice (International Society for Traumatic Stress Studies, 1998). The summary and conclusions of this report are reproduced here:

Childhood trauma involving interpersonal violence occurs frequently and plays an important role in latter adult maladaptive functioning. Correspondent with a general increase in trauma-focused scholarship has been has been an increase in the knowledge about delayed recall of traumatic events and about memory processes relevant to an understanding of traumatic memories. We know that people forget childhood traumas and that this is not limited to people whose trauma is sexual abuse. We also know that people can accurately recall memories of documented childhood trauma that they report having previously forgot-

---

[3]The author was a contributor to this report.

ten, and that a wide range of triggers seems to be associated with these memories. Most memory recovery appears to be precipitated in situations that include cues that are similar to the original trauma and does not occur as a direct result of psychotherapy. However, it is possible, and indeed many would argue likely, that therapists who fail to conform to accepted standards of practice may promote a "recovered memory" of an event that never occurred.

While there is some evidence that recovered memories of childhood abuse can be as accurate as never-forgotten memories of childhood abuse, there is also evidence that memory is reconstructive and imperfect, that people can make very glaring errors in memory, that people are suggestible under some circumstances to social influence or persuasion when reporting memories for past events and that at least under some circumstances inaccurate memories can be strongly believed and convincingly described. While traumatic memories may be different than ordinary memories, we currently do not have conclusive scientific consensus on this issue. Likewise, it is not currently known how traumatic memories are forgotten or latter recovered. These are all fundamental questions that have stimulated a great deal of important research on the memory process in general and on traumatic memories in particular.

Trauma-focused approaches to assessment and treatment have also promoted a sophisticated articulation of the purpose, process, and standards of care. While competent therapists must provide a therapeutic environment in which recovered memories of childhood trauma can be addressed, they must also recognize that memory is fallible and that certain therapeutic approaches may increase the likelihood of distortion or confabulation. Professionals agree that there is no standard procedure for establishing the accuracy of recovered memories in individual cases and that in clinical practice, it is up to the patient to come up with his or her own conclusions about whether or not he or she was previously traumatized and about the specific details of such events. Professionals also agree that it is not the role of the therapist to instruct or pressure patients to take a particular course of action with the accused offenders and/or family members during the course of the therapy for childhood abuse.

There is a strong commitment in contemporary society to accurately identify perpetrators of child abuse, and it is as important that innocent people not be accused of such crime as it is that victims see their perpetrators held responsible. In the efforts of our legal and judicial systems to balance the rights and protection of both alleged victims and alleged perpetrators, the current scientific controversy concerning recovered memory has received considerable forensic attention and has led to a number of legal initiatives. Both alleged perpetrators and those held responsible for alleged false accusations, including therapists, have been targets of legal action. While there is not a standard protocol for the determination of the validity of the individual reports of recovered memories of childhood trauma, our current scientific knowledge base provides consensual and balanced information that can be essential in forensic practice.

In addition to all of these, a number of other documents and sets of general and specialty guidelines have been prepared or are currently in press. They are not included with the above either because they are not specific to the topic of recovered/false memory issues (e.g., The International Society for the Study of Dissociation, 1994, 1997, "Guidelines for the Treatment of Dissociative Identity Disorder"), are published by a committee or division of a major professional organization rather than the organization itself, are written by single or multiple authors rather than an association (Courtois, 1997a, 1997b; Enns, et al., 1998; Nagy, 1994) and/or are in preparation. The reader is directed to these (and others as they are released) for the most recently prepared professional consensus statements on issues of recovered/false memory. In all likelihood, they will continue to develop and shift according to emerging research and clinical findings and in response to the various political forces in effect. As suggested by the New Zealand Psychological Society report (included in Appendix B), a joint consensus statement from allied mental health bodies would be a beneficial undertaking at this point.

CURRENT STATUS OF SCIENTIFIC AND CLINICAL ISSUES

Taken alone and together, these task force reports identify and delineate the fundamental scientific and clinical issues and the unanswered questions in need of continued research. They are in agreement with the statement made by Pezdek and Banks (1996) from their review of the literature:

It is no longer productive to debate whether recovered childhood memories are true or false. It now seems clear that *some* recovered memories for childhood abuse are true and *some* are suggestively planted. We feel that the most compelling course for future research on the recovered memory/false memory debate is in the direction of investigating the conditions under which traumatic events are or are not likely to be repressed and the conditions under which recovered traumatic memories are or are not likely to be true, using, whenever possible, memory for real world traumatic events. (authors' italics) (p. 1)

Some of the core scientific issues are in this vein. Evidence has been gathered that substantiates the actuality and possibility of recovered memory and false memory (both in and outside of the context of psychotherapy), but relative prevalence of these occurrences have not been determined and are subject to very divergent speculation. Yet, as stated by the American Psychological Association Working Group, "the mechanisms by which they occur are not well understood" and "knowledge gaps exist about what leads to accurate and inaccurate recollections of abuse." Research substantiation of memory loss (or traumatic amnesia) in the aftermath of different types of trauma has also been forthcoming and is accumulating. Much remains to be learned, however, about the mechanisms of forgetting and later recovering memories of trauma, especially trauma that is complex and occurs repeatedly over an extended period of time. The study of memory in the aftermath of trauma has only been undertaken in recent years and clearly warrants much additional research to determine similarities to and differences from normal event memory.

It is recognized that memory is malleable but that conditions of encoding, storage, and retrieval might differ during an event that is traumatic versus one that is neutral or moderately stressful. It is also clear that memory can be influenced in a number of different ways and that recovered memory is not veridical. Issues of suggestibility need more research attention, particularly concerning conditions related to the acceptance of suggestion and whether whole, complex memories and associated psychiatric conditions can be suggested or implanted. Another vexing question concerns whether research on these issues in a laboratory setting are wholly generalizable to the conditions of psychotherapy. It is also unclear at present how frequently pseudomemories can be created and whether they can be created by other sources of ongoing influence besides psychotherapy and therapists. Finally, more research needs to be conducted to distinguish false memories and false beliefs and the conditions that might be related to the development of each.

As more balanced perspectives have taken hold, a synthesis is developing. The partial truths of both the false memory and trauma accuracy positions are being emphasized by a number of writers, among them Brown et al. (1998), Ceci (1994), Nash (1994), Pezdek and Banks (1996), Pope and Brown (1996), and Schooler (1994). It is also increasingly recognized that professionals engaged in different activities with different

Figure 2.1

2 x 2 Table of Abuse Versus Memory Status

Abuse Status

	Not abused	Abused
No Recall	True Negatives I	False Negatives II
Recall	False Positives III	True Positives IV

Memory Status

From "Perspectives on Adult Memories of Childhood Sexual Abuse: A Research Review," by L.A. Williams and V.L. Banyard, 1997. In D. Spiegel, Section Editor, *Repressed Memories, Section II of Review of Psychiatry, 16* (p. II–132), 1997, Washington DC: American Psychiatric Press. Copyright 1997 by American Psychiatric Press, Inc. Reprinted with permission.

goals have different vested interests. Both Nash (1994) and Williams and Banyard (1997b) discussed this in terms of a 2x2 table (see Figure 2.1). As the controversy has been set up, researchers have tended to be more interested in false positives (belief in abuse when it did not occur) and clinicians in false negatives (belief in no abuse when, in fact, it did occur). Obviously, both are important and, as the field develops and more synthesis occurs, both should be of equal concern to researchers and clinicians.

Ceci (1994) and Nash (1994) also used this false positive and false negative conceptualization in addressing the complexities of clinical practice with recovered memory issues. Therapists have the difficult task of increasing (or not suppressing) disclosure of genuine abuse while simultaneously decreasing the risk of false memory production. In other words, therapists must navigate with caution and steer clear of both false positives and false negatives.

Other issues in clinical practice warrant investigation. Research is needed to determine with more specificity what conditions and procedures are more rather than less likely to be suggestive and ways to control for them in clinical practice. Studies are also needed that provide data about memory recovery per se. How often does it occur and under what conditions? What gives rise to the spontaneous emergence of memories?

At the present time, no study has been conducted that tests the specific benefit of recovering memories that were previously unavailable. (Personal testimonies [Cheit, 1997; Fitzpatrick, 1997] have given a subjective perspective on both the pain the and perceived benefits of recovering memories and integrating emotions associated with past abuse. These, of course, could be counterbalanced by personal testimonies where individuals found the recovery of memories of past abuse to be harmful rather than beneficial.) Preliminary outcome studies have been conducted that support the utility of encouraging patients to address issues (including memories) of childhood trauma in individual and group treatment (Alexander, 1992; Jehu, 1988; Linehan, 1993; Pennebaker & Susman, 1988; Roth & Batson, 1997); however, much more detailed investigation is needed.

SUMMARY

This chapter has reviewed the major points made by both sides of the recovered/false memory controversy. The early years of the controversy were marked by intense polemic with little middle ground. Recently, the tone has shifted and a more collaborative and less adversarial approach has taken hold in professional circles. A number of professional task forces organized to study the issues involved and make recommendations for clinical, research, and forensic practice have issued their reports. These were reviewed in this chapter. By and large, they support aspects of each side of the controversy (i.e., recovered and delayed memories are possible, as are the creation of false memories) and urge clinicians, researchers, and forensic experts to practice conservatively within established professional standards and ethics and to not exceed the available scientific data in their respective endeavors. They also call for more collaborative study of memory in the aftermath to traumatization. All caution that the current controversy must not be used to obscure or deny the reality, prevalence, and seriousness of child abuse as a social issue but also indicate concern for the seriousness and destructiveness of false accusations.

Chapter 3

TRAUMA AND MEMORY

This chapter presents information about memory for traumatic events, the heart of the recovered/false memory controversy. At issue is whether such memory is encoded at the time of the trauma and later forgotten and recovered; what mechanisms are involved and in what form memory is recovered; the nature of traumatic memory and whether it differs from memory for nontraumatic events; and whether memory for trauma occurring in childhood differs from memory of trauma in adulthood. As discussed in chapter 2, the issue is contested between memory and trauma scientists. Among memory researchers, the prevailing view is that traumatic memory is not special and constitutes a variant of normal remembering and forgetting for stressful or emotional events. It must, therefore, follow the rules of normal event memory and not some special mechanism. From the perspective of many trauma researchers, however, traumatic memory is essentially different from normal event memory and so does not follow the same rules. Trauma proponents further believe that memories can be out of consciousness for years but still be present in the mind, especially when memory loss is due to dissociative amnesia and various forms of repression and suppression.

The literature reviewed in this chapter offers support for the view that traumatic memories can differ considerably from normal event memories due to the heightened psychobiological and physiological processes associated with the traumatization that affect how memories are encoded, stored, and retrieved. But, by the same token, they are not totally independent of the rules governing normal event memory and can contain inaccuracies. It is clear that additional research is needed to uncover the essential similarities and differences between traumatic and nontraumatic memories and the memories of children as opposed to those of adults.

This chapter begins with a description of the characteristics of traumatic events that differentiate them from events that are personally stressful but nontraumatic. This is followed by information on the continuum of possible posttraumatic reactions including posttraumatic stress disorder and the dissociative disorders. Of particular import to this discussion is the inclusion of memory impairments in the criteria for these diagnoses and the psychobiological and psychophysiological mechanisms of posttraumatic stress disorder that might relate to memory difficulties. This chapter also includes information on normal event memory against which to compare and contrast emerging information on traumatic memory. All of this information serves as background for understanding some of the memory disturbances that might result from experiences of traumatic child sexual abuse. Achieving a better understanding of memory for traumatic events in general and for childhood trauma in particular will enable us to address many of the issues raised in the controversy. This understanding will assist researchers and clinicians who study and treat trauma, provide bases for cases that reach the forensic setting, and establish the agenda for future research.

THE NATURE OF TRAUMA AND POSTTRAUMATIC REACTIONS

Defining Trauma

Before defining responses to trauma (including memory for the experience), let us discuss the nature of trauma, since the definition might affect the way the issue is understood and interpreted. Reviere (1996) noted:

> Trauma is defined in various ways that may differ among clinicians and between the clinician and laboratory scientist. On one end of a continuum, the clinician may consider "traumatic" any experience, intrapsychic or external, fantasied or real, that is subjectively felt or labeled as traumatic by the client. Of course, the wide range, subjectivity, and lack of clarity of this definition create significant difficulties for objective study of the phenomenon. On the other end of a continuum are laboratory definitions of trauma such as unpleasantness, task failure, affective intensity, stress, or other "negative" emotional states. While these def-

initions operate under a loose umbrella of "psychic pain" (which is assumed to be the motivation underlying differential memory responses), their narrowness, variety, and specificity are of questionable utility in the consideration of traumatic states. (p. 2)

A trauma or traumatic stressor is, by definition, an event or experience that is not merely stressful—it is also shocking, terrifying, and overwhelming to the person who experiences it. The *DSM-IV* (American Psychiatric Association, 1994) definition of an extreme traumatic stressor (criterion A (1) for the diagnosis of posttraumatic stress disorder) indicates that it involves the following objective elements:

> actual or threatened death or serious injury, or other threat to one's physical integrity; witnessing an event that involves death, injury, or a threat to the physical integrity of another person; or learning about unexpected or violent death, serious harm, or threat of death or injury experienced by a family member or other close associate (p. 424).

According to the *DSM* description, traumatic events may be experienced directly, witnessed, or learned about after they have been experienced by others (usually someone significant):

> Traumatic events that are experienced directly include, but are not limited to, military combat, violent personal assault (sexual assault, physical attack, robbery, mugging), being kidnapped, being taken hostage, terrorist attack, torture, incarceration as a prisoner of war or in a concentration camp, natural or manmade disasters, severe automobile accidents, or being diagnosed with a life-threatening illness. For children, sexually traumatic events may include developmentally inappropriate sexual experiences without threatened or actual violence or injury. Witnessed events include, but are not limited to, observing the serious injury or unnatural death of another person due to violent assault, accident, war, or disaster or unexpectedly witnessing a dead body or body parts. Events experienced by others that are learned about include, but are not limited to, violent personal assault, serious accident, or serious injury experienced by a family member or a close friend; learning about the sudden, unexpected death of a family member or a close friend; or learning that one's child has a life-threatening disease. The disorder may be especially severe or long lasting when the stressor is of human design (e.g., torture, rape). The likelihood of developing the disorder may increase as the intensity of and physical proximity to the stressor increase. (p. 424)

According to criterion A (2), a stressor is also traumatic by virtue of subjective response it elicits. The person's response must involve intense reactions of fear, helplessness, or horror. In children, the response must involve disorganized or agitated behavior.

Other authors have developed definitions of trauma that offer additional specificity and that expand upon the rather narrow *DSM* criteria. McCann and Pearlman (1990a) wrote that trauma: "(1) is sudden, unexpected, or non-normative, (2) exceeds the individual's perceived ability to meet its demands, and (3) disrupts the individual's frame of reference and other central psychological needs and related schema" (p. 10). They wrote:

> The first part of the definition serves to exclude the chronic difficulties of life, which, although themselves important and at times severe, must be distinguished from trauma if the construct is to serve any heuristic purpose. Our definition includes experiences which may not be unexpected for the individual, such as ongoing incest, but which, from the perspective of the larger society, are non-normative. (pp. 10-11)

Pearlman and Saakvitne (1995) further offered some of the subjective elements of trauma in their process definition:

> We define it as the unique individual experience, associated with an event or enduring conditions, in which (1) the individual's ability to integrate affective experience is overwhelmed or (2) the individual experiences a threat to life or bodily integrity. The pathognomonic responses are changes in the individual's (1) frame of reference, or usual way of understanding self and world, including spirituality, (2) capacity to modulate affect and maintain benevolent inner connection with self and others, (3) ability to meet his psychological needs in mature ways, (4) central psychological needs, which are reflected in disrupted cognitive schema, and (5) memory system, including sensory experience. (pp. 60-61)

Figley (1985) offered the following, mainly subjective, definition of trauma and further discussed traumatic stress reactions and posttraumatic stress disorder: *Trauma* represents "an emotional state of discomfort and stress resulting from memories of an extraordinary, catastrophic experience which shattered the survivor's sense of invulnerability to harm" (p. xviii). *Traumatic stress reactions* give indication of the presence of a trauma and are natural behavioral and emotional responses to the trauma. *Posttraumatic stress reactions* are defined as a "set of conscious and unconscious behaviors and emotions associated with dealing with the memories of the stressors of the catastrophe and immediately afterwards. . . . A *posttraumatic stress disorder* is the clinical manifestation of problems associated with trauma induced during the catastrophe and represented by the posttraumatic stress reactions" (p. xix, author's italics).

As these definitions suggest, trauma consists of a variety of objective and subjective elements that interact. Several researchers, notably Pearlman and Saakvitne (1995), Pynoos et al. (1997), and Wilson (1989), have considered the process of traumatization as an interactive process involving the unique variables or dimensions of the traumatic stressor, the individual, and the context surrounding them. These interact in a complex interplay of objective, subjective, and contextual factors to determine the strength and severity of the outcome. (See Figure 3.1 for the Person x Environmental/Situational variables that make up Wilson's interactive theory of traumatic stress reactions).

According to Wilson's theory, on average, the more of the objective dimensions of the trauma that are present as environmental and situational variables, the greater the potential for producing a pathological outcome. It is noteworthy that incest and other forms of child sexual abuse often include many of the most serious of the dimensions as posited by Wilson and other researchers. They involve a stressor of human design, repeated exposure and physical proximity to the stressor that often increases in severity and physical intrusion over time and over the course of childhood, when the individual is physically and emotionally immature and dependent on caretakers and with whom there is a conflicted relationship and ambivalent attachment (discussed further in chapter 4). Thus, they can be considered psychologically complex stressors and have high potential for serious consequences including PTSD (per the *DSM* definition included above).

Last but not least, another dimension of traumatization that deserves mention is its social context. At present, all forms of traumatization/victimization are documented as ubiquitous problems not only in Western culture but worldwide; yet, trauma goes largely unrecognized because it is quite consistently denied, ignored, and dismissed at both the societal and the personal level (Herman, 1992b). The inability to acknowledge or speak of the trauma (Lister, 1982 coined the term "forced silence" and identified it as a hidden dimension of trauma) can be, in and of itself, part of what makes an experience traumatic (Brown, 1995; Caruth, 1995; Elin, 1997; Herman, 1992b). By failing to acknowledge, witness, and/or intervene, those surrounding the victim allow human-induced traumatic acts and traumatization to continue unabated, another source of traumatization to those already injured (termed the "second injury" by Symonds,

Figure 3.1

Interactive Theory of Traumatic Stress Reactions: Elements for a Theory of Traumatic Stress Reactions

INPUTS TO THE PROCESSING OF TRAUMA   FORMS OF STRESS RESPONSE DETERMINED BY PERSON-ENVIRONMENT INTERACTION

Person Variables ⇄ (PXE) ⇄ Environmental and → Individual Subjective → Post-Trauma Adaptation
(P)   Situational Variables (E)   Responses to Trauma

Person Variables (P)	Environmental and Situational Variables (E)	Individual Subjective Responses to Trauma	Post-Trauma Adaptation
Motives	I. Dimensions of the Trauma	I. Emotional	I. Acute
Traits	a. Bereavement/Loss	a. Affective distress	a. Pathological
Beliefs	b. Imminence	b. Affective numbing	1. PTSD
Values	c. Duration/Severity	c. Affective balance	2. Other disorders
Abilities	d. Displacement		b. Non-pathological
Cognitive Structure	e. Exposure to death, dying, etc.	II. Cognition	
Defensive Style	f. Moral conflict	a. denial/avoidance	II. Chronic
Genetic propensities	g. Role in trauma	b. distortion	a. Pathological
	h. Potential for re-occurrence	c. accurate appraisal	1. PTSD
	i. Life-threat	d. dissociation	2. Other disorders
	j. Complexity of stressor	e. intrusion	b. Non-pathological
	k. Impact on Community		1. Personality alteration
		III. Motivational	2. Character change
	II. Experience of Trauma	a. aroused	
	a. alone	b. non-aroused	III. Life-Course Development
	b. with others		a. Intensification of
	c. community based (collective)	IV. Neurophysiological	developmental stages
		a. hyperarousal	b. Retrogression
	III. Structure of Trauma	b. depressed-avoidant	c. Psychological acceleration
	a. single stressor	c. balanced	
	b. multiple stressor		
	c. complex vs. simple	V. Coping	
	d. natural vs. man-made	a. instrumental	
		b. emotional	
	IV. Post-Trauma Milieu	c. cognitive re-structure	
	a. level of support	1. positive	
	b. cultural rituals for recovery	2. negative	
	c. societal attitudes towards event	d. resilient	
	d. opportunity structures		

From *Trauma Transformation and Healing: An Integrative Approach to Theory, Research, and Post-traumatic Therapy* (p. 7), by J. Wilson, 1989, New York: Brunner/Mazel. Copyright 1989 by Brunner/Mazel. Reprinted with permission.

1980). Trauma also has impact beyond the individual victim to significant others, some of whom might suffer from secondary or vicarious forms of traumatization; furthermore, patterns of intergenerational transmission and cyclical effects have been associated with all forms of family violence. It is important that these crucial facts—the high prevalence of traumatization and its devastating toll on the individual, the family, and society—not be lost in the current debate.

A Continuum of Posttraumatic Reactions Including Posttraumatic Stress Disorder

Both Figley's and Wilson's theoretical models imply that traumatic events inevitably cause posttraumatic symptoms or reactions, although they are not always problematic, severe, or long-lasting; however, when the symptoms are of sufficient strength or duration, they may meet criteria for a diagnosis of acute stress disorder, posttraumatic stress disorder, one of the dissociative disorders, or a personality disorder (most commonly borderline personality disorder). As *DSM-IV* criterion A (1) implies (and in line with Wilson's model), severe and long-lasting reactions are especially likely when the stressor is of human design and intent (and is therefore premeditated and not accidental, as is the case in assault, torture, rape, and all forms of family violence, including child abuse). Moreover, the likelihood of developing PTSD increases as the intensity and the physical proximity to the stressor increase (American Psychiatric Association, 1994, p. 424), a situation found in ongoing family violence, including sexual abuse. Of special interest and pertinence to this discussion are the posttraumatic reactions that emerge years after the initial trauma and that meet criteria for posttraumatic stress disorder, chronic and/or delayed form, and severe dissociative disorders. These are often associated with the return of memory for the traumatic event after a delay and/or a period of absence.

   Kardiner (1941), who researched soldiers' responses to war trauma or "war neurosis," provided the original conceptualization of the essential features of the human posttraumatic stress response as it is currently understood. Kardiner labeled this syndrome a "physioneurosis" because he found that it involved both psychological and physical or psychosomatic reactions (as Charcot, Freud and Breuer, and Janet had discovered at the turn of the century as they studied the psychological and psychosomatic responses of patients diagnosed with hysteria). Kardiner's formulation is also consistent with data documenting that the ordinary human response to stress involves both body and mind in a complex system of psychophysiological processes and reactions (Selye, 1976); however, important data have recently emerged to indicate that the neurobiological response to trauma-based stress has distinctive features that differentiate it from the response to normal stress (Yehuda & McFarlane, 1997b).

The trauma response has been documented to occur fairly consistently in the aftermath of a wide range of overwhelming trauma-based stressors, alternating between intrusive/reexperiencing and numbing/avoidance phases of response expressed both psychologically and physiologically. This model was developed, in part, from psychiatrist Mardi Horowitz's conceptualization of the traumatic stress response as an information-processing model (Horowitz, 1976/1986). In his now classic book, *Stress Response Syndromes*, Horowitz described the human response to traumatization as involving a disruption in ordinary information-processing and a disturbance of the individual's personal schemata about self and others. The physical and emotional shock of the trauma and the schema disruption that result require a period of adjustment and readjustment through what Horowitz identified as five predictable stages: outcry, denial, intrusive reexperiencing, working through, and completion. In progressing through these stages, the traumatized person attempts to "come to grips with" the emotions and memories associated with the traumatic experience. With successful resolution, the individual goes through this progression (a process that might meet diagnostic criteria for acute stress disorder, a short-term variant of posttraumatic stress disorder) and achieves relative completeness and integration (the updating of personal schemata via the cognitive process of assimilation/accommodation) of the traumatic material over an attenuated period of time. With a less successful resolution, the material does not assimilate and the individual continues to alternate between symptoms associated with the intrusive and numbing phases, meeting the criteria for posttraumatic stress disorder. In this case, symptoms might become chronic and/or might emerge in delayed fashion.

As research has accumulated about the traumatic stress response and the diagnosis and prevalence of PTSD, it has become apparent that full-blown PTSD is the less, rather than more, typical response in the aftermath of traumatization, occurring in a minority of individuals who have been traumatized (Yehuda & McFarlane, 1995) (however, the range estimate for PTSD given in the *DSM-IV* for individuals exposed to a Criterion 1 (A) stressor is between 3-58 percent). Yet, given the amount of traumatization that occurs, rates of PTSD in the general population are higher than would have been expected a decade ago (Stein, Hanna, Koverola, Torchia, & McClarty, 1997). It seems likely that most individuals who are traumatized work through their posttraumatic reactions in some naturalistic way over time, via some form of information-processing along the lines proposed by Horowitz or through social support and normalizing responses. From epidemiological data gathered to date, it appears that approximately one-quarter to one-third of those individuals exposed to a traumatic stressor will develop PTSD in the immediate or longer-term aftermath. Thus, even if PTSD is not the normative response to exposure to traumatization, it still occurs in a substantial and significant percentage of exposed individuals. As discussed above, the probability of developing PTSD varies according to the nature and severity of the trauma (including its duration). In adults who report experiencing childhood abuse, symptoms of PTSD and Complex PTSD have been found across studies at high rates of prevalence (Albach & Everaerd, 1992; Beitchman et al., 1992; Polusny & Follette, 1995; Roth & Batson, 1997; Rowan & Foy, 1993). This finding is expanded upon in chapter 4.

PTSD has also been found to have distinctive physiological characteristics (described below) that both validate it as a discrete disorder and provide the basis of an explanatory model for memory disturbance and the inhibition of information-processing, symptoms that are incorporated within the diagnosis. Concerning the diagnostic criteria for PTSD, according to the *DSM*, the reexperiencing response can involve "recurrent and intrusive distressing *recollections* of the events, including images, thoughts, or perceptions" (p. 428, italics added), recurrent distressing dreams, *a sense of reliving* the experience, and intense psychological distress and physiological reactivity at exposure to internal or external cues that symbolize or resemble some aspect of the trauma. Experiences of selective hypermnesia have been identified that involve the activation of total episodes, partial scenes, or small disjointed components or fragments of an experience (often, but not always, in the form of nightmares and flashbacks). Many of these reexperiencing reactions also involve a sense of depersonalization and a loss of time sense and reference, such that a memory of a past event feels like a present-day occurrence of great immediacy.

In contrast, the numbing phase of the PTSD response involves emotional and cognitive constriction and "persistent avoidance of stimuli associated with the trauma and numbing of general responsiveness (not present before the trauma)" (p. 428), indicated by *efforts to avoid reminders of the trauma*, including aversive stimuli, *recollections*, and emotions; *the inability to recall* an important aspect of the trauma; and a general detachment from events, behaviors, or social contacts. This inability to recall all or parts of the trauma may be due either to unconscious processes and defensive operations, or to conscious attempts to forget the traumatic material (i.e., intentional forgetting, motivated forgetting, voluntary thought suppression).

The current description of PTSD therefore acknowledges that trauma can result in extremes of retention (hypermnesia) *and* forgetting (amnesia) and oscillations between the two: traumatic experiences are often remembered and even relived in great detail and vividness in one phase of the trauma response and avoided, numbed out, and shut down in the other. Additionally, the difficulties associated with traumatic memories and responses are generally more diverse than all-or-nothing categories. At times, they are quite idiosyncratic and even paradoxical. For example, some individuals experience difficulties at only one end of the memory spectrum, being either hypermnestic or amnestic, while others experience a combination of remembering and forgetting, sometimes having intrusive imagery that they seemingly "can't turn off" while knowing they do not recall other important aspects of the event (van der Kolk & Fisler, 1995). Christianson and Engelberg (1997) wrote that traumatic memories might be available but not always accessible to conscious retrieval but might nonetheless influence or control behavior.

It is routine to hear descriptions of survivors simultaneously "knowing and not knowing" (Courtois, 1988; Freyd, 1996; Grand, 1995; Laub & Auerhahn, 1993; Roth & Batson, 1997) or "knowing more than they know they know" (Courtois, 1992) from researchers and clinicians who work with individuals who have experienced massive psychic trauma. Caruth (1995) spoke of this paradox in the introduction to her book, *Trauma: Explorations in Memory:*

> It is indeed this truth of traumatic experience that forms the center of its pathology or symptoms; it is not a pathology, that is, of falsehood or displacement of meaning, but of history itself. If PTSD must be understood as a pathological symptom, then it is not so much a symptom of the unconscious, as it is a *symptom of history.* The traumatized, we might say, carry an impossible history within them, or they become themselves the symptoms of a history that they cannot entirely possess. (Italics added) (p. 5)

To summarize, then, pathologies of memory have been repeatedly observed as a response to psychic trauma and constitute an essential element of the posttraumatic response and the diagnostic nomenclature for PTSD.

The Emerging Data on the Psychobiology and Psychophysiology of PTSD

The biological and physiological changes and dysregulations associated with PTSD are believed to be integrally connected to its psychological phenomenology, including memory impairment. A body of research is emerging that documents the psychobiological and psychophysiological alterations involved in both the arousal and numbing phases of PTSD that might underlie the psychological and psychosomatic responses to trauma described above (Everly, 1995; van der Kolk & Fisler, 1995; Friedman, 1994; Friedman, Charney, & Deutch, 1995; Giller, 1990; Kolb, 1987; Yehuda & McFarlane, 1997b). These changes include abnormalities of stress hormone regulation, hyperarousal of the autonomic nervous system, chronically increased levels of cortisol, and changes in the central nervous system (CNS) catecholamine, serotonin, and endogenous opioid systems (Cahill, Prins, Weber, & McGaugh, 1994; Charney, Deutch, Krystal, Southwick, & Davis, 1993; Shalev, 1996; Southwick, Krystal, Johnson, & Charney, 1995; van der Kolk, 1996; Yehuda & Harvey, 1996; Yehuda & McFarlane, 1997b; Yehuda et al., 1994). Preliminary research supports the fact that traumatization can lead to measurable, sometimes permanent, alterations in brain neurophysiology and neurochemistry (Cahill et al., 1994; McGaugh, 1992; Pitman & Orr, in press; Rauch et al., 1996; van der Kolk, 1988; van der Kolk & Fisler, 1995; van der Kolk & Saporta 1993). Those alterations can, in turn, account for the production of symptoms of chronic hyperarousal and intrusive symptomatology. Griffin, Nishith, Resick, and Yehuda (1997) recently proposed that a biological approach holds promise for a better understanding of the etiology, maintenance, and treatment of PTSD. See Tables 3.1 and 3.2 for a listing of brain psychobiology and physiology affected by traumatization.

In their review of the literature, Yehuda and Harvey (1996) cautioned that studies of the neurobiology of PTSD have found and made the distinction between trauma survivors *with* PTSD and trauma survivors *without* PTSD. They suggest that the study of memory impairment in PTSD must include attention to individual characteristics that potentially modify the risk or vulnerability for PTSD following exposure to a traumatic event, since not everyone who is exposed goes on to develop PTSD, and hence it is not only exposure to the traumatic event that results in PTSD. These scientists also noted that, since many of the biological changes observed in individuals with PTSD occur in systems intimately involved in memory processing, an understanding of these biological alterations may lead to an understanding of the cognitive deficits associated with PTSD.

Table 3.1
Psychobiological Abnormalities in PTSD

I. Psychophysiological effects
    A. Extreme autonomic responses to stimuli reminiscent of the trauma
    B. Hyperarousal to intense but neutral stimuli (loss of stimulus discrimination)
        1. Nonhabituation of the acoustic startle response
        2. Response below threshold to sound intensities
        3. Reduced electrical pattern in cortical event-related potentials

II. Neurohormonal effects
    A. Norepinephrine (NE), other catecholamines
        1. Elevated urinary catecholamines
        2. Increased plasma NE metabolite response to yohimbine
        3. Down-regulation of adrenergic receptors
    B. Glucocorticoids
        1. Decreased resting glucocorticoid levels
        2. Decreased glucocorticoid response to stress
        3. Down-regulation of glucocorticoid receptors
        4. Hyperresponsiveness to low-dose dexamethasone
    C. Serotonin
        1. Decreased serotonin activity in traumatized animals
        2. Best pharmacological responses to serotonin uptake inhibitors
    D. Endogenous opioids
        1. Increased opioid response to stimuli reminiscent of trauma
        2. Conditionability of stress-induced analgesia
    E. Various hormones: Memory effects
        1. NE, vasopressin: Consolidation of traumatic memories
        2. Oxytocin, endogenous opioids: Amnesias

III. Neuroanatomical effects
    A. Decreased hippocampal volume
    B. Activation of amygdala and connected structures during flashbacks
    C. Activation of sensory areas during flashbacks
    D. Decreased activation of Broca's area during flashbacks
    E. Marked right-hemispheric lateralization

IV. Immunological effects
    A. Increased CD45 RO/RA ratio

From "The Body Keeps the Score: Approaches to the Psychobiology of Posttraumatic Stress Disorder," by B. A. van der Kolk, 1996. In B. A. van der Kolk, A. C. McFarlane, and L. Weisaeth, Editors, *Traumatic Stress: The Effects of Overwhelming Experience on Mind, Body, and Society* (p. 220), 1996, New York: Guilford Press. Copyright 1996 by Guilford Press. Reprinted with permission.

Table 3.2
Physiological Alterations Associated with PTSD

1. Heightened Sympathetic Arousal
    a. Elevated resting heart rate and blood pressure
    b. Increased reactivity to neutral stimuli
    c. Increased reactivity to traumaminetic stimuli

2. Exaggerated Startle Response
    a. Lowered threshold
    b. Increased amplitude
    c. Loss of startle inhibition

3. Disturbed Sleep and Dreaming
    a. Poor quality of sleep
        1. Increased sleep latency
        2. Decreased sleep time
        3. Increased movement
        4. Increased awakenings
    b. Possible abnormalities in sleep architecture (decreased slow wave sleep)
    c. Traumatic nightmares are unique

4. Abnormal Evoked Cortical Potentials
    a. Reducer pattern in response to neutral stimuli

From "Biological and Pharmacological Aspects of the Treatment of PTSD," by M. J. Friedman. In M. B. Williams and J. F. Sommer, Jr., Editors, *Handbook of Post-Traumatic Therapy* (p. 496), 1994, Westport, CT: Greenwood Press. Copyright 1994 by the Greenwood Press. Reprinted with permission.

Dissociative Reactions and Disorders

Beginning with the observations of Charcot, Freud and Breuer, and Janet, dissociative reactions and symptoms (including psychogenic amnesia, depersonalization, derealization, fugue states, conversion reactions, reexperiencing phenomena, and fragmented identity) have been associated with traumatization, especially childhood abuse. Dissociative amnesia—where information is not available to conscious awareness for an extended period of time, although it may have an influence on behavior—is consistent with Janet's original formulation and thought to play an important role in the memory loss for episodes of childhood abuse. A resurgence of interest in dissociation over the past two decades has led to a growing body of clinical observation and empirical research documenting the prevalence, phenomenology, psychophysiology, neurophysiology, and neurochemistry of dissociation and the treatment of dissociative disorders. (See reviews by Klein & Doane, 1994; Lynn & Rhue, 1994; Putnam, 1989a, 1993b, 1997; Spiegel, 1993, 1994a; Spiegel & Cardena, 1991.)

According to Cardena (1994), "In its broadest sense, 'dissociation' simply means that two or more mental processes or contents are not associated or integrated. It is usually assumed that these dissociated elements would be integrated in conscious awareness, memory, or identity" (p. 15). Dissociation has also been defined as: "a mechanism that constructs a noticeable change in a person's thoughts, feelings, or actions so that for a period of time, certain information is not associated or integrated with other information as it normally or logically would be" (West, 1967). Dissociation has typically been described by many authorities as a relatively continuous phenomenon ranging from normal to pathological variations; however, recent research has indicated that, similar to what has been noted about the stress response and PTSD, as described above, the continuum model may not accurately reflect the relationship of normal to pathological. Yates and Nasby (1993) made such a distinction in their definition of dissociation: "[the] disconnection, independence or separation of one part of memory from another. 'Normal' dissociation implies a dynamic and fluid ability to access memory." In contrast, in pathological dissociation, "specific memories are inaccessible because they are associated with a highly charged negatively toned affective component. Dissociation is not forgetting. In dissociation, *the item is encoded but cannot be retrieved*" (Yates & Nasby, 1993, p. 309, italics added). Dissociative pathologies are thus differentiated from normal dissociation by the unbridged or unbridgeable compartmentalization of experiences in memory storage and retrieval (Nemiah, 1985). Such a distinction has also been found to differentiate patients with posttraumatic or dissociative disorders from those without (Putnam, Carlson, & Waller, 1994).

A strong relationship between trauma exposure and dissociative disorders has been reported consistently across studies and types of trauma ranging from combat to natural disasters to interpersonal victimization of all sorts (e.g., Chu & Dill, 1990; Coons & Milstein, 1986; Marmar et al., 1994; Noyes & Keltti, 1977; Putnam, 1989a; Saxe et al., 1993; Spiegel, 1984, 1986). Exposure to trauma has been shown to increase prevalence of certain dissociative symptoms. These include detachment, alterations in perception, and alterations in memory (Spiegel, 1993, 1994b; Spiegel & Cardena, 1991). As discussed in chapter 2, peritraumatic dissociation (or the involuntary separation of affect and cognition during the experience) has been reported by one-quarter to one-half of traumatized individuals (Spiegel, 1993) and has been found to be an important long-term predictor for the later development of PTSD. It also has implications for how memories are encoded at the time of the trauma (van der Hart, Steele, Boon, & Brown, 1993).

The prevalence of dissociation has come under investigation in both general and clinical population epidemiological studies. In one study, 5 percent of a general population sample exhibited a high degree of dissociative symptoms (Ross, Joshi, & Currie, 1990), a prevalence figure that does not appear to be an overestimate given the prevalence of exposure to traumatic events in the general population (Elliott, 1997). In several clinical studies, the rates of *DSM-IV* dissociative pathologies in the psychiatric inpatient population have been investigated. Depending upon the sample, between 15 and 30 percent of studied inpatients met diagnostic criteria for one of the dissociative disorders (Chu & Dill, 1990; Ross, Anderson, Fleisher, & Norton, 1991; Saxe et al., 1993; Swett & Halpert, 1993). Additionally, in comparing dissociation in abused versus nonabused populations, Chu and Dill (1990), studying 98 female psychiatric patients, found that dissociation scores were significantly higher for those patients with a reported history of childhood intrafamilial sexual or physical abuse than for those with no such history.

Children may be especially prone to dissociate during traumatic circumstances. Putnam (1993a, 1993b) suggests that this connection between trauma and dissociation—as well as evidence demonstrating that children, as a group, display greater dissociative capacities than adults—may indicate that childhood trauma enhances the child's normatively elevated capacity to dissociate and/or preserves that capacity into adulthood as dissociative pathology.

Four distinct dissociative disorders are recognized in the *DSM-IV*—dissociative amnesia, dissociative fugue, dissociative identity disorder, depersonalization disorder, and a fifth category, dissociative disorder not otherwise specified (DDNOS). According to *DSM-IV*, the essential features of the dissociative disorders are a disruption in the usually integrated functions of consciousness, memory, identity, or perception of the environment, with the disturbance being sudden or gradual, transient or chronic.

Complex Posttraumatic Stress Disorder

As research data on traumatic stress and posttraumatic reactions have accumulated over the last two decades, they have made it clear that PTSD as it is currently defined does not account for much of the symptomatology that emerges following repeated experiences of chronic traumatization. This is especially the case for childhood victimization spanning years of the child's physical maturation and psychosexual development, thereby creating the need for a psychological adaptation to the traumatization (Briere, 1989, 1996b; Courtois, 1988; Herman, 1992b). Roth and Batson (1997) addressed this issue in their book on the treatment of incest survivors. Their viewpoint is applicable to other victims of chronic traumatization as well:

> First, while it is true that a wide array of symptoms and disorders are likely correlates of childhood sexual abuse, there is something lost in treating those symptoms without some understanding of their relationship to a *traumatic adaptation*. Second, the complex adaptation to trauma necessary in cases of ongoing, familial sexual abuse requires a distortion of reality that often involves the recruitment of altered states of consciousness. Third, the *complex adaptation to trauma* necessarily disrupts normative self and social development. (italics added) (p. 6)

As currently defined, PTSD is categorized within the Axis I disorders in the *DSM*, where developmental disruptions and disorders are not included or accounted for, rather than within the Axis II disorders, where they are. In recent years, a new diagnostic category that spans both axes to include attention to developmental issues and symptoms has been proposed (Herman, 1992a, 1992b) and tested in a field trial at five different research sites (Pelcovitz et al., 1997; Roth, Newman, Pelcovitz, van der Kolk, & Mandel, 1997). Although researchers found evidence in support of the symptom categories included in the diagnosis, complex posttraumatic stress disorder or disorder of extreme stress, not otherwise specified (DESNOS) has not been formally included in the current edition of the *DSM*, except as *associated features* of "simple" PTSD.

The seven symptom categories described by complex PTSD (see Table 3.3) reflect the idea of a traumatic adaptation that disrupts important developmental processes, including the ability to regulate affect and impulses, and alterations in self and object relations. The data that have been collected thus far suggest that patients with complex PTSD represent the more severely affected PTSD patients, many of whom have been the most chronically sexually or physically abused and whose abuse began at a young age. A related finding is that patients diagnosed with borderline personality disorder (BPD) represent the more severely affected complex PTSD patients (Roth & Batson, 1997). BPD has itself been found to be a posttraumatic personality and relational adaptation in the aftermath of severe abuse and other crises or difficulties during childhood, including disruptions in parenting and parent-child bonding (Kroll, 1993; Linehan, 1993). Some writers have suggested that BPD is really a post-abuse syndrome (Briere, 1984).

Table 3.3
Symptom Categories and Diagnostic Criteria for Complex PTSD

I. Alterations in Regulation of Affect and Impulses

     A. Affect Regulation   D. Suicidal preoccupation
     B. Modulation of anger   E. Difficulty modulating sexual involve-
     C. Self-destructive   ment
                                    F. Excessive risk taking

     A and one of B-F required

II. Alterations in Attention or Consciousness

     A. Amnesia
     B. Transient dissociative episodes and depersonalization

     A or B required

III. Alterations in Self-Perception

     A. Ineffectiveness   D. Shame
     B. Permanent damage   E. Nobody can understand
     C. Guilt and responsibility   F. Minimizing
     Two of A-F required

IV. Alterations in Perception of the Perpetrator

     A. Adopting distorted beliefs   C. Preoccupation with hurting perpetrator
     B. Idealization of the perpetrator

     Not required

V. Alterations in Relations with Others

     A. Inability to trust   C. Victimizing others
     B. Revictimization

     One of A-C required

VI. Somatization

     A. Digestive system   D. Conversion symptoms
     B. Chronic pain   E. Sexual symptoms
     C. Cardiopulmonary symptoms
     Two of A-E required

VII. Alterations in Systems of Meaning

     A. Despair and hopelessness   B. Loss of previously sustaining beliefs
     A or B required

From "Development of a Criteria Set and a Structured Interview for Disorders of Extreme Stress (SIDES),"
by D. Pelcovitz, B. A. van der Kolk, S. Roth, F. S. Mandel, S. Kaplan, and P. A. Resick, 1997, *Journal of
Traumatic Stress, 10*, p. 9. Copyright 1997 by The International Society for Traumatic Stress Studies. Adapted
with permission.

THE NATURE OF MEMORY FOR TRAUMATIC EVENTS

Traumatic memory has been defined in a number of ways. Butler and Spiegel (1997) use the term *traumatic memory* in the broadest and most obvious way to refer to memories of traumatic events. Yet, they note that some of the clinical literature is more particular and designates traumatic memories as specific types of posttraumatic memory disturbance (such as intrusive memories). These authors further comment on the fact that much of the clinical and experimental research employs different terms or similar terms with different meanings. The standardization of terminology would provide a useful starting point in bridging some of the most obvious differences in the controversy.

Here we review several definitions and descriptions that have been offered by traumatic stress researchers. "Traumatic memories is a descriptive term for recall of negative personal experiences. . . . Traumatic memories are always formed under high levels of emotional arousal" (Tromp, Koss, Figueredo, & Tharan, 1995, p. 608). "Traumatic memories are the unassimilated scraps of overwhelming experiences, which need to be integrated with existing mental schemes, and be transformed into narrative language. It appears that, in order for this to happen successfully, the traumatized person has to return to the memory often in order to complete it" (van der Kolk & van der Hart, 1995, p. 176). Traumatic memories have been repeatedly observed to have more perceptual and emotional elements than declarative (verbal) elements and perhaps to be encoded differently from memories for normal events (van der Kolk, 1997).

A number of writers beginning with Pierre Janet have commented on the apparently paradoxical nature of traumatic memories. Janet (1889) described the memories of overwhelming experiences as different and more rigid than memories for normal or less stressful events. Such memories are not flexible and not easily accommodated into existing mental schemata, are dissociated outside of conscious control, and return unbidden as intrusive recollections and experiences. Christianson and Engelberg (1997) commented on the seemingly contradictory findings about memories for traumatic events. On one hand, these memories tend to be accurate and persistent with respect to the central, critical detail information about the emotion-laden traumatic event (although these authors were careful to note that traumatic memories are not always fully accurate). On the other hand, the memories might be available but *not always accessible to conscious retrieval*. Christianson and Engelberg further comment on the adaptive and even survival benefit for humans of being able to identify and recognize situations of high threat (thus to remember them), as well as the contradictory but equally important need to "forget" unpleasant events in order for life to be bearable (p. 230). In a similar vein, Freyd (1996) noted:

> One gap in our knowledge that fuels the current debate about the accuracy of recovered memories concerns the apparent paradox that traumatic memories are both the least forgettable of all memories (causing intrusive recollections and excruciatingly detailed remembrances in some cases) and the most forgettable of all memories (leading to all forms of avoidance/suppression and resulting in memory failure). (author's italics) (p. 29)

Many writers have also commented on the persistence of traumatic memories and the distress that they cause. Charcot called traumatic memories "parasites of the mind" (quoted in van der Kolk, 1997, p. 243) and van der Kolk and van der Hart (1995) termed them "the memories that plague people" (p. 175). Brown et al. (1998) wrote that, "Traumatic memory can be distinguished from memory for events of impact by the occurrence of posttraumatic stress symptoms" (p. 154). They go on to summarize the variety of trauma-related problems that have been identified in the literature when traumatic memory remains split off from conscious awareness/control rather than processed and integrated: (1) sustained chronic hyperarousal; (2) vulnerability to intrusive reexperiencing symptoms; (3) generalized numbing or responsiveness; (4) vulnerability to dissociative symptoms; (5) sustained propensity to reenact elements of the traumatic experience in everyday relationships including in the transference in therapy; (6) increased vulnerability to subsequent retraumatization; (7) arrest in self and self-esteem development; and/or (8) failure to transform everyday beliefs that have been shattered by the trauma and/or internalized trauma-related pathological beliefs (pp. 445-446). These problems are important to keep in mind since they suggest the rationale for the treatment of traumatic memories. These are discussed in considerable detail in chapters 5 to 9.

Principles of Normal Event Memory

Siegel (1995), in an article entitled "Memory, trauma, and psychotherapy: A cognitive science view," made a meaningful observation reflecting back to the findings of Janet (1889) and his contemporaries, namely, that memory is intertwined with other cognitive processes and that both may be impacted by trauma in complex ways. He began his discussion with a review of basic principles of normal memory as an anchoring framework and reference from which to discuss traumatic memory. These principles are important for clinicians to understand as they work with memories in a therapeutic context and thus are the starting point of our discussion of traumatic memories as well. Yapko (1994a, 1994b), in surveying clinicians regarding their knowledge of human memory processes (and hypnosis), found many to be woefully uninformed about the workings of memory. Erroneous beliefs might impact negatively on how clinicians work with their clients regarding their memory productions; therefore, it is imperative that they have a basic understanding of principles of normal memory as a foundation for their work (Chu, Matthews, Frey, & Ganzel, 1996; Courtois, 1997a, 1997d; Lindsay & Read, 1994; Ornstein, Ceci, & Loftus, 1996a; Yapko, 1994a, 1994b).

SOME GENERAL PRINCIPLES OF NORMAL EVENT/AUTOBIOGRAPHICAL MEMORY.   Memory has been extensively studied for the last hundred years and a considerable body of information has accumulated, including general principles and information on normal event/autobiographical memory, developmental and maturational issues in memory acquisition, retention, and retrieval, and memory for emotional events (for reviews, see Brown et al., 1998; Roediger, 1980; Schacter, 1996). Information of most importance to clinicians is presented here.

1. Memory is a process, not an event, and is imperfect and fallible. The comparison of the mind to a computer or a video camera that records events and plays them back in full reproduction is not accurate. Memory is not a simple unitary process but rather involves complicated processes across different regions of the brain. Remembering, like other cognitive processes, has been found to be the result of interactions between networks of nerve cells in the brain. It also involves stages of sensory encoding, organizing and consolidation, storage and retrieval, and an information flow between them (Ornstein et al., 1996a). According to Siegel, "Remembering can be thought of as the activation of a neural net profile that represents the things being recalled. Thus, memory can be thought of as a verb, not a noun" (p. 97).

2. A corollary principle is that memory is generally reconstructive rather than reproductive and is dynamic and fluid rather than static (although traumatic memory is believed to have reproductive qualities by some researchers). Each of the stages of mental processing is influenced by a variety of other cognitive processes and issues, including personal schema, emotional arousal, beliefs,

associated learning and memories, motivations, expectations, etc., as well as external influences and processes. The details of a memory may be accurate or not and can be influenced by ques tioning and other processes after the event, including the time elapsed since the memory's formation and retrieval conditions. Memory is therefore both fallible and malleable.

According to Ornstein et al., key issues revolve around (a) the encoding processes that lead to the establishment of a trace or representation in storage; (b) the factors that influence these rep-resentations over time; and (c) the variables that affect the later retrieval of the information represented in the memory. Ornstein, Larus, and Clubb (1991) further defined the remem-bering process into four general themes about memory perfor-mance: (a) not everything gets into memory; (b) what gets into memory may vary in strength; (c) the status of information in memory changes; and (d) retrieval is not perfect (not all that endures in memory is retrieved and different retrieval strategies might affect what is recalled). Memory in both children and adults may be impacted by retrieval strategies, particularly how questions are asked, the presentation of new and misleading information, multiple attempts at retrieval, and prior knowledge on the part of the individual.

3.   Memory and consciousness are not the same and memory is not a unitary process; rather, it is composed of multiple processes and systems (Tulving & Schacter, 1990). The memory of a specific event is not stored or processed in a single location in the brain but is instead distributed across a network of different brain areas. Research has identified different forms of memory, explic-it and implicit memory. Each has been found to involve different brain structures. The hippocampus and related midbrain struc-tures are important in the formation and consolidation of explic-it memory also known as episodic, declarative, and late memory). Explicit memories involve information that is available to con-scious and verbal recall. Implicit (or nondeclarative and early) memories refer to those not available to consciousness that might nevertheless be demonstrated through behavior. They often involve non-conscious emotional memories embedded within a conditioned emotional response, such as the conditioned fear response. The amygdala and other diverse neocortical and sub-cortical systems are brain structures related to emotional condi-tioning and implicit memory. Explicit and implicit forms of memory may be dissociated from each.

4. Memory involves monitoring processes regarding origin and accuracy. The sources of memories may be mistaken and influenced. The role of suggestibility in the malleability of memory has been demonstrated in laboratory experiments on the role of two significant mechanisms: the misinformation effect and source misattribution. The misinformation effect involves the incorporation of inaccurate postevent information into memories for previous events (Loftus, 1992); however, whether the postevent information actually impairs memory for the original event (especially an emotionally experienced and salient event) has been questioned by some researchers (Zaragosa & McCloskey, 1989). Source misattribution refers to the tendency for individuals to claim that they remember actually experiencing events that they only thought about or that were made available to them by others or through other sources such as media accounts. Confusion of this sort is especially evident in young children and highly suggestible adults. Age and individual differences in suggestibility have been found, with younger children, on average, more suggestible and susceptible to memory distortion effects than older children and adults (Ceci & Bruck, 1993).

5. Memory completeness and accuracy are not to be confused. A memory may be incomplete but accurate and, conversely, complete yet highly inaccurate. "The relative accuracy of the memory needs to be assessed independently from the issues of memory completeness or incompleteness, full or partial amnesia, or from the methods of recovery of the memory" (Brown et al., 1998, p. 82).

6. In a similar vein, memory and narrative are not the same, and vividness, emotionality, and confidence in a memory should not be confused with accuracy. The verbal telling of an event is an approximation that can be influenced by a number of factors. Also, the vividness of recall, the amount of emotionality accompanying it, and the certainty that it is true do not mean that it actually is. Some clinicians have too readily confounded these factors with a memory's accuracy (McConkey, 1997). As in point 5, independent corroboration is called for in determining reality and accuracy.

7. Despite information about memory distortion and malleability, the bulk of memory research supports the accuracy of memory for events known to have occurred. Recent memories are significantly more likely to be remembered and remote memories less

likely. Adults generally do not have much recall of early child-hood experence (before age four) due to childhood or infantile amnesia. Exact dates are not well retained and dating of remote memories may be highly inaccurate, unless the event was espe-cially relevant and tagged in some way.

8. Autobiographical memories for remarkable and personally signif-icant events can be well retained over long durations. In general, the gist of the memory is highly accurate and durable while peripheral details may be less so. However, research has also shown that psychologically motivated forgetting or voluntary thought suppression may cause the opposite to occur. Some remarkable personal events may be less likely to be recalled due to their association with internal conflict and distress and due to the use of avoidance and suppression mechanisms.

9. Evidence is also available that individuals can remember events that did not occur and that pseudo-memories can be induced through repeated suggestion and rehearsal (especially when sug-gestions come from a person with perceived authority), repeated attempts at retrieval, and the use of imagery and imagination. Young children and individuals who are fantasy prone and high-ly suggestible, hypnotizable, or dissociative may be the easiest to influence.

10. Memory disturbances and amnesia are involved in a number of psychiatric and neurological conditions in addition to PTSD and the dissociative disorders. Memory disturbances are found to be associated with the diagnoses of depression, Korsakoff's disease, Alzheimer's dementia, and acute alcoholism, among others. Memory disturbances may also be due to specific brain injury and damage.

DEVELOPMENTAL ISSUES IN MEMORY.   Developmental studies investi-gate normal changes in the processes of coding and retrieving informa-tion due to the child's age and level of physical and emotional matura-tion. This area of inquiry is relatively new and, at present, understudied. Its importance (in general and due to the controversy) obviously requires additional research attention. Although different theories have been put forth, several principles have emerged from this field of inquiry:

1. Some research data suggest the development of two parallel yet independent memory systems, a behavioral memory system and a verbal or narrative memory system (Pillemer & White, 1989). According to these researchers, the behavioral memory system

develops earlier. Memory in very young children is expressed primarily in imageryand behavioral reenactment. Studies suggest that children ages two to three (and possibly younger) retain relatively complete and mostly accurate behavioral memory for play events even when they are unable to verbalize memory of the event due to infantile or childhood amnesia. The verbal memory system begins, on average, in the second year and is highly organized by the third year. Three and four year olds can verbally describe events with a reasonable degree of accuracy, even though the descriptions might not be complete. After the fourth year, verbal memory can be shared with others, and by roughly the eighth year, the child is capable of verbalizing and elaborating on specific autobiographical memories.

Until recently, researchers believed that memories from early childhood were predominantly if not exclusively implicit and that explicit memory was not developed in infants and young children; however, in a recent review article, researcher Rovee-Collier (1997) challenges this perspective. She writes:

Contrary to the assumption that the memory system of very young infants is exclusively implicit, evidence amassed from a large number of studies that were conducted over the past 25 years reveals that very young infants display experimental dissociations in memory performance that exactly mirror the memory dissociations displayed by adults with normal memory on analogous tests in response to manipulations of the same independent variables. This evidence disputes claims that implicit and explicit memory follow different developmental time lines and challenges the utility of conscious recollection as the defining characteristic of explicit memory. It seems unlikely that any simple dichotomy could adequately characterize a process as complex as memory, even during the infancy period. Should a dichotomy eventually prove to be the most satisfactory account, than at a minimum, both implicit and explicit memory must be viewed as primitive systems that are simultaneously functional very early in development. (p. 468)

Similarly, some memory researchers suggest that children's memory is not structurally different from that of adults, but that forgetting childhood events may be related more to other aspects of social and cognitive development and emotion than to the developmental immaturity of the child's memory systems. Nevertheless, these perspectives on child memory do not run counter to the viewpoint that children are unable, on average, to explicitly and consciously remember complex memories that occur before four years of age (Williams & Banyard, 1997b).

2. Accurate verbal memory for experiences in early childhood (before the ages of two or three, possibly later) is generally not available due to maturational reasons and lack of verbal skills; however, behavioral memory may be available and accurate. The absence of verbal memory for much of childhood in adults is normal and may be explained by aspects of cognitive and social development that affect the memory system. Many researchers have argued that children must develop a degree of neurophysiological maturation, a sense of self, a social context for discussion and rehearsal, as well as content knowledge by which to understand and describe events (Fivush & Hammond, 1990; Goodman, Rudy, Bottoms, & Aman, 1990; Howe & Courage, 1993; Nelson, 1993, 1994). Recent research has suggested that children are sometimes able at a later stage of development to go back to earlier times and put words and comprehension to their experiences.

3. In general, children can remember accurately and retain information for long periods of time, although their spontaneous recall is often incomplete and inconstant. Age-related differences in performance consistently have been found. Older children, on average, remember more and are less suggestible than younger children. Individual differences, including emotional response to an event, may have an impact on a child's ability to remember or to report an event. Also, children's ability to distinguish between fact and fantasy is generally better than has been assumed and improves with age (Ceci & Bruck, 1993).

4. The development of memory is heavily influenced by interpersonal experiences. Social support and shared constructions of stories about remembered events may assist in their retention, especially for childhood events (Fivush, 1991; 1996; Nelson, 1993; Tessler & Nelson, 1996). Events that are secret and not discussed may therefore be less well retained and recalled. Events may be forgotten in order to maintain a significant attachment if retention of the memory interferes with the relationship (Freyd, 1996).

5. Repeated questioning of a young child may result in the elaboration of a story with fictional elements accompanied by conviction about having experienced the fictional events (Ceci & Bruck, 1993; Ceci, Huffman, Smith, & Loftus, 1996); however, in many respects, children of school age and older are not signif-

icantly more suggestiblethan adults, especially when asked to recall stressful or personally remarkable events (Ornstein, 1995).

Studies of normal memory processes in both adults and children have ramifications for the study of traumatic memories. Williams and Banyard (1997b) summarized their review of this literature as follows:

> What are the implications of these studies of general memory process-es for memories of traumatic events such as child sexual abuse? Again, this area of study is characterized by considerable controversy and dis-agreement. Some researchers suggest that memories for traumatic events are the same as for other events, suggesting that normal devel-opmental differences in memories for childhood events may explain why some survivors of abuse have no impaired recall of the trauma. Others provide evidence for a distinction, stating that trauma has unique effects on memory that may result in impaired recall. One avenue of investigation has examined the effect of emotion on memory based on the notion that the emotional salience of traumatic events may exert particular effects on memory. (p. II-127)

We now turn to a review of some of the data concerning the effect of stressful and emotional events on memory.

MEMORY FOR STRESSFUL AND EMOTIONAL EVENTS.   In the late '80s, memory researchers began to conduct studies outside of the laboratory in order to achieve more ecological validity by investigating real life rather than analog situations. Investigators studied the effects of highly stress-ful or emotional events on memory ("events of impact" according to Yuille and Tollestrup, 1992, some of which might be considered traumat-ic). In contrast to the viewpoint held by some memory researchers that high levels of emotional arousal interfere with the encoding and reten-tion of memory, Yuille and Tollestrup reported that events of this sort may involve special or preferential processing resulting in better reten-tion. Koss, Tromp, and Tharan (1995) reviewed the literature on this topic and concluded that "emotional memories have been characterized as 'detailed, accurate, and persistent' and ratings of intense emotional reaction are predictive of better, not worse, recall" (p. 124). In general, the central and critical details of stressful/emotional events appear to be better remembered than those of nonstressful events, but peripheral details may not be as well remembered (Christianson, 1992a, 1992b). This should not, however, be taken to mean that memory for emotional events is not malleable or is always accurate in its entirety. Research has demonstrated that the emotional intensity of an experience does not guarantee that memory is indelible. Some important aspects of the experience might be forgotten or misremembered even as memory of the central event is well retained.

At this point, considerable multidisciplinary research has been conducted on memory for personally salient and experienced emotional events (Christianson, 1992a). It seems fair to conclude from available data that memory for emotional events differs in some significant ways from memory for nonemotional events and that the more emotionally impactful and remarkable an event, the better its retention in terms of central detail. Some researchers even hold that emotion is a form of memory (LeDoux, 1992). Yet, what accounts for the better retention remains unclear. Several hypotheses have been proposed including that remarkable events have more rehearsal when they are in the public domain and discussed with others, that they are more memorable due to personal salience and impact, possibly that they may be encoded differently from more mundane and less remarkable personal experiences (Elin, 1997; Yuille & Tollestrup, 1992), and that brain structures and biology are involved (Bremner, Krystal, Southwick, & Charney, 1995; Bremner, Krystal, Charney, & Southwick, 1996; LeDoux, 1992; McGaugh, 1992).

Studies have also been undertaken regarding "events of impact" for children. Their findings support the fact that children can accurately recall personally salient events, especially if they are asked about the gist of the event in question. They are generally not very accurate about peripheral details. Memory processes occur in interaction with physical maturation and the level of psychosexual development, the nature of the event and its meaning to the child, and the type of questions asked (Ceci & Bruck, 1993; Perry, 1993a, 1993b). Cued (or assisted) versus free recall is often needed for younger children to more accurately report their memories of stressful situations (Pynoos, Steinberg, & Aronson, 1997).

Does Traumatic Memory
Differ from Normal Event Memory?

At the center of the controversy are the issues of whether traumatic memory differs from memory for ordinary events, whether both types operate under different rules of memory, whether memories can be forgotten for an extended period of time before returning, and whether they are veridical representations of past events. Until fairly recently, information on traumatic memory has been available mainly from field and clinical observations rather than from research studies. These mostly naturalistic studies have repeatedly and consistently reported on abnormalities in memory across a range of traumata. Formal research studies on memory for traumatic events have only been undertaken in recent years (results are summarized in chapter 4). These and future studies, involving more sophisticated methodology and collaboration between memory and trauma experts, will hopefully provide information to settle many of the vexing questions that are in contention at present (American Psychological Association, 1996b; Butler & Spiegel, 1997; Conway, 1997; Lindsay & Briere, 1997; McConkey, 1997; Schooler, Bendiksen, & Ambadar, 1997; Toglia, 1997).

For the most part, memory and trauma researchers are split on questions involving traumatic memory and have approached the issue from very different perspectives. Indeed, they may even be split on the definition of trauma, as noted earlier in this chapter. Trauma researchers have identified the tendency of some memory scientists to misunderstand or minimize the nature of trauma and to not differentiate it from events that are emotional, stressful, or aversive but that nevertheless do not qualify as traumatic (Alpert, Brown, & Courtois, 1996b, 1996c; Butler & Spiegel, 1997; Putnam, 1997; Reviere, 1996). Additionally, the issue of ecological validity has been raised repeatedly to challenge the notion that findings from laboratory studies of normal individuals (often nonclinical samples of college students exposed to mildly to moderately stressful events) are comparable and generalizable to traumatized individuals who witnessed or directly experienced overwhelming events and emotions (see Brown et al., 1998 and Butler & Spiegel, 1997 for considerable discussion of this issue). It would obviously be unethical to traumatize individuals in the laboratory in order to study their responses. Memory researchers must therefore find ways to conduct studies of individuals who have been traumatized, in either the immediate or long-term aftermath of the trauma, in order to have more direct ecological validity.

THE PERSPECTIVE OF THE MEMORY RESEARCHERS. Many of the most vocal of the memory researchers involved in the debate do not believe that memories for traumatic events differ from memories for more neutral events and contend that they must follow the laws identified for normal event memory. They tend to be more concerned with the malleability of human memories and the many ways that memories can be influenced and distorted (i.e., through suggestions, misinformation, etc.) (Loftus, 1993; Ornstein, Ceci, & Loftus, 1996a; Shobe & Kihlstrom, 1997). These experts argue that traumatized individuals have normal memory systems unaffected by trauma and that failure to recollect traumatic events is due to "normal forgetting" rather than any kind of special mechanism (Loftus, Garry, & Feldman, 1994). Moreover, they take the position that, since traumatic memories are not distinct, they are not immune from the laws of memory that have been identified over the course of the last hundred years of study. In particular, they take issue with the idea of the indelible fixation and inflexibility of traumatic memory described by some trauma researchers and argue instead that even traumatic memory is subject to error and modification. Shobe and Kihlstrom (1997) summarized their article entitled "Are traumatic memories special?" as follows:

> Maintaining the conviction that traumatic memories have special properties requires that one reject laboratory evidence as irrelevant to cases of clinical trauma, and accept instead evidence from clinical case studies of actual trauma victims. However, as we have shown, the clinical evidence is itself highly ambiguous. What on initial inspection appear to be exceptions to the rule of enhanced emotional memory are either poorly documented or else explicated by other, normal, memory processes. Nothing about the clinical evidence suggests that traumatic memories are special, or that special techniques are required to recover them. (p. 74)

Taking a similar perspective, McConkey (1997) wrote: "there is no reason that memory for traumatic events should follow entirely different psychological principles from those followed by memory for nontraumatic events. Although a case for that possibility is made by some . . . , evidence suggests that traumatic memories can be influenced by the same range of cognitive and social events that influence nontraumatic memories" (p. II-58). Nor are memory researchers impressed by the physiological data that trauma researchers are accumulating to possibly account for differences in encoding, retention, and retrieval. According to Ornstein et al., (1996a):

> Although everyone would agree that physical and psychological sequelae to trauma can and do occur, there is no compelling biological or social evidence to support the view that once-viable memories of traumatic experiences can be submerged and then recovered after intervals that extend many years . . . The claim of repressed memory has little evidence to support it, and efforts to bolster it with allusions to neurophysiology are ill-wrought . . . . (p. 108)

These memory researchers point to the literature on human memory, particularly the flow of information within the memory system (from preliminary encoding to storage, consolidation, and alteration/degradation over time, to retrieval) to underscore the points at which memory might not be registered or might be influenced. They highlight the potential for variability and fallibility at each stage of the process and note particularly that failure to remember may be due to lack of encoding in the first place rather than to retrieval failure. It might also be due to the normal degradation of memory over time. They also highlight important developmental issues such as age-related differences, including infantile/childhood amnesia, in the encoding, retention, and retrieval of memory. Children's source monitoring and developmental susceptibility to suggestion and to post-event misleading information are particular concerns (Bruck & Ceci, 1997). Memory researchers cite evidence from recent research studies that support both the creation of pseudomemories and the purported ease with which pseudomemories can be suggested. These studies demonstrate that false memory production is possible in a nontrivial minority of individuals investigated (approximately 20 to 40 percent depending on the strength and repetition of the experimental procedure) (Hyman, Husband, & Billings, 1995; Loftus & Coan, 1994; Loftus & Pickrell, 1995). Of greatest interest, of course, is the creation of false memories for sexual abuse in psychotherapy through suggestive influences both within and outside of treatment setting, including confirmatory bias on the part of the therapist (Hyman & Loftus, 1997; Loftus, 1993).

In contrast to the perspective exemplified by the writings of Loftus (1993) and Ornstein et al. (1996a), some memory researchers are more open to the idea that traumatic memories are different in some significant ways from normal event memories (Christianson, 1992a, 1992b; Christianson & Engelberg, 1997) and have gathered data that support this perspective (Schooler, Ambadar, & Bendiksen, 1997; Schooler, Bendiksen, & Ambadar, 1997). Some are also more open to the possibility and reality of recovered memory of trauma after a delay (Lindsay, 1997). Others have researched brain psychobiology and structure and identified changes associated with trauma that might impact coding, retention and accessibility, and retrieval (LeDoux, 1992; McGaugh, 1992, 1995). These authors tend to emphasize the need for greater ecological validity in studying traumatic memory than is currently the case with laboratory studies and analogs of stressful events. They also herald the opportunity to extend memory study in this largely unexplored area.

THE PERSPECTIVE OF THE TRAUMA RESEARCHERS.   In contrast to the more conservative of the memory viewpoints, many trauma researchers are of the opinion that enough data have accumulated to support the position that traumatic memory is different from ordinary event memory and that recovered memories are possible (although not necessarily accurate in their entirety). They cite clinical and field observations across a range of traumatic circumstances from the turn of the century. These findings are now being tested and supplemented by formal research studies of traumatization and its effect on memory. For example, in an important recently conducted random population study, amnesia for some or all of a traumatic experience has been found across many different types of trauma, including accidents and natural disasters, combat trauma, situations of captivity and torture, experiences of sexual and physical abuse, and witnessing a murder or a suicide of a family member (Elliott, 1997). Also of note was the finding that 72% of the respondents reported having experienced some form of trauma, and of these, 32% reported delayed recall of the event.

To date, evidence has accumulated from the study of trauma to suggest that traumatic memory differs in some significant ways from normal event memory. Van der Kolk recently wrote that the study of traumatic memory raises questions about at least four basic notions concerning the nature of human memory derived from laboratory study of memory for ordinary events:

> (1) that memory is flexible and integrated with other life experiences, (2) that memory generally is present in consciousness in a continuous and uninterrupted fashion, (3) that memory always disintegrates in accuracy over time, and (4) that memory is primarily declarative, i.e., that people generally can articulate what they know in words and symbols. A century of study of traumatic memories shows that (1) they generally remain unaffected by other life experiences, (2) they may return, triggered by reminders, at any time during a person's life with a vividness as if the subject is having the experience all over again, and (3) these memories are primarily sensory and emotional; they frequently leave victims in a state of speechless terror, in which they may be unable to precisely articulate what they are feeling and thinking. (1997, pp. 245-246)

It has long been recognized that trauma may singularly impact memory processing, as well as personal functioning. Moreover, according to Siegel: "Cognition and interpersonal experiences during and after trauma may uniquely affect the ways in which memories for these events are processed and later accessed" (p. 98). The memory of trauma is encoded under conditions of heightened physiological and emotional arousal. The traumatic experience itself, as well as its associated effects, is difficult to incorporate into existing mental schemata about self, others, and the world. This lack of fit results in the inability to process or integrate the experience and its impact (Horowitz, 1986). This, along with the distinctive neurobiology of PTSD that results in emotional and physiological dysregulation, may be related to the alternation between reexperiencing and vivid recall, on the one hand, and numbing and amnesia, on the other. Psychophysiologic and neural processes may also affect memory. Evidence has accrued from the study of a variety of traumatized populations that individuals with stress-related disorders such as PTSD show differences in memory function relative to traumatized individuals without PTSD and nontraumatized normals (Bremner et al., 1996a, 1996b; Golier, Yehuda, & Southwick, 1996). Butler and Spiegel (1997) have discussed another dimension of traumatic memory, namely, the intrusion symptoms that include sensory, affective, and motoric reliving experiences, flashbacks, nightmares, and behavioral reenactments as representing a distinct departure from normal memory processing:

> The unbidden, vivid, and absorbing experience of a flashback or reliving of the traumatic event is one of the most profoundly disturbing intrusion symptoms in posttraumatic reactions. During these episodes, which may last from a few seconds to several hours, the traumatic event is not just remembered but reexperienced in the moment. This event presumably reflects a state of absorption into the content or fragment of a memory or belief and its attendant affect that is so profound that the current environment is largely ignored and the individual temporarily does not distinguish memory from present experience. (p. II-24)

Additionally, recollection of the trauma may well be at the implicit rather than explicit level of awareness, with emotional/perceptual/sensorimotor components more prominent than declarative ones. Reports of the memories of traumatized individuals indicate that they emerge more often in unintegrated and fragmented somatosensory and emotional form with little verbal representation, often in response to environmental and emotional triggers and cues that are somehow reminiscent of the trauma, including the emotional state in which it was encoded. These characteristics contrast markedly with those of memories for nontraumatic events (van der Kolk and Fisler, 1995).

Trauma researchers also point out that available research indicates that trauma can influence the encoding, retention, and retrieval of memory due to its effect on psychobiology and physiology. For example, from their review of the literature Chu et al. (1996) summarized:

> There is considerable evidence that traumatic memory may be associ-

ated with psychobiologic features and cognitive characteristics that are quite different from ordinary memory. The characteristics of traumatic memory are quite varied and are dependent on the nature of the traumatic events and the age when they were experienced. Clinical evidence and some studies suggest that brief or limited traumatization results in increased clarity or recall (hypermnesia) and a high level of accuracy concerning the central details of the experience. On the other hand, severe and chronic early traumatization may be correlated with denial, dissociation, and amnesia. (p. 2)

Bremner et al. (1996) reviewed neural mechanisms in dissociative amnesia for childhood abuse and concluded:

What is known about the neurobiology of memory supports the idea that special mechanisms may be operative in recall of traumatic events, such as childhood abuse. Neuromodulators released during stress have both strengthening and diminishing effects on memory traces, depending on the dose and the particular type of neuromodulator. Changes in brain regions involved in memory may underlie many symptoms of stress-related psychiatric disorders, including symptoms of amnesia. (p. 72)

Van der Kolk is a vocal supporter of this position and the first author of the earliest contemporary paper on memory for traumatic events (van der Kolk & van der Hart, 1991). He has emphasized the prominence of emotional and perceptual elements in traumatic memories. This viewpoint is founded upon and concordant with the original findings of Janet regarding traumatic memories ("fixed ideas") operating at an implicit rather than explicit level and having the potential to "have a life of their own" and to affect behavior outside of awareness or consciousness. From findings derived from a number of laboratory (animal and human) and clinical studies, van der Kolk and associates have come to believe that trauma (especially prolonged and intense trauma) can affect brain psychobiology and brain structures such as the hippocampus in ways that alter normal memory processes (Bremner et al., 1995; Rauch, et al., 1996; van der Kolk & Fisler, 1995; van der Kolk & van der Hart, 1991).

These researchers believe that memory for trauma may have been encoded differently from memory for ordinary events, impeding the formation of explicit memory "perhaps via alterations in attentional focusing, perhaps because extreme emotional arousal interferes with hippocampal memory functions" (van der Kolk,1997, p. 248). The alterations found in traumatic memory include strengthened memory traces as well as absent memory. They further believe that, because these memories exist apart from (or are dissociated from) memories for normal events and normal memory processes, they may resist integration and not be subject to the rules found to govern normal memories (van der Hart et al., 1993).

Golier et al., (1996) have cautioned that these findings do not apply to all individuals exposed to trauma but rather are only applicable to those with PTSD:

> Patients with PTSD differ from other trauma survivors in their recall of the traumatic event, in the ways in which memory for the event is altered, and in the ways they continue to process information related to victimization. The extent of these memory alterations remains to be elucidated, as there is evidence that a broad range of cognitive functions may be affected. Given the differences between PTSD and non-PTSD survivors, however, the abnormalities seen in PTSD should not be considered synonymous with the effect of trauma on memory. (p. 240)

At the present time, several neural mechanisms that are relevant to the effects of traumatic stress on memory, such as fear conditioning (and other emotional conditioning as well), stress sensitization, and the failure of extinction, are posited as related to traumatic memory processes, including dissociative amnesia (Bremner, et al.,1995). The reader interested in more information about the psychobiology and neurophysiology of traumatization and PTSD and their possible effect on memory processes is referred to Bremner et al. (1996), Bremner et al. (1995), Bremner, Southwick, & Charney (1991), Chu et al. (1996), Friedman et al. (1995), Metcalfe and Jacobs (1996), LeDoux (1994), McGaugh (1989), Siegel (1995), van der Kolk (1996, 1997), and Yehuda and McFarlane (1997).

Brown et al. (1998), from their review of the extant memory and trauma literatures, make an interesting observation regarding whether traumatic memory must follow the laws of ordinary event memory. In contrast to the position taken by some influential memory researchers, they speculate that it is premature to assume that memory for trauma follows the available conceptualizations used to understand normal memory processes (the trace and reconstructive schools). They suggest instead that the mechanisms by which memory for trauma are processed will be better understood once trauma is studied under laboratory conditions. They refer specifically to the partially constructive theory of memory described by Brewer (1986) as a type of hybrid theory that might be needed to accommodate findings about traumatic memory. In Brewer's model, the

gist of the memory for an important autobiographical event is retained at
the expense of less important details that are subject to reconstruction
when the event is repeatedly recalled. Brown et al. conclude: "It is conceivable that a partially constructive theory might apply to trauma, where
a traumatized individual preserves the gist of the traumatic experience
but reconstructs, and thereby distorts, the details upon each recall" (p.
71). These speculations show how collaboration between memory and
trauma scientists might lead to new understandings and hybrid formulations about the mechanisms involved in traumatic memory.

Brown et al. (1998) completed an exhaustive review of the normal
event and traumatic memory literatures, to which the reader is referred
for more comprehensive information on these topics. Included in Table
3.4 are 13 summary points they identified from the available literature on
memory performance in traumatized individuals.

Traumatic Memory in Children

The study of memory in traumatized children is a subcategory of the
study of trauma and children, a relatively recent (and as yet understudied) area of scientific investigation. It is clear that children interpret and
respond to trauma according to their developmental level and maturity,
but it has only been in the last two decades that a description of PTSD
in children has been available (Eth & Pynoos, 1985; Pynoos & Eth, 1985;
Terr, 1979, 1981, 1983a , 1983b). Recent studies of traumatized children
and their reactions have led to a number of conceptual developmental
models of memory, in general and of traumatic memory in particular
(Elin, 1997; Perry, 1993a, 1993b; Putnam, 1997; Pynoos & Nader, 1989;
Pynoos et al., 1997; Pynoos et al., 1996; Trickett & Putnam, 1993).

In order to understand traumatic memory in children, it is necessary to
place it in the context of the development of normal event memory in
children, as described earlier in this chapter, and in the context of children's physical and psychosexual development as well. The child's
behavioral memory system, available from infancy, is supplemented and
supplanted by the narrative memory system in later childhood (starting
approximately at age three), as the child acquires greater facility with language and representational skills. This behavioral expression is consistent with research on infant memory showing the nonverbal and behavioral manifestations of remembered experiences by preverbal infants
(Rovee-Collier, 1993) and with studies of childhood memory in cases of
documented early trauma (before the age of two and a half) (Hewitt,
1994; Terr, 1988). It should be noted that some children between the
ages two and three have been able to accurately verbally describe trau-

Table 3.4
Conclusions Drawn from Studies of Traumatic Memory in Adults

1. Traumatizing events differ from events of impact by the *occurrence of posttraumatic stress symptoms.*

2. The data on *completeness* of memory for trauma suggest a bimodal distribution, with a larger sample who always remember the trauma, often vividly and accompanied by intrusive reexperiencing symptoms, and a smaller sample who are amnestic for the trauma for some period in their lives and may or may not later recover the memory.

3. The subsample of traumatized individuals who are amnestic for the trauma can be differentiated into those who are *fully* or *partially* amnestic for specific traumatizing event(s) versus those whose amnesia also encompasses personal autobiographical memory or memory for socially shared events. The difference between *trauma-specific amnesia* and *general functional retrograde amnesia* subsequent to traumatization may in part be determined by the type of traumatization, with limited amnesia being more characteristic of single-incident trauma and general amnesia more common of multiple or cumulative trauma.

4. There are few data available on whether traumatic memories are stored in the form of *specific* or *generic memories* for cumulative abuse experiences.

5. Functional, psychogenic, and organic amnesia sometimes overlap, especially where the traumatization involved injury or intoxication.

6. When failure to remember a traumatic event and later remembering is reported, it is difficult to distinguish genuine traumatic *amnesia* from *denial* (i.e., remembering the event and not wanting to think about or talk about it).

7. The *predictors* of amnesia subsequent to traumatization represent a complex interaction of a number of variables, some of which have been identified: biological, cognitive, affective, duration, number of perpetrators, injury and threat to life, and relationship to the perpetrator. Predictors of traumatic amnesia represent a complex interaction of multiple factors. No data are available on predictors of continuous memory for a traumatic experience.

8. There is no consensus on the *mechanisms* by which trauma-specific amnesia occurs.

9. *Recovery of memories* for trauma in those who are amnestic occurs through expectable retrieval strategies such as free recall, context reinstatement, or reinstatement of emotional arousal. Recovery of CSA memories occurs much less frequently inside, as compared to outside, psychotherapy.

10. Hypermnesia and amnesia for the trauma pertain to the relative completeness or incompleteness of the memory and have little to do with its *accuracy.* Accuracy and completeness are independent constructs.

Continued on following page

Table 3.4 (continued)
Conclusions Drawn from Studies of Traumatic Memory in Adults

11. Nearly all of the available data on the completeness and accuracy of memory for trauma is limited to one category of memory, namely, verbal and autobiographical memory. Clinical, developmental, and neurobiological studies document the existence of a behavioral or implicit memory for trauma, which may be the primary memory system in which traumatic experiences are stored.

12. A significant subpopulation of traumatized individuals retain little or no narrative memory for the trauma. When the trauma recollection is recovered, it is often initially recovered in a somato-sensory, imagistic, and affective form. *The initial narrative memory is often fragmented, incomplete, and overly general.* Over time a more organized form of the narrative memory is likely to be reported, although fragmented or dissociated aspects of the trauma memory may persist.

13. There has been little research on how different traumas may impact on memory differently.

From *Memory, Trauma, Treatment and the Law* (pp. 198-200), by D. Brown, A. W. Scheflin, and D. C Hammond, 1998, New York: W. W. Norton & Company, Inc. Reprinted with permission.

matic events (Sugar, 1992; Terr, 1988), but that the majority of children cannot verbalize their memory and instead manifest it behaviorally. This finding is captured in the *DSM-IV* (American Psychiatric Association, 1994) notation for the diagnosis of PTSD that traumatized children are more likely to reenact or behaviorally manifest traumatic experiences than to describe them verbally.

It appears that memory for single traumas occurring in later childhood is relatively well retained, particularly concerning the gist of the event, and that memory is available in behavioral as well as verbal representation, depending upon the age of the child at the time of the traumatization. The memory, however, is not always accurate and represents a reconstruction rather than a reproduction of the event. In an important study of the response of children to a sniper attack at an elementary school, Pynoos and Nader (1989) found memory retention and unassisted reporting to be highly idiosyncratic, related to what they termed anchor points or memory markers that varied according to the experience of the particular child. These researchers found that the organization of memory and strategy of recall differed as the children focused on different anchor points and their idiosyncratic meaning and, furthermore, that the anchor points were associated with imagined or intended interventions (influenced by age and level of maturity) that became part of the memory network surrounding the experience.

Perry (1993a, 1993b, 1994) has described the neurophysiological and neurodevelopmental implications of maltreatment during the course of childhood. His findings are consistent with those of researchers studying neurobiological and psychophysiological impact in traumatized adults but he adds another dimension, namely, that chronic traumatization during the course of childhood alters the child's neurological response and affects subsequent development. This, in turn, may relate to the child's symptoms and, in some cases, may actually be implicated in additional abuse and traumatization (e.g., the learning disabled, oppositional-defiant, or dissociative child who is taunted or punished). Perry also describes specific risk and protective factors that can exacerbate or ameliorate the traumatized child's reactions. These involve the child's age and salient developmental tasks; degree of threat; disruption of social and family support; number, nature, and pattern of traumatic events; early intervention and "sensitization;" and the child's loss of control.

Conceptual models have also been developed by Elin (1997) and Pynoos and his colleagues (Pynoos, et al., 1997). Both of these models stress the complexity of traumatic experiences and reactions and, according to Pynoos et al., "the extreme activity of children's minds in the experience and remembering of traumatic events" and the necessity to understand children's memory of traumatic experiences from both functional and developmental perspectives:

> By *functional*, we refer to how such experiences contribute to a child's evolving schematization of the world, especially of threat, danger, security, safety, risk, injury, loss, protection, and intervention. By *developmental*, we refer to maturational and experiential processes that govern the mental representation of external and internal dangers. These include a progressive capacity for the metacognition of emotions, the acquisition of cognitive competencies, and plasticity and consolidation of neuroanatomical structure within memory systems of the brain. (authors' italics) (pp. 272-273)

Amnesia for childhood trauma (occurring after the offset of and therefore not due to infantile or childhood amnesia) has been documented as quite variable. It has been found to be more likely to occur in situations involving repeated severe traumatization (Burgess, Hartman, & Baker, 1995; Corwin, 1997; Grassian & Holtzen, 1996; Terr, 1991) and in some cases where the traumatization and previous detailed verbal descriptions have been documented and where variable memory occurs between individuals exposed to the same traumatic stressor. Importantly, even in the absence of verbal memory for the traumatization, children have been found to retain some sort of behavioral representation over a period of years.

Terr (1991, 1994) has developed the most detailed model of memory loss in traumatized children from her years of study of children who experienced a variety of traumatic events. She proposed a model of two primary types of childhood trauma, each with a corresponding pattern of memory encoding and retrieval. Type I consists of a sudden, external, single traumatic event that, if stressful enough, results in stereotyped symptoms of childhood PTSD along with detailed memories but some misperceptions and mistimings regarding characteristics of the event. In contrast,

> Type II traumas follow from long-standing or repeated exposure to extreme external events. . . . The subsequent unfolding of horrors creates a sense of anticipation. Massive attempts to protect the psyche and to preserve the self are put into gear. The defenses and coping operations used in the type II disorders of childhood—massive denial, repression, dissociation, self-anesthesia, self-hypnosis, identification with the aggressor and aggression turned against the self—often lead to profound character changes in the youngster. . . . The emotions stirred up by type II traumas are 1) an absence of feeling, 2) a sense of rage, or 3) unremitting sadness in addition to fear. (1991, pp. 15-16)

Memory loss is common in this type of trauma. Terr also described a cross-over type between the two involving a one-time trauma of such objective and subjective intensity (e.g., witnessing the murder of one parent by the other) that the response is closer to the type II effect. In both type II and cross-over type situations, the traumatic response becomes intertwined in the child's personality development and sets the stage for continued difficulties later in life. Although in need of additional substantiation, Terr's model is consistent with and receives preliminary support from the study of dissociative children (Putnam, 1997). It is also concordant with and supported by the studies of adults documenting amnesia and recovered memories for child sexual abuse that are reported in the next chapter.

Brown et al. (1998) also provided summary points regarding traumatic memory in children. These are included in Table 3.5.

Butler and Spiegel (1997) concluded their review of the research and clinical literature on emotional stress and memory with the following observation that is quite useful to our discussion of normal event versus traumatic event memory:

Table 3.5
Conclusions from the Studies on Memory for Trauma in Children

1. The *behavioral* or *implicit* memory system is the primary medium for storage of memory for trauma in younger children. . . . Although memory for trauma is also encoded as a verbal memory system, a behavioral memory for trauma evidently persists in older children and adults, and may represent the primary mode of memory for traumatic experiences. Behavioral memory for trauma may manifest in the form of behavioral reenactments in relationships, posttraumatic play, trauma-specific fears, or somatic symptoms. *Behavioral* or *implicit memory for trauma* is a robust finding across all available studies.

2. Nevertheless, children as young as 35 months and sometimes as young as 18 months, manifest a *verbal memory for trauma*, as do older children and adults. This verbal memory, however, is likely to be *fragmented* and incomplete, especially in younger children, but often in older children and adults, too.

3. As of yet, there are virtually no data on what *predicts* whether a traumatic experience in childhood is stored and manifested primarily as a behavioral memory, a narrative memory, or both.

4. In contrast to the adult studies on memory for trauma, some child studies on single-incident trauma fail to find evidence for *amnesia for trauma* at least up to several years after traumatization. However, *selective amnesia for bodily injury* does occur in some traumatized children exposed to single-incident trauma over relatively short retention intervals. Moreover, full or partial amnesia for multiple, repeated sexual abuse does occur in some children over longer retention intervals and into adolescence. Combining the child and adult data, there is some indication that amnesia for trauma in childhood does not typically manifest itself shortly after the event and may not manifest itself until later childhood or adolescence.

5. The specificity of a behavioral reenactment of a trauma is not necessarily an indicator of *accuracy* . . . . Children's narrative memories for trauma vary in their degree of completeness and accuracy. Although there are exceptions, most studies demonstrate that the gist of the child's verbal memory for a real traumatic experience is generally accurate, although the details may be distorted.

6. The child studies demonstrate very specific *psychologically motivated distortion* of memory for trauma, especially when traumatization involves injury or threat to life, and possibly betrayal-trauma.

7. Some of the *predictors* of completeness and accuracy of memory for traumatic events in children are similar to those in adulthood, except that age, quality of interaction with caregivers and other forms of social support, level of understanding, and coping ability are significant predictors of at least the child's verbal memory for the trauma.

From *Memory, Trauma, Treatment and the Law* (pp. 210-211), by D. Brown, A. W. Scheflin, and D. C Hammond, 1998, New York: W. W. Norton & Company, Inc. Reprinted with permission.

In summary, the experimental psychological literature on emotion/ stress and memory seems to be correct up to a point. In general, *memory for the central details and overall theme of a traumatic event may be enhanced by the increased negative affect associated with an event, whereas memory for peripheral or contextual information may be diminished.* . . . The clinical literature, on the other hand, suggests that with respect to individuals with posttraumatic conditions, the quantitative association (of increasing stress and improved retention/recall) may be replaced by a qualitatively different one in which intense fear, helplessness, or horror overwhelms the individual and exerts a destabilizing effect on the process of memory consolidation and/or accessibility. Individuals who have experienced significant trauma, especially with PTSD symptomatology, seem to represent a different population, exhibiting a contrasting response, in what are likely incomparable conditions, when compared with subjects in experimental studies of emotional arousal and memory. (italics added) (p. II-29)

Mechanisms for Forgetting Trauma: Repression, Dissociation, Amnesia

The concept of "repressed memory" (versus dissociated memory) is also a core feature of the controversy. Repression and dissociation have been posited by trauma researchers as the mechanisms most related to memory loss. The terms have been used interchangeably, adding another level of conceptual confusion to the debate (Freyd, 1996).

The concept of repression as related to or responsible for absent memory has been challenged by some memory researchers and false memory critics (Loftus & Ketcham, 1994; Ofshe & Watters, 1994), largely on the basis of one review article by Holmes (1990) in which he argues that the concept of repression is not empirically supported (even though Holmes later admitted that his perspective was a distinctly minority viewpoint) (Holmes, 1994). Nevertheless, his article has been used by false memory proponents and some memory researchers to contend that repression does not exist and is a myth (Loftus and Ketcham titled their book *The Myth of Repressed Memory*). This contention has been used, by extension, to suggest that memories cannot be repressed; therefore, repressed/recovered memories are not possible and are also a myth (a.k.a. false memories).

At present, among many trauma researchers and clinicians, the preferred term for memory loss is *traumatic* or *dissociative amnesia* and for the mechanism underlying the loss, dissociation (both encompassed in the *DSM* diagnosis of dissociative amnesia). Dissociation is favored for a number of reasons. It relates to the diverse memory systems that are being identified and researched by both trauma and memory scientists. It supports the idea of state-dependent memory where events experienced and encoded in a particular emotional state may be more subject to recall in a similar state. Furthermore, as discussed by Yates and Nasby (1993), dissociation is the preferred term because it can be empirically demonstrated to occur, can be experimentally induced, is atheoretical (versus repression, which is associated with psychoanalytic theory), and has been found to be implicated in the storage and retrieval of traumatic events. Butler and Spiegel (1997) commented on the non-random distribution of dissociative amnesia among adults survivors of childhood sexual abuse in the currently available studies as arguing against normal forgetting as the most likely mechanism for memory loss: ". . . the greater the predictable psychological or developmental effect, the more likely the life experience will be forgotten by these individuals—clearly, this is contrary to what might be predicted from normal processes of memory failure, and it is inconsistent with the extensive cognitive literature on increased memorability of emotional events in nonclinical subjects" (p. II-32).

Yet, is it quite evident that the terms "dissociation," "repression," and "amnesia" have been used interchangeably and that currently there is no overarching consensus on the mechanisms by which trauma-specific memory loss occurs. Hypothetically, the mechanisms may include dissociation, repression, failure to encode, motivated or intentional forgetting, normal forgetting, thought suppression, conditioned extinction, betrayal of attachment, state-dependent learning and retrieval failure, and long-term depression (Brown et al., 1998; Koutstaal & Schacter, 1997; Roth & Friedman, 1998). In addition, these mechanisms might not be mutually exclusive (Freyd, 1996). What seems most important is not the terminology used per se (although perhaps the mechanism(s) will be more articulated as research findings accumulate), but rather that particular terminology not obscure the data on memory loss for traumatic events.

Numerous observers have commented that the remembering of trauma is not an all-or-nothing phenomenon (Alpert et al., 1996c; Brown et al., 1998; Gold, Hughes, & Hohnecker, 1994; Harvey & Herman, 1994; Herman & Harvey, 1997). It has been found to range from continuous to relatively continuous to absent, with a fairly bimodal distribution. It appears that a majority of traumatized individuals retain memory for the traumatization, although possibly not in full detail (those individuals who have relatively continuous or partial memory), and a smaller group forget the trauma for long periods of time (those who have relatively complete to complete amnesia). Individuals in the middle of the continuum of remembering can be described as having either relatively continuous or relatively absent memory for traumatic events. It seems that the descriptor applied by the researcher can determine the interpretation of the memory accessibility or loss and that, as with other issues, standardization of terms and concepts would be beneficial.

Brown et al. (1998) provided more specificity by subdividing the partial amnesia category into a number of more detailed subcategories (all of which might be seen in clinical practice), as follows:

1. memory for the gist but not the details of the trauma, with or without intrusive/numbing PTSD symptoms;
2. memory for the peripheral details but not for the gist of the central information about the trauma, with or without intrusive/numbing PTSD symptoms;
3. patchy memory for the trauma, i.e., some episodes/details are clear but not others . . .
4. memory for at least the gist of the trauma is somewhat clear (although not necessarily the details), but the patient . . . is dissociated from the affects associated with the trauma;
5. memory for at least the gist of the trauma (although for neither the details nor affects) is clear and the patient has no clear understanding of its meaning, the impact of the trauma on current life, or any possible causal relationship to current symptoms;
6. very partial memory, i.e., simply a general sense of previous trauma background, without memory of specific incidents or memory for the gist or details of such incidents . . . . (pp. 443-444)

Laub and Auerhahn (1993), from their clinical work and review of relevant literature, wrote a seminal paper entitled "Knowing and Not Knowing Massive Psychic Trauma: Forms of Traumatic Memory." These authors went beyond simply describing amnesia patterns to describing a continuum of behavioral and verbal manifestations of knowledge about traumatization, ranging from least to most integrated according to the distance the individual is able to get from the traumatic event. In essence, they proposed that forms of knowing may differ from forms of remembering. They described the following as points along such a continuum and illustrated each with case examples:

1. Not knowing but paradoxically knowing simultaneously. The patient demonstrates no conscious knowledge of the trauma that is defended against through a variety of primitive defensive operations, e.g., denial, splitting, amnesia, derealization, and depersonalization. Memory for the trauma coexists paradoxically with normal autobiographical memory but in a split-off form without integration.

2. Reactivation of memory of the trauma in flashbacks, fugues, and other intrusive experiences. The memory is kept from conscious awareness but returns via these various types of fragments of experience or behavior.

3. Fragmented and decontextualized verbal memory that remains devoid of meaning and integration into consciousness and narrative memory. Verbal memory with no conscious representation.

4. Behavioral and object relations reenactment of trauma in the transference. "This form of knowing involves the grafting of isolated fragments of the past onto current relationships and life situations which become coloured by these 'memories'. The fragmentary quality of these transplants is responsible for the resulting absurdity, inappropriateness, and distortions in present experience" (p. 294).

5. Overpowering narratives. A more conscious knowing is involved here as the "memory can be described and the event narrated . . . The present form does consist of a memory; one which, however, crowds current reality out and occupies a great deal of psychological and emotional space. The individual is stuck with images and affect with which he cannot cope" (p. 295). In essence, the individual is hypermnestic and overpowered by the narrative of the trauma.

6. Living out life themes. The patient has partially sublimated the trauma and has less immersion in the concrete details of the trauma but reenacts it in life themes.

7. Witnessed narrative. "On this level, knowing takes the form of a true memory. When the individual narrates on this level, there is a distance, a perspective retained by the observing ego" (p. 297). The patient has integrated the trauma and can describe it objectively.

8. Trauma as metaphor. ". . . The motive for this form of traumatic memory comes more from a need to organize internal experience than, as with the previous forms, from a need to organize the external historical reality" (p. 298). It nevertheless impacts the resolution of developmental tasks and conflicts.

One final issue deserves consideration. Although a number of mechanisms for forgetting traumatic memories have been posited, they are not, as yet, conclusive. Similarly, the mechanisms by which such memories might be later recovered are not, as yet, well-determined and need much additional investigation. It is expected that once the mechanisms behind the loss of traumatic memories are better understood, the mechanisms by which recovery occurs will also be better understood (Roth & Friedman, 1998).

SUMMARY

This chapter has reviewed information about memory for traumatic events in both adults and children, as well as information about pertinent aspects of normal event memory. We began with a review of aspects of the traumatic stressor (or what makes trauma traumatic) and descriptions of a continuum of posttraumatic reactions. Pathologies of memory have long been found in the aftermath of serious traumatization and in association with PTSD. Psychobiological and psychophysiological alterations as a consequence of trauma are believed to be related to patterns of extreme memory retention and memory loss associated with traumatic events. Whether traumatic memory differs from normal event memory is a core issue in the controversy, and we have considered both sides of this issue in this chapter.

Despite data supporting the differences in memory of the traumatized, practitioners must incorporate information about normal event memory in their clinical work and understand that traumatic memory (like normal memory) is reconstructive, subject to error, and influenced by conditions of memory retrieval. They must also understand that the mechanisms behind traumatic amnesia and behind memory recovery and its relation to historical reality are, at present, not fully understood. Caution must therefore be taken in the clinical approach to traumatic memories, especially those that are only partially available to consciousness and/or recovered after a period of unavailability. These cautions must be counterbalanced, so that vague or partial accounts of abuse and trauma are not prematurely dismissed or automatically assumed to be false. In the next chapter, we review the evidence in support of delayed and recovered memory of sexual abuse before moving to more detailed discussion of issues of clinical practice.

Chapter 4

CHILD SEXUAL ABUSE
AND MEMORY

Incest is the most serious and damaging form of child sexual abuse. Since its characteristics and dynamics are found to varying degrees in all forms of child sexual abuse, it is presented here as the prototype against which other forms can be compared. The severity of incest is largely due to the many dynamics that contribute to both its occurrence and maintenance in a family, and the potential for numerous serious consequences initially and in the long-term. In chronic forms of incest, the child is subjected to repeated and escalating sexual intrusions in circumstances of entrapment and conflicted family relationships, a situation that usually compels the child to mount extensive defensive operations (including dissociation) to maintain ego integrity and attachment. It is theorized that many of these dynamics, effects, and defenses relate to memory disturbance at the time of the abuse or later. They may contribute to lack of memory encoding, retention, and/or retrieval in a number of different ways.

Variable memory accessibility and recovered memories of incest/child sexual abuse have been observed in clinical settings beginning with the observations of Freud and Janet and their contemporaries and continuing with the recent renewed focus on abuse issues in clinical practice. These observations have contributed to the controversy and have stimulated numerous research investigations. Findings of the studies conducted to date regarding incest/child sexual abuse and memory document the clinical observations regarding different degrees of amnesia for traumatic memory. A continuum of memory possibilities, ranging from full amnesia to continuous memory with many points between these two poles, is a constant finding in these studies and is consistent with information presented in the previous chapter. Besides reviewing the available studies, this chapter includes discussion of the mechanisms and processes identified thus far relating to remembering and forgetting, as well as factors associated with amnesia.

DYNAMICS AND SYMPTOMS ASSOCIATED WITH INCEST/CHILD SEXUAL ABUSE AND THEIR POSSIBLE RELATION TO MEMORY

Child sexual abuse refers to:

> a sexual act imposed on a child who lacks emotional, maturational, and cognitive development. The ability to lure a child into a sexual relationship is based on the all-powerful and dominant position of the adult or older perpetrator, which is in sharp contrast to the child's age, dependence, or subordinate position. Authority and power enable the perpetrator, implicitly or directly, to coerce the child into sexual compliance. (Sgroi, 1982, p. 9)

Sexual abuse is both intrafamilial and extrafamilial; substantial overlap exists between the two types, although it is generally acknowledged that incestuous abuse is more psychologically complicated due to familial bonds and patterns of attachment/dependence between the child and the caretaker/abuser (Cole & Putnam, 1992; Courtois, 1988; Freyd, 1996; Herman, 1981).

Child sexual abuse can vary dramatically in frequency (ranging from a one-time occurrence to very frequent and ongoing contact) and in seriousness of sexual activity (ranging from no physical contact—as in observation and exhibitionism—to fondling, oral stimulation, and vaginal, oral, or anal penetration involving violence and resulting in physical injury). Most commonly, it involves multiple sexual contacts that intensify over time. The average duration of incest is four years, with onset usually occurring in early childhood and before latency when the child is especially accessible, immature, lacking in power, and dependent on caretakers. Of particular importance is that the abuse occurs over the course of child's formative years and usually occurs within the context of repeated injunctions and threats to maintain secrecy. It is generally not acknowledged and/or discussed within the family or elsewhere. Attempts at disclosure are usually unsuccessful, with the child blamed for lying and/or scapegoated for causing the problem in the first place. Unfortunately, children who disclose often learn that they will not be believed or receive the hoped-for assistance; as a consequence, they often recant their disclosures and are additionally wounded by the betrayal inherent in the lack of assistance (Summit, 1983). In a circumstance such as this, sexual abuse is likely to continue unabated and to escalate. It thus continues as a chronic and inescapable stressor that, by and large, goes unacknowledged, and that can impact, become entwined with, and distort the child's development in a number of significant ways, including the development and maintenance of memory (Cole & Putnam, 1992; Courtois, 1988; Elin, 1997; Freyd, 1996; Pynoos et al., 1997).

On average, the child who is more genetically hardy and personally resilient usually fares better in such circumstances. This child may be able to achieve perspective on what is happening and why, and to engage in some positive means of coping. Responses such as this might, in some cases, provide psychological insulation or inoculation against the repeated stressor. Unfortunately, these are not the most likely responses and circumstances; consequently, the abused child is usually quite bereft and left to endure as best she or he can, most often by developing a psychological adaptation of some sort and a host of symptoms at the time of the abuse or later. Although this adaptation provides a defense against the emotionally overwhelming nature of the experience, it does not usually end the abuse, nor does it resolve its aftermath; moreover, it may impact the encoding of the abuse trauma and later memory accessibility.

Until the resurgence of interest and investigation in recent years, sexual abuse was not considered particularly traumatic, a viewpoint that is challenged by the emerging data. Sexual abuse is now identified as a stressor of such emotional complexity that it has a high potential to traumatize. Incest has the greatest risk for traumatization due to its prominent and complicated dynamics, which include its occurrence within the family (usually in the context of other major dysfunction and impaired relationships) and its duration and chronicity.

It is important to note, however, that not all sexual abuse is traumatic or results in traumatization and that some children and adults suffer few or no ill effects. This is especially true if the child was very young when the abuse occurred and did not register it and/or understand its meaning, or if it constituted such mild or unthreatening contact or behavior that fear responses were not elicited. It may also be the case if disclosure was met with belief rather than blame, and if the abuse was stopped. Carlson, Furby, Armstrong, and Schlaes (1997), in a review article proposing a conceptual framework for the long-term psychological effects of traumatic childhood abuse, took pains to articulate the defining features of a traumatic experience. They wrote: "By *traumatic abuse*, we mean experiences of abuse that involve the threat of death, serious injury, or harm and that produce overwhelming fear responses and feelings of helplessness" (p. 273). They also were careful to note that they were not implying that abuse that is not traumatic is not harmful or does not have detrimental psychological effects. Differentiating abuse experiences that are truly traumatic from those that are not is important because the effects of those experiences may be quite different from one another. Traumatization may well result in symptoms meeting the criteria for posttraumatic stress disorder or dissociative disorder at the time of the abuse or later. These diagnoses include as essential components criteria that address variable memory accessibility ranging from hypermnesia to amnesia.

Traumagenic Dynamics and Their Possible Relationship to Memory

In an important review article, Finkelhor and Browne (1985) postulated four trauma-causing factors, or "traumagenic dynamics," associated with the unique impact of incest/childhood sexual abuse. They took pains to note that, while these same four dynamics could very well occur in other types of trauma, they may have a particularly damaging synergistic effect in childhood sexual abuse. These authors were careful to point out that these dynamics are not narrowly defined; in fact, each one is a cluster of harmful influences with a common theme. Furthermore, reactions to abuse are multiply determined and are only rarely reliant upon one factor or dynamic. These four, along with the secrecy and lack of social discourse that most often accompany its occurrence, continue to be identified as the most salient dynamics associated with sexual abuse. They are of additional interest due to their possible relationship to and implications for memory disturbance, which are discussed here.

Betrayal refers to the dynamic that accompanies a child's discovery that a trusted individual has caused harm by abusing him or her, by disbelieving or denying that the event(s) occurred, or by failing to offer assistance or intervention. When the abuser is a relative, the child is usually in prolonged and confusing contact and, in fact, may be quite attached to the very person who is exploiting and causing harm. Abandonment or disregard by those who should have noticed or who could have intervened is also implicated in betrayal. Freyd (1994, 1996) has recently developed a conceptualization of how personal betrayal can lead to psychogenic amnesia for abuse. In her book, *Betrayal Trauma: The Logic of Forgetting Childhood Abuse*, Freyd describes the need—even the necessity—for a child to block information (and thereby not know about) ongoing abuse, especially in a family context, because that information would interfere with the child's ability to function reasonably well within a relationship of dependence with a caretaker who is also an abuser.

A related dynamic may be at work. Recent research has suggested a social-interactive effect on children's encoding and later recall of a situation shared with an adult (Tessler & Nelson, 1994) and greater recall of stressful or traumatic events that are discussed and explained to a child by a caretaker (Goodman, Quas, Batterman-Faunce, Riddlesberger, & Kuhn, 1996). Discourse (and related linguistic encoding) may thus shape better memory retention of a traumatic event, and lack of discourse may lead to less retention. Much more research is needed on this point—see Fivush (1996). Extrapolated to sexual abuse, the joint dynamics of secrecy and betrayal often impede acknowledgment and discourse and may lead a child to understand and encode the event differently, a point relevant to the recovered memory issue. Abused children often have their perceptions and feelings repeatedly challenged and shaped by the abuser and others in the direction of ignoring or not acknowledging the reality of what is happening. This form of social influence needs more research, as it may also interfere with later recollection of the abuse.

Powerlessness refers to the dynamic that renders the child helpless, fearful, and/or in terror, emotions that may be reinforced by threats of or actual violence and by other forms of coercion (including threats of abandonment) and injunctions to secrecy. Chronic abuse that is accompanied by violence and/or a high degree of threat and coercion is likely to lead to traumatization and resembles Terr's conceptualization of Type II trauma (Terr, 1991), described in chapters 2 and 3, and Carlson et al.'s description of a defining element of traumatic abuse. Such circumstances would necessitate the mobilization of very strong defenses, including extensive denial, repression, dissociation, self-anesthesia, self-hypnosis, identification with the aggressor, and aggression turned against the self. These, in turn, could interfere with memory encoding and retention and result in memory loss and delayed and fragmentary recall (Terr, 1991). This type of defensive mobilization is also suggested from the studies of dissociative identity disorder, where extreme and coercive forms of abuse have been reported, most often in the context of massively dysfunctional and double-binding relationships with caretaker/abusers in which the child is trapped. The child's coping may be reduced to peri-dissociation and splitting from the experience, defenses that could also interfere with memory encoding and retention (Chu & Dill, 1990; Freyd, 1996; Herman, 1992b; Putnam, 1985a, 1985b; Putnam, Guroff, Silberman, Barban, & Post, 1986).

Stigmatization refers to the process by which negative connotations, such as personal badness, shame, self-blame, and responsibility for the abuse become incorporated into the child's self-image. In order to maintain attachment and dependency, the child holds him/herself responsible for the occurrence of the abuse while simultaneously and paradoxically exonerating the caretaker/abuser. Shame and extremely negative self-worth, self-blame, and irrational guilt are among the most common self-representations of children (and later on, of adults) who have been sexually abused. These are related to the development of depression and psychological adaptation in response to ongoing abuse (Carlson et al., 1997; Fiering, Taska, & Lewis, 1996; Herman, 1981). Extreme shame is related to a sense of personal badness and fear of exposure and judgment by others, representations that could certainly interact with other dynamics to cause a child to deny and disavow knowledge of abuse through dissociation or other psychic mechanisms such as avoidance and motivated forgetting. Depression may also be implicated in poor memory encoding and retention.

Traumatic sexualization refers to the manner in which the experience of having been sexually abused may shape the child's sexuality in developmentally inappropriate and interpersonally dysfunctional ways. Degree of physical penetration and the use of force (and any accompanying physical damage) and related shock reactions are factors related to severity of response. When these occur in chronic situations, they necessitate the use of extreme defenses, which might interfere with memory encoding and retrieval. Terr (1991) has also described the anticipatory dread that accompanies chronic abuse involving physical contact, use of force, and pain. The child who fears for her life or anticipates a repeat of painful abuse must mount extensive defenses, often those involving splitting and dissociating from the experience as it occurs.

The child's defenses and psychological adaptations to the abuse situation are also related to severity and memory retention. As discussed by Freyd (1994), not knowing and not responding may be the safest options available to the child caught in a situation of ongoing betrayal-trauma. A number of studies have documented that a subset of child victims appear to be asymptomatic (Beichtman et al., 1992; Finkelhor, 1990; Kendall-Tackett, Williams, & Finkelhor, 1993). These children may truly be without symptoms or they may be masking them to appear normal and/or to maintain attachment. The façade of normalcy is often maintained at a price. Not uncommonly there is a "sleeper effect," with symptoms emerging in adult life as defensive operations break down and/or as post-traumatic and dissociative reactions are triggered in some way (Courtois, 1988). This process may well be related to the recovered memory phenomenon. It is consistent with the delayed onset formulation of posttraumatic stress disorder as defined in the *DSM-IV* (American Psychiatric Association, 1994) and with the diagnostic criteria and the natural history of dissociative disorders, especially DID and DDNOS.

The Correlates of Incest/Child Sexual Abuse and Their Relationship to Memory

The effects summarized above are not unique to individuals who have experienced incest/sexual abuse, yet they are problems commonly observed in sexually abused patients. In the clinical literature, the symptom pictures that emerge most strongly and consistently include those associated with emotional and relational distress; autonomic hyperarousal (somatic symptoms, affective dyscontrol, chronic anxiety); behavioral indices including reenactment of early behavior (often trauma-related and involving noncognitive or procedural memories—e.g., sexual avoidance or acting-out, stereotyped relational responses, startle responses, phobias, patterns of self-harm and revictimization); attempts at management of hyperarousal or numbing/derealization (depression, emotional numbness or flatness, relational avoidance, sexual dysfunction, psychogenic amnesia, self-harm and suicidality, compulsions and addictions); and dissociation (detachment, distortions of memory and cognition, flashbacks).

At present, a substantial body of research derived from clinical, non-clinical, and community samples correlates a history of childhood sexual abuse with a wide range of potential aftereffects and diagnosable mental conditions in approximately 20-40 percent of victims. These have been documented and cross-referenced in a series of review articles (Beitchman, Zucker, Hood, daCosta, & Ackman, 1991; Beitchman et al., 1992; Briere & Elliott, 1994; Briere & Runtz, 1988; Browne & Finkelhor, 1986; Carlson et al., 1997; Cole & Putnam, 1992; Finkelhor, 1990; 1994; Finkelhor & Browne, 1985; Green, 1993; Kendall-Tackett et al., 1993; Lipovsky & Kilpatrick, 1992; Neumann, Houskamp, Pollock, & Briere, 1996; Polusny & Follette, 1995; Silverman, Reinherz, & Giaconia, 1996).

In their review of the available research, Kendall-Tackett et al. (1993) concluded that, while no one symptom or set of symptoms has yet consistently emerged as pathognomic of an abuse history, "There is virtually no domain of symptomatology that has not been associated with a history of sexual abuse . . . and . . . some sexually abused children may also . . . have no apparent symptoms" (p. 173), a viewpoint echoed in other reviews (Carlson et al., 1997). Later in their review, Kendall-Tackett et al. stated that ". . . the absence of one dominant and consistent set of symptoms suggests that the impact of sexual abuse is more complicated because it produces multifaceted effects" (p. 174). A lack of symptoms in childhood cannot be used to conclude a lack of symptoms in adulthood— some effects emerge later and still others have been found to emerge and abate at different times across the individual's lifespan. By the same token, sexual abuse should not be inferred or definitively diagnosed on the basis of one symptom or set of symptoms when memory is absent; however, these symptoms may legitimately generate an index of suspicion in the clinician (see chapters 7 and 8 for additional discussion).

RECOLLECTIONS OF
CHILD SEXUAL ABUSE:
A REVIEW OF THE SCIENTIFIC LITERATURE

At the root of the recovered/false memory debate is the issue of whether experiences of sexual abuse can be forgotten and remembered after a period of time has elapsed and whether such memories are accurate and credible. As discussed earlier, memory researchers/false memory proponents have argued that the loss of memory for abuse that occurred after the offset of childhood amnesia (i.e., approximately three years of age) is infrequent and that repeated abuse would be expected to be remembered rather than forgotten since "Traumatic experiences are memorable" (Pope & Hudson, 1995a, p. 715). Nevertheless, enough research has now accumulated documenting the forgetting of traumatic childhood abuse (as well as other forms of trauma as described in chapter 3) that memory researchers have come to acknowledge its occurrence while continuing to question its prevalence, the mechanisms by which it occurs, and its accuracy. As Harvey and Herman (1997) put it: "The occurrence of amnesia following traumatic exposure runs counter to intuition and prediction. If terrifying events are unforgettable, how can they be completely forgotten?" (p. 558). This is the question to be researched.

At the present time, more than 35 scientific studies have been published and a number of clinical observation studies and corroborated case reports compiled that independently and collectively document various degrees of forgetting (or amnesia) for experiences of child sexual abuse. These studies, as discussed below, also document various degrees of memory retention and a wide variation of possibilities between the two. Other studies are currently underway and in press and additional case reports are being accumulated. The findings of the available research studies are reviewed and summarized in this section along with information from clinical observations and case reports.

Taken together, the results of these studies and cases suggest that a significant subset of adults (ranging from 4.5 percent to 68 percent depending on the study) who report a history of childhood sexual abuse also report some period of time in their lives when they were partially or fully amnestic for the memory of the abuse. These adults fit into quadrant II (false negatives) of the 2 x 2 table on abuse and memory presented in chapter 2. These data also document another finding that should not be ignored, namely, the subset of adults who report continuous memory of past abuse and who therefore are likely to fit into quadrant IV (true positives) of the table. This continuous memory subset averages 50 percent across all studies, with a range of 23 percent to 72 percent (Brown et al., 1998).

These continuous memory data suggest a problem of a different magnitude than false memory proponents have publicized and one that should not be lost in the heat of the controversy, namely that "Most people who were sexually abused as children remember all or part of what happened to them" (American Psychological Association, 1996b). Recovered memory issues arise predominantly with those individuals who have no recollection or who have experienced partial or full amnesia for past abuse, not those with continuous memory. *The issue of false memory therefore applies more to the subsample of adults who report amnesia and recovered memory for past abuse rather than to the entire population* (Courtois, 1997a).

Yet continuous memory does not necessarily mean full or perfectly accurate memory. Research studies and clinical observations (Binder, McNiel, & Goldstone, 1994; Gold et al., 1994; Harvey & Herman, 1996, 1997) have documented individuals with continuous memory and delayed recall. As Gold et al. write, "Many clients who enter treatment believing that they have full memory of the sexual abuse they experienced as children come to realize that their recollections are much more fragmentary than they originally thought" (p. 441). Many have been found to retrieve additional memories and detail over time. Gold et al. also found that when they broke down questions about repression or the absence of memory to form a continuum marked by degrees of memory (i.e., a vague sense of suspicion but no definite memory, partial memory only, remembered at least one episode of abuse in its entirety but not all of them, always retained a fairly complete memory of all or most episodes of abuse, and completely blocked out any recollection of sexual abuse), a different and more complex picture of memory retention and loss emerged.

It is noteworthy, however, that although these studies document reports of absent memories, they do not (with some exceptions discussed below) address either the accuracy or the authenticity of the memories under discussion. This, however, does not mean that recovered memories are necessarily inaccurate, as false memory critics often propose. Review of the available documentation regarding the accuracy of recovered memories has thus far found the crux of the memory to be generally accurate, even though memory for peripheral details might not be (Brown et al., 1998).

Table 4.1 contains a summary of the available studies conducted to date on the base rate of amnesia for childhood sexual abuse. This table is organized by categories of studies (clinical, nonclinical, random, prospective, others) and includes clinical observations and naturalistic studies and case reports as well as research reports. It describes the type of amnesia and continuous memory and the percentage of the sample where some sort of independent corroboration was available. As is the case with research studies in general, many of these investigations have methodological and design flaws; however, the more recent studies correct for the most glaring of the past deficiencies. The research methodology is increasingly sophisticated as the field matures and evolves. Naturalistic and volunteer retrospective clinical samples have been supplanted by nonclinical samples and by random samples of varied clinical and nonclinical groups. Prospective studies of documented past abuse have also been undertaken and counterbalance the limitations found in retrospective studies of self-reported abuse where tno corroboration is reported and/or available.

The aggregate findings across all of these studies cannot be dismissed on the basis of methodological weakness alone, as was suggested by Pope and Hudson (1995a, 1995b) in two review articles. Since these authors based their conclusions on a review of four of the earliest studies, their conclusions should not be generalized to those that were not yet published or that were not included in the review. The currently available studies *each document* some degree of full or partial amnesia for abuse and *none fails to document* amnesia in at least some of the sample, regardless of the type of study. This cross-referencing of findings across different types of samples using different research designs is significant, provides some cross-validation, and meets the demands of scientific inquiry.

According to Brown et al. (1998):

> In our opinion, these studies meet the true test of science, namely that the finding holds up across quite a number of independent experiments, each with different samples, each assessing the target variables in a variety of different ways and each arriving at a similar conclusion . . . . When multiple samples and multiple sampling methods are used, the error rate across studies is reduced. Even where a small portion of these

Table 4.1
Studies Documenting Amnesia for Childhood Sexual Abuse

Source	N	FA	PA	C	NA	IC	Rx	c/nc	r/nr	Sample
Clinical Studies										
Herman & Schatzow 1987	53	28	36	64	36	74	100	c	nr	outpatient tx
Draijer, 1990	1,054			57						national survey
Ensink, 1992	100	29	28	57	43		100	c	nr	incest & tx groups (hi DID)
Cameron, 1994 (1996)	60 (46)	42 (57)	23	65 (57)	35 (43)	(65)	100 (100)	c (c)	nr (nr)	women in tx with hx of csa: (longitudinal follow-up)
Gold et al., 1994 (1995)	105 (160)	30 (29)	40 (42)	70 (71)	30 (28)			c (c)	nr (nr)	intake interview in tx
Loftus et al., 1994	105	19	12	31	69			c	nr	women in drug tx
Albach et al., 1996	97e 65c			35 1	65 99		100	c	nr	women w/hx of csa/ normal controls
Masters and Dalenberg, 1996	40e 32c	43			57			c	nr	therapist-recruited incest victims, and non-abused client controls
Roe & Schwartz, 1996	52			77	23	44	68 32	c	nr	women in inpatient tx
Non-clinical Samples										
Bernet et al., 1993	624	36			64		30	nc	nr	college undergrad- uates
Belicki et al., 1994	68			55	45			nc	nr	college undergrad- uates
Binder et al., 1994	30			44	57		5	nc	nr	women in self-help groups for incest victims
Elliot & Fox, 1994	484	30	14	44	56		19	nc	nr	college undergrad- uates
Roesler & Wind, 1994	228	28			72					triggered by M. van Derber disclosure
Kristiansen et al., 1995	113	25	26	51	49	61	93	nc	nr	community sample, women
van der Kolk & Fisler, 1995	36			42	58	75		nc	nr	volunteers, & terrible life experi- ences
Grassian & Holtzen, 1996	42	19	28	47	53			nc	nr	triggered by Father Porter disclosure
Random Samples										
Briere & Conte, 1993	450			59	41			c	r	in tx for csa

Continued on following page

Table 4.1 (continued)
Studies Documenting Amnesia for Childhood Sexual Abuse

Source	N	FA	PA	C	NA	IC	Rx	c/nc	r/nr	Sample
Feldman-Summers & Pope, 1994	330			40	60	47	56	nc	r	psychologists
Elliot & Briere, 1995	505	20	22	42	58		7 13	nc	r	general population
Fish & Scott, 1995	423	17	38	55	45		44	nc	r	counselors
Melchert, 1996	553			18	82			nc	r	introductory psychology students
Elliot, 1997	357	15	17	32	68		14	nc	r	general population
Melchert Parker, 1997	429			20	80			nc	r	vocational and college students
Westerhof et al., in press	500	22	17	39	61	69	68	nc	r	psychologists
Prospective Studies										
Femina et al, 1990	69			73	27	100	0	nc	nr	incarcerated youth; physical abuse
Williams, 1994	129	38			62	100	0	nc	nr	women with clinic documentation of csa
Burgess et al., 1995	22	14	27	41	59	100	0	c	nr	daycare csa
Widom & Morris, 1997	1196	37			63	100		nc	nr	court substantiated csa
Widom & Shepard, 1997	1196			40	60	100		nc	nr	court substantiated physical abuse
Other Studies										
Goodman et al., 1995	1,652	45	45	50	50			c	nr	ritual abuse allegations
Dalenberg, 1996; 1997	17			100		>50	100	c	nr	women csa victims with some continuous memories and some memories recovered in tx
Andrews, 1997	100	56	44	100		(40)	100	c	nr	outpatients w/ recovered memories of trauma in tx; 60% csa
Herman & Harvey, 1997	130	16	17	33	53	(43)	28	c	nr	outpatients with memories of trauma; 77% csa
Kluft, 1997	34	68			32	100	100	c	nr	DID patients in tx; confirmed abuse
Case Studies										
Wickramasekera, 1994	1			100		100	100	c	nr	Therapy client

Continued on following page

Table 4.1 (continued)
Studies Documenting Amnesia for Childhood Sexual Abuse

Source	N	FA	PA	C	NA	IC	Rx	c/nc	r/nr	Sample
Tayloe, 1995	1	100		100		100		nc	nr	Case study of adult w/ amnesia for murder of his wife
Corwin & Olafson, 1997	1	100		100		100			nr	Videotaped csa victim describing abuse and recovering memories of same abuse 11 years later
Schooler, Ambadar, & Bendiksen, 1997	4	75	25	100		100			nr	4 case studies
Duggal & Sroufe, 1998	1	100		100		100			nr	Prospective report of documented csa, memory loss, and recovery
Cheit, 1998	33			100		100			nr	Archive of recovered memories in corroborated cases of csa; 33 of current 36 are csa

Key:

N = sample size

FA = percentage of abused reporting full amnesia/no memory for a significant period of time

PA = percentage of abused reporting partial amnesia

C = combined percentage of full and partial amnesia

NA =percentage of abused with no amnesia; continuous memory

IC = percentage of abuse cases for which some sort of independent corroboration existed; ( ) = subject-reported independent corroboration

Rx = percentage of abused for whom memory recovery was associated with (but not necessarily caused by) therapy; percentage of sample where memory initially recovered in therapy

c/nc = clinical vs. non-clinical sample

r/nr = random vs. non-random sampling

e = experimental group

c = control group

hx = history

tx = treatment

c = control group

csa = childhood sexual abuse

DID = dissociative identity disorder

Adapted and Updated From "Repressed Memory or Dissociative Amnesia: What the Science Says," by A. W. Scheflin, & D. Brown, 1996, *The Journal of Psychiatry and Law, 3*, p. 180-181. Copyright 1996 by Federal Legal Publications, Inc. Reprinted with permission.

cases of reported amnesia may be associated with abuse that may not have occurred or at least could not be substantiated, the great preponderance of the evidence strongly suggests that at least some subpopulation of sexually abused survivors experience a period of full or partial amnesia for the abuse. Moreover, for a good portion of these amnestic subjects some sort of corroboration of the abuse was available . . . . Dawes (1994) argues, however, that the type of corroborative evidence sought in at least some of these studies does not constitute an adequate determination of accuracy. (p. 194)

Clinical Samples—Survey Studies

As of this writing, at least eight studies of amnesia for childhood sexual abuse in clinical samples have been conducted (see Table 4.1), the earliest conducted by Herman and Schatzow (1987). Starting with the findings of this study, all of the others have documented (at varying percentage rates) that many adults with recollections of childhood sexual abuse report prior time periods when they did not remember the abuse. Herman and Schatzow reported "severe memory deficits" in 28 percent of their sample of women in a therapy group for incest survivors. Approximately two-thirds of these women (64 percent) reported some degree of lost memory for past abuse. In this study, the majority of women (74 percent) were able to find corroborative evidence of some sort to support their memory. The researchers concluded their write-up of these findings by cautioning that recovered memory should not be attributed only to fantasy and by further suggesting that memory loss (full or partial amnesia) for a period of time was the norm for a significant subpopulation of adult incest survivors. The findings of all of the other published clinical studies support these conclusions, namely that a significant minority of victims of child sexual abuse in treatment report varying periods and degrees of forgetting; furthermore, the rates of amnesia are fairly consistent across the studies, with two exceptions. See Table 4.1 for information on the additional studies.

A variety of legitimate criticisms have been leveled at studies in this category (Lindsay & Read, 1994; Loftus, 1993; Pope & Hudson, 1995a, 1995b): e.g., that they used biased samples of individuals in psychotherapy; that subject selection was not specified; that experimenters collecting the data were also clinicians who could have biased expectations that would, in turn, influence results; that questions about memory were flawed; and that findings were based on retrospective self-reports of abuse. An additional criticism of significance is that the design of these clinical surveys does not consistently make a distinction between what is meant by full, partial, and no amnesia for childhood sexual abuse and instead treats traumatic memory as an all-or-nothing phenomenon (Scheflin & Brown, 1996). The more recently conducted studies are better designed and correct for some of the major limitations of the earlier ones. It is expected that future studies will continue to improve.

Nonclinical Samples—Survey Studies

In response to the criticism of selection bias and to test the generalization of findings from clinical samples, several studies have been conducted on nonclinical convenience or volunteer samples drawn from different populations (college students, community samples, self-identified Father Porter victims, volunteers who identified themselves as survivors of childhood sexual abuse or as "haunted by memories of terrible life experiences") (see Table 4.1). Various advances and innovations are evident from the different studies included in this category. These include: the use of a control group of "simulators" of childhood sexual abuse (subjects who reported no history of abuse but who "were asked to complete all questionnaires as if they had been sexually abused") in one study (Belicki, Correy, Boucock, Cuddy, & Dunlop, 1994); a study of ways subjects initially remembered the trauma when the memory was recovered (van der Kolk & Fisler, 1995); and a study of a convenience sample of self-identified victims (the majority of them male) of one perpetrator, Father Porter, who admitted to abusing many boys. For the majority of Father Porter's victims, the abuse was short-term (68 percent reported five episodes or less) and differential patterns of remembering and not remembering were correlated with later psychiatric distress (discussed in more detail later in this chapter).

Although this category of studies improves on the clinical category by correcting for sampling bias and the possibility of iatrogenic effects of the therapist/researcher studying clinical samples, another significant source of bias remains, namely, retrospective self-reporting. Self-reports of abuse are largely uncorroborated and make the validity of the reports unknown. It is therefore noteworthy that several of the studies in this category reported on the availability of some form of evidence to corroborate self-reports. Van der Kolk and Fisler reported a 75 percent corroboration rate for the subjects in their volunteer sample who had experienced childhood trauma. Belicki et al. (1994) found no significant differences in response to questions between those subjects who reported corroboration of the abuse and and those who did not. Also, they found no significant differences in corroborative evidence in those who had disrupted memory and those who had continuous memory. Kristiansen,

Felton, Hovdestad, and Allard (1995) reported corroborative evidence of some sort in 61 percent of the women in their sample who reported a history of childhood sexual abuse. The limitations of the retrospective self-report design are counterbalanced to some extent by the availability of corroborative evidence in several of the studies.

As a group, this category of studies documents a sizable rate of forgetting child sexual abuse for a period of time across different nonclinical populations, a finding that cross references those of the clinical studies and, as is seen below, those of other categories as well.

Random Samples

Random sampling eliminates problems of selection bias. A number of randomized studies have been conducted on different clinical and nonclinical populations (subjects in therapy for child sexual abuse, counselors and psychologists, general population, college students in the psychology department pool). Briere and Conte (1993) were the first to conduct and publish a study of this type. They randomly sampled 450 individuals in treatment for sexual abuse through a national network of therapists. Their findings from a larger and randomly selected clinical sample are in accord with those of Herman and Schatzow (59 percent of their subjects, versus 64 percent of Herman and Schatzow's, reported a period of time before their 18th birthday of having forgotten the abuse).

Despite the advances of a random survey methodology, the studies in this category have other limitations and weaknesses in terms of the wording of the questions asked about remembering and forgetting, about recruitment of the study sample through therapists, or the study sample consisting of therapists (4 of the studies of this category were of clinical samples of therapists) (Pope & Hudson, 1995a, 1995b). An important, more recently conducted survey reported by Briere and Elliott (1995) and Elliott (1997) remedied these limitations by using a stratified random sample of general population subjects and using more neutrally worded open-ended questioning. The findings of this study are noteworthy, because, although only 7 percent of the subjects were in therapy, they reported rates of forgetting similar to those found in the other, more clinically based studies that are included within this category. Among respondents who reported some form of trauma (72%), delayed recall of the event was reported by 32%. The severity of the trauma was predictive of memory status, but demographic variables were not. Quite significantly, the most commonly reported trigger for delayed recall of the trauma was some form of media (i.e., TV show, movie); the *least commonly reported trigger was psychotherapy*. These findings suggest that a history of trauma is relatively common and delayed recall may not be uncommon and is not limited to sexual abuse. Memory is usually cued outside of psychotherapy, in contrast to the perspective put forth by false memory proponents.

Melchert (1996) and Melchert and Parker (1997) recently reported on two large random sample studies of college students. Their findings add another dimension of complexity to the issue of memory for childhood abuse. Both studies found proportions of individuals with histories of sexual, emotional, and physical abuse reporting that they had periods without memory (21 percent and 19.8 percent, 18 percent and 11.5 percent, and 18 percent and 14.9 percent, respectively). Participants in both studies appeared to be referring to both a lack of conscious access to their abuse memories and the intentional avoidance of the memories for some period. Variance was also found in the reported quality of general childhood memory, unrelated to reporting a history of child abuse, suggesting that it is normal to recover general memories of childhood. Melchert and Parker offered the following summary:

> These findings have important implications for future research and for current practice regarding child abuse and memory. The data do not support the view that poor childhood memory or even amnesia for one's childhood is associated with a history of sexual abuse or, indeed, the experience of any type of child abuse, either singly or in combination. It also appears that individuals commonly report recovering childhood memories, and that doing so is actually a normative experience that is not associated with a history of child abuse. When individuals report recovered child abuse memories, they may be referring to a lack of conscious access to their abuse memories for a period or to having intentionally avoided their abuse memories for some period. There is also very limited evidence regarding gender effects in childhood memory generally, or in recovered memories of child abuse specifically . . . .
>
> The findings of the present study offer useful data for understanding aspects of the relationship between childhood abuse and memory . . . . Nevertheless, the limitations of the current data along with the complexity of the phenomena under study strongly suggest that research employing a variety of methodologies be conducted before specific conclusions are drawn regarding the question addressed in this study. (p. 134)

To summarize the findings of the random sampling category: Consistent with the results of the other categories of studies, a subpopulation of subjects in the random sample studies reported a significant period of forgetting of childhood sexual abuse; however, data from the

Melchert and Melchert and Parker studies suggest that these findings are not complete and must be examined against the broader background of recovered memory for other types of previously forgotten childhood events.

This category of studies has also been criticized for its major limitation of relying on retrospective self-reports. Commentators have questioned whether findings based on reported (retrospective and largely unsubstantiated) abuse measure true abuse and are generalizable. Although prospective studies offer another methodology to correct for this difficulty and are discussed next, it is nevertheless worth discussing some findings about adult retrospective memory that counter this specific criticism. While it is true that retrospective reports have limitations, this should not be taken to mean that retrospective reports are always in error and never to be believed, as some of the critics seem to suggest. Brewer (1994) and Brewin, Andrews, and Gotlib (1993) reviewed the literature on retrospective memory and independently concluded that autobiographical memory is relatively accurate, even though, wherever possible, steps must be taken to overcome the limitations of retrospective reports to enhance their reliability and to check their accuracy. Williams and Banyard (1997b) discussed another dimension of retrospective reports that has not received enough mention: ". . . retrospective designs are unable to examine instances in which sexual abuse experienced in childhood continues to be forgotten. Obviously, researchers cannot survey adults and ask whether they were abused in childhood but have now forgotten" (p. II–135). It is for this reason and others that prospective designs have particular utility.

Prospective Studies

Five prospective studies of amnesia for documented sexual abuse and/or physical abuse have been published thus far. They counterbalance retrospective research designs by studying cases that are documented and correct for some of the design limitations found in the other categories of studies.

Williams (1994a, 1994b, 1995) conducted a follow-up interview study (17 years post-abuse of a nonclinical sample) of women and Williams and Banyard (1997a) of women and men whose sexual abuse and its immediate effects were documented in hospital records. Using a free-recall and cued-recall interview about childhood experiences with sex, interviewers asked questions about reports of sexual abuse and other forms of abuse but did not explicitly ask about the index abuse. Thirty-eight percent of the women and 55 percent of the men did not recall the abuse or did not report it to the interviewer, even though it had been serious enough to require medical intervention and documentation; 32 percent of the women said they had never been abused. Some described periods of forgetting and remembering the abuse prior to the time of the interview. The researchers also found that women who were younger at the time of the abuse, who were molested by someone they knew, and who had the clearest documentation of abuse were more likely to be more amnestic and to have no recall of the abuse. A number of criticisms have been made of this study's methodology and of the use of the term "amnesia" for what Loftus, Garry, and Feldman (1994) suggest might be "simple forgetting" and Pope and Hudson suggest is infantile or childhood amnesia (both viewpoints rejected by Williams (1994b) after several reanalyses of her data). Nevertheless, the critiques do not negate the importance of its findings in providing a different methodological approach to the issues of forgetting and later remembering past sexual abuse.

Widom (reported in Widom, 1997; Widom & Morris, 1997; and Widom & Shepard, 1996) conducted an important large-scale (n=1,144) prospective study that satisfies many of the objections made to the Williams study. This study consisted of a long-term follow-up of children with a documented history of physical abuse, sexual abuse, and neglect severe enough to have warranted judicial involvement. This cohort of abused children was compared to a demographically matched control group of nonabused children. The study groups were followed over a 20-year time period. Two-hour nonleading interviews were conducted after 20 years with both groups. The interviewers and interviewees were blind to the study's purpose. In these interviews, 61 percent of the sexually abused subjects reported other experiences of sexual abuse, but 39 percent did not report abuse that had been previously documented (the index abuse). Thus, substantial underreporting (possibly due to nonremembering) of documented past physical abuse and sexual abuse was found, the sexual abuse underreporting at a rate concordant with the findings reported by Williams (1994a, 1995). No differences in age at time of abuse and subsequent remembering/reporting were found in either investigation, findings discordant with those of Williams and Banyard. Males were even less likely than females to report sexual abuse and sex against their will, a significant gender difference similar to the gender-related findings of Williams and Banyard. Widom concluded: "For both types of childhood abuse, there was substantial underreporting of abuse among known victims of childhood abuse. This is particularly impressive since these are court substantiated cases of childhood abuse" (p. 64).

Widom also commented on the the difficulties with retrospective self-reports from a different perspective than addressed by false memory critics. Her emphasis was on the *underreporting (or nonremembering)* of significant personal events *that occurred and are documented as to their occurrence.* Underreporting or nonremembering of the target abuse occurred even when experiences of abuse were inquired about in a sensitive but non-leading interview (this finding of underreporting/nonremembering of documented prior abuse was reported previously by Femina, Yeager, and Lewis in their 1990 prospective study of physical abuse).

Widom suggests that patients' perceptions and cognitive appraisals of their early childhood experiences at the time and later are important to the encoding, retrieval, and later reporting of such information and that information from collateral sources can be important to making a determination of accuracy of retrospective remembering/reporting. This viewpoint is supported by the research findings of a random sample prospective cohort study reported by Friedrich, Talley, Panser, Fett, & Zinmeister (1997). Using a questionnaire, these researchers, on two occasions separated by an average of 20 months, asked a random sample of 610 adults about unwanted sexual experiences, physical abuse, and psychological abuse that might have occurred when they were younger. Relatively high rates of concordance between the responses at the two intervals were found, with variance in rates related to type of abuse. Despite the year-and-a-half lag time, a large nonclinical, community-based sample provided relatively consistent reports of sexual and physical abuse but less consistent reports of psychological abuse. The researchers commented on the obvious limitations of retrospective self-report data in the study but also noted the importance of the individual's interpretation of both abusive acts and questions about them to the responses that were obtained.

A prospective study conducted by Burgess and her colleagues (Burgess et al., 1995) examined a total of 34 children who had been physically, psychologically, and sexually abused at the time of the initial report. The purpose of the study was to follow the natural presentation over time of childhood traumatic memories in a sample of children. A follow-up interview with 22 children and their parents was conducted either five or ten years after the index abuse. The majority of the children (59 percent) retained relatively complete verbal memory of the abuse, yet 14 percent were fully amnestic and 27 percent partially amnestic—despite the fact that their abuse had been previously documented in some detail in investigative interviews. These authors also inquired about other dimensions of memory besides verbal narrative memory. Upon interview, the parents reported that, over the years from the time of the abuse, the children had exhibited somatic, behavioral, and visual manifestations of the abuse whether or not verbal narrative memories were available to them.

These findings are consistent with those reported by Terr (1991) based on her investigations of traumatized children and those of van der Kolk and Fisler (1995) concerning somatosensory manifestations of memory in the absence of verbal narratives.

Prospective Case Reports

A report by Corwin and Olafson (1997) of a videotaped interview in which a previously unrecallable memory of documented child sexual abuse was recalled in vivo eleven years later, gives a fascinating example of how such recall might be manifested in individuals who were amnestic for a period of time. During the second interview (conducted at the request of the subject and videotaped), her memory of the forgotten abuse began to return as she discussed the reasons for the original video-taped interview before watching it. This case was published with commentaries from a variety of different trauma and memory experts in which they discuss the case and the possible mechanisms related to the recovered memory.

Another prospective case report was recently published by Duggal and Sroufe (1998). In it, both the abuse and the lack of memory for the abuse were documented during the course of a longitudinal developmental study not related to memory processes or child abuse. Spontaneous recovery of memory for a subject's abuse that had been previously corroborated along with the evidence that she had forgotten it for a number of years was documented and described.

Taken together, the Femina, Williams, Widom, and Burgess prospective studies and the Corwin and Duggal case reports provide documentation of memory loss and/or nondisclosure among adolescents and adults with documented childhood physical and sexual abuse histories. The Friedrich study supports the concordance of reports in adulthood in response to questions about past abuse. The studies thus *substantiate both underreporting and recovered memories, provide evidence that these can occur independent of a therapeutic context and therapeutic influence, and demonstrate that such reports can have consistency over time.*

The findings of these different prospective studies also contradict the viewpoint that retrospective reports are always inaccurate. To the contrary, they have been found to be accurate a fair amount of the time (Brewer, 1994; Brewin et al., 1993). Moreover, the inaccuracy can be in both the false positive and false negative directions. This is an important point to note in the current debate, which tends to emphasize the unreliability of retrospective reports as always indicative of a false positive position. The findings are consequential in their own right and point the way for future investigations of the many factors that might be associated with forgetting, recall, and nondisclosure, with different forms of memory, and with different forms of abuse. Williams's concluding comment about her results are equally applicable to those of the other studies:

> While these findings cannot be used to assert the validity of *all* recovered memories of child abuse, this study does suggest that recovered memories of child sexual abuse reported by adults can be quite consistent with contemporaneous documentation of the abuse and should not be summarily dismissed by therapists, lawyers, family members, judges or the women [and men] themselves (1995, p. 670)

Other Studies: Clinical Observations and Studies and Case Reports

CLINICAL OBSERVATIONS.   In a 1996 paper and again in a 1997 version, Harvey and Herman wrote that clinical experience suggests the variety of ways that adult survivors of trauma arrive at their memories, with varying degrees of associated distress and uncertainty and, in some cases, after memory lapses of varying durations and degree (Harvey & Herman, 1996; Harvey & Herman, 1997). They identified three general patterns of traumatic recall among patients who enter psychotherapy as a result of early abuse: (1) relatively continuous and complete recall of experiences of childhood abuse coupled with changing interpretations (delayed understanding) of these experiences; (2) partial amnesia for abuse events, accompanied by a mixture of delayed recall and delayed understanding; and (3) delayed recall following a period of profound and pervasive amnesia. These authors also identified variations among and between the three and suggested that the phenomena underlying traumatic recall are complex and continuous rather than dichotomous. They further suggested that "clinical observation is a reasonable starting point for scientific inquiry into the nature of traumatic memory" (Harvey & Herman, 1996, p. 31).

CLINICAL STUDIES.   These same authors recently completed a clinical study to investigate the memory presentation of adult psychiatric outpatients (Harvey & Herman, 1997). Their findings were remarkably in line with their previous observations and research findings: of 77 patients, 53 percent reported continuous memory only, no delayed recall; 17 percent reported continuous memory and delayed recall; and 16 percent reported complete amnesia and delayed recall (14 percent did not give specific information). Additionally, 43 percent of these patients spontaneously described some type of corroboration. The study was undertaken to investigate the role of psychotherapy in memory retrieval by studying patients at the point of entry into therapy as they spontaneously described memories of childhood trauma. This method is consistent with that employed by Gold et al. (1994), in which research questions were asked as early in contact with prospective patients as possible to minimize the likelihood of the interference of treatment effects on subjects' responses. The interviews were conducted in a free recall manner, with assessors instructed to record information that the patients volunteered rather than asking any specific or probing questions. Although Harvey and Herman acknowledged the possible selection biases and limitations to their study, they also noted that their main findings were congruent with those of previous studies documenting memory disturbances in a sizable proportion of patients with histories of childhood trauma. They wrote on another dimension of their findings:

> Our data also suggest that delayed recall of childhood trauma is often a process that unfolds over time rather than a single event, and that it occurs most commonly in the context of a life crisis or developmental milestone, with a trauma-specific reminder serving as the proximate cue to new recall. Psychotherapy was not implicated in the early stages of delayed recall in most cases. *However, the retrieval of traumatic memories, once begun, proved to be a powerful incentive for entering psychotherapy. Patients rarely sought treatment with a goal of recovering more memories; rather, they wished to gain more control over intrusive, involuntary reliving experiences and to make sense of the fragmented, confusing and disturbing recollections they already had.*
>
> These data remind us that remembering autobiographical material is normally an active process, characterized by shifting emphases, changing interpretations, and repeated evaluation of the meaning of particular events in relation to an ongoing life narrative. (p. 567) (italics added)

In an innovative study that sought to verify memories disclosed during the course of treatment with corroborative evidence, Dalenberg (1996) recruited 17 subjects who had previously completed psychotherapy with her. All therapy sessions had been audiotaped and tapes were analyzed for memory-related material and for the point in therapy when memories were disclosed and/or retrieved. Most of these subjects and their families located evidence confirming or disconfirming about 65 percent–75 percent of the memories, with an identical mean accuracy for both recovered memory and continuous memory. These findings are significant in demonstrating that recovered memories may be as accurate as continuous memories and should therefore not be automatically discounted. Interestingly, Dalenberg also found support for the possibility that the identification of recovered memories and their accuracy might be related to different phases and issues that emerge in the therapy process, an area certainly deserving of further investigation.

Andrews (1996) reported preliminary results from an in-depth telephone interview survey of 100 qualified therapists in Great Britain who reported working with clients who had recovered memories of trauma while in treatment with them. The tape-recorded interviews covered such topics as the features of recovered memories, the process of memory recovery, and the consequences for the clients in terms of the effect on symptoms and current relationships, among other things. Approximately 60 percent of the recovered memories involved child sexual abuse, and 40 percent, other traumas. Over half of the memories were recovered from a position of total amnesia. Corroborating evidence was found in 40 percent of the cases. Memories for sexual abuse took significantly longer to recover than memories of other traumas and involved vivid reliving and fear as a predominant emotion.

Kluft (1997) conducted a "naturalistic pilot study" on 34 patients (32 females, 2 males) in his therapy practice, with the purpose of finding evidence to either document or disconfirm the memories recovered during psychotherapy by patients with dissociative identity disorder (DID). All patients met *DSM-IV* criteria for DID and had been in treatment with the investigator for an average of five and a half years. Through chart review of available disclosed corroboration and other evidentiary sources, he confirmed the occurrence of abuse for 19 patients (56 percent). Of these 19 corroborated cases, 10 (53 percent) reported continuous abuse memory, compared to 9 (47 percent) who had not remembered the abuse prior to treatment. In all but two cases, the first discovery of the abuse incidents occurred in connection with the use of hypnosis, a noteworthy finding. Another finding of significance was that, even in corroborated cases, the recollections of the index abuse were not always pristine but rather contained an admixture of accurate and inaccurate information. Furthermore, of the 34 patients, 3 (9 percent) had instances of alleged abuse disconfirmed. Kluft concluded:

> In contradiction to positions taken by numerous proponents of the extreme false memory perspective, these findings seem to indicate that memory of genuine trauma can be absent from awareness for protracted periods of time and then recovered, and that genuine trauma can be documented in the childhood and adulthood of many adults with DID. Furthermore, these findings cast doubt on the argument that materials

emerging from hypnotic exploration should be discounted in a peremptory manner. It seems that there are indeed many systems and/or forms of memory, and that they may have very different characteristics. Treating memory as a unitary phenomenon that can be discussed in glib generalizations is a dangerous oversimplification. (p. 35)

CASE REPORTS.   Individual case reports of repressed memories for authenticated traumatic events have appeared sporadically in the popular and professional literature (i.e., Corwin & Olafson, 1997; Duggal & Sroufe, 1998; Horn, 1993; Mehren, 1993; Schooler, Bendiksen, & Ambadar, 1997; Stanton, 1997; Tayloe, 1995; Terr, 1994; van der Kolk & Kadish, 1987). Some of the most recent and compelling cases are those involving the sexual abuse of multiple victims, usually by clergy or other professionals and/or pedophiles who have access to children through their occupations or hobbies. Cases of this sort provide substantiation of the reality of repressed memories for traumatic incidents through documentation of both the target abuse and the later return of memory long lost to the individual. Cases involving multiple victims of the same perpetrator(s) provide unique opportunities to compare memory retention and memory loss in the victims in a naturalistic study, as was done by Grassian and Holtzen (1996) in the Father Porter case in New England.

Schooler, Ambadar, and Bendiksen (1997) have reported initial findings of an innovative cognitive corroborative case study approach they devised for investigating cases involving discovered memories (their term) of abuse. They investigated the characteristics of the memory discovery experiences and of prior forgetting, in addition to corroboration of the abuse in four cases. They found "reasonably compelling evidence that discovered memories of sexual abuse may sometimes correspond to actual events" (p. 384). They also identified possible clues into the nature of discovered memories, in particular, the conditions under which they occur, their phenomenological quality and the manner in which they may distort estimations of prior forgetting. These mechanisms include matches between abuse experiences and retrieval conditions, the involvement of an insight regarding a memory that was previously absent or obscured in some way (the "a-ha" effect), and the misconstrual of prior forgetting, suggesting a new type of hindsight bias they termed the "forgot it all along effect" (as opposed to the "remembered it all along effect"). Although they offer cautions about limitations of their study method, they also propose a strong conclusion as being warranted from their initial findings: "A corroborative case study approach, grounded in an understanding of basic cognitive mechanisms, is likely to provide an important tool for furthering our understanding of how individuals can have the shocking experience of discovering memories of seemingly unknown trauma" (p. 386).

Other efforts are currently underway to gather examples of corroborated cases of recovered memory. Professor Ross Cheit of Brown University is compiling an archive of such cases (Cheit, 1998). The archive includes verified cases of recovered memory where strong corroborative evidence is available in the form of abuser confession, guilty plea, or self-incriminatory statement; testimony from other victims or eyewitnesses, or documentary evidence; or significant circumstantial evidence. Thus far, more than one form of corroborative evidence is available for almost all of the 36 cases that currently make up the archive.

MECHANISMS FOR REMEMBERING OR FORGETTING AND PREDICTORS OF AMNESIA FOR CHILD SEXUAL ABUSE

Williams and Banyard (1997b) and others have reviewed some of the mechanisms that may play a role in remembering or forgetting child sexual abuse and other traumas. Some of these were discussed in chapters 2 and 3 and in the first section of the current chapter. It appears that various explanations are likely and that others will emerge as this field of study develops.

Although some memory experts continue to reject the notion of any type of special mechanism for the lack of recall documented in these studies, others, such as Schooler, Bendiksen, and Ambadar (1997), entertain the possibility of special mechanisms. They suggest, however, that these mechanisms should be considered *only* after first considering and ruling out standard factors typically associated with variations in the accessibility of normal memories. These researchers note that recovered memory experiences seem to have some unusual characteristics that distinguish them from standard memory recollection experiences. Some of those that have been identified are: the phenomenology of the experiences described by recovered memory subjects as "suddenly and vividly coming out of nowhere" and involving a great onrush of emotions; the capacity to forget about a period in which one was aware of the memory and even discussed it with others (what the authors term the "forgot it all along effect"); the effect of shame on triggering self-defense mechanisms that enhance memory distortion and forgetting; and other special mechanisms such as repression, dissociation, and trauma-induced physiological processes proposed by trauma researchers and, at present, not well examined by or acceptable to the cognitive psychologists. Interestingly, it is mechanisms such as these that Williams and Banyard suggest are implicated and that are increasingly supported by the pooled data from these studies.

In another article, Schooler (1996) reviews the issues along with the evidence surrounding recovered accounts of sexual trauma. He concludes that evidence exists that individuals can actually forget trauma (child sexual abuse as well as other forms such as war trauma) and that there are fluctuations in the accessibility of the memory. Schooler identifies the following as mechanisms that might lead to recovered memory experiences: the fact that these situations cause shame or embarrassment, so that they are less likely to be shared and talked about or more likely to be avoided or suppressed, resulting in their temporarily reduced accessibility; general forgetting and processes more specific to trauma such as dissociation, physiological processes, and even repression, that might contribute to the decreased accessibility of the traumatic memory; and, in terms of recall, the existence of a situation or cue that has some fundamental similarity to the original traumatic experience with respect to either context or affective/physiological state. Schooler's summary comment is consistent with views of traumatic memory and memory retrieval reviewed in chapter 3:

> Once access to the memory is increased, to the degree that the suppression processes were involved in the initial reduction in accessibility to the memory, rebound effects may be experienced in which there is a flooding of the previously suppressed thoughts. . . . The resulting prevalence of thoughts about the trauma may powerfully contrast with the prior relative absence of such thoughts. From the perspective of this current flooding of thoughts about the trauma, the previous relatively reduced accessibility of the memory may be construed as a complete unavailability. The above account provides a highly feasible characterization of the recovered memory process without having to draw on the notion that traumatic memories are ever completely unavailable. This is not to say that traumatic memories may not be completely unavailable for some period of time, but merely that we do not need to postulate such a memory state in order to account for sincere reports of recovered memory experiences corresponding to actual incidents of trauma. At the very minimum, we cannot argue against the possibility of recovered memory experiences on the basis that there is no existing way to explain them. (p. 462)

Brown et al. (1998) reviewed the literature to produce a useful tripartate list of what they termed "predictors of amnesia for childhood sexual abuse." These are (1) background or predisposing factors under the headings of biological factors (intoxication, head injury, personality factors, memory-vulnerable diagnoses, level of intelligence, use of dissociation at the time of trauma, previous history of amnesia, previous history of trauma), developmental factors such as the age of onset of the trauma, and relational factors, particularly the degree of relationship between victim and offender; (2) factors associated with the traumatic event, including the intensity of emotional arousal, degree of physical violence, physical injury, and ability to cope during the event; and (3) factors that intensify or perpetuate effects, including duration and repetition of the trauma, number of perpetrators, injunctions and threats to insure secrecy, victim's cognitive appraisal of the abuse, and victim's accommodation and consent. These factors resemble those articulated by Wilson (1989) in his Interactive Theory of Traumatic Stress Reactions (see Figure 3.1) and the Pynoos et al. (1997) child model, discussed in chapter 3. These models account for the variability in individual response to traumatization and might also account for the variability of factors related to memory retention and amnesia.

MEMORY AS RELATED
TO SYMPTOMATOLOGY

Are there mental health consequences associated with forgetting abuse for a period of time? Williams and Banyard (1997b) wrote that "Theories that address this issue are closely linked to discussion of mechanisms that underlie the forgetting" (p. II–143). Paraphrasing them: If normal forgetting is the proposed mechanism for the loss of memory for abuse, then it would seem that mental health status would not be very negatively impacted. If forgetting is hypothesized as the result of avoidance or suppression that might be adaptive, survivors who avoid or suppress memory might be expected to have relatively good mental health and functioning. And, if forgetting were the result of special mechanisms put in place due to the severity of the stressor (such as repression, dissociation, physiological and neurochemical alterations), higher levels of psychological symptomatology might be expected. Available data both support and challenge these positions and suggest that people are not so easily categorized.

Some studies have reported that continuous memory may result in significant ongoing symptomatology and dysfunction (Grassian & Holtzen, 1996, from their Father Porter sample). In contrast, these researchers found that those subjects who had no thoughts about the abuse had less distress over time than those with continuous memory, but that the latter group showed an intensification of symptoms when they recovered memories (through media exposure or some other trigger). Elliott and Briere (1995a) found that individuals with more recent recall of previously unremembered abuse reported the highest levels of symptomatology, and that symptoms and distress tended to remit over time in conjunction with the processing of the traumatic material. Their findings match the phenomenological descriptions of shock and an onrush of feelings and distress reported in the Schooler et al. and Andrews samples. They also match the descriptions given by clinicians of patients who seek treatment in states of distress and intrusive symptoms after having recovered memories of abuse in response to a trigger of some sort.

SUMMARY

The findings of all of these studies and case reports establish that *a significant subpopulation of victims of childhood sexual abuse (as well as other forms of childhood abuse and trauma) are, for some period of time in their lives, partially or fully amnestic for the abuse/trauma. These individuals may, at a later time, recover these lost memories, which will contain a combination of accurate and inaccurate features.* As noted throughout this discussion, data are unfortunately lacking about the accuracy or inaccuracy of memories in the currently available research, although this situation is improving as more sophisticated research is undertaken. The lack of data should not be used to support the claim that recovered memories of sexual abuse are necessarily inaccurate or false, since research specifically includes attention to the accuracy of recovered memories has consistently found them to be reasonably accurate in the main features of the event in question. By the same token, accuracy cannot be definitively verified without corroborative evidence of some sort.

This chapter has also reviewed some of the mechanisms that might be related to the remembering and forgetting of sexual abuse, beginning with salient traumagenic dynamics associated with abuse. It has also reviewed and highlighted the complexity of the issues involved and the obvious need for additional research—optimally collaborative research by experts in the fields of memory and trauma. We summarize this chapter and lead into the next section with a quote and cautions to practitioners from Chu et al. (1996) from their review of the literature on the nature of traumatic memories for childhood trauma:

> It appears that horribly abused children do forget. However, this forgetting does not necessarily support the concept of repression as opposed to simple dissociation of traumatic experience. When individ-

uals begin to recover memories of past traumatic events, it remains unclear as to what extent these memories reflect the actual events. Recall of single events of childhood trauma have been observed to have an unusual clarity. However, until there is further research, we cannot assume that there is a similar clarity for recovered memories of chronic traumatization. In fact, the defenses used to cope with chronic traumatization—denial, depersonalization, and derealization—may make encoding of memory substantially less accurate. After all, even single events of trauma are often recalled with misperceptions and distortions. It is reasonable to assume that chronic traumatization is likely to result in an even greater degree of inaccuracy.

Despite the uncertainties concerning the processes of traumatic memory encoding and recall, recovered memories of severe childhood abuse cannot be dismissed out-of-hand. Although chronic traumatization may negatively affect the accuracy of memory, several clinical studies do support the validity of some recovery [*sic*] memories of childhood abuse. However, more investigation is required to bridge the rift between clinical observations of traumatic events, and research and the empirical observations of the laboratory. (p. 12)

Chapter 5

EVOLVING STANDARDS OF PRACTICE AND THE STANDARD OF CARE

Philosophy and Principles of Practice

A t the present time, neither the treatment of posttraumatic conditions resulting from any type of trauma (including incest/child sexual abuse) nor treatment involving delayed/recovered memory is well substantiated in terms of efficacy and outcome. This deficit is not unique to the diagnosis or the issue. The entire field of psychotherapy has been slow in the empirical testing of treatment outcome and the provision of treatment guidelines. Major efforts are currently underway to document the effectiveness of treatment approaches for various diagnoses and disorders and to provide guidelines for practice (Rainer, 1996; Saunders & Williams, 1996; VandenBos, 1996). The American Psychiatric Association has recently published guidelines for the treatment of several psychiatric conditions, including eating disorders, major depressive disorder, bipolar disorder, panic disorder, and substance abuse disorders (American Psychiatric Association, 1996, 1998). Preliminary efforts are underway within the American Psychological Association to develop criteria for evaluating the efficacy of assessment and intervention efforts for various diagnoses and disorders (American Psychological Association, 1995; Chambless, 1996; Chambless et al., 1996).

Such efforts to substantiate applied practice are becoming increasingly important to working clinicians due to the growth and developing sophistication of the behavioral and mental health fields, to changes that are occurring in the health-care delivery system requiring greater accountability, and to the demands of consumers and interested or affected third parties (i.e., insurance companies and especially managed care companies). They are particularly critical in terms of the treatment model under discussion here, where greater validation and accountability are being sought by false memory/recovered memory commentators, the courts, and state licensing boards (Applebaum & Zoltek-Jick, 1996; Brown & Scheflin, 1996; Hedges, Hilton, Hilton, & Caudill, 1997; Knapp & VandeCreek, 1997).

Empirical substantiation and related clinical guideline efforts are not without critics, however. Concerns have been raised about such important issues as what criteria to establish for the investigation, what validation level to meet, how many studies are needed, whether the findings achieved in highly structured research settings readily apply to practice, and whether they will lead prematurely or needlessly to a restriction of practice and a devaluation of clinical observation (Abrahamson & Saakvitne, in press; Garfield, 1996; Kovacs, 1995; Nathan, 1998). Other critics, some of them feminists, weigh in from a different perspective (Brown, 1996; Harvey and Herman, 1996, 1997; Stricker and Trierweiler, 1995). They dispute the concept of neutrality and objectivity implied in scientific formulations and data-driven investigations and challenge that they are not the only method by which to gather information about human behavior. They decry losing the voice, authority, or needs of the individual to scientifically-derived one-size-fits-all formulas. They also challenge the superiority of "science" in understanding human experience and point out how often this outlook has advantaged the powerful in defining experience of those less powerful, often causing harm in the process. This perspective should not be taken to mean that these critics are against science or standards to practice by, only that they question some of the closed-end methods of empirical investigations and support other ways of deriving information and substantiation about aspects of human experience. These commentators also point out that information derived from naturalistic and/or clinical studies are often important in their own right and may raise the issues that investigators later study empirically.

In terms of the effects of past abuse and its treatment, literature on this subject has been growing since the early 1980s. In aggregate, this information has resulted in theoretical conceptualizations and the development of preliminary treatment principles, guidelines, and recommendations, a considerable advance over what was available prior to that time; however, as I noted when my model was published (Courtois, 1988), little empirically-derived substantiation was available, a situation that has not changed much in the intervening years. It is fair to say that the treatment of past abuse (whether professional or lay, but especially the type espoused in the lay and self-help literature) has exceeded available efficacy data. Conversely, research has not kept up with the clinical descriptions and suggested applications. Across the field as a whole, much more outcome research is needed. This conclusion was stated by the participants at the National Institute of Mental Health research workshop on treatment of adult victims of child sexual abuse held in March of 1990:

> Clinical accounts of the treatment of adults who have experienced childhood sexual abuse are numerous, but there is little controlled treatment research with this clinical population. Such research would be of value if it prompted clinicians to empirically assess the efficacy of their treatment approaches. (Gordon & Alexander, 1993, p. 307)

Both outcome and process research efforts are underway. Thus far, evidence has accumulated that short-term, time-limited individual and group treatments can be effective in reducing some core PTSD and depressive symptoms and that some short- and longer-term individual treatments are successful in modifying specific coping mechanisms, cognitive schema, and psychological and somatic symptoms (Alexander, Neimeyer, & Follette, 1991; Alexander, Neimeyer, Follette, Moore, & Harter, 1989; Cahill, Llewelyn & Pearson, 1991; Cameron, 1993, 1994; Follette & Alexander, 1991; Jehu, 1988; Koraleski & Larson, 1997; Lundberg-Love, Marmion, Ford, Geffner, & Peacock, 1992; Roth & Batson, 1997). Treatment success has been reported in the amelioration of symptoms such as anxiety (Foa, Rothbaum, Riggs, & Murdock, 1991), and conditions underlying the diagnoses of dissociative identity disorder (Ellason & Ross, 1995) and borderline personality disorder (Linehan, 1993). Specialized and novel treatment approaches are under investigation (F. Shapiro, 1995). Models that measure the acquisition of particular skills, treatment dimensions, or healing tasks according to stage of treatment (such as those provided by Kepner, 1995; Kluft, 1994; and Lebowitz, Harvey, and Herman, 1993) readily lend themselves to empirical study and are increasingly under investigation.

As discussed in the first section of this book, the literature and research base is rapidly expanding and the treatment model has shifted considerably over the course of the last decade (especially the last five years) due to the memory controversy. The observation made by van der Kolk et al. (1996) in their recently published review article on the treatment of posttraumatic stress disorder applies equally well to the treatment of past sexual abuse: "Until more comprehensive treatment outcome studies are available, we continue to be critically dependent on clinical wisdom in treating these patients. Thus we must remain aware of the caveat that there can be significant gaps between clinical impressions and scientific data" (p. 418). These authors further noted that: "The treatment of PTSD has this in common with other areas of psychotherapy practice: Much of the required research information does not exist. Therefore, the treatment must in large part be derived from clinical judgment and drawn from the available knowledge about the etiology and longitudinal course of this condition" (p. 419).

In sum, it is reasonable to conclude that, at the present time, "the systematic investigation of what constitutes effective treatment [for PTSD] is still in its infancy" (van der Kolk et al., 1996, p. 417) and "there are no well developed guidelines for the treatment of anxiety and post-traumatic stress disorders" (Abrahamson & Saakvitne, in press) (although treatment guidelines for PTSD are currently under development by the International Society for Traumatic Stress Studies and other organizations and review articles on PTSD treatment have been published in recent years by Shalev, Bonne, & Eth, 1996, Sherman, 1998, and Solomon, Gerrity, & Muff, 1992). These reviews strongly suggest the necessity for multi-modal or multi-dimensional treatment given the complexity of PTSD (with or without associated and comorbid conditions). Much additional work is needed. In the absence of outcome research regarding treatment effectiveness and guidelines for treatment of abuse/trauma, therapists must proceed cautiously and pay particular attention to standards of care and standards of practice and to the emerging literature having to do with abuse and posttrauma treatment, particularly to issues pertaining to traumatic memory.

EVOLVING STANDARDS OF PRACTICE AND THE STANDARD OF CARE

Standards of Psychological Practice

"Standards of psychological practice" refer to general bounds set on practice that are consistent with current scientific evidence and accumulated knowledge. They encompass hortatory or prescriptive standards describing what a practitioner "ought to do" as well as minatory or proscriptive standards describing "what not to do" (Dawes, 1995). Developing a scientific basis for specific practice interventions is part and parcel of the treatment substantiation effort described above. It is a complex and multidetermined endeavor, at once a practical and rational process (as well as an aspirational one) but very difficult to operationalize in terms of evaluation criteria (Chambless, 1996; Chambless et al, 1996). Typically, the task of setting practice standards and making practice recommendations is undertaken by working groups of recognized experts in a topic area, who review the available authoritative literature to determine the "state-of-the-art" in terms of applied outcome. The findings of a review of this sort then form the basis for recommended assessment and intervention efforts for a particular condition or disorder and suggest areas where additional research is needed (Hayes, 1995).

The Standard of Care

"Standard of care" is a legal term applied in malpractice cases where the burden is on the plaintiff to prove that treatment was below standard and was the proximate cause of harm. Standard of care thus refers to the overall treatment of the patient, including assessment and choice and efficacy of specific therapeutic interventions, in addition to professional and ethical practice issues. At present, the standard of care is determined by professional peer and expert opinion and testimony, as well as authoritative research and applied clinical literature, all within applicable regulatory statutes and general professional practice standards and ethical codes (Brown, 1995; Knapp & VandeCreek, 1997).

In considering the standard of care for trauma treatment, Brown wrote that the standard "is defined by the evolving literature on diagnosis, as defined by *DSM-IV*, and on trauma treatment written by trauma experts" (Brown, 1995, p.16). This encompasses a review of the available literature on the "state of the science" and "state of applied science and practice" in the field of traumatic stress studies. In terms of delayed/recovered memory issues, it also takes into consideration and encompasses the pertinent findings, recommendations, and cautions of cognitive memory experts as well as those of professional task forces and working groups.

EVOLVING STANDARDS FOR TRAUMA TREATMENT AND DELAYED/RECOVERED MEMORY ISSUES

Currently, it is generally acknowledged that both standards of practice and the standard of care for trauma treatment and for treatment of recovered memory are evolving and that more outcome research, empirical substantiation, and expert consensus are needed before standards can be conclusively established (Brown et al., 1998; Courtois, 1997a, 1997d; Knapp & VandeCreek, 1997; Pope & Brown, 1996; van der Kolk et al., 1996). Nevertheless, enough agreements exist between expert researchers and practitioners and enough consistency is found within the research and applied clinical literature, in the recommendations of the

professional task forces, and in therapist and consumer satisfaction surveys to suggest a beginning consensus standard of practice and standard
of care. Keeping in mind the caveats offered by van der Kolk and his colleagues, the remainder of this chapter and book is devoted to an articulation of aspects of the consensus model of posttrauma treatment, especially involving treatment for lost or recovered memories of childhood
abuse. My aim is not to provide a definitive and unchangeable model;
rather, it is to suggest principles and guidelines to assist ethical and competent practice. It is expected that the model will undergo continuous
updating and revision as new information becomes available.

PHILOSOPHICAL FOUNDATIONS AND PRINCIPLES OF PRACTICE

Attention to the philosophical foundations and practice principles that
have been devised for working with suspected child abuse and issues of
delayed/recovered memories will help therapists to reduce risk and provide state-of-the-art treatment for individuals who, for a variety of reasons, constitute a high-risk clinical population. A portion of the risk
comes from the population itself. As discussed in chapter 4, a significant
number of survivors of chronic forms of interpersonal violence have
symptoms noteworthy for their complexity and tenacity and have higher
than average potential for impulsivity, relational instability, substance
abuse, and violence to self or others. Additional risk is associated with the
patient's degree of memory and what techniques, if any, are (or were)
used for memory retrieval. Patients who never forgot the abuse, who
spontaneously recovered memory outside of therapy, and/or who have
corroboration pose the least risk. Some risk is associated with those
whose memory returns during the course of the psychotherapy. The
highest risk comes with individuals who have no prior memories of abuse
and who, due to the use of unsubstantiated and/or suggestive therapy
techniques, develop highly detailed memory they believe to be accurate
(including memory for quite improbable or even impossible events).

Still more risk comes from the social milieu and the memory controversy itself. The last several years have witnessed a rapid rise in the number of ethics and licensing complaints and lawsuits against therapists who
treat adults alleging childhood abuse (Applebaum & Zoltek-Jick, 1996;
Hedges et al., 1997; Knapp & VandeCreek, 1997). Adherence to sound
principles of professional practice and ethical standards, development of
competence to treat abuse-related effects and syndromes, and attention
to recommendations regarding work with delayed/recovered memories

help safeguard both the practitioner and the patient. It is hoped that they will also satisfy the most legitimate of the critiques, allowing vital work with this population to continue. As noted by Knapp & VandeCreek in their recent book on legal risk management in treating patients with memories of abuse:

> Psychotherapists who treat adult survivors of childhood abuse provide a valuable public service. Their patients may be among the most needy, vulnerable, and traumatized of all psychotherapy patients. Psychotherapy may play a crucial role in facilitating the recovery of these survivors. The work of psychotherapists who treat adult survivors of childhood abuse is especially commendable given the way that the society has historically denied or neglected its reality. (p. 2)

Philosophical Foundations

The philosophy of treatment for working with delayed/recovered memory issues is in sharp contrast to the treatment model that has received so much publicity and condemnation from the false memories critics. Quite ironically, the model espoused here constitutes a therapeutic approach that is likely to be acceptable to the majority of critics, especially those most inclined toward finding a middle ground position and not seeking to suppress reports or suspicions of abuse. This very point has been made repeatedly by a number of writers in the field who have been seeking to diffuse the polemics and to find points of commonality between the involved parties (Alpert, Brown, & Courtois, 1996c; Briere, 1996a, 1996b, 1997a; Brown et al., 1998; Courtois, 1995b, 1997a, 1997d; Lindsay & Briere, 1997; Pope & Brown, 1996).

   This treatment model has as its foundation the standards of practice and codes of ethical conduct that have been developed over the years by the mental health professions to guide the responsible practice of psychotherapy. The treatment of past abuse or of delayed/recovered memory is not exempted from following these accepted generic standards and ethics. In fact, they may be even more salient in this work because of the many difficult issues and uncertainties that come into play, including many occasions when legal and ethical requirements contradict each other (Briere, 1996a; Dalenberg & Carlson, in press; Daniluk & Haverkamp, 1993; Knapp & VandeCreek, 1997). In particular, the standards attend to the broad-based principles upon which the specific ethics codes are founded: autonomy, fidelity, justice, beneficence, nonmaleficence, and therapist self-interest (Beauchamp & Childress, 1983; Daniluk & Haverkamp, 1993). The principle of *autonomy* refers to freedom of action and choice, with the promotion of patient autonomy a central goal of therapy. *Fidelity* involves faithfulness and loyalty to the patient, protecting his/her best interests. *Justice* implies equality in treatment, in terms of access and quality. *Beneficence* relates to doing good, a core value of all helping professions and *nonmaleficence*, to doing no harm. *Self-interest* relates to the moral and ethical responsibility of self-knowledge and self-protection on the part of the therapist. These principles form a backdrop for clinical judgement and decision making in circumstances where the ethics code is not specific or detailed enough.

In this therapy, memory retrieval is not the guiding strategy or the goal, and remembering abuse is not equated with recovery (Gold & Brown, 1997). Instead, treatment is broad-based complex, and multifaceted. It is directed towards the stabilization of the presenting symptoms and personal healing over time, with empowerment as an organizing focus. The recollection of trauma is not the *sine qua non* of treatment, and the patient is not told that s/he has forgotten past abuse and/or must therefore retrieve previously unavailable memories of abuse in order to get better. The therapist understands and avoids the suggestive implications of such a treatment approach. There is high potential to recreate dynamics associated with any past abuse by implying that the therapist is the authority figure who knows best.

Memories of abuse are worked with as they are naturally presented by the patient. Early in treatment, a cognitive/educational approach is used to validate and normalize the patient's experience, but the predominant emphasis is on self management and the stabilization of any intrusive memories and debilitating symptoms. Only after the patient has gained more control and mastery does the content and affect of any traumatic material become the direct focus. Even then, the intensity is carefully titrated to the capacities of the patient and traumatic material is worked primarily in terms of its significance, geared towards its gradual resolution. The aim is not to develop deeper and deeper memories of more and more abuse; rather, the patient must gradually face and accommodate the occurrence and meaning of any abuse as it is known and resolve associated feelings.

The therapy model is explicitly founded on professionalism, professional behavior, and a scientific attitude. The therapist strives to be as objective as possible to avoid getting caught in false dichotomies. S/he maintains ongoing awareness of the possible effects of personal beliefs and values in terms of confirmatory bias, works to achieve and maintain a stance of technical neutrality regarding abuse memories, and strives to improve knowledge and skills on an ongoing basis. Therapeutic approaches are data-based whenever possible, and information is evaluated and used properly (for example, the therapist does not rely on media reports or lay literature for accuracy, nor are these sources used for professional discourse or therapeutic decision-making). Where the patient is confused by therapeutic material and memories that are indefinite or contradictory, the therapist encourages evaluation over a period of time to avoid arriving at hasty or premature conclusions. The therapist must be able to tolerate ambiguity and must assist the patient to do the same.

The therapist counsels caution and thoughtfulness versus impulsive or premature action, especially on the basis of recovered memory alone. As noted by Herman (1992b), technical neutrality does not equate with moral neutrality regarding the reality and prevalence of sexual abuse, nor does it mean ignoring the politics surrounding such abuse or its grave personal and societal ramifications, as discussed by Brown (1996). The therapist is also under obligation to continuously review the treatment and its effectiveness for the individual patient. Treatment plans are essential and require frequent review and modification, especially when treatment stalemates or the patient is not showing expected therapeutic gain (Pope & Brown 1996).

The model is organized around recognition of the primacy and uniqueness of the individual who seeks treatment and the maintenance of his/her welfare (the ethical principle of beneficence, "first, do no harm"). Treatment is not one-size-fits-all; rather, each individual must be differentially assessed and treated under the umbrella of accepted therapeutic practice and ethical standards. The therapeutic approach is determined in a decision-tree fashion (see chapter 9 for a decision model and discussion). A generic treatment strategy is followed when abuse is not specifically recalled and the patient has no posttraumatic symptoms. A more trauma-oriented treatment is instituted when posttraumatic symptoms are manifest, whether abuse is known or unknown, or when strong reasons exist to suspect abuse or other trauma. In either treatment approach, an individualized treatment strategy is devised that initially focuses on the amelioration of symptoms and the strengthening of personal functioning. Where the exploration and resolution of abuse/trauma-related material are warranted, they occur later in the process.

The "whole person" philosophy prevails: Although symptoms, deficits, and disorders are reasons for seeking treatment and are targets of intervention, the individual's strengths, resources, and reliance are identified and reinforced. Similarly, where an abuse history is disclosed, suspected, or uncovered, it is not considered the sole issue of significance in the patient's life, nor is it the sole focus of intervention. The therapist understands that many other life experiences, independent of or in concert with abuse experiences, must be considered. Additionally, through strategies designed to educate and inform the patient about treatment, s/he is made a partner in the endeavor, with ultimate responsibility for doing the work and making changes that hopefully lead to symptom and life improvement.

In a related vein, a philosophy of personal empowerment and self-determination also undergirds this treatment. The patient's unique phenomenological experience and its specific meaning are the province of the individual and are reinforced. *The individual has the authority over the meaning and interpretation of his/her personal life history.* These should not be exported to or appropriated by the therapist, especially when the patient is uncertain as to specific content or meaning (a situation that is quite routine when struggling with delayed/recovered memories with their quite variable degrees of fragmentation, clarity, and continuity) or when a patient is especially dependent, suggestible, inexperienced, or naive. The therapist functions as an active and empathetic listener and a guide in working with the emotional material that is the primary domain of psychotherapy. He or she also works to enable the patient to openly voice and examine all material, especially that which is confusing and shameful, and/or was previously suppressed or forbidden.

The clinician is further invested in creating conditions within the therapeutic relationship that are as egalitarian as possible. S/he establishes conditions conducive to a collaborative relationship that is neither *laissez faire* nor authoritarian in style. The responsibilities and power differentials inherent in the roles of the therapist and patient are explicitly acknowledged and the therapist strives to use power effectively on the individual's behalf and to encourage the patient's development and autonomy (Courtois, 1997b; Enns, 1996). The therapist further conveys an openness to the patient's questioning of authority (including the therapist) and the patient's ultimate authority over his/her life and therapeutic engagement and progress. The clinician is careful to maintain appropriate boundaries and limitations and is responsible for avoiding dual relationships with the patient.

The treatment relies on a foundation of professional training, suitable qualifications, and competence to treat. As discussed in Chapter 1, the delayed/recovered memory controversy emerged, in part, due to charges of incompetence and malpractice on the part of therapists. They were accused of misdiagnosing patients, attributing all of their problems to past sexual abuse, and using unsubstantiated and suggestive methods to recover false memories of abuse. It appears that a sizable portion of the most problematic and suggestive treatment has been provided by uncredentialed and unqualified individuals who nevertheless practiced as therapists or counselors; however, it is also evident that substandard care was provided, in some cases, by licensed practitioners (not infrequently by those with the least amount of training, those who resist supervision or consultation, or by those who were unaware of issues of suggestibility but sometimes by those with high levels of training and experience) (Brenneis, 1997; Knapp & VandeCreek, 1997).

The problem is compounded by the fact that issues of interpersonal violence and traumatization have not been included in the curricula of the various mental health professions, nor has specific training or supervision been readily available in the treatment of posttraumatic conditions. Unfortunately, this situation continues to prevail in professional training. Consequently, practitioners working with patients who report or suspect abuse must be appropriately credentialed so that they are bound by professional standards and ethics. They must take the initiative to supplement their generic psychotherapy training with specialized information to develop the needed proficiency to treat. In addition, clinicians must have emotional maturity and intellectual competence to work with potentially difficult and painful material (Pope & Brown, 1996) and with patients whose symptom pictures may be complex, multifaceted, longstanding, and vexing (Chu, 1998). It has become increasingly recognized that individuals who have been interpersonally victimized, especially chronically and in the context of ongoing relationships, often have characterological and attachment disturbances that pose great challenges in psychotherapy. Therapists who have not been training to anticipate or manage these issues may have great difficulty managing transference and countertransference reenactments, which might result in their making therapeutic errors they might not otherwise make. It is additionally recommended that all professionals working with these issues engage in continuing education to stay abreast of the new developments in this clinical specialty and in ongoing supervision or consultation in order to monitor their functioning and capability.

Finally, the treatment of the abused or possibly abused is planful and systematic. It closely follows the evolving consensus model that is organized around careful and comprehensive assessment and a planned sequence of interventions that are hierarchically ordered (presented in chapter 6). Any in-depth work with abuse or other trauma occurs in the middle phase of treatment and is not haphazard; it is undertaken after the patient is assessed for readiness and emotional tolerance and only if necessary. This treatment is thus not a hunt for missing memories, nor is it an archeological expedition for long-hidden trauma.

Principles of Practice

Principles of practice for treatment involving suspected childhood abuse and delayed/recovery memories flow from and support these philosophical foundations. They also continuously reference major ethical principles as they attend to the primary issues and dynamics associated with sexual abuse and its recollection.

INFORMED CONSENT.   Informed consent begins prior to the initiation of treatment, optimally from the initial contact. At that time, the therapist provides a prospective patient with an explanation of the process of psychotherapy and the potential risks and benefits of the procedures involved. The latter is especially important when the therapist is using a technique whose effectiveness for a specific purpose is unproven. Informed consent is an ongoing process rather than a one-time event, designed for dialogue about the treatment process and active collaboration by the patient. The code of ethics of the American Psychological Association (1992) contains the following description of informed consent:

> Psychologists make reasonable efforts to answer patients' questions and to avoid apparent misunderstandings about therapy. Whenever possible, psychologists provide oral and/or written information, using language that is reasonably understandable to the patient or client. (Standard 4.01d)
>
> Psychologists obtain appropriate informed consent to therapy or related procedures, using language that is reasonably understandable to participants. The content of informed consent will vary depending on many circumstances; however, informed consent generally implies that the person (1) has the capacity to consent, (2) has been informed of significant information concerning the procedure, (3) has freely and without undue influence expressed consent, and (4) consent has been appropriately documented. (Standards 4.10d and 4.02a)

Information should be imparted to the patient in both verbal and written form. A general informed consent form signed by the patient is used to document that information has been conveyed and that the patient indicates understanding and agreement. Additionally, it is recommended that a specialized informed consent form be used with any technique that is experimental, controversial, possible suggestive, or unproven, or that carries a greater than average degree of risk. The patient is thus given an explanation of the technique and advised of the implications and risk/benefits of its use. Examples of such specialized forms for use with hypnosis and eye movement desensitization and reprocessing (EMDR) are found in Hammond et al. (1994), Scheflin and Shapiro (1989), and F. Shapiro (1995). The therapist should be sure to discuss the efficacy and limitations of any technique used for memory retrieval or processing *per se*.

Brown (1994) has proposed the concept of "empowered consent," which goes beyond standard informed consent. Empowered consent communicates that the treatment process is collaborative and has personal empowerment as a central goal. Inherent in the process of informed consent is the option of refusal, the choice not to engage in treatment or agree to the use or application of a specific technique. Pope and Brown (1996) offered this description of the empowered consent process:

> A goal of the empowered consent process is that the client gains access to the kind of relevant knowledge that the therapist already has about the therapist's training and background, and about the various risks and benefits of therapy. Empowered consent clarifies that the client is the ultimate arbiter of what is helpful and has the right to refuse any intervention, seek a second opinion, request that the therapist get consultation, or terminate treatment at any time without punitive consequences or having the refusal labeled as a form of pathology. This empowerment of the client as a partner in decision-making does not abrogate the therapist's responsibility for careful treatment planning; rather, it underscores respect for the autonomy and adulthood of clients and for their right to challenge interventions that feel wrong and may be countertherapeutic. This form of consent demonstrates that the therapists seek to avoid unilaterally and dictatorially imposing their own goals on the client. . . . The net effect of this sort of empowered consent should be a strong communication to clients that this is their therapy and they have rights and privileges that do not disappear no matter how frightened or vulnerable they feel, which includes a collaborative participation in plans for what will happen in therapy. (pp.165-166)

Obviously, this type of informed consent and the option of informed refusal support the philosophical foundation of personal empowerment, as well as the ethical principle of autonomy described earlier in this chapter. Informed consent is an especially critical issue for abuse survivors and individuals who struggle with delayed/recovered memories. Abuse involves disempowerment of the victim, who often becomes mistrustful yet compliant towards authority figures. A strategy that encourages self-determination and discourages an overdependant/compliant stance contradicts a major abuse dynamic and, over time, can be very therapeutic. Similarly, individuals who grapple with unclear memory must be supported in both their uncertainty and their right to determine its personal meaning. Therapists should not present themselves as the "knowers" or arbiters of their patient's experience and should instead model the ability to be uncertain.

THE TREATMENT FRAME   Issues that fall under the general rubric of the psychotherapy treatment frame (i.e., conditions for treatment) are especially critical in working with this population and provide risk management for both therapist and patient. Attention to and communication about issues should occur from the preliminary contact. It is advantageous for the therapist to convey his/her approach to these issues in writing and for the patient to sign a statement of understanding and consent that becomes an essential component of the treatment record. A "rights and responsibilities" statement, individually tailored to meet the needs of the practitioner's practice philosophy, therapeutic orientation, areas of specialization, and treatment methods, addresses a variety of routine professional and business issues such as:

- a general introduction to psychotherapy, including the mutual roles, rights, and responsibilities of the therapist and patient
- professional boundaries and limitations
- professional privilege and confidentiality and its limits (i.e., child abuse reporting statutes, duty to warn, duty to protect,etc.)
- scheduling and attendance requirements
- therapist accessibility outside of session and means of contact
- back-up arrangements during vacations and other absences
- fees and billing
- insurance issues (i.e., reporting requirements, issues of confidentiality)
- payment schedule and expectations
- issues pertaining to the personal safety of both patient and therapist
- general approaches to hospitalization and medication,
- approaches to collateral consultation and adjunctive treatment, and
- special issues tailored to the needs or philosophy of the therapist or the needs of the specific treatment population

The "information for patients" (or "rights and responsibilities") document should be routinely updated to communicate any significant changes (i.e., fees, insurance/managed care information, schedule modifications) and to incorporate newly available pertinent information (for example, I amended my statement with the American Psychiatric

Association "Statement on Memories of Sexual Abuse" when it was first published in 1993 to provide information to patients who had questions about the memory controversy or who wanted information about how I worked with memory issues). Practitioners might consider adopting a similar strategy and attaching the guidelines or recommendations made by their respective professions or something that particularly fits their practice (I continue to use the American Psychiatric Association Statement for its succinctness and continued relevance; however, I occasionally supplement it with material from the American Psychological Association Working Group on Memories of Childhood Abuse). Model "information for patients" and "rights and responsibilities" statements are available as handouts in many professional risk management workshops and books. One that I have developed for my practice, along with an informed consent form, is available in Appendix C.

We now move to an expanded discussion of some of the most salient treatment frame issues and principles of practice in psychotherapy involving memory of abuse/trauma.

PROFESSIONAL ROLES, BOUNDARIES, AND LIMITATIONS.   Clear role definition and boundary maintenance are especially relevant in the treatment of abuse survivors. Interpersonal victimization, by definition, involves the violation of personal boundaries. Chronic victimization further involves conditioning into a relationship with overlapping roles, boundary slippage, ambivalent attachment, and ambivalent emotions. This affiliative conditioning may play out in other relationships, including therapy. Consequently, the clinician must be scrupulous about defining and maintaining appropriate roles and boundaries and must further refrain from dual relationships that would interfere with the objectivity required of a professional psychotherapy relationship. The most common dual roles for therapist and patient are personal friendships, mentoring/training relationships, business partnerships, sexual/intimate relationships, and the confounding of therapist, investigatory, and expert witness roles.

The therapist also has an obligation to be conscientious about the maintainance of professional boundaries. Practically speaking, this means that the therapist must continuously monitor other aspects of the therapeutic relationship, including his/her emotional attunement, attachment, and availability and the patient's patterns of relating, while steering clear of the aforementioned dual relationships. Empathic attunement continues to be recognized as an essential (and possibly the critical element) of the healing process (Chu, 1998; McCann & Colletti, 1994; Wilson & Lindy, 1994). A balancing act is called for. Enough closeness must be developed for therapeutic engagement, while enough distance must be maintained for therapeutic observation and objectivity. A dance of empathy and attunement occurs throughout the process, often with repetitive patterns of connecting and distancing.

Abuse survivors are notoriously mistrustful of authority figures. They may hide their mistrust under a facade of superficial compliance or overdependence or, alternatively, resist the development of any relationship or attachment in a counterdependent fashion. A position of supportive neutrality that is neither overindulgent nor overly abstinent helps to develop a therapeutic relationship with enough safety to anchor treatment and rework issues of past abuse. Like other psychotherapy patients, abuse survivors transfer relational patterns and feelings onto their therapists; however, they tend to do so with more intensity than other patients and in posttraumatic role reenactments (Courtois, 1988; Davies & Frawley, 1994; Pearlman & Saakvitne, 1995). They often "invite" the therapist to play roles complementary to those they experienced in the past and that they play out in present-day relationships (the predominant abuse roles are victim, victimizer, rescuer, and bystander). The therapist must expect these relational dynamics and role enactments yet not succumb to them. S/he must also assist the patient in understanding rather than reenacting them. These issues are discussed in more depth in chapter 9.

The stance of supportive neutrality takes on additional significance with the issues of delayed/recovered memory. On the one hand, it establishes enough professionalism and distance to offset the criticisms regarding therapists' overidentifying with patients and working their own personal agendas regarding abuse. It also removes the therapist from the role of rescuer/interpreter and advocate, while countering the patient's overreliance on the therapist for validation of recovered memory. On the other hand, this stance provides enough support for patients struggling with memories of real abuse to openly explore their recollections. Studies of abuse disclosure routinely report that empathic connection and openness on the part of the therapist are critical elements in patients' being able to examine personal evidence and to arrive at conclusions, whether in the direction of believing that abuse occurred or that it did not (Dalenberg, 1997; Josephson & Fong-Beyette, 1987). Issues of assessment and disclosure are discussed in more detail in chapter 7.

Accessibility and limitations are other important boundary issues for therapists to consider and convey. Therapists have a responsibility to be generally accessible, particularly in the event of an emergency or crisis; however, they must guard against fostering regression or overdependence by being too available or eager to help or by taking on too much responsibility. The role of rescuer may be particularly compelling when working with a patient who is compliant, idealizing, and dependent, one who is needy and engaged in ongoing crises, or one whose behavior leads the therapist to feel anxious and threatened. The therapist may find that s/he overidentifies with or wishes to protect certain patients. The therapist may also be drawn to the rescuer role if s/he is overanxious or is consciously or unconsciously looking toward patients for the fulfillment of narcissistic or professional needs. Overinvolvement may be a particular "treatment trap" for the novice therapist who is simultaneously in search of professional affirmation and in the process of honing skills and professional judgment (Chu, 1988; Pearlman & Saakvitne, 1995) or of the therapist who is also an abuse or trauma survivor and who might be prone to overidentify with the patient.

It is generally countertherapeutic for therapists to overgratify their patients. An indulgent stance does not hold patients responsible for their behavior and can promote unhealthy dependence; moreover, therapists who do not have appropriate boundaries and limits often experience burnout and become enraged at what they perceive to be the insatiable demands of their patients. They may thus move from the role of rescuer to victim and ultimately to victimizer/bystander if, in their exhaustion and rage, they become either hostile or rigidly inaccessible or indifferent. It is up to therapists to monitor and titrate their availability and responses according to the patient's diagnosis, condition, susceptibility to influence, and characterological structure, taking care to be neither too obliging nor too distant. As discussed above, the therapist will optimally provide a balance in response to the patient, maintaining both an empathic connection and professional distance and limits in order to rework rather than reenact relational issues. It is the responsibility of the therapist to continuously monitor transference and countertransference dynamics in terms of boundary management and to address problematic boundary and role issues as they occur.

THERAPIST RELIABILITY AND CONSISTENCY.   All other issues notwithstanding, therapists must strive to maintain consistency and reliability in their work with these patients, who, although they may anticipate inconstancy and mistrust the therapist, are simultaneously very sensitive and reactive to instability and change. The therapist should, as much as possible, explicitly spell out scheduling issues, attendance expectations, and accessibility outside of session, along with expectations and means of contact. Some abuse survivors are prone to overreliance and misuse of therapist availability, calling for trivial reasons or "just to check in." In contrast, others do not call, even when they are in situations of desperate need, such as a suicidal or self-mutilative crisis. The therapist must help the patient to achieve a comfortable balance between these two extremes, i.e., making contact when a legitimate need exists to do so and not waiting until a situation is critical.

Separations and absences pose special difficulties for this treatment population and should also be conscientiously attended to. Often, separations call up instances of painful past abandonment and neglect, resulting in increased anxiety and frantic efforts to either reconnect or sever the connection with the therapist. Separations might also serve as triggers to previously inaccessible memories, due to the fact that instances of abuse may have occurred in the context of emotional or physical abandonment or both (Courtois, 1988). Therapists must be knowledgeable about and sensitive to these possibilities and help prepare patients for any planned absences. They can help modulate these reactions somewhat by insisting that patients have sources of support besides the therapist and by helping patients to anticipate and manage change as a normal rather than catastrophic human experience. Additionally, the therapist might devise his/her own methods for working with these issues. For example, I communicate in my initial sessions and throughout the course of therapy about planned absences. I indicate in my "rights and responsibilities" statement that I will be out of the office an average of eight weeks per year for consulting/conferences/writing/vacation purposes. I also provide my patients with a quarterly schedule indicating when I will be unavailable and why, and coverage arrangements. In general, unless on vacation or traveling far from home where timely response would be problematic, I maintain telephone accessibility. Otherwise, my patients are given the name and number of another professional as back-up.

Professional coverage is essential during any times of prolonged unavailability or inaccessibility (childbirth and family leave, illness, planned leave, sabbatical, etc.) and when absences occur suddenly (due to illness, death, other personal or family crisis). As noted above, it is during such times that some of these patients have the most difficulty managing, due to the myriad of meaning, projections, interpretations, and memories that might be stirred by change and, more specifically, by absences. Backup therapists can provide support and comfort to patients while giving them the opportunity to verbalize their reactions. They may offer interpretations of patients' responses while simultaneously allaying their fears of total abandonment and rejection.

OTHER RELATIONSHIP ISSUES.   The therapist also communicates that therapeutic relationships, like all human relationships, have their ups and downs and times of disagreement and discord, and that the therapist is not perfect. S/he indicates an openness to all feelings about the relationship and treatment, not just the positive, and further invites discussion about the process and its "fit" for the individual. Treatment difficulties and even impasses are expected and are not treated as signs of failure. In fact, when handled successfully, they can be opportunities for great therapeutic gain (whether the treatment continues or ends). The therapist must own rather than deny his/her mistakes or missteps when a patient brings them up or questions them and, furthermore, must take them seriously and not blame them on the patient. In particular, the therapist must aim for honesty in the relationship but must not confuse honesty with loss of boundaries, especially unnecessary and potentially harmful self-disclosure. For example, if a patient comments about a therapist's lapse of attention and responsiveness, the therapist acknowledges its occurrence and may identify something about its origin (the therapist is tired); however, she does not go on to disclose a great deal of personal information (the therapist is not sleeping well because s/he is in the midst of a painful divorce and child custody evaluation). The therapist thereby maintains personal privacy and does not engage the patient in any kind of role reversal, thus not reenacting a dynamic of the past.

Expectations regarding ongoing impasses in treatment that do not resolve and the decision to terminate should also be discussed beforehand. Patients should know that they have the right to end treatment at any time without penalty, but should also be urged not to terminate abruptly or without attempts at problem-solving or resolution. These patients are often hypersensitive to interpersonal cues, prone to misunderstandings and misinterpretations, and further prone to impulsive actions in response to feelings. They should, therefore, be encouraged to verbalize their concerns and perceptions before acting on them and be taught communication, problem-solving, and conflict resolution skills. Therapists should make every effort to be respectful of patients during times of disagreement and impasse. As noted by Hilton (1997), most complaints against therapists for actual or perceived transgressions do not begin with the transgression itself; rather, most are undertaken because the response on the part of the therapist was unsatisfactory and the patient felt unheard, was further wounded, and/or was blamed or abandoned. In the event that termination is the option of choice (by either party or by mutual agreement), the therapist offers referrals to other practitioners and ongoing contact for a specified period of time (as appropriate) until a transfer to another therapist occurs. Regardless of the circumstances, the therapist must guard against patient abandonment and must terminate responsibly and ethically.

ENGAGEMENT IN THE TREATMENT PROCESS AND RESPONSIBILITY FOR PROGRESS. A related issue involves the patient's engagement in the treatment process and ultimate responsibility for its outcome. Although the therapist maintains professional responsibility for the structure and conduct of the psychotherapy itself, the therapist is not and cannot be responsible for the patient's motivation, commitment, and resultant progress or lack thereof. The patient must willingly engage in the process in order for change to occur and might have to struggle with many personal fears, defenses, and resistances before being able to do so. As Chu discussed in his 1988 article, some resistances arise from and are related to a therapeutic impasse and some cause the impasse. The therapist must monitor whether s/he seems more invested in the treatment or is taking on more responsibility than the patient.

This issue is particularly pertinent to delayed/recovered memories and their interpretation. Although the therapist may have suspicions that the patient was abused or traumatized in childhood based upon his/her diagnosis and constellation of symptoms and may further believe that the symptoms are related to the patient's clinical condition, s/he has a duty to responsibly raise these speculations with the patient. It is the patient's prerogative to explore the possible reality basis and meaning of childhood abuse. Some patients will make a deliberate choice not to explore (even when compelling reasons to do so exist and, in some cases, when corroboration is available). The therapist should not underestimate the difficulty that some individuals have in exploring–much less accepting–the possibility of past abuse, especially abuse perpetrated by a family member. This issue is often overlooked or downplayed by false memory critics who instead emphasize the ease with which abuse can be suggested by a therapist.

PROFESSIONAL PRIVILEGE AND THE LIMITS OF CONFIDENTIALITY.   From the time of intake, prospective patients must be apprised of issues of privilege and the limits of confidentiality in psychotherapy. Again, these issues have particular significance for patients who are abuse survivors or who are sorting out abuse-related memories. These individuals often have higher than average concerns about the privacy of their communication and about safety and clear boundaries within the therapeutic relationship. And, they often have higher than average situations of the sort that require breaches in confidentiality, for example, disclosure of possible current abuse of children in the patient's family, direct threats of violence to or from others, attempts or threats of suicide or other life-threatening behaviors. An additional threat to confidentiality is a rather recent development associated with the memory controversy: attempted breaches of confidentiality from those outside of the treatment process, e.g., those accused of perpetration against the patient or someone else on the basis of a patient's report; individuals from whom the patient has severed contact, often family members who may or may not contend that they have been falsely accused. It is therefore advisable that therapists impart general information to the patient regarding all of these circumstances, e.g., that confidentiality may be broken in the event of direct reports or strong suspicions of ongoing abuse of children (and adults in some jurisdictions), or in the event of imminent threat or danger to the patient or to others. Otherwise confidentiality is maintained and breaking it is at the discretion of the patient, not the therapist.

These issues are often thorny and difficult ones for therapists and require a high degree of clinical acumen and judgment. Whenever possible, therapists should consult with other professionals when these issues arise. Therapists must be aware of the statutes in his/her particular jurisdiction that require mandated or discretionary reporting, including duties to warn or to protect third parties. Therapists should consider developing ongoing consultative relationships with attorneys who have experience and expertise with these issues in their particular jurisdiction. Some professional organizations include legal consultation as part of their membership benefits and some insurance companies make it available as a part of their liability plans.

THE BUSINESS RELATIONSHIP AND ISSUES OF CONFIDENTIALITY.   Issues of confidentiality also arise in connection with the business aspects of the psychotherapy relationship, particularly regarding insurance and collection efforts. It behooves the therapist to spell out the terms of the relationship, in this instance expectations regarding fees, billing, insurance submissions, and timely payment. It is also helpful to inform the patient of the requirement of insurance and managed care companies for information about the patient's diagnosis, condition, and treatment and the limits of confidentiality/privacy once information is submitted. It is generally acknowledged that confidentiality cannot be assured once such information has been disclosed; therefore the therapist should discuss with the patient what specific information is to be submitted. The release of certain types of information is restricted in some jurisdictions; so the practitioner must be aware of pertinent state and local statutes concerning disclosure.

The terms of the business aspects of the therapy relationship should also be detailed in advance, and modified as needed throughout treatment; the course and intensity of treatment are determined, in part, with careful consideration of the patient's resources (this issue is discussed further in chapters 7 and 8). It is advisable that billing and payments occur on a regular schedule, with any difficulties discussed as they arise.

In general, it is not recommended that patients be allowed to build up large debts or be treated for free. In either instance, the power differential is further unbalanced. This may lead to resentments, countertransference errors, and treatment failures. In circumstances involving exhaustion of benefits, ongoing inability to pay, or nonpayment (for whatever reason), the therapist may choose to end treatment but must not abandon the patient and must make referrals to other practitioners or agencies. In the event that a large unpaid debt has accrued and payment is not forthcoming or a payment plan has not been agreed upon, the therapist may choose to write off the loss or send the debt to collection. Collection as an option to be used in the event of nonpayment should be communicated clearly at the outset of treatment.

ISSUES OF PERSONAL SAFETY OF BOTH PATIENT AND THERAPIST.   As discussed earlier, abuse survivors have a higher than average risk of interpersonal violence whether in the form of self-harm or at the hands of others. They may consciously or unconsciously reenact abuse dynamics and scenarios both within and outside of therapy, and move among the roles of victim, victimizer, rescuer, or bystander. Reenactment dynamics may put them in considerable danger. In turn, they may put others, including the therapist, in danger. Therapy must be predicated upon safety, with safety underscored as an expectation and a condition of treatment. The therapist must maintain a firm stance about personal security–that of the office and staff, and that of home and family. Therapists cannot work comfortably when threatened or when actively aggressed against. In general, serious threats or actions should be the cause for the immediate termination of treatment or, at the very least, must be understood and controlled before treatment continues. Moreover, in most cases, charges should be filed and restraining orders sought when personal assault, destruction of property, or other aggressive behavior or serious threat is involved.

Suicide gestures and attempts, self-mutilation, and other forms of self-harm, including high-risk activities, involvement in abusive relationships, and ongoing threats of violence are quite prevalent in this population. These issues must be taken very seriously and should not be minimized by the therapist; rather, the patient must be enjoined to work towards personal safety as an essential goal and component of the treatment. The point being made here is that the therapist must communicate the need for safety from harm and must engage the patient in actively working against all forms of violence, whether inflicted by self or others. Some abused and traumatized patients have lived their lives in conditions of fear and danger (some even seem to be "addicted to" risk and chaos) and may actually have little understanding of the concept of personal safety; nevertheless, the therapist must persist in gaining a commitment from the patient to work on these issues as a core issue and as a foundation of recovery.

Regarding delayed/recovered memories, many reenactment dynamics may come into play in a variety of different ways and may lead to additional risk or actual harm. In some cases, the potential for suicide, self-mutilation, and other forms of self-injury increases as the patient struggles with the possible reality of past abuse on the basis of recovered memory. This is yet another reason why insistence on personal safety and the development of strategies for safety are critical and are undertaken early in treatment.

INITIAL, ONGOING, AND COLLATERAL ASSESSMENT.   Potential patients are advised from the point of initial contact that treatment is predicated upon assessment and diagnosis that are undertaken over time and not arrived at in short order (i.e., no "instant assessment and diagnosis"). Critics have specifically highlighted the malpractice of therapists who have described, in the absence of any memory or disclosure on the part of the individual, being able to identify a sexual abuse survivor on sight by his/her demeanor and posture, or over the phone without having met the individual face to face, or through the use of symptom checklists or one major presenting symptom (e.g., eating disorder). The responsible therapist makes assessments over time and after weighing a variety of information, including prior diagnoses and treatment. However, prior diagnoses are not automatically accepted without further inquiry and assessment. This is especially important in situations where individuals have carried diagnoses of schizophrenia, schizoaffective disorder, bipolar depression, and dissociative identity disorder–diagnoses identified as having high potential for misdiagnosis among this population (Ross, 1997).

Additionally, the therapist should inquire about who made the diagnosis. In some cases, individuals have self-diagnosed after having seen a television show or read a book or after having received "treatment" and a diagnosis from a lay practitioner. One of the most egregious examples of the latter circumstance is a patient admitted to my hospital program who carried a dissociative identity disorder diagnosis. She showed no dissociative symptoms while on our unit, leading staff to inquire as to the origins of the diagnosis. It turned out that it had been suggested by the patient's massage therapist(!) and reinforced by members of a survivors' support group that she joined subsequent to receiving the "diagnosis" (ergo, if she had a DID diagnosis, it meant that she must have been abused even if she did not remember, so she joined a survivors' group to help her remember).

Patients should also understand that a general treatment plan is established after a period of pretreatment assessment (this issue, procedures,
and instruments are described in chapter 7) and that assessment may be
ongoing throughout the course of treatment as more material or symptoms become accessible. It is not uncommon, for example, for dissociative symptoms to remain hidden and emerge when the therapeutic
alliance has been established and some trust has started to build. At that
point, the therapist would undertake a detailed assessment of these
symptoms.

The possible need for collateral assessments should also be explored
beforehand. Neuropsychological, neurological, medical and psychiatric
testing may be required for a wide variety of symptoms in an effort to differentiate organic from psychological conditions and to further suggest
appropriate directions for treatment. Similarly, testing for other conditions, such as learning deficits and disabilities, substance abuse, obsessive-compulsive disorder, and eating disorders, might prove helpful in distinguishing causation and in establishing a treatment course. As described
in chapter 2, survivors of abuse have been found to be at risk for a host of
initial and long-term injuries and medical conditions and may have suffered actual physical damage (e.g., head injury from physical abuse either
in childhood or adulthood, gynecological damage from sexual abuse). The
possibility of such damage should not be overlooked, especially since
some, such as head injury and resultant neurological impairment, might
be related to the individual's cognitive capacity and memory.

ADJUNCTIVE OR COLLATERAL TREATMENT INCLUDING HOSPITALIZATION
AND MEDICATION.   It is also useful at the initiation of psychotherapy for
the practitioner to describe his/her approach to adjunctive treatment and,
related to this, the possible use of hospitalization and medication.
Adjunctive treatment might be necessitated as follow-up to the types of
assessments described in the previous section or might be suggested as
part of the overall treatment plan (e.g., referral to a group, for a psychopharmacological or neurological evaluation, to couples therapy, to a
medical specialist or acupuncturist). Collateral treatment might also be
undertaken independently by the patient, in some cases without the
knowledge and agreement of the primary therapist. It is important to
convey that all adjunctive treatment initiatives should be coordinated
within the main treatment. Although this stance may seem to contradict
the principles of empowerment and autonomy discussed earlier in this
chapter, this is not the case. Instead, it underscores the principles of coordinated and collaborative treatment under the professional direction and
responsibility of the primary therapist.

Any treatment that is undertaken independently, especially without the therapist's knowledge, may lead to splits in the treatment and conditions of additional liability. Splits between treaters may play out the dynamics of secrecy and the allying of one family member against another that are often legacies of family abuse. In such a circumstance, whether consciously or not, the patient may pit one practitioner or treatment against the other in an effort to gain control, to self-sabotage, or to avoid facing difficult issues such as communication, trust, and anger. Additional liability may be created if adjunctive treatments contradict the main treatment approach and/or cause the patient to become more symptomatic, to regress, or to decompensate. Adjunctive treatments are especially problematic if they involve suggestive strategies undertaken with the specific intention of retrieving or enhancing memories of abuse. I contend that the therapist must insist that any and all adjunctive treatments (whether professional, lay medical, or nonmedical) be brought to the main treatment for discussion and decision-making within the established treatment plan. When the decision is made to include an adjunctive treatment, it is a good policy for the therapist to make contact with the outside practitioner and to carefully coordinate the treatments. Such coordination and the back-and-forth flow of communication allow for informed as well as coordinated treatment.

The therapist should also communicate his/her standard approach to hospitalization and the use of psychotropic medications. In general this includes the position that hospitalization is reserved as an option in the event of serious suicidal and parasuicidal threats and gestures, acute threats of violence to others, and unmanageable symptoms and associated inability to function. Many patients (primarily those who were abused in childhood and/or were previously hospitalized, especially if involuntarily) fear hospitalization and often associate it with any previous abuse involving confinement or threat (e.g., threats of being locked up with the key thrown away). These are frequently reality-based fears that the therapist must handle in an empathic and forthright way. Nonetheless, the option of hospitalization must be retained to insure that safety and protection are not compromised. I tell my patients that hospitalization is an infrequent intervention in my outpatient practice due to the initial treatment emphasis placed on stabilization, skill-building, and functioning. This usually has the benefit of offsetting the need for hospitalization; yet, on occasion, it is necessary and/or recommended for safety and intensive intervention and therefore must be retained as an option. Also, except in extreme circumstances, admission is on a voluntary basis, with the patient involved in discussing the need and suitability of hospitalization as well as other possible strategies for safety and containment (i.e., more intensive outpatient treatment, more frequent sessions and phone calls during a time of crisis, partial or day hospital programs and offerings, etc.). Wherever possible and suitable, hospitalization on a unit with expertise in treating patients with posttraumatic issues is advisable unless the patient has no abuse memories, in which case a general unit is the more appropriate and less suggestive choice.

The therapist also provides a general orientation to psychopharmaco-logical evaluations and consultations related to the possible need for psy-chotropic medications. Abuse survivors in clinical samples have been found to have primary diagnoses and comorbid conditions and symptoms such as PTSD, depression, and anxiety that benefit from rational and tar-geted psychopharmacological interventions. Although the option of tak-ing medication might be quite threatening (particularly for the patient whose abuse involved the administration or ingestion of drugs, who has had previous negative experiences with overmedication and/or negative side effects, or who is in recovery from substance abuse), its usefulness should be carefully explained. It is ultimately the patient's choice as to whether to try a medication or not but it is the therapist's responsibility to keep it open as a possibility, especially for serious symptoms and diag-noses that are responsive to medication or where the potential exists for the worsening of symptoms without such treatment.

THE PATIENT IN RELATIONSHIP.   Finally, the patient is understood with-in and not apart from a familial, relational, and cultural context. The client's interpersonal world must be taken into consideration by the ther-apist. The impact of the treatment may be felt not only by the primary patient but by the family members and significant others; the treatment, in turn, may also be affected by their influence. Although, at present, no formal duty is owed to third parties (i.e., family member, spouses/part-ners, children, or others), this situation has been challenged in the recov-ered memory debate. As noted by Appelbaum & Zoltek-Jick (1996), "It is no accident that a spate of successful efforts to extend duties to third parties has come along now, as concern is growing about the treatment of patients with memories of childhood sexual abuse" (p. 463). Up until recently, only patients had the right to sue caregivers for negligence, but in the bellwether 1995 case, *Ramona v. Ramona*, a California court allowed a father accused of abusing his daughter to sue his daughter's therapists for malpractice as a "direct victim" of their negligent and sug-gestive practice (Appelbaum & Zoltek-Jick, 1996; Ewing, 1994). At pre-sent, it does not appear that this case establishes a broad precedent; how-ever, legislation introduced in several states by a coalition of state false memory syndrome associations under the title "The Mental Health

Consumers Protection Act" would create a duty to third parties and permit lawsuits by those who perceive themselves to be injured by psychotherapy (whether filed individually or in conjunction with the patient). Professional groups and therapists have opposed bills of this sort due, among other concerns, to their inhibitory effect on the confidentiality of communication in psychotherapy (Hinnefeld & Newman, 1997; Knapp & VandeCreek, 1997).

Expanded discussion of this issue is beyond the scope of this chapter. At the very least, therapists must remain cognizant of the potency and complexity of family/intimate relationships and the variable loyalty and attachment dynamics that are possible. They must also be aware of the possible effects of various courses of action on significant others (e.g., disclosures, confrontations, reports to the police or child protection agencies, lawsuits, public acknowledgments, emotional and physical cut-offs from family). As a consequence, therapists do not independently pursue any of these courses of action or advise the patient to do so (except in circumstances such as ongoing battering or sexual violence, where protective strategies are primary and are ethically and professionally required, or in a case of ongoing child abuse, where reporting is mandated). Instead, they might work with a patient to assess the advantages and disadvantages of alternative courses of action, with the patient in control of his/her own decision-making. Even in cases of mandated reporting, it is usually advisable to inform the patient before the action is taken and, in some cases, to encourage the patient to make the report in the therapist's presence.

The therapist has another reason to be concerned about these various courses of actions, namely, liability. It is prudent for the therapist to make explicit to the patient that disclosures, confrontations, lawsuits, and family cut-offs should not be undertaken impulsively and/or in unplanned fashion without the therapist's knowledge (and, in some cases, the therapist's approval). Any such course of action should be a deliberate choice made after careful consideration and a weighing of pros and cons. For example, in the statement I have developed for my practice, I require *as a condition of treatment* that patients not make an impulsive and/or unplanned disclosure of abuse (whether known or suspected), especially to the alleged perpetrator or other family members. Any decisions to confront or disclose must be carefully discussed, decided upon, and planned, since it carries considerable risk potential to both the practitioner and the patient. If a patient does not abide by this agreement, I reserve the right to discontinue treatment and make a referral.

I also routinely ask potential patients whether they have been, or are currently involved in or considering involvement in any legal action—for any cause but especially pertaining to abuse. The decision to treat is sometimes predicated upon whether a lawsuit is in the works—some therapists chose not to provide treatment if there is any possibility of their becoming involved in a forensic proceeding. Furthermore, choice of therapeutic strategies is affected. With a patient who has any forensic involvement, therapists are advised to not utilize hypnosis or any related intervention, because courts have maintained a skeptical view of the reliability of hypnosis and have rejected hypnotically refreshed memory (Giannelli, 1995; Scheflin & Shapiro, 1989).

THERAPIST ATTENTION TO TRANSFERENCE, COUNTERTRANSFERENCE, AND VICARIOUS TRAUMATIZATION.   The therapist must be aware of transference patterns that commonly occur in working with abuse and those that have been identified when memory-related issues are in play. The transference projections of interpersonally victimized patients can be very challenging and difficult to manage and are often similar (if not identical) to those identified with personality disturbances, notably borderline personality. Transference reactions related to memory issues can be intertwined with these more generic issues and can result in a situation that is cumulatively daunting to the therapist. Common countertransference patterns have also been identified that often occur in complementary fashion with similar degrees of intensity. The therapist's ability to identify and control his/her countertransference reactions is critical to the success or failure of the treatment process. Failure to adequately attend to these issues can result in therapeutic blunders, misalliances, and misadventures. Additionally, as discussed in the first section of this book, it is likely that countertransference errors made by therapists engaged in work with abuse issues in the last decade have contributed to the memory critiques. Thus, it is crucial for the practitioner to be knowledgeable about "treatment traps" involving transference and countertransference in order to anticipate their occurrence and to manage them therapeutically. When well-handled, they have great potential for the resolution of many of the interpersonal reenactments that so often occur as consequences of abuse. As these resolve, the individual is able to separate and individuate from some of the most pervasive and damaging aspects of the abuse experience. And with patients who have either not been abused or who remain uncertain as to their experience, the therapist is less likely to be negatively impacted or enmeshed in the patient's uncertainty.

An ancillary issue that has been identified in work with this population is the personal impact of the material and the process on the therapist. This process has been labeled in a number of descriptive ways, as "vicarious traumatization" (McCann & Pearlman, 1990a; Pearlman &

Saakvitne, 1995), "secondary traumatic stress" (Stamm, 1996), or "compassion fatigue" (Figley, 1995). Whatever the term used, this process refers to the personal reactions of the therapist and the ways s/he might be affected by hearing about abuse and other forms of trauma and by working with what are often high-intensity symptoms and emotional reactions. These therapist reactions can also be prompted by uncertainty regarding memory issues, which bring with them additional risks and challenges. Therapists must therefore observe their reactions above and beyond countertransference and monitor whether and how they are being affected personally. They must establish mechanisms to maintain their own physical and mental health and ways to get relief from the intensity of the work. As mentioned earlier in this chapter, one such mechanism is to have professional outlets, such as supervision and consultation, to provide information, perspective, and support. Another is to have personal outlets for sustenance and recreation away from the work setting. These issues are discussed more thoroughly later in this text.

SUMMARY

This chapter summarizes the philosophy and principles of practice for the treatment of adults abused as children where memories are in question. At present, the treatment model is developing but is firmly anchored in established professional standards of practice and codes of ethics. The current model derives primarily from clinical practice and observation and from reviews of available literature on abuse, trauma, and memory in the absence of a sizable body of evaluation data. Research on the effectiveness and efficiency of this treatment will contribute to the continued development and maturation of the model. The philosophy and principles reviewed in this chapter thus constitute a preliminary and evolving standard of care and standard of treatment for this population.

Chapter 6

THE EVOLVING CONSENSUS MODEL OF POSTTRAUMA TREATMENT

Sequenced, Titrated, Focused on Symptom Relief and Functioning

This chapter introduces and outlines the evolving consensus model of posttrauma treatment (PTT). A trauma-responsive model is used when the individual has posttraumatic and/or dissociative symptoms that appear to be related to a history of reported and known abuse or trauma. It might also be considered for the individual who exhibits these symptoms and has valid reason to suspect past abuse/trauma even in the absence of clear memory. However, it is *not* the orientation of choice and should not be used when an individual lacks memory for abuse/trauma and does not have posttraumatic symptoms. It the latter case, it could be deemed suggestive. See chapter 9 for a decision model of therapeutic strategy according to the availability of memory and posttraumatic symptomatology.

The model of treatment presented in this chapter is a consensus version of the various models developed by experts on the treatment of a variety of posttraumatic conditions. It has an articulated sequence that addresses the individual's ability to function along with symptom stabilization, management, and resolution. Different tasks and therapeutic strategies are associated with the different phases of treatment. Any work with memories of trauma and the resolution of traumatic material takes place mid-treatment, as needed, after the patient has first been stabilized and taught coping and self-management skills. The post-resolution phase involves a re-working of life issues to accommodate changes that have been wrought both by the trauma and its outcome. This model is quite different from and must be differentiated from the model of "memory recovery therapy" that has been most criticized by false memory advocates.

POSTTRAUMA THERAPY

Over the course of the past two decades, experience in the treatment of the mental health consequences of many types of traumatization has led to the development of contemporary professional approaches to post-trauma therapy (Figley, 1985, 1986; Foy, 1992; Herman, 1992b; Ochberg, 1988, 1993; Parson, 1984; van der Kolk, 1987; Williams & Sommer, 1994; Wilson, 1989). The treatment model was initially developed for use with combat trauma in returning Vietnam veterans. It incorporated approaches used earlier in the century during the two world wars, namely, a rapid stabilization model based upon reexperiencing and abreaction of the trauma, allowing a quick return to the battlefield. Elements of this approach were later applied to the treatment of more chronic forms of posttraumatic reactions and to those patients identified here as suffering from complex posttraumatic reactions resulting from child abuse. In many cases, such a strong focus on the trauma, to the exclusion of the assessment and acknowledgment of other symptoms and diagnoses, was premature. Instead of rapidly stabilizing patients, it overwhelmed and retraumatized them, and many regressed and even decompensated (Chu, 1998). The differences between types of traumatization and patient groups was soon noted. A modified treatment approach was developed for use with "simple" PTSD (whether acute and/or chronic) and particularly for use with complex forms of PTSD (i.e., those with associated chronic Axis I and Axis II diagnostic comorbidity).

The reconfigured model is now clearly sequenced, task- and skill-focused, and multimodal. It has been labeled as phase-oriented treatment by Brown et al. (1998) to emphasize its sequence of addressing therapeutic tasks. It places initial emphasis on personal safety and stabilization, the strengthening of self and ego capacities, and the development of self-management and interpersonal skills, along with pharmacotherapy of the most onerous of the biological/psychiatric symptoms associated with PTSD and comorbid conditions. The patient is initially taught skills to manage and cope with any spontaneous reexperiencing and abreacting of traumatic material. Work with the trauma and traumatic memories is undertaken only as needed and solely with adequate preparation and planning, usually in the middle phase of treatment.

The model also acknowledges the wide variance between posttraumatic reactions and each individual's unique response and capabilities;

thus, "treatment trajectories" (Kluft, 1994) and treatment duration and intensity can vary markedly. On average, uncomplicated forms of PTSD require a shorter-term treatment and are amenable to specialized techniques (as described later in this chapter); in contrast, complex, comorbid forms are lengthier, require more intensive multimodal treatment, and may require treatment on an ongoing basis with periodic intensification due to cyclical decompensation (Wang, Wilson, & Mason, 1996). Evidence has also accrued to suggest that, in some cases, posttraumatic symptoms recur even after intensive treatment and that transtheoretical, multimodal treatments and those that are orientated towards stabilization and skill-building may yield more effective (although not curative) results (Shalev et al., 1996).

At the present time, this modified treatment model has achieved fairly widespread consensus among therapists and clinical researchers who specialize in the treatment of posttraumatic conditions in different trauma populations (Briere, 1996a, 1996b, 1997a; Brown et al., 1998; Chu, 1998; Courtois, 1992, 1997a, 1997c, 1997d; Herman, 1992b; Parson, 1984; Roth & Batson, 1997; van der Kolk et al, 1996); yet it is expected to mature as the results of clinical investigations become available. Although additional research is required and few controlled treatment trials have been reported, early investigations of the efficacy of the posttraumatic approach have shown it to hold promise, per the findings of the reviews reported by Shalev et al. (1996), Sherman (1998), and Solomon et al. (1992).

Characteristics of Posttrauma Therapy

What makes posttrauma therapy different from less specialized therapy? One of the most notable differences is the reversal of the traditional perspective taken on the traumatic event(s) and its aftermath. Rather than disregarding or minimizing trauma and its significance, traumatic stress theory puts it front and center as having high potential as a pathologic agent. An individual's symptoms are not in and of themselves pathological; rather, they develop as natural and healthy responses to out-of-the ordinary, catastrophic and overwhelming events. Bloom (1994) articulated this shift as moving from a position of "What's wrong with you?" to "What happened to you and what did you have to do to cope?" It doesn't matter whether the coping was short term or long term. It is further assumed that repetitive trauma, especially if it occured during the course of childhood, can have a significant impact on the individual's psychosexual maturation.

It should be stated explicitly that the posttraumatic perspective is not the "abuse excuse," not intended to make a victim out of everyone, and not an attempt to "infantilize" individuals or make them less responsible for their behavior (Kaminer, 1993). Instead, it is an alteration in perspective that encompasses events that have often been ignored or minimized to the detriment of the affected individual and a corresponding reframing of overwhelming and damaging experiences that is empathic to the individual who experienced them. In psychotherapy, this shift in viewpoint can often be seen in an attitudinal change toward the patient. The therapist understands symptoms, defenses/resistances, object relations, and transference reactions from a different perspective and, as a consequence, works with them differently.

Ochberg, in his seminal book on trauma-focused treatment, put it this way:

> The advantages in what I will now call post-traumatic therapy (PTT) are its assumption of psychological health, its fundamental assumption that the victim is not to blame *[for the victimization, even when it is repetitive and chronic]*, and its ability to facilitate a working relationship between victim and therapist through partnership and parity in respect and power. (phrase in italics added) (1988, p. 10)

In later writing, Ochberg (1993) identified three principles of this treatment approach:

1. The normalization principle: "There is a general pattern of post-traumatic adjustment and the thoughts and feelings that comprise this pattern are normal, although they may be painful and perplexing, and perhaps not well understood by individuals and professionals not familiar with such expectable reactions" (p. 773).

2. The collaborative and empowering principle: "The therapeutic relationship must be collaborative, leading to empowerment of one who has been diminished in dignity and security. This principle is particularly important in work with victims of violent crime. The exposure to human cruelty, the feeling of dehumanization, and the experience of powerlessness create a diminished sense of self" (p. 774).

3. The individuality principle: "Every individual has a unique pathway to recovery after traumatic stress. . . . This principle suggests that a unique pathway of post-traumatic adjustment is to be

anticipated and valued, and not to be feared or disparaged." (p. 774).

Ochberg also identified the main techniques of posttraumatic therapy: education and teaching about the human stress response and trauma; holistic health techniques for physical as well as emotional healing (since victims often neglect their physical and emotional well-being as part of a pattern of posttraumatic decline); techniques for enhanced and restitutive social support and social integration; and clinical techniques to work through some of the major aftereffects associated with victimization such as grief, fear, betrayal, autonomic arousal, and negative intimacy.

Other technical dimensions of this treatment have been articulated. Briere (1996a, 1996b) and others have discussed the necessity to titrate the pace and intensity of the psychotherapy and to specify the focus of various interventions. Since avoidance, motivated forgetting, dissociation and other defenses are so commonly used by abuse/trauma survivors to keep painful material at bay, the psychotherapeutic process must proceed slowly and carefully to avoid overwhelming the client's personal capacities and to keep from stimulating further avoidance responses or even decompensation (Briere 1996a, 1996b; Cornell & Olio, 1991). The treatment must be anchored in techniques that are initially supportive and that strengthen the patient and consolidate his/her skills and capabilities. Once a base of support, personal security, and stabilization has occurred and the patient has developed the ability to identify, tolerate, and modulate emotions, he or she can then be gradually and more safely exposed to material that was previously overwhelming. The trauma survivor must not be overly challenged to the point of shutdown, but must not be underchallenged, since the latter will result in stagnation, little or no therapeutic gain, and the continuation of distress. Exposure is titrated according to the individual's capacity and tolerance, and treatment goals must be organized in a sequential, hierarchical, and progressive fashion.

The clinical techniques that are most in use at present in posttraumatic therapy broadly fall into the categories of psychodynamic approaches, behavior treatments, cognitive-behavioral treatments, and psychopharmacologic approaches in both inpatient and outpatient settings (Marmar, Foy, Kagan, & Pynoos, 1994). These authors recently reviewed and commented on the relative contribution of each of these approaches to the treatment of PTSD:

> *Psychodynamic approaches* stress associative meanings for the trauma registered from a wider network, including unconscious as well as conscious representations, unconsciously motivated defenses against remembering,

the contribution of early psychological development to trauma-based self- and other representations, and the management of transference, countertransference, and resistance in the treatment setting.

Behavior treatments focus in-depth on overt behavioral avoidance and reenactment, stimulus and response components that have become part of the fear memory or signal for danger, and a detailed understanding of biological and psychological conditioning occurring during trauma exposure. *Cognitive-behavior treatments* emphasize revision of pathogenic beliefs in the course of direct therapeutic exposure. *Pharmacotherapy* targets underline psychobiological mechanisms regarding chronic hyperarousal, cue-specific hyperreactivity, insomnia, and comorbid anxiety and depressive disorders. (Italics added) (pp.127–128)

Additionally, these same authors listed the common goals and change mechanisms involved in posttrauma therapy. This list gives a fair reading of what is different and unique about it. The goals and change mechanisms of PTT are:

- To increase the capacity to respond to threat with realistic appraisal rather than exaggerated or minimized responses
- To maintain normal levels of arousal rather than hypervigilance or psychic numbing
- To facilitate return to normal development, adaptive coping, and improved functioning in work and interpersonal relations
- To restore personal integrity and normalize traumatic stress response, in part by validating the universality of stress symptomatology and by establishing a frame of meaning
- To conduct treatment in an atmosphere of safety and security to ensure that the threat of retraumatization is modulated
- To regulate level of intensity of traumatic aspects to facilitate cognitive reappraisal
- *To increase capacity to differentiate remembering from reliving of the trauma, for both external reminders and internal cues*
- *Neither to eradicate the memories of the trauma nor to avoid and overreact rigidly to reminders, but rather to place trauma in perspective and regain control over life experiences*
- To attend to early risk factors that shape trauma response
- To intervene actively to address secondary adversities and prevent future complications, including the risk for spreading comorbidities
- To regard self-concept as impacted by changes in dynamic, cognitive, behavioral, and neurobiological systems

- To facilitate a transformation from a victim identity to a sense of constructive engagement in daily life and future goals
- To enhance a sense of personal courage in approaching the memories and reminders of the trauma (Italics added) (p. 127).

Finally, these authors summarized in tabular form the comparative features of dynamic, cognitive-behavioral, and pharmacological approaches according to the specific forms of traumatic stress categories and diagnoses (see Table 6.1). As can be seen from this table and as it pertains to the patients under discussion in this text, the necessary treatment approach is transtheoretical and multimodal and of longer rather than shorter duration due to complexity of the symptom picture and associated comorbidity.

Models of Posttrauma Therapy

A number of sequenced posttrauma treatment models have been proposed and developed, forming the foundation of the treatment discussed in the remainder of this chapter. See the following sources for more information about these different models and their application to different trauma populations: Briere (1996a, 1996b, 1997a), adult survivors of child abuse; Brown and Fromm (1986), general trauma; Chu (1998), adult survivors of childhood abuse; Courtois (1988, 1991, 1993, 1997c), adult survivors of incest/child sexual abuse; Harvey (1996), an ecological model of trauma and recovery; Herman (1992b), complex PTSD secondary to child abuse and other forms of chronic traumatization; Horowitz (1986), general trauma; Kepner (1995), adult survivors of childhood abuse; Kluft (1990) and Kluft and Fine (1993), dissociative identity disorder; Kroll (1993), PTSD/borderline personality; Lebowitz, et al., (1993), sexual trauma; Linehan (1993), borderline personality disorder; Loo (1993), war internment; McCann and Pearlman (1990a), adult survivors of childhood trauma and general trauma; Marshall (1995) and Parson (1984), war veterans; Meichenbaum (1994), general trauma; Putnam (1989a, 1997), multiple personality disorder/dissociative identity disorder in adults and children; Ross (1995), satanic ritual abuse; Ross (1989, 1997), multiple personality disorder/dissociative identity disorder; Roth and Batson (1997), incest survivors; Sgroi (1988, 1989); child victims and adult survivors of sexual abuse; Wang et al. (1996), complex PTSD with cyclical decompensation secondary to war trauma. For a much more detailed description of the historical origins and development of the phase-oriented treatment model than is provided below, the interested reader is referred to chapter 13 in Brown et al. (1998).

Table 6.1

Comparative Treatment Approaches for Posttraumatic Stress Disorder (PTSD)

Traumatic Stress Category	Dynamic	Cognitive-Behavioral	Pharmacologic
Normal stress response	Debriefing	Debriefing	None
Acute catastrophic stress reaction	Debriefing, abreaction, support, self-cohesion, adjunctive pharmacotherapy	Debriefing, restructuring of erroneous ideas, prevention of avoidant behavior	BZDs for sleep and anxiety, adrenergic blockers for intrusion and arousal
PTSD without comorbidity	Time-limited dynamic psychotherapy, establish therapeutic alliance, focus on self-concepts, working through conflicts, linkage to prior trauma, attention to transference and countertransference	Desensitization to trauma, restructuring of erroneous beliefs, gradual activation of avoidant behaviors	None or BZDs, adrenergic blockers for intrusion/arousal, TCAs/MAOIs for intrusion/arousal serotonin re-uptake inhibitors
PTSD with Axis I comorbidity	time-limited dynamic therapy, treat alcohol and substance abuse first, treat other comorbidities concurrently	treat comorbidity first, then cognitive-behavior treatments	treat comorbidity as usual, then medication for PTSD if needed
Chronic PTSD with secondary Axis II comorbidity	multimodal; longterm dynamic group and pharmacologic; inpatient at times for uncovering or crises, individual, marital, family treatment; vocational rehabilitation and social skills training	Cognitive behavior treatments, chronic intermittent skills training, relapse prevention	TCAs/MAOIs, serotonin re-uptake inhibitors, BZDs with caution, neuroleptics for hallucinations, lithium/carbamazepine for irritability/aggressivity

BZDs = benzodiazepines. TCAs = tricyclic antidepressants. MAOIs = monoamine oxidase inhibitors. From "An Integrated Approach for Treating Posttraumatic Stress," by C.R. Marmar, D. Foy, B. Kagan, and R. S. Pynoos, 1994. In R. Pynoos, Editor, *Posttraumatic Stress Disorder: A Clinical Review* (p. 129), 1994, Lutherville, MD: The Sidran Press. Copyright 1994 by The Sidran Press. Reprinted with permission.

THE SEQUENCED POSTTRAUMA TREATMENT MODEL

The sequenced or phase-oriented model of trauma treatment traces its origins to the work of Pierre Janet (1889, 1977) in which he described the process as consisting of three phases: (1) stabilization, containment, and symptom reduction; (2) modification and integration of traumatic memories; and (3) personality reintegration and life enhancement. As discussed above and as exemplified by these treatment approaches for various traumatized populations, the critical importance of sequencing and the utility of conducting work in phases has been recognized and widely implemented. As clinical experience has accumulated, it has become ever more evident that survivors of trauma require "an initial (sometimes lengthy) period of developing fundamental skills concerning maintaining supportive relationships, developing self-care strategies, coping with symptomatology, improving functioning, and establishing some basic positive self-identity" and that "building a solid foundation of ego functioning is essential prior to embarking on any extensive exploration of . . . trauma or abreactive work" (Chu, 1998, p. 77). In this sequencing, the restoration of self and functioning, the restoration of trustworthy relationships with others, and the development of social supports are important preliminary foci that take precedence over the processing of traumatic material, although they are often interlinked, as described in the next section. The patient is cautioned against premature unplanned work with traumatic material without adequate emotional and coping resources in place (including social support) and without sufficient preparation. This orientation and structure work against an ambiguous and unfocused treatment format that runs the risk of creating conditions of regression and overdependence on therapy, on the one hand, or flooding/retraumatization and decompensation, on the other. It also works against those conditions that are suggestive or conducive to memory elaboration (Courtois, 1997b, 1997d).

The rationale for this structured approach is also to avoid chaos in the treatment as much as possible, to make sense of the process, and to have a clearly demarcated and somewhat hierarchical and progressive course to follow (Herman, 1992b; Kepner, 1995). The sheer number of different issues that may need to be addressed and their relative complexity mandate an articulated, structured therapeutic strategy. As discussed in Chapter 5, this therapy is not laissez-faire, nor is it focused solely on traumatic memories to the exclusion of other issues and tasks. In contrast, it is quite complex and more broadly focused than false memory critics imply and requires a sophisticated articulation of treatment goals that are progressively addressed.

Although sequenced treatment is presented as a model with identified and demarcated stages, it is not linear, nor is it static. Instead, it is helpful to conceptualize it as dynamic, fluid, and building upon itself in a back-and-forth recursive fashion. It is a focused process of healing tasks and issues that are reworked and that deepen as the therapy progresses (Bass & Davis, 1988; 1994; Kepner, 1995; Wang et al., 1996). Kepner is most eloquent in describing the sequenced treatment model as a growth cycle:

In healing as *growth*, as opposed to a linear progression toward cure, we address and readdress certain issues in ever more accomplished and more differentiated ways, in much the same way as we learn any complex task—speaking, reading, or writing, for example. We do not achieve one stage and move on to the next, leaving the previous stage behind. Rather, the healing process is more like the creation of an oil painting: the background is painted in, and then details are added, and then washes and tone are overlaid on the whole. But the painting is not yet done, for the background still has to be refined in light of the emerging details, and then more details will be added and shifted, and as these elements take on new weight and interactions, the tone and the cast of the canvas will be shifted and refined by the artist. Each part of the painting supports and refines the previous part and is supported and refined in turn.

To put this idea another way, growth proceeds in a spiral fashion. We visit and revisit complex issues and tasks with increasing mastery, breadth, and capacity. We approach previously intolerable risks at each new level of the spiral. At each round, at each pass, a new reorganization of the whole field, the whole *gestalt*, occurs as new capacities are integrated and assimilated, old traumas are undone, and a new self emerges in engagement with the world. (pp. 2–3)

Titration and Modulation

The sequenced model also calls for a strategy of modulation in addressing the symptoms and issues of each stage and pacing of the work to the individual's needs and capacities. The patient is carefully monitored as to his/her reactions to the work at hand and the intensity and pace are adjusted accordingly. Several writers (Briere, 1996a, 1996b; Cornell & Olio, 1993; Courtois, 1988; Horowitz, 1986) have identified the need for such titration/pacing in work with traumatized patients in order to not overwhelm or flood them, on the one hand, nor to underwhelm them or understimulate change on the other. Kluft (1994) has addressed another issue concerning treatment pacing and progress. He identified twelve dimensions that he was able to link to the pace and progress of treatment (or what he labeled treatment trajectories) in a sample of dissociative identity disorder patients in his practice. Through the rating of these different dimensions, he was able to define and classify patients into different treatment trajectory subgroups. He found that reasonable expectations for the scope, progress, and pace of treatment varied widely according to the trajectory subgroup in which a given patient was classified. In other words, not all patients are capable of the same degree of therapeutic focus, pace, or accomplishment. While Kluft's work is preliminary, it may offer a way to determine early on a particular patient's response to therapy and a corresponding adjustment in therapeutic strategy, scope, and intensity. It also reminds us of the heterogeneity of PTSD/DD patients and the necessity of assessing individual differences at the outset and throughout the course of treatment. The twelve dimensions used by Kluft to assess his patients' capacity for therapeutic progress and process are:

1. Therapeutic alliance
2. Integration
3. Capacity for adaptive change
4. Management of life stressors
5. Alters' responsibility for self-management (in the case of a non-DID patient, this would refer to the individual's responsibility for self-management)
6. Restraint from self-endangerment
7. Quality of interpersonal relationships
8. Need for medication
9. Need for hospital care
10. Resolution of transference phenomena
11. Intersession contacts
12. Subjective well-being

For the reader interested in learning more about this approach, Kluft's article contains additional information on defining and rating these dimensions.

Hierarchy of Issues, Goals, and Interventions

The posttrauma therapy model also acknowledges that the resolution of one issue is often necessary before another can be addressed (Jehu, 1988) and that relapse is to be anticipated and planned for (Kepner, 1995; Wang et al., 1996). It is not unusual for these patients slip back to tried and true (and often maladaptive) coping skills when stressed and exposed (or reexposed) to material that is overwhelming and emotionally intolerable. This response must be expected by the therapist and should not be viewed as a treatment failure as much as a setback leading to an opportunity for relearning. In fact, it is now recommended that both the disorder and the treatment model be conceptualized and organized dynamically so as to anticipate what Wang et al. (1996) have identified as cycles of decompensation and recompensation in complex PTSD patients. In this cyclical model, following careful and ongoing assessment and observation, therapists are encouraged to anticipate with their patients the precipitants to decompensation. They are then urged to intervene actively and intensively as soon as possible in order to interrupt and reverse the decline before it accelerates into greater degrees of danger and risk. Wang et al. also comment on the need for different intervention and stabilization strategies chosen according to the patient's degree of decompensation and emotional dysregulation, on one hand, and resilience and capacity for insight, on the other. These authors included the illustration found in Figure 6.1 to illustrate their model.

Figure 6.1

Progressive Stages of Decompensation and Recompensation in Severe Combat-Related PTSD

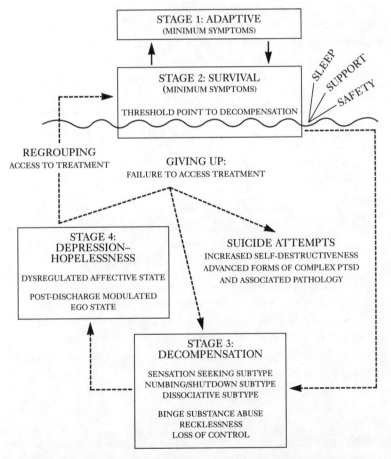

From "Stages of Decompensation in Combat-Related Posttraumatic Stress Disorder: A New Conceptual Model," by S. Wang and J.W. Mason, 1996 July-September, *Integrative Physiological and Behavioral Science, 31* (3), p. 245. Copyright 1996 by Transaction Publishers. Reprinted with permission.

The posttrauma treatment model is usually conceptualized as consisting of three or four main phases, each with different subphases, tasks, and emphases, in addition to a comprehensive pretreatment assessment (the latter described in the next chapter). Here the model is discussed in three main phases: (1) the initial or early phase of stabilization, safety, alliance-building, support, and self functions; (2) the middle phase of deconditioning, mourning, and resolution of past trauma and associated losses (past and present); and (3) the late phase of reconsolidation consisting of self and relational development and life enhancement. Brown et al. (1998) helpfully described the phases of the sequenced model as follows:

> Each phase is defined by a unique set of treatment problems and symptoms that become the focus of treatment at that stage only. Each phase of treatment is characterized by a specific set of treatment procedures. Each phase of treatment requires a certain type of treatment alliance. Transference manifestations also differ at each stage. Each stage is characterized by its own unique benchmarks of progress and also by certain treatment challenges and special problems typical to that stage. (p. 437)

These authors also comprehensively reviewed the trauma treatment literature to arrive at a detailed synthesis of the phase-oriented posttrauma treatment model. The reader in search of more in-depth information than presented here should refer to their book, *Memory, Trauma, Treatment, and the Law.*

Early Phase: Pre-Treatment Issues, Treatment Frame, Stabilization, Safety, Alliance-Building, Self-Care, Self Functions, and Support

Since many patients enter treatment in a state of crisis or extreme distress and/or without the knowledge or personal capacity to engage in a collaborative relational endeavor, it is vitally important for the therapist to spend the time and effort to create an adequate foundation for the work to come. It appears that many of the treatments with traumatized patients that later foundered did so because they inadequately addressed this important phase. Sufficient preparation has been found to be so crucial to the successful treatment of patients with borderline personality self and relational difficulties that Linehan (1993) incorporated a pretreatment phase in her model with the aim of (1) stopping suicidal and other self-injurious behavior; (2) changing therapy-intefering behaviors (constant chaos and crises, tardiness, cancellation or "no-show's" for therapy sessions, non-payment, excessive requests for extra-session involvement on the part of the patient); and (3) addressing lifestyle issues that impact treatment such as financial mismanagement, general lifestyle chaos, significant addictions or chemical dependency issues, an inadequate or destabilizing social system, etc. In this model, a written behavioral contract is drawn up and the patient is expected to successfully address these issues and modify problem behavior as a condition of continuing treatment. If the patient is unable or unwilling to do so within a reasonable time period, the treatment is discontinued. Otherwise, a treatment contract is then negotiated that is in accord with the model presented here.

The critical and foundational importance of early phase work to the establishment of parameters for the treatment (whether it has a pre-treatment component à la Linehan model or not) is emphasized in all trauma-focused models. As Kluft (1993) has commented:

> I try to emphasize the importance of the initial stages of therapy by citing what I call Belafonte's Law: "House built on a weak foundation, it will fall. Oh, yes! Oh, yes! Oh, yes!" The security of the recovery process will be profoundly influenced by the manner in which treatment is begun. Once an [abused/traumatized] . . . patient comes to believe that the therapy is not a sufficiently safe place in which his or her pain can be contained and addressed, even the most skillful therapist is hard-pressed to help the overwhelmed patient restabilize and avoid significant regression. . . . (p. 146)

The following are issues to be addressed at the outset of treatment:

ESTABLISHING THE TREATMENT AND REINFORCING THE TREATMENT FRAME   Critical tasks of this phase are: The continued establishment of the parameters of the treatment frame (see chapter 5 for additional information about issues that make up the treatment frame) along with the sequencing of treatment, the development of the therapeutic relationship and working alliance, the maintenance of personal safety and relative life stability, the development of additional sources of support, and attention to self functions and symptom management skills. The objective of clarifying expectations and contracting with the patient is to avert disruption and acting out later in the treatment process. The therapist communicates clearly what will and will not be tolerated, as a condition of treatment. This approach places considerable responsibility on the patient and communicates that therapy is not unconditional or a place where "anything goes." In general, the majority of patients are able to work within the treatment parameters (albeit at times with difficulty and with a need for flexibility on the part of the therapist in negotiating relapses) but a minority will be unable to do so. In some cases, such a patient has not achieved a degree of readiness or acknowledged the seriousness of his/her difficulties and, in the parlance of Alcoholics Anonymous, may not have "hit bottom."

In many ways and in many of these tasks, the therapeutic emphasis of this phase resembles that of generic, nontrauma therapy; however, the patient's posttraumatic aftereffects, including deficits in functioning, victimization-related schema about self and others, and episodes of revictimization, often compound it. For example, the development of the therapeutic alliance, a more or less straightforward process with a non-traumatized patient, is often a daunting challenge with one who has been severely interpersonally victimized. The patient may be beset by shame and anxiety and terrified of being judged and "seen" by the therapist. The therapist, in turn, may be perceived as a stand-in for other untrust-worthy and abusive authority figures to be feared, mistrusted, challenged, tested, distanced from, raged against, sexualized, etc., or may be perceived as a stand-in for the longed-for good parent or rescuer to be clung to, deferred to, and nurtured by, or the two may alternate in unpredictable, kaleidoscopic shifts (especially when the patient is highly dissociative and is easily triggered). In a related vein, issues of personal safety and revictimization are typically much more pronounced in this treatment population versus one that is more general.

The beginning of this phase extends the education of the patient that was begun during the assessment process and additionally fosters active ownership of and collaboration in the treatment process. It includes continued attention to treatment frame issues and the therapeutic relationship, including the mutual voluntary participation of both parties (mutual rights and responsibilities of therapist and patient), discussion of the assessment and diagnostic findings as related to the proposed course of treatment, and the establishment of an agreed-upon treatment contract, including preliminary goals. With these discussions, empowered informed consent and informed refusal are ensured (see discussion of these issues in chapters 5, 7, and 8).

Despite these detailed deliberations and the preliminary agreement to the treatment plan, a degree of noncompliance is to be anticipated (Kluft, 1993; van der Kolk et al., 1996). Traumatized individuals can be quite difficult to engage in treatment due to their profound mistrust of others and other trauma-based symptoms, associated characterological issues, emotional and cognitive constriction, and what is often a heightened ability (whether conscious or unconscious) to avoid and otherwise defend against painful material. The problem of therapeutic engagement requires that the therapist perform something akin to a juggling act of adhering to the parameters of the treatment contract while maintaining flexibility, sensitivity, and a capacity to enter into mutual negotiation and problem-solving. The patient's motivation and capacity to do the work must be constantly assessed and treatment tasks paced and accomplished accordingly.

INITIAL TASKS AND GOALS OF TREATMENT.   The specific tasks and goals of the early phase of treatment are determined according to the assessment findings and the patient's unique character structure, defensive patterns, concerns, symptoms, social support, and personal resources, including motivation and insurance coverage/financial resources (Gil, 1988; Horowitz, 1986; Turkus, 1995; Wells et al., 1995). On average and in keeping with the information presented earlier in this chapter and in chapters 3 and 4, patients who meet the criteria for complex PTSD and who exhibit a borderline ego structure and/or who have a comorbid dissociative disorder (i.e., those who lack a stable identity, observing ego, object constancy, relational stability, and the ability to identify, tolerate, and regulate their affective states) need more intensive stabilization and character-building work than patients with more developed ego capacities and ability to relate to others.

Early phase work is generally measured in terms of the mastery of skills and the development of ego resources and personal stability, not time (Turkus & Courtois, 1996). In fact, it is usually the lengthiest of the three phases, encompassing many therapeutic issues, some of which ebb and flow as progress is made (often slowly). Much of this work is focused on the development of a sense of self and what have been called self functions (affect recognition, tolerance, and management; separation of emotion from action; learning grounding, self-care, and self-soothing skills; identity formation, personal stabilization, and self-esteem development; mood regulation, object constancy, etc.). The treatment is also continuously focused on issues of personal safety, along with symptom stabilization and self-management achieved through education, cognitive restructuring, and skill development.

DEVELOPMENT OF THE THERAPEUTIC RELATIONSHIP.   The development of a therapeutic relationship is a task of crucial importance in this phase and a process that occurs over the entire course of treatment (Courtois, 1988). The relationship provides an interpersonal context and foundation for the various healing tasks and also provides "grist for the mill" about the patient's object relations. As discussed previously, object relations and interpersonal attachments are often seriously compromised by the relational insults of abuse, in particular all forms of chronic intrafamilial victimization, especially incest. The relational challenges inherent in working with interpersonally victimized individuals have been increasingly recognized, and a literature addressing these issues has become available in recent years (Chu, 1988; Davies & Frawley, 1994; Figley, 1995; Pearlman & Saakvitne, 1995; Saakvitne & Pearlman, 1996; Stamm, 1996; Wilson & Lindy, 1994). A relational approach to stabilization of the patient that attends to the patient's primary attachment and relational dynamics is espoused by these writers.

Issues having to do with interpersonal relationships (or self in relationship to others) are frequently projected onto the therapist, providing a form of coded communication about object relations and about past relationships. The clinician must expect these projections and strive to analyze and interpret their antecedents and meanings as they present and are re-enacted in the therapeutic relationship; however, caution is in order regarding interpretation and delayed/recovered memories: Some therapists have tended to overinterpret transference projections and behavioral reenactments (as well as other material such as dreams and flashbacks), as though they are literal and accurate representations of historical reality, an interpretive stance that does not have adequate research support (Brenneis, 1997). Relational challenges and the possible overinterpretation of transference/countertransference responses when delayed/recovered memories are at issue are discussed in more detail in chapters 8 and 9.

Over time, as the relational challenges lessen somewhat and the therapeutic relationship and alliance grow, the goal is for patients to learn new relational and attachment skills, such as assertiveness, empowerment, boundary management, mutuality, connection and intimacy with others, and the ability to negotiate their needs. They are also expected to deepen their capacity to begin to trust others after first learning to test their trustworthiness. It is now understood much more than previously that patients will not learn needed relational skills in a therapy that is overly caretaking, that does not stress personal responsibility, and that is noncollaborative. While reassurance and some caretaking are needed and will necessarily occur, numerous authors have cautioned that patients cannot be reparented or "loved into health" (Chu, 1998) and that relying exclusively on such as strategy is misadvised and potentially quite dangerous for both the patient and the therapist. As discussed previously, a strategy designed to foster empowerment of the patient will discourage regression and overdependence on the part of the patient, again countering some of the charges against therapists made by the false memory critics.

DISCUSSION OF ABUSE/TRAUMA IN THE INITIAL PHASE OF TREATMENT. Although the exploration and addressing of abuse and trauma are generally contraindicated in this phase of treatment due to the potential to destabilize the patient, issues pertaining to abuse/trauma will nevertheless come up in a variety of ways. As much as possible, any direct work with abuse material in the early stage of treatment should be educational and cognitive in focus. In this stage, the opportunity exists to give the patient information about the process and aftermath of traumatization, the management of symptoms and affect, and cognitive and emotional schema molded by the abuse. Many traumatized individuals are lacking in such information and interpret their reactions and symptoms as abnormal or crazy. As documented by Jehu (1988), the provision of information can be powerfully therapeutic. The normalization of posttrauma reponses can have the effect of beginning to shift core beliefs and cognitions associated with abuse/trauma that have reinforced symptoms of depression. The change in perspective and understanding may therefore begin to ameliorate depression. Cognitive protocols have been developed by Jehu, 1988; McCann and Pearlman (1990a) Linehan (1993) and Meichenbaum (1994) to correct predominant cognitive distortions associated with victimization.

One of the most difficult initial situations occurs when a patient presents for treatment with florid symptoms of PTSD/DD involving intrusion and/or numbing (some of which may be due to delayed/recovered memories) and unmodulated hyperarousal (and possibly an associated panic condition). Most often and quite understandably, this patient expresses the need to alleviate his/her distress by addressing the trauma intensively and directly "to get it over and done with" and for relief from the taxing symptoms. In such circumstances, intense reexposure is not recommended due to its potential to retraumatize rather than help. It is necessary therefore for the therapist to explain in some detail the rationale for not immediately plunging into the traumatic content; simultaneously, the therapist must offer reassurance that this does not mean that he or she is unaware of or uncaring about the patient's suffering. To the contrary. In order to prevent more distress, traumatic material is specifically not restimulated until the patient has some skills to be able to slow down and manage the powerful affects that get unleashed. Patients are taught that the sequenced model of progressive skill-building is the safe way to proceed and that they will be better off by "making haste slowly" (Turkus, 1995). The patient's acute discomfort is not neglected, however. Patients must be actively taught skills with which to manage their symptoms. The most common, in addition to cognitive interventions, are cognitive-behavioral strategies such as behavioral self-monitoring, regular exercise and/or relaxation-based interventions, and relaxation-based interventions paired with those that involve exposure. Additionally, rational and targeted pharmacotherapy is recommended for use in stabilizing distressing mood and physiological states.

All the while, the therapist must acknowledge the significance of abusive and traumatic events and empathize with the patient's misery (providing the relational "holding" context for the work). Both the acknowledgment of remembered abuse (or the possibility of suspected abuse) and the normalizing of reactions and coping skills are crucial. These responses rebut what often are erroneous beliefs held by the survivor about being crazy and defective and offer a significantly different viewpoint from what was available at the time of the abuse and quite possibly throughout the individual's life. According to Chu (1998):

> To ignore the role of abusive experiences is to tacitly collude in patients' denial of the impact of the abuse, as well as in their erroneous beliefs of personal defectiveness. The simple acknowledgment of the possible role of early traumatic experiences begins the process of helping survivors to understand many of their current difficulties as normally adaptive responses to extraordinarily overwhelming events. Therapists must reiterate that although patients must shoulder the responsibility of the recovery process, they are not responsible for the abuse itself. (p. 81)

This message may not be initially heard, much less integrated, and the therapist may have to present it many times from a variety of different perspectives before it sticks. Abuse/trauma survivors are rather notorious concerning their capacity for denial, minimization, self-depreciation, shame, and resultant self-blame, in addition to their tenacious attachment to caregivers, even those who hurt them. They may intellectually understand the therapist's posttraumatic reframe but continue in their emotional adherence to a position of denial, ambivalent attachment, and loyalty. Therapists walk a fine line in these acknowldgement responses: They must firmly validate both the reality and aversive consequences of abuse while understanding these attachment dilemmas and not scapegoating abusers, especially those who are family members and primary caretakers (Blizard & Bruhn, 1994; Courtois, 1988).

ISSUES OF SAFETY.   Early in this phase of treatment, the assessment of the patient's personal safety is made a priority. The lives of many victimized individuals are often rife with danger and traumatic reenactments and revictimizations of all sorts. They are consequently crisis-ridden and chaotic. Of necessity, a focus on safety must take precedence and any ongoing life-threatening and/or crisis circumstance—including but not limited to active suicidality, self-mutilation, homicidality, major risk-taking, violence to and from others, addictions and compulsions (eating, drug and alcohol, sex, relationships), and debilitating degrees of dissociation and reenactment/reexperiencing—must be addressed and managed early on. Because these behaviors and symptoms may well have developed as ways to cope with the painful effects of the original trauma and, in fact, may be mechanisms of reenacting (usually unconsciously but sometimes quite consciously and deliberately) abuse dynamics even after the original abuse has ceased, restricting or dismantling their use must proceed slowly and cautiously. As the patient begins to feel what has been avoided/split off, it is not unusual for relapse and even decompensation to occur. These behaviors may also have developed because the traumatized individual had no words and no social context or holding environment in which to express distress. In such circumstances, behavioral and somatic expression replaces verbalization and must be reversed over time (Straker & Waks, 1997). Thus, a plan must be in place to counteract such deterioration and to prevent and reverse relapse. According to the findings of a research study by Straker and Waks, the plan must not be initially too rigid or ambitious regarding the limitations imposed, lest it reinforce the feeling behind the action.

Nevertheless, personal safety must be insisted upon as an early focus of treatment, which is not to say that it is easily managed or achieved. Since it is a foundation of and a precedent for further therapeutic work, emotional and physical safety must be addressed with diligence and revisited repeatedly. Yet, the therapist must not expect that unsafe or risky behavior will be easily given up or readily changed. Not uncommonly, a great deal of time and effort, along with changes in other areas (including resolution of the abuse/trauma in some cases), is needed before safety issues can be settled.

Working on personal safety can be a most disheartening and difficult task. It causes the therapist to come face to face with often terrifying and repulsive self-abusive and self-endangering behavior, made all the more difficult when the patient rationalizes or justifies it and actively resists attempts to change it. While such resistance may be difficult to tolerate, it is understandable in its own right, given that many of these patients have little or no idea about the concept—much less the implementation—of personal safety and are frequently caught in cyclical reenactments of abuse-related behaviors and emotions over which they feel they have little control. These reenactments may be perceived as "normal" because they conform to what the patient has learned and known. They may also have a physiological basis associated with early abuse and/or attachment failures (van der Kolk, Perry, & Herman, 1991) and be related to an inability to verbalize affect rather than to take action on it. Self-harm, risk-taking, and addictions and compulsions may have been learned and reinforced as ways to cope with and avoid the pain associated with the original abuse/trauma; paradoxically, they often serve as simultaneous means of self-punishment and self-soothing.

The ongoing insistence on safety can be taxing to both therapist and patient, but, as discussed above, its importance must not be ignored or minimized. It may become a major area of disagreement between them, but the therapist must be consistent in supporting the position that "no abuse is OK" and "no abuse is a primary goal and condition of this treatment" versus "you are bad because you engage in these behaviors." Patients for whom safety is an issue are invited to engage in a strategy of ongoing safety planning both in pre-treatment and early in the process. According to Chu (1998), this can take the form of the therapist's asking for agreement on a therapeutic agenda regarding safety, e.g., "I know that hurting yourself has been a longstanding coping mechanism for you, and that you may not feel that self-care is important. However, if we are to get anywhere in this therapy, you will have to make a commitment to work very hard to take care of yourself, even when you may not want to" (p. 80). He further discusses the necessity of keeping these issues at the top of the agenda and his approach is very consistent with that espoused by Linehan (1993):

> In many situations, lapses will occur and patients may retreat to self-destructive behavior. However, such lapses are only tolerable when patients are able to demonstrate a commitment to the principles of self-care over time. It is essential to the treatment that patients ally with their therapists around preventing self-harm, oppose their own self-destructive impulses, and understand the mechanisms of their vulnerability to revictimization. They must also begin to learn how to soothe themselves using alternative and less self-destructive ways of coping with stress. (p. 80)

Safety planning is an active and collaborative process in which the patient agrees to address issues of risk and danger in incremental steps and to implement various self-soothing and safety actions according to the degree of risk and instability. As an example, a chronically suicidal patient might agree to activate this order of behaviors: (1) to not keep lethal materials or objects in the home (at all times); (2) to use positive affirmations, to write feelings in a journal, and to engage in activities as distraction to counter random thoughts of suicide (numerous times daily); (3) to take antidepressant medication, as prescribed, and to actively implement stress management strategies and exercise (daily); (4) to not drink or take drugs (ongoing); (5) to activate a phone tree for support from friends when feeling lonely and beginning to have thoughts of suicide (as needed); (6) to be honest with the therapist and other caregivers about any active or passive suicidal plan (on an ongoing basis); (7) to call the therapist, back-up therapist, predetermined family member, or crisis resource when suicidal actions are being seriously considered or a plan has been drawn up; and (8) to enter a hospital if suicidal impulses become unmanageable and/or the elements of the plan have been activated.

Such planning teaches the significance of safety and provides the patient with alternative means of self-management to replace dangerous and addictive behaviors and practices. Planning for relapse anticipates and destigmatizes setbacks but also structures mechanisms by which the patient is able to recoup and regroup. This collaborative approach also removes the therapist from the role of limit-setter/rescuer and fosters responsibility on the part of the patient. By close attention to safety issues, the therapist demonstrates active concern while refusing the role of passive bystander, an aspect of the abuse experience of many patients that contributed to the original traumatization (discussed further in chapters 4 and 9).

ISSUES OF SELF-CARE AND SYMPTOM STABILIZATION.   Many abuse and trauma survivors are ambivalent, unconcerned, or negligent in their self-care as well as their personal safety. These issues are often related. Some survivors present for treatment in a condition of posttraumatic decline due to chronic and debilitating PTSD symptoms, associated comorbid conditions, and ongoing personal neglect and episodes of self-harm, re-enactments, and revictimization. They may exhibit an array of behavioral and health problems, such as poor eating and sleeping, as well as patterns of physical and medical neglect. Stress management strategies for trauma survivors are discussed in Merwin & Smith-Kurtz (1988). Interestingly, the management or resolution of some issues might have a cascading impact on others (i.e., taking medication as prescribed might lessen symptoms and assist with sleep, adequate sleep might, in turn, dramatically improve personal functioning and lessen interpersonal irritability). Yet, the therapist must understand that even seemingly small and simple self-care issues may have major traumatic antecedents and associations and may not resolve easily (e.g., poor sleep may be the result of the terror of being abused at night that, in turn, resulted in a longstanding pattern of nocturnal hypervigilance; poor dental hygiene may be due to an aversion to having a foaming white substance in the mouth, secondary to experiences of forced fellatio).

Other destabilizing behaviors and symptoms should be given treatment priority to help the patient achieve control over symptoms they perceive are controlling them. Patients can be taught relaxation and deescalation skills to manage physical hyperarousal and intrusive symptoms and taught grounding and refocusing skills to control dissociation. Specific cognitive-behavioral interventions have been recommended as a preliminary strategy in challenging maladaptive schema about self and others and in treating mood disturbances (Jehu, 1988; Linehan, 1993; McCann & Pearlman, 1990a; Meichenbaum, 1994; Roth & Batson, 1997). Many of these educative and cognitive-behavioral interventions do not work instantaneously and require diligent practice and/or a structured treatment protocol. The reward is well worth the effort when the patient gains mastery over previously crippling symptoms and intrusions of the trauma and learns how to achieve personal control that was lacking.

Psychotropic medications are recommended to lessen or manage the most debilitating emotional symptoms of depression, anxiety, and hyperarousal, along with other active mental conditions. Specific types of medications are now recommended for PTSD symptoms (Davidson & van der Kolk, 1996); however, the therapist must prepare the patient adequately for their use and must simultaneously guard against overmedication—unfortunately, a common occurrence among women patients. The ultimate goal of all of these interventions is to stabilize the patient's mood and symptoms sufficiently to improve and maintain functioning.

SELF FUNCTIONS.   Attention to what have been labeled "self functions" also contributes to emotional development and the ability to function. Numerous authors have discussed the necessity of working various self functions pertaining to: identity and self-worth, both as they have been affected by the trauma and apart from it; ego, structural, and characterological issues; personal schema about self and others; boundary issues or the differentiation of self from others; and affect regulation (including affect modulation and tolerance), as a prelude to any directed work with traumatic material or memories (Briere, 1996a, 1996b; Courtois, 1997c; Linehan, 1993; McCann & Pearlman, 1990a; Roth & Batson, 1997; Wells, et al., 1995). Chronic abuse in childhood quite commonly deforms and derails psychosexual maturation and leads to gaps in the individual's development. Many survivors have missed essential developmental psychosexual stages and processes that must be reworked to whatever degree possible during the course of treatment.

PERSONAL FUNCTIONING.   Personal functioning in abuse survivors ranges from a total inability to function to exceptional competence; however, it is not unusual for individuals beset by posttraumatic and other acute symptoms to regress and deteriorate in their ability to function. At times, decompensation may be paradoxically associated with and even prompted by the psychotherapy. Patients may become much more symptomatic and their functioning may suffer as they face what they have previously denied or otherwise warded off. Wherever possible, the therapist should slow the pace of treatment and make any exposure to traumatic material gradual enough that it is tolerable and patients can maintain or even improve their level of functioning. For those patients who are too disabled to engage in educational or vocational training or to maintain employment, alternatives such as volunteer activities, partial hospitalization, day programs, and group therapy and support groups should be considered to assist in structuring the patient's time, building self-esteem, fostering social support and skill-building, and supplementing the individual treatment.

A subset of patients may be predisposed to strive to make therapy their life rather than their temporary lifeline. Highly dependent patients engage in regressive-dependent transference patterns, where they essentially trade off their independence and capabilities in return for therapeutic attention and gratification. They long for the therapist's attention above all else and wish to be "loved into health" through merger with the therapist. Since being in therapy is not the same as living one's life, the therapist must challenge this stance and not overgratify the patient's dependency needs (discussed further in chapter 9). I tell my patients that I understand that therapy might be a linchpin in their lives for a while, but that it is not a substitute for their life and should not be viewed that way. Nor should they engage in treatment compulsively on a 24-hour-a-day basis (as some survivors are prone to do because they are trying to "get it over with quickly" or feel the need to please and be compliant with those in authority), to the exclusion of other life activities and relationships.

A focus on the maintenance of functioning is essential. The therapist should actively discourage regressive dependency, instead, encouraging patients to maintain their lives and their social supports. As with many of the other issues discussed in this section, this must be done tactfully, with appreciation of the patient's needs and perspective. It should also be attended as it pertains to the memory controversy. Lief and Fetkewicz (1995), in questioning a cohort of 40 self-identified retractors of false memories, found that a high percentage reported an enormous positive dependent transference on the therapist whose "attention and support meant everything to the patient" and who rewarded the emergence or recovery of memories with positive attention. These therapies were also characterized as excessively caretaking and as lacking in appropriate therapeutic limits and boundaries and suggest a caution to all.

DEVELOPMENT OF INTERPERSONAL RELATIONSHIPS AND A SUPPORT SYSTEM. In a related vein, the patient must be encouraged to develop relationship skills and to build healthy relationships and a system of support apart from the therapist. Optimally, the therapeutic relationship serves as a model of a healthy affiliation and provides a safe arena for learning and practicing skills that can be applied to other relationships. Much therapeutic time must be spent identifying and unlearning the "relational rules of abuse and victimization" and replacing them with skills and attitudes necessary for healthy, interdependent connections with supportive others. Relational work proceeds slowly and may have many false starts and stops. As described earlier, the negotiation (and renegotiation) of the therapeutic relationship and alliance is an important task that involves repeated testing and cyclical patterns of affiliation and disenchantment. It certainly models the development of process skills, including the ability to negotiate and to give and take.

In keeping with the discussion of the previous section on functioning, therapists must be clear in their expectation that the patient develop sources of personal support apart from treatment and additionally that s/he work to cultivate social contacts and activities. This is an enormously difficult challenge for some patients, especially those who coped with abuse through social isolation and withdrawal and whose experiences with others have been predominantly negative, abusive, and revictimizing. As with all other issues, the pace of progress in relationship skills may be excruciatingly slow, but the expectation of some degree of affiliation with and connection to others must be maintained nevertheless. The therapist cannot be and should not be the patient's only source of relationship and affiliation.

Group therapy is an especially useful setting in which to address relational issues; however, abuse survivors may not be able to productively participate in a group until preliminary stabilization and relational work has been accomplished. Group treatment can be problematic if undertaken too early in the treatment process and is not recommended unless the survivor has adequate ego resources and relational skills to engage safely and productively. If group involvement is considered or mandated early in the treatment process (e.g., some insurance companies and mental health centers require that treatment be provided only in a group format), a structured educational group organized around specific themes or issues is far preferable to an unstructured process-oriented therapy group. Courtois (1993) and Linehan (1993) have provided structured didactic models of group treatment and Harris and colleagues (1998) recently published a sequenced and graduated group treatment model for chronically abused and traumatized women.

Whatever the type of group and whatever point it is undertaken in the recovery process, it is advisable to carefully screen potential group members as to their suitability and motivation. Group treatment is usually much more stimulating and intense than individual treatment and the patient and therapist have much less ability to control its pace and content. The patient must therefore be stable enough for the additional challenges as well as the additional gains that can result from group participation (Courtois, 1988, 1993). A specialized group for abuse/trauma survivors is also not a suitable modality for those individuals who have no memory of abuse, because it may create conditions of social compliance and suggestion (refer to chapter 9 for more on this issue).

The emphasis on functioning and outside support and relationships discussed in these sections is important vis-à-vis delayed/recovered memory concerns. One of the most common charges has been that the treatment (especially so-called recovered memory therapy) has caused massive deterioration in functioning and mental health as patients focus on the past at the expense of the present and the future. Working from this orientation, therapists encourage their patients in their ongoing search for repressed abuse memories and foster unhealthy dependence on treatment, resulting in conditions of severe personal and interpersonal regression. A therapeutic agenda that is demonstrably organized around self-care and safety, self-management and skill-building, a social contract, and present-day personal and interpersonal functioning obviously demonstrates a totally different philosophy of treatment and therefore works against these criticisms.

SCOPE, INTENSITY, AND DURATION OF THE INITIAL PHASE.   Clearly, the scope, intensity, and duration of this first phase of the treatment process vary considerably. It should not be assumed to be the same for all, nor should it always be assumed to be long-term. Such assumptions of homogeneity have been critiqued with good reason (Haaken & Schlaps, 1991). Patients with sufficient ego resources and adequate relationship skills may, following the development of the therapeutic alliance, move through this phase and into middle phase work in relatively short order. More compromised patients may literally require years of stabilization, skill-building, and alliance-building (Chu, 1998; Kluft, 1994; Wells et al., 1995) and may, in fact, never go any further in the process. Recent research and literature reviews on the treatment of chronic PTSD suggests that some patients may not progress beyond rehabilitation and some may periodically decompensate as part of their chronic posttraumatic condition (Shalev et al., 1996; Wang et al., 1996).

Some patients may exercise the option of stopping treatment once they have mastered the tasks of this phase and their lives are back on track. For example, several of my patients made enough progress in this phase to be able to develop committed relationships and begin families. They were stable enough to be out of treatment, enjoy their accomplishments, and focus on family and childrearing. They chose not to work on the trauma during a relatively happy and placid time in their lives. They left open the option to return to treatment if symptoms returned or worsened or any other circumstance warranted therapeutic attention.

Other patients discontinue because they lack the personal, motivational, familial, or financial resources to continue. In essence, they exercise their option of informed refusal. This is particularly difficult in those situations where, in the therapist's judgment, it is not in the patient's best interest to leave treatment; nonetheless, the choice is the patient's to make (hopefully, after first discussing it with the therapist) and the consequences then become his/her responsibility.

Chu (1988) and other writers have discussed the difficulties of treatment with unmotivated and/or uninvolved and resistant patients. Discussion is needed to try to work through impasses when they occur (Pearlman & Saakvitne, 1995) but, in keeping with the remainder of the treatment philosophy espoused here, it is ultimately the patient's choice whether to continue or not and continuance should not be pressured. Whatever the reason for terminating treatment at this point, the patient who is successful in mastering the major tasks of this phase leaves therapy with more personal and interpersonal resources and life stability than when treatment began (Courtois, 1997d), a major gain and a perspective likely to satisfy to some of the predominant concerns regarding false memory production in never-ending treatment that fosters dependency and regression.

The Middle Phase:
Deconditioning, Mourning,
Resolution and Integration of the Trauma

Van der Kolk (1996) had the following to say about the decision to continue treatment and critical purpose of the middle phase:

> When patients have gained stability, control, and perspective, treatment can be terminated. There is no intrinsic value in dredging up past trauma if a patient's current life provides gratification . . . . However, if . . .

involuntary emotional, perceptual, or behavioral intrusions continue to interfere with people's current functioning, controlled and predictable exposure to the traumatic memories can help with regaining mastery . . . . A therapist's natural proclivity is to help a patient avoid experiencing undue pain; however, learning to tolerate the memories of intense emotional experiences is a critical part of recovery. The psychotherapist who understands the nature of trauma can aid the process of integration by staying with the patient through his or her suffering; by providing a perspective that the suffering is meaningful; and by helping in the mastery of trauma through putting the experience into symbolic, communicable form (i.e., through putting perceptions and sensations into words). (p. 428)

Chu (1998) offered a viewpoint consistent with van der Kolk's, but included an important caveat about the working-through process of this phase:

It is premature at this point in time, to estimate what proportion of survivors of chronic and severe abuse will be able to abreact[1] and successfully work through early traumatic experiences. Clinical evidence suggests that although many are able to do so, others may be able to achieve resolution and integration of traumatic backgrounds only to a minimal or partial extent. For such patients, stabilization and symptom management remain the long-term (sometimes life-long) goals of treatment. (p. 86)

The primary goal of the middle phase of trauma resolution and integration is for the patient to gradually face and make sense of the abuse/trauma and to experience associated emotions at a pace that is safe, manageable, and not overwhelming. The work of this phase is not devoted to high intensity "reliving" that retraumatizes and results in decompensation, nor does it involve *digging for or active solicitation of memories*. Patients are not encouraged to do this work to foster regressive dependency or to get stuck in a morass of more and more serious abuse, and certainly not to *create* traumatic memories.

Waites (1996) commented as follows on the risks and the choice of whether to focus on traumatic memories:

The pitfalls of psychotherapy can be compared with those of other consequential interventions, including medical interventions, that must be

---

[1] As used in this chapter, abreaction refers to the cognitive and emotional processing of traumatic material, not just to its revivification/re-experiencing.

evaluated for risk factors but that should not necessarily be avoided just because they are risky. In many instances, intensive psychotherapy is the most sensible approach to difficult problems. Prudent therapists, nevertheless, will be sensitive to the pitfalls and strive to avoid them. It is not necessary to become unduly defensive in this regard, just vigilant, careful, and informed.

A corollary of these considerations is that, in matters of remembering, individuals must have their own timetable. Readiness to remember is as important as the ability to remember. In the long run, it is not the therapist's interpretation, but the client's comprehension that makes the difference between memories that injure and those that, even though painful, contribute to healing. (p. 231)

Careful assessment, timing, and rationale are therefore important considerations in choosing to tackle the therapeutic work of this phase of treatment.

RATIONALE FOR WORK WITH TRAUMATIC MEMORIES.   Before discussing specifics of this phase, we first review the reasons for working with traumatic memories. Clear rationale exists in the clinical literature across therapeutic orientations for addressing and reworking available and newly accessible memories of trauma. The primary rationale is for the individual to feel better, to feel whole, and to be free of the symptoms and life interruptions that are the direct result of trauma. The patient is encouraged to re-incorporate split-off aspects of the self that may have taken on a life of their own, causing the misery associated with chronic posttraumatic stress, dissociative disorders, and related comorbid psychological and medical conditions. The patient is also encouraged to verbalize or "narrativize" available memories, since trauma disrupts narrative processing, by interfering with psychophysiological coordination, social connections, and cognitive processes (van der Hart et al., 1993; van der Kolk & van der Hart, 1991; Waites, 1996; Wigren, 1994). Brown et al. (1998), drawing from a number of authors from different theoretical perspectives, offered the following composite description of memory integration:

Memory integration entails a process of "translating" or "verbally encoding" heretofore "unsymbolized" trauma-related symptoms and implicit behavioral reenactments into a coherent narrative, as well as a process of "making meaning" and "realization" of the trauma as part of the personal history of the self. (authors' italics) (p. 481)

Some research is available at the present time that supports the therapeutic utility of "dredging up past trauma," to quote the title of a research report by Brabin and Berah (1995). These authors reported that the majority of their research subjects found it helpful to be interviewed about a traumatic experience and its aftermath. Only a small percentage found it distressing. I reported a similar finding from my interview study of a volunteer sample of women who disclosed a history of incestuous abuse (Courtois, 1979). While many subjects said it was stressful at first, they also found it helpful to talk in some detail to someone who wanted to know about their experience, a markedly different response from what most of these women had experienced throughout their lives. Roth and Batson (1997) also reported positive outcomes concerning the discussion and processing of abuse-related cognitions. Foa, Rothbaum, and Molnar (1995) found a decrease in psychiatric symptomatology and emotional relief.

Pennebaker and his associates (Harber & Pennebaker, 1992; Pennebaker, 1989, 1993; Pennebaker, Kiecolt-Glaser, & Glaser, 1988) have engaged in a long-term course of research about the cost benefits of disclosing traumas verbally or in writing. They have reported significant improvements in physical health and immune function when individuals write or talk about personally upsetting experiences. Pennebaker has also found that verbal or written "confession" or the construction of a coherent story, including the expression of negative emotions about traumatic experiences, versus inhibition of the story and associated emotion is linked to health improvement.

It is not only the re-association of what has been dissociated that is needed (Courtois, 1992) or the reconstruction of what is occluded or unavailable (Laub & Auerhahn, 1993); rather, processing, desensitizing, resolving, and synthesizing/integrating of traumatic memories allow for completion and resultant symptom alleviation and relief (Brown et al., 1998; van der Hart et al., 1993). Siegel (1995) has written that "The symptoms of unresolved trauma are themselves traumatizing; the patient may not be aware of why they are occurring and may again feel helpless to control them. In addition, the content of the memory may be frightening. When the patient is ready, there may come a time when he or she needs to recount the details of the experienced trauma" (p. 117). He goes on to explain:

> The retrieval of a memory by itself is not therapeutic, nor does it necessarily alter the form in which the memory is stored. A flashback or abreaction that does not involve therapeutic processing only exposes the patient to a repeated experience of being overwhelmed, helpless,

and in pain. A "therapeutic abreaction" emphasizes processing, both cognitive and emotional, of dissociated elements of a previously inaccessible or partially accessible memory. Two basic axioms based on the hypotheses presented in this article are as follows:

1. Therapeutic interventions that allow implicit memories to be processed in an explicit manner, including desensitization, self-reflection, and narrativization, will be essential in the resolution process.

2. Self-reflection during an abreactive experience will provide additional reflective components to a previously perceptually rich and reflectively poor memory profile. This increase in reflective processes will then permit source monitoring to assess the origin of the memory accurately and not misinterpret it (as in a flashback) as a presently lived experience. (p. 117)

Here, Siegel addresses the shifting of memory from sensorimotor and implicit form to verbalized and explicit form as part of what allows processing and more control to be exerted over the memory process. As opposed to fragmented, dissociated, unmetabolized memory that drives the symptoms, processed memory is much more under the conscious control of the individual. In Harvey's (1994) terminology, the patient "regains authority over the memory."

And what about the issue of therapeutic "truth" of memory for trauma? A number of writers have cautioned therapists about the difference between the individual's narrative construction of truth and its historical analog (Brenneis, 1997; Ganaway, 1989; Spence, 1994). Obviously, work with memory (especially as concerns trauma) in the context of psychotherapy is enormously complicated. Reviere (1996) commented on the fact that it is ". . . a complex psychological operation further complicated by the psychotherapeutic process of reconstruction of life narrative through interpersonal dialogue" (p. 96). The therapist must carefully weigh belief in the reality of trauma with the understanding that discussion of trauma involves a translation of sorts. Memories and constructions are not necessarily veridical representations of the original event but encompass subjective elements and understandings (or systems of meaning, fantasies, developmental issues, etc.) that must be given consideration (Galatzer-Levy, 1997; Levine, 1997). The purpose of facing trauma, of accessing material originally split off in the interest of self-integrity and defense (and, in some cases, sanity), is to allow the gradual reconstruction and deconditioning of the traumatic material along with a restructuring of trauma-related cognitions and schema about self and others, all to achieve resolution and personal integrity.

APPROACHES TO TRAUMATIC MEMORY.   A number of techniques have thus far been identified and developed to work with traumatic memories. Before discussing some of them, it is useful to underscore the fact that access to memory of traumatic events can quite often be accomplished without special techniques—free narrative and recall in response to therapist inquiry may constitute all that is required. The therapist must provide a relational context in which it is safe for the individual to lessen defenses and face and discuss memories that have previously been hidden or warded-off (Courtois, 1992; Olio, 1989). A number of triggers, including transference responses and emotional states reminiscent of the time of traumatization, may cue recall and should therefore be noticed by the therapist (and, where advisable, brought to the patient's attention) (Davies & Frawley, 1994; Waites, 1996). In general, it is best if the traumatic material is addressed "from the top down" (Kluft, 1996). Working with and resolving consciously available material first allows other (often unconscious or defended against) material to emerge. The therapist might want to begin by having the patient describe in his or her own words what is remembered and work from there (Courtois, 1992). As discussed earlier, many traumatized individuals have been found to be highly avoidant, yet "know more than they know they know" and keep information segregated or dissociated in the interest of defense, resulting in patterns of partial accessibility and amnesia (Courtois, 1992; Laub & Auerhahn, 1993; Harvey & Herman, 1996, 1997). Simply asking patients to describe (verbally or in writing) what they know or to think about what happened to them may be enough for them to describe or acknowledge knowing more. They may also remember more by focusing rather than avoiding and by responding to specific questions or neutral prompts such as "Tell me," "I'd like to know," "Is there more?" "Uh-huh," "And then . . ."

Briere (1996b) also provided helpful commentary and insight on the self-perpetuating aspects of ego strengthening psychotherapy (or what he has labeled the Self-Trauma Model, which is in concordance with the treatment model described in this chapter) in terms of memory recovery. From his perspective, specialized techniques to attain memories are usually unnecessary since memory tends to become more accessible as the patient stabilizes and as the need for strong defenses decreases.

> In combination, decreasing stress levels and increasing self resources can lead to a relatively self-sustaining process: As the need to avoid painful material lessens with treatment, memories previously too overwhelming to address become more available for processing. As this new material is, in turn, desensitized and cognitively accommodated, self capacity is further improved and the overall stress level is further

reduced—thereby permitting access to (and processing of) even more unavailable material. Ultimately, treatment ends when traumatic material is sufficiently desensitized and integrated, and self resources are sufficiently learned and strengthened, that the survivor no longer experiences significant intrusive, avoidant, or dysphoric symptoms.

This progressive function of Self-Trauma therapy removes the need for any so-called "memory recovery" techniques. Instead of relying on hypnosis or drug-assisted interviews, for example, to somehow increase access to unavailable material, Self-Trauma therapy allows these memories to emerge naturally as a function of the survivor's reduced need for avoidance. Whereas authoritarian memory recovery techniques might easily exceed the therapeutic window and flood the survivor with destabilizing memories and affects, the . . . dynamic only allows access to dissociated material when, by definition, the therapeutic window has not been exceeded. The Self-Trauma model reverses an assumption of those who advocate aggressive memory retrieval: It holds that clients do not get better when they remember more, but rather, that *they may remember more as they get better.* (p. 154) (italics added)

Despite this naturalistic emergence during the course of treatment described by Briere and others, a number of techniques have been developed for the processing of memory. They can be very useful in addressing and resolving traumatic material in terms of content and meaning. A sampling of some of the most common techniques, grouped by therapeutic orientation, is included in Table 6.2. In the remainder of this section, we discuss some of the technical issues and approaches that have been identified that are conducive to the processing and integration of traumatic memories.

Horowitz (1986) was the first to suggest an information-processing strategy for the resolution of traumatic symptoms and Litz and Keane (1995) have recently reviewed the literature on information-processing approaches to the processing and resolution of trauma. Horowitz wrote that the resolution process for trauma involves an approach-avoid strategy that initially mimics the phasic alterations of the posttraumatic response and that simultaneously reverses the dissociative response (as well as other defensive operations and adaptations). Over time, the patient is encouraged to gradually increase his/her approach or exposure to traumatic material in manageable doses while simultaneously lessening avoidance, numbing, and dissociation to enable deconditioning to occur. In following this strategy of graduated exposure, the therapist offsets approach strategies with slowdown or temporizing ones, modulating the pace according to the patient's response, including degree of distress and any decompensation.

Table 6.2
Techniques for Memory and Narrative Integration

Psychoanalytic/Psychodynamic	Cognitive-Behavioral	Experiential/Somatic	Hypnotic/Guided Imagery
"Talking cure"/testimony/catharsis/insight free recall Inquiry about events and details - inviting discussion Development of therapeutic relationship – restorative function – providing object constancy Assessment of psychological structure, defenses, and functioning Identification of dissociation and other defenses – lifting repression through Identification of schema/themes about self and others Attention to behavioral reenactments Attention to transference and countertransference Building of affect tolerance Building of coping/functioning skills Interpretation – analyze conscious and unconscious – invite re-connection Titrate to "therapeutic window" of patient's tolerance (Briere, 1997a &b) – increase approach – decrease avoid Reconstruction – "memory as recombinant experience" (Kafka, 1995) Reconnection, synthesis, and realization Abreaction – planned with the goal of emotional processing and integration Completion and integration of narrative (cognitive and perceptual change and integration of memory and affect) – in writing – verbally Meaning-making and resolution of existential crises Integration and shift in self-concept and authority over memories	Education about trauma, trauma response, PTSD Identification and deconditioning of triggers/cues Teaching and strengthening of coping skills/self-resources Identification of cognitions and beliefs for restructuring and processing – correct cognitive distortions – direct therapeutic exposure – imaginal – in vivo – inhibition and confrontation of traumatic memories – systematic desensitization – stress inoculation training – dialectic-behavior therapy-DBT (Linehan, 1993) – cognitive-processing therapy-CPT (Resick & Schnicke, 1992) – eye movement desensitization and reprocessing-EMDR (Shapiro, 1989) – thought-field therapy-TFT – counting method (Ochberg, 1996) writing/"confession"/association/ assimilation/narrative construction (Harber & Pennebaker, 1992) Information and emotional processing (Litz & Keane, 1989) Information processing for children (Hartman & Burgess, 1993) – anchor for safety – strengthen resources – resurface the trauma – process the trauma – unlink sensory, perceptual, and cognitive information – transfer to past memory – terminate intervention	Writing – direct – creative writing; poetry/metaphor – list advantages/disadvantages of remembering (Calof, 1994) Art Sand Tray Psychodrama High Risk Model for Threat Perception/Psychophysiological Psychotherapy (Wickramasekera, 1994) – analysis of somatic symptoms in absence of pathophysiology Movement Medical evaluation of somatic symptoms Massage Corroboration	Ego strengthening/self-soothing/self-control Imaginal exposure and desentization (labeled by some authors as abreaction) – controlled access to memories – alter meaning/meaning-making Stategic use of Eriksonian techniques (Kingsbury, 1992) Affect bridge (Watkins, 1981) Memory reconstruction (Gravitz, 1994)

Briere (1996a, 1996b) and Cornell and Olio (1991) have discussed similar titration strategies. Briere discusses the utility of a focused goal sequence and the concept of a "therapeutic window" of emotional tolerance within which optimal therapeutic work is done. Undershooting the window (or not making a strong enough approach to the traumatic material) keeps the patient from adequately addressing and processing the trauma and thus maintains avoidance/dissociation. Overshooting (making too strong an approach) results in overwhelming the patient's capacity and increases reexperiencing and flooding. Finding a middle ground in the patient's ability to tolerate the traumatic material allows it to be processed and "metabolized." In a similar vein, Cornell and Olio discuss an "affective edge"—the maintenance of increasing degrees of emotional expression, cognitive understanding, and bodily awareness when facing traumatic material, without resorting to the same degree of denial, dissociation, and other common blunting/numbing strategies. By working on the affective edge, patients can first acknowledge and then begin to integrate previously split-off aspects of their experience with the ultimate goal of processing the material to achieve some emotional resolution.

"Controlled or graduated exposure" is another way to describe aspects of this process. In controlled exposure, traumatic memory is reactivated along with its associated affect, with the therapeutic intent of modifying it, to make it less rigid and distressing and more like memories for nontraumatic events (van der Kolk, et al., 1996). The objective of this stage of treatment is for the patient to achieve mastery over the trauma imagery and emotions, i.e., to be able to evoke traumatic material but to process it in a sufficiently different way that it loses its potency and spontaneous and uncontrolled/unbidden emergence. The fact that the patient reexperiences the trauma not in isolation but in the presence of the therapist who provides the experience of empathic response and secure attachment helps to neutralize the traumatic loading (Courtois, 1992; Olio, 1989; Phelps, Friedlander, & Enns, 1997).

It is the back-and-forth nature of a gradual and controlled exposure strategy within the support provided by the therapeutic relationship that help to produce the reconstruction, reworking, and ultimately the resolution of the trauma. Patients must be directly supported as they struggle with their ambivalence and doubt their perceptions and memories. Feelings of shock, rage, anguish, and grief often accompany facing interpersonal trauma, its betrayals and lack of protection, as well as its life consequences. Thus, this process involves the grieving of losses and a cycle of mourning. Individuals may appear to be shell-shocked as the defenses of denial and minimization give way and as previously unacknowledged incidents of trauma surface and the full extent of the victimization and its toll become evident.

Group therapy specific to abuse and trauma is especially useful in this treatment phase, where the intent is to help the patient to process the material that is available or that emerges (Chew, 1997; Courtois, 1988; Donaldson & Cordes-Green, 1995; Herman, 1992b; Herman & Schatzow, 1987; Webb & Leehan, 1996). Group participation relieves feelings of emotional isolation and stigmatization by providing a context of support from individuals with similar experiences and reactions. It serves as an interpersonal catalyst and container for the exploration of the abuse memories, beliefs, cognitions, and emotions and offers a unique forum for grieving. At times, participation in a group may restimulate memory (new memory as well as details) and provide the forum for working with new information or nuances. Additionally, group provides a safe context for exploring and changing abuse-related interpersonal dynamics. Group members assist and support each other as they struggle with issues of connection, respect, trust, conflict, and intimacy (Courtois, 1988). The resolution of these issues may often stimulate the emergence and resolution of additional traumatic material.

An existential crisis of major proportions often occurs as survivors try to understand how and why sexual abuse (and/or other victimization) happened to them. Intense mourning may result. During this phase, some survivors again contemplate suicide but for different reasons than before. As part of the resolution of their existential anguish, patients must decide if they can live with the knowledge and pain of what was done to them and the losses they suffered. Schema about self and others developed in the context of trauma must be processed and changed for resolution to occur. Core self schema such as shame, powerlessness, and a sense of having deserved the abuse, along with irrational guilt and self-blame and "secondary secrets" such as liking the attention or physical contact, sexual response during abuse, and/or a sense of power (or special relationship) with the abuser or others, must be addressed (Courtois, 1988). Brown et al., 1998 discuss "representational integration" as a subphase of the integration stage where the goal is to facilitate integration of the dissociated trauma-related self-representations into a conscious system of self-representations. Core relational schema, including mistrust and powerlessness/compliance must also be addressed and shifted (Pearlman & Saakvitne, 1995) and transference/countertransference reenactments identified and worked through to resolution (Davies & Frawley, 1994).

Nonverbal as well as verbal strategies can be used productively at this time (Cohen, Barnes, & Rankin, 1995; Cohen & Cox, 1995; Simonds, 1994). Expressive strategies such as writing, movement and physical expression, and drawing may provide means to symbolize and communicate what the patient has difficulty verbalizing. Nameless emotional states are better understood as they are processed and verbalized. Once the survivor has faced the abuse and experienced the resultant emotions with less denial or dissociation, assimilation can occur as he or she expands personal understanding of what happened in childhood and why it happened and attaches new meaning to the experience and its personal implications. At its most basic, a resolution of issues of self-blame and associated self-hatred is achieved as the patient develops a deeper understanding of the abuse scenario, including the abuser's motivations and any contributory family dynamics and characteristics. Over time, posttraumatic responses lose their intensity and their power to overwhelm the individual, who is then freed to develop additional personal and interpersonal perspective and competence.

MEMORY RETRIEVAL.   Brown et al. (1998) also discuss the utility and even necessity for some patients with partial or complete amnesia to engage in a process of memory retrieval during this treatment phase. They wrote:

> While trauma experts agree that memory integration is the main goal of the integration phase . . . , most also acknowledge that a clinically important subpopulation of trauma patients enter treatment with a relatively incomplete narrative memory for the trauma. These fully or partially amnestic patients present a special challenge, in that recovery or enhancement of their incomplete memory may be a necessary prerequisite to memory integration. We disagree with false memory advocates who claim that memory recovery should never be done, or who claim that all treatment that addresses recollections of trauma is memory recovery and not memory integration. We recognize, however, that some false memory advocates will strongly disagree with our position and interpret it as justification for memory recovery, at least under certain circumstances.
>
> Our position, which is supported by the professional trauma literature, is that memory recovery has a legitimate place within the overall trauma treatment plan, provided that memory recovery, in the narrow sense, is restricted to those patients in whom full or partial amnesia for trauma is a fundamental clinical problem. In this sense, memory recovery is well matched to the problem. Avoidance of memory enhancement in certain instances is an avoidance of clinical responsibility. (Authors' italics) (pp. 481–482)

For additional detailed information about memory retrieval and memory integration (much beyond the scope of what has been presented here), the interested reader is referred to Alpert (1996); Appelbaum et al. (1997); Brown et al. (1998); Gartner (1997); and Waites (1996).

PREPARATION FOR THIS TREATMENT PHASE.   The therapist should discuss his/her approach to working with traumatic memories and make explicit that the patient must come to a personal understanding and acceptance about them and that considerable uncertainty may remain. Patients must struggle with their own doubts and ambivalence about what they "know" and "don't know"—the struggle about what is real and what is not belongs to them rather than to the therapist. The therapist cannot define their reality for them; rather, his or her job is to offer support, encouragement, and perspective. In the absence of corroboration, the therapist has no way of knowing the reality of what did or did not happen in the past.

Thus, the work of this phase is undertaken with caution and with ongoing attention to the patient's ability to tolerate the emotional load that accompanies this approach. The rate and intensity of the work should be carefully monitored and titrated so that the patient can maintain his/her level of functioning to whatever degree possible. That said, it is important to understand that second phase work is inherently destabilizing and even retraumatizing to some degree, and that the patient may well lose some personal equilibrium and ability to function during this time period.

Patients and their supportive others should be informed ahead of time about the rigors of this phase, both to prepare them for it and to solicit additional support for the patient. It is likely to be the most painful part of the therapy, and the individual may, for a time, appear to get worse instead of better. It often helps for patients to understand that facing formerly warded-off realities and previously intolerable feelings will make them feel worse in the short run, but is undertaken in the interest of long-term resolution and of ultimately feeling and functioning better. Patients should also know that the option of informed refusal is available and that decisions can be made throughout this phase about whether to continue to work with the trauma or to modify the approach that is being used.

The therapist must also be personally and professionally prepared for the additional demands of this phase. The therapist may be personally impacted by the material and its intensity in a process that has been labeled contact or vicarious traumatization (as discussed more fully in chapter 9). Additionally, patients may require more by way of availability, reassurance, and support as they struggle with the traumatic material, its impact, and its meaning. The therapist's willingness to address and work with the traumatic material (rather than denying or suppressing it in repetition of dynamics of the past) is itself reparative. It provides a relational context for experience made all the more traumatic by being experienced in isolation. As one of my patients has told me repeatedly, "I don't want to go there if you're not there with me. I don't want to be alone as I was in the past." Phelps, Friedlander, and Enns (1997) conducted research on elements of the therapeutic process and their association with the retrieval of sexual abuse memories from the patient's viewpoint that supports this perspective. Reviere (1996) discussed the therapist's role and function in considerable detail:

> The therapist must be able (1) to establish in the client a trust in the therapist's ability to accept, label, and hold strong emotions; (2) to structure and pace the therapy work in a manner that enhances client safety and minimizes risk of retraumatization; (3) to bear witness to the reexperience of often horrific traumatic events; (4) to maintain clear, consistent, and safe boundaries; and (5) to contain the initial chaos and fear in facing the traumatic events. Finally, the therapist should normalize and validate the client's early and current responses to known traumas and provide education about traumatic sequelae and the process of trauma work, including possible risks and benefits. (p. 112)

Trauma resolution is furthered by addressing any related issues and weighing the need for any specific courses of action. In this phase of treatment, patients might struggle with such diverse issues as seeking corroboration or outside evidence that the abuse/trauma occurred, disclosing and being open about their abuse history with selected friends and associates, breaking silence and maintaining assertiveness in the family (especially if abuse was intrafamilial and in the face of ongoing responses of denial and scapegoating), attempting mediation and reconciliation with family members, deciding whether or not to forgive family members, developing self-protection strategies when faced with ongoing mistreatment, reporting past or current abuse, and initiating criminal or civil proceedings. Whenever possible, all of these courses of action are best decided after the major trauma work is completed and the patient is in a stable enough emotional state to be able to implement actions and deal with any repercussions without decompensating. Interestingly, however, these strategies might lead to additional memory accessibility or the confirmation or clarification of what has been remembered. Corroboration and/or discussion with family and friends sometimes provides additional detail to what is already available.

The Late Phase:
Self and Relational Development and
Life Reconsolidation and Restructuring

The gains achieved over the course of treatment, development of a self less encumbered by traumatic intrusions and effects, and continued development of interpersonal connections are consolidated and built upon in this third phase. Nevertheless, in keeping with the view of this model as spiraling and recursive rather than linear, attention continues to be directed to personality issues, self and emotional development, mood stability, personal safety, self-care, and personal boundary management as they are needed. These issues tend to mature and resolve in this phase of the process as they become more meaningful and understandable to the patient, but they might require further therapeutic attention in the aftermath of phase two. Additional major foci of the late stage are the establishment and continuance of secure social connections, an accumulation of restitutive emotional experiences both with the therapist and with trustworthy others (van der Kolk, 1996), and a revitalization of the individual. Physiological stabilization and the amelioration of the most distressing symptoms continues in this phase. With the resolution and integration of the trauma, some patients become relatively symptom free while others find that their physiological arousal and symptoms lessen but don't entirely remit.

Unfortunately, it is not unusual for this phase to involve additional losses along with its substantive gains. Pockets of unexpected and unresolved trauma and trauma-related issues may emerge and require supplementary second phase work. This should not be interpreted as signifying therapeutic failure; rather, it is in a sense "mopping up." Previous relationships (those with parents, siblings, and other relatives, spouses/intimate partners, children, friends, colleagues, and coworkers) may need rebalancing to accommodate the patient's newfound personal and interpersonal maturation and assertiveness. Some relationships will adaptively grow and change, while others will falter and end. Additional issues, such as sexual difficulties and dysfunctions and addictions and compulsions, may become amenable to therapeutic influence only during this phase, once core traumatic issues have been resolved. These issues are best treated with modified therapeutic strategies designed to include attention to their traumatic etiology or posttraumatic adaptation. For example, specialized techniques to treat sexual difficulties, addictions, and eating disorders have been developed for abuse survivors with these concerns (Evans & Sullivan, 1995; Maltz, 1991; Schwartz & Cohn, 1996; Westerlund, 1992).

Finally, in this phase, survivors may begin or accelerate the development of aspects of their lives that were attenuated by the trauma and its aftermath. Educational and occupational endeavors, friendships and intimate relationships, spiritual and religious activities, recreational activities and hobbies may all develop in a way that was not previously possible. Trauma resolution can open many prematurely foreclosed avenues, and the growth and development achieved in this phase of treatment can be very gratifying to both therapist and patient. Survivors might also have a need to take some sort of action to commemorate their experience or to help others. "Survivor missions" often serve an important function by allowing patients to do something active and meaningful to memorialize and share their experience with others who were similarly mistreated.

The final task of treatment is its ending, a most poignant, exhilarating, and difficult endeavor. The therapeutic relationship is especially significant and restorative for individuals who resolve the interpersonal betrayals of abuse; therefore, its ending is usually profound. Termination frequently stirs up feelings of abandonment, grief, fear, and related feelings, so sufficient time must be allotted for emotional ventilation and assimilation. Quintana (1993) has recently suggested a modification in the view of termination of psychotherapy from loss to transformation that is very applicable to this population. In his words:

> In short, the termination-as-transformation approach focuses less narrowly on loss and more broadly on the view that termination is a critical transition that can promote transformations in the therapist-client relationship and in how clients view themselves, their therapists, and their therapies. These transformations may promote therapeutic internalizations. . . . Thus, the most important transformation in therapist-client relationship is not that it is lost or ended but that it becomes progressively updated. Termination is a particularly critical opportunity for clients and therapists to update or transform their relationship to incorporate clients' growth. For this transformation to occur, clients need to acknowledge the steps they have taken toward more mature functioning. . . . With encouragement, clients may internalize this positive view of themselves and internalize images of their therapists that support these newly developed self-concepts. These positive internalizations

could supply clients with resources to confront future crises. Rigid adherence to uncovering loss reactions during termination may unnecessarily detract from clients' internalization of these positive achievements. (pp. 429–430)

This view supports the perspective that is taken throughout this book. The therapeutic process should be set up as a collaborative and empowering one that allows temporary dependence on the therapeutic relationship as a foundation for personal growth and transformation and for relational development. Patients are expected to grow and develop at their own pace over the course of treatment and should be able to own and be proud of their therapeutic and life accomplishments. They leave treatment with the resources to be more in control of their lives.

Although termination should be clearly demarcated for both therapeutic and liability purposes, a return for additional work in the future should not necessarily be precluded. The patient might need an occasional "tune-up" or "check-in" for minor concerns that might arise. More extensive work might be called for if the individual experiences a major resurgence of symptoms or period of destabilization. These often result from unanticipated triggers, a crisis of some sort, latent developmental precipitants, or the cyclical decompensation associated with chronic PTSD identified by Wang et al., (1996). Because of the possibility of a patient's return, the therapist should scrupulously guard against blurred boundaries or the development of a dual relationship after the formal treatment has ended. Abuse/trauma survivors, more than any other therapeutic population, must be assured that the therapeutic relationship is unencumbered by conflicted role relationships, so that a return to the "safe place" is possible if needed (Herman, 1992b).

SUMMARY

This chapter has outlined the philosophy underlying posttrauma treatment (PTT) for patients who have memories of abuse accompanied by posttraumatic and dissociative symptoms. Its use might also be properly considered with patients who exhibit characteristic symptoms and who have reasons to suspect abuse, but whose memory of abuse is variable or hazy. The consensus model of posttrauma treatment is evolving as new clinical and research findings become available. As it is currently conceptualized, it has three main phases in addition to the pretreatment assessment: (1) the initial or early phase of stabilization, alliance-building, safety, self-care, self-functions, and support; (2) the middle phase of deconditioning, resolution and personal integration of past trauma; and (3) the last phase self and relational development and reconsolidation. Each of the three phases has associated therapeutic tasks. The model is best conceptualized as a spiral rather than a straight line, with progress expected to occur in hierarchical, stepwise, and recursive fashion.

We now turn to a discussion of clinical guidelines and risk management for assessment and treatment of traumatized and possibly traumatized individuals in the next two chapters.

Chapter 7

CLINICAL GUIDELINES AND RISK MANAGEMENT FOR ASSESSMENT AND DIAGNOSIS

A buse and other forms of trauma are commonly found in the background of a significant percentage of individuals who seek mental health services. A therapist who is a generalist and provides psychotherapy for a range of psychological issues is likely to come across cases of past sexual abuse and recovered memory (however, a trauma specialist is obviously more likely to come across these cases). This is due to the high proportion of individuals who seek treatment for mental health concerns that are a direct or indirect consequence of a previous history of childhood abuse and traumatization. Available statistics from a number of studies indicate a high percentage of reported prior abuse in the general population and in both outpatient and inpatient psychotherapy populations. Moreover, as discussed in previous chapters, certain diagnoses (PTSD, the dissociative disorders, depression, anxiety, and borderline personality) have been found to have a significant correlation with a history of childhood abuse and trauma.

Therapists have the responsibility to conduct a comprehensive and factual assessment of individuals who seek psychotherapy and to diagnose accurately, especially important endeavors in light of the current controversy. Therapists have been accused of being simplistic and reductionistic in assessing a past history of abuse by relying on symptom checklists or an individual's appearance and presentation style to make a diagnosis (i.e., "I could tell just by looking at her that she was an abuse survivor") or by offering an "instant" diagnosis after a preliminary meeting or even over the phone without the benefit of a face-to-face meeting

(Loftus, 1993). Obviously, these are not professionally endorsed methods of assessment and diagnosis. Therapists are expected to conduct a formal assessment in line with professional standards and ethics. They must, however, "walk a fine line" and conduct an assessment that neither suppresses nor suggests a history of abuse or other trauma.

Historically, therapists have not included questions about these issues as part of their assessments or have routinely disregarded or negated disclosures of abuse due to their own denial or discomfort. As a result, issues of abuse and trauma have been substantially underreported and suppressed, often to the detriment of the individual in treatment (Courtois, 1988; Gelinas, 1983; Jacobson & Herald, 1990; Rieker & Carmen, 1986). However it occurs, this nonrecognition or suppression of a real abuse history is problematic because it reinforces one of the most insidious and damaging dynamics associated with abuse, namely secrecy, forced silence, and the resultant lack of validation. In contrast, therapists are now accused of going to the other extreme and suggesting abuse where none exists. Some critics have gone so far as to imply that even asking about abuse constitutes suggestion, a criticism rejected as overwrought by most clinicians. The present consensus on the subject is in accord with Lindsay's view that ". . . research does not support the notion that people are likely to develop illusory memories of traumatic events in response to a few straightforward questions" (Lindsay, 1997, p. 6).

A more systematized assessment approach is clearly needed to remedy errors of suppression or suggestion, one that is based upon neutrality and a broad-based assessment as a starting point. While such a strategy is recommended, it is not feasible in every clinical setting. It may be limited by an individual's unwillingness to spend the time, by insurance coverage limitations and the individual's ability to pay or, alternatively, by the therapist's theoretical orientation or cultural and professional norms (Peter Dale, personal communication, 1996) or other factors. Nevertheless, even when the opportunity to evaluate is attenuated for some reason, it still behooves the therapist to spend some time on a wide-ranging preliminary assessment and to maintain as comprehensive a record as possible of the same.

Assessment should be conceptualized as a process that occurs over time rather than as a one-time event. Recurrent assessments build upon the original evaluation and should be routinely undertaken when the treatment plan is reviewed and updated. They are also required if and when new symptoms and problems emerge. It is now well recognized that, early on, abused and traumatized individuals can be difficult to assess accurately (Briere, 1997a, Carlson, 1997; Courtois, 1995a). They often present with masked symptoms and/or nondisclosure of their history due to a number of psychological and posttraumatic defenses, the most prominent being shame, mistrust, denial, and dissociation. Some issues and symptoms become evident or are disclosed only after therapy is underway, often when some trust has developed. Symptoms (and memories) may emerge when the individual is triggered in some way or defenses lessen or fail (either within or outside of treatment) or, paradoxically, when the individual begins to get better (Briere, 1996b, 1997b). Whatever the case, the therapist should consider recurrent assessments as a routine part of the treatment process, both to monitor progress and to assess newly available symptom, clues, and memories.

ASSESSMENT AS A BASELINE AND AS A PROCESS

Assessment begins with an intake interview and a comprehensive psychosocial evaluation undertaken from social, behavioral, psychosexual, and biological perspectives (and may possibly warrant a medical examination as well to rule in or rule out physical illness). Notes of the intake assessment provide a baseline of information about the individual's status at the start of treatment. They thus make up an important foundation of the clinical record and provide documentation of the therapist's careful attention to assessment as the basis of the treatment plan versus a rush to premature diagnosis and treatment.

As part of the initial assessment, most therapists conduct at least a limited mental status examination and record their observations about the individual's presentation, including appearance, behavior, personality traits, and general cognitive functioning. This is expanded upon, when indicated. The overall evaluation encompasses questions about a range of issues, beginning with basic demographic information; the individual's reason for seeking treatment (the chief complaint); a review of predominant symptoms—their onset, sequence, course and duration; previous episodes and treatment; and past and current stressors. A second major area of inquiry involves the individual's personal and social history, including an overview of major personal events and developmental milestones across the lifespan; family history and status; past medical history (including gynecological/obstetrical history for women, major illnesses or injury); and any involvement in the legal/criminal justice system. Also included is attention to the individual's cultural background, social class, religion, ethnicity, sexual orientation (if disclosed), or any other issue that might shape the presentation or the individual's perspective. A third area of inquiry gives attention to clinical signs, symptoms, and personality and diagnostic indicators (e.g., mood disturbances; reality-testing and psychosis; predominant defensive operations and characterological structure; substance use and abuse; personal, relational, sexual, and social/vocational problems; anxiety and associated problems; suicidality and other forms of self-harm; risk of interpersonal violence) and their respective onset, duration, intensity, degree of disruption, and subjective level of distress. It is also very important to assess the individual's personal assets, strengths, and resiliency factors as well as significant supports.

It is essential that questions about past or current abuse (physical, sexual, and emotional), current safety and risk of violence to or from others, domestic violence and other important family dysfunction such as substance abuse and history of major mental illness, and additional crises and trauma during the individual's lifetime (e.g., significant losses, accidents or disasters, major illnesses and medical emergencies and/or trauma) are asked routinely, interspersed within the general areas of questioning. Inquiries about interpersonal violence and trauma are quite sensitive. They may generate strong affect in both therapist and patient. Since attention to these issues has not been habitually included in professional training, asking about them may be uncomfortable for the practitioner. As a consequence, these topics have generally been underassessed, bypassed, or omitted entirely. Omission has several untoward consequences. It conveys to the prospective patient that these topics are unimportant and/or so shameful or aberrant that they cannot be discussed. Unfortunately, this usually results in the nondisclosure of potentially crucial information. Recent studies of disclosure patterns in psychiatric patients have found that nondisclosure of abuse and other trauma was oftentimes due to the fact that these issues were never asked about. Nondisclosure is sometimes the result of the patient protecting the clinician from discomfort or distress. Alternatively, some respondents reported disclosing abuse/trauma only to have the clinician ignore, disregard, downplay, or otherwise minimize it (Courtois, 1988; Jacobson & Herald, 1990; Josephson & Fong-Beyette, 1987). For individuals who experienced abuse, a context of nonrecognition and nonacknowledgement may replicate early experiences and reinforce nondisclosure and silencing. Similarly, protecting authority and/or attachment figures through silence may constitute a replay of old abuse dynamics.

Inquiries about abuse, violence, and trauma must be in keeping with inquiries about other issues or symptoms so that they are unobtrusive and don't stand out. It is best that they are asked neutrally using descriptive, behavioral language and an open-ended format (i.e., "did you ever experience such and such?"; "did such and such ever happen to you?"; "please tell me about it"; "can you tell me any more about it?") to counter the view that all questions about abuse/trauma are suggestive. Open-ended questions are designed to elicit free recall—the interviewee describes the situation in his/her own words, which are then recorded verbatim by the therapist. The style of questioning should be objective yet supportive and the therapist must be prepared to ask for details in follow-up questioning and to hear responses without minimizing them or downplaying their significance. A number of research studies have been consistent in showing that disclosure of past abuse and trauma is influenced by what terminology is used, how questions are phrased, and the attitude and manner of the examiner (Dalenberg, 1996; Josephson & Fong-Beyette, 1987). Disclosure of difficult and shameful material occurs most readily when the interviewer is perceived to be open to the revelations, empathic, and nonjudgmental. At the same time, the therapist must be objective and neutral rather than leading or overinvested in finding abuse when making these inquiries and should avoid repetitive questions. The importance of the patient's controlling disclosure cannot be overstated. "Time spent discussing fears and fantasies about disclosure is time well-spent: patients are reassured that *they* can decide when, where, and how much to disclose" (Brainin-Rodriguez, 1997, p. 142). This strategy has the additional advantage of avoiding any appearance of being suggesting or leading.

A number of other areas of exploration are recommended in conducting a broad-based assessment, especially when abuse or possible abuse and recovered memories are at issue. It behooves the therapist to ask about other therapy experiences, past and present, and to request a release of information for records. Inquiry should also be made concerning the reason for seeking treatment in the past, diagnosis (if known to the individual), the duration, course, and type of therapy, whether the individual found it helpful and improved while in treatment (or alternatively, found it unhelpful and deteriorated), conditions of termination, and why the individual is seeking a different therapist. In particular, the evaluator should ascertain whether the previous therapist seemed overinvested in an abuse hypothesis or diagnosis (i.e., past incest, ritual abuse, DID) or pushed one on the patient, whether the treatment involved the (extensive) use of suggestive techniques, and/or whether the individual recovered memories while in treatment. If so, the therapist should record in some detail the therapeutic approach that was taken, the memories that emerged, and the patient's perspective on the previous treatment and the recovered memories. This information should be included along with the previous therapist's records in the patient's chart, to provide baseline documentation.

Another area to be queried involves personal and financial resources.

Inquiries need to be made about the individual's living situation, personal support network, financial and job security, and health-care funding. A treatment plan must be built that is in keeping with available resources. The plan should start with attention to deficit areas that, once bolstered, provide a foundation upon on which to proceed (i.e., building up a personal support system, finding stable housing, finding steady employment, getting health insurance or disability coverage, getting additional case management or social services). It is clearly not helpful if a treatment is proposed that exceeds the individual's ability to manage or to pay for it or that further destabilizes an already precarious living situation. Both therapist and patient must be aware of and realistic about any funding limitations and must work collaboratively on a plan that supports the best use of available resources. Strategizing in this way counters the criticism that therapists are overly invested in long-term treatments that fully deplete the patient's personal and insurance resources and that result in personal and lifestyle deterioration.

In the assessment phase and throughout the treatment process as necessary, the therapist should consider adjunctive consultations and testing for corollary medical, psychiatric, substance abuse, or neurological conditions. Any and all of these might have implications for memory impairment that should be ruled out wherever necessary. Other adjunctive services to be considered pertain to rehabilitation and vocational services or testing for learning difficulties and disorders. A second opinion might prove useful even after a comprehensive assessment work up in cases that remain complicated or perplexing and when the therapist has residual concerns about the scope of the symptom picture, the diagnosis, and treatment recommendations. It might additionally prove useful to provide another professional perspective on any recovered memory material.

Suggestibility, hypnotizability, and any other risk factors associated with the production of false memories (such as dependent and hystrionic personality, fantasy-proneness, a high need to please and to comply with authority figures) should be evaluated in a general way as part of the initial assessment and in more detail where it seems warranted. Scales for the evaluation of hypnotizability (Hammond, 1990; Spiegel & Spiegel, 1978) and suggestibility (Gudjonsson, 1984) are available and personality characteristics can be assessed using generic personality measures such as the Minnesota Multiphasic Personality Inventory-2 (MMPI-2) and the Millon Clinical Multi-axial Inventory-III (MCMI-III), as described below. The therapist will want to be especially cautious and circumspect in working with the highly suggestible patient. Once this information is evident, the therapist should inform the patient of the vulnerability for the production of false memories that is found with high levels of suggestibility/hypnotizability and with various personality factors. These issues are discussed more in the next chapter as they relate to memory recovery.

One final area of exploration is recommended: determining whether the individual has undertaken, is currently involved in, or is contemplating a lawsuit or other legal action, for any reason but particularly for past abuse on the basis of recovered memory. Until recently, this has not been a standard area of inquiry; however, it is now prudent and expedient to ask because the stakes have been raised by the controversy. The therapist needs to know about litigation that might, at some point in time, call for his/her involvement in the forensic setting and that might affect the decision to treat in the first place. At present, some therapists choose not to provide treatment that will involve any forensic involvement on their part. A worse case scenario involves an individual who, at assessment, is in the process of litigation (of any sort but especially having to do with previous abuse and/or recovered memory issues) but does not disclose it to the therapist, who, once the treatment is underway, is then later called upon to provide testimony. This situation is further complicated if the memories forming the basis of the lawsuit were recovered during therapy (past or present) and if the defense strategy involves the therapist being accused of creating conditions or using techniques that suggested or implanted the memories.

Inquiry about forensic involvement is mandated due to another area of potential risk: the restriction of the use of certain therapeutic techniques while a forensic case is open due to their potential to undermine the case. Courts have taken a fairly consistent stance in disqualifying testimony based on memories that were hypnotically refreshed. Consequently, the therapist should not use hypnosis or a similar technique when a patient is involved in any type of litigation. Therapists have been sued for causing the disqualification of testimony through the use of hypnosis, even when it was not used for the purposes of memory retrieval or refreshment (see Scheflin & Shapiro, 1989 for a graphic example of such a lawsuit against a therapist by a patient for the inadvertent disqualification of the individual's ability to provide testimony. Hypnosis was used for symptom relief after a rape and its use unfortunately undermined the criminal rape case).

We now consider some of the special issues concerning abuse/trauma disclosure that arise during the assessment process.

When Abuse/Trauma Is Disclosed during the Assessment

When abuse or other trauma is made known during the course of the assessment, the therapist should *record the information factually and objec-*

tively as reported. This provides documentation in the individual's own words and works against the implication of therapist suggestion. A description of the abuse/trauma should be obtained in as much detail as is feasible without unduly overwhelming or destabilizing the individual. As discussed earlier, questions are best asked in an open-ended, matter-of-fact, and objective manner, from a position of empathy, concern, and support. The therapist inquires about the nature and particulars of the abuse/trauma (who, what, when, where, how long, severity, progression, use of force, any physical injury, the individual's role, actions taken or not, and subjective thoughts and feelings about its occurrence and its effects, etc.). Since even questions about the details can be very upsetting, the therapist must monitor the individual's responses and reactions and be prepared to slow or even curtail the questioning.

Inquiry is also made as to whether memory for the reported abuse has been continuous, whether there have been or are memory gaps, and/or whether there have been periods when memory was inaccessible or unavailable. The therapist should also ascertain whether the individual has experienced other traumatic events and circumstances, including past and current revictimizations (Courtois, 1988; Scurfield, 1985; van der Kolk, et al., 1996) and the degree of memory intactness for these events.

When past abuse/trauma is disclosed, the therapist evaluates for possible posttraumatic reactions (intrusive reexperiencing, autonomic hyperarousal, numbing of responsiveness and affect, substance abuse and other addictive/compulsive behaviors, intense emotional states, learning difficulties, memory disturbances and dissociation, medical problems and psychosomatic reactions, interpersonal difficulties, and criminal justice or legal difficulties). Inquiry should also be made about the individual's current level of safety in terms of self-harm and violence to and from others. As discussed in chapter 3, it is quite common to discover further victimization and trauma along with suicidality, self-injury, and extreme personal disregard and risk-taking in a subgroup of abuse survivors. Reports of ongoing interpersonal violence such as battering are fairly common and thus also need assessment attention. Physical damage sustained via self-injury or interpersonal violence may be implicated in memory loss and should be assessed.

The therapist must ask questions regarding these issues in direct but supportive fashion, all the while staying attuned to the toll the questioning might be taking and modifying the pace and intensity accordingly. Some victimized individuals have the capacity to respond to such detailed questioning without much discomfort (this may be due to their well-honed ability to separate cognition from affect—to present "just the facts" without the emotions), but others experience strong reactions and need to answer the questions slowly over a more extended period of time. Others show no outward reactions but report delayed or rebound responses either in the session or later. And others dissociate all or part of the assessment and later deny or are confused about their responses to the questions. In addition to the therapist's ongoing titration of the detail, intensity, and range of the questioning according to the individual's observable response, it is good policy to offer cautions about the possibility and the normalcy of delayed reactions and to offer suggestions for managing any that arise.

At some point, the therapist might wish to follow up this preliminary and more generic assessment of the traumatic event(s) with one that has a more organized and formalized format. A number of structured assessment measures are now available. These are identified and discussed later in this chapter.

A most difficult circumstance arises when, upon assessment, the patient reports abuse based on recall mechanisms that were not available at the time and/or reports abuse that is improbable or clearly impossible. Where such a disclosure is made in terms of erroneous information about memory ("I remember being abused in my crib when I was 3 months old"), the therapist should give corrective information about memory (the offset of infantile or childhood amnesia does not occur until approximately age 2½ or later) and can still offer to explore family and historical circumstances with the individual. It is possible (given that prevalence studies have found that much sexual abuse occurs preverbally and that sexual abuse of neonates have been reported) that abuse in the crib occurred at 3 months of age and should not be entirely discounted. Patterns of family dysfunction, other abuse that occurred later in childhood and is remembered, symptoms of PTSD/DD might all favor the abuse hypothesis. Both the misinformation about memory and the provision of correct information should be noted in the chart.

Where less probable, improbable, or impossible forms of abuse are reported ("I was abused in a cult and forced to participate in rituals involving murdering and eating babies"; "I was repeatedly raped and used as a baby breeder in a cult—I had four babies pulled from me by the time I was 9 years old"; "I was abused over and over in a past life"; "My current abuse is punishment for my activities in a past life") the therapist has an even more complex assessment task that involves not discounting the patient while not accepting the information as factual and in this way validating or reinforcing it. Schwarz (1996) has warned against what he has labeled *magnification*, where the therapist takes a report either of improbable abuse or suggests it to the patient in the first place. It is known that organized, ritualistic, religiously-based, and satanic abuse does occur but that available evidence suggests that satanic abuse occurs with much less frequency than many have assumed and, further, that assumptions about frequency may depend more on the perspective and belief of the treating psychotherapist than on objective circumstances (Goodman, Bottoms, Qin, & Shaver, 1993; Mulhern, 1994). Research findings also suggest that religiously-based abuse may be more common than has been previously assumed. In any event, with improbable and highly improbable abuse reports, the therapist must maintain a position of informed skepticism yet remain open to the possibility that parts of the report are true or that the report is actually a screen memory for other abuse experiences that are more difficult for the patient to face (i.e., incestuous abuse). In cases of this sort, the seeking of collateral information that might confirm or discomfirm such a report should be seriously considered. Also, where allegations of ongoing current abuse are made, the therapist should consider duty to warn and duty to protect responsibilities, including reporting or encouraging a report to police. Extensive notes of the patient's verbatim statements about the alleged abuse should be maintained in the chart.

When Abuse/Trauma Is Not Disclosed during the Assessment

Abuse/trauma is often not disclosed for a variety of reasons. The abuse might be known but deliberately not divulged due to shame, guilt, self-blame, fear, mistrust, the protection of others, family loyalty, and previous negative experience with disclosure. Or, it might not be known or even suspected due to memory suppression or disruption or not be known explicitly, but suspected. Additionally, as Lindsay has pointed out, there may be no disclosure because abuse did not occur and therefore there is no abuse to report (D. Stephen Lindsay, personal communication, 1994). Where uncertainty is the case, the individual's expectations in seeking treatment must be carefully assessed and may need to be reworked or even challenged. For example, some expectations are realistic (e.g., "I want help determining if there is any basis to my suspicions," or "I want to determine if something I'm not sure about is causing my symptoms"), while others are unrealistic and even potentially hazardous to the individual or the therapist (e.g., "I want you to *tell me* that I was abused so that I understand my problems or so that I can sue my parents;" "My friends/support group tell me I act like I was abused but I don't remember, so I might as well find out"; "I want to find out if I was really abused so then I'd have a reason to kill myself").

As a general matter, the therapist should not make assumptions regarding the meaning of a lack of disclosure—the most obvious meaning is that the individual does not have an abuse/trauma history to report. Yet, when the individual's symptom picture is acute and/or has a strong resemblance to the comorbid complex dissociative PTSD formulation discussed earlier or when the therapist observes certain behavioral and response patterns commonly associated with trauma (such as dissociation in the session or a high degree of personal risk-taking, substance abuse, chronic self-harm and suicidality, and/or a history of revictimization), the possibility of undisclosed or unrecognized abuse or other trauma or forms or abuse that often go unrecognized (extreme neglect, attachment abuse, or emotional abuse) should be considered. In such a case, the therapist might maintain a degree of suspicion or develop a hypothesis but must also accept the patient's not knowing and/or not disclosing. In some highly traumatized individuals, the story will emerge only in a disguised and fragmented manner that requires patience and diligence on the part of the therapist. It may also only emerge when the individual has advanced enough in the treatment tasks of early stage treatment to have the ego resources and self capacities to support recall. Campbell, Courtois, Enns, Gottlieb, and Wells (1995) discussed these issues:

> In cases of long-term trauma, the client may not have experienced the necessary conditions for acquiring a coherent, consolidated sense of self or may have encountered ongoing abuse in adulthood that resulted in significant disruptions of the client's self structure. The consequences of long-term abuse may be manifested through a wide range of problems in defining and integrating aspects of the self, including identity confusion or fragmentation, the tendency to experience normally integrated process as separate aspects of the self, and distortions of body image or personal esteem. Furthermore, the client may exhibit behaviors such as either-or thinking, affective instability, impulsivity, rapid shifts in emotional or cognitive states, or self-injurious behavior. Careful assessment regarding the strength and nature of the client's self-structure is necessary for planning optimal interventions and establishing whether the client is prepared to deal with traumatic memories. (p. 3)

The therapist must be especially circumspect and cautious when abuse is not known but is suspected, even when the basis for suspicion is quite compelling (e.g., when dream content is replete with abuse scenarios or when diagnostic formulations and behavioral reenactments and abreactions within or outside of the therapy seem to point to past abuse) (Brenneis, 1997). It is expedient to inquire about how the individual came to suspect abuse in the absence of specific memory and to assess possible personal and interpersonal motivations, including secondary gain, loss, and/or revenge, malingering, whether certain diagnoses are egosyntonic to the individual and why, and any sources of suggestion and misinformation (e.g., social influences, media reports, books, previous suggestive therapeutic activities, etc.). It may, at times, be necessary for the therapist to explain to the individual that his/her memory has been possibly influenced and to urge an open-ended exploratory stance. The therapist must also be prepared to correct misinformation about abuse and memory processes and to clarify appropriate goals of treatment (and should explicitly note both the misinformation and the correction in the chart).

Additional evaluation of other risk factors associated with possible false memory production, such as personal motivation to find abuse, and fantasy-proneness, hypnotizability, interrogatory suggestibility, paranoia, malingering, and psychosis, is called for in some cases. It is necessary to underscore that psychosis does not automatically rule out the occurrence of abuse. Positive symptoms of psychosis have been documented in samples of PTSD patients (Butler, Mueser, Sprock & Braff, 1996) and abuse has been documented as a common occurrence in the background of a subset of psychotic patients (Read, 1997). Psychotic and posttraumatic symptoms can co-occur, and/or psychotic symptoms might, in reality, be posttraumatic intrusion/reexperiencing of real abuse. Many posttraumatic and dissociative patients have been misdiagnosed as schizophrenic and the reality of their past experiences downplayed or ignored (Ellason & Ross, 1995; Ellenson, 1986; Kluft, 1987).

Yet, *when specific memory is absent, it is crucially important that the therapist not speculate about, fill in, or confirm suspicions of a nonremembered abuse history.* The individual needs to come to a personal understanding and may need to withstand considerable uncertainty, especially when corroboration is lacking. The clinician must avoid leading or assumptive questions that put the individual in a double bind and must also abstain from a premature focus on sexual abuse as the only possible explanation of an individual's distress (e.g., "You *must have been* sexually abused to have those symptoms"; "You have all the characteristics of an abuse survivor. You *must have repressed* the abuse and are in denial"; "You have a 70 % chance of having been sexually abused due to your substance abuse/eating disorder—can you remember the abuse?"). Alternatively, as discussed above, exploration should not be curtailed in such a way that reports of abuse or other trauma are dismissed prematurely. Many survivors may never have been in an interpersonal context that supported their phenomenological knowing about abuse on a consistent basis (Courtois,

1992; Roth & Batson, 1997). Therapy can provide such a context, but the establishment of adequate self-capacities and trust in the therapist, of necessity, take time.

Where no conscious memory of suspected abuse is available, the therapist needs to maintain a middle-ground stance and an exploratory approach that is conveyed to the prospective patient. This can be done verbally and through written material such as the American Psychiatric Association statement outlining recommended therapeutic approaches to delayed memories (APA, 1993). Some individuals, especially those seeking therapy and techniques for the explicit purpose of "finding their missing memories," may be resistant to information about memory processes that counters their beliefs and unwilling to work within an exploratory framework. Perhaps the best recourse when such a discrepancy in perspectives arises is for the individual to seek out other practitioners with whom s/he may be more compatible. Hopefully, at some point, the individual will arrive at the conclusion that s/he is better off with a therapist who does not insist on a certain perspective or a certain reality, who "honestly holds judgment in abeyance," and "who is not afraid to express uncertainty about the etiology of a particular problem" (Knapp & VandeCreek, 1997, pp. 60-61). In any event, the individual's disagreement with the therapist's unwillingness to provide a certain perspective or to offer speculations should be documented in the record.

Assessment during Crises

An especially difficult circumstance arises when the individual initially seeks treatment in a state of crisis, making assessment at once more imperative and more difficult. The crisis may be of a general sort, brought on by stressful events, substance abuse, relationship discord and loss, mood disorders, the emergence or worsening of symptoms, problems in functioning, etc., and resulting in a range of standard crisis responses. Or, it may be more posttraumatic, brought on by acute, chronic, or delayed reactions to all forms of trauma (current or past, whether remembered or not) and delayed/recovered memory triggered by a wide variety of external events and cues and/or internal reactions. The posttraumatic type of crisis usually develops from the onset of a range of intrusive symptoms (including flashbacks and recollections that may or may not have been previously available), numbing symptoms (including memory loss, depersonalization, derealization), and intolerable hyperarousal and startle reaction in response to both continuous and recovered memories. The posttraumatic presentation also typically includes past and current episodes of revictimization (including family violence of all sorts), acute self-harm and suicidality, homicidality, substance abuse, in addition to general life chaos and recurrent periods of destabilization. Dissociative reactions may be prominent in crisis presentations and include complaints of loss of identity/consciousness/personal memory, time loss, and fugue states. In dissociative identity disorder, a lack of control over dissociative processes (e.g., uncontrollable rapid switching of personality states, the emergence and functioning of personality states outside of the individual's control, behavior that is contradictory to the individual's normal behavior, fugue episodes, conversion symptoms, etc.) may be apparent. The emergence of delayed/recovered memories of previously unremembered abuse/trauma can be extremely unnerving and destabilizing in its own right and even more so when accompanied by florid posttraumatic and dissociative symptoms (sometimes accompanied by profound depression, panic, hallucinations, and/or strong urges to self-harm and suicide). Individuals in this situation might present with the objective of either having the therapist confirm or deny the reality of the memory to make the symptoms go away.

With a crisis presentation, the therapist is placed in the difficult circumstance of assisting someone in an urgent situation with little or no knowledge to work from. The therapist must make a rapid, broad-brush assessment of the individual's distress and symptoms and the degree of danger to or from self and others, with the immediate aim of safety, stabilization, and containment. In such a compelling situation, the therapist might be tempted to bypass or forego the type of assessment described above in favor of beginning treatment straightaway. While de-escalation and stabilization are certainly the primary tasks during a crisis, assessment prior to treatment is still necessary. The therapist is better off conducting whatever assessment is possible during the crisis stabilization phase (however long that takes and whatever strategies must be utilized) and then moving back into an assessment mode to establish both a diagnosis and a treatment plan.

In particular, with a crisis precipitated by or involving posttraumatic, dissociative, and delayed/recovered memory issues, the therapist must avoid prematurely confirming or denying the possibility of an abuse history, joining with the patient and taking on his/her perspective while abdicating a stance of professional objectivity and evaluation, and, in the heat of the crisis, using techniques and approaches that are suggestive. In such a circumstance, the therapist might be tempted to take a self-reported experience or diagnosis at face value, especially when presented with an individual in a state of extreme distress and decompensation who is experiencing florid symptoms.

Several examples serve to illustrate situations of this sort. In one case, an individual reported very distressing recovered memories of having been in a cult and being abused in a group setting from a very early age. She also reported memories of having participated in killing babies from a young age as part of the cult's indoctrination. This young woman presented for treatment in a suicidal crisis over these memories, saying she couldn't live with her guilt. The therapist took this individual's recovered memories at face value. He offered reassurance by telling her that she had engaged in these activities due to coercion and mind control and that children were never to blame for anything they did as children, especially anything involving abuse. He made no effort to learn more about how the individual had come to believe that she had been abused in a cult, for how long, and under what circumstances, before responding in ways that conveyed that her beliefs represented historical reality. He also did not make a diagnostic assessment.

In another case, an individual sought treatment while in a suicidal crisis, telling the therapist that she had been diagnosed with dissociative identity disorder and that one of her alter personalities was about to kill off another and in the process kill her. She further told the therapist that she had no control over the situation. Without inquiry as to when the DID diagnosis was made and by whom and without much further assessment, the therapist instructed the individual to "map her system" and worked with the ostensible alternate personalities involved in the suicide plan to stabilize them. While such a strategy is often used in the treatment of DID patients, in this case, the therapist prematurely accepted the diagnosis and then worked with it in a way that could be deemed reinforcing and suggestive, since no attempt was made to ascertain whether other factors or diagnoses could be at play.

In a third case, an individual sought treatment for uncontrollable abreactions that were reported to have begun spontaneously and that involved horrific abuse experiences. These were presented to the therapist as experiences of past life abuse. The therapist was swayed to believe them by their graphic presentation and the intensity of the individual's reactions and psychic pain. Past life abuse was accepted as factual and treated without consideration of other information or diagnoses.

As these examples show, a crisis situation does not exempt the therapist from making a preliminary evaluation, nor should it keep him/her from following the principles and recommendations made in this and the previous chapter. Furthermore, a crisis requires the use of interventions that de-escalate the situation while not inadvertently reinforcing it or supporting a diagnosis or a history that has not been formally evaluated. Standard interventions, including determinations of risk, safety, ego strength, and ability to tolerate affect and control impulses, the need for additional support and monitoring (e.g., family, friends, hotline contact, partial hospitalization, inpatient stabilization), should be made with the intention of steadying the individual and defusing the situation while not contributing to another difficulty.

Available instruments for assessing abuse and trauma are discussed next. Some of these are concise instruments with a limited number of items that require little time to complete. They are especially useful for rapid evaluation during a crisis situation.

TRAUMA ASSESSMENT: STRATEGIES, ISSUES, AND INSTRUMENTS

In recent years, increased attention has been given to the assessment of trauma in terms of rationale, strategies, and issues. A number of trauma-specific instruments have been developed and are useful when abuse/trauma has been disclosed or when the individual reports symptoms that appear to be posttraumatic and/or dissociative (with or without memory of precipitating events). They can be used to assess the circumstances of reported abuse/trauma and to screen for symptoms that accompany both disclosures and suspicions. Information derived from these trauma-sensitive and symptom-specific instruments might support or rebut suspected abuse when distinct memory is not available; yet, like other forms of indirect evidence, they obviously do not prove the reality of abuse suspicions.

The Process of Assessing Trauma

Successful psychological assessment of posttraumatic states, whether by diagnostic interview or formal psychological testing, typically includes the following characteristics: a neutral or positive, nonintrusive evaluation environment, inquiry that extends beyond the detection of trauma symptoms alone, awareness that clients may underreport or overreport traumatic events and symptoms, and an understanding of potential constraints on the interpretation of trauma-relevant psychological assessment data. (Briere, 1997b, p. 57)

As this quote implies, a number of issues and challenges are inherent in the assessment of both a possible trauma history and trauma symptoms. The evaluator must maintain a delicate balance in terms of the general stance and approach to the individual and in terms of neutrality of questions asked. Traumatized individuals can be difficult to engage due to many factors, some of which have to do with their posttraumatic history, reactions, and symptoms, as discussed previously. Some victims are closed and suspicious of the assessment and may resist offering any information that is a painful reminder of things they would rather not focus on and have actively avoided. Others may find direct questions overwhelming and destabilize during the course of an assessment, especially one that is badly paced or too focused on details. Their responses may, in turn, affect the assessor and cause countertransference and/or vicarious traumatization responses that must be carefully monitored and managed lest they interfere with or influence the assessment process and data (Pearlman & McCann, 1994). It is also the case that some individuals are immediately and obviously relieved to be asked about their trauma history and experience. The assessment may be the first time anyone has indicated interest in their experience and they may find the interview or testing (especially when conducted with sensitivity and attention to pacing and reactions) to be immediately cathartic and therapeutic.

In general, it is best if the practitioner approaches the assessment (whether a clinical interview or a testing session using structured instruments and self-report measures) from a position of supportive neutrality. A supportive yet neutral posture is recommended because the individual may be unable to disclose the trauma or its effects unless support and encouragement are offered during the assessment and yet impartiality must also be maintained. It is necessary for the evaluator to be carefully attuned to the individual and his/her clinical status during and after the process. S/he should strive to have a very calm and respectful demeanor and be prepared to be regarded with suspicion if not outright mistrust or hostility by some interviewees. By definition, trauma victims (especially those who have suffered severe and/or repeated interpersonal victimization, whether past, present, or both) have experienced danger and intrusion at the hands of others and may be quite guarded as a result. Being in a situation where they are asked to discuss highly personal events and reactions may feel invasive and like "salt in an open wound." This may, in turn, generate a protective, cautious, noncooperative, or even antagonistic stance on the part of the interviewee. Urquiza, Wyatt, and Goodlin-Jones (1997) and Pearlman and McCann (1994) have commented on the risks to the interviewer when assessing trauma victims in the countertransference or via vicarious traumatization. These responses on the part of the therapist may result from the difficult interpersonal context, from hearing about atrocities, and from identifying their painful and damaging consequences. These authors recommend the opportunity for training, debriefing, and support as necessary.

It is also useful for the practitioner to understand that the assessment process is likely to be quite stressful for many traumatized individuals no matter how gently or sensitively it is conducted. It is therefore essential to create assessment conditions and a testing environment that are as safe as possible and to develop a reasonable amount of rapport. This sometimes requires additional time at the outset, time well-spent if it allows the assessment to proceed. Interviewees should be encouraged to maintain as much control as possible and to engage in a collaborative assessment effort. They should be told directly that there is no right or wrong answer and that the assessor is not expecting particular responses. It is also helpful to advise them that although the testing circumstance is not intended to be hurtful, it may, by virtue of focusing on painful episodes, cause discomfort and upset. The request to describe traumatic events in some detail (whether verbally by interview or in written form via structured testing) can restimulate disturbing and painful material, in some cases causing distress where none had been previously, or in others, producing additional distress. Provision of information of this sort meets informed consent requirements.

The attentive evaluator must closely monitor the individual's reactions. At times, it will prove necessary to change the pacing or to suspend the assessment because it is overly unsettling but also because the individual's level of distress has the possibility of influencing or even contaminating the results. Shifting the pace and/or extending the testing time is thus in the interest of both the safety of the individual and the attainment of a valid and accurate assessment of the individual's status. When destabilization occurs in the session or in its aftermath (evidenced by flashbacks, regressive behaviors, numbing/dissociation, anger, anxiety, panic, suicidal ideation or action, episodes of self-harm, etc.) despite the evaluator's best efforts, the primary task is to restabilize the individual and to insure personal safety. In some cases, the testing can resume (with continued monitoring) after a return to stabilization; in other cases, the better course of action is to halt the process.

The assessment should be comprehensive and not only focused on trauma symptoms. In some cases, the assessment is necessarily oriented towards a determination of whether a traumatic experience is likely the proximate cause of posttraumatic reactions and symptoms as well as the individual's diagnosis and clinical status. This is especially the case when the evaluation is conducted for forensic purposes (e.g., civil litigation for psychological damages; criminal proceedings for an assault) and requires that the assessor carefully document the temporal emergence and sequence of reactions following the trauma and the nature and severity of the symptoms. The individual's clinical picture may not definitively correlate with prior abuse/trauma. Conditions of chronic or delayed PTSD, dissociative, or personality-related symptoms may develop in the aftermath of a number of the etiological circumstance(s) that occurred much earlier in the individual's life and, additionally, may have been influenced by a range of more recent events and issues. The evaluator can assess the general validity of the individual's abuse/trauma history and can only speculate about its relation to his/her symptoms and diagnosis. A comprehensive assessment should include attention to the individual's entire symptom and diagnostic picture, not only the posttraumatic. As discussed throughout this text, individuals with PTSD/DD often have a number of other coexisting or comorbid Axis I and Axis II disorders that create a complex clinical picture requiring ongoing monitoring and assessment.

Traumatized individuals may underreport or overreport their histories and symptoms, a circumstance that must also be anticipated. Adults' retrospective reports of trauma are subject to error from several sources. They may not report or may underreport past abuse or traumatic life experiences if questions about these experiences are imprecise, missing, or misunderstood. For example, when asked if she has even had "a traumatic experience" or an "experience outside the range of usual human experience," an individual might respond "No" if what happened is not understood as either traumatic or unusual. For this reason, it is necessary that questions be asked in behavioral and precise terms in open-ended form, yet as neutrally and calmly as possible (e.g., "Did you, as a child, ever have a sexual experience with an adult? . . . with a family member? . . . with another child?"; "Have you ever been exposed to violence between members of your family?"; "Have you ever been pressured into unwanted sexual contact of any sort?"). Individuals might also underreport in an attempt to hide the shameful and/or painful material from the evaluator or to protect the evaluator, especially if s/he gives any indication of aversion, judgment, or personal distress at hearing details about abuse/trauma.

Underreporting might obviously also result from memory difficulties ranging from poor encoding, storage, or retrieval of trauma memories; to motivated forgetting and avoidance; to partial or more continuous amnesia or lack of recall; to dissociation or the splitting off of aspects of the experience, including memory of its occurrence. Overreporting might also occur. Some of the following reasons have been identified for over-reporting: the desire for secondary gain (such as sympathy, attention, compensation and financial gain; retribution/vindictiveness; an explanation for life's problems—labeled the "abuse excuse" by some critics); delusions due to psychosis or other severe personality disturbance; memory errors, misunderstandings, and misperceptions; and personal traits of suggestibility or fantasy proneness that would increase the likelihood of compliance with suggestions from an authority figure. At present, it is unknown how often past trauma is overreported or reported in error, how much constitutes false memory or false belief, and how often it is under-reported or denied. The implication is that the practitioner must conduct the assessment with attention to possible exaggeration, on one hand, or underreporting, on the other.

Issues of gender, ethnicity, and culture are important to take into consideration and to address openly at the outset of the assessment. All may impact the interviewee's comfort level, ability to relate, interpretation of questions, and assignment of meaning. Optimally, the evaluator is someone with whom the individual can attain some degree of comfort and matching should be considered wherever practical or possible (for example, an interviewer of the same race, gender, or cultural background). Where this is not possible, additional care must be taken to be sensitive to the individual's comfort level and safety and to how the interview might be impacted. For example, a female sexually abused by a male might be markedly uncomfortable being asked questions referring to the sexual violation by a male interviewer. The interviewer might also be impacted and shift in his/her ability to ask detailed questions. Continuing with this example, the male interviewer may go to great lengths to avoid appearing voyeuristic and intrusive and fail to ask important questions about abuse experiences and subjective responses. Structured interviews and self-report measures can provide scripted and neutral but precise questions that offset personal responses. Additionally, care must be taken to make sure the individual is able to understand the rationale for the assessment and the questions. This might be an especially important consideration in cross-cultural interviews. Again, close monitoring is called for as the assessment progresses to determine the individual's ability to comprehend the questions and to phrase them in a way that they are understandable and tolerable. As with other issues, there may be times when misunderstanding, cultural meanings, or the stress are too great for the assessment to proceed and it is best to terminate the activity.

Assessment of both traumatic experiences and trauma-related symptoms will be more accurate if the evaluator uses instruments that have been constructed to assess psychological conditions and traumatization, that are psychometrically sound in terms of reliability and validity, and that are neutral and precise in terms of the questions asked. As discussed above, neutrality on the part of the evaluator and of the measurement items and questions helps minimize the effects of interviewer and client bias and expectations. Precision in the wording of measure items and interview questions also helps to reduce confusion and misunderstanding about what is being asked. In forensic cases in particular, where accuracy and neutrality are especially important, the assessment and treatment should be conducted by different professionals so that bias can be minimized and roles are not confounded.

Four types of abuse- and trauma-specific assessment instruments and strategies are available: (1) generic psychological testing and supplemental measures of traumatic response and symptoms; (2) measures of traumatic events and experiences; (3) structured interviews to provide detailed information about the traumatic event(s) or for the purposes of diagnosis; and (4) psychophysiological, biological, and neurological/neuropsychological assessment of posttraumatic response/PTSD. These can also be supplemented with the assessment of substance abuse and with information from collateral sources.

Generic Psychological Testing and Trauma-specific Measures

As part of the assessment process, the therapist might choose to use psychological testing to measure symptoms and personality variables. Generic and widely accepted measurements, such as the Minnesota Multiphasic Personality Instrument (MMPI), the Millon Clinical Multi-Axial Inventory (MCMI-III), the Psychological Assessment Inventory (PAI), the Symptom Checklist-90—Revised (SCL-90-R), and the Rorschach, are useful in assessing general psychological issues and symptoms. For the most part, they are not abuse or trauma specific and do not specifically assess symptoms associated with traumatic response. Although PTSD-oriented subscales have been included in the MMPI-2 and the MCMI-III, they are quite general and are more specific to symptoms of adult-onset and war trauma from which they were derived than to childhood abuse. In general, they have not been found to provide an accurate measure of the complexities of abuse-specific symptomatology. Moreover, abuse- and trauma-related symptomatology that shows up on these instruments may be misconstrued. According to Briere (1997b, p. 53), misinterpretation can occur for a variety of reasons: (1) the pervasiveness of abuse- and trauma-related symptomatology and its peripheral relation to a variety of forms of psychological disturbance; (2) the potential for intrusive, avoidant, hypervigilant, and disorganizing trauma-related symptomatology to be tapped by measures of psychosis and personality disorder; and (3) the fact that generic instruments were originally developed without reference to abuse-related or posttraumatic phenomena, making them unlikely to be very sensitive to distress related to them.

When abuse and other trauma are either reported or are strongly suspected, the therapist should consider supplementing generic instruments with measures that are more sensitive and responsive to these issues. These include symptom scales and structured diagnostic interviews that typically extend beyond the usual symptoms of depression, anxiety, and personality disturbance to assess the more trauma-related symptoms of dissociation, posttraumatic stress, somatization, and enduring personality characteristics and relational and sexual difficulties. Although a number of abuse and trauma symptom scales are now available, they must be selected knowledgeably and interpreted with caution because of their psychometric limitations and because they cannot and should not be used to assume past abuse or trauma in the absence of memory. On the former point, only several of these scales have satisfactory psychometric properties and most lack adequate normative or validity data; their use and usefulness are thereby restricted by these limitations. Regardless, they can be useful for screening purposes and as a point of departure for additional inquiry. Concerning the latter, one of the most oft-repeated and vocal criticisms of the memory controversy has to do with therapists diagnosing an abuse history on the basis of the individual's symptom profile at intake and in the absence of any memory of past abuse or additional assessment. Therapists have been cautioned that no one symptom or set of symptoms is pathonomic of sexual abuse (or other trauma) (Alpert et al., 1996c; American Psychological Association, 1994), making it critical that symptom scales not be used to make a diagnostic determination of these events. When an individual responds affirmatively to a set of symptoms that have some correlation with abuse, all that can be definitively said is that they intimate the possibility of, but do not prove, prior abuse/trauma.

The most methodologically developed and sound measures of posttraumatic symptoms are listed in Table 7.1.

Table 7.1
Measures of Posttraumatic Symptoms

Measure	Reference(s)
The Dissociative Experiences Scale	Bernstein & Putnam, 1986
The Impact of Events Scale-Revised	Weiss, Marmar, Metzler, & Rondfelt, 1995; Marmer, Weiss, Metzler, & Delucchi, 1996
The Los Angeles Symptom Checklist	Foy, Sipprelle, Rueger, & Carroll, 1984
Revised Civilian Mississippi Scale for PTSD (R-CMS)	Norris & Perilla, 1996
Structured Interview for Disorders of Extreme Stress (SIDES)	Pelcovitz, van der Kolk, Roth, Mandel, Kaplan, & Resick, 1997
The Trauma Symptom Checklist-40	Briere & Runtz , 1989; Elliott & Briere, 1992
The Trauma Symptom Inventory	Briere, 1995; 1997b
The Traumatic Stress Institute Belief Scale	Pearlman, 1996

Measures of Traumatic Events and Experiences

Measures are now available to explore trauma events and experience, in general and by particular trauma. They are available in different formats, usually as structured interviews and structured sets of questions posed by the interviewer who records responses verbatim, or as paper-and-pencil self-report measures completed by the patient. They are designed to provide specific information about the event(s) and are most often used when an abuse/trauma history is disclosed during the assessment and a more detailed description is sought. These measures of traumatic events and experiences are particularly useful in the detailed assessment of Criterion A (the stressor), one of the three criteria that must be met in diagnosing PTSD (*DSM-IV,* APA, 1994). Criterion A is made up of two dimensions (the experiencing or witnessing of the traumatic event or stressor and associated reactions of intense fear, horror, or helplessness), both of which are required for the assignment of the diagnosis. The therapist should be aware that most of the measures that are currently available to detail traumatic events and experiences place more emphasis on the stressor event than on subjective reactions and thus do not typically provide enough information to definitively make the diagnosis of PTSD (or Acute Stress Disorder, ASD). As new measures are developed, it is expected that this deficit will be rectified and more attention will be paid to the subjective responses dimension of Criterion A. In the interim, the therapist should supplement any measure of the stressor event with questions about the subjective responses of intense fear, helplessness, and horror at the time of the trauma (Briere, 1996c; Carlson, 1997; Norris & Riad, 1997).

Maintaining strict adherence to the diagnostic criteria is good clinical practice in any event. This is especially so when PTSD is the diagnosis under consideration. It serves to offset one of the charges made by the memory critics, namely, that PTSD has been overdiagnosed and diagnosed in error. This criticism has been leveled in general (Bowman, 1997) but more particularly in cases when memory of the index trauma is not available or becomes available due to memory retrieval/recovery after a period of inaccessibility. Similar criticism has come from some insurance companies. In some plans, the diagnosis of PTSD is scrutinized more carefully than less controversial diagnoses and is subject to claim rejection (and, more seriously for the therapist, charges of malpractice and/or fraud) if the full criteria for the diagnosis are not met.

Measures of traumatic events and experiences have another potential. In selected cases, they might be used as a screening instrument to rule in or rule out a trauma history. The therapist should proceed cautiously when using an interview for either purpose since, on the one hand, it could be deemed suggestive because it includes detailed questions about abuse/trauma and, on the other, it could prematurely rule out an abuse history if the respondent has little or no memory or is unable to disclose. When conducting an interview of this sort, the therapist should routinely conduct a preassessment orientation to advise the respondent to answer the questions to the best of his/her ability and to convey that the therapist holds no expectations about his/her responses. This counters any belief or mind-set on the part of the respondent that he or she should have something traumatic to report or disclose (Briere, 1997b, p. 83) or that the therapist is searching for or expecting disclosure. The respondent can also be advised that the interview can be updated in the future if needed.

One other assessment option in this category should be mentioned: a customized interview that includes attention to lifetime traumatic events as well as other areas of interest. As the name implies, an interview of this sort has questions customized to the individual's reported history about which the evaluator seeks to gain additional information. Suggestions and strategies for such an interview are available in Briere (1997b), Carlson (1997), and Wilson and Keane (1997).

The various instruments that are currently available for evaluating traumatic events and experiences are listed by category in Table 7.2.

Table 7.2
Measures of Traumatic Events

Measure	Reference(s)
Traumas Occurring in Adulthood or Across the Lifespan	
The Evaluation of Lifetime Stressors	Krinsley, Gallagher, Weathers, Kaloupek, & Vielhauer, 1997
The Harvard Trauma Questionnaire	Mollica et al., 1992; Mollica et al., 1995
The Trauma Assessment for Adults	Resnick, 1996
The Trauma History Questionnaire	Green, 1996
The Traumatic Events Scale	Elliott, 1992
The Traumatic Memory Inventory	van der Kolk & Fisler, 1995
The Traumatic Events Questionnaire	Vrana & Lauterback, 1994
The Traumatic Stress Schedule, Revised	Norris, 1992
Traumas Occurring in Childhood	
Assessing Environments III, Form SD	Rausch & Knutson, 1991
The Childhood Trauma Interview	Fink, Bernstein, Handelsman, Foote, & Lovejoy, 1995
The Traumatic Events Scale	Elliott, 1992
The Child Maltreatment Interview Schedule	Briere, 1992
The Childhood Maltreatment Questionnaire	Demaré, 1993
Specific Stressors	
Incest	Courtois, 1979; 1988
Rape	Koss & Gidycz, 1992
Spouse Abuse	Shepard & Campbell, 1992

Structured Trauma and Diagnostic Interviews

Structured interviews have been developed to generate detailed information about the specific traumatic experience and the circumstances surrounding it. Interviews of this type normally include more direct and in-depth questions about a particular type of trauma than are found in a less specialized interview. These interviews are not for the purpose of diagnosis and are generally not psychometrically derived. They can be considered for use on an as-needed basis and to customize the assessment process. For example, The Incest History Questionnaire (Courtois, 1979, 1988) is a structured interview I developed about the specifics of incestuous abuse. The questions in this structured interview were culled from the clinical literature on incest and include items that refer to the objective characteristics and dynamics of its occurrence, the respondent's subjective views and observations on its occurrence, roles and relationships within the family, relationship with the perpetrator(s), attempts at disclosure and whether intervention occurred, personal beliefs and self-perceptions, and seven categories of initial and long-term aftereffects. Interviews of this sort are used to generate details that might not otherwise be disclosed and that often underlie the individual's subjective distress and require therapeutic attention (Courtois, 1988; McCann & Pearlman, 1990a; Roth & Batson, 1997).

A second form of structured interview does have as its purpose the generation of objectively derived PTSD/DD diagnoses, per *DSM* criteria. Although a number of structured diagnostic interviews have been developed, the most methodologically sound at this point are the Clinician-Administered PTSD Scale (CAPS) (Blake et al., 1996; Blake et al., 1990), the Dissociative Disorders Interview Schedule (DDIS, which uses *DSM-III* diagnostic criteria) (Ross et al.,1989; Ross et al, 1990), and the Structured Clinical Interview for *DSM-IV* Dissociative Disorders (SCID-D) (Steinberg, 1994, 1995). Additionally, the Office Mental Status Examination for Complex Dissociative Symptoms and Multiple Personality Disorder (Loewenstein, 1991) is an organized set of questions about issues relevant to the diagnosis of the dissociative disorders.These questions have been found to have great clinical utility but have not been organized into a structured interview and have no psychometric properties. Where the clinician requires a psychometrically tested instrument for the diagnosis of the dissociative disorders, Steinberg's SCID-D is the instrument of choice. Additionally, the Structured Interview for Disorders of Extreme Stress (SIDES) is available (Pelcovitz et al., 1997). It is quite useful clinically in determining whether a patient meets criteria for Complex PTSD (DESNOS); however, the reader is reminded that DESNOS is not yet included as an official diagnosis in the *DSM* but rather is listed as associated features of PTSD.

Psychophysiological, Biological, and Neurological Assessment

In some cases, generic or more specialized psychophysiological, biological, and/or neurological assessment might be warranted to supplement and clarify psychological and medical data. While detailed discussion of these types of assessment is beyond the range of this chapter, they are mentioned here to inform the reader of their ongoing development for the assessment of PTSD. As discussed in chapters 2 and 3, a substantial amount of research has been conducted on the psychobiological and psychophysiological patterns of PTSD. This research has provided a consistent picture of greater physiological reactivity and startle response and biological alterations in individuals who developed PTSD versus those who did not (Orr & Kaloupek, 1997). The most wide ranging presentation of the findings concerning the psychobiology of PTSD is found in a recently published issue of the *Annals of the New York Academy of Sciences* edited by Yehuda and McFarlane (1997b).

These research findings have also resulted in new, more objective, physiological and biological methods to diagnose PTSD and to measure treatment process and outcome. According to Newman, Kaloupek, and Keane (1996), psychophysiological measures typically include heart rate, blood pressure, muscle tension, skin conductance level and response, and peripheral temperature as well as challenge tests in response to standardized or personalized cues of potentially traumatic experiences. Griffin et al., (1997) described objective psychophysiological and psychoendocrine assessment and treatment outcome indicators in PTSD. Friedman (1995), following his review of the literature on the biological alterations and neurobiological concomitants associated with PTSD, proposed several biological approaches to the diagnosis of PTSD and to its differential diagnosis from major depressive disorder and panic disorder. The biological assessment procedures he reviewed (none of which is necessarily definitive of PTSD but which help with differential diagnosis) include psychophysiological assessment, the dexamethasone suppression test (DST), the sleep EEG, sodium lactate infusion, and the sodium amytal interview. The reader should be aware that the latter is especially controversial for recovered memory purposes and should not be used for memory retrieval except in situations of great urgency and with peer review. Additional information on psychophysiological assessment of PTSD can be found in Friedman (1994), Giller (1990), Lating and Everly (1995), Orr and Kaloupek (1997), and the aforementioned text by Yehuda and McFarlane (1997b). Some of these methods are beyond the purview of most practitioners but are mentioned in the event that objective measures are sought.

Neuropsychological assessment provides another valuable means of evaluating the possible neurocognitive concomitants of PTSD symptoms and of making differential diagnoses (Horton, 1993; Knight, 1997). Horton framed three postulates about neuropsychological impairment related to PTSD in terms of its potential clinical significance as well as its complexity and the need for differential diagnosis: Postulate 1: PTSD causes neuropsychological impairment; Postulate 2: PTSD does not cause neuropsychological impairment, but neuropsychological assessment can be helpful; Postulate 3: PTSD may coexist with neuropsychological impairment (Horton, 1993). He further discussed the possible advantages of this form of assessment in some cases:

It might be suggested that neuropsychological assessment contributes to the comprehensive multiaxial assessment of PTSD by both identifying concentration problems and memory problems caused by PTSD and assessing neuropathology, and its neuropsychological effects (which may or may not be attributable to PTSD). First and foremost there is the concern that the patient may have associated neurological conditions that may or may not be related to the stressor experience (e.g., head trauma from a motor accident). (Horton, 1993, p. 154)

In the case of child abuse and other interpersonal victimization, associated neurological conditions may be related to past and/or present physical abuse or battering.

Knight, in his review article, further summarized some of the benefits of neuropsychological assessment:

Functional recommendations from neuropsychological evaluations will need to be integrated more effectively with clinical treatment protocols. At present, if impairments are detected, typical test findings are less likely to be interpreted from a PTSD framework and more likely summarized as performances showing a diffuse patterns [sic] of neurocognitive deficits, ranging in severity from mild to moderate, similar to organic-psychiatric or general psychiatric groups . . . some samples, and some individuals within PTSD samples, will exhibit greater degrees of functional impairment in cognitive domains resembling other brain syndromes because of coexisting closed head injuries, learning disabilities, attention deficit disorder, seizure disorders, medical problems, and substance abuse. In chronic PTSD samples with coexisting mood disorders, the effects of depression will likely be evident in the test findings as well. (Knight, 1997, p. 483)

Thus, neurological assessment might provide additional diagnostic clarity and suggest treatment direction.

Assessment of Substance Abuse

Substance abuse is prevalent in traumatized populations (Stewart, 1996) in general and in women with reported histories of childhood sexual abuse (Wilsnack, Vogeltanz, Klassen, & Harris (1997). Trauma histories are reported very frequently in substance abuse treatment populations (Evans & Sullivan, 1995), and patients often have comorbid psychiatric conditions. Although these patients are usually labeled as dual diagnosis, in reality, they are more accurately described as multiple diagnosis. Since substance abuse is so often comorbid with PTSD, the therapist should consider specialized alcohol and drug assessments as warranted (including, at times, neuropsychological testing especially for patients with second- and third-stage alcoholism, where cognitive impairment is likely to occur). Memory deficits including blackouts are often major indicators of later stage physical deterioration and functional impairment.

Substance abuse might also be implicated in the suppression or loss (via numbing or chemical dissociation) and recovery of an individual's memory for past abuse and trauma. One of the clinical dilemmas in substance abuse treatment is the frequent emergence of abuse/trauma memories as the individual achieves sobriety. The shock and upset that accompany these memories often challenge the recovering individual's ability to sustain sobriety and induce him/her to relapse and return to the substance of choice. Many survivors of all sorts of trauma have used alcohol and other drugs (often from an early age during the course of the traumatization during childhood and adolescence or immediately afterwards) to cope with its occurrence and/or to suppress or avoid associated memories and emotions (Evans & Sullivan, 1995; Stewart, 1996).

Substance abuse is implicated in some cases of memory loss and later recovered memories and is therefore important to consider as a possible explanatory mechanism. As an example, in a study of substance-abusing women early in their sobriety, Loftus, Polonsky, & Fullilove (1994), found that 19% of the women reported recovering memories of past abuse that they had previously forgotten. Although this study has been criticized for not addressing the confounding effects of early sobriety on memory processes, it nonetheless provides some preliminary data on recovered memories of sexual abuse in this population.

To summarize: As recovered memory issues are comprehensively assessed, the therapist should not ignore the possibility of memory impairment due to substance abuse; however, even in addicted populations suffering from memory impairment and blackouts, substance abuse does not rule out and, in fact, may provide a mechanism for the loss and recovery of memories of past abuse.

Collateral Assessment:
Interviews and Information-Gathering

In some instances, collateral information-gathering has been found to be important in the determination of an abuse/trauma history and in assessment and diagnosis of PTSD/DD. It has been recommended as a strategy for gaining external information in the case of recovered memories; however, it should not, in all cases, be expected to definitively determine the reality and veracity of these memories. Information from collateral sources may be mandated in a forensic case or a disability determination but should be otherwise used selectively on a case-by-case basis as clinically indicated.

Collateral interviews with spouses, partners, family members, friends, teachers, employers/coworkers, and former therapists can, at times, provide valuable input. Individuals with PTSD/DD diagnoses often have difficulty with accurately reporting their condition and symptoms due to factors such as numbing, avoidance, denial, amnesia, minimization, rationalization, cognitive impairment, etc. Collateral reports and interviews may be able to fill in memory gaps and provide more objective, observational information. They can also provide information about events for which the individual has no recollection (or variable recollection). Additionally, they might help an evaluator assess or understand the impact the individual is having on others and ways the individual interprets personal experiences and symptoms and can provide supplementary data not otherwise available within the parameters of the assessment process (Newman, et al., 1996).

As Carlson (1997) and Shapiro (1995) independently noted, information from outside sources must be sought and used judiciously since it may be counterproductive and even damaging to the patient and the therapeutic relationship. In such a circumstance, it may cause the individual to feel disbelieved and out of control and reinforce alienation from and mistrust of others. The solicitation of collateral information from sources external to the treatment is best decided and undertaken collaboratively and only with the individual's consent.

Prior records can provide a rich source of supplemental information. They may serve to corroborate and elaborate on the individual's reports of prior symptoms and functioning. These include medical, school, police, legal, child protective services, psychotherapy, work, and military records, as well as information from other sources such as diaries, pictures and photo albums, and newspaper reports. Patients may seek out the information themselves or it may be sought by the therapist/evaluator. Obviously, such sources should be solicited only with the patient's permission and with the recognition that the information derived from these sources can be upsetting and/or relieving to the patient. In my practice, I have had patients seek and gain outside corroboration that supported the abuse hypothesis. This information turned out to be both validating but very upsetting to them. On the other hand, I have had other patients seek outside information and not gain any. This outcome was, in some cases, upsetting. In others, it was relieving.

Considerable controversy has surrounded the strategy of seeking information from collateral sources to substantiate or disconfirm recovered memories of abuse, especially abuse perpetrated by family members who are then accused of abuse (and possibly sued). Several false memory advocates have suggested that therapists have a duty to seek out corroborative information in all cases of recovered memories of abuse (McHugh, 1992) while other commentators have argued against this position (Brown et al., 1998). Still others have commented that seeking corroboration is not a strategy without risk. This was made evident in the *Ramona* case where attempts at corroboration were made by the defendant therapists but the interpretations they applied to the evidence were challenged in the malpractice lawsuit by the alleged victim's father (Appelbaum & Zoltek-Jick, 1996).

An additional point deserves mention. While on the surface the strategy of seeking corroboration seems quite reasonable, therapists with specialization in the dynamics of abuse and in the treatment of perpetrators point out that it has major shortcomings. The most obvious are that perpetrators deny and minimize their behavior and that family members, due to their attachment, loyalty, and the dysfunctional family relationships that accompany abuse, usually close ranks around the perpetrator and blame the accuser/victim for fabricating the abuse and for having false memories. Thus, in a situation where abuse really occurred, collateral interviews of the alleged perpetrator and other family members can serve to obscure rather than support the reality of its occurrence, supporting false memory for true abuse (Carlson, 1997; Rubin, 1996). In discussing this issue, Rubin pointedly subtitled her article "False accusations of 'false memory'" and criticized the asymmetrical attention and weight given to the false memories of alleged victims versus those of alleged perpetrators. Courtois (1997a) and Whitfield (1995) have also discussed the tendency on the part of some false memory critics to accord more credence to the alleged abuser's denials than to the alleged victim's memories, without adequate assessment.

When and if collateral interviews are undertaken, the therapist must have an understanding of these dynamics and must not automatically take the family's word over the accuser's. Like other aspects of assessment, the therapist must weigh the evidence at hand and not be too hasty at drawing a conclusion. At times, collateral interviews of family members and others clearly support an allegation of abuse (e.g., a sibling who witnessed incestuous abuse by a parent; a neighbor who witnessed beatings; a teacher who noticed and reported bruises), but at other times nothing conclusive is available, making a clear determination difficult if not impossible. Fees for collateral interviews should be paid by the patient to insure that family members do not become patients in their own right (and thus be owed the therapist's primary duty of care) if they pay.

Whitfield (1995) differentiated between external corroboration (what he labeled "external verification") from factors associated with the individual (labeled "internal verification"). According to Whitfield, internal verification refers to common diagnoses associated with an abuse/trauma history, behavioral indicators and interpersonal dynamics, along with the characteristics of the memories themselves. Although his approach is helpful in making a preliminary versus a conclusive assessment of the possibility of abuse, his use of the term "verification" is problematic since most of the factors (other than witnesses and confession by the abuser) do not verify the occurrence of abuse. They may offer support for the probability of the abuse hypothesis but are generally inconclusive in *proving* its occurrence. Nevertheless, Whitfield's factors can be useful to a comprehensive assessment if used broadly as a way to determine likelihood or probability of abuse. These factors are listed in Table 7.3. They can be further supplemented with an assessment of family functioning, including factors often associated with abuse such as parental alcoholism and mental illness, patterns of major family secrets, other abuse in the family, etc.

At the present time, a few questionnaires and interviews are available for collateral information-gathering regarding PTSD/DD and past abuse in adults, and for parents to complete in the assessment of children. Several interviews and self-report forms have been devised for the assessment of family members accused of abuse on the basis of recovered memories and of retractors. Few of these are psychometrically sound and their use has been criticized on this basis. The development of additional collateral assessment measures that follow methodological principles would make a substantial contribution to comprehensive assessment.

Diagnosis

To reiterate points made earlier, a diagnosis should be considered over time and made only after careful consideration of all the information obtained from the assessment and only if all of the criteria for the diagnosis are met (otherwise, the diagnosis is made provisionally, per *DSM* guidelines). A diagnosis can be modified following the emergence of additional information and symptoms, whether they come directly from the patient and/or are the result of additional assessment efforts. It is use-

Table 7.3
Summary of the Documentation of Traumatic Memories

External Verification	Date Recorded
Witnesses	
Photographs	
Diaries, Journals or Letters	
Medical or Clinical Records	
Other Person(s) Abused	
Confession by Abuser	
Other Statements or Evidence	

Internal Verification	
High Risk Disorder Present	
Post-traumatic Stress Disorder	
Age Regression, Abreactions, and Flashbacks	
Repetitions and Repetition Compulsions	
Characteristics of the Memories	
Other Dynamics, Patterns, Observations, and Aftereffects	

Write in the features of each of the above, with the page number or other reference from the clinical record or elsewhere. Where possible, include the date when the observation was made and also when you recorded it on this summary page.

From *Memory and Abuse: Remembering and Healing the Effects of Trauma* (p. 165), by C. L. Whitfield, 1995, Deerfield Beach, FL: Health Communications, Inc. Copyright 1995 by Health Communications, Inc. Reprinted with permission.

ful to complete all five axes listed in the *DSM* (American Psychiatric Association, 1994) since they take into account a wide range of issues and concerns pertinent to inclusive treatment planning: psychological/psychiatric symptomatology, characterological/ developmental issues, medical conditions, past and current stressors, and past and current levels of functioning.

Adults with a trauma history who have had previous therapy often carry numerous diagnoses, so the therapist may have to sort through these to see which, if any, apply. Complications related to diagnosis are that traumatized patients tend to be comorbid as well as misdiagnosed. Research has found that among patients with PTSD, 80% have at least one associated disorder (Brady, 1997) and that traumatic or dissociative symptoms are frequently misdiagnosed, most often as bipolar, schizoaffective, or psychotic (Kluft, 1987; Read, 1997; Ross, 1997). Common concurrent Axis I disorders include panic and anxiety, unipolar and bipolar depression, alcohol/substance abuse and eating disorders, obsessive compulsive disorder, dissociative disorders, atypical psychosis and schizophrenia, and somatization along with a range of Axis II personality disorders and Axis III medical conditions. Multiple diagnoses are often necessary to cover the full range of symptoms and should be listed in order of their severity and treatment sequence. This is in keeping with recommendations made concerning the assessment of PTSD: "In order to assess PTSD accurately, it is imperative to recognize that other DSM-IV diagnoses are frequently associated with trauma and must be differentiated from PTSD or diagnosed concomitantly with it" (Lating, Zeichner, & Keane, 1995, p. 115).

Concerning diagnosis and recovered memories of abuse, a number of common mistakes have been identified that the therapist should scrupulously avoid (Knapp & VandeCreek, 1997). Most of these are discussed throughout this book so will be touched upon only briefly here. First of all, "abuse," "post-abuse syndrome," "repressed memory syndrome," or "false memory syndrome" are not diagnoses and therefore should not be given as though they were. Second, a history of past abuse and trauma may, or may not, be related to the individual's current difficulties. A cause and effect link should not be assumed nor should it be assumed that past abuse is always traumatic. Third, the therapist *should not assume or conclude*, on the basis of certain symptoms alone ("syndrome evidence"), that abuse occurred or that abuse is the *only possible explanation* for the individual's symptoms and distress. A more broad-based consideration of etiology is needed. Memory researchers have identified assumptive reasoning as resulting from "confirmatory bias" on the part of the therapist. Certainly, many other issues, including other personal or family difficulties as well as other forms of trauma, may be implicated in the individual's distress and must be carefully determined.

The diagnoses of PTSD and DID, in particular, are quite controversial and have been challenged by some of the critics as largely inaccurate, exaggerated, iatrogenic, and socially-induced (particularly DID). Quite recently, the issue of misdiagnosis has been raised in several malpractice lawsuits and one criminal fraud case, particularly the diagnosis of DID (along with allegations of associated satanic ritual abuse for which the patient is also treated) (Belluck, 1997; Grinfield, 1995, 1997).

As discussed in earlier chapters, PTSD has come to be used as an overarching diagnosis for many types of traumatization since it destigmatizes many posttraumatic symptoms and is inclusive of associated features of depression and anxiety symptoms so often seen in traumatized patients. But, PTSD must be carefully differentiated from other diagnoses, as discussed in the *DSM:*

> Not all psychopathology that occurs in individuals exposed to an extreme stressor should necessarily be attributed to Posttraumatic Stress Disorder. Symptoms of avoidance, numbing, and increased arousal that are present before exposure to the stressor do not meet criteria for the diagnosis of Posttraumatic Stress Disorder and require consideration of other diagnoses (e.g., a Mood Disorder or another Anxiety Disorder). Moreover, if the symptom response pattern to the extreme stressor meets criteria for another mental disorder (e.g., Brief Psychotic Disorder, Conversion Disorder, Major Depressive Disorder), these diagnoses should be given instead of, or in addition to, Posttraumatic Stress Disorder. (American Psychiatric Association, 1994, p. 427)

To properly diagnose PTSD, the symptoms from all three categories of criteria must be met, including Criterion A, involving exposure and response to a traumatic event (Blank, 1994). The assignment of the PTSD diagnosis is therefore problematic when the traumatic event is in question, as occurs when the patient has no conscious memory of abuse/trauma or when a history of trauma is not otherwise well-established. Therapists *should not assume that abuse constitutes the missing trauma* and make the PTSD diagnosis on the basis of that assumption. Of course, the problem of unremembered trauma is paradoxical and the specifications of Criterion A may not be met due to memory loss, not because the traumatic event did not occur. Since numbing responses may result in memory repression, suppression, and/or dissociation and, in fact, "the inability to recall an important aspect of the trauma" is listed under Criterion B of the PTSD diagnosis, it is conceivable that a patient has

PTSD but is amnestic for the traumatic antecedent. In such a situation, psychological testing and structured interviewing might be useful in eliciting more information to help with memory and to establish the diagnosis. If memory continues to be absent, however, it is advisable for the therapist to err in the direction of caution and either not make the diagnosis, make it only provisionally, or consider whether the patient meets criteria for dissociative amnesia or one of the other dissociative disorders. In chapter 2, the diagnostic formulation of Complex PTSD (or DESNOS, Disorder of Extreme Stress, Not Otherwise Specified,) was discussed in terms of its development to account for Axis I and II symptoms not included in the diagnosis of "simple" PTSD. The therapist who utilizes DESNOS to help conceptualize the patient's symptoms and organize the treatment must be aware that it is not an official *DSM* diagnosis and so should not be assigned as such.

Dissociative disorders also pose a diagnostic conundrum because symptoms of the condition and diagnostic criteria involve memory loss. "The essential feature of the dissociative disorders is a disruption in the usually integrated functions of consciousness, *memory*, identity, or perception of the environment" (American Psychiatric Association, 1994, p. 477, italics added). In the past decade, dissociative disorders have been increasingly diagnosed as their relationship to abuse and trauma has been identified and as therapists have become more familiar with them. Critics contend that they have been grossly overdiagnosed due to extensive media attention, beginning with the publication of *Sybil* and *Three Faces of Eve*. Dissociative identity disorder (formerly multiple personality disorder), in particular, has been highlighted in the memory controversy, especially as concerns patient suggestibility, therapist overfascination, its treatment with hypnosis, and its purported origins in severe sadistic abuse, possibly including satanic ritual abuse. Professionals are deeply divided about this diagnosis, with some strongly believing in its existence (Kluft, 1984a, 1984b, 1985; Putnam, 1989a, 1997; Ross, 1989, 1997), others challenging it as nonexistent, iatrogenic, and socially constructed (Aldridge-Morris, 1989; Mersky, 1992; Spanos, 1996), and still others viewing it as a valid but rare diagnosis (Cormier & Thelen, 1998) or viewing it with skepticism (Dell, 1988). Despite these strong personal and professional divisions, criteria for the diagnosis of DID as well as other dissociative disorders have enough accumulated evidence to be included in the *DSM-IV* (American Psychiatric Association, 1994).

The *DSM* includes the following concerning the differential diagnosis of DID:

Dissociative Identity Disorder must be distinguished from symptoms that are caused by the direct physiological effects of a general medical condition (e.g., seizure disorder) . . . This determination is based on history, laboratory findings, or physical examination. Dissociative Identity Disorder should be distinguished from dissociative symptoms due to complex partial seizures, although the two disorders may co-occur. Seizure episodes are generally brief, and do not involve the complex and enduring structures of identity and behavior typically found in Dissociative Identity Disorder. Also, a history of physical and sexual abuse is less common in individuals with complex partial seizures. EEG studies, especially sleep deprived and with nasopharyngeal leads, may help clarify the differential diagnosis.

Symptoms caused by the direct physiological effects of a substance can be distinguished from Dissociative Identity Disorder by the fact that a substance (e.g., a drug of abuse or a medication) is judged to be etiologically related to the disturbance.

The diagnosis of Dissociative Identity Disorder takes precedence over Dissociative Amnesia, Dissociative Fugue, and Depersonalization Disorder. (American Psychiatric Association, 1994, p. 486)

The controversy over the diagnosis and some general guidelines regarding making the diagnoses are also discussed in the *DSM:*

Controversy exists concerning the differential diagnosis between Dissociative Identity Disorder and a variety of other mental disorders, including Schizophrenia and other Psychotic Disorders, Bipolar Disorder With Rapid Cycling, Anxiety Disorders, Somatization Disorders, and Personality Disorders. Some clinicians believe that Dissociative Identity Disorder has been underdiagnosed (e.g., the presence of more than one dissociated personality state may be mistaken for a delusion or the communication from one identity to another may be mistaken for an auditory hallucination, leading to confusion with the Psychotic Disorders; shifts between identity states may be confused with cyclical mood fluctuations leading to confusion with Bipolar Disorder). In contrast, others are concerned that Dissociative Identity Disorder may be overdiagnosed relative to other mental disorders based on the media interest in the disorder and the suggestible nature of the individuals. Factors that may support a diagnosis of Dissociative Identity Disorder are the presence of clear-cut dissociative symptomatology with sudden shifts in identity states, reversible amnesia, and high scores on measures of dissociation and hypnotizability in individuals who do not have the characteristic presentations of another mental disorder. (American Psychiatric Association, 1994, p. 487)

Therapists should be meticulous in documenting symptoms and behaviors that lead them to consider the diagnosis of DID, and conservative in making the diagnosis. It is of note that even among those who believe in and specialize in treating the diagnosis, concern has been voiced about misdiagnosis as well as overdiagnosis (Chu, 1991). DID has been diagnosed when another dissociative disorder is more accurate and should have been considered. Put another way, one can have a dissociative disorder and not have dissociative identity disorder, a fact that has escaped some therapists. It is advisable that, once dissociative behaviors and symptoms have been observed or reported, the therapist make a preliminary screening of these symptoms through a clinical interview and/or with the Dissociative Experiences Scale (Bernstein & Putnam, 1986). If the score is elevated and the responses seem valid, the therapist can follow up by conducting a structured interview such as the SCID-D (1994, 1995), the DDIS (Ross et al., 1989), or using the mental status examinations questions proposed by Loewenstein (1991).

Conservative criteria for diagnosis include the therapist's observation of "switching" or recurrent changes in executive control between at least two alternate identities or personality states on several occasions and amnesia between them, along with the "inability to recall important personal information that is too extensive to be explained by ordinary forgetfulness" (American Psychiatric Association, 1994, p. 487). As an additional precaution and due to the complex and serious ramifications of this diagnosis, the therapist (especially if s/he is professionally inexperienced and/or has not had training or experience working with dissociative disorders) should consult with a more senior colleague versed in the treatment of dissociative disorders or request a collaborative diagnostic consultation for the patient. The therapist should furthermore gain additional training and consultation in working with this condition and, barring that, should consider the merits of referring the patient to a therapist with expertise.

In response to these different diagnostic challenges, the therapist is well-advised to be as careful in ascribing a diagnosis as in making an overall assessment of the patient's concerns and symptoms. To be redundant, the patient is hurt equally when either a false positive or a false negative assessment is made and when s/he does not receive the appropriate diagnosis and treatment. Assessment that attends to the strategies and cautions presented above hopefully reduces the risk of assumptions and erroneous diagnoses in either direction. In situations where the patient remains uncertain or ambiguous about the past, the therapist should be more cautious in making a diagnosis of either PTSD or DID (or other dissociative disorder) without documenting strong symptoms that meet all criteria of these diagnoses. The patient should also be assessed as to outside influences or personality characteristics that might cause him/her to seek a particular diagnosis or to subscribe to a belief in sexual abuse in the absence of any memory. In cases of this type, it is certainly more conservative to diagnose Axis I and II disorders other than PTSD/DD and to highlight these as treatment foci. This strategy supports a treatment that is symptom and functioning focused. It further sidesteps the criticism that some therapists are on a "fishing expedition" for trauma or operate on a "no pain, no gain" philosophy about the treatment of traumatic circumstances, especially in the absence of memory for the trauma and at the expense of the patient's current functioning and mental health.

SUMMARY

This chapter has reviewed strategies and issues in conducting a psychological assessment that neither suggests nor suppresses an abuse/trauma history. Therapists have the responsibility to conduct a comprehensive psychosocial assessment of individuals who seek psychotherapy, an especially important undertaking when memories of abuse/trauma are in question or at issue. This chapter also reviewed issues that might arise during the assessment process. Various strategies have been devised and instruments developed to assist in the assessment of traumatic events and effects. Finally, issues of diagnosis were presented.

Chapter 8

CLINICAL GUIDELINES AND RISK MANAGEMENT FOR WORKING WITH MEMORY ISSUES

This chapter presents recommended strategies and techniques in working with traumatic memories and memory issues in clinical practice. It describes, in the form of guidelines, the types of recommended responses and strategies and also mentions those that are contraindicated in work with traumatic memories. This material consolidates much of the available authoritative writing on the topic. It references the reports of the various professional task forces, the observations and cautions of clinicians, and the critiques of memory researchers and proponents of the false memory position in an attempt to arrive at a broad-based and less polarized position espoused by many writers in the field (Berliner, 1997; Briere, 1997b; Lindsay & Briere, 1997; Courtois, 1995c, 1997d; Lindsay, 1997, 1998). These recommendations make up part of the currently evolving standard of care (described in chapter 5) and constitute risk management for clinicians working with abuse and memory issues. These guidelines and the treatment process will continue to develop as new research and clinical information become available.

CLINICAL GUIDELINES AND RISK MANAGEMENT

In a recently published chapter, Grunberg and Ney (1997) provided a review and comparative analysis of the then-available reports of the major professional organizations regarding recovered memory issues and recommendations for clinical practice. Since then, several other professional reports have been released (many of which were reviewed in chapter 2 or are included in Appendix B). Grunberg and Ney's original table comparing and contrasting the various reports is reproduced in Table 8.1,

Table 8.1

Categories of Recommendations in Professional Reports on Recovered Memories

	CPA	C. Psychiatric A.	APA	ASCH	BPS	APA Div. 17	ISSD	AMA	APS	A. Psychiatric A.	RA&NZCP	NZPS	ISTSS	RCP
Specialized knowledge and competence	✓	✓	✓	✓	✓	✓	✓	✓	✓	✓		✓		✓
Consideration of alternative diagnoses		✓	✓	✓	✓	✓	✓	✓	✓			✓	✓	
Memory enhancing techniques	✓	✓	✓	✓	✓	✓	✓	✓		✓		✓	✓	✓
Emotional competence						✓	✓			✓		✓		
Objectivity/Neutrality in forensic context	✓	✓											✓	
Record-keeping	✓	✓		✓	✓	✓			✓			✓		✓
Informed consent	✓	✓	✓	✓	✓	✓			✓				✓	✓
Confrontation/Legal Action	✓		✓	✓	✓	✓	✓	✓			✓	✓		✓
Awareness of personal beliefs	✓	✓		✓	✓	✓	✓	✓	✓		✓	✓		✓

Note – The presence of a check-mark indicates that this issue is referred to in the guidelines

*Association Guidelines & Key:

CPA = Canadian Psychological Association (1996)
C. Psychiatric A. = Canadian Psychiatric Association (1996)
APA = American Psychological Association (1996)
BPS = British Psychological Society (1995)
ASCH = American Society of Clinical Hypnosis (1995)
APA Div. 17 = American Psycological Association Div. 17, Committee on Women – Draft (1995)
AMA = American Medical Association

APS = Australian Psychological Society (1994)
A. Psychiatric A. = American Psychiatric Association (1993)
RA&NZCP = Royal Australia and New Zealand College of Psychiatrists (1996)
NZPS = New Zealand Psychological Society (1995)
ISTSS = International Society for Traumatic Stress Studies (1998)
RCP = Royal College of Psychiatrists (1998)

From "Professional Guidelines on Clinical Practice for Recovered Memory: A Comparative Analysis," by F. Grunberg, and T. Ney, 1997. In J.D. Read and D.S. Lindsay, Editors, *Recollections of trauma: Scientific evidence and clinical practice* (pp. 541–556), New York: Plenum Press. Copyright 1997 by Plenum Press. Adapted and updated with permission.

supplemented with material from the newly published reports. The reader will note that all of these categories are included in the material in the remainder of this chapter, augmented by additional (and in many cases more detailed) recommendations for working with memories in clinical practice culled from other professional writings.

In summarizing their review, Grunberg and Ney wrote: "Generally, as the guidelines indicate, there is developing concern (albeit with increasing consensus) among clinicians about how memory works and how clinicians should conduct themselves in their work with trauma survivors and with clients who may or may not be trauma survivors" (p. 543). They further noted that consensus was not achieved in all nine categories across the reports of the various professions, possibly due to the need for different perspectives by different disciplines. This suggests that, at a minimum, the practitioner should be familiar with and follow the recommendations made by his/her respective profession. Another statement made by these authors in summarizing their comparative analysis provides additional perspective and guidance:

> In many cases there is no "right" or "wrong" way to act; aspects of the situation must be weighed and a combination of sensitivity and realism must be considered in all clinical practice. We anticipate that guidelines will evolve in conjunction with developments in clinical practice and research in this area. There is still much that is not yet understood, and guidelines which are overly prescriptive will not likely survive the test of time; however, without sufficient detail and rationale in the guidelines, the clinician is left without adequate reason for acting in particular ways. (p. 543)

The recommendations discussed below are also presented against the backdrop of the meta-issues concerning the practice of posttrauma treatment presented in chapters 5 and 6. Although every attempt has been made to minimize redundancy between the two, some is unavoidable. The intent here is to impart in more detail information concerning clinical work with memory and memory issues, whether memory is continuous or reinstated. In a general way, these guidelines are an attempt to answer the practical practice questions posed by Meichenbaum (1994):

> But where does all this controversy leave the practicing clinician? How do clinicians who do not have independent corroborating data . . . operate? How does the therapist provide a supportive therapeutic environment, but reduce the likelihood of iatrogenic influences? How can the clinician remain responsible to his/her clients, but reduce the likelihood

of "insinuating memories." with the risk of clients eventually "retract-ing" their accounts and possibly bringing lawsuits again their therapist? (p. 268)

They are also an attempt to be both prescriptive and proscriptive (Dawes, 1995), by providing general and quite specific guidance to the therapist about "what to do and not to do" (Courtois, 1997d). They thus constitute guidelines for risk management as well.

The Therapist "Walks a Fine Line" between an Overly Endorsing Stance and an Overly Defensive Stance

The therapist must practice in ways that are responsible and within accepted professional standards in working with traumatic memories and memory issues but must simultaneously avoid practicing in an overly defensive manner. On the one hand, the therapist can err in the direction of suggesting abuse by practicing one of the many types of unconventional therapies, by having tunnel vision and being overzealous in concluding that unremembered past abuse is always at the root of certain symptoms, and by practicing advocacy instead of psychotherapy. On the other hand, the therapist can be too conservative and defensive by automatically disbelieving or refusing to treat anyone who reports having been abused or having delayed/recovered memories of past trauma (with or without corroboration) and by refusing to include questions about abuse and other forms of trauma as part of a standard psychological assessment. In a recent article, Gutheil and Simon (1997) addressed another dimension of this issue, namely, risk management efforts that are overly stringent and defensive and that put questionable restrictions on traditionally accepted forms of psychotherapy. They write:

> Several attempts at managing liability risks associated with recovery of memories constitute "cures" that may be worse than the alleged "disease" of inappropriate therapies. These efforts include stringent legislation governing informed consent in which only those forms of psychotherapy that have empirically proven effects on particular maladies may be used . . . . Would-be reformers also show poor discrimination between ordinary psychotherapy and alternative, nonmainstream therapies such as past life regression. It is unclear at this point what goal these efforts at reform will accomplish. (pp. 1403-1404)

The Therapist Practices Fairly
Conservatively within the Mainstream

It is recommended that the therapist make every effort to stay within the accepted mainstream practice of psychotherapy (with the understanding that what is mainstream may vary by therapeutic orientation and by culture) and to use techniques that carry the lowest amount of risk. The therapist seeks to apply interventions conservatively and in step-wise fashion from those with the least risk or potential to be suggestive to those with more risk, and chooses professionally accepted interventions. The therapist must also try to avoid an ideological, advocacy-based approach and instead to practice from a stance of impartiality to avoid unduly influencing the patient. Gutheil and Simon (1997) addressed this issue as follows:

> Confounding all this activity is the fact that all psychotherapy, by encouraging self-directed attention, involves voluntary or involuntary recovery of memory. The distinction among repression, suppression, avoidance, and simple forgetting or redirection of attention is often hard to establish. Thus, many of the problems, fears, and recommendations about recovered memory overlap problematically with issues about psychotherapy itself. Hence any risk management guidelines for proper conduct should be constructed to leave appropriately conducted psychotherapy intact. (p. 1404)

Where new, relatively unproven and possibly unconventional treatments are introduced that seem to hold promise for symptom amelioration and the resolution of traumatic material [e.g., Eye Movement Desensitization and Reprocessing (EMDR), Thought Field Therapy (TFT)], the therapist utilizes these methodologies only after having considered alternatives and having been trained in their use; furthermore, the therapist does not exceed their stated purposes or apply them to populations and conditions for which their use is contraindicated, informs patients of their experimental status and the possible risk/benefits associated with them, and gains the patient's informed consent beforehand. The patient must also be given the opportunity to refuse treatment with these procedures. The therapist does not practice in isolation, hidden from peers, in order to use techniques that are outside of the norm or to practice a "special form of therapy" or in a "special way that no one would understand." S/he should make it a practice to seek peer review, consultation, and support in general but especially before utilizing any unconventional strategy or technique for any circumstance that is atypical and/or holds greater-than-average risk.

Additionally, the therapist must strive to associate with other professionals who are similarly informed and are cautious about practicing within accepted standards. In a number of situations (i.e., employment and supervision of other clinicians, group practice settings) therapists can carry vicarious as well as direct liability and should make every effort to avoid unnecessary risks. It is therefore very important (and good risk management) to have a working knowledge of the philosophy and practices of associated individuals. At times, therapists may need to confront peers, employees, or supervisees about their practices (Briere, 1997b). If those associated individuals continue to utilize suggestive practices or to otherwise practice with an unacceptable degree of risk, disaffiliation is the best strategy, since vicarious liability and increased risk accrue from their actions (Caudill, 1997; Gutheil & Simon, 1997).

The Therapist Develops
Specialized Knowledge and Competence
and Stays Updated

Although the general practitioner is not expected to be an expert in issues of abuse and in posttrauma treatment, any therapist whose patient reports abuse and/or who has memories of abuse emerge during the course of treatment has a responsibility to gain knowledge about these issues and to develop a general level of competence in the treatment of these concerns. As discussed earlier in this text, in all likelihood issues related to abuse/trauma and memory were not addressed during the practitioner's formal clinical training. As a result, they must be learned through supplemental focused training via continuing education offerings, professional reading, and participation in consultation, supervision, and peer study/support groups. As well, the knowledge base for this area of practice has expanded and evolved rapidly in the past decade (and seemingly exponentially in the past few years!) and will continue to do so. What constituted the prevailing standard of practice five to ten years ago is quite different and much more developed today. It is necessary for the therapist to stay current with new research and practice developments and to have specific training, competence, and credentialing, where available, in any specialized techniques that are used and to utilize opportunities for consultation and supervision.

Different types of competence to conduct psychotherapy also come into play in this work. In addition to the intellectual competence derived from an adequate knowledge base, Pope and Brown (1996) have discussed two other forms: emotional competence and the competence (and willingness) to treat. Therapists who work with abuse and trauma (whether memory is at issue or not) must be able to emotionally tolerate both the material and the patient's reactions and to respond in ways that are therapeutic. It should be acknowledged that, for a wide variety of reasons, not all therapists have the knowledge, temperament, inclination, or willingness to treat cases involving abuse/trauma (whatever the degree of memory and/or corroboration). Some are overly fearful of these topics and the controversy and some have an active aversion or antagonism to the issues. Therapists who hold these perspectives have a professional responsibility to honestly self-assess, not attempt to treat, and instead refer the patient to a more willing and knowledgeable practitioner.

Competence and knowledge have special pertinence for students or novice therapists who, due to their apprentice status, may have neither the understanding nor the skills to work effectively with the demands, complexities, and high-risk situations inherent in many of these cases and for whom trainers/supervisors are vicariously liable. The trainee/novice's ability to understand and manage dynamics must be closely supervised, as must the strategies and techniques that they employ. Wherever possible, trainees and new practitioners should be assigned cases that are commensurate with their knowledge and developmental progression as a therapist. It is advisable for them to maintain adequate supervision and consultation and to make special efforts to not treat cases of this sort in isolation.

The Therapeutic Approach Is Determined According to Available Memory and Symptoms

The therapist utilizes a generic model of psychotherapy when a trauma history is either not known or not disclosed at intake or during the course of treatment and/or where no posttraumatic/dissociative symptoms are in evidence. When a trauma history is known and reported (possibly with corroboration) or is strongly suspected, and the patient has posttraumatic/dissociative symptoms in need of therapeutic focus, the phase-oriented model of posttrauma treatment described in chapter 6 is implemented.

A decision model of therapeutic options according to memory accessibility is provided in chapter 9.

The Therapist Stays in Role

The therapist must be especially scrupulous about the maintenance of the treatment frame and about insuring that the relationship remains a professional one with appropriate and reasonable boundaries in place. As discussed in chapters 5 and 6, a therapeutic contract is established that is nonauthoritarian, empowers the patient, and fosters collaboration in the treatment process, yet simultaneously distinguishes psychotherapy (with its special restrictions and obligations) from other types of interpersonal relationships. The responsibility for the conduct of the treatment is with the therapist and the responsibility for engaging in the treatment is with the patient. Treatment is explicitly organized around goals and objectives. It is not organized around ongoing dependency on therapy nor is organized solely around the retrieval of absent memory.

The clinician must be cautious regarding invitations or inclinations to engage in dual relationships with the patient. S/he does not function as friend, advocate, surrogate parent, rescuer, forensic examiner or expert, or get involved in extratherapeutic activities; rather, s/he keeps to the role of therapist and forgoes other roles, while maintaining an ability to respond to and interpret the patient's attempts to engage him/her in mixed or dual roles. Such attempts and needs are quite common among individuals who have suffered chronic abuse of some sort; they may be in the interest of reenacting past relational dynamics or be a contemporary example of how the patient best knows how to relate or to achieve homeostasis in a relationship.

Additionally, many individuals with histories of interpersonal trauma make heavy relational demands on caretakers, who, as a result of the pressure of these demands, may end up losing their perspective and acting on their countertransference. Often, such countertransference responses find therapists becoming overly lax about boundaries, inappropriately interfering and intruding in the patient's life, and making attempts to rescue, caretake, or compensate the patient rather than remaining in the more objective therapist role. Responses of this type are also the result of inexperience (according to Pearlman and Saakvitne, 1995, the most likely countertransference response to this population that has been identified in trainees and novice therapists is overinvolvement and rescuing), naivete, and overidentification. The latter may be a particular concern, especially for the therapist with a personal history that has parallels to the patient's.

Therapists have a responsibility to seek consultation or even to refer patients to other practitioners if they are unable to reasonably stay within their therapeutic role and tasks and where there is significant risk that they will seriously transgress ethical boundaries due to their countertransference. Knapp and VandeCreek (1996) discuss another potential problem arising from this type of overinvolvement:

> The failure to maintain appropriate boundaries not only can undermine therapeutic effectiveness, but also can anger the patient enough to pre-

cipitate a lawsuit. Many patients with an apparent history of abuse enter therapy with a background of unstable interpersonal relationships, sometimes varying between idealization and vilification of others, including their therapists. (p. 455)

Chu (1988) and others have also written about the boomerang reaction and the pitfalls that often follow overinvolvement with and overgratification of the patient. When the patient continues to expect the same degree of involvement and effort and/or fails to get better or take personal responsibility, the therapist often comes to resent and withdraw from the patient. In some situations, this withdrawal is extreme, with the depleted/angry therapist terminating treatment abruptly and without adequate warning or preparation, abandoning the patient in the process. In such a scenario, the patient can be left worse off than when treatment began and, furthermore, may be grief stricken, enraged, and ready to seek revenge on the abandoning and disillusioning therapist.

The therapist must also maintain role clarity and avoid mixing roles. The therapist stays within the clinical setting and does not get involved in outside issues (except where mandated by statutes requiring the breaking of confidentiality, such as child abuse reporting requirements, Tarasoff-type responsibilities to warn or protect against credible threats of violence against others, or in the case of clear and present danger to the self). A most important issue arises in distinguishing between the consulting room and the courtroom. The therapist must be cognizant of the differences between clinical and forensic settings and roles [see Greenberg and Shuman (1997) and Melton (1994) for a thorough discussion of the differences in these settings and their associated roles] and must not agree to serve as a forensic examiner or expert witness while in the primary role of therapist. Not only are these dual roles, but they are in conflict with one another and, according to Gutheil and Simon (1997), "may well represent a form of disloyalty to the patient" (p. 1406).

Another important issue involving mixed roles and settings arises when a patient indicates a wish or desire to take some sort of extratherapy action (i.e., lawsuit, confrontation of the alleged abuser or others, cut-off from a family member or the entire family). As a general rule, the therapist can indicate a willingness to explore the reasons and motivations underlying the urge but should also communicate the serious potential consequences of actions of this sort. In particular, the therapist should encourage (or require) that any such action be decided upon after careful consideration and discussion in therapy (including attention to the motivation for, anticipated consequences of, and preparation for any course of action), rather than being undertaken haphazardly or impulsively, since it holds potential risk and liability for both patient and therapist. The therapist should also convey that, for the most part, actions such as these occur outside of the therapeutic setting and without the direct involvement of the therapist (Scheflin, 1998). The patient must therefore plan to undertake them alone or in the context of supportive others (spouse, partner, family members, friend), not the therapist. On an additonal note, *any extratherapeutic action (but especially a lawsuit) is generally ill-advised if it is undertaken solely on the basis of recovered memory without any corroboration* due to the major forensic challenges that have been mounted against the validity of recovered memories. In the current atmosphere, situations of this sort pose additional risk and liability. Grunberg and Ney (1997) made the following observation regarding confrontations:

> Arguably, confrontations with clear/available memory are risky enough . . . they are all the more so when there is not corroborative evidence available, which is sometimes the case with a recovered memory. Although primary concern for the welfare of the client is always paramount, a secondary consideration of harm must also be given to third parties. . . . In the interest of all parties, confrontations should probably not be undertaken if the evidence/corroboration is not available. In response to increasing numbers of legal suits against therapists by their clients, Caudill (1996) suggests that all confrontations be done by a third party. Or, if done by the client's therapist, it should be done after signing a Waiver of Conflict which informs the third party of the potentially distressing situation. While primary duty is to the client, therapists must also consider the degree of distress that is being inflicted upon third parties when confronting. A combination of sensitivity and realism is necessary with confrontation: confrontation is a choice, not a necessity. (p. 550)

Gutheil and Simon (1997) address another aspect of extratherapy actions, namely termination of the treatment when the therapy contract has been violated. Although their discussion in the following quote involves only lawsuits, it may pertain to other forms of extratherapy actions that violate the therapeutic agreement and that further signal treatment noncompliance:

> If a patient rushes blindly ahead with the intent to sue a parent for long-ago abuse recalled in current therapy, and the therapist's advice militates against this course, therapy should not go forward until this difference of opinion is taken up as a treatment issue. In this situation, the patient has violated the therapeutic contract to explore in therapy the likely consequences of an action before acting or acting out. The

> patient should be reminded of this contract and be given an opportuni-
> ty to weigh the alternatives. If the patient persists with the intention to
> sue, the clinician should refer the patient to another therapist, if neces-
> sary, and terminate therapeutic work with that patient. (p. 1407)

Of course, in such a circumstance, the therapist carries an obligation to not abandon the patient and should arrange for a reasonable time frame for termination, in addition to making referrals to other suitable practi-tioners.

One other type of mixed or dual role relationship is worth mentioning. Whenever possible, when abuse has been reported or is suspected, the therapist does not treat members of the same family due to issues of enmeshment, role conflict, triangulation, and divided loyalty that might ensue, often in replication of past relationship dynamics (Courtois, 1988). In such a situation, where the therapist is acting on behalf of several patients and not only one, his/her therapeutic neutrality and effective-ness are compromised. Such role segmentation may be nearly impossible in some settings and circumstances (e.g., isolated and rural settings and/or any community with limited mental health resources). The prac-titioner who ends up treating several members of a family where abuse is an issue should be especially attentive to informed consent and the main-tenance of confidentiality and have consultation and supervision readily available (even if these are conducted long-distance by phone).

The Therapist Is Aware of Transference, Countertransference, Secondary Traumatization, and Self-Care Issues

Transference has long been understood as a reflection of autobiographical memory and attachment issues from the patient's life projected onto the therapist. It can also be understood as a form of coded communication about the past and thus a form of implicit memory (Brown et al., 1998; Waites, 1997). The therapist, at times, gains understanding about possible past abuse/trauma through a patient's reenactments, repetition compul-sions, and behaviors that make up the patient's transference reactions to the therapist (Brown et al., 1998; Galatzer-Levy, 1997; Levine, 1997). Yet, as with other forms of indirect or indistinct information, absent corrobora-tion, the therapist must not overinterpret the material or take it to be the exact reconstruction or replication of historical reality (Brenneis, 1997). Instead, it should be considered more broadly as a representation of aspects of the patient's past and present, including schemata, fantasies, and object relations that are subject to discussion and examination within the therapy (Hegeman, 1995; Levine, 1997). (Transference and counter-transference are discussed more specifically in chapter 9).

Self-monitoring, self-analysis, and supervision/consultation assist in therapeutically managing rather than inappropriately reacting to or enacting patient transference material. The practitioner should, whenever possible, maintain a varied caseload, avoiding one that is overly taxing and/or one comprising only abuse and trauma cases. Furthermore, the practitioner would be well advised to avoid becoming isolated in work with these patients and to engage in adequate self-care, including a variety of social, recreational, and spiritual outlets. It is crucial for the therapist to monitor the status of his/her mental health, seeking additional support and personal therapy during times of heightened stress or crisis. When a therapist has a personal history similar to the patient's in terms of abuse/trauma and/or recovered memories, over- or underidentification may be problematic and additional consultation may be necessary to maintain a therapeutic role and perspective. Especially when the therapist has not resolved abuse-related issues, it is generally better to not treat cases that are overly similar and/or that elicit reactions that interfere with the ability to practice professionally and objectively.

The Therapist Utilizes
General and Specialized Informed Consent

As discussed earlier, information presented verbally and in writing at the initiation and throughout the course of treatment, along with forms signifying the individual's consent to treatment, are especially important. The provision of information and informed consent educate and empower the patient regarding voluntary participation in psychotherapy. Informed consent establishes conditions of the treatment frame, defines the focus and goals of the treatment and the methods to be used and their rationale, all the while encouraging a joint endeavor. Moreover, it serves another important function vis-à-vis memory and memory issues: It explains and demystifies the therapeutic process, thus reducing the stress and uncertainty that are often features of psychotherapy. Highly hypnotizable/suggestible/fantasy-prone patients and/or those who are immature/compliant/dependent tend to rely on others for definition or direction. As a result, they may be at higher-than-average risk for false memory production when in conditions of interpersonal uncertainty. They may be unduly influenced by or eager to please a real or perceived authority figure/powerful other/parental stand-in by producing what they believe is expected or desired. They may also overrely on the authority figure for answers or, as so cogently stated by David Calof (1994), they may attempt "to export the locus of authority" for their experience (including memories) to the therapist in return for attention and support.

When a prospective patient seeks therapy for abuse-related issues or reports suspicions and/or recovered memories of abuse, preliminary information about how the practitioner works with issues of abuse/trauma and memory-related issues should be included in the initial informed consent procedure (to be signed by the patient). This can later be supplemented, on an as-needed basis, with specifics. For example, the American Psychiatric Association "Statement on Memories of Sexual Abuse" (1993), a concise but comprehensive overview of these issues, or any similar document (perhaps written by the therapist) can be given to the prospective patient at the time of intake. This introductory material provides the basis of a mutual understanding of the practitioner's approach that is addressed in greater depth and detail during the course of treatment. Brown et al. (1998) recommend the following as part of more detailed informed consent regarding memory:

> If the trauma treatment potentially may involve enhancement of memory or the integration of memory components, the therapist should provide the patient with detailed and accurate information about memory. This information should correct myths, for example, that recovered memories are necessarily accurate. The patient needs to know that memory is imperfect, that most memories contain a mixture of accurate and inaccurate information, and that some memories, however emotionally compelling, may be quite inaccurate with respect to historical truth. It is advisable to inform the patient that emotionality about, vividness of detail about, and confidence in any given memory, have little relationship to its accuracy or inaccuracy. Moreover, patients should know about common errors in memory, such as detail reconstruction, source misattribution, dating errors, and filling in the gaps. (pp. 501–502)

These authors further suggest that the main points outlined here about trauma treatment and memory-related issues, including its fallibility and suggestibility, and the legal implications of treatment be given to the patient in writing. In addition, if any specialized or experimental memory enhancement or integration technique is given consideration (e.g., hypnosis, EMDR, TFT), it should be fully explained to the patient along with the potential benefits and risks associated with its use. More specific informed consent documents should be used for these techniques and signed by the patient to indicate understanding, agreement, and voluntary participation.

Treatment Is Planned and Periodically Reviewed

A treatment plan involves ongoing monitoring of treatment progress or lack thereof, with attention to the achievement of stated goals, the mastery of skills and the lessening of symptoms, the treatment of remaining symptoms and problem areas, and the risk of possible relapse. Through planning and periodic updating, the therapist demonstrates attention to ongoing assessment and to treatment progress and compliance. Among other things, this attention to goals serves to counter the oft-repeated criticism that abuse-related treatment is overly vague and open-ended and that patient dependence is encouraged (until insurance benefits run out). Ongoing treatment planning is in accord with treatment guideline initiatives across the various mental health and medical professions. It is further compatible with the approach fostered by managed care and, as such, helps with meeting the criteria for ongoing insurance review and benefits. As pertains to recovered memory issues in particular, Table 8.2 lists some of the elements that are useful for the therapist to review in creating and updating the treatment plan.

The Therapist Strives to Practice from a Neutral Perspective Regarding Memory

Since personal beliefs, assumptions, cognitive distortions, and knowledge gaps can easily lead therapists into positions of bias (as reflected in premature cognitive commitment, hindsight bias, confirmatory bias, or premature conclusions due to illusory correlations—i.e., between certain symptoms and an unremembered history of abuse), it is important for them to engage in honest self-appraisal regarding their operative biases and relevant knowledge. Therapists must develop a broad knowledge base from which to approach memory issues in clinical practice and make every attempt to keep major prejudices and ideologies out of the consulting room. They must, instead, strive to maintain an open, reflective, and objective point of view while remaining personally supportive to the patient. They must be inquisitive about the material at hand, bring a perspective of "unbiased curiosity" to its exploration or meaning to the patient, and must themselves be able to tolerate ambiguity and uncertainty. This stance is far preferable to one that represents an overly narrow focus on abuse and premature cognitive commitment to the abuse hypothesis above all others (Pope & Brown, 1996).

The therapist must attempt to remain neutral vis-à-vis memory mate-

Table 8.2
Elements to Consider in Developing and Updating
the Treatment Plans and Recovered Memory Issues

Preliminary Development of the Treatment Plan

- Preliminary treatment contract (information for patient's statement) signifying general informed consent to treatment. Reviewed with and signed by the patient.

- Preliminary assessment completed to determine:
  - symptoms and deficit areas
  - strengths and resources
  - priority areas to be addressed first
  - risk areas requiring immediate or potential intervention
  - medical or other issues requiring assessment/attention
  - areas requiring immediate (or potential) mandatory or discretionary reporting (i.e., continuous or recovered memories of past abuse or reports of current abuse or violence). Reporting requirements vary by state.

- Preliminary treatment plan specifying goals and objectives drawn up and reviewed with the patient, including:
  - discussion of strategies for intervention and their risks/benefits
  - discussion of alternative strategies

- Determination of need for coordination of services with any other provider/s
  - signed release/s of information

Review and Update of the Treatment Plan

- Review of chart notes to determine:
  - whether notes are current, complete, and accurate
  - whether release of information forms and informed consent forms are current

- Review of treatment to date to determine:
  - progress on and/or resolution of the treatment goals (symptoms or problem areas)
  - new symptoms and/or problems
  - need for additional assessment/consultation

- Have any treatment issues emerged that therapist is not prepared for or competent to treat? If so, have provisions been made for supervision, consultation, and/or referral to someone with relevant expertise?

- Review of any reactions to the patient that might interfere with treatment and provisions for consultation/supervision

- Revision and updating of treatment goals and objectives
  - reviewed with the patient

Recovered Memory Issues

- Review of approaches to memory issues before or during course of treatment

- Notation of having provided specific written and verbal information to the patient (in chart notes)
  - about memory processes for normal event memory, traumatic memory, and recovered memory

Continued on following page

Table 8.2 (continued)
Elements to Consider in Developing and Updating
the Treatment Plans and Recovered Memory Issues

- about approaches to treatment and risks/benefits
- about how the therapist works with memory

- Notation of correction of any patient misunderstanding/misinformation regarding treatment (and memory) (noted in chart notes)
  - at start of treatment
  - during course of treatment

- Assessment and review of patient's available memories of abuse/trauma
  - access to, whether continuous or sporadic
  - quality and degree of completeness of memories
  - conditions of recovery and triggers
  - spontaneous emergence of memories within or outside of treatment setting
  - beliefs, interpretations about memories
  - whether memories emerged in prior treatment or self-help efforts or due to media exposure
    - under what circumstances?
    - patient's perspective on them

- Assessment and review of risk and suggestibility factors
  - personality factors or diagnoses
  - hypnotizability
  - suggestibility
  - social compliance/other-directedness/external locus of control
  - dependence
  - naivete

- Assessment of any forensic involvement

- Request and receipt of records of prior treatment

- Request and receipt of other records (possibly notarized)

- Review of any reactions to the patient and/or recovered memory issues that might interfere with treatment and provisions for supervision/consultation

- Audiotapes, videotapes, transcripts and/or notes of sessions where memories reported

rial. Being neutral and exploratory/open-ended in technique does not mean that the therapist is in denial about abuse/trauma as serious and quite common, about its possibility in the patient's past, or about its possible traumatic impact. Individuals with positive abuse/trauma histories often struggle with differentiating what is real and what is not, experience strongly ambivalent emotions, and require a supportive context in which to consider various perspectives. Similarly, individuals with suspicions but no memories and those with incomplete and reinstated memories must have the latitude to explore all possibilities without constraint.

Suspicions of abuse are best explored via open-ended questioning and free narrative to lessen the possibility of suggestion. It is recommended that therapists avoid: the use of language that is overly defining (i.e., labeling impressions or sensations conclusively as abuse/memories of abuse); leading and close-ended questions (especially when posed repeatedly); specific suggestions or allegations; premature conclusions and/or the closure of further exploration; and an uncritical acceptance of an individual's recollections of abuse as always representing historical truth. Additionally, therapists are encouraged to practice in ways that minimize suggestion effects, especially concerning the use of strategies involving more suggestion. According to Brown et al. (1998), the most suggestive activities are those that involve conditions of (1) psychophysiological destabilization of the individual, (2) information control, (3) repetition of misleading suggestions both within and across interviews, (4) emotional manipulation, and (5) interrogatory bias. None of these belongs in the consulting room.

Equally important, as the patient is cautioned against "jumping to conclusions" or premature closure, the therapist must not "fill in," "confirm," or "disconfirm" suspicions of a nonremembered abuse history; rather, the therapist should help the patient explore the content and its possible meaning while guarding against suggestion, pro or con. Although the clinician keeps to this stance as much as possible, there are times when it is both important and necessary to educate or challenge the patient on material that is clearly impossible, improbable, seems delusional, and/or in which the patient is overinvested. In such circumstances, return to more formalized assessment might also be in order. On the other end of the spectrum, there may be times when the therapist needs to share or even confront the patient with evidence of abuse when remaining in denial/avoidance is clearly interfering with the patient's ability to function or is related to danger and/or life threat. For example, a therapist was contacted by a sibling of the patient's after the patient made a quite serious suicide attempt. The attempt came in the aftermath of the sudden recovery of abuse memories and debilitating intrusive posttraumatic symptoms triggered by a recent cancer diagnosis. The sibling provided information to corroborate past abuse in order to spare the patient ongoing uncertainty about the recovered memories, in the belief that the uncertainty was fueling the suicidality. The therapist also thought that the uncertainty was sufficiently stressful that the corroboration could prove beneficial. Without disclosing the content, she told the patient that she had received important information that could be of help to her. She asked the patient's permission to invite the sibling into a session to disclose the information.

The Therapist Understands the Malleability of Human Memory and the Difference between Historical and Narrative Truth

The therapist understands that human memory is fluid rather than static and that conditions at the time of encoding, storage/consolidation, and retrieval may affect memory retention and accessibility. The therapist uses this knowledge to provide the patient with education regarding the malleability and reconstructive nature of human memory processes and the possibility that memories may represent reality, fantasies, confabulation, or some combination thereof. The therapist further conveys that there can be differences between historical and narrative truth, that what is remembered may be quite variable, and that the gist of the memory and its possible meaning to the individual are more important than the peripheral details (although in some cases of traumatic memory remembrance, it may be the return of peripheral details focused on during the traumatic episode that suggest or lead the way to the return of the gist of the memory, e.g., the return of memories of sexual abuse by first remembering the wallpaper pattern in the bedroom where the abuse occurred, rather than the event itself).

Where delayed/recovered memories are at issue, the therapist helps the patient to develop critical judgment regarding their possible interpretation and meaning and further recommends the development of a scientific attitude over time (Brown, 1995). The patient is encouraged to not rush to conclusions and to avoid premature closure or certainty. S/he can be given additional counsel and reassurance regarding the possibility that no "right answer" or conclusion is available and that struggling with uncertainty and developing tolerance for ambiguity are often part of the process and are quite acceptable to the therapist.

As part of this understanding, the therapist does not definitively confirm/validate the reality of a memory (whether continuous or recovered) when there is no evidence or corroboration; however, therapist and patient might arrive at a shared conclusion/belief about the reality and probability of the occurrence of abuse or the patient might make such a determination independent of the therapist (and at times contrary to the belief of the therapist). The therapist might also arrive at hypotheses about past abuse/trauma that might be shared or withheld from the patient, depending upon the circumstances. Making and sharing hypotheses regarding possible past abuse/trauma requires careful clinical consideration and judgment, as discussed by Sauzier (1997) and Uyehara (1997). Uyehara further offers the reminder that the therapist is not all-knowing and "needs to take a humble position regarding knowledge of a patient's history" (p. 417).

The Therapist Develops a
Variety of Clinical Approaches for
Work with Recovered Memories

Perhaps one of the most difficult clinical situations arises when the patient who is struggling with what to believe regarding memories of past abuse (especially when memories are fragmentary, unclear, partially accessible, etc.) asks: "Do you believe me?" or similar questions that seek the therapist's validation. This is a quite legitimate question from individuals who may have had repeated experiences of being disbelieved; however, it may also be an attempt by the patient to circumvent the difficult process of arriving at his/her own understanding and beliefs about the memory. In general, the therapist faced with such a query must maintain a stance of supportive encouragement towards the patient while simultaneously assessing clinical status, motivation, how the patient is asking the question, and what is being asked for. The response offered to the query depends upon what the therapist knows about the individual and his/her story and personality dynamics and motivation. Calof (1994) suggested a number of approaches and responses that are useful for the therapist to consider for use in such a situation. The following list paraphrases some of his suggestions:

- The therapist honestly accepts/expresses that s/he can neither bear witness to the patient's disputed memories nor prove them wrong, and considers the possibility of real memory as well as false memory.
- The therapist works in the context of the therapy frame that has been developed and that includes emphasis on the patient's personal authority regarding memories and other productions by:
  - Reflecting back the patient's doubt and uncertainty and not being too quick to join one side or the other to offset the patient's struggle with ambiguity
  - Accepting/framing/regarding/aligning with the patient's doubt and confusion as having a valuable underlying function, worthy of exploration
  - Focusing on the dynamics surrounding the surfacing and subsequent confusion over memories of abuse, as much as on the memories themselves
  - Gently confronting the patient's attempt to export the locus of authority and inviting the him/her to consider the motivation behind the attempt

- Directing the patient back to his/her own internal validation mechanisms
- Directing the patient to a consideration of the "advantages" or "disadvantages" that would accompany the resolving of doubts over the accuracy of his/her memories
- Mirroring back to the patient disowned and disavowed issues and aspects
- Encouraging the seeking of corroborative evidence and/or memory triggers/cues
- Stating the legitimacy and possibility of "not knowing" or "never knowing"
- Accepting and supporting the patient's frustration and wish to know/not know

- The therapist monitors transference carefully for indicators of patient dependence on the therapist as the arbiter of experience, for an over-focus on "memory work" to the neglect of overall treatment goals directed at functioning and self-management, for objectification and role inducement of the therapist, etc. The therapist can also monitor how a patient asks a question such as "Do you believe me?"in order to understand the underlying motivation or hope. For example, some patients ask in a demanding, close-ended, and even hostile way, whereas others are more plaintive and dependent in their inquiry. Noting the style, the therapist can engage the patient in a discussion of expectations and motivation.
- The therapist also monitors countertransference for indicators of complementary role enactment, role slippage and loss of objectivity, and compensatory validation.

Kepner (1995) has discussed another aspect of the response dilemma, one that is not mentioned very often in the current climate: that of the therapist indicating belief in the patient's memories and story. He reminds the therapist that, at times and depending upon the circumstances, it is quite appropriate to indicate belief in the patient as well as in his/her reports of abuse (again without confirming that such belief indicates that all details are historically accurate or true). From my perspective, a response indicating general belief on the part of the therapist is appropriate when the individual has had continuous memory, has been consistent in the abuse story over the course of treatment, and has some corroboration. It is not appropriate when an individual is struggling with fragmentary/uncertain memory, amnesia, and recovered memory, and there is no corroboration. In this circumstance, neither the patient nor the therapist has clarity (although they may hold opinions or share strong suspicions) yet the therapist has no basis for providing a definitive or confirmatory response.

The Therapist Attempts to Ascertain
What the Patient Remembers

Elsewhere (Courtois, 1988, 1992), I have commented that many adult survivors of incest and sexual abuse will disclose information that is known to them only when directly asked to do so. It can therefore be most beneficial for the therapist to ask the patient (using open-ended inquiry aimed at eliciting free narrative) to describe or write what is known as a baseline and to record verbatim any additional memories or details as they might emerge (this strategy is further described in chapter 6 in the discussion of the mid-phase of the posttrauma treatment model). Korn (Leeds and Korn, 1998) has described this as "daring to ask." It is not unusual for patients to be able to produce more information upon such direct inquiry or with permission to do so. Many then express surprise at what they know and are able to remember more spontaneously when they are in a supportive context that is open to their personal exploration.

The Therapist Utilizes a
Variety of Strategies with
Posttraumatic Symptoms and Memories

Gold and Brown (1997) address therapeutic approaches to patients who have numbing or intrusive/reexperiencing symptoms and/or whose memories of new details emerge spontaneously during the course of therapy. They specifically caution therapists about undermining the spontaneous emergence of memories and instead suggest:

> Both client and therapist can have greater confidence in the accuracy of abuse memories that emerge spontaneously from the client rather than in response to prompting by the therapist. Recollections surfacing in this manner are less vulnerable to the potentially distorting influences of leading or suggestion on the part of the therapist. (p. 186)

These authors further emphasize the importance of empowering the patient and teaching a variety of skill-building and self-care skills, in general and to gain control when in the throes of intrusive/reexperiencing and numbing symptoms. They recommend as well that therapists help patients identify any triggers or prodromal symptoms (those that typically precede flashbacks or other posttraumatic or dissociative reactions that may, in turn, be the harbinger of a new memory or detail). Identification might be an important step in managing reactions, with the goals of facilitating recall "in the least retraumatizing fashion," and of beginning "to pair active self-care and self-awareness with the process of memory recovery" (Gold & Brown, 1997, p. 188).

Finally, these same authors give important advice on the therapist's response in-session to a patient's spontaneous recall, a topic that has not yet received much discussion in the literature. The therapist must respond calmly and from a stance of empathic neutrality and inquisitiveness to any material that emerges, even when it is in highly emotional form, as is sometimes the case with in-session spontaneous abreactions. The therapist must avoid overreacting and underreacting to the material and its emotional presentation. By overreacting, s/he may express overfascination and, in this and other ways, reinforce an expectation that therapy work only occurs when it involves new material and a highly emotional presentation. On the other hand, by underreacting or attempting to deflect the patient from the material and any related strong affect, the therapist may signal to the patient that the material is unacceptable and imply that s/he should to return to a position of silence. Therapists must also learn a strategy of progressive asking for details, still using an open-ended format (Courtois, 1988, 1992).

Various strategies currently described in the literature help to stabilize symptoms and empower the patient and thus should be considered by the therapist when issues of this sort are in evidence. Many of these were presented in chapters 5, 6, and 7. A listing of different strategies by therapeutic orientation is included in Table 6.2 on page 209.

The Therapist Keeps Accurate Records

Each patient file is a medical-legal chart. Record-keeping is necessary in the provision of all psychotherapy and is especially important when memory recovery is at issue. The therapist is obligated to keep records in sufficient detail to document the main issues and events in the treatment; to articulate and track symptomatology, the treatment plan, and progress in achieving goals; and to chronicle all major communications and interventions with the patient. Most professional organizations offer their members guidelines for record-keeping that can be consulted for more information on this topic. The importance of documentation was underscored by attorney Brandt Caudill (1997) who, in a chapter on risk management, labeled good documentation "the therapist's shield."

The file should contain the patient's history, presenting concerns, assessment information, diagnosis, treatment goals and objectives, progress notes, and other documentation, such as copies of materials given to patients, signed copies of informed consent forms, and releases of information. Each session's progress notes, at minimum, include the date on which treatment was provided, major issues, and any specific interventions. Progress notes should be brief, neutral in tone, and based on fact and behavior rather than on the therapist's speculations. They contain information about the patient's mood, areas of concern or progress, and action taken by the therapist. Examples of behaviorally-oriented therapy notes are included in table 8.3.

The patient's file is also the place for the therapist to record discussions about memory and the information given to patients verbally and in writing. It further makes mention of any erroneous expectations and misinformation regarding abuse and memory held by the patient. It should contain specific documentation of the provision by the therapist of accurate information and the discussion of process issues regarding memory. Additionally, notes should document memories and events as "by report," "by history," "reported by," or "believed by" the patient, rather than as factual or as historical reality. They should also document any attempts by the patient to get the therapist to confirm or indicate belief in an abuse history (whether or not it is based on recovered memory and/or lacks corroboration).

Brown et al., (1998) suggest the following for inclusion in the record:

> Where memory enhancement or integration is done, the notes should document efforts to encourage critical evaluation of therapeutically elicited material, minimize suggestive influences, discourage confrontation with alleged perpetrators, and explore the potential negative ramifications of such controntation. (p. 504)

Knapp and VandeCreek (1996) further suggest that notes include the patient's recollections before, during, and after any specific efforts at memory recovery. Therapists might also consider additional forms of documentation when conducting exploratory sessions utilizing specialized techniques. These include detailed process notes and audio- and videotaping of the session to record information as reported by the patient and to record the intervention (Brown et al., 1997; Courtois, 1996; Nagy, 1994). Finally, as suggested in the guidelines put forth by the American Society for Clinical Hypnosis, the more serious or unusual the memories and allegations of the patient, the more detailed and thorough the treatment note documentation should be (Hammond et al., 1994).

Table 8.3
Record-Keeping Suggestions*

General Records (Patient Chart)**

- Client name, address, and telephone number
- Location of treatment, evaluation, or consultation
- Client complaint on intake
- Medical history recognized as to its potential significance
- Past and current medications
- Significant social history
- Findings on appropriate examinations
- Raw data and interpretation of psychological tests administered
- Current functional impairments and rating levels thereof
- Diagnostic impression(s)
- Contemporaneous and dated progress or session notes including specific components of treatment, evaluation, or consultation
- Dates of all treatment evaluations, or consultation sessions
- An evaluation of progress (if applicable)
- A prognosis
- Fees charged and paid
- Identity of each provider of treatment, evaluation or consultation (and supervisor, if any)
- If services are rendered by a permit holder
- Written disclosures form signed by the client

Progress/Process Notes

- Client identity on each page
- Date
- Patient clinical status/symptoms
- Intervention(s)
- Topic areas discussed/theme or focus of session
- Treatment plan change(s)
- Should be written in behavioral and descriptive/factual terms,
- Should be written in more detail and verbatim if abuse is discussed and/or memory material is new or emerges spontaneously

Sample Progress/Process Notes

Patient Name:_____Date: _____

Patient was late to session due to work schedule. Reported feelings of suicidality this week in relation to thoughts and memories of abuse and in relation to a call from her brother. Suicidal risk assessed and determined to be low. Patient utilized safety plan this week and referenced it in session, agrees to continue to utilize, as needed. Patient continues on medication, as prescribed.
Standing appointment.
Clinical status: stable with support systems in place.

Continued on following page

Table 8.3 (continued)
Record-Keeping Suggestions*

---

*Patient Name:*_____*Date:* _____

Emergency Session. Patient reports ongoing thoughts of suicide and a plan. Assessed suicidality. Patient at high risk, with available lethal means, few available resources, tunnel vision re: options, and serious hopelessness. Describes suicidality as response to upsetting phone call from brother who challenged patient's memories and intrusive visual images of abuse. Attempts to stabilize unsuccessful; patient unable to agree to a safety plan. Hospitalization recommended for safety/stabilization. Patient pre-certified by insurance company and admitted. Communication initiated with treatment team—information re: clinical status and treatment goals imparted.

*Patient Name:*_____*Date:* _____

Patient destabilized from last session. Very upset re: the emergence of memories this week after seeing a television show on sexual abuse. Patient reports intrusive and fragmented memories of abuse that occured in a group context. Patient reports that she "can't turn off these memories, like pictures," which she further described as "a group of people around me smiling or glancing at me and making me do sex things with them". Does not know what this means and questioned me as to its possible interpretation. Offered support for her feelings and ongoing exploration— cautioned against jumping to conclusions. Images as reported are not consistent with her previous memories. Reviewed stabilization strategies including specific grounding skills, people she can call for support. Safety plan reviewed and in place.
Patient described herself as less agitated and frightened at the end of session.
Standing appointment.

*Therapist should be aware of any requirements mandated by state law.

**General Records (Patient Chart) Requirements From "Forensic Corner: Record Keeping in Cases of Suspected Sexual Abuse," 1998 Spring, *NJ Advisor: The American Professional Society on the Abuse of Children-New Jersey Newsletter,* 3(1), p.5. Copyright 1998 by The American Professional Society on the Abuse of Children. Reprinted with permission.

The Therapist Is Alert to
Suggestion and Suggestibility Issues and
Assesses Risk for False Memory Production

The therapist must maintain an awareness of suggestion and suggestive influences as well as a patient's degree of malleability. As discussed earlier, the therapist monitors interactions with the patient for suggestion and confirmatory bias on an ongoing basis and is neutrally supportive.

Additionally, the therapist asks quite specifically about different types of suggestive influences and activities in the patient's life that may have predetermined or prejudiced him/her about memory, past abuse/trauma, and even about diagnosis. It can be crucially important to know about what a patient has been exposed to, whether in the family environment growing up, in the course of previous therapy or through participation in self-help activities (especially if unconventional or suggestive techniques were used, or a nontraditional or even erroneous perspective espoused), or due to exposure via the media and reading (including information found on the internet and in "chat rooms"). The therapist should simultaneously assess the possibility of secondary gain or loss (e.g., maintaining membership in a self-help group by virtue of having abuse memories or carrying a particular diagnosis or, conversely, losing membership by not having them).

As part of the overall assessment and where it seems especially warranted, the therapist should evaluate the patient's level of hypnotizability, interrogatory suggestibility, and other risk factors associated with the production of memories (Brown, 1995; Brown et al., 1998; Gudjonsson, 1984; Lynn, Myers, & Malinoski, 1997), as well as personality factors such as immaturity/naivete/dependence/external locus of control/social compliance and Axis II diagnoses (e.g., hysteria, antisocial, borderline, dependent, paranoid, mixed personality disorders), along with Axis I diagnoses (depression, dissociative disorder) that might make the patient more suggestible to outside influence. Specific assessment of these diagnoses might also be warranted.

Brown et al. (1998) recommended the following if a high level of suggestibility is determined:

> When the assessment shows that a given individual is in the high range of suggestibility, specifically memory suggestibility, the therapist needs to properly inform the patient of this vulnerability. With such patients we recommend that therapists avoid memory recovery. When memory recovery cannot be avoided, we recommend that the therapist explicitly discuss the patient's memory vulnerability with him or her and secure appropriate informed consent that the patient understands that any of his or her memories, recovered or not, are significantly vulnerable to external suggestive influences . . . . We also recommend that treatment sessions be videotaped, so that if subsequent allegations of undue therapeutic suggestions arise an independent assessment can be made of alleged claims.
>
> *It is very important, however, that the capacity for accepting hypnotic or interrogatory suggestions not be considered to be directly correlated with the like-*

lihood that a particular memory is true or false. In other words, the fact that a person scores high on an hypnotic or interrogative suggestibility scale does not prove that his/her memories are false. At the opposite end of the continuum, people with low suggestibility should not be assumed to have only real memories. No matter what the susceptibility level, there is no substitute for independent corroboration. . . . (p. 506) (italics added)

The Therapist Avoids Regressive Techniques

It is recommended that therapists generally avoid techniques that foster the patient's regression, in particular with highly malleable/dependent individuals. Regressive dissociative techniques are especially to be avoided because they add degrees of suggestibility.

Elsewhere, we have discussed encouraging the highest degree of functioning in patients and the development of a support system besides the therapist. This position helps to equalize responsibility for the treatment and works against overdependence and associated regressive tendencies. The therapist must recognize that some individuals who were abused/neglected in childhood are searching for reparenting of sorts. The need may match the tendency of some therapists to overattach and overgratify the "wounded child parts" (or the child alters in the case of DID) of their patients. To do so is well-documented as a treatment trap that needs to be avoided. Although the therapist may serve in the capacity of a parenting figure, s/he should not take on a parenting/rescuing role and must encourage the patient (including the DID patient) to function at an adult level. This is discussed further in chapter 9.

The Therapist Utilizes Techniques Carrying the Lowest Degree of Suggestive Risk First

Of necessity, the therapist utilizes different strategies depending on the various memory presentations and the individual patient's dynamics and needs. In general, aggressive methods used to surface hidden memories are contraindicated unless a specific circumstance mandates their use (and even this is controversial—see Lynn et al., 1997, for further discussion). The therapist begins with what is available and encourages free recall. As described by Brown et al. (1998) paraphrasing other authors and discussed in chapter 6, the best "technique" for recall is no technique at all other than free recall. Kluft (1996) also suggested that the therapist work with memory from the "top on down," from what is available first and perhaps with detail emerging later. The therapist keeps in mind a hierarchy of interventions and begins with those that have the lowest degree of risk for suggestion, moving "step-wise" to those with greater intensity and suggestibility only where clinically warranted (and possibly only after consultation, supervision, and/or peer review).

Whatever the specific method, memory-focused integration (and sometimes memory enhancement) work occurs in the middle phase of the sequenced treatment model (see chapter 6 for details). As a general rule and wherever possible, any exploratory work involving traumatic memories ought to be undertaken within the context of the main therapy and ought not be parceled out (e.g., to another practitioner who "knows about abuse and knows how to get at lost memories," or to a weekend workshop or group where a specific focus is placed on the retrieval of unremembered material related to a past history of abuse).

The Therapist Should Not Use Hypnosis (Or Related Techniques) Specifically for Memory Retrieval

Hypnosis is probably the most controversial technique in the entire false/recovered memory debate, especially when its explicit purpose is memory recovery. At present, available research is conclusive that memories that emerge as a result of hypnosis can be compelling yet inaccurate, that they nevertheless can be held with confidence by the patient, and that the veridicality of memories retrieved under hypnosis should not be assumed (although some may well be accurate). Additionally, risk for the development of pseudomemories increases with the use of hypnosis, especially among high- to medium-hypnotizable subjects, and such memories, once instated, are difficult to reverse (Lynn et al., 1997). The potentially confounding nature of hypnosis and the hypnotic process (or any similar technique) makes its use generally inadvisable as a method for memory retrieval; however, it has an important place in such therapeutic tasks and endeavors as ego-strengthening, coping-enhancement, self-soothing, temporizing and pacing, etc.

The American Society for Clinical Hypnosis guidelines concerning clinical hypnosis and memory (Hammond et al., 1994), recently have been criticized as too lenient regarding the use of hypnosis specifically for memory retrieval (Lynn et al., 1997). Although these authors found much to commend in the ASCH guidelines that would deter therapists from engaging in a number of potentially risky therapy practices, they also signaled the following as problems:

We are concerned that clinicians will interpret the guidelines to imply that if the practices suggested are adhered to, false memory risk will be completely eliminated. It would be unfortunate if clinicians did not fully appreciate that whatever advantage in accurate recall hypnosis provides, it is accompanied by a tradeoff in recall errors. Furthermore, contrary to the implication in the ASCH guidelines . . . the available evidence indicates that hypnosis provides no special recall benefit in terms of improving memories associated with relatively arousing situations. Before implying that hypnosis might be of particular benefit in helping trauma victims recall information, it would be prudent to await convincing experimental data that supported this contention. Although the ASCH report may be correct that hypnosis improves so-called emotional or traumatic memories, this still remains a speculative proposition. (pp. 324-325)

These same authors, following their review of the literature on hypnosis and pseudomemories, concluded the following regarding the role of hypnosis in memory recovery and in trauma treatment in general:

> In conclusion, hypnosis is not a reliable means of helping clients recall either traumatic or nontraumatic memories. Hence, hypnosis should not be used to recover memories in psychotherapy. Nevertheless, hypnosis does have a role in the treatment of persons with continuously available memories, preferably in the context of a present-centered, mastery-based treatment . . . . Yet even in these instances, great care should be taken to avoid leading procedures, and the therapist should have an appreciation for the difficulty, if not impossibility, of completely eliminating inappropriate and counter-therapeutic suggestive influences.
>
> It would be unfortunate if hypnosis comes to be singled out as a particularly risky procedure, somehow more "dangerous" than many other interventions . . . . If hypnosis were to be scapegoated in this fashion, and we can see some indications that it has already begun to occur, it would be most unfortunate. Whether geared to memory recovery or not, no psychotherapy or treatment technique protects against pseudomemory formation. All therapies contain many of the elements that our review indicates are associated with false memories in the hypnotic context. Clinicians would do well to evaluate their practice of psychotherapy in light of the proposition that there is no such thing as risk-free therapy. (p. 327)

Brown et al. (1998) took a different perspective. They differentiated memory retrieval from memory enhancement undertaken in the interest of integration and argue that, at times, memory enhancement (and even retrieval, in limited circumstances), with or without the use of carefully considered and applied hypnotic process, is warranted in the treatment of trauma. They offer quite extensive rationale and discussion, as well as cautions, concerning the use of clinical hypnosis for memory enhancement for the specific purpose of memory integration in the ultimate interest of trauma resolution. They state their position as follows: "We do not agree with those advocates of the false memory position who would have clinicians abandon memory enhancement altogether. . . . The issue is not whether it is done but *how* it is done. To put it another way: *the task of memory enhancement is to decrease memory omission errors without increasing memory commission errors*" (authors' italics) (p. 516). They further elaborate this point:

> The main issue is not whether or not hypnosis can be used, but how it is used, under what conditions, in what type of treatment relationship, for what type of treatment goal. The hypnotherapist whose use of hypnosis is informed by available scientific research about appropriate uses and limitations, who has carefully considered this information in the treatment plan, and who carefully documents these variables or videotapes the hypnotic treatment sessions, has made every effort to practice within the standard of care. (p. 515)

Kluft (1995, 1997) recently offered clinical documentation and discussion in support of this view. He reported the confirmation of 56% of recalled episodes of abuse in a sample of 34 DID patients, the first discovery of which occurred in therapy in connection with the use of hypnosis. As a result, he cautioned: " . . . these findings cast doubt on the argument that materials emerging from hypnotic exploration should be discounted in a peremptory manner" (Kluft, 1997, p. 35) and he argued that hypnosis has an important and appropriate use in the treatment of the traumatized: "Many dissociative and posttraumatic symptoms respond well to therapies facilitated by hypnosis. Hypnosis is often a most useful modality with which to facilitate their restructuring and resolution. It would be a shame to throw the baby out with the bathwater by unduly restricting the use of hypnosis in traumatized populations" (p. 42).

To summarize the current consensus regarding the use of hypnosis: In general, it should not be used specifically for the retrieval of memory, but it does have a place in memory enhancement when it is in the interest of memory integration and resolution and when undertaken in an informed way, with rationale considered, and with appropriate cautions in place. Memory that emerges under hypnosis should not be disregarded or summarily dismissed as always inaccurate but it should be recognized that its use entails a higher degree of risk for memory production. Moreover, hypnosis should not be used if a patient is involved in a legal proceeding of any type or has any likelihood of taking any legal action in the future (whether related to past abuse or not), since its use may result in the inadmissibility of material and/or the disqualification of the individual's ability to testify. The therapist could end up facing a malpractice action for such disqualification (Scheflin & Shapiro, 1989). Similar to any other specialized technique, hypnosis should only be used if the therapist has been trained in its use and following the provision of informed consent and a signed informed consent document.

The Therapist Uses EMDR
Only with Proper Training

A recently developed technique, Eye Movement Desensitization and Reprocessing (EMDR), shows promise for resolving traumatic memories and ameliorating symptoms; however, it, too, should be used conservatively and with caution in keeping with the following:

> EMDR should be used by a trained and licensed clinician . . . . It is noted for reprocessing (emotional resolution and cognitive restructuring) of memory and many clinicians report that previously unrecalled memories may arise during treatment. While this means that many associated events can be effected rapidly . . . images emerging during treatment cannot be assumed to be historically accurate. (Shapiro, personal communication, 1996)

In following this restrained stance, EMDR (or any similar technique) should not be used if the individual has current or future forensic involvement, at least not without the advice of counsel. Although the admissibility of material emerging from EMDR has not yet been ruled on by the courts, the process may well be viewed as similar to hypnosis because of its potential to elicit and change memories. Clinicians should stay aware of court rulings on this matter and bring questions to the attention of counsel to avoid the potential of disqualification.

The Therapists Does Not Unequivocally
Accept Reports of False Memories or
Recantations as True

Therapists must be as cautious about accepting recantations or retractions at face value and believing they indicate conclusively that abuse/trauma did not occur as they are about accepting all recovered memories as historically true. Formal studies of recanters who deny abuse recollections arising during the course of treatment are scarce. On the other hand, in cases of proven abuse, recantation has long been identified as a common response in both children (Summit, 1983) and adults (Courtois, 1988).

Many reasons and motivations have been identified as the basis of recantation. In their preliminary study, Lief and Fetkewicz (1995) found that the life themes of many recanters were organized around a search for personal meaning and explanation for their mental and emotional disturbances. Many were externally focused dependent personalities who ended up in therapeutic relationships that fostered dependence and that traded off the approval and attention of the therapist with memory production. A number of first person accounts are now available that offer a similar description of the process (Goldstein & Farmer, 1993; Hauser-Hines, 1997; Jeffery, 1997). Some recantations result from later disillusionment with the treatment and with the therapist and/or with belated realization of the therapist's influence on the patient's (false) belief of abuse. This is the basis of many malpractice lawsuits at the present time, whether initiated by patients or by third parties.

At other times, retractions occur to deny or otherwise obscure the occurrence of real abuse and/or retractors have histories of remembered abuse but recant on other abuse incidents that emerged during a course of psychotherapy (whether it was suggestive or not). Grand (1995) writes that many of these are individuals who are highly malleable and who have previously been conditioned into nonremembering of real abuse by caretaker-perpetrators in order to maintain attachment [in keeping with the betrayal-trauma thesis of Freyd (1996)]. As in the case of memory production where the therapist cannot make a determination of historical truth absent corroboration, the therapist similarly cannot make a determination of falsity in the absence of corroboration. Greater weight should not be given to the possibility of false memory than to the possibility of real memory (Berliner & Williams, 1994). When a patient struggles with a recovered memory of abuse and/or the possibility of false memories of abuse due to past suggestive influences (including therapy), the present therapist must offer support and a context for exploration and keep open the possibility of real or illusory memories.

The Therapist Is Careful in Recommending Self-help Books and Groups

The therapist should recommend self-help books and groups only when familiar with their content and perspective. Where abuse is suspected in the absence of clear memory, a generic book on the effects of a painful childhood is preferable to a book on signs and symptoms of sexual abuse or a book on repressed memories that offers suggestive methods for retrieving missing memories. Similarly, the patient with absent autobiographical memory for abuse is best referred to a heterogeneous group for general mental health concerns or an educational or skill-building group rather than a homogeneous abuse-focused one. As discussed earlier, a difficult circumstance arises when a patient with suspicions of abuse and sketchy memory has read books, viewed media presentations, or participated in individual or group therapy or self-help formats that pushed an abuse-focused perspective based on misinformation. The clinician must seek to reeducate the patient and correct skewed content and erroneous beliefs. In some cases, the patient has been so influenced that it is virtually impossible to sort out and disentangle the information from the various sources of influence.

The Therapists's Goal in Attending to Traumatic Memories Is to Facilitate Mastery and Resolution

As part of the informed consent procedure and throughout the course of treatment, the therapist can explain that work with memories is not for the purpose of achieving additional recollections or of finding additional abuse. The therapist should communicate that s/he has no pre-set agenda regarding memory and that to have no recollection and/or to be uncertain is an acceptable (although at times frustrating) outcome. Instead, the therapist can explain the model articulated by Harvey (1994), which is in keeping with the perspective offered here, that work with memory is in the interest of (1) achieving new or renewed authority over the remembering process, acknowledging that:

> Traumatic memory is remarkable for the control it assumes over daily life, turning that life into a literal minefield of disturbing associations, unbidden intrusions and amnestic gaps that render the intrusions incomprehensible.
>
> The aim of psychotherapy with trauma patients is to change the balance of power between the survivor and her memories: to enable her to recall or not recall the events of a distant past, *as she chooses*, and to know that she can reach into a rich storehouse of remembrances and select what to look at now. Part of the work is to assure that whatever may have been stored at time one is made available for voluntary remem-

brance at time two. Another part of the work is to place once fragmented and incomprehensible images into a narrative and associative context that adds meaning to these remembrances even as it deprives them
of their post-traumatic hold. (Italics added) (p. 9)

(2) integrating memory and affect; that is, "to place traumatic remembrances in an affective as well as a narrative context" so that *"the recovered
survivor will feel her or his history"* (p. 9); and (3) resolution of whatever
memory is available and personal meaning-making:

> By this we mean that survivors will in their recovery process come to
> know not only more of what happened, but also something more about
> why, how, when and where it happened. They will find in their review
> of the past the kind of context and flow of events that we believe can
> transform traumatic memory to normal memory. They will be able to
> acknowledge and grieve what happened and they will be able to leave
> it behind. They will be able to approach the future with some kind of
> self-affirming, life-affirming understanding of their history. Making
> meaning of the past is for each survivor deeply personal and psycholog-
> ically grueling work. The clinician's role in the process is not to shape it
> or impose upon it our own understanding of things, but rather to bear
> witness to it. (p. 9)

The Therapist Supports a Patient's Search
for Corroboration When Warranted

Controversy exists about whether it is the therapist's responsibility to
seek corroboration for recovered memories of abuse. Dr. Paul McHugh is
the main proponent of the position that therapists should interview the
patient's parents and others to ascertain the accuracy of recovered memories and that not seeking outside corroboration constitutes malpractice
(McHugh, 1992). Uyehara (1997) has challenged this viewpoint—"A
pointed objection to the clinician's demand for outside corroboration is
that the level of skepticism implied about the patient's reliability is inim-
ical to establishing a therapeutic relationship" (p. 401)—and role as
being "closer to Gutheil's characterization of a forensic expert witness
than to a therapist" (p. 401), concluding that "when patients pursue their
own searches for external validation during the course of therapy, many
of the problems engendered by the therapist's search for evidence are
obviated" (p. 403).

I agree with Uyehara. Her perspective leaves open the option of the
patient's seeking corroboration and at times even encourages such a

search as a means of gaining potential material to be assessed and weighed in determining what might have happened. It should also be noted that, although the issue of corroboration usually comes up when memories are delayed/recovered rather than continuous, "the 'always held' memory is not above suspicion and has not been exempted from demands for corroboration" (Uyehara, 1997, p. 403). Such corroboration is required in the forensic setting and is sometimes useful in the clinical setting.

When a patient seeks to gain corroboration, it is advisable that the motivations and ramifications for doing so first be discussed in treatment. Optimally, a search should be undertaken only after the patient has achieved a relative degree of symptom stability and after adequate preparation. In particular, the patient should be encouraged to consider the range of possible consequences of a search, from positive to negative, and the relative probability of each. Possible scenarios should also be anticipated and prepared for—finding or not finding corroboration can be very unsettling (Alpert, 1995; S. Shapiro, 1995). It is helpful for a support system to be in place to assist the patient with the results and the emotional consequences of a search.

Whitfield (1995) brings another dimension to the discussion of corroboration by differentiating external verification from internal verification. His viewpoint is that corroboration comes not only from external sources (such as witnesses; photographs, diaries, journals, or letters; medical or clinical records; other person(s) abused; confession by the abuser; other statements or evidence) but from information gleaned from patient and his/her diagnosis and presentation (such as the presence of a high-risk disorder, PTSD, age regressions and flashbacks, reenactments and repetition compulsions, characteristics of the recovered memories and other dynamics, patterns, observations, and aftereffects. These are listed in Table 7.3 on page 251). In general, the therapist should pay attention to all of these issues as the patient struggles with their possible reality but should continue in a stance of caution regarding conclusive determinations, absent external evidence. Therapist and patient may come to a shared hypothesis or understanding about what might have happened that is worked with clinically but not used for any extratherapeutic purpose.

The Therapist Does Not Recommend
Family Separations, Cut-offs, or Lawsuits

As discussed previously, the therapist keeps to the role of therapist and, as a general rule, does not encourage or get involved in extratherapeutic activities or advocacy. S/he must also maintain a regard for the welfare of third parties while maintaining a primary obligation for the welfare of the patient. The therapist should not suggest that a patient limit or cut off contact with the family on the basis of recovered memories of abuse; however, in cases of a positive and validated abuse history and reports of ongoing abuse or other clear and present danger, the therapist is responsible for helping the patient to assess the cost/danger of continuing contact (and may further have a duty to report). The therapist must keep the patient's safety paramount while helping him/her to deal with ambivalent attachments, to recognize ongoing danger, and to learn assertive and self-protective strategies with unsafe or abusive others.

One other issue should be considered: At times, the patient enters therapy having previously broken off contact with the family. The therapist should make note of this in the clinical record as having occurred prior to the initiation of treatment and by the patient's decision. Decision-making regarding contact with family members occurs routinely during treatment. The therapist can assist the patient to explore options, including the option of family arbitration and mediation (Barrett, 1997; London, 1994), as alternatives to total family cut-offs. It is generally advisable that such a dispute resolution effort occur apart from the main therapy and involve professionals responsible to all parties. In this way the therapist continues to work solely on behalf of his/her patient and does not enter a situation of dual roles and loyalties.

It is not within the purview of the therapist's role to suggest or encourage a lawsuit—doing so may constitute giving the patient legal advice and "Most practitioners are not trained to provide legal advice" (Enns et al., 1998). If a patient chooses to investigate this option, the therapist should encourage the exploration of associated feelings, wants, needs, fantasies, etc., as well as the gathering of comprehensive information on which to base decision-making. Litigation should not be undertaken blindly, as it is enormously stressful and requires the commitment of extensive time as well as the allocation of significant personal and financial resources. The plaintiff in a legal proceeding (whether civil or criminal) must meet a standard of proof that is not required in a clinical setting. This standard has become more stringent (even when recovered memories are not an issue) due to defense strategies alleging false memory, and developed in the context of the recovered memory controversy; thus the likelihood of prevailing in such a lawsuit is slim (even less than when such suits were first allowed). Finally, patients should be explicitly cautioned about initiating a lawsuit on the basis of recovered memory alone where no corroboration is available and the therapist should not agree to serve as a forensic evaluator or expert witness in any case involving a patient.

The Therapist Is Alert to a
Number of "Red Flag Issues" before
Agreeing to Undertake Treatment.

We end this discussion by including a table containing "red flag" issues and circumstances regarding recovered memory that were highlighted in the ASCH guidelines (Hammond et al., 1994). They are included here in Table 8.4 in the interest of alerting the therapist to the need for extra caution and possibly to extended discussion aimed at shared mutual understanding with a potential patient about treatment, its purposes, and goals, especially *before* treatment starts. The authors of the report were careful to point out that these "red flag" items should be regarded as situations where extra circumspection is required and not as circumstances where it is impossible that a recalled memory has validity. However, it is also important that therapists understand that they have the right to refuse to embark on a course of treatment that they believe to be especially problematic and/or risky, an important consideration in dealing with issues of abuse/trauma and memory at the current time.

SUMMARY

The material in this chapter provides the therapist with guidelines for clinical practice and risk management with traumatic memories and memory issues. They are derived from the various professional guidelines on the topic and interwoven with available authoritative literature. The issues at hand are complex and there are few pat answers, but the therapist can utilize these guidelines to assist in providing competent and balanced psychotherapy within the existing and developing standard of care.

Table 8.4

Red Flags: Situations Warranting Therapist Cautiousness Regarding the Validity of Recovered Memories

The following items are based primarily on clinical intuition, rather than established research, and should be regarded strictly as situations where therapist cautiousness is encouraged and not as circumstances where it is impossible that a recalled memory has validity.

A. A patient has a history of switching therapists or doctor shopping. It may be wise to have such patients provide a detailed history of prior therapy in their own handwriting and to provide a release of information for all prior therapists. A patient unwilling to do this may not want unfavorable information in prior treatment records to be available.

B. When the possibility of litigation is raised, especially early in therapy or when an attorney has been consulted prior to the onset of therapy. Similarly, when the patient demonstrates an overfamiliarity with psychological terminology and litigation concepts, it implies substantial prior experience that should be explored by the therapist.

C. In the treatment of highly manipulative patients with characterological issues.

D. Caution should be exercised in uncritically accepting memories in a patient coming for treatment to "confirm" if he/she were abused in the past. The therapist cannot make that determination without independent factual corroboration. The therapist cannot act as a judge or jury.

E. Caution should be observed when a previous therapist has suggested that abuse may have occurred.

F. When uncovered memories are from before the age of 3.

G. In persons remembering amnestic memories from adolescence or adulthood, or who claim to have a lack of memories for significant blocks of time after the middle of childhood, but who do not demonstrate evidence of a dissociative disorder on objective evaluations (e.g., with the Dissociative Experiences Scale, the SCID-D, and the HIP) (Bernstein & Putnam, 1986; Frischholz, Lipman, Braun, & Sachs, 1992; Steinberg, 1994; Steinberg, Cicchetti, Buchanan, Hall, & Rounsaville, 1993).

H. In instances where the past relationship with the alleged perpetrator was an entirely positive one, not associated with ambivalent feelings, aloofness or conflicts.

I. When patients have previously seen unlicensed therapists or lay hypnotists. Likewise, extra caution is indicated when a previous therapist has used non-traditional forms of therapy, such as (but not limited to) crystals, energy balancing, muscle testing, reading auras, past life therapy, or expelling entities from the patients. In such circumstances, the potential for patients to be inappropriately influenced in their expectations and to misunderstand and misinterpret such techniques is much higher.

J. When patients have participated in lay support or self-help groups which are unsupervised by licensed professionals, and where a topic of discussion is often trauma, sexual abuse, or incest. Likewise, extra caution is indicated when the patient's memories are subject to contamination because the patient has participated in seminars on abuse, read literature on abuse, or viewed television or video presentations on abuse.

K. When the therapist has a personal history similar to the patient, potentially leading to the increased possibility of unconscious bias, misinterpretations, and countertransference.

From *Clinical hypnosis and memory: Guidelines for clinicians and for forensic hypnosis* (pp. 34–35), by D. C. Hammond, R. B. Garver, C. B. Mutter, H. B. Crasilneck, E. Frischolz, M. A. Gravitz, N. S. Hibler, J. Olson, A. Scheflin, H. Spiegel, and W. Wester, 1994, Chicago: American Society for Clinical Hypnosis Press. Copyright 1994 by American Society for Clinical Hypnosis Press. Reprinted with permission.

Chapter 9

COUNTERTRANSFERENCE ISSUES AND A TREATMENT DECISION MODEL

Application to Ten Clinical Memory Scenarios

Although clinical guidelines and recommendations are useful in creating boundary conditions and assisting in risk management, there are no simple answers in working with traumatic memory issues and their myriad presentations. Ultimately, it is the therapist sitting with the patient in the consulting room who must use professionalism, clinical judgment, and specialized knowledge to deal with whatever recollections and symptoms are presented. The territory remains largely uncharted. Therapists face unique challenges in working with memory issues, in addition to the patient's transference reactions. They are further challenged to keep countertransference and vicarious traumatization responses under control, lest they interfere with the treatment. Historically, transference and countertransference have been identified as difficult issues in the treatment of interpersonal victimization. How countertransference reactions are managed by the therapist often accounts for whether the treatment succeeds or fails. These issues have become more complicated due to the pressures of the controversy.

In this chapter, we begin by discussing common transference responses in traumatized individuals, as well as countertransference responses that have been identified in therapists, both generally and specifically in work with recovered memory issues. Individuals who have not been traumatized will, in all likelihood, not exhibit these same transference responses; however, they might when recovered memories are at issue. The therapist must know how to respond to them and not get into treatment traps that cause the loss of impartiality in response to emerging memories. Transference and countertransference issues are discussed as they support or detract from the treatment and as they affect the therapist's ability to work from a stance of supportive neutrality.

This chapter also includes discussion of the choice of treatment approach, depending on the degree of memory, whether it is disclosed, withheld, suspected, or recanted, and the individual's predominant symptoms. A decision model of treatment options that references the treatment approaches discussed in chapters 5 through 8 is presented. These are applied in step-wise fashion, starting with those that entail the least amount of risk. These options are then applied to ten clinical scenarios involving traumatic memory, each illustrated with case material. These scenarios are presented in somewhat hierarchical order in terms of the degree of intactness or continuity of memory of past abuse (or other trauma) and corresponding disclosure to the therapist. This order of presentation roughly corresponds to the degree of risk each entails in the current atmosphere. In general, previously inaccessible or absent memory followed by recovered memory (especially highly detailed memory of severe or implausible abuse following the use of techniques deemed to be suggestive) involves the most risk. These ten scenarios are likely to evoke different countertransference responses in the therapist, responses that are also important to the determination of therapeutic strategy and technique. Along with the data derived from assessment, they form the basis for decisions about therapeutic options. Each scenario is discussed in terms of clinical choices and strategies and in terms of prominent transference and countertransference dynamics.

TRANSFERENCE AND COUNTERTRANSFERENCE ISSUES

It is now well-recognized that abused and traumatized individuals present special challenges to therapists by virtue of the verbal, behavioral, and existential material they bring to treatment, along with relational patterns that can interfere with the development of a therapeutic alliance. In working with traumatized individuals, therapists have to cope with and respond to verbal content and behavioral manifestations that may be emotionally overwhelming and that induce reactions of horror, fear, and heightened existential anxiety in helpers. Secondly, individuals who have been repeatedly abused (and especially those victimized throughout childhood and adolescence) usually present major hurdles to the development of a stable working relationship. As often as not, relationships (in general and with authority figures in particular) are perceived as a source of hurt, danger, and betrayal, rather than as a source of connection and solace. Disturbances of attachment and object relations are brought to bear in the treatment, in some cases creating major interpersonal impediments that must be overcome before a working alliance is possible.

Traumatized individuals often manifest their trauma interpersonally, in transference reactions from the past projected onto the therapist and the treatment and in other, more contemporaneous (or "here and now"), cognitive or emotional responses. In parallel process, the therapist responds countertransferentially and contemporaneously to the presentations of the patient. These responses are derived from the therapist's own life experiences and personality and from the impact of the patient and his/her presentation. In discussing these issues, Elliott and Briere (1995b) state that contemporaneous and transferential responses frequently occur together in the therapeutic relationship:

> In fact, it is usually not *whether* transference or countertransference is present, but rather the extent to which it dominates contemporaneous awareness and influences client or therapist behavior, and the extent to which such processes are a help or a hindrance. The interplay between transferential and contemporaneous responses is not always readily apparent. (p. 188)

The implication is that the therapist needs to maintain an ongoing awareness of each and to attempt to use them therapeutically to better understand the patient. These responses can then be a rich source of information that helps to direct the treatment.

TRANSFERENCE REACTIONS

Transference can, additionally, be understood as a form of indirect communication by which the patient "speaks" that which may be outside of conscious awareness and hence has remained unspoken. Davies and Frawley (1994), Reviere (1996), Waites (1997), and other clinicians have described how transference might, in fact, be a form of memory about the past and might inform the therapist about past abuse/trauma. Yet, as discussed previously in this text, the therapist must be careful to not overinterpret the meaning of particular transference responses, except in a general way. Instead, out of the ordinary/out of context transferential responses can be useful to the development of hypotheses to be considered and tested over time, as additional confirming or disconfirming information emerges.

A number of contemporary writers have identified abuse- and trauma-related transference responses and issues. Following a major review of the literature on trauma available at the time, McCann and Pearlman (1990a) described common schema about self and others that are impacted or disrupted by abuse and other trauma. The schema they identified involve: (1) the individual's frame of reference related to the ability to envision a meaningful (just, predictable, and controllable) world; (2) safety, or the belief in personal security or invulnerability from harm; (3) trust/dependency, the need for support from others and the expectation that other people are reliable and can be depended upon to provide connection and support; (4) independence, the need to have personal authority and the ability to exert control and have initiative; (5) power, a related ability to have control, self-determination, and personal agency; (6) esteem, the belief in one's worth or value; and (7) intimacy, or the importance of human connection and bonding versus isolation and alienation. Abused and otherwise traumatized individuals develop their sense of self and sense of others through the filter of these abuse-related schema. It is quite common that most, if not all, of these seven schema are disrupted in the negative direction in individuals who have suffered severe interpersonal traumatization (i.e., they usually expect that the world is unfair and dangerous, that personal safety is compromised, that people are not trustworthy and are instead hurtful and self-serving, that independence is not possible—or, conversely, that extreme self-sufficiency is the only option—and that they are powerless, worthless, and existentially doomed to a life of isolation and alienation from others). These reactions are often projected onto the therapist and certainly present a challenge to the development of a stable working relationship.

Elsewhere (Courtois, 1988), I have discussed some of the most common transference reactions related to these schema that are found in incestuously abused patients. Because of the betrayal inherent in child abuse, previously victimized patients are often massively disillusioned with others (especially caretakers/authority figures), have a compromised ability to trust, and experience a profound sense of betrayal. They often exhibit what has been labeled "traumatic transference" by Spiegel (1986). This transference response occurs when "the patient unconsciously expects that the therapist, despite overt helpfulness and concern, will covertly exploit the patient for his or her own narcissistic gratification" (p. 72) in much the same way that the abusive caretakers originally did. Formerly abused adults have been found to have predominantly negative self-esteem and to view themselves with loathing and self-hatred. A sense of shame is often abundantly in evidence, as well. Abused individuals usually (if not always) hold themselves responsible for and deserving of the abuse. These negative self-perceptions are quite often projected onto the therapist from whom the patient expects treatment similar to what was experienced in the past, all the while hoping for something different.

In addition, transference reflects attachment issues and object relations. Abused individuals doubt that others can believe or support them. Interpersonal and intimacy difficulties are ever-present and are related to various problematic attachment styles that have been found to be the consequence of unstable parenting and bonding patterns and abuse/trauma in childhood. These attachment disturbances were first researched by Ainsworth and her associates (Ainsworth, Blehar, Waters, & Wall, 1978), following the work of John Bowlby on attachment and loss (Bolwby, 1969, 1973, 1980, 1988). The following predominant attachment styles were identified through this line of research: (1) secure-autonomous; (2) dismissing/avoidant; (3) preoccupied/resistant-ambivalent; and (4) unresolved-disorganized (Main, 1996). The last three have been found by clinical researchers [among them Alexander (1992) Barach (1991), Liotti (1992) and deZulueta (1993)] to correlate with abuse, neglect, and other forms of problematic parenting. These attachment and bonding difficulties tend to play out later in significant relationships, including therapy. Attachment dynamics have come to be seen as especially important in the treatment process and give clues to some of the predominant relational modes in the patient's past. They further are useful in suggesting appropriate treatment strategies, as discussed by Alexander and Anderson (1994).

Relational and attachment dynamics may also signal the expectations (conscious or unconscious) the patient holds of the therapist (i.e., as potential parent, perpetrator, rescuer, lover) and the role relationship that is played out (i.e., victim, victimizer, rescuer, passive bystander) (Davies & Frawley, 1994). It is imperative, to the degree possible, that the therapist identify these relational dynamics and not engage solely in role reenactments with the patient. To do so can have the tragic effect of retraumatizing rather than assisting the patient to understand and resolve the historical origins and dynamics of these transference patterns. It can also have the unfortunate effect of causing significant missteps regarding recovered memory issues. Genova (1993) gives an example of a therapist pressured by his patient to believe all of her memory productions and how, at the time (early 90s), this stance was reflective of the cultural milieu surrounding the treatment of sexual abuse (i.e., the survivor was *always* to be believed). He correctly points out that by giving in to the patient's demands in such a situation, the therapist is appropriating the patient's independence and ability to decide, taking on the role of all-knowing parent (as well as victim), enacting a "transference cure," and depriving the patient of the important task of determining her own experience. He wrote:

> No amount of external approval can ever substitute for inner accep-
> tance, no matter how much uncertainty and incomprehensible pain
> such acceptance of self entails. If an honest relationship is to survive,
> then the "doubting" therapist's only alternative is to bear his uncer-
> tainty and to help the patient bear hers, hoping thereby to recall to
> them both a deeper experience of self-acceptance. (p. 37)

Consequently, it behooves the therapist to study and understand these relational dynamics as potential treatment traps, both in general and as they play out regarding recovered memories. Chu (1988) made the obser-vation that knowing about them does not keep them from happening; however, it makes it easier to identify them and to extricate from them sooner, more therapeutically, and with less anxiety. It also behooves the therapist to develop an understanding of his/her interpersonal needs and vulnerabilities and how they are most likely to be countertransferential-ly "hooked." In terms of recovered memory issues, familiarity with these issues assists the therapist in avoiding some of the additional traps inher-ent in this treatment.

Other predominant transference issues have been identified. Formerly abused adults often hold themselves responsible for the abuse and have great feelings of complicity and associated guilt. Unfortunately, irrational guilt is usually reinforced by abusers who have a vested interest in trans-ferring responsibility to the child. The child who felt favored, special, or powerful during the abuse and/or who experienced a sexual response or sexual pleasure is likely to be additionally guilt-stricken. Some abused children, due to the skewed relationship and power roles that character-ize abusive families, are called upon to be caretakers (commonly identi-fied as the "adult child" role) and to engage in role reversals with their parents. These and other relational patterns might be replicated within the transference relationship, where the patient attempts to caretake the therapist and is counterdependent. Alternatively, caretaking deficits from the past may cause the patient to be overdependent on the therapist' approval and attention in an attempt to find a parent substitute.

Transference reactions involving feelings of loss and grief, which may or may not have a concrete association with the past, may nonetheless be transferred to the present, including the therapeutic relationship. Strong reactions, including feelings of abandonment and rejection during times of separation from the therapist (due to vacation, conference leave, maternity leave, or other absence), may allude to past abandonments and losses. Abandonment is almost always implicated in child abuse. Leave-takings or separations in therapy can function as triggers to memories of abuse and abandonment as the patient grapples (at a conscious or unconscious level) with the therapist's ostensible abandonment and rejection. Feelings of anger and rage may also surface but be masked and disavowed. Typically, angry feelings are associated with the abuser and are seen as uncontrollable, dangerous, and forbidden to the victim. Yet, anger and rage responses are elicited by abuse and may very well be expressed passively or in disguised fashion. These are the emotions that most often fuel suicidal and parasuicidal ideation and attempts, and that may also be implicated in the victimization of others.

Elliott and Briere (1995b) discussed transference as typically manifesting itself in one or more of four abuse/trauma-related responses: (1) cognitive perceptual distortions generalized from abuse/trauma-era learning about self, others, and the environment; (2) responses associated with early attachment disruption that are elicited by the relational aspects of the treatment; (3) specific abuse-related effects and sensory experiences that are restimulated by therapist characteristics or behaviors; and (4) reenactment of childhood behaviors arising from unresolved traumatic experiences, triggered by current interpersonal events or aspects of the therapeutic relationship (p. 191).

Davies and Frawley (1994) further discussed what they refer to as four major traumagenic complications to analysis of the transference and countertransference in work with adult survivors of incest and childhood sexual abuse: (1) the extent to which the patient presents with unorganized, unsymbolized (unspoken or with no words attached) experiences that begin to emerge during treatment. (These authors refer to these experiences as sometimes representing unformed memories. They have the effect of frightening and confusing the patient and, as a result, may cause them to flee treatment); (2) the individual's use of dissociation as a coping skill, defense, and vehicle of communication that serves to keep intolerable memories, cognitions, and affects at bay; (3) the additional and more general defensive structure common to sexual abuse survivors, of splitting, denial, acting out, omnipotence, and projective identification; and (4) countertransference reactions related to the therapist's personal attitudes or experiences with trauma. These authors also highlighted the enormously complicated and ever-shifting presentations and relational dynamics of these fragmented and dissociative patients, which they described as kaleidoscopic and difficult for the therapist to understand and respond to. They suggest that these presentations and dynamics may hold clues to the patient's abusive or traumatic background.

In a similar vein, Loewenstein (1993) commented on what he labeled the posttraumatic and dissociative relational matrix between therapist and patient. The therapist is faced with "transference fields" of continuously shifting and alternating patterns of reality, symptoms, and relational patterns. Patients with posttraumatic diagnoses alternate between states of numbing, emotional avoidance, and shut-down, on one hand, and flooding, intrusions, hyperarousal, and other somatic sensations, on the other. Those with additional dissociative diagnoses manifest absorption, focused attention, amnesia, trance-like phenomena, trance logic, altered perceptions, discrete ego states, and at the far end of the continuum, alternate personalities, as found in dissociative identity disorder. Loewenstein's description resembles the kaleidoscopic presentation described by Davies and Frawley.

Obviously, reactions of this type, in addition to whatever verbal descriptions of abuse and trauma are given, can be very disconcerting to the therapist and result in a variety of countertransference reactions, as described below. Although both transference and countertransference reactions may be discomforting and perplexing, they should not be considered as necessarily always neurotic, problematic, or undesirable (Elliott & Briere, 1995b). Instead, they should be regarded as sources of information and hypothesis-building and as the opportunity for therapeutic insight into the individual. Yet, as has been stressed throughout this text, *in the absence of memory, neither transference or countertransference, no matter how compelling, should be interpreted as always indicative of past abuse, nor should flashbacks, abreactions, or other types of posttraumatic or dissociative reactions be taken only as veridical memory or historical truth.* Instead, their content and process contain information to be explored and assessed. These might, for example, generally represent historical events, provide an indication for additional exploration as to their meaning to the individual, and/or necessitate additional assessment.

Transference Reactions to Recovered Memory Issues

The controversy has added another level of transferential complexity to what is already a minefield. Not only do patients have the general and abuse-related transferential reactions, but they have reactions to the controversy itself and to the therapist's perspective on the controversy, approach to treatment, and countertransference reactions. Although little research has been conducted to date on the impact of the controversy on patients, some observations drawn from clinical practice can be made. In general, it seems to have created additional self-doubt and fear in some patients, causing roadblocks in their treatment and slowing its pace. It has also, in some cases, made patients who report abuse more wary of the therapist, as well as guarded, angry, and despairing. To these patients, the controversy is viewed as another form of societal denial, another attempt to silence victims. The therapist may be additionally mistrusted regarding memory and belief and trust issues (i.e., "Will you believe me if I disclose to you?"; "Do you know how to deal with false or true memories?"; "How do I know you won't try to implant false memories of abuse in me?"; "Will you be willing to work with me?"; "Are you afraid that I will sue you?"). The therapist is certainly challenged to try to stay open rather than defensive in discussing and working with these issues.

Tranference reactions need not be negative. Some patients have indicated that the discussion of these issues gives them additional confidence in their therapist, especially one who works from a stance of reasoned caution and who is informed about the major issues in the controversy. In general, the best course of action seems to be to address these issues and fears in a straightforward manner at the initiation of treatment, as discussed in chapters 5, 6, and 7, and to revisit them as needed and as they surface throughout the course of treatment.

COUNTERTRANSFERENCE REACTIONS TO ABUSE AND TRAUMA

Countertransference emerges not only in direct response to the patient but in response to social influence as well. Mental health professionals are influenced by and operate within dominant societal and cultural contexts. Historically, during the first two-thirds of this century, labeled "The Age of Denial" by Armstrong (1978), society was largely ignorant about abuse and all other forms of trauma, as were mental health professionals. As discussed in chapter 1, most therapists followed Freud's lead in repudiating the seduction theory in favor of the oedipal theory. This shift in perspective allowed real abuse to be ignored and real victims to be unprotected and unacknowledged. In another trauma domain, war and related atrocities gained the attention of the general public and mental health professionals during the two World Wars and the Korean conflict. Once these conflicts were over, interest waned until Vietnam, when the study of combat trauma reemerged. This was followed by the resumption of attention to other forms of human traumatization, notably rape and all forms of child abuse and family violence.

In some of the earliest writings on countertransference responses to incest during the years following the Freudian reversal, Renshaw (1982) categorized the reactions of therapists into three dominant themes:

avoidance, attraction/approach, and attack/aggression. Each of these themes plays out quite routinely in the treatment of incest and other forms of trauma, and each can be quite problematic if left unaddressed and unmanaged. In such a situation, it has the possibility of interfering with appropriate and ethical care, since it may lead to serious errors and transgressions, including countertransference acting out. In contrast, when acknowledged and thoughtfully considered by the therapist, it can be used as information about complementary transference issues and as information that aids in a better understanding of the patient. This, in turn, contributes to shaping the treatment in such a way that transference issues and relational patterns are addressed rather than only reenacted with the patient. Reenactment alone, without interpretation and understanding, is often not helpful and may well be retraumatizing to the formerly abused patient. In the case of a non-abused patient, countertransference errors may lead to an overzealous search for missing memories of abuse, which can traumatize the patient in quite a different way.

The "Age of Denial," as the label implies, is best characterized by the countertransference theme of *avoidance,* a position on the part of therapists that was supported by prevalent data available at the time that suggested that incest was an extreme rarity (occurring at a rate of 1 in 1.4 or 1.6 million individuals per year) (Weinberg, 1955). Thus, it was considered an aberration and its victims stigmatized by association. During this period, reports of abuse were predominantly treated with horror, disdain, skepticism, disavowal, and aversion. At the other extreme, however, some therapists showed responses related to poor boundary management and exploitation: privileged voyeurism, overfascination, and sexual misuse (demonstrating the *attraction* category). Instead of understanding incest as victimization, they tended to be mesmerized by it. Incest victims were especially enthralling due to having been involved in the most taboo of sexual relationships, and some therapists sexually exploited patients they viewed as "soiled virgins"—sullied but available and enticing. Still others reacted with indignation and rage, attacking the alleged victim's credibility and the threat she posed to the social order and the privacy of the family. Many patients who alleged abuse and who had significant posttraumatic symptomatology were pathologized for their symptoms and further stigmatized (demonstrating the *attack/aggression* theme). During this time period, compassionate and empathic care was hard to come by, if not impossible to find.

The "Age of Validation" (Armstrong, 1978) began in the late 1960s with the recognition of the society-wide prevalence of child physical and sexual abuse and with the attention given to combat trauma and posttraumatic reactions. In terms of recognition, these were important times for real victims. Their experiences of abuse and other forms of trauma were acknowledged as important and as related to their mental health concerns. Psychological survival mechanisms were identified, not as symptoms of psychopathology, but rather as normal human coping mechanisms and adaptations to abnormal events. They were thus destigmatized. New treatment options incorporating attention to the trauma offered hope for resolution and recovery.

During this same time period, the significance of countertransference issues in the treatment of the traumatized was again recognized. The therapist's ability to manage personal reactions to the patient's transference reactions and trauma was credited with either sustaining or impeding the therapeutic process. Unacknowledged and/or unmanaged countertransference and related countertransference-based errors were identified as perhaps the single greatest obstacles to successful treatment. The avoidance, approach, and attack themes first identified by Renshaw were further developed and their importance to treatment outcome stressed in a major article by Danieli (1984) and later in books by Courtois (1988), Wilson and Lindy (1994), and Pearlman and Saakvitne (1995). A sophisticated new treatment literature began to develop, as discussed in chapter 1. In it, clinicians identified the complex transference issues and relational dynamics that were so difficult to manage and that Chu (1988) was the first to label "treatment traps." Simultaneously, a similar but distinct deterrent to successful treatment was identified: the emotional toll of hearing about trauma and the therapist's subsequent reactions resulting from working with the challenges of the "posttraumatic and dissociative relational fields" identified by Loewenstein (1993). It encompassed such common responses as being overwhelmed by the work, rage, sadness and horror regarding stories of abuse, and vulnerability in personal relationships (Knight, 1997). This process was labeled "vicarious traumatization" by McCann and Pearlman (1990a) and recognized for its ability to interfere with the conditions necessary for effective trauma treatment, namely, a stable and reliable therapeutic relationship. Turkus (Joan Turkus, personal communication, 1998) described a *secondary rescuer syndrome*, referring to the tendency of overwhelmed therapists to seek out more experienced colleagues with the expectation of being rescued by them.

Yet, it was during this time period, as societal attention to abuse and other trauma accelerated to the point of sensationalism and exaggeration, that the predominant theme regarding abuse shifted. What began as acknowledgment and an attempt to make up for past denial moved into overfascination and voyeurism. In parallel, therapists' countertransference shifted to the *attraction* theme as it became "fashionable" and even required to treat incest/sexual abuse survivors. As part of the attraction, it quickly became the norm for some therapists (professionals as well as lay) to overemphasize abuse to the exclusion of other life and therapy issues, and to rely prematurely and almost exclusively on exploratory approaches to traumatic memory that were inherently destabilizing. When patients exhibited symptoms associated with a history of sexual abuse but had no memory, repressed memory for the abuse came to be viewed as the rule and non-remembering as constituting dissociative amnesia and denial. As the atmosphere of zealotry accelerated, more and more serious and bizarre forms of abuse were regarded as the norm, accepted uncritically, and, in some cases, reinforced. A number of therapists acted out on their countertransference, suspended critical judgment, developed dual-role relationships with patients, and functioned as advocates (and sometimes zealots), rather than remaining in their roles as therapists. Complicating the matter further was the overlap between professional and lay recovery services and the unavailability of training in the treatment of abuse and trauma, especially regarding the complexities and management of transference and countertransference reactions.

The "Age of the Backlash" (Armstrong, 1994) brought another societal shift. Therapists were criticized and, in some cases, scapegoated for the excesses, charged with implanting false memories of nonexistent abuse, and with uncritically accepting reports of incredible forms of abuse. The extensive publicity given the critique (including egregious case examples) gave legitimacy to the false memory perspective and de-legitimized the posttraumatic and recovered memory viewpoint. Adults abused as children found themselves again in the position of having the reality and accuracy of their abuse reports challenged, particularly those based upon recovered memories. The zeitgeist of disbelief returned. As therapists experienced societal disapproval and came to perceive these patients and their treatment as dangerous, the countertransference themes of attack and avoidance were once again in evidence.

Countertransference and Vicarious Traumatization Reactions to Recovered Memory Issues[1]

How else are therapists responding to issues raised in the controversy and how are their responses affecting the care they offer individuals who seek treatment for remembered or suspected abuse? In this section, we review

---

[1] I thank Drs. Constance Dalenberg and Laurie Anne Pearlman for discussing their views on countertransference responses to recovered memory with me. Each graciously gave time that I know is in short supply to share her perspective.

some of the major countertransference issues and vicarious traumatization
(VT) responses that have been identified to date, and how they can interfere with even-handed treatment. Little by way of literature is available
on these topics at the present time, so this discussion is in many ways preliminary. Undoubtedly, more attention will be given to them as this field
of study continues to develop. The countertransference reactions and VT
responses identified here are discussed within Renshaw's categories of
avoidance, attack, and *attraction* for consistency with the earlier discourse.
We then move to a discussion of more balanced responses and strategies
for working with the many uncertainties that are involved when the
patient's memories and memory productions are in question.

Avoidance Theme

FEAR AND ANXIETY RESULTING IN CYNICISM AND CLOSE-DOWN.   In general, predominant (if not the most predominant) reactions are fear and anxiety, both of the current environment and the new risks it holds (especially
in terms of malpractice lawsuits and the opening of lawsuits to third-party
plaintiffs) and of the patients themselves (who are now perceived by some
therapists as unwanted sources of risk). The patients who evoke the most
fear and anxiety are those who have no clear memories yet have suspicions
of past abuse based on symptoms or other factors; those who have been in
past suggestive treatment and who report the recovery of abuse memories
during that treatment (i.e., those who have source contamination); those
who report memories of terrible and horrific abuse; those who believe
themselves to have been victims of organized sadistic abuse, satanic ritual
abuse, and/or forms of implausible abuse; those who are litigious; and
those with borderline personality-type dynamics. Patients may be split
into those who are "good" (i.e., who retain memory) and those who are
"bad" (i.e., those who do not). Both Kluft (1997) and Bronheim (Ben
Bronheim, personal communication, 1998) have independently decried
the fact that therapists have come to regard memories of abuse (as opposed
to other autobiographical memories) with suspicion and a degree of skepticism that is anything but therapeutic or conducive to exploration. In
essence, they ask why these memories are any different or any more suspect than other memories brought to treatment.

Obviously, fear and anxiety reactions can create major impediments to
the calm objectivity needed to successfully work with these issues. These
unmodulated emotions can result in a cynical and doubting stance on the
part of the therapist. Dalenberg (in press) identified the tendency of therapists to make what she helpfully termed "distancing errors." This distancing, in turn, can lead to what has been described as "lawsuit therapy,"

the overly cautious, nonexploratory treatment where the patient is doubt-ed, or it can lead to responses of disbelief and related attacks on the patient's credibility and personal integrity. In response, the patient who has an abuse history may close down and may be harmed by the reenact-ment of abuse dynamics of disbelief, denial, blame, and stigmatization.

AVOIDANCE AND DENIAL RESULTING IN SUPPRESSION.   Therapists may deliberately choose not to ask about abuse or trauma-related issues, either at intake/assessment or during the course of treatment. Any attempt to focus on abuse is redirected by the therapist, who instead encourages the patient to attend to other issues. This is done to such a degree that any discussion of abuse is curtailed, the result being sup-pression of the topic and any discussion of its relevance to the patient. As discussed in chapter 7, several studies of abuse inquiries by psychother-apists have found in some a propensity to never return to the topic once it has been asked about and/or disclosed. Also, as discussed in an article entitled "Interpretations that feel horrible to make and a theoretical uni-corn," Sinason (1990) described the difficult task of responding to abuse reports and especially to transference manifestations. The current con-troversy makes it easier for therapists to avoid considering abuse or mak-ing interpretations or comments about it, and thus easier for them to join the patient in the defensive operations that keep abuse unknown and unknowable. For many real abuse survivors, this has the effect of rein-forcing their defenses and curtailing further attempts at disclosure/dis-cussion, while continuing the pattern of silence predicated on unavail-able and unwilling listeners/responders.

ANXIETY, CONFUSION, AND PARANOIA, RESULTING IN PARALYSIS.   Many therapists are very anxious and even paranoid about recovered memory issues and are thoroughly confused about what to do and what not to do. These feelings may result in paralysis. The therapist ends up in an over-ly defensive, passive bystander role, unable to maintain an assertive and exploratory stance. Patients who sense their therapists' anxiety and dis-comfort may attempt to protect them through nondisclosure and become paralyzed in parallel process, a recreation of past harmful dynamics in patients who were abused. They may also adopt the therapist's paranoia and become fearful of powerful outside forces that require suppression of the abuse history, reinforcing the forced silence dictum.

SELF-PROTECTION, HELPLESSNESS, AND BETRAYAL RESULTING IN SHAME. Related feelings are of sadness and shame associated with being a helpless bystander or otherwise betraying the patient. Psychoanalyst Dr. Sue Grand wrote what has become a rather classic (perhaps because so many therapists resonate with it) description of the countertransference conundrum of the therapist:

On this particular day, I have read yet another media exposé on the false-memory controversy. I realize that this outspoken, serious, and assertive woman would confront her stepfather if thoroughly convinced that had [sic] incested her; this litigious volatile man would lie and very possibly sue me for "implanting" an incest memory. Her stepfather suddenly appears to me powerful, vindictive, and relentless in his retaliation; I am helpless, vulnerable, small. I feel exposed. There is a dangerous secret about what is going on in her analysis. I will be implicated. Financially ruined, professionally humiliated. I am a little girl, terrorized with a shameful secret. Even as she weeps, she does not yet know, but she has lost me. I hear the howls of judicial accusation: Have I suggested this? How can I demonstrate that I haven't? Should I start taping to protect myself, and how to explain this to the patient? Have I allowed her to be too literal in her interpretation of her dreams and symptoms? How can I demonstrate in court that I have not led the patient into this? Suddenly I feel I must demonstrate to the patient that these images may be more symbolic than literal, expressive of other issues and anxieties. I must document my effort to explore other explanations besides incest for her dreams and symptoms. Even as she weeps, I question her differently, drawing her away from the image of actual incest. She attempts to follow me where I am going, desperate for us to stay together, willing to be confused, deflected. Inside of my secret terror, I know I have betrayed her. . . . It is one of my worst moments as an analyst. I don't want her or anyone else to see me.

The next day, I receive a rare call of protest from my patient; fortunately, I have been trustworthy until now. By the time she calls, I have worked myself through this countertransferential moment. She says that she felt I did not believe her. She has never felt so alone and bewildered with me before. Despite my inquiry, she cannot allow herself to attribute this to any failure of mine, but rather must attribute this to her own lack of clarity and poor communication. This sophisticated woman, who is fully informed about the false-memory controversy and its attendant lawsuits, cannot access any of her knowledge about what might have actually occurred inside *me* during her session. This is familiar analytic ground for us; we have often seen a surge of panic attacks when she is refusing to know what she knows about being betrayed and in danger. In the transference, she resurrects an object tie of mendacity and submission, after I have enacted a subtle form of domination by redirecting the definition of reality about incest. She has returned to exclusive bond with her stepfather, a bond in which all dangerous knowledge must be falsified and denied, in the hopes that she can hide from the impact of trauma and ultimately be safe and know. (author's italics) (Grand, 1995, pp. 249–251)

This quote illustrates how even the therapist's fears and subtle shaping responses can have a pronounced impact and can cause harm (in this case, the patient's symptoms increase, along with her silence and her discontinued exploration). This quote also shows the seepage of the controversy into the therapist's psyche and her panicked reactions to possible outcomes, including the devastation of her personal/professional life. Such worries distract from the work at hand and the therapist's ability to therapeutically "stay with the patient."

DISEMPOWERED AND DEFENSIVE ABOUT WORKING WITH AND BELIEVING ABUSE.   In the current atmosphere, many therapists struggle with continuing to believe their patients. They may feel disempowered and deskilled by the critique and feel that they have to defend a stance of belief about abuse-related issues (this is not a new issue—therapists who believe patients' reports of abuse have long been viewed with suspicion, as discussed by Spiegel (1988) in a commentary on the treatment accorded those who treat patients with multiple personality disorder). Defensiveness can certainly occur in the treatment room and other professional contexts but increasingly occurs in nonprofessional settings as well. The effect of the media coverage has been such that therapists may find themselves questioned in social settings as to what they believe and how they work with abuse memories, particularly given that "false memory syndrome is so prevalent." An atmosphere of challenge and disbelief may put the therapist on the defensive and adversely affect the ability to work impartially with memory issues. Patients who pick up on this defensiveness may react with anger. They may also close down or terminate treatment, again feeling betrayed by an unseeing, self-protective authority figure.

Attraction/Approach Theme

OVERCOMPENSATION, OVERBELIEF, AND RESULTANT RESCUER/ADVOCATE ROLE.   Some therapists (probably the minority) have responded to the controversy by intensifying their efforts and overcompensating in the direction of uncritical belief. They persist in the position that recovered memories and other presentations such as transference reactions and flashbacks are always veridical representations of historical truth. These therapists may use information about traumatic memories (i.e., that these memories are "burned in" or engraved on the brain in pristine form, are unlike other memories, are stored differently and do not degrade with the passage of time) to buttress their position and how they work. In this stance, the patient may be "saved" from the uncertainty that might otherwise be required as the therapist becomes the arbiter of what is true. Dalenberg (in press) has labeled this type of response an "intrusion error." Working from this position, the therapist may foster regression in the patient, and thus "up the emotional ante," especially in the dependent/suggestible patient, who may trade independence and critical judgment (and possibly "create" memories of abuse) in order to gain the therapist's continued approval, attention, and involvement. This stance may also result in the therapist's recommending specific courses of action and becoming an advocate for the patient, possibly creating boundary violations and a dual-role relationship (i.e., therapist and expert witness in the case of a therapist-recommended lawsuit).

IGNORANCE/NAIVETÉ, INEXPERIENCE, AND RESULTANT OVERINVOLVEMENT. The countertransference error of overinvolvement is often due to ignorance and naiveté resulting from inexperience. As discussed previously, novice therapists and trainees are the least prepared to deal with the challenges associated with the treatment of abuse and trauma. The same is true, only to a greater degree, where recovered memories are involved, particularly if these issues were not included in training. Inexperienced and untrained therapists may mismanage recovered memory issues as part of their general stance of overbelief and overinvolvement. They may be unable to take the more sophisticated but technically difficult position of sitting with the patient and tolerating uncertainty. The inexperienced therapist may feel unsuccessful if the patient does not achieve certitude. The patient who works with this therapist may therefore be encouraged in premature closure while discouraged in ambiguity.

Attack/Aggression Theme

ANGER, IRRITATION, AND INTOLERANCE RESULTING IN WITHDRAWAL/HOSTILITY. Therapists may experience anger, irritation, and intolerance of abuse-related issues, both in general and more specifically as they pertain to recovered memories. Therapists may find themselves angered at being de-skilled and disempowered in the controversy, their clinical wisdom derided especially by viewpoints that overvalue empirically derived data. Anger may also be heightened by the perception that confused/

uncertain patients or those who report recovered memories (of abuse of any sort but especially of bizarre and/or implausible forms) are dangerous and put the therapist at risk. These feelings, when unmanaged, may compound the already strong negative reactions that might accompany a report of incest, as discussed by MacCarthy (1988) in his provocatively entitled article "Are Incest Victims Hated?" It can result in the therapist's withdrawal from the patient and subtle or not so subtle redirection away from abuse-related issues. The therapist may also seek to remove such a patient from his/her caseload by encouraging referral to another practitioner. In a worse case scenario, it might also involve direct attacks on the patient's credibility and character and harsh, punitive treatment. Responses of this sort would be damaging to any patient; with those with an abuse history and/or a posttraumatic diagnosis, they would be retraumatizing and highly damaging.

SKEPTICISM AND DOUBT, RESULTING IN DISBELIEF. An overly strong stance of skepticism and of related disbelief of the patient is found in this countertransference reaction. Therapists who work from this perspective may be unwilling to tolerate the patient's uncertainty and exploration and become overly rigid in demanding corroboration. The patient may be put on the defensive and feel that s/he will not be believed, unless evidence is forthcoming. In the most egregious cases, patients with recovered memories are diagnosed with "false memory syndrome" (even though this is not yet a proven syndrome nor is it a diagnosis). The labeling and diagnosis can be destructive and even life-threatening. A recent report of a young woman who committed suicide in despair after having been told that she suffered from false memory syndrome attests to this danger. It is also of note that the treating therapist was recently sued by the patient's mother for inappropriate diagnosis and for being an accessory to the patient's death.

Achieving Balance in Countertransference and VT Responses to Recovered Memory Issues

In the current atmosphere, with its many challenges, it is quite likely that therapists will find themselves more reactive to their patients' memory presentations and transference issues. Strong countertransference and VT responses are to be expected and cannot (or should not) be necessarily suppressed or rejected out of hand. But they must be actively identified and managed. Responses that are uncharacteristic of the therapist or are at an unusually high or low level need monitoring. As discussed above, if maintained at a balanced level, countertransference need not be damaging and may provide insight about both patient and therapist that can guide the treatment. For example, "realistic paranoia" and a cautious, conservative, and educative stance regarding memory issues are reasonable; overly strong paranoia leading to an unwillingness to entertain the possibility of abuse and accusing the patient of having false memories is not.

Some of these reactions are best handled apart from the patient, in a supportive atmosphere conducive to ventilation and redirection, such as consultation and supervision with colleagues. Yet, some are best handled with the patient and have the potential to be reality-based and therapeutic. Dalenberg is currently studying patients' reactions to therapists' countertransference. She recommends enough countertransference disclosure so that the patient can understand the therapist's reactions and not incorporate them in a self-blaming way, as abuse survivors are so prone to do. She also recommends that therapists have a general discussion of memory issues and the therapeutic approach taken to these issues with patients right from the start of treatment and later as the need arises, in keeping with the approach that has been stressed throughout this text (Constance Dalenberg, personal communication, 1998).

Grand (1995), in the final paragraph of her case description quoted above, discusses and illustrates the benefit of validating the patient's perception of the countertransference reaction(s) and how doing so can prove restorative to the patient. She wrote:

> In subsequent sessions, she does not mention either incest or the moment of analytic rupture . . . . Her symptoms increase. She has retreated from what she was beginning to know about him, and what she knows about me, because of the transferential reenactment of memory falsification. Her inability to know what she knows becomes the focus of her analysis. What she cannot yet afford to discover is that, unlike her father, I am willing to see myself and for her to see me, for her to see and know my betrayal, and for her to be angry, for her to regain her memory and her history in this transferential moment. When she is able to discover this aspect of me, she may feel the despair and liberation of separation. (p. 251)

When the therapist discloses her response error, the patient is encouraged to have genuine feelings in response, a marked contrast to what happens in abuse situations. The patient is then free to have reactions, unencumbered by threats to her reality or her well-being.

A DECISION MODEL OF THERAPEUTIC OPTIONS

Let us now shift gears to attend to another aspect of the treatment process, namely, the choice of therapeutic option depending upon degree and type of memory and disclosure by the patient. These options are outlined in a decision model illustrated by Figure 9.1.

It is generally recommended that the posttraumatic (PTT) model of treatment (described in chapter 6) be implemented when past abuse/trauma is identified at intake, during the course of the assessment, or later in the process, especially when the patient exhibits associated posttraumatic and dissociative symptomatology (and, in some cases, even in the absence of this specific symptomatology). The first phase of the PTT treatment approach is educative and cognitive/behavioral. It is designed to offer the patient information about human traumatization (especially interpersonal violence) and normative posttraumatic responses and reactions. It is also designed to foster skill development for the management and stabilization of symptoms. It is only in the second stage of the model that the focus of therapeutic work becomes the identification and resolution of specific trauma material. As discussed in chapter 6, second phase trauma resolution work is decided on an as-needed basis, based upon the patient's motivation and stability as well as his/her clinical status and symptomatology. In any event, the focus on abuse/trauma comprises only one focus of the treatment. As Dalenberg (1996) has counseled, the therapist should "beware overestimating the role of abuse in the maintenance of symptoms" and should be broad-based rather than only abuse-focused in the treatment.

The PTT approach can also be implemented when posttraumatic and dissociative symptoms are in evidence, even if memory of the index abuse/trauma is not available to the patient. Use of the PTT model in this situation requires a clinical judgment call on the part of the therapist, and is based upon the findings of the comprehensive assessment at the outset of treatment or reassessment during the course of treatment (as outlined in chapter 7). The early phase of the PTT model can be made generic enough (by focusing it on symptom stabilization, skill development, and increasing the ability to function) that it is not oriented toward or suggestive of abuse. The PTT model can also be considered and implemented when a patient recovers memories of abuse/trauma (or otherwise receives third-party information that confirms its occurrence, in the absence of the patient's specific memory, possibly causing the reinstatement/recovery of memory). This patient may then develop posttraumatic/dissociative symptoms, the other major indicator to consider in implementing the PTT model.

Table 9.1
Decision Model of Therapeutic Options

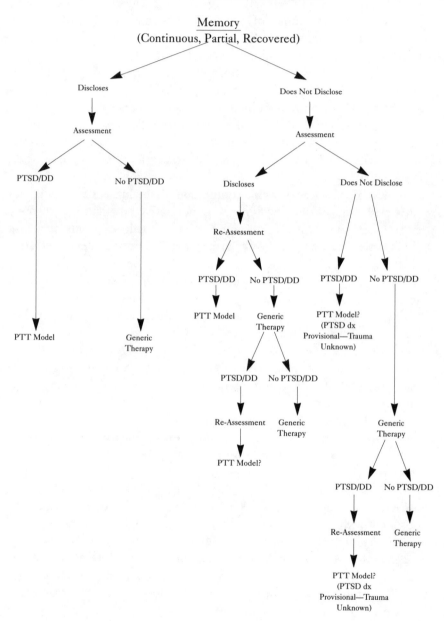

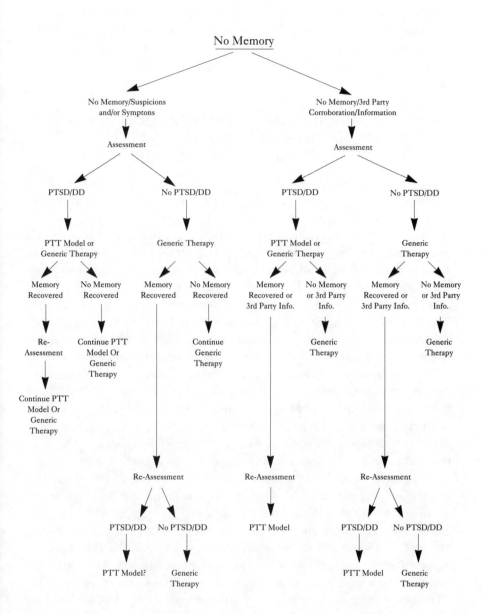

In contrast, where abuse/trauma is not remembered and the patient does not show posttraumatic/dissociative symptoms, a generic model of treatment is recommended. The approach can be reassessed and a PTT model implemented if the patient later recovers memories of abuse/trauma and/or develops the aforementioned symptomatology.

APPLICATIONS: TEN COMMON CLINICAL SCENARIOS INVOLVING TRAUMATIC MEMORY AND MEMORY ISSUES

We now consider the choice of therapeutic strategy and countertransference responses as applied to a variety of clinical scenarios involving traumatic memory and memory issues. Presented below is a representative sample of ten such scenarios that the practitioner is likely to encounter, some more commonly than others. For our purposes, they are offered to suggest the complexity of issues and the myriad potential clinical presentations, which are not always as mutually exclusive as these separate descriptions imply. Each scenario includes an explanation and a case, followed by a commentary on the choice of overall treatment strategy, the application of specific techniques, and some of the transference, countertransference, and vicarious traumatization issues that might arise.

These scenarios are offered in somewhat hierarchical order in terms of the degree of intactness or continuity of memory of past abuse or other trauma and their disclosure to the therapist. Except for scenarios 3, 4, and 8, where third-party information/corroboration is available, outside evidence of occurrence may or may not be present. This order of presentation also roughly corresponds to the degree of risk to the practitioner that each scenario entails in the current atmosphere. In general, the most risk is found in cases of recovered memory with one or more of these features: detailed memory of extremely severe, improbable, or impossible forms of abuse in a very dependent or suggestible patient that occurs in the aftermath of previously absent or inaccessible memory and following the repeated use of suggestive and/or authoritarian techniques. The reader is reminded, however, that each case must be individually assessed, that recovered memory after a period of unavailability has been found to be no less valid than continuous memory (Brown et al., 1998; Dalenberg, 1996; Kluft, 1997), and that corroboration has been found in some cases of seemingly improbable forms of abuse (S. Shapiro, 1995). It is also important to note that the availability of evidence or independent confirmation reduces risk considerably, although it does not remove it entirely.

In general, relatively continuous memory of abuse and disclosure at time of intake is the least complicated and vexing of all of the scenarios. It may also be more common than implied by false memory critics, whose writings emphasize highly elaborated recovered memory following a *total absence* of prior memory. It is this type of circumstance that has been most heavily (and justifiably) criticized. It appears, however, that it is *not* the most likely scenario and that the majority of individuals who were abused as children remember all or part of what happened to them (American Psychological Association, 1994, 1996b; British Psychological Society, 1995), but that their memories may be discontinuous or variably accessible over time (Gold et al, 1994; Williams, 1994a, 1995).The reader is referred back to the discussion of traumatic memory and abuse in chapters 3 and 4, specifically to the descriptions of a continuum of memory accessibility/traumatic amnesia described by Brown et al. (1998), Harvey and Herman, 1996), Herman and Harvey (1997), and Laub and Auerhahn (1993).

In terms of recommending principles and guidelines for working with delayed/recovered memory issues, we are most concerned with scenarios 4 through 10, those that require the most clinical judgment and acumen on the part of the therapist, those that may elicit the greatest degree of countertransference and vicarious traumatization, and those for which the least information and training have been available.

Scenario 1: Continuous/Relatively Continuous Memory of Abuse (Physical, Sexual, Emotional) or Other Trauma and Disclosure at the Initiation of Treatment

The individual seeks treatment reporting continuous or relatively continuous memory for incidents of childhood abuse or other trauma that has never been forgotten and that is disclosed at intake or during assessment. The abuse may or may not have been previously disclosed. In this scenario, the abuse and its aftermath are frequently, although not always, the explicit reasons for seeking therapy. On the other hand, the individual may not be seeking abuse-related treatment and/or may not associate the presenting symptoms with past abuse (Courtois, 1988). Indeed, previous abuse and the need for treatment may or may not be related, thus calling for careful assessment. In this scenario, as in many of the others, additional memory may emerge during the course of therapy. Corroboration may be available, or not.

CASE EXAMPLE. *Ms. A. sought treatment for her recurrent debilitating symptoms of depression and her difficulty establishing an intimate relationship. In the initial interview, she readily disclosed a history of several years of forceful incestuous abuse (including intercourse) by her older brother that began when she was approximately 8 (the time period was vague to her). Upon inquiry, she stated that she had never forgotten this activity, but that she had never told anyone after having told her mother at the time. Her mother had disbelieved her yet paradoxically blamed her. She had also had a lock installed on the inside of her daughter's bedroom door without any acknowledgment that doing so had anything to do with the disclosure. Ms. A. wondered whether or not the incest and her mother's reaction were related in any way to her chronic depression and ongoing relationship problems. She also stated that she would rather not think about the situation in hopes that it was all a bad dream that would "just go away."*

COMMENTARY ON ASSESSMENT, APPROACH, STRATEGIES, AND COUNTER-TRANSFERENCE.   A broad pretreatment assessment to determine Ms. A.'s family and psychosocial history, her memory of the abuse (including its quality and accessibility over time), additional family violence and trauma, and her psychological (including posttraumatic) symptoms and their relative severity is in order. At this juncture, the therapist can also attempt a preliminary determination of the relative weight of the incestuous abuse versus other life events to Ms. A.'s symptoms and functioning. Because the incest began at a relatively young age, was described as involving force and repeated intercourse, the therapist can safely speculate about its likely association to the presenting symptoms (based on literature about sibling abuse). Also, the degree to which Ms. A. has integrated her knowledge of the abuse into the remainder of her personal history is worth assessing. As I noted in a previous discussion of memory in incest survivors (Courtois, 1992), many individuals who have relatively complete and/or continuous memory of their abuse wish that they did not and use psychological defenses to deny, suppress, or split off their knowledge. They may also utilize other mechanisms (i.e., drug use, somatization, and compulsive behaviors, including self-injury, risk-taking, overwork, and relationships) to blunt the memories and keep them at bay. In cases such as this, work with the trauma cannot be undertaken until better coping mechanisms are developed and the symptoms stabilized.

With the determination of a high degree of depression and other posttraumatic symptomatology, an evaluation for psychotropic medication is recommended. The patient's relative degree of safety and functionality should also be assessed. The PTT treatment model is appropriate in this case, with initial treatment focused on decreasing depressive symptoms (and any associated self-harm or safety issues); defining the treatment and safety contracts and developing the treatment alliance; providing general education regarding trauma, posttraumatic symptoms, sibling incest (and any other family dysfunction identified in the assessment); identifying posttraumatic beliefs and cognitions as the focus of early intervention; and teaching preliminary affect modulation and self-management skills.

At this point, the therapist can begin to identify evident and possible traumatic and transference themes. Given that Ms. A. described an ambivalent relationship with her mother who provided mixed responses to her initial disclosure, that her brother was the perpetrator, and that relationship problems are part of the reason for seeking treatment, themes of mistrust, fear, betrayal, and "being seen" by the therapist can be anticipated. The therapist, in turn, might be watchful for counter-transference responses that suggest a need to "be a better mother" to Ms. A. and to rescue her, possibly by colluding with her wish to avoid the situation and make it a bad dream that just goes away.

Scenario 2: Continuous/Relatively Continuous Memory of Abuse or Other Trauma and No Disclosure at the Outset of Treatment

Scenario 2 involves an individual who has continuous/relatively continuous memory for past abuse/trauma yet does not disclose this information during intake and assessment. Numerous reasons have been identified for nondisclosure, a circumstance that is quite typical for abuse/trauma survivors, as discussed in chapter 4. The individual may seek treatment for major symptoms or symptom constellations that have been found to correlate with an abuse history. This scenario fits the "disguised presentation" outlined by Gelinas (1983) and may lead to the therapist's developing an "index of suspicion" regarding the possibility of past abuse/trauma. In this situation, the therapist reassesses the possibility of abuse over time but must be careful that the "index of suspicion" does not result in influence or suggestion, however subtle. This scenario also calls for additional assessment once the abuse/trauma is disclosed. As in scenario 1, more details or memory accessibility may occur during treatment as the individual focuses on past events and attempts to remember them in an atmosphere that is accepting and supportive. The individual may also make attempts to forget things that have been remembered, especially when painful, conflictual, and uncomfortable. Corroboration may be available, or not.

CASE EXAMPLE.   *Mr. B. sought treatment reluctantly, due only to his wife's concerns and threats to leave him if he did not do so. He described a recent history of compulsive sexual activity, online and in person, with an ever expand-*

ing number of anonymous male partners. His wife had recently discovered the
extent of the activity and was betrayed/outraged and concerned about the risk of
HIV. Mr. B. had suffered a career setback that he identified as the precipitant to
his behavior–having sexual conversations and contacts with other men tem-
porarily stopped what he described as major anxiety reactions bordering on
panic. He had maintained a furtive life of occasional sexual contacts with other
men, but the activity had accelerated dramatically of late when he discovered
online sex-oriented "chat rooms."

Upon assessment, it was clear that Mr. B. was clinically depressed and alco-
hol dependent. During the assessment, when asked directly whether he had ever
had sexual experiences as a child with an adult, Mr. B. did not disclose the
fondling and mutual masturbation that his parish priest had initiated during
his childhood and that had persisted into adolescence, even though he had never
forgotten it. He felt ashamed and believed that, because he was male, he should
have been able to defend himself and put a stop to the activity. Not having been
able to do so meant to him that he had really liked it and had done something to
deserve it. Mr. B. also suspected that the priest had singled him out as a child
because he had somehow determined that he was a homosexual. He feared that
the therapist would blame him for what had happened and would further tell
him he was a homosexual and should get a divorce, something he did not want.

Mr. B. mentioned the sexual abuse with great shame and trepidation several
months into treatment and into sobriety, inquiring whether it might be associat-
ed with his addictions and his depression. He also expressed fear about disclos-
ing the abuse to his wife and to his family, all of whom were very religious and
maintained close ties to the church.

COMMENTARY ON ASSESSMENT, APPROACH, STRATEGIES, AND COUNTER-
TRANSFERENCE. Despite the nondisclosure of sexual abuse at intake and
upon specific inquiry during the assessment, the therapist is justified by
the patient's presenting symptoms (and gender) in suspecting and maintaining a hypothesis about an undisclosed abuse history. A comprehensive general assessment is a mandatory starting point, with specialized
evaluations for substance abuse, sexual addiction, and depression.
Corollary testing for HIV is also a consideration. If assessment reveals
serious problems with substance abuse, sexual compulsion, and major
depression, or if the the HIV testing is positive, treatment geared to
these issues takes precedence. Corollary sessions with Mr. B.'s wife
might be used to stabilize the immediate crisis. If the couple were
amenable, marital therapy would be recommended but deferred until
after the treatment of these initial concerns is underway and Mr. B. is
more stable.

In a clinical scenario such as this one, it is quite usual (and unfortunately very uncomfortable) for the individual struggling to recover from substance abuse or compulsive activities to have traumatic memories emerge and/or major posttraumatic/dissociative symptoms develop as sobriety is maintained. At that point, the therapist must reassess for a history of past abuse/trauma, and the re-inquiry may well lead to disclosure. The therapist might find that the individual always remembered all or part of the abuse, but chose not to disclose due to shame and fears of being judged, disbelieved, and rejected. The motivation for nondisclosure might also be fear of retribution from the perpetrator and/or a desire to protect him/her. Transference responses of mistrust, shame, and self-blame often come to the fore. The potential for a rescuing, overprotective, and overzealous countertransference response is usual in a case such as this one. The therapist might feel very angry and outraged about the damage in the patient and feel a related wish for restitution when faced with abuse perpetrated on a child by a "man of the cloth" or "in God's name."

Over time, a more abuse/trauma-oriented treatment can be introduced. Initially, it should be kept low-key and informative because the therapeutic goals of sobriety and symptom stabilization take therapeutic precedence. Relapse planning and personal safety need priority attention post-disclosure, given the patient's intense shame, fear of judgment, and sense of self-blame. Additionally, during early-stage sobriety, the patient is only beginning the process of learning alternative means of self-soothing and anxiety management. Preliminary education about abuse and abuse reactions, especially concerning themes of shame and self-blame among male victims, is appropriate at this time. It is also appropriate to offer information about same-sex and clergy abuse and how they might generate confusion about sexual orientation and contribute to sexual compulsivity. Therapy proceeds step-wise as the patient gets sober and is less depressed.

Scenario 3: Discontinuous Memory or Partial Amnesia of Abuse/Other Trauma with Disclosure at the Outset of Treatment

In this scenario, the individual reports discontinuous or variable memory for experiences of past abuse/trauma but makes a disclosure at the outset of treatment. Such a situation, as described earlier, relates to the patient's simultaneously "knowing and not knowing" (Courtois, 1988; Gold et al., 1994; Grand, 1995; Roth & Batson, 1997). Variable patterns of partial amnesia are routinely observed in clinical settings. These may include memory for the gist but not the details of the trauma, memory for the peripheral details but not the gist, and patchy memory, each with or without intrusive/numbing symptoms of PTSD, and symptoms of primary or secondary dissociation (Brown et al., 1998). Memory might return after a period of absence when cued by some external event or internal response (Elliott & Briere, 1995b) or when the individual tries to remember (as described by Fitzpatrick, 1997). It is not unusual for some individuals to report abuse in response to direct questions, and to later not remember or deny having reported it, a circumstance that can be very confusing to the patient as well as to the clinician unaccustomed to the vageries of dissociative amnesia. As in scenario 1, the abuse may or may not have been revealed previously and may or may not be associated with the individual's present-day concerns or the reason for seeking treatment. Here, too, corroboration is variable.

> CASE EXAMPLE.   *Ms. C. sought treatment for acute symptoms associated with intrusive recollections related to incestuous abuse by her stepfather and physical abuse and neglect by her mother. Although Ms. C. had never totally forgotten about the abuse and neglect, she had lived her life "trying to pretend it hadn't happened" and she had largely succeeded. She described keeping it in the back of her mind, mostly out of her awareness, and "getting on with her life." On occasion, she thought of it, but only fleetingly, and had learned that she could "make it go away" if she so willed it. She could even spend "pleasant enough" time with her stepfather and "not focus on it much." She had a loving husband with whom she had a happy marriage and a grown family of several well-adjusted children, and she had just opened a small specialty shop in fulfillment of a long-held occupational goal.*
>
> *Upon the sudden death of her mother, she began to be flooded with memories of the sexual contacts with her stepfather and the things that he had told her at the time (that she enjoyed it and wanted it, that he preferred her sexually to her mother/his wife, that she had better not disclose because no one would believe her, and that her mother would put her up for adoption if she found out). She further learned that her stepfather had abused her younger sister (whom she had actively tried to protect from him) and that her sister had once observed him abusing her. She was overcome with feelings of rage, grief, betrayal, anxiety, dread, and guilt and was actively suicidal at the time of intake. She also indicated an urge to kill her stepfather for his transgressions and betrayals.*

COMMENTARY ON ASSESSMENT, APPROACH, STRATEGIES, AND COUNTER-TRANSFERENCE.   Immediate crisis management and a preliminary risk assessment are called for in such an acute situation. Where a high risk for suicide and/or homicide is determined (i.e., the individual cannot give assurances regarding her own safety or that of someone else, and furthermore has access to lethal means), a hospital admission (voluntary or involuntary) is called for. During even a brief hospital stay, a comprehensive assessment, including evaluation for medication, can be undertaken. After resolution of the immediate crisis, a period of stabilization, and the development of a safety plan, the patient can be discharged to outpatient treatment.

The PTT model is appropriate for outpatient treatment in a case such as this one, given the patient's extreme crisis and posttraumatic symptomatology. The initial focus of treatment would be reinforcement and extension of the work done in the hospital, as well as attempts to stabilize the patient's mood and functioning. Preliminary education might be around the role of triggers in the emergence of symptoms and methods for managing distressing emotions. More detailed assessment of what the patient remembers is also a consideration at this time.

Transference themes of mistrust and disillusionment are likely, especially around times of separation, since they might also be a time where the patient is flooded with new memories and abandonment fears and simultaneously enraged with the therapist for leaving and for "causing the pain." Strong back-up coverage and safety planning during times of separation are mandatory for such patients.

Countertransference feelings of shame and guilt for abandoning the patient and causing her additional distress can be expected. These feelings, in turn, might tempt the therapist to overcompensate or overextend herself in some way (for example, giving the patient her phone number while on vacation). Instead, it would be more beneficial for the therapist to empathize with the patient's distress at the impending leavetaking and to help her associate it to the trigger of her mother's death. It would also be helpful to remind herself and the patient of the patient's strengths and competence and the availability of her personal support system in addition to the back-up therapist.

Scenario 4: New Memories (Delayed/Recovered) of Abuse/Other Trauma While Not in Therapy and Without Therapeutic Intervention

In this scenario, the individual presents for treatment reporting new (delayed/recovered) memories of abuse/trauma that emerged outside of therapy and in the absence of therapeutic intervention. Prior memories (continuous or with variable accessibility/amnesia) may or may not have been available. Specific triggers or cueing events, whether internal or external to the individual, may be identified. As described above, the memories may constitute the reason for seeking treatment and/or may be associated with the individual's present-day concerns. Corroboration may be obtainable, or not.

> CASE EXAMPLE. *Ms. D. sought a consultation when she began to have memories of a traumatic medical procedure in late childhood after reading an account of a similar event in her local newspaper. Her parents confirmed her memory of the procedure, which had never been discussed in hopes that she wouldn't remember it and therefore wouldn't be distressed by it. Her memories felt upsetting but not overwhelming and she continued to function well at the time of her consultation. She was generally in good mental health and described her upbringing as rather carefree and devoid of any major problem or disruption. Her stated reason for seeking a therapy consultation was that she wanted to know how she could have forgotten/not thought about something for so long, only to have it come back so suddenly and with such immediacy. She was also concerned that there were other events in her background that she had forgotten and that would begin to emerge and upset her.*

COMMENTARY ON ASSESSMENT, APPROACH, STRATEGIES, AND COUNTER-TRANSFERENCE.   A situation such as this one usually requires a more general assessment/consultation and focused, brief, generic treatment unless symptoms accompany the recovered memory or additional recovered memories are reported. In the scenario described here, the individual can be given a supportive context within which to discuss her reactions and questions about her reinstated memories; she can also be provided with information about trauma, posttraumatic responses, and recovered memories. With discussion, the impact of the event might be connected to other life events and themes (for example, in this case, the parents' tendency to keep secrets in order to protect their children, as evidenced by their never mentioning the medical procedure).

Little by way of high intensity transference reactions would be expected in such a situation where the patient was not highly distressed, did not have an additional trauma history or other psychological distress, and was mainly in need of support and information. Contemporaneous feelings of gratitude to the therapist for listening and providing information might be a predominant reaction. In terms of countertransference, the therapist might be tempted by reactions of attraction to and overfascination with recovered memories or the confirmatory belief that other memories might be right beneath the surface. In the absence of any outstanding symptoms or distress, treatment is not indicated. Termination could be predicated upon the individual returning at a later time if she had additional questions, experienced any untoward symptoms, and/or recovered any other memories.

Scenario 5: New Memories (Delayed/Recovered) While in Past Therapy

The individual describes the emergence of new (delayed/recovered) memories of abuse during the course of previous therapy. Prior memories (continuous or with variable amnesia) may or may not have been available. New memories may have arisen spontaneously without the use of any specific therapeutic technique (as described by Briere, 1996b, 1996c; Gold & Brown, 1997, and other clinician researchers) or as the result of therapeutic suggestion, influence, reinforcement, pressure, etc., from the therapist, adjunctive treatment (i.e., group therapy and self-help groups), and outside influences such as the media. Specific triggers or cueing events, whether internal or external to the individual and possibly involving the therapeutic context and relationship (Dalenberg, 1996), may or may not be identified. Corroboration is available for some recovered memories and not available for others.

CASE EXAMPLE. *Ms. E. sought treatment after having taken a hiatus from therapy for several years. Her stated goal was to determine the reality of memories of past sexual abuse, memories that she had recovered during her previous therapy. Prior to that time, she had had no memory whatsoever of having been abused, although her family was quite dysfunctional during her childhood and was positive for a number of risk factors associated with abuse. Both parents had been alcoholics during the course of her childhood and she had basically raised herself and her siblings. Her parents had divorced, had shared custody, and both had multiple partners over the years.*

Ms. E.'s initial treatment during her college years had been for depression following a failed relationship and a history of bulimarexia. She described the treatment as quite helpful to her and said that the therapist had helped her to "grow up and face my life." Early into her treatment, her therapist had inquired about the possibility of sexual abuse, which she had denied and for which she had no memory. The therapist took a detailed history, was convinced that abuse had occurred, and utilized hypnosis quite extensively to assist her with retrieving her abuse memories. She had also encouraged Ms. E. join one of her incest survivor groups to help her with her memories. During the course of this treatment, Ms. E. had recovered memories about one of her mother's boyfriends fondling her.

Recently, after having had oral sex with her husband, she began to remember that her mother's boyfriend had also forced her to fellate him. She now feels sick to her stomach and gets numbed out whenever she thinks about oral sex and/or sexual abuse. She is confused and is seeking therapy hoping the new therapist will help her sort out what's true.

COMMENTARY ON ASSESSMENT, APPROACH, STRATEGIES, AND COUNTER-TRANSFERENCE. This case is more complex regarding delayed/recovered memory, its relation to historical truth, and the possible suggestibility of the previous therapy. The therapist's job is to help the patient to evaluate (and reevaluate) both past and present situations and to "not convey too much certainty or uncertainty" (Dalenberg & Carlson, in press). A comprehensive assessment includes attention to the degree of suggestibility in the previous therapy and the degree to which the patient seems suggestible or reliant on authority figures to determine her reality. In a case such as this one, records of the previous therapy might well reveal that the therapist had good reason to suspect abuse (even though unremembered) by virtue of risk factors in the family history (the alcoholism of both parents, general family dysfunction and marital conflict resulting in divorce, the patient's role as caretaker to her siblings, exposure and vulnerability to the parents' subsequent partners). However, since the initial recovered memories occurred in the context of treatment utilizing activities and strategies that were possibly suggestive, more evaluation is called for. The patient can be assisted in assessing available internal and external evidence (including seeking out information from siblings or other third parties). Additionally, the new memory might well provide additional information and another reason for suspecting the reality of past abuse. Its retrieval, years after the original treatment when the Ms. E. was not in treatment, was related to a quite specific trigger and was of a different experience of abuse than previously remembered. Complicating the matter still further is the possibility that one of the recovered memories represents an experience of genuine past abuse, while another does not (or that both do or do not). The therapist has no concrete way of knowing without corroboration, and so must offer the patient empathy and support as she explores the prospect of past abuse.

In discussing cases of memory recovered in previous therapy, especially with regard to strategy and transference issues, Dalenberg and Carlson (in press) have offered this advice:

> The greater the possibility that the former therapist has improperly influenced the client's doubt or certainty (perhaps by claiming privileged knowledge or overreliance on unvalidated checklists), the more important the new therapist's respect for the patient's capacity for independence will come to be. As both client and therapist come to understand any such processes of influence, they can be used to define the boundaries of the existing relationship. Such discussions can and should be quite explicit, recognizing that patient-therapist interactions are interactions and may replicate abusive dynamics if the therapist does

not recognize the "transference test" and step out of the reality-defining authority role.

In a case such as this one, the therapist must also sidestep the inclination to paint the past therapist as all good or all bad, but rather must work towards a balanced perspective that is in the interest of the patient. Countertransference might therefore involve overfascination, self-righteousness, or anger at the therapeutic approach of the past. The therapist might also be fearful of the "recovered memory" patient who is perceived as bringing increased liability into the treatment room. Fear responses might lead to premature suppression without adequate examination. Responses of fear and anxiety need to be processed away from the patient in order to maintain a stance of support and an even-handed appraisal of all possibilities.

Scenario 6: New (Delayed/Recovered) Memories of Abuse/Other Trauma While in Current Therapy

The individual describes the development of new (delayed/recovered) memories of abuse during the current therapy. Prior memories (continuous or with variable amnesia) may or may not have been available. As discussed previously, there are a number of reasons that memories might be more accessible during the course of psychotherapy. Therapy provides a context for the discussion of autobiographical events and may otherwise provide specific and nonspecific prompts to recollection. For example, questions asked in therapy, the lessening of dissociative or other numbing mechanisms, and explicit and implicit permission to remember and discuss long-suppressed or forgotten events may prompt the return of association and memory. New memories may arise due to the therapeutic context and relationship (Courtois, 1992; Dalenberg, 1996). This may happen spontaneously as the patient gets better (Briere, 1996b, 1996c; Gold & Brown, 1997) or develops trust (Courtois, 1988), or it may be induced by state-dependency and specific triggers or cueing events, whether internal or external to the individual. Alternatively, memories may arise in therapy, as false memory critics imply, with the presence of suggestion, influence, pressure, reinforcement, etc. Corroboration for memories recovered in current treatment may or may not be available.

CASE EXAMPLE. *Ms. F. sought treatment for unremitting depression, failed relationships, and a history of discord with and harassment by coworkers at a variety of jobs. In describing her family history, she portrayed her mother as having been uncaring and neglectful and her father as mostly benign but absent;*

she minimized the significance of these parenting deficits to her current concerns because she currently felt close to both parents. She remembered being constantly picked on and scapegoated by other children during elementary and middle school, with no one to protect her, and believed that these experiences negatively affected her and related to her current distress

Her therapy was marked by profound mistrust and testing of her female therapist. Times of separation and absence (such as vacations and holidays) were especially problematic for Ms. F.—they resulted in rage and anguish of noteworthy intensity and associated episodes of self-harm. In her second year of treatment and during her therapist's vacation, Ms. F. began to have strong physical sensations of having been held down by someone whose face she could not see and who "did something bad" to her. She was highly distressed that her therapist was unavailable at the time of this recovered memory episode. Ms. F. had a number of recurrences of this experience, always in association with the therapist's unavailability or absence. Additional physical sensations were experienced with some vague sense of remembering something bad happening when she was quite young and of screaming "no, no!" She felt intense shame and remorse after having these experiences.

Ms. F. and her therapist hypothesized the possibility of abuse or assault of some sort. Her older sister vaguely remembered something about a dirty old man in the neighborhood and a police investigation involving her family and neighbors, but her parents denied knowing anything about it. Ms. F. was considering checking police and newspaper archives for possible information.

COMMENTARY ON ASSESSMENT, APPROACH, STRATEGIES, AND COUNTER-TRANSFERENCE. This case involves fragmentary information without clear memory and transference dynamics and some third-party information that implies the possibility of victimization of some sort (not necessarily sexual abuse). Reviere's advice is especially pertinent in a case such as this one:

> Direct work with partial memory should be embedded in a general exploration of other events and circumstances in the client's past and current life. . . . Within this context the *available* memory fragments, along with the client's reactions to these memories, can be explored, rather than focusing exclusively on the excavation of unavailable memories. (author's italics) (Reviere, 1996, p. 121).

The patient's interpersonal difficulties could certainly emanate from the neglect and estrangement she experienced with both parents during her childhood, possibly in conjunction with an experience of victimization that was either ignored or not well-managed by the parents. The abandonment dynamics that play out in the transference could be the result of nonvalidation and nonresponse to an episode of victimization, all within the larger context of the impoverished parent-child relationship. Thus, although abuse or assault is a distinct possibility in this scenario, it is not the sole explanation for the patient's history of relational discord.

The therapist must "hold the line" with Ms. F.'s strong transferential and contemporaneous reactions by not underreacting or overreacting to them. Instead, gentle guidance and support are called for as Ms. F. sifts and weighs available evidence and considers searching for additional corroboration. Because of the strong mistrust and a past history of problematic relationships (including with both parents), the therapist should remain attuned to relational nuances and their possible meaning to the patient. Being trustworthy and maintaining a stance of empathy can assist Ms. F. with object constancy and a sense of ongoing support, providing a new relational experience that is ultimately restorative.

Scenario 7: No Memory of Abuse/Other Trauma But the Individual Suspects or Believes It Occurred

The individual reports suspicions or beliefs that past abuse occurred, but without any available memory. He or she may seek treatment with the specific goal of finding the missing memories and confirming abuse beliefs/suspicions or may have a more open-ended, exploratory agenda. The suspicions or beliefs may be derived from a variety of sources (e.g., symptoms and diagnosis, the media, a support or self-help group, a lay or professional caregiver's belief or suggestion, personality variables such as suggestibility or dependence, reactions to cues or triggers, available corroboration or witnesses, etc.) and may involve a specific agenda.

CASE EXAMPLE. *Ms. G. sought therapy with the stated goal of retrieving her repressed memories of incest by her father. She had no specific memories but strong suspicions of its occurrence. She had some vague recollections of discomfort when with her father. When asked what led her to believe she had been abused, she replied that it was the only possible explanation for how badly things had gone in her life. She believed that, if she could remember, everything would make sense and she would feel better. She had heard all about repressed memories of trauma and how not remembering could be associated with having been traumatized, especially through incest. She requested hypnosis to quickly "get at the memories" and also asked about some sort of truth serum test that she had heard discussed in her incest self-help group. She wanted to know if the therapist believed in repressed memories and whether the therapist believed her story.*

Alternative Scenario 7:
No Memory of Abuse/Other Trauma
But Passionate Belief in Its Occurrence and
Past Involvement in Suggestive Self-Help
and Alternative Healing Activities

CASE EXAMPLE. *Ms. H. was convinced that she had been sexually abused as a child by many members of her immediate and extended family, although she had no conscious memory of any abuse. She sought psychotherapy to help her find her missing memories. She described a long history of alternative "treatments" (aura readings, tarot card readings, regression-oriented group hypnotic work, massage therapy/body work), during which it had been suggested that she had many characteristics and body symptoms/body memories of someone who had been seriously abused. She had been voraciously reading literature on how to access repressed abuse memories and thought they were finally beginning to emerge.*

COMMENTARY ON ASSESSMENT, APPROACH, STRATEGIES, AND COUNTER-TRANSFERENCE.   In both of these cases, the individual is highly invested in finding incest memories but has no memory of having been abused. Rather than viewing incest as shameful or upsetting, these two women see it as the explanation for their problems or for their ostensible symptoms. Sexual abuse has been suggested or is seen as the only logical conclusion and these individuals are attempting to recover memories via therapy. These cases represent the type of case where, obviously, the therapist must be excessively cautious. Broad-based, unbiased assessment is called for as a starting point. The therapist should ascertain whether the individual has any memories of abuse (given that they may not be divulged unless asked about directly and may be "known but not known") *and* should ascertain the individual's beliefs about abuse and recovered memory and the source of these beliefs. The therapist must then seek to educate the individual about open-ended exploratory treatment versus *a priori* assumptions of abuse and about memory processes and recovered memory. Informed consent based on a clear mutual understanding about the course of treatment and agreement to the therapist's approach regarding memories is especially important in cases such as these. Should such an agreement not be possible, the best (and safest) course of action for the therapist is not to agree to treat and to refer instead to other practitioners (with whom the individual may be better able to arrive at a collaborative understanding). Quoting again from Dalenberg and Carlson (in press) regarding therapist missteps (due to lack of knowledge or transference/countertransference issues) at the initiation of treatment with a case of this sort:

> The therapist who responds that the existence of doubt or prolonged amnesia is a conclusive sign of the truth or falsity of the recovered memory is not only making an empirically indefensible statement, but also may be missing the point for this client, as well as imposing his or her own version of reality. Other reported sources for client beliefs in their own abuse (absent memory) are media, popular texts, friends, or support groups who claim the ability to identify abuse victims from unvalidated checklists or list of multidetermined symptoms. . . . Again, the client's passionate belief can push the therapist toward premature confirmation, just as the therapist's knowledge of the unreliability of such instruments might push toward premature disconfirmation. The question "Was I abused?" is not one that should be answered in a first session for a patient without memories, despite the press to do so from a client in pain from the disequilibrium such doubt may cause.

These clinicians go on to assert: "The clinician must keep in mind that the client's disclosed reasons for suspicion may be inadequate, but this does not mean that other undisclosed reasons are not more adequate or that firm statements can be made that the client was not abused." And, "Insufficient evidence for presence is not evidence for absence, and should not be presented as such to the patient." These statements contain a great deal of wisdom. They alert the therapist to the dilemmas and difficulties inherent in maintaining a stance of openness to all possibilities and the necessity of ongoing assessment and weighing of available information. It is strongly recommended that whatever exploration is undertaken begin with a strategy of free-recall. Subsequent strategies can be applied in step-wise fashion, as discussed in chapter 6 and as recommended by Brown et al. (1998). Strategically and countertransferentially, the therapist must be mindful of not reinforcing any production or recovered memory by being overly invested or attentive. Memory content ought to be received with a demeanor of calm consideration to the degree possible, to avoid reinforcing the patient for "upping the ante" and recovering "more and better" memories to keep the therapist's attention (Gold & Brown, 1997).

Patients such as these are likely to elicit strong countertransference responses, ranging from fear/aversion/avoidance to obsession/voyeuristic interest. Support for the therapist is recommended in working with cases of this sort in order to have an outside source of consultation and a counterbalance to work through prominent emotional reactions.

Scenario 8: No Memory of Abuse/Other Trauma
But with Third-Party Information/Corroboration
That It Occurred

The individual reports no memory for the occurrence of past abuse that has been substantiated by third-party information or other outside evidence. He or she may seek treatment to recover memories or to deal with the emotional impact of the disclosure and substantiation of past abuse, or s/he may seek support in disputing or disqualifying the evidence.

CASE EXAMPLE.   *Recently, Mr. I. was surprised to receive a phone call from a man who had attended summer camp with him as a child. This man inquired whether Mr. I. had any memory of a specific camp counselor and whether anything out of the ordinary had ever happened with him. Mr. I. remembered the counselor in question with great fondness as someone who had helped him with his acute homesickness by giving him special attention. He was startled and saddened to learn that this counselor had recently been charged with molesting a number of boys over many years. A lawsuit was in the works against the camp for covering up his activities and for continuing to employ him, even after receiving a number of reports and complaints of molestation. He was further shocked when the caller told him that he had observed the counselor molest Mr. I. on several occasions, events for which Mr. I. had no memory.*

Mr. I. subsequently sought therapy to sort out what might have happened to him and to help him with his reactions. He had been mostly asymptomatic throughout his life but following the phone call began to experience depression, episodes of panic, nightmares and sleep disturbance, but not memories. Additionally, he was angry that the phone call had disrupted his heretofore "peaceful existence, blissful innocence, and good thoughts about everyone."

COMMENTARY ON ASSESSMENT, APPROACH, STRATEGIES, AND COUNTER-TRANSFERENCE.   Depending upon the individual's status and symptoms at intake, this scenario may require only a consultation or, alternately, more extensive therapeutic attention. The therapist might be tempted to prematurely push the individual to accept the third-party information at face value. It is more helpful if the therapist can assist the individual to evaluate the information, come to terms with its implications, and decide on a course of action. In this case example, Mr. I. indicates that major life themes about self and others have been disrupted and a previously cherished relationship upended. Such disillusionment and the shock of learning about unremembered abuse require immediate therapeutic attention and stabilization. As in all cases, early assessment is called for. Information derived from a detailed psychosocial, family, and developmental history might provide information that is useful in beginning to assess the third-party report. Information from additional corollary sources might also be available and helpful in weighing the evidence. It is also likely that, in a case such as this, basic education about abuse/trauma and memory processes would prove useful.

Transference themes of dependence, avoidance, shame, and anger might be anticipated. Some individuals might expect the therapist to function as the "arbiter of reality" who makes a determination about the information. Others might well attempt to close down or split off the information that has been conveyed to maintain their previous equilibrium. Still others might express anger at the disruption caused by abuse and its unexpected disclosure. The therapist must decline the invitation to determine the individual's reality or even to determine the credibility of the third-party information. Rather, the individual must struggle with the information and with making a personal determination of its accuracy and ramifications. Circumstances such as this one sometimes result in reactions of relief at "having found the missing piece to the puzzle" of lifelong problems and symptoms for which no cause could previously be identified (as described by Fitzpatrick, 1997). On the other hand, they sometimes upset an otherwise well-adjusted life (as described by Cheit, 1997).

Scenario 9: Memory (Usually Recovered) of Improbable, Obviously False, or Seemingly False Memory

The individual in this scenario seeks treatment for improbable, obviously false, or seemingly false memory (terminology used by Dalenberg and Carlson, in press) based on memory that is usually, but not always, recovered, or on the basis of realistic revivifications, "abreactions," and intrusive/reexperiencing symptoms. Such memory may be reported within the context of a therapy where suggestive practices were employed or may have developed independently, possibly due to other suggestive influences. In this scenario, the therapist is faced with the task of offering the individual a forum for sorting out improbable abuse circumstances from those that may appear to be seemingly or obviously false, while assessing the individual's reality-testing, characterological and defensive structure, possible sources of suggestion or pressure, and any secondary gain. It is worth noting that reports of improbable abuse or seemingly false memory must not be dismissed out of hand. Valid corroborative evidence has sometimes been found that supports the occurrence of implausible forms of abuse (Dalenberg & Carlson, in press), and some documented cases of abuse meet the criteria of being way out of the ordinary and quite bizarre. On the other hand, some situations are patently impossible and obviously false and should be so identified. Complicating the matter further, some impossible abuses may actually be screen memories or covers for real experiences of abuse, a circumstance that must be considered and assessed.

> CASE EXAMPLE. *Ms. J. sought treatment for what she reported as past life abuse that she was reexperiencing in the form of highly distressing and detailed flashbacks. She traced the onset of these flashbacks to her recently completed course of past life regression therapy, where she had undergone hypnosis several times a week in individual and group sessions. During these sessions, on the basis of physical reactions and flashbacks involving scenes of horrible abuse, Ms. J. had come to believe that she was multiply abused over the course of several past lives. She felt increasingly out of control as her flashbacks intensified and increased in frequency and interfered with her ability to function at school and in her job. She became seriously depressed, desperate, and suicidal. She wondered what she had done to have been so viciously abused so many times over and wanted the therapist's help in understanding.*

> ALTERNATIVE CASE EXAMPLE. *Ms. K. initially sought treatment for a severe postpartum depression. She was so depressed at the time that she was vegetative, fairly unresponsive, with marked memory and concentration impairment, and appeared "numbed out." Her therapist evaluated her as suffering from major depression and a dissociative disorder. She was prescribed medication for her depression and her overwhelming anxiety. Over time, the therapist focused on Ms. K.'s lack of memory and the postpartum depression, seizing on the hypothesis that the birth of her child was a trigger to past memories involving babies. The therapist began a search for memories of past abuse involving babies. Following the use of extensive hypnosis, Ms. K. recovered memories of being a baby breeder in a satanic cult and being forced to sacrifice her babies on religious holidays. She was grief-stricken and guilty and became suicidal "to atone for what she had done." She also was experiencing difficulty bonding with her child.*

COMMENTARY ON ASSESSMENT, APPROACH, STRATEGIES, AND COUNTER-TRANSFERENCE.   In cases such as these, the immediate circumstance takes precedence over the evaluation of the reality of reported past abuse. Once the individual is stabilized, then assessment can be undertaken to ascertain the individual's history and background, including the quality of past treatment. In particular, in a case like the first example, it would be important to find out why the patient sought out past life treatment and what belief system was operative and what (if any) symptoms were present at the time.

Each therapist must make a judgment call as to how to respond to reports of patently impossible abuse, a difficult issue with ethical ramifications. Some choose to communicate their disbelief in the type of abuse being reported by the patient, while others do not. Reasons for either response should be included in the chart notes. The patient's abuse reports should be recorded in the chart as "reported by," "believed," or "alleged," so the record conveys that they are not accepted uncritically as events that really took place. Whatever the position taken, it is still not the therapist's purview to determine the reality of the patient's beliefs, and s/he must guard against closing down the patient's communication and examination of past and current material. Instead, the therapist can first offer education about memory and memory processes and, in both of these cases, about how the use of repeated regressive hypnosis in individual and group contexts might cause false memory (and influence both memory production and the individual's confidence in the memory), as well as about how flashbacks and other intrusive/reexperiencing phenomena differ from historical reality. In the alternative case example, the therapist might provide information about postpartum depression. Second, the therapist might explore the patient's belief systems and how beliefs might be related to or causative of psychic pain. (For instance, referring to the first case example, a rather common belief among some psychically inclined individuals who believe in past life phenomena is that abuse in any lifetime—including the current one—is a payback for the individual's badness or bad behavior in another.) Third, the therapist provides corrective or alternative information about improbable forms of abuse and urges examination of clues and evidence over time. S/he teaches hypothesis-testing over time while working to refocus the patient on current life issues, especially personal safety, parenting, symptom management, and improved functioning.

Cases such as these might lead to a knee-jerk reaction on the therapist's part. The predominant reaction in the current atmosphere is disbelief/disparagement/rejection. The therapist is likely to be on the defensive with such a presentation and, in parallel process, likely to put the patient on the defensive. On the other hand, some therapists are overinvested in the forms of abuse represented in these case examples. Both perspectives may lead to inadequate evaluation of the patient's current condition and of the past. The therapist's job is to maintain a calm, evaluative stance over time and to start with attention to the risk for suicide and stabilizing the patient's status.

Scenario 10: Memory Discussed or Recovered in Previous or Current Therapy Recanted as False

In this scenario, the individual doubts and recants memories that were discussed or recovered in past or current therapy. Such a recantation may result from additional consideration of new information that calls into question or discredits past beliefs or memories and/or the conclusion that elements of past or current treatment were suggestive or had an abuse-related agenda. Recantation may also be the result of an unwillingness or inability to tolerate the pain, losses, family pressures, and disruptions that attend memories of abuse (whether they are continuous or recovered). Just as true and false recovered memories are possible, recantations of true and false memories are also possible.

> CASE EXAMPLE.   *On the basis of a number of symptoms and relationship patterns that have been found to be associated with a history of abuse, Ms. L., over the course of several years of psychotherapy, had come to believe that she had been sexually abused as a child. She felt that too many of her issues and symptoms pointed in the direction of past abuse for it to not have happened, even though she had no specific or even vague memories of abuse. Her therapist neither suggested nor refuted her beliefs but encouraged her to try to piece together a possible scenario and to make inquiries of family members and neighbors who might be able to provide her with information. No substantiation was forthcoming and Ms. L. gradually recanted her previous belief as erroneous. She was also quite upset at having spent so much therapy time focused on the possibility of and belief in past abuse.*

> ALTERNATIVE CASE EXAMPLE.   *Same initial situation, but Ms. M. had, through extensive regressive and abreactive hypnotherapy developed memories of having been raised and abused in a multigenerational satanic cult. She was diagnosed as having poly-fragmented DID. Her therapist was very alarmed by the material that came out during these hypnotic sessions and believed that Ms. M. had been programmed to turn her own children over to the cult. She urged Ms. M. to cut off all contact with her "satanist family" and to go into hiding with her children in order to escape them. Following several years on the run, Ms. M. began to question the reality of her memories. She and her parents reconciled and they later sued the therapist for implanting false memories and for the infliction of harm.*

COMMENTARY ON ASSESSMENT, APPROACH, STRATEGIES, AND COUNTER-TRANSFERENCE.   Preliminary research on recanters suggests that they may be unusually needy and susceptible to social pressure and likely to be especially responsive to both suggestive forms of psychotherapy and the therapist's approval in reaction to memory production (Lief & Fetkewicz, 1995). Thus, they might very well develop false beliefs or false memories within a psychotherapy that is suggestive and/or one that fosters dependence. However, just as "true" and "false" memories are possible and cannot be determined definitively without evidence, "true" and "false" recantations are possible and might be equally difficult to determine. The therapist whose patient recants memory from a past or current therapy must not automatically believe the racantation, but must explore it and the motivations for it, along with a broader-based asssessment of the individual's history. And, as noted by Dalenberg and Carlson (in press): "The therapist who 'specializes' in recovered memory or in recanter therapy owes a special duty of care to the . . . client, who is likely to know of the therapist's biases and fear the possibility of being a disappointment." In such a case, it is especially important for the patient to be made aware that the therapist is not expecting one scenario over another, and furthermore, that the therapist can tolerate uncertainty and exploration. In any event, it is still recommended that the therapist attempt to contact the previous therapist for records and for a determination of techniques that were employed.

Recantation of material brought to the fore during the current therapy presents special challenges, especially if the therapist has become overinvested in the abuse hypothesis or has reason to believe that the patient is reverting to a position of denial about the likelihood of abuse, possibly due to internal and outside pressures (i.e., feelings of guilt, a strong need for forgiveness and reconciliation, the illness or death of the alleged perpetrator or other family member). These can and should be discussed candidly and without pressure on the patient. At times, therapist and patient might be at odds in their assessment of what they believe really happened and an "agreement to disagree" might need to be explicitly acknowledged. In any event, the therapist must continue in the position that it is the patient's right to make the determination and to have authority over his/her beliefs and memories, even if they are contrary to what the therapist believes. Situations of this sort elicit major countertransference responses, again indicating outside consultation and support.

SUMMARY

This chapter reviews predominant transference, countertransference, and vicarious traumatization issues in the treatment of abused or possibly abused patients. Depending on whether they are identified and how they are managed, they have the potential to support or confound the treatment process, especially where recovered memory is at issue. Treatment strategies for recovered memories are also reviewed in this chapter. Different strategies are suggested by the patient's degree of memory, disclosure, and symptomatology. Transference issues and therapeutic strategies were illustrated and discussed in ten different clinical scenarios, each involving a different memory/disclosure presentation.

AFTERWORD

The recovered memory controversy has changed the landscape of psychotherapy quite dramatically. Although the full impact of the controversy has yet to be determined, it has already been profound. It has irrevocably altered (in both positive and negative directions) the general practice of psychotherapy and the specialty area of incest/sexual abuse treatment. In many ways, the issues raised regarding the veracity and accuracy of adults' memories of past sexual abuse (especially when recovered after a period of inaccessibility) and questions about suggestive therapeutic practice recapitulate those raised at the turn of the last century. Now, as then, societal denial of abuse and its victims gave way to validation and then moved back to a position of skepticism. Today's version differs significantly, however, in that it has influenced and been influenced by the mass media and newly emerging information technology; furthermore, it has entered the courtroom. False memory critics have been enormously successful in influencing public opinion and in instituting forensic and policy changes. The debate is far from over, and data on both sides of the issue are far from complete. New findings are emerging almost daily, and researchers and practitioners are challenged to interpret and apply them in a timely and responsible fashion.

The early years of the recovered memory controversy were marked by extreme positions and high emotion. Recently, a more rational middle ground has developed, but some of the professionals who espouse extreme perspectives refuse to occupy it. It is clearly unacceptable to false memory critics and abuse/trauma advocates who support a

341

"scorched earth" policy regarding whether recovered memories are always false or always veridical. In contrast, the perspective taken in this book (and in recent work by clinicians and researchers, as well as in the recommendations of task forces of various professional organizations impaneled to study these issues) is that a balanced perspective is needed that allows for the continued development of the study and treatment of traumatized individuals. In particular, how trauma affects memory processes needs much additional investigation. A centrist position provides fertile ground for collaborative efforts and new discoveries about memory and consciousness as they are affected by traumatization. It also affords room to study the mechanisms by which recovered memory and false memory might develop.

The debate and the issues involved are not trivial, whether in terms of the individual, the family, or the larger society. Whatever the true or absolute statistics concerning the incidence and prevalence of sexual abuse (and this issue comes under considerable debate as well, with some commentators arguing that current prevalence statistics are much too high and abuse definitions much too inclusive, and others arguing that they are much too low and don't capture individuals who continue to not know or not disclose their abuse experiences), all forms of child abuse and family violence are prevalent enough to pose a serious societal problem that must not be ignored or minimized in this debate. At the present time, despite calls for research data and substantiation (Pope, 1996; Pope & Vaughn, 1998), the prevalence of false memory and false accusations of sexual abuse derived from suggestive practice (or "memory work") in psychotherapy remains largely unquantified (although Lindsay and Read [1994, 1995] have provided estimates based upon therapist surveys suggesting that "memory work" of the sort likely to lead to false memory production is not an insignificant problem and is practiced by a "nontrivial minority" of psychotherapists). Nevertheless, there are those who charge that false memory of sexual abuse is at epidemic levels and who attribute its prevalence solely to suggestive psychotherapy practices. In contrast, others argue that false memory is not a problem of the magnitude implied by the critics and that data have not been forthcoming to support that false memories (as opposed to false beliefs) result from psychotherapy (Alpert et al., 1996c; Courtois, 1997a). Others have called for data to support the claims of the critics and for an end to some of the most unprofessional and offensive tactics (Pope, 1996). The position that the scope of the problem of false memory is exaggerated is bolstered by sociological and statistical analyses that suggest that the rate of false negatives for child sexual abuse history poses a larger epidemiological and social problem than the rate of false positives (Finkelhor, 1994; Fish, 1998).

These dissimilar viewpoints regarding false negatives and false positives lead us back to the 2 X 2 table of abuse versus memory introduced in chapter 2 and reproduced here. As discussed in the final conclusions of the American Psychological Association Working Group on the Investigation of Memories of Childhood Abuse (1996b), an important starting point in trying to achieve some consensus and collaboration is to acknowledge the fundamental differences between clinicians and cognitive scientists (or traumatologists and memory critics) in terms of the basic definitions of the issues under investigation and the profound epistemological differences between the two groups. As Nash (1994), Williams and Banyard (1997) and many others have recognized, cognitive scientists and clinicians are likely to be more focused on one quadrant over another by virtue of their divergent areas of professional interest and application. Thus, the memory researchers are more likely to be concerned with quadrant III (false positives) and the clinicians, with quadrants II and IV (false negatives and true positives). The clinicians, however, are the ones who have to face the real life dilemmas of working with patients when their memories are less than pristine. They must grapple with the difficult issues presented when the patients fall somewhere "in

Figure 2.1

2 x 2 Table of Abuse Versus Memory Status

Abuse Status

		Not abused	Abused
Memory Status	No Recall	True Negatives I	False Negatives II
	Recall	False Positives III	True Positives IV

From "Perspectives on Adult Memories of Childhood Sexual Abuse: A Research Review," by L.A. Williams and V.L. Banyard, 1997. In D. Spiegel, Section Editor, *Repressed Memories, Section II of Review of Psychiatry, 16* (p. II–132), 1997, Washington DC: American Psychiatric Press. Copyright 1997 by American Psychiatric Press, Inc. Reprinted with permission.

the gray zone," that is, somewhere between the false positive and false negative quadrants.

Before moving to a more detailed discussion of the clinical dilemmas involved in working with recovered memory, let us first address how to bridge some of the differences between the clinicians and memory researchers. Many of the professional task forces organized to study these issues have commented on these significant between-group differences. The American Psychological Association Working Group report (1996b) offered perhaps the most detailed commentary and proposed the following as ways to bridge the gap:

> . . . one important implication of our deliberations is that psychologists who work in the field of trauma and those who study memory would benefit from working collaboratively to (a) develop paradigms for research; (b) search for consensual definitions of constructs that speak to the issues of how trauma affects memory; and (c) develop models that will be scientifically sound while being well-grounded in the realities of clinical practice. (p. 3)

They further wrote:

> The epistemological foundation from which one evaluates clinical out-comes or research findings affects the meaning given to those out-comes/findings. Because the entire Working Group converges on the belief that a science-informed practice will be the most effective strat-egy for treatment, we believe that practice-informed research will enhance the integration of knowledge about memory into the overall field of trauma treatment. This direction in research may also help us to answer the still unclear questions about the nature of various observed human behaviors in response to trauma. (p. 4).

This perspective has obvious significance for professional training. One of the major issues leading to the current state of affairs is that clin-icians across all mental health disciplines have had too little training regarding either trauma or human memory processes and cognitive sci-entists have had too little exposure to trauma and applied practice issues. Cross-referencing these separate areas of research and practice is there-fore of critical importance "in avoiding harm to all those who are affect-ed by the consequences of both accurate and false recollections of abuse" (American Psychological Association, 1996b, p. 12). Training issues are returned to below.

DILEMMAS OF CLINICAL PRACTICE

The controversy and its "political surround" (Seligman, 1997) have made this a daunting and disconcerting time to be a psychotherapist. The excitement generated by the discoveries and advances of the 70s and 80s has been tempered by the critiques and challenges of the 90s (Armstrong, 1978, 1994; Brown, 1996). The pendulum has swung. Yet, one difficulty for today's practicing therapist is that the treatment population of previously abused individuals has not disappeared. If anything, due to the "Age of Validation," it is larger and more visible than ever before. As I have frequently noted, abused children don't just disappear—they grow up. And many of them grow up compromised, carrying and living the legacy of their abuse. As reviewed in chapter 4, research is conclusive in identifying serious and life-interfering effects of sexual abuse across the lifespan in a significant number of victims. Many suffer from symptoms meeting criteria for a host of psychiatric diagnoses (including posttraumatic and dissociative disorders) and a sizable number have additional medical conditions. Many are in need of psychotherapy. As discussed in the introduction to chapter 7, even the generalist therapist is likely to see survivors of all forms of child abuse, because these individuals make up a substantial percentage of the inpatient and outpatient mental health population.

The challenge for psychotherapists is how to practice responsibly and ethically, especially when recovered memories are involved and uncertainty reigns. In a recent article describing clinical dilemmas posed by the controversy, Jonathan Slavin asked the rhetorical question, "Who shall the therapist believe?" (Slavin, 1997). This question comes to life in the consulting room every time a therapist treats a patient who suspects or claims abuse but lacks continuous or conclusive memories or corroboration (but may have signs and symptoms indicative of possible abuse), and every time the therapist treats someone who claims to have been falsely accused but lacks corroboration. It also comes to life when a therapist tries to help a patient determine his/her own reality, especially in the face of ongoing internal and external pressures to deny and not remember. Social and clinical researchers who have extensively studied trauma and its effects, such as Caruth (1995), Krystal (1995), and Laub and Auerhahn (1993), describe how the very nature of trauma makes its recognition and remembrance psychologically intolerable and leads to conscious and unconscious efforts to keep it at bay. Tendencies to deny and suppress trauma are reinforced by the "social and political surround." The social context is particularly influential in determining what is acceptable to know on an individual basis and what can be revealed to others.

Brenneis (1994) described the dilemma that accompanies two compet-
ing therapeutic paradigms concerning recovered memory. The first is
that of the therapist's *suggestion:* "belief in the existence and ultimate
accessibility of repressed memories of early trauma [that] creates the
potential for the suggestions of memories" and the second, *belief:* "that
precisely the same beliefs are a necessary condition for their emergence"
(p. 1028). Expanding on this, he wrote:

> Clinically, the analyst [therapist] confronts a serious dilemma. Leaning
> in the direction of doubt, from the belief paradigm, threatens betrayal;
> leaning in the direction of belief, from the suggestion paradigm, pro-
> motes fabrication. On the other hand, if one does not believe, no mem-
> ory can be tolerated; and if one does believe, whatever memory appears
> is suspect.
>   . . . Vivid, affectively charged, and apparently genuine presentations
> of repressed memory do not guarantee authenticity. Similarly, even
> directly expressed belief and blatantly suggestive questioning do not
> conclusively invalidate authenticity. We cannot, as yet, discriminate
> false from genuine recovered memory either on the basis of process or
> presentation. (p. 1049)

Brenneis concluded his commentary as follows:

> When the possibility of an early trauma experience comes into view,
> this balancing becomes more difficult and carries greater implications
> for real people in the real world. At some points, we may find ourselves
> forced to choose between bearing false witness or failing to bear true
> witness without knowing with any certainty which we are doing.
> Neither of these alternatives is without potent clinical consequences.
> Until this area is more clearly understood, our moral propensities may
> decide which way we lean clinically, and our personal qualities may help
> us to believe skeptically and doubt empathically. (p. 1050)

Yet another clinical dilemma has to do with memories themselves,
especially those that are submerged and inaccessible to the individual
and that might make their presence known through symptoms and
behaviors, including transference, as discussed in chapter 9. Is it better or
necessary for the patient who is amnestic to remember? Or, is it better for
memories to remain unavailable? Is it advisable to help the patient
remember and is it possible to assist the patient to resolve and integrate
the traumatic memory in a way that does not retraumatize? As discussed
in chapter 6, the answer might be a judgment call on the part of the ther-

apist in consultation with the patient. If the patient is free of major symptoms and/or otherwise does not have the personal motivation or resources
to address traumatic memories, they can be left unaddressed (to be
returned to later, if the need arises to do so). If, on the other hand, the
patient is highly symptomatic and wants to know and resolve the trauma,
then the memories are explored in the interest of integrating them into
the individual's life narrative. Some laboratory and clinical research is
available that substantiates the benefits of working with and processing
available memories of trauma and, in selective cases, supports the utility
of retrieving and enhancing previously inaccessible memories (Brown et
al., 1998). Much more research is needed to address this topic.

IMPLICATIONS FOR CLINICAL
PRACTICE AND TRAINING

When recovered memories are at issue, the therapist must tread cautiously. The failure to recognize abuse can be as harmful as overzealousness in attempting to find it. How the therapist works with these issues
has come to be seen as critical. At the present time, it is unclear how
many therapists are practicing on the basis of erroneous beliefs about
memory and trauma and how many are practicing in ways that are problematic and suggestive. Available survey data (Andrews, 1997; Palm &
Gibson, 1998; Polusny & Follette, 1996; Poole, Lindsay, Memon, & Bull,
1995; Pope & Feldman-Summers, 1992; Yapko, 1994a, 1994b) indicate
that therapists do use some of the techniques that have been identified
as the most suggestive, but these surveys are not sophisticated enough to
make clear how they are used, how often and in what circumstance. At
present it is also unclear and unproven whether it is possible for therapists to implant memories in their patients and to further cause them to
develop full-blown posttraumatic conditions. Clearly, additional study is
needed regarding what constitutes suggestive practice, how it works, and
ways to limit undue influence in psychotherapy.

These surveys have identified another very salient issue: Most therapists reported receiving little, if any, education about human traumatization, interpersonal victimization, family violence and child abuse in their
professional curricula; nor were they exposed to information on human
memory processes. They also did not receive any training in the treatment of abuse and trauma, much less training in working with recovered
memory issues. As discussed previously, this is especially problematic
given the high likelihood that the majority of therapists will see abuse
and trauma survivors in their practices. It is further problematic because

of the inherent ethical difficulties and clinical dilemmas that attend treating traumatized individuals, in general and in the current atmosphere (Chu, 1998; Dalenberg, in press; Wilson & Lindy, 1994). This is especially the case when memories are not continuous and/or when recovered memories emerge somewhere along the line. The naive or inexperienced therapist or the practitioner unduly compromised by unrecognized and unaddressed countertransference reactions is at considerable risk, as are his/her patients (Chu, 1988; Pearlman & Saakvitne, 1995).

It is very important to recognize that some of the current problems stem directly from the lack of inclusion of these issues in professional training, a major lacuna that has followed the societal lead on denial of abuse and other forms of traumatization. A number of clinical researchers have commented on the irony that chronically traumatized individuals suffering from complex dissociative PTSD require the most skilled and knowledgeable therapists yet therapists receive inadequate formal training to provide the treatment and must rely instead on continuing education offerings, professional reading, and personal consultation (Briere, 1996b; Chu, 1998; Courtois, 1988). It is in the interest of all concerned for the mental health professions to change this situation posthaste and to incorporate a balanced presentation of these issues (including their clinical complexity) into the training curriculum. This recommendation has been made by many, if not all, of the professional task forces that have addressed recovered memory issues. Some initial efforts have been reported (Campbell & Carlson, 1995; Cohen & Mannarino, 1998; Leifer et al., 1995; Payne, 1995; Weiss & Marmar, 1993), but many more are needed. As demonstrated in this text, much professional material is available on all of these issues that can easily be incorporated into professional training.

SUMMARY

This aim of this book has been to provide practicing clinicians with essential information for treating patients where memories of sexual abuse or other trauma are at issue. It reviewed the sociohistorical context of the recovered memory controversy in order to put contemporary practice issues into perspective. It also reviewed available information on sexual abuse and traumatization and their relation to memory processes, including variable accessibility to memories over time. Clinical principles and guidelines for working with patients when memories of abuse/trauma are at issue were discussed in considerable detail. The contemporary phase-oriented post trauma treatment model was introduced, with particular attention to recommended and contraindicated approaches by degree of memory accessibility and symptoms. It is hoped that the material provided in this book will assist and support the clinician in working with trauma and memory issues, in the interest of allowing this important area of practice to continue to develop. The needs of traumatized individuals and the societal impact of trauma are too critical for them to be dismissed or for treatment efforts to be discontinued.

APPENDICES

PROFESSIONAL TASK FORCE REPORTS

American Medical Association
575 North State St.
Chicago, IL 60610
(312) 464-5000
CSA Report 5-A-94: *Memories of Childhood Abuse*

American Psychiatric Association
1400 K St., N.W.
Washington, DC 20005
(202) 682-6000
Statement on Memories of Sexual Abuse

American Psychological Association
750 First St., N.E.
Washington, DC 20002-4242
(202) 336-5000
c/o Public Interest Directorate
Working Group on the Investigation of Memories of Childhood Abuse Final Report

American Society of Clinical Hypnosis
c/o American Society of Clinical Hypnosis Press
2200 E. Devon Avenue
DesPlaines, IL 60018
(708) 297-3317
Clinical Hypnosis and Memory: Guidelines for Clinicians and for Forensic Hypnosis

Australian Psychological Society
natl-off@aps-nho.mhs.compuserve.com
or
lisselle@aps-nho.mhs.compuserve.com
Guidelines Relating to the Reporting of Recovered Memories

British Association for Counseling
1 Regent Place
Rugby, Warwickshire CV21 2PJ
01788 550899
bac@bac.co.uk
False Memory Syndrome: A Statement

British Psychological Society
http://www.bps.org.uk/
Report of the Working Party of the British Psychological Society

Canadian Psychiatric Association
http://cpa.medical.org/cpa/
public2/papers/position papers/
memory.htm
Adult Recovered Memories of Childhood Sexual Abuse

New Zealand Psychological Society
http://www.massey.ac.nz/
Memory of Traumatic Childhood Events

The International Society for
Traumatic Stress Studies
60 Revere Drive, Suite 500
Northbrook, IL 60062
(847) 480-9028
istss@istss.org
Childhood Trauma Remembered: A
Report Based on the Current Scientific
Knowledge Base and Its Applications

National Association of Social
Workers
750 First St., N.E.
Washington, DC 20002-4241
(202) 408-8600
Office of Policy and Practice
Evaluation and Treatment of Adults
with the Possibility of Recovered
Memories of Childhood Sexual Abuse

Royal College of Psychiatrists
17 Belgrave Square
London, England
Reported Recovered Memories of
Child Sexual Abuse:
Recommendations for Good Practice
and Implications for Training.
Continuing Professional Development
and Research

The Royal Australian and New
Zealand College of Psychiatrists
309 La Trobe St.
Melbourne, VIC 3000
Australia
Clinical Memorandum #17:
Guidelines for Psychiatrists Dealing
with Repressed Traumatic Memories

Appendix B

SUMMARIES OF SELECTED REPORTS OF PROFESSIONAL TASK FORCES ON DELAYED/ RECOVERED MEMORIES*

THE AUSTRALIAN PSYCHOLOGICAL SOCIETY

The Australian Psychological Society's Guidelines Relating to Recovered Memories were published in 1994 (Australian Psychological Society, 1994). The guidelines on scientific issues and clinical practice are reproduced here.

Scientific Issues

Memory is a constructive and a reconstructive process. What is remembered about an event is shaped by what is observed of that event, by conditions prevailing during attempts to remember, and by events occurring between the observation and the attempted remembering. Memories can be altered, deleted and created by events that occur during and after the time of encoding, and during the period of storage, and during any attempts at retrieval.

Memory is integral to many approaches to therapy. Repression and dissociation are processes central to some theories and approaches to therapy. According to these theories and approaches, memories of traumatic events may be blocked out unconsciously and lead to a person having no memory of the events. However, memories of these traumatic events may become accessible at some later time. Although some clinical observations support the notion of repressed memories, empirical research on memory generally does not. Moreover, existing scientific evidence does not allow global statements to be made about a definite relationship between trauma and memory. "Memories" that are reported either spontaneously or following the use of special procedures in therapy may be accurate, inaccurate, fabricated, or a mixture of these. The presence or absence of detail in a memory report does not necessarily mean that it is accurate or inaccurate. The level of

---

*Summaries of other reports appear in Chapter 2.

belief in memory or the emotion associated with memory does not necessarily relate directly to the accuracy of the memory. The available scientific and clinical evidence does not allow accurate, inaccurate and fabricated memories to be distinguished in the absence of independent corroboration.

It is established by scientific evidence that sexual and/or physical abuse against children and adults is typically destructive of mental health, self esteem, and personal relationships. It is also the case that people who suffer these experiences may use various psychological mechanisms to reduce the psychological severity of the painful events in an attempt to help them cope with the experience and its consequences.

Just as psychologists should be familiar with this evidence, so should they recognize that reports of abuse long after the events are reported to have occurred are difficult to prove or disprove in the majority of cases. Independent corroboration of the statements of those who make or deny such allegations is typically difficult if not impossible. Accordingly, psychologists should exercise special care in dealing with clients, their family members, and the wider community when allegations of past abuse are made (pp. 2–3).

Clinical Issues

Psychologists should evaluate critically their assumptions or biases about attempts to recover memories of trauma-related events. Equally, psychologists should assist their clients to understand any assumptions that they have about repressed memories. Assumptions that adult problems may or may not be associated with repressed memories from childhood cannot be addressed by existing scientific evidence.

Psychologists should be alert to the ways in which they may unintentionally overlook or minimize reports of experiences of abuse or events that may have had a significant impact on a client. They should also be alert to the ways that they can shape the reported memories of clients through the expectations they convey, the comments they make, the questions they ask, and the responses they give. Psychologists should be alert that clients are susceptible to subtle suggestions and reinforcements, whether those communications are intended or unintended. Therefore, psychologists should record intact memories at the beginning of therapy, and be aware of any possible effects from outside the therapeutic setting (e.g., self-help groups, popular books, films, television programs).

Psychologists should be alert not to dismiss memories that may be based in fact. Equally they should be alert to the role that they may play in creating or shaping false memories. At all times, psychologists should be empathic and supportive of the reports of clients while also ensuring that clients do not jump to conclusions about the truth or falsity of their recollections of the past. They should also ensure that alternative causes of any problems that are reported are explored. Psychologists should recognize that the context of therapy is important as is the content.

Psychologists should not avoid asking clients about the possibility of sexual or other abusive occurrences in their past, if such a question is relevant to the problem being treated. However, psychologists should be cautious in interpreting the response that is given. Psychologists should not assume the accuracy or inaccuracy of any report of a recovered memory.

Psychologists should recognize that the needs and well-being of clients are their essential focus and they should design their therapeutic interventions accordingly. Relatedy [*sic*], psychologists should recognize that therapeutic interventions may have an indirect impact on people other than the client they are treating. They should seek to meet the needs of clients who report memories of abuse, and should do this quite apart from the truth or falsity of those reports. Psychologists should be cautious about conveying statements about the accuracy of memory reports given by clients. In particular, psychologists should understand clearly the difference between narrative truth and historical truth, and the relevance of this difference inside the therapy context and outside that context. Memory reports as part of a personal narrative can be helpf....l [*sic*] in therapy independent of the accuracy of those reports. But, to be accepted as accurate in another setting (e.g., court of law), those reports will need to be shown to be accurate. (p.3)

THE ROYAL AUSTRALIAN AND NEW ZEALAND COLLEGE OF PSYCHIATRISTS

Clinical Memorandum #17: "Guidelines for Psychiatrists Dealing with Repressed Traumatic Memories" was issued by the Royal College in 1996 (The Royal Australian and New Zealand College of Psychiatrists, 1996). It included the following commentary:

1. Although the role of traumatic sexual experiences during childhood in influencing adult psychopathology has been a part of clinical psychiatry for some 100 years, there has recently been an upsurge of popular interest in what is being termed in the lay press "Recovered Memory Syndrome". The clinical and ethical issues involved in the present circumstances pose a real issue for psychiatrists and for the college.

2. There is general agreement about the following matters:
    (a) Clinical experience, supported by relevant research, has shown that both physical and sexual abuse in early and later childhood occur with disconcerting frequency.
    (b) Children who are subject to such developmentally inappropriate experiences are, in most (if not all) cases, adversely affected by such experience in respect of their mental development and evidence varying degrees of psychological damage which can be attributed to their experience of the abuse.
    (c) Memory of such abusive experiences may be absent for considerable and varied periods of life and may be recalled under any variety of circumstances, including as a vicissitude of undergoing psychiatric treatment for (at least initially) apparently unrelated reasons.

3. In these circumstances psychiatrists should be mindful of the following:
    (a) Modern day understanding of the nature of memory itself is that it is highly susceptible to influence and revision from the time of encoding up to and including the time and relationship context of the memory being retrieved.
    (b) It is an appropriate role for the psychiatrist to facilitate and maximize the therapeutic potential of any memory recovery process on behalf of the patient.
    (c) Psychiatrists must respect the right of patients to secure their own memory—free, as far as possible, from contamination by external influences.

(d) It is important that psychiatrists maintain a position of clinical neutrality in the consulting room—no matter what personal views they may have formed. This is no different from the stance which psychiatrists must take on many other matters raised by patients.

(e) It is not generally the clinical role of the psychiatrist to advocate for the victim—but, where necessary and possible, to support a process whereby the patient comes to feel able to deal with the experience of having recovered hitherto forgotten aspect of their history, in a way which they themselves deem appropriate.

4. The scientific literature carries a growing number of studies in this field and, in turn, a growing number of reviews in this literature. In addition, there is an explosion of books being published taking polemic positions in the controversy—there are instances of extremist positions on each side.

5. Regrettably, the legal consequences of this have been a disturbing increase in the number of court cases (especially in America), where the concept of "repressed memory" and the counterclaim of "false memory" have been tested more in the style associated with television courtroom drama, than in a spirit of seeking the truth—difficult as that may be.

6. As a further consequence, the airing of these vexed issues in the popular press can only serve to entrench the fixed views held by the various proponents.

7. In a climate of such complexity, where psychologically positive outcomes are largely made impossible by the adversarial nature of the legal arena and the sensationalist nature of the popular press, it is important that psychiatrists maintain at least the hope of a clinical haven for those who need the opportunity to explore their own relevant issues in a neutral, supportive environment.

8. The only thing that we can know for certain in this complex field is that it is almost impossible to know for certain what transpired privately between two individuals—especially if one of them is a child.

THE ROYAL COLLEGE OF PSYCHIATRISTS

In 1994, the Royal College of Psychiatrists in Great Britain convened The Working Group on Reported Recovered Memories of Child Abuse to examine: (a) current views on the psychology of memory; (b) current beliefs and practices on the recovery in adult life of previously forgotten memories of childhood sexual abuse; (c) the effectiveness of memory enhancement techniques; (d) the validity of memories of long-forgotten childhood sexual abuse; (e) the consequences of memory recovery; and (f) the distinction between true and illusory memory. The working party submitted its report in the summer of 1996. Following months of internal arguments over details of the report (Hall, 1997), the College decided not to publish the report under its imprimatur and instead agreed to the publication of consensus recommendations for good practice (Royal College of Psychiatrists' Working Group on Reported Recovered Memories of Child Sexual Abuse, 1997). A paper entitled "Recovered memories of childhood sexual abuse: Implications for clinical practice," a revised version of the report originally submitted to the Royal College was recently published in the British Journal of Psychiatry, *not as a College document (and hence not endorsed by all members of the Working Group) but as a paper by individual authors (Brandon, Boakes, Glaser, & Green, 1998). It includes a summary of the evidence on recovered memories of childhood sexual abuse in addition to the previously released recommendations. The interested reader is referred to that publication to compare and contrast the two.*

The recommendations made by the Working Party in the formal report include:

(a) The welfare of the patient is the first concern of the psychiatrist. Concern for the needs of family members and others may also be necessary, within the constraints imposed by the need for confidentiality.

(b) In children and adolescents, symptoms and behaviour patterns may alert the clinician to the possibility of current sexual abuse, but these are no more than indicators for suspicion. Previous sexual abuse in the absence of memories of these events cannot be diagnosed through a check-list of symptoms.

(c) Psychiatrists are advised to avoid engaging in any "memory recovery techniques" which are intended to reveal evidence of past sexual abuse of which the patient has no memory and should regard with extreme caution memories of this kind whenever they appear. There is no evidence that the use of consciousness-altering techniques, such as drug-mediated interviews or hypnosis, can reveal or elaborate evidence of childhood sexual abuse. Techniques of "regression therapy" (age regression, guided imagery, "body memories," journaling, or literal dream interpretation, where this is used as evidence of fact) are of dubious provenance.

(d) Forceful or persuasive interviewing techniques are not acceptable in psychiatric practice. Doctors should be aware that patients are susceptible to subtle suggestions and reinforcements, whether or not these communications are intended.

(e) The psychiatrist should alert the patient to any doubts about the historical accuracy of recovered memories of previously unknown sexual abuse. This is particularly important if the patient intends to take action outside the therapeutic situation. Memories, however emotionally intense and significant to the individual, may not necessarily represent historical truth. Memories may be historically true, metaphorical representations, caused by the psychological state of the patient or be the result of unintentional suggestion by the practitioner.

(f) It may be legitimate not to question the validity of a recovered memory while it remains within the privacy of the consulting room, although this introduces the risk of colluding in the creation of a life history based upon a false belief.

(g) Action taken outside the consulting room, including the revelation of accusations to any third party, must depend on circumstances and the wishes of the patient, but the full implications of such actions must always be considered. Adults who report previously forgotten childhood abuse may wish to confront the alleged abuser. Such action should not be mandated by the psychiatrist and it is rarely, if ever, justifiable to discourage or forbid the patient from having contact with the alleged abuser or other family members. The psychiatrist should help the patient think through the consequences of any confrontation. In these circumstances it is important to encourage a search for corroborative evidence before any action is taken. The truth or falsity of the underlying memories cannot be known in the absence of such evidence.

(h) Once an accusation is taken outside the consulting room, especially where any question of confrontation or public accusation arises, there is rarely any justification for refusal to allow a member of the therapeutic team to meet family members.

(i) Where an alleged abuser is still in touch with children, serious consideration must be given to informing the appropriate social services. This must be done where there are reasonable grounds for believing the alleged assault took place and that children may still be at risk. The psychiatrist must also be prepared to state clearly whether he or she believes that the grounds for any accusation are unlikely or impossible.

(j) The patient may wish to take legal advice with a view to the prosecution of, or litigation against, the alleged abuser. It is inappropriate to make any decision about this as a condition of continuing treatment.

(k) Alongside reports of recovered memories of sexual abuse there have been growing numbers of cases of multiple personality disorder (also known as dissociative identity disorder). There seems to be little doubt that many of these cases are iatrogenically determined. Any spontaneous presentation of multiple personality disorder should be sympathetically considered but should not be made subject of undue attention nor should the patient be encouraged to develop "alter personalities" in whom to invest aspects of their personality, their fantasies or their current life problems. Psychiatrists should be particularly aware of the unreliability of the memories reported in these cases and of the close association both with prolonged therapy and with recovered memories of sexual abuse, particularly alleged satanic abuse. Since there is not settled view of the validity of multiple personality disorder, and because of the very strong correlation with recovered memories of sexual abuse which is itself a disputed concept, there is a strong case for a consensus paper on multiple personality disorder based upon a substantial review of the literature.

THE BRITISH ASSOCIATION FOR COUNSELLING

In late 1997, The British Association for Counselling (BAC) issued its report on false memory syndrome authored by Alec McGuire, chair of the Research & Evaluation Committee (British Association of Counseling, 1997).

The principal conclusions of the report are:

- The incidence of episodes of remembering events of childhood sexual abuse is not at presently known.
- Many cases of remembering childhood sexual abuse are straightforward.
- Amnesia for periods of childhood sexual abuse is possible.
- The recovery of memories of abuse for which the person has been previously amnesic is possible.
- False memories must be accepted as occurring in at least some cases.
- The incidence of false memory is at present unknown but appears to be low.
- A low incidence of false memory is consistent with a substantial actual number of cases.

The following implications for practice were also included in the BAC Report:

- It is good practice for counsellors to familiarise themselves with the issues relating to the nature of memory generally.
- Practitioners should not use methods which are deliberately intended to induce memories of abuse. Such methods run considerable risks of eliciting false rather than actual memories.
- It is not good practice to diagnose that sexual abuse occurred to a client on the basis or reported symptoms unaccompanied by clear pre-existing memories. In general, counsellors should be careful not to say anything to a client which suggests that abuse may have occurred.
- The impetus for discussions of abuse as a possibility should come from the client.
- When clients retrieve memories of abuse spontaneously during the counselling process, counsellors should proceed with caution. Nothing should be done which might encourage the client to elaborate beyond what has actually been recalled. Counsellors should be aware that the details of memories are not always reliable.

- Having said that, counsellors should also bear in mind that the majority of memories of abuse are clear and reliable and they should not be afraid to work with the many issues that childhood sexual abuse arouses for the client.
- In these matters, it is paramount for the counsellor to discuss the issues with his/her supervisor.

THE NEW ZEALAND PSYCHOLOGICAL SOCIETY

The New Zealand Psychological Society established a working party in 1995 to report on research and practice issues concerning memory for traumatic childhood events. The terms of reference for the Report were: (1) to report on conclusions that can be drawn from current research and clinical practice knowledge concerning memory for childhood traumatic events; (2) to describe relevant areas where facts are as yet uncertain and further research is required; (3) to present guidelines for clinical practice where memory for childhood traumatic events is an issue; and (4) to make recommendation to the New Zealand Psychological Society regarding education of the profession and the public on issues of memory for childhood traumatic events and to investigate the possibility of a joint statement from allied mental health professional bodies. The following conclusions concerning memory and clinical practice were made. The reader is referred to the full report for additional discussion (New Zealand Psychological Society, 1997).

Conclusions from Research and Clinical Practice Knowledge Regarding Memory for Trauma

Evidence on memory for traumatic events has been based on naturally occurring traumas, and therefore lacks the degree of experimental control found in laboratory based research. Nevertheless, this evidence suggests that traumatic experiences may be remembered in detail, partially forgotten, or even completely forgotten over very long delays. There appears to be no simple relation between the degrees of negative emotion associated with an event. It cannot be assumed that traumatic experiences will always be better remembered than other experiences or, alternatively, that they will necessarily be remembered less well than other experiences. There are a number of factors that may determine whether and how well particular traumatic experiences are remembered over very long time periods, including the age at which the experience occurred (e.g., during or after the period of infantile amnesia), whether the traumatic experience was discussed or thought about, whether there were attempts to suppress thinking about the experience, whether the experience occurred only once or repeatedly, the emotional impact of the experience, the way in which the information was encoded at the time of the experience, and exposure to appropriate retrieval cues. Not all experiences, whether traumatic or not, result in coherent, well-organized narrative descriptions. A number of factors may influence how detailed, elaborate, organized, and coherent the accounts of early memories are, which in turn may influence how accessible the memories are for later recall.

Memories that have been for all intents and purposes forgotten, in that they have not been brought to conscious awareness for long periods of time, often may be retrieved given the appropriate conditions for recall. The phenomenon of memory recovery, in this sense, is well established. There is no reason to believe that traumatic experiences that have been forgotten might not later be retrieved given the appropriate retrieval cues.

Memories might also be modified, for example by intervening similar experiences, or by discussion following the event that results in memory "blends" or confusion between sources of information or between particular experiences. There is some evidence that memories are more vulnerable to modification following very long delays, and that extreme modifications will be more likely when the experiences occurred a long time ago.

Many procedures that are supposed to facilitate memory retrieval have not been systematically evaluated with respect to their effectiveness, and in particular, to their effects on accuracy. Given that memories may be particularly vulnerable to modification following very long delays, there is reason to be cautious of any element of suggestion or coercion.

Clinical Practice Guidelines

Issues Concerning the Practitioner

The practice of therapy is built on the sound scientific basis of psychological knowledge. The scientist/practitioner model of clinical psychology requires that therapeutic techniques be based on empirical knowledge. . . .

Practitioners who work with clients who may have been subjected to traumatic experiences during childhood, need a sound knowledge of theory and research relating to memory processes, child abuse and traumatic stress. To work with this group may therefore require special competency and training. It is especially important for practitioners to be aware that memory is a fragile, constructive process that need not provide accurate information about past events, especially if those events occurred a long time ago.

Practitioners should also be aware of their power, beliefs, assumptions, and how these factors may affect their clients. They need to be aware that they may be viewed by their clients as figures of authority, and that they are in a position where they could inadvertently influence their clients in ways that might prove harmful to them. The risk is heightened if, as is likely, the client is in a vulnerable state of mind. Measures need to be taken so that the practitioner's assumptions and conclusions are not imposed on their clients. It is a matter of sound clinical practice that the practitioners do not bring personal or political agendas to bear in the course of therapy.

Issues Concerning Assessment

The assessment of the client should be careful and comprehensive. It may include questions about violence, trauma and abuse. The form, content and timing of the questions that are used to assist the client in describing experiences need to be carefully considered. It is important that questions do not confuse or lead the client through suggestion. It is better to use free recall and open ended questions rather than questions that may constrain or bias the client's answers. Premature conclusions about causality or the existence of childhood trauma may improperly influence the client and may not be supported by further in-depth inquiry. Trauma and/or abuse should not be assumed without the client making a clear disclosure.

Practitioners should attempt to create a climate of acceptance for their clients without losing the scientific base to their assessment. There is a need to accept what the client says, without colluding with the information that is not supported by other data. Practitioners should be able to tolerate ambiguity and contradictions and help their client cope with these as well. Practitioners should be able to hold a neutral but supportive position and adopt a scientific attitude, testing hypotheses rather than jumping to conclusions. Information that is not supported should not be endorsed as accurate.

If the client suspects abuse but cannot remember it, or remembers only fragments, the practitioner should adhere to the following aspects of good practice. They should ask what has led to suspicions, without assuming an abuse history or confirming suspicions. Leading or repeated questions or suggestions should be avoided, and contradictions identified. If the client holds mistaken beliefs, for example, about the nature of memory or the causes of particular symptoms, these should be corrected. The practitioner may need to educate the client about memory processes. In instances where the client suspects abuse and there is no clear memory, a move to other issues that have emerged in the course of therapy is recommended, although it may be necessary to re-consider the possibility that the client may have suffered trauma or abuse as therapy proceeds.

Practitioners should be aware of the different requirements of the therapeutic and legal domains. Forensic and clinical assessments need to be distinguished, with accurate records made up of what the client says in either circumstance. It is good practice to establish and clearly document what a client remembers about childhood and traumatic experiences before therapy begins. Clearly if a memory of trauma or abuse is disclosed at the beginning of therapy, then it cannot have been induced by the therapy itself. Documentation of what a client remembers at the beginning of therapy protects both client and practitioner.

Issues Concerning Therapy

The goal of therapy for clients who have experienced childhood trauma is to enable them to function more effectively in the present and future. To achieve this, therapy may focus on all aspects of psychological functioning—thoughts, behaviors and feelings, including memories of past experiences. The emphasis should not be just on recovery from trauma, but should embrace all aspects of the client's psychological and interpersonal well-being.

Recovery from trauma may involve exposure to memories of the trauma, in order to reduce symptoms through the process of habituation, and to integrate past experiences into the present sense of self. Nevertheless, the active pursuit of memory should not be a goal of the therapy. The majority of clients already remember most of the trauma. Further recall may occur as the client gains psychological and emotional strength. The evidence suggests that hypnosis does not increase the accuracy of memory, or provide access to memories that are otherwise inaccessible, although it may increase the subject's belief that some episode occurred. Hypnosis is therefore a potential source of distortion, and even of false memories, and its use is not recommended for memory recall. Complete recall of all memories associated with trauma or abuse is not necessary, or even possible. Distortions and inconsistencies are present in many essentially accurate memories.

To promote a feeling of safety, therapy sessions need to be structured and predictable. The therapist needs to be reliable and consistent. It is especially important to maintain personal and professional boundaries when dealing with clients who may have suffered from trauma or abuse, as they are likely to be especially vulnerable to inconsistencies in the therapist's attitudes and behaviors. The relationship between the therapist and the client should be collaborative and non-authoritarian, but at the same time the therapist needs to retain responsibility and control of the therapy. The nature of this work means that the emotions that the client and the therapist may experience toward each other (transference and countertransference) may be intense, unexpected and difficult to deal with. Regular clinical supervision acts to protect clients and therapists in this respect.

It is the role of the practitioner to facilitate an informed decision-making process, by helping clients identify possible consequences of their actions. The effects of legal action and confrontation with an abuser need to be considered carefully, as in many cases these may not be essential for recovery.

MODEL FORMS: POLICIES AND PROCEDURES AND INFORMED CONSENT

INFORMATION FOR PROSPECTIVE AND ONGOING PATIENTS*

The following information is provided to establish a clear mutual understanding of the professional and business aspects of our relationship. Please read this information carefully and feel free to ask about anything that is unclear to you, to ask for additional information, and/or share any concerns about these issues. Bring this policy statement with you to your next session for discussion.

I. General Information

A. PSYCHOLOGICAL SERVICES.   Psychotherapy varies depending on the personalities of both therapist and patient, the particular problems and issues being addressed, the length of the treatment, and the strategies used. Psychotherapy has both benefits and risks. Risks sometimes include experiencing uncomfortable feelings and/or working with unpleasant life events. Psychotherapy often leads to a significant reduction of distress, better relationships, and the resolution of specific problems. In order to be most successful, hard work on your part is required, both during our sessions and between them.

B. INTAKE AND ASSESSMENT.   The first few sessions (intake) is the time during which we: (1) discuss your presenting problem(s) and symptom(s), current and past personality and interpersonal functioning, any past treatment and its outcome, family background and history, personal strengths and assets, and preliminary goals, sequencing, and planning of treatment; (2) get to know something about each other, each

---

*Given to prospective patients during the first meeting or sent to them prior to the meeting and reviewed and updated periodically with ongoing patients.

other's styles, and whether I can treat the problem as presented; (3) inquire about any special circumstances that might affect our work, e.g., in process or anticipated legal actions, medical conditions and prescribed medications, time limits, general schedules and travel schedules; (4) determine whether we can effectively work together and/or whether another referral would be appropriate; (5) determine appointment times and the number of sessions weekly and whether a group might be useful presently or at some later time (as appropriate or as available); and (6) any other recommendations, suggestions, or necessities, such as the need for a physical, medical, or neurological examination, psychological testing, psychiatric evaluation for medication, or records from past therapy. In addition to the verbal exchange of information, I request that each new patient complete a one-page intake form and a personal history questionnaire and request a release of information for summary records of any previous psychotherapy.

C. CONFIDENTIALITY. In general, the confidentiality of all communications between a patient and a psychologist (or other mental health practitioner) is protected by law, and I can only release information about our work to others with your written permission. Under the law, I am limited in what information can be released.

In most judicial proceedings, you have the right to prevent me from providing any information about your treatment. However, in some circumstances such as child custody proceedings and proceedings in which your emotional condition is an important element, a judge may require my testimony if he/she determines that resolution of the legal issues demands it.

There are some situations in which I am legally required to take action to protect others from harm, even though that requires revealing information about a patient's treatment. If I learn that a child, an elderly person, or a disabled person is being abused, I must file a report with the appropriate protective services agency. If I learn that a patient is threatening serious bodily harm to another, I am required to take protective actions, which may include notifying the potential victim, notifying the police, or seeking appropriate hospitalization. If a patient threatens self-harm, I may be required to seek hospitalization, or to contact family members or others who can provide protection.

These situations have rarely arisen in my outpatient practice. Should such a situation occur, I will make every effort to discuss it with you fully before taking any action and to involve you in the action.

I occasionally find it helpful to consult about a case with other professionals. In these consultations, I do not reveal the identity of my patient.

The consultant is, of course, also legally bound to keep all information confidential. Unless you object, I will not tell you about these consultations unless I feel that it is important to our work together.

D. PROFESSIONAL RECORDS.   I maintain records regarding treatment strategies and progress as a professional obligation and often take notes in the course of a session.

E. PATIENT RIGHTS.   You have the following rights in therapy: (1) to ask questions about my philosophy of therapy, my experience with the problem at hand, your treatment plan, and the procedures used. I will explain my usual methods to you; (2) to seek a consultation regarding your treatment from another credentialed professional. I ask that you discuss this with me prior to seeking such a consultation. At times, a meeting involving the consultant and both of us is advisable and helpful; (3) to end therapy at any time without moral, legal, or financial obligation beyond payment due for completed sessions. Should you decide between sessions to withdraw from therapy, I request that you attend at least one additional session to discuss your reasons with me. Therapy termination can sometimes be the result of misinterpretation, miscommunication, and the painfulness of the material under discussion. I encourage open communication before a final decision is made. Should you decide to terminate therapy with me but wish to continue with someone else, I will provide you with names of other qualified therapists.

F. OTHER.   If a problem of any type (e.g., financial, scheduling, therapy approach, communication) arises during the course of our work, please bring it up for discussion.
It may be useful or necessary to invite a spouse, partner, or friend to attend a session. This is only done if you give consent, except in an emergency.
As a *condition of being in treatment with me*, please do not undertake any other form of simultaneous therapy without first bringing it up for discussion and mutual decision-making. When another form of mental health treatment is undertaken, I *require* that open mutual releases of information be maintained with the other treating professional(s) to facilitate communication and to avoid miscommunication or splitting. As your primary therapist, I have professional responsibility for your overall psychological treatment and additional therapy should be coordinated within the main treatment.
Another *condition of treatment with me* involves no unplanned major disclosures and/or confrontations (involving any significant issue such as

abuse or neglect) of family members or other significant individuals. Such action should be discussed, decided upon, and prepared for to minimize adverse outcomes and should not be undertaken impulsively. Also, any significant break or detachment from family members should not be undertaken impulsively without careful deliberation.

My practice has a specialization in the treatment of adults abused as children and the treatment of post-traumatic conditions. If your therapy involves treatment of abuse/trauma and the issues of delayed/recovered memories, I will provide you with additional written and verbal information on these topics. Considerable controversy surrounds these topics, making it very important that we have a mutual understanding about how these issues will be addressed in treatment.

II. Fee Information and Scheduling

A. INDIVIDUAL THERAPY.   Fees are $XXX per 50-minute session.

B. GROUP THERAPY.   Fees are $XXX per 90-minute session.

C. INTAKE SESSION.   The intake session is $XXX per 50 minutes or, in the case of sliding scale clients, billed at the same rate as the negotiated sliding scale fee.

D. CONSULTATION.   Fees are $XXX per 50-minute session.

E. SLIDING SCALE.   I am able to see a limited number of clients on a sliding scale, ability-to-pay basis, $XXX per 50-minute session minimum. This is negotiated on an individual basis. When a sliding scale slot is not available, I am happy to provide referrals to my associates, other therapists and/or clinics providing services on a low-cost basis.

F. FEE STRUCTURE.   My fee structure will be reassessed annually. Fees are kept within the usual and customary schedule.

G. OTHER.   Other professional services you may require, such as report writing, telephone conversations that last longer than 10 minutes, attendance at meetings or consultations with other professionals that you have authorized, preparation of records or treatment summaries, or the time required to perform any other service, are billed on a prorated basis of the individual therapy fee.

In unusual circumstances, you may become involved with litigation that may require my participation. In that event, you will be billed for my professional time even if I am compelled to testify by another party. Fees for these services will be negotiated separately; my fee for testimony is higher than for psychotherapy due to the additional demands imposed by work of this type.

H. INSURANCE REIMBURSEMENT. In order for us to set realistic treatment goals and priorities, it is important to evaluate your available therapy resources. If you have a health benefits policy, it will usually provide some coverage for mental health treatment. I will help facilitate your receiving the benefits you are entitled to by filling out forms as appropriate; however, you, and not your insurance company, are responsible for full payment of the mutually agreed upon fee. Therefore, it is very important that you find out exactly what mental health services your insurance policy covers and the conditions of coverage. You should carefully read the mental health section of your insurance booklet and call your carrier with your questions. I will provide you with whatever information I have based on my experience and will assist you to understand the information you receive. If necessary, I am willing to call the carrier on your behalf.

The escalation of the cost of health care has resulted in an increasing level of complexity about insurance benefits that sometimes makes it difficult to determine exactly how much mental health coverage is available. "Managed Health Care Plans" such as HMOs and PPOs often require advance authorization before providing reimbursement for mental health services. These plans are usually oriented towards a short-term treatment approach designed to resolve specific problems. It may be necessary to seek additional approval after a certain number of sessions. In my experience, while quite a lot can be accomplished in short-term therapy, patients may feel that more services are necessary after insurance benefits expire. Some managed care plans will not allow me to provide additional services once your benefits are used. If this is the case, I will do my best to find you another provider who will help you continue your psychotherapy.

Once we have all of the information about your insurance coverage, we will discuss what we can expect to accomplish with the available benefits and what will happen if the insurance benefits run out before you feel ready to end treatment. Please be aware that you always have the right to pay for services yourself and avoid these insurance complexities. I am willing to negotiate my fee in such a situation.

You should also be aware that most insurance agreements require you to authorize me to provide a clinical diagnosis, and sometimes additional clinical information such as a treatment plan or summary, or in rare cases, a copy of the entire record. Under current state law, I cannot provide the entire record and will so inform your carrier. If you request it, I will provide you with a copy of any report that I submit. Please note that whatever information is released will become part of the insurance files, and, in all probability, some, if not all, of it will be computerized. Insurance companies claim to keep such information confidential, but once it is submitted, I have no control over its status. In some cases, it may be shared with a national medical information data bank.

I. PAYMENT. *All fees are payable at the time of service or when billed or by other arrangement determined on an individual basis.* Please note that this requires you to await insurance reimbursement. I am unable, for professional and personal reasons, to allow large back balances to build. Please discuss with me when financial circumstances make it difficult to pay your bill on a weekly or monthly basis.

If your account is more than 60 days in arrears and suitable arrangements for payment have not been made, I have the option of suspending or discontinuing treatment and after a brief time period devoted to the termination of our work, will provide the names of other therapists or clinics.

In the event of an unpaid bill, legal means can be used to secure payment, including collection agencies or small claims court. (If such legal action is necessary, the costs of bringing that proceeding will be included in the claim.) In most cases, the only information that is released is the patient's name, the nature of the services provided, and the amount due.

J. SCHEDULING.   Scheduling presents a special problem in private therapy because once a given hour is blocked out over a period of time, it cannot be filled again on short notice. Consequently, fees will be charged for all missed sessions, regardless of the reason for the absence, except:

1. If you give sufficient forewarning, usually 24 hours in non-emergency situations. Leave a message on my voice mail if you are unable to contact me directly.
2. Three sessions per calendar year which you might use in the case of vacation, business trips, illness, etc. This three-session limit will be waived in the event of prolonged illness or work-related absence and by discussion, or if I can schedule the hour when you've given me notice of a cancellation.
3. "Snow days" or other circumstances beyond our mutual control.

Please note that insurance companies will not pay for sessions that are missed and billed as absences; you are responsible for the entire fee when this occurs.

Should you need to cancel your regularly scheduled session, I will attempt to find another appointment time during the same week. I cannot guarantee that this will always be possible since I am generally tightly booked; however, I will be as flexible as possible. A phone session might be possible as an alternative.

Occasionally, telephone contact is needed when issues come up or a crisis develops between regularly scheduled sessions. (In emergencies, you can try me at my home office number.) I am often not immediately available but I monitor my voice mail frequently. I will make every effort to return your call on the same day you make it with the exception of late nights, weekends, and holidays. If you are difficult to reach, please leave some times when you will be available. If you cannot reach me, and you feel that you cannot wait for a return call, you should call a local hotline or the emergency room at the nearest hospital and ask for the psychologist or psychiatrist on call.

Phone calls over ten minutes' duration are billed at the normal hourly rate; they are added to your bill when 50 minutes of telephone time accumulates. Phone contact is usually kept brief unless you are in a crisis or unless a session by phone has been scheduled in advance.

K. VACATION. My schedule includes approximately 6–8 weeks of professional and vacation time each year during which I am out of the office. I usually take Christmas and New Year's weeks as vacation, summer vacation in July and/or August, and several weeks for conferences, consulting trips, and writing. You will receive a quarterly schedule for your information and planning. Please try to schedule your absences and vacations to correspond with mine whenever possible.

Occasionally, I need to reschedule due to other professional commitments or for personal reasons. I attempt to give notice for changes wherever possible. For short notice changes, you will be contacted by me or by my secretary.

It is my policy to be available by phone during absences required for consulting trips, except when I travel to the West Coast or out of the country. I am not available when on vacation. Whatever the absence, another therapist will always be available for back-up coverage. You will be notified of coverage in advance and information to that effect will be on my voice mail.

CONSENT TO TREATMENT

I acknowledge that I have received, have read, and understand "Information for Prospective and Ongoing Patients." I have had my questions answered adequately at this time. I understand that I have the right to ask questions throughout the course of my treatment and may request an outside consultation. (I also understand that the therapist may provide me with additional information about specific treatment issues and treatment methods on an as-needed basis during the course of my treatment and that I have the right to consent to or refuse such treatment.) The therapist might also seek or suggest outside consultation.

I understand that I will be involved in the development of the initial and ongoing treatment plans and can expect regular review of treatment to determine whether treatment goals are being met. I agree to be actively involved in the treatment and in the review process. No promises have been made as to the results of this treatment or of any procedures utilized within it.

I further understand that I may stop my treatment at any time, but agree to discuss this decision first with the therapist. My only obligation, should I decide to stop treatment, is to pay for the services I have already received.

I have been informed that I must give 24 hours' notice to cancel an appointment and that I will be charged if I do not cancel or show up for a scheduled appointment.

I am aware that I must authorize this therapist to release information about my treatment but that confidentiality can be broken under certain circumstances of danger to myself or others. I understand that once information is released to insurance companies or any other third party, that my therapist cannot guarantee that it will remain confidential.

My signature signifies my understanding and agreement with these issues and with the additional information conveyed in "Information for Prospective and Ongoing Patients."

_____   _____
        Patient signature   Date

REFERENCES

Abrahamson, D. J., & Saakvitne, K. W. (in press). Quality management in practice: Re-visioning practice guidelines to improve treatment of anxiety and traumatic stress disorders. In G. Stricker, W. Troy, and S. Shueman (Eds.), *Handbook of quality management in behavioral health*. New York: Plenum Press.

Adshead, G. (1996). Seekers after truth: Ethical issues raised by the discussion of "false" and "recovered" memories. In J. D. Read & D. S. Lindsay (Eds.), *Recollections of trauma: Scientific evidence and clinical practice* (pp. 435–440). New York: Plenum Press.

Ainsworth, M. D. S., Blehar, M. C., Waters, E., & Wall, S. (1978). *Patterns of attachment: A psychological study of the strange situation.* Hillsdale, NJ: Erlbaum.

Albach, F., & Everaerd, W. (1992). Postraumatic stress symptoms in victims of childhood incest. *Journal of Psychotherapy and Psychosomatics, 57,* 143–151.

Aldridge-Morris, R. (1989). *Multiple personality: An exercise in deception.* Hillsdale, NJ: Erlbaum.

Alexander, P. C. (1992). Application of attachment theory to the study of sexual abuse. *Journal of Consulting and Clinical Psychology, 60,* 185–195.

Alexander, P C., & Anderson, C. (1994). An attachment approach to psychotherapy with the incest survivor. *Psychotherapy, 31,* 665–675.

Alexander, P. C., Neimayer, R. A., & Follette, V. M. (1991). Group therapy for women sexually abused as children: A controlled study and investigation of individual differences. *Journal of Interpersonal Violence, 6*(2), 218–231.

Alexander, P. C., Neimayer, R. A., Follette, V. M., Moore, M. K., & Harter, S. (1989). A comparison of group treatments of women sexually abused as children. *Journal of Consulting and Clinical Psychology, 57*(4), 479–483.

Allen, C. V. (1980). *Daddy's girl.* New York: Berkley Books.

Alpert, J. L. (Ed.). (1995). *Sexual abuse recalled: Treating trauma in the era of the recovered memory debate.* Northvale, NJ: Jason Aronson Inc.

377

Alpert, J. L., Brown, L. S., Ceci, S. J., Courtois, C. A., Loftus, E. F., Ornstein, P. A. (1996a). Final conclusions of the APA working group on investigation of memories of childhood abuse. In J. Alpert, L. Brown, S. Ceci, C. Courtois, E. Loftus, & P. Ornstein. (Eds.), *Working group on investigation of memories of childhood abuse* (pp.1–14). Washington, DC: American Psychological Association.

Alpert, J. L., Brown, L. S., Ceci, S. J., Courtois, C. A., Loftus, E. F., Ornstein, P. A. (Eds.). (1996b). *Working group on investigation of memories of childhood abuse: Final report.* Washington, DC: American Psychological Association.

Alpert, J. L., Brown, L. S., & Courtois, C. A. (1996a). The politics of memory: A response to Ornstein, Ceci, and Loftus. In J. Alpert, L. Brown, S. Ceci, C. Courtois, E. Loftus, & P. Ornstein. (Eds.), *Working group on investigation of memories of childhood abuse* (pp. 132–149). Washington, DC: American Psychological Association.

Alpert, J. L., Brown, L. S., & Courtois, C. A. (1996b). Response to "Adult recollections of childhood abuse: Cognitive and developmental perspectives." In J. Alpert, L. Brown, S. Ceci, C. Courtois, E. Loftus, & P. Ornstein. (Eds.), *Working group on investigation of memories of childhood abuse* (pp. 198–220). Washington, DC: American Psychological Association.

Alpert, J. L., Brown, L. S., & Courtois, C. A. (1996c). Symptomatic clients and memories of childhood abuse: What the trauma and child sexual abuse literature tells us. In J. Alpert, L. Brown, S. Ceci, C. Courtois, E. Loftus, & P. Ornstein. (Eds.), *Working group on investigation of memories of childhood abuse* (pp.15–105). Washington, DC: American Psychological Association.

American Humane Association. (1988). *Highlights of official child neglect and abuse reporting, 1986.* Denver, CO: Author.

American Medical Association Council on Scientific Affairs (1994). *Memories of childhood abuse, CSA Report 5-A-94.* Chicago: Author.

American Psychiatric Association. (1980). *Diagnostic and statistical manual of mental disorders* (3rd ed.). Washington, DC: Author.

American Psychiatric Association. (1987). *Diagnostic and statistical manual of mental disorders* (3rd ed. rev.). Washington, DC: Author.

American Psychiatric Association. (1994). *Diagnostic and statistical manual of mental disorders* (4th ed.). Washington, DC: Author.

American Psychiatric Association. (1996). *Practice guidelines.* Washington, DC: Author.

American Psychiatric Association. (1998). Practice guidelines for treatment of patients with panic disorder. [Supplement]. *American Journal of Psychiatry, 155*(5).

American Psychiatric Association Board of Directors. (1993). *Statement on Memories of Sexual Abuse.* Washington, DC: Author.

American Psychological Association. (1992). Ethical principles of psychologists and code of conduct. *American Psychologist, 47,* 1597–1611.

American Psychological Association. (1994). *Interim report of the Working Group on Investigation of Memories of Childhood Abuse.* Washington, DC: Author.

American Psychological Association. (1996a). *Analysis of the "Truth and Responsibility in Mental Health Practices Act" and similar proposals.* Washington, DC: Author.

American Psychological Association. (1996b). *Final report of the Working Group on Investigation of Memories of Childhood Abuse.* Washington, DC: Author.

American Psychological Association ad hoc Committee on Legal and Ethical Issues in the Treatment of Interpersonal Violence. (1996a). *Potential problems for psychologists working with the area of interpersonal violence.* [Brochure]. Washington, DC: Author.

American Psychological Association ad hoc Committee on Legal and Ethical Issues in the Treatment of Interpersonal Violence. (1996b). *Professional, ethical, and legal issues concerning interpersonal violence, maltreatment and related trauma.* [Brochure]. Washington, DC: Author.

American Psychological Association Task Force on Psychological Intervention Guidelines. (1995). *Template for developing guidelines: Interventions for mental disorders and psychosocial aspects of physical disorders.* Washington, DC: American Psychological Association.

Andrews, B. (1997). Forms of memory recovery among adults in therapy: Preliminary results from an in-depth survey. In J. D. Read & D. S. Lindsay (Eds.), *Recollections of trauma: Scientific evidence and clinical practice* (pp. 455–460). New York: Plenum Press.

Appelbaum, P. S., & Zoltek-Jick, R. (1996). Psychotherapists' duties to third parties: Ramona and beyond. *American Journal of Psychiatry, 153,*(4), 457–465.

Appelbaum, P. S., Uyehara, L. A., & Elin, M. R. (Eds.). (1997). *Trauma and memory: Clinical and legal controversies.* New York: Oxford University Press.

Armstrong, L. (1978). *Kiss daddy good-night: A speakout on incest.* New York: Hawthorne Books.

Armstrong, L. (1994). *Rocking the cradle of sexual politics: What happened when women said incest.* New York: Addison-Wesley Publishing Company.

Armstrong, H., Barker, E., Bright, B., Bergljot, B., Coll, P. G., Curtis, J. C., Dean, M. S., Fraser, G., Froese, A. P., Gutowski, W. D., Hunter, M., Korzekwa, M., O'Neil, J. A., Pain, C., Robitaille, G., & Wheelwright, D. (1996, September 10). [Letter to colleagues in response to Canadian Psychiatric Association, *Position statement: Adult recovered memories of childhood sexual abuse.*].

Australian Psychological Society Limited Board of Directors. (1994). *Guidelines relating to the reporting of recovered memories.* Sydney, New South Wales, Australia: Author.

Barach, P. M. (1991). Multiple personality disorder as an attachment disorder. *Dissociation, 4,* 117–123.

Barden, R. C. (1994). A proposal to finance preparation of model legislation titled: Mental health consumer protection act. Unpublished manuscript.

Barnier, A. J. & McConkey, K. M. (1992). Reports of real and false memories: The relevance of hypnosis, hypnotizability, and context of memory test. *Journal of Abnormal Psychology, 101,* 521–527.

Barrett, M. J. (1997, November/December). Resolving the irresolvable: Constructing a way out for families torn apart by struggles over recovered memories. *Family Therapy Networker,* 81–86.

Bass, E., & Davis, L. (1988). *The courage to heal: A guide for women survivors of child sexual abuse.* New York: Harper & Row.

Bass, E., & Davis, L. (1994). *The courage to heal: A guide for women survivors of child sexual abuse* (3rd Ed.). New York: Harper & Row.

Bass, E., Thornton, L., Brister, J., Hammond, G., & Lamb, V. (Eds.). (1983). *I never told anyone: Writings by women survivors of child sexual abuse.* New York: Harper & Row.

Beattie, M. (1989). *Beyond codependency: And getting better all the time.* New York: Harper & Row.

Beauchamp, T. L., & Childress, J. F. (1983). *Principles of biomedical ethics* (2nd ed.). Oxford, England: Oxford University Press.

Beckett, K. (1996). Culture and the politics of signification: The case of child sexual abuse. *Social Problems, 43*(1), 57–76.

Beitchman, J., Zucker, K., Hood, J., daCosta, G., & Ackman, D. (1991). A review of the short-term effects of childhood sexual abuse. *Child Abuse and Neglect, 15,* 537–556.

Beitchman, J. H., Zucker, K. J., Hood, J. E., daCosta, G. A., Akman, D., & Cassavia, E. (1992). A review of the long-term effects of child sexual abuse. *Child Abuse and Neglect, 16,* 101–118.

Belicki, K., Correy, B., Boucock, A., Cuddy, M., & Dunlop, A. (1994). *Reports of sexual abuse: Facts or fantasies?* Unpublished manuscript. Brock University, St. Catherines, Ontario.

Belluck, P. (1997, November 6). "Memory" therapy leads to a lawsuit and big settlement. *The New York Times*, pp. A1, A14.

Benedict, J. G., & Donaldson, D. W. (1996). Recovered memories threaten all. *Professional Psychology: Research and Practice, 27*, 27–428.

Benward, J., & Densen-Gerber, J. (1975). Incest as a causative factor in anti-social behavior: An exploratory study. *Contemporary Drug Problems, 4*(3), 323–340.

Berliner, L. (1997). Introduction to the special commentary: The memory wars: Detente, anyone? *Journal of Interpersonal Violence, 12*(5) 629–630.

Berliner, L., & Williams, L. M. (1994). Memories of child sexual abuse: A response to Lindsay and Read. *Applied Cognitive Psychology, 8*(4), 379–389.

Bernstein, E. M., & Putnam, F. W. (1986). Development, reliability, and validity of a dissociation scale. *Journal of Nervous and Mental Disease, 174*, 727–735.

Beutler, L., & Hill, C. (1992). Process and outcome research in the treatment of adult victims of childhood sexual abuse: Methodological issues. *Journal of Consulting and Clinical Psychology, 60*, 204–212.

Binder, R. L., McNiel, D. E., & Goldstone, R. L. (1994). Patterns of recall of childhood sexual abuse as described by adult survivors. *Bulletin of the American Academy of Law, 22*(3), 358–366.

Blake, D. D., Weathers, F. W., Nagy, L. M., Kaloupek, D. G., Klauminzer, G., Charney, D. S., & Keane, T. M. (1990). A clinician rating scale for assessing current and lifetime PTSD: The CAPS-1. *Behavior Therapist, 18*, 187–188.

Blake, D. D., Weathers, F. W., Nagy, L. M., Kaloupek, D. G., Charney, D. S., & Keane, T. M. (1996). *The Clinician-Administered PTSD Scale (CAPS)*. Boston: National Center for PTSD, Boston VA Medical Center.

Blank, A. S. (1994). Clinical detection, diagnosis, and differential diagnosis of posttraumatic stress disorder. *Psychiatric Clinics of North America, 17*(2), 351–383.

Blizard, R., & Bruhn, A. (1994). Attachment to the abuser: Integrating object-relations and trauma theories in treatment of abuse survivors. *Psychotherapy, 31*, 383–390.

Bloom, S. L. (1994). The sanctuary model: Developing generic inpatient programs for the treatment of psychological trauma. In M. B. Williams & J. F. Sommer (Eds.), *Handbook of post-traumatic therapy* (pp. 474–494). Westport, CT: Greenwood Press.

Blume, e. s. (1990). *Secret survivors: Uncovering incest and its aftereffects in women*. New York: John Wiley & Sons.

Bottoms, B. L., & Goodman, G. S. (Eds.). (1996). *International perspectives on child abuse and children's testimony: Psychological research and law*. Thousand Oaks, CA: Sage.

Bowlby, J. (1969). *Attachment and loss: Vol. 1: Attachment*. New York: Basic Books.

Bowlby, J. (1973). *Attachment and loss: Vol. 2: Separation: Anxiety and anger*. London: Penguin Books.

Bowlby, J. (1980). *Attachment and loss: Vol. 3: Loss: Sadness and depression*. London: Penguin Books.

Bowlby, J. (1988). *Parent-child attachment and healthy human development*. New York: Basic Books.

Bowman, M. L. (1997). *Individual differences in posttraumatic response*. Hillsdale, NJ: Erlbaum.

Brabin, P. J., & Berah, E. F. (1995). Dredging up past traumas: Harmful or helpful? *Psychiatry, Psychology, and Law, 2*(2), 165–171.

Bradshaw, J. (1988). *The family: A revolutionary way of self-discovery*. Deerfield Beach, FL: Health Communications.

Brady, K. T. (1997). Posttraumatic stress disorder and comorbidity: Recognizing the many faces of PTSD. *Journal of Clinical Psychiatry, 58*(Suppl. 9), 12–15.

Brainin-Rodriguez, J. E. (1997). Assessment of trauma in the female psychiatric inpatient: Impact and treatment implications. In C. Prozan (Ed.), *Construction and reconstruction of memory: Dilemmas of childhood sexual abuse* (pp. 135–150). Northvale, NJ: Jason Aronson Inc.

Brandon, S., Boakes, J., Glaser, D., & Green, R. (1998). Recovered memories of childhood sexual abuse: Implications for clinical practice. *British Journal of Psychiatry, 172*, 296–307.

Braun, B. G. (Ed.). (1986). *Treatment of multiple personality disorder.* Washington, DC: American Psychiatric Press, Inc.

Bremner, J. D., Krystal, J. H., Charney, D. S., & Southwick, S. M. (1996). Neural mechanisms in dissociative amnesia for childhood abuse: Relevance to the current controversy surrounding the "False Memory Syndrome." *American Journal of Psychiatry, 153*, 71–82.

Bremner, J. D., Krystal, J. H., Southwick, S. M., & Charney, D. S. (1995). Functional neuroanatomical correlates of the effects of stress on memory. *Journal of Traumatic Stress, 8*, 527–553.

Bremner, J. D., Scott, T. M., Delaney, R. C., Southwick, S. M., Mason, J. W., Johnson, D. R., Innis, R. B., McCarthy, G., & Charney, D. S. (1993). Deficits in short-term memory in posttraumatic stress disorder. *American Journal of Psychiatry, 150*, 1015–1019.

Bremner, J. D., Southwick, S. M., & Charney, D. S. (1991, Fall). Animal models for the neurobiology of trauma. *PTSD Research Quarterly, 2*,(4), 1–3.

Brenneis, B. (1994). Can early trauma be reconstructed from dreams?: On the realtionship of dreams to trauma. *Psychoanalytic Psychology, 11*, 429–447.

Brenneis, C. B. (1997). *Recovered memories of trauma: Transferring the present to the past.* Madison, CT: International Universities Press, Inc.

Breuer, J., & Freud, S. (1959).On the psychical mechanism of hysterical phenomena: Preliminary communication. In J. Riviere (Trans.), *Sigmund Freud: Collected papers* (Vol. 1, pp. 24–42). New York: Basic. (Original work published 1892).

Brewer, W. F. (1986). What is autobiographical memory? In D. C. Rubin (Ed.), *Autobiographical memory* (pp. 25–49). New York: Cambridge University Press.

Brewer, W. F. (1994). Autobiographical memory and survey research. In N. Schwarz & S. Sudman (Eds.), *Autobiographical memory and the validity of retrospective reports.* New York: Springer-Verlag.

Brewin, C. R., Andrews, B., & Gotlib, I. H. (1993). Psychopathology and early experience: A reappraisal of retrospective reports. *Psychological Bulletin, 113*, 82–98.

Briere, J. (1984, April). The effects of childhood sexual abuse on later psychological functioning: Defining a post-sexual abuse syndrome. Paper presented at the annual meeting of the American Psychological Association, Los Angeles, CA.

Briere, J. (1989). *Therapy for adults molested as children: Beyond survival.* New York: Springer Publishing Co.

Briere, J. (Ed.). (1991). *Treating victims of child sexual abuse.* San Francisco: Jossey-Bass, Inc.

Briere, J. (1992). *Child abuse trauma: Theory and treatment of the lasting effects.* Newbury Park, CA: Sage.

Briere, J. (1993). Methodological issues in the study of sexual abuse side effects. *Journal of Consulting and Clinical Psychology, 60*, 196–203.

Briere, J. (1995). *Trauma Symptom Inventory (TSI) Professional Manual.* Odessa, FL: Psychological Assessment Resources, Inc.

Briere, J. (1996a). A self-trauma model for treating adult survivors of severe child abuse. In Briere, J., Berliner, L., Bulkley, J. A., Jenny, C., & Reid, T. (Eds.), *The APSAC handbook on child maltreatment.* Thousand Oaks, CA: Sage.

Briere, J. (1996b). *Therapy for adults molested as children: Beyond survival* (2nd Ed.). New York: Springer Publishing Co.

Briere, J. (1997a). An integrated approach to to treating adults abused as children with specific reference to self-reported recovered memories. In J. D. Read & D. S. Lindsay (Eds.), *Recollections of trauma: Scientific evidence and clinical practice* (pp. 25–48). New York: Plenum Press.

Briere, J. (1997b). *Psychological assessment of adult posttraumatic states.* Washington, DC: American Psychological Association.

Briere, J., Berliner, L., Bulkley, J. A., Jenny, C., & Reid, T. (Eds.). (1996). *The APSAC Handbook on Child Maltreatment.* Thousand Oaks, CA: Sage.

Briere, J., & Conte, J. (1993). Self-reported amnesia for abuse in adults molested in childhood. *Journal of Traumatic Stress, 6,* 21–31.

Briere, J., & Elliott, D. M. (1994). Immediate and long-term impacts of child sexual abuse. *The Future of Children, 4,* 54–69.

Briere, J. & Runtz, M. (1987). Post-sexual abuse trauma: Data and implications for clinical practice. *Journal of Interpersonal Violence, 2*(4), 367–379.

Briere, J. & Runtz, M. (1988). Symptomatology associated with childhood sexual victimization in a non-clinical sample. *Child Abuse and Neglect, 12,* 51–59.

Briere, J., & Runtz, M. (1989). The Trauma Symptom Checklist (TSC-33): Early data on a new scale. *Journal of Interpersonal Violence, 4.* 151–163.

British Association of Counseling (1997). *False memory syndrome: A statement.* Rugby, Warwickshire, England: Author.

British Psychological Society (1995). *Recovered memories: The Report of the Working Party of the British Psychological Society.* London: Author.

Brown, D. (1995). Pseudomemories: The standard of science and the standard of care in trauma treatment. *American Journal of Clinical Hypnosis, 37,* 1–24.

Brown, D., & Fromm, E. (1986). *Hypnotherapy and hypnoanalysis.* Hillsdale, NJ: Lawrence Earlbaum Associates.

Brown, D. & Scheflin, A. W. (Eds.). (1996). *The Journal of Psychiatry and Law, 24*(2).

Brown, D., Scheflin, A. W., & Hammond, D. C. (1998). *Memory, trauma treatment, and the law: An essential reference on memory for clinicians, researchers, attorneys, and judges.* New York: W. W. Norton & Company.

Brown, L. S. (1994). *Subversive dialogues: Theory in feminist therapy.* New York: Basic Books.

Brown, L. S. (1995). Not outside the range: One feminist perspective on psychic trauma. In Caruth, C. (Ed.), *Trauma: Explorations in memory* (pp. 100–112). Baltimore, MD: The Johns Hopkins University Press.

Brown, L. S. (1996). Politics of memory, politics of incest: Doing therapy and politics that really matter. In S. Contratto & M. J. Gutfreund (Eds.), *A feminist clinician's guide to the memory debate* (pp. 5–18). New York: Haworth Press.

Browne, A., & Finkelhor, D. (1986). Impact of child sexual abuse: A review of the research. *Psychological Bulletin, 99*(1), 66–77.

Brownmiller, S. (1975). *Against our will: Men, women, and rape.* New York: Simon and Schuster.

Bruck, M., & Ceci, S. (1997). The suggestibility of young children. *Current Directions in Psychological Science, 6,* 75–79.

Bruck, M., Ceci, S. J., & Hembrooke, H. (1998). Reliability and credibility of young children's reports: From research to policy and practice. *American Psychologist, 53*(2), 136–151.

Burgess, A. W., Groth, A. N., Holmstrom, L. L., & Sgroi, S. M. (1978). *Sexual assault of children and adolescents.* Lexington, MA: Lexington Books.

Burgess, A. W., Hartman, C. R., & Baker, T. (1995). Memory presentations of child sexual abuse. *Journal of Psychosocial Nursing, 33,* 9–16.

Burgess, A. W., & Holmstrom, L. L. (1974). Sexual trauma of children and adolescents: Pressure, sex and secrecy. *Nursing Clinics of North America, 10,* 554–563.

Butler, K. (1996, November/December). The latest on recovered memory. *Family Therapy Networker, 6,* 36–37.

Butler, L. D., & Spiegel, D. (1997). Trauma and memory. In L. J. Dickson, M. B. Riba, & J. M. Oldham (Series Eds.) & D. Spiegel (Vol. Ed.), *Section II of American Psychiatric Press review of psychiatry: Volume 16. Repressed memories* (pp. 13–54). Washington, DC: American Psychiatric Press.

Butler, R. W., Mueser, K. T., Sprock, J., & Braff, D. L. (1996). Positive symptoms of psychosis in posttraumatic stress disorder. *Society of Biological Psychiatry, 39,* 839–844.

Butler, S. (1978). *Conspiracy of silence: The trauma of incest.* New York: Bantam Books.

Byrd, K. R. (1994). The narrative reconstructions of incest survivors. *American Psychologist, 49,* 439–440.

Cahill, L., Prins, B., Weber, M., & McGaugh, J. L. (1994, October 20). B-adrenergic activation and memory for emotional events. *Nature, 371,* 702–704.

Calof, D. (1993, September/October). Facing the truth about false memory. *Family Therapy Networker,* 39–45.

Calof, D. (1994). *Clinical issues: Delayed memories of abuse: Managing clients requests for validation of delayed-memories of child abuse.* Unpublished manuscript.

Calof, D. (1997). Notes from a practice under seige. In *Science and politics of recovered memories.* Symposium conducted at the 105th Annual Meeting of the American Psychological Association, Toronto, Canada.

Cameron, C. (1993, April). *Changed lives: A longitudinal report on recovering sexual abuse survivors.* Paper presented at the Western Psychological Association Convention, Phoenix, Arizona.

Cameron, C. (1994, July). *Recovery from childhood sexual trauma: A longitudinal report.* Paper presented at the 23rd International Congress of Applied Psychology, Madrid, Spain.

Campbell, J. A., & Carlson, K. (1995). Training and knowledge of professionals on specific topics in child sexual abuse. *Journal of Child Sexual Abuse, 4*(1), 75–86.

Campbell, J., Courtois, C. A., Enns, C., Gottlieb, M., & Wells, M. (1995). *Psychotherapy guidelines for working with clients who may have an abuse or trauma history.* Washington, DC : American Psychological Association Division 17 (Counseling Psychology) Committee on Women.

Canadian Psychiatric Association (1996). *Position statement: Adult recovered memories of childhood sexual abuse.* Toronto: Author.

Cardena, E. (1994). The domain of dissociation. In S. J. Lynn & R. W. Rhue (Eds.), *Dissociation: Theoretical, clinical and research perspectives* (pp. 15–31). New York: The Guilford Press.

Carlson, E. B. (1997). *Trauma assessments: A clinician's guide.* New York: The Guilford Press.

Carlson, E. B., Furby, L., Armstrong, J., & Shlaes, J. (1997). A conceptual framework for the long-term psychological effects of traumatic childhood abuse. *Child Maltreatment, 2,* 272–295.

Caruth, C. (1995). *Trauma: Explorations in memory.* Baltimore, MD: The Johns Hopkins University Press.

Caudill, O. B. (1997). Repressed memory and the attack on the therapist: Pitfalls in practice from the legal perspective. *Journal of Child Sexual Abuse, 6*(3), 123–128.

Ceci, S. J. (1993, August). *Cognitive and social factors in children's testimony.* Paper presented at the 101st Annual Meeting of the American Psychological Association, Toronto, Canada.

Ceci, S. J. (1994, August). *Cognitive and social factors in children's testimony.* Paper presented at the 102nd Annual Meeting of the American Psychological Association.

Ceci, S. J., & Bruck, M. (1993). The suggestibility of the child witness: A historical review and synthesis. *Psychological Bulletin, 113*(3), 403–439.

Ceci, S. J., & Bruck, M. (1995). *Jeopardy in the courtroom: A scientific analysis of children's testimony.* Washington, DC: American Psychological Association Press.

Ceci, S. J., Huffman, M. L., Smith, E., & Loftus E. F. (1996). Repeatedly thinking about non-events. *Consciousness and Cognition, 3,* 388–407.

Ceci, S. J., Loftus, E. F., Leichtman, M., & Bruck, M. (1994). The role of source misattributions in the creation of false beliefs among preschoolers. *International Journal of Clinical and Experimental Hypnosis, 62,* 304–320.

Chambless, D. L. (1996). In defense of dissemination of empirically supported psychological interventions. *Clinical Psychology: Science & Practice, 3*, 230–235.

Chambless, D. L., Sanderson, W. C., Varda, S., Johnson, S. J., Pope, K. S., Crits-Christoph, P., Baker, M., Johnson, B., Woody, S. R., Sue, S., Buetler, L., Williams, D. A., & McCurry, S. (1996). An update on empirically validated therapies. *The Clinical Psychologist, 49*, 3–18.

Chapman, J. R., & Gates, M. (Eds.). (1978). *Sage yearbooks in women's policy studies: Volume 3. The victimization of women.* Beverly Hills: Sage.

Charney, D. S., Deutch, A. Y., Krystal, J. H., Southwick, S. M., & Davis, M. (1993). Psychobiologic mechanisms of posttraumatic stress disorder. *Archives of General Psychiatry, 50*, 294–305.

Cheit, R. E. (1997, March 21). *The experience of dissociative amnesia.* Presented at Harvard Medical School Department of Continuing Education and Massachusetts Mental Health Center, Psychological Trauma Conference, Boston, MA.

Cheit, R. E. (1998). False representations about true cases of recovered memory. *Ethics and Behavior, 8*(2).

Chew, J. (1997). *Women survivors of childhood sexual abuse: Healing through group work: Beyond survival.* New York: The Haworth Press, Inc.

Christianson, S. A. (1992a). Emotional stress and eyewitness memory: A critical review. *Psychological Bulletin, 112*, 284–309.

Christianson, S. A. (Ed.). (1992b). *The handbook of emotion and memory: Research and theory.* Hillsdale, NJ: Erlbaum.

Christianson, S. A., & Engelberg, E. (1997). Remembering and forgetting traumatic experiences: A matter of survival. In M. Conway (Ed.), *False and recovered memories* (pp. 230–250). Oxford, England: Oxford University Press.

Christianson, S. A., & Loftus, E. F. (1987). Memory for traumatic events. *Applied Cognitive Psychology, 1*, 225–239.

Christianson, S. A., Loftus, E. F., Hoffman, H., & Loftus, G. R. (1991). Eye fixations and memory for emotional events. *Journal of Experimental Psychology, 17*, 693–701.

Chu, J. A. (1988). Ten traps for therapists in the treatment of trauma survivors. *Dissociation, 1*(4), 24–32.

Chu, J. A. (1991). On the misdiagnosis of multiple personality disorder. *Dissociation, 4*, 200–204.

Chu, J. A. (1992). The therapeutic roller coaster: Dilemmas in the treatment of childhood abuse survivors. *Journal of Psychotherapy Practice and Research, 1*, 351–370.

Chu, J. A. (1998). *Rebuilding shattered lives: The responsible treatment of complex post-traumatic and dissociative disorders.* New York: Wiley.

Chu, J. A., & Dill, D. L. (1990). Dissociative symptoms in relation to childhood physical and sexual abuse. *American Journal of Psychiatry, 147*, 887–892.

Chu, J. A., Matthews, J., Frey, L. M., & Ganzel, B. (1996). The nature of traumatic memories of childhood abuse. *Dissociation, 9*, 2–17.

Classen, C. (Vol. Ed.) & Yalom, I. D. (Series Ed.). (1995). *Treating women molested in childhood: A volume in the Jossey-Bass library of current clinical technique.* San Francisco: Jossey-Bass.

Cohen, B. M., Barnes, M., & Rankin, A. B. (1995). *Managing traumatic stress through art: Drawing from the CENTER.* Lutherville, MD: The Sidran Press.

Cohen, B. M., & Cox, T. C. (1995). *Telling without talking: Art as a window into the world of multiple personality.* New York: W.W. Norton & Company.

Cohen, G. (1990). Reality monitoring. In M. W. Eysenck (Ed.), *The Blackwell dictionary of cognitive psychology.* Great Britain: Basil Blackwell, Inc.

Cohen, J. A., & Mannarino, A. P. (1998). Creating a curriculum on childhood traumatic stress. *Child Maltreatment, 3*(1), 53–62.

Cohen, L., Berzoff, J., & Elin, M. (Eds.). (1995). *Dissociative identity disorder.* Northvale, NJ: Jason Aronson Inc.

Cohen, N. J. (1996). Functional retrograde amnesia as a model of amnesia for childhood sexual abuse. In K. Pezdek & W. P. Banks (Eds.), *The recovered memory/false memory debate* (pp. 81–100). New York: Academic Press.

Cole, P. & Putnam, F. (1992). Effect of incest on self and social functioning: A developmental psychopathology perspective. *Journal of Consulting and Clinical Psychology, 60,* 174–184.

Conway, M. A. (Ed.). (1997). *Recovered memories and false memories.* Oxford, England: Oxford University Press.

Coons, P. M., Bowman, E. S., & Milstein, V. (1988). Multiple personality disorder: A clinical investigation of 50 cases. *Journal of Nervous and Mental Disease, 176,* 519–527.

Coons, P. M., Bowman, E. S., & Milstein, V. (1997). Repressed memories in patients with dissociative disorder: Literature review, controlled study, and treatment recommendations. In L. J. Dickson, M. B. Riba, & J. M. Oldham (Series Eds.) & D. Spiegel (Vol. Ed.), *Section II of American Psychiatric Press review of psychiatry: Volume 16. Repressed memories* (pp. II-153–172). Washington, DC: American Psychiatric Press.

Coons, P. M., & Milstein, V. (1986). Psychosexual disturbances in multiple personality: Characteristics, etiology, and treatment. *Journal of Clinical Psychiatry, 47,* 106–110.

Cormier, J. F., & Thelan, M. H. (1998). Professional skepticism of multiple personality disorder. *Professional Psychology: Research and Practice, 29*(2), 163–167.

Cornell, W. F., & Olio, K. A. (1991). Integrating affect in treatment with adult survivors of physical and sexual abuse. *American Journal of Orthopsychiatry, 61,* 59–69.

Corwin, D. L., & Olafson, E. (1997). Videotaped discovery of a reportedly unrecallable memory of child sexual abuse: Comparison with a childhood interview videotaped 11 years before. *Child Maltreatment, 29*(2), 91–112.

Courtois, C. A. (1979). Characteristics of a volunteer sample of adult women who experienced incest in childhood and adolescence. *Dissertation Abstracts International, 40A,* Nov–Dec. 1979, 3194–A.

Courtois, C. A. (1988). *Healing the incest wound: Adult survivors in therapy.* New York: W. W. Norton & Company.

Courtois, C. A. (1991). Theory, sequencing, and strategy in treating adult survivors. In J. Briere (Ed.), *Treating victims of child sexual abuse.* San Francisco: Jossey-Bass.

Courtois, C. A. (1992). The memory retrieval process in incest survivor therapy. *Journal of Child Sexual Abuse, 1*(1), 15–31.

Courtois, C. A. (1993). *Adult survivors of child sexual abuse: A workshop model.* Milwaukee, WI: Family Services International.

Courtois, C. A. (1994). Treatment of incest and complex dissociative traumatic stress reactions. In L.Vandecreek, S. Knapp, & T. L. Jackson (Eds.), *Innovations in clinical practice: Volume 13. A source book* (pp. 37–54). Sarasota, FL: Professional Resource Press.

Courtois, C. A. (1995a). Assessment and diagnosis. In C. Classen (Vol. Ed.) & I. D. Yalom (Series Ed.)., *Treating women molested in childhood: A volume in the Jossey-Bass library of current clinical technique* (pp. 1–34). San Francisco: Jossey-Bass.

Courtois, C. A. (1995b). Foreword in J. L. Alpert (Ed.), *Sexual abuse recalled: Treating trauma in the era of the recovered memory debate* (pp. vii–xiv). Northvale, NJ: Jason Aronson, Inc.

Courtois, C. A. (1995c). Scientist-practitioners and the delayed memory controversy: Scientific standards and the need for collaboration. *The Counseling Psychologist, 23,* 290–293.

Courtois, C. A. (1996). Informed clinical practice and the delayed memory controversy. In K. Pezdek & W. P. Banks (Eds.), *The recovered memory/false memory debate* (pp. 355–370). New York: Academic Press.

Courtois, C. A. (1997a). Delayed memories of trauma: Theoretical perspectives and clinical guidelines. In M. Conway (Ed.), *False and recovered memories* (pp. 206–229). Oxford, England: Oxford University Press.

Courtois, C. A. (1997b). Guidelines for the treatment of adults abused or possibly abused as children. *American Journal of Psychotherapy, 51,* 497–510.

Courtois, C. A. (1997c). Healing the incest wound: A treatment update with attention to delayed memory issues. *American Journal of Psychotherapy, 51,* 464–496.

Courtois, C. A. (1997d). Informed clinical practice and the standard of care: Proposed guidelines for the treatment of adults who report delayed memories of childhood trauma (pp. 337–361). In J. D. Read & D. S. Lindsay (Eds.), *Recollections of trauma: Scientific evidence and clinical practice* (pp. 337–370). New York: Plenum Press.

Courtois, C. A., & Watts, D. L. (1982). Counseling adult women who experienced incest in childhood or adolescence. *Personnel and Guidance Journal, 60,* 275–279.

Crews, F. (1993, November 18). The unknown Freud. *The New York Review of Books,* 55–66.

Crews, F. (1994, November 17–December 1). The revenge of the repressed. *The New York Review of Books,* Part I: 54–60; Part 2: 49–58.

Crews, F. (1995). The memory wars: Freud's legacy in dispute. *The New York Review of Books.*

Dalenberg, C. J. (1996). Accuracy, timing and circumstances of disclosure in therapy of recovered and continuous memories of abuse. In A. W. Scheflin & D. Brown (Eds.), *Psychiatry and the Law, 24*(2), 229–276.

Dalenberg, C. J. (1997). The prediction of accurate recollections of trauma. In J. D. Read & D. S. Lindsay (Eds.), *Recollections of trauma: Scientific evidence and clinical practice* (pp. 449–454). New York: Plenum Press.

Dalenberg, C. J. (in press). Ethical issues in the assessment and treatment of child abuse victims. In S. Bucky (Ed.), *The comprehensive textbook of ethics and law in the practice of psychology.* New York: Plenum Press.

Dalenberg, C. J., & Carlson, E. (in press). Ethical issues in the treatment of recovered memory trauma victims with false memory of trauma. In Bucky, S. (Ed.), *The comprehensive textbook of ethics and law in the practice of psychology.* New York: Plenum Press.

Dammeyer, M. D., Nightingale, N. N., & McCoy, M. L. (1997). Repressed memory and other controversial origins of sexual abuse allegations: Beliefs among psychologists and clinical social workers. *Child Maltreatment, 2*(3), 252–263.

Danieli, Y. (1984). Psychotherapists' participation in the conspiracy of silence about the Holocaust. *Psychoanalytic Review, 1,* 23–42.

Daniliuk, J. C., & Haverkamp, B. E. (1993). Ethical issues in counseling adult survivors of incest. *Journal of Counseling & Development, 72,* 16–22.

Davies, J. M. (1997). Dissociation, repression, and reality testing in the countertransference. In R. B. Gartner (Ed.), *Memories of sexual betrayal: Truth, fantasy, repression and dissociation* (pp. 45–76). Northvale, NJ: Jason Aronson Inc.

Davies, J., & Frawley, M. G. (1994). *Treating the adult survivor of childhood sexual abuse: A psychoanalytic perspective.* New York: Basic Books.

Davis, L. (1991). *Allies in healing: When the person you love was sexually abused as a child.* New York: Harper Perennial.

Davis, S. L. (1998). Social and scientific influences on the study of children's suggestibility: A historical perspective. *Child Maltreatment, 3*(2), 186–194.

Dawes, R. M. (1994). *House of cards: Psychology and psychotherapy built on myth.* Toronto: Maxwell Macmillan.

Dawes, R. M. (1995). Standards of practice. In Hayes, S. C., Follette, V. M., Dawes, R. M., & Grady, K. E. *Scientific standards of psychological practice: Issues and recommendations*. Reno, NV: Context Press.

Dell, P. F. (1988). Professional skepticism about multiple personality. *The Journal of Nervous and Mental Disease, 176*(9), 528–531.

Demaré, D. (1993). *The Childhood Maltreatment Questionnaire*. Unpublished manuscript, University of Manitoba, Winnipeg, Canada.

De Zulueta, F. (1994). *The traumatic roots of destructiveness: From pain to violence*. New York: Jason Aronson Inc.

Dobson, R. (1998, April 5). Abused lose out over false memory scares. *The Independent*, p. 2.

Dolan, Y. M. (1991). *Resolving sexual abuse: Solution-focused therapy and Ericksonian hypnosis for adult survivors*. New York: W. W. Norton & Company.

Donaldson, M. A., & Cordes-Green, S. (1995). *Group treatment of adult incest survivors*. Thousand Oaks, CA: Sage.

Donaldson, M. A., & Gardner, R. (1985). Diagnosis and treatment of traumatic stress among women after childhood incest. In C. Figley (Ed.), *Trauma and its wake: The study and treatment of post-traumatic stress disorder.* (pp. 356–377). New York: Brunner/Mazel.

Draucker, C. (1992). *Counseling survivors of childhood sexual abuse*. Newbury Park, CA: Sage.

Duggal, S., & Sroufe, A. (1998). Recovered memory of childhood sexual trauma: A documented case from a longitudinal study. *Journal of Traumatic Stress, 11*(2), 301–321.

Dutton, M. A. (1998, May–June). Trauma assessments. *Centering. Newsletter of The CENTER: Post-traumatic & Dissociative Disorders Program, 3*, 1–4.

Elin, M. R. (1997). An integrative developmental model for trauma and memory (pp. 188–224). In P. S. Appelbaum, L. A. Uyehara, & M. R. Elin (Eds.), *Trauma and memory: Clinical and legal controversies*. New York: Oxford University Press.

Ellason, J. W., & Ross, C. A. (1995). Positive and negative symptoms in dissociative identity disorder and schizophrenia: A comparative analysis. *Journal of Nervous and Mental Disease, 183*, 236–241.

Ellenberger, H. F. (1970). *The discovery of the unconscious: The history and evolution of dynamic psychiatry*. New York: Basic Books.

Ellenson, G. S. (1986). Disturbances of perception in adult female incest survivors. *Social Casework, 67*, 149–159.

Elliott, D. M. (1992). *Traumatic Events Survey*. Unpublished psychological test. Los Angeles: Harbor-UCLA Medical Center.

Elliott, D. M. (1997). Traumatic events: Prevalence and delayed recall in the general population. *Journal of Counseling and Clinical Psychology, 65*(5), 811–820.

Elliott, D. M., & Briere, J. (1992). Sexual abuse trauma among professional women: Validating the Trauma Symptom Checklist-40 (TSC-40). *Child Abuse and Neglect, 16*, 391–398.

Elliott, D. M., & Briere, J. (1995a). Posttraumatic stress associated with delayed recall of sexual abuse: A general population study. *Journal of Traumatic Stress, 8*, 629–648.

Elliott, D. M., & Briere, J. (1995b). Transference and countertransference. In C. Classen (Vol. Ed.) & I. D. Yalom (Series Ed.)., *Treating women molested in childhood: A volume in the Jossey-Bass library of current clinical technique* (pp.187–226). San Francisco: Jossey-Bass.

Engel, B. (1989). *The right to innocence: Healing the trauma of childhood sexual abuse*. Los Angeles: Jeremy P. Tarcher, Inc.

Enns, C. Z. (1996). The feminist institute code of ethics: Implications for working with survivors of child sexual abuse. In S. Contratto & M. J. Gutfreund (Eds.), *A feminist clinician's guide to the memory debate* (pp. 79–92). New York: Haworth Press.

Enns, C. Z., Campbell, J., Courtois, C. A., Gottlieb, M. C., Lese, K. P., Gilbert, M. S., & Forrest, L. (1998). Clients who experienced childhood abuse: Recommendations for assessment and practice. *Professional Psychology, 29*(3), 245–256.

Enns, C. Z., McNeilly, C. L., Corkery, J. M., & Gilbert, M. S. (1995). The debate about delayed memories of child sexual abuse: A feminist perspective. *The Counseling Psychologist, 23*, 181–279.

Eth, S., & Pynoos, R. (Eds.). (1985). *Post-traumatic stress disorder in children.* American Psychiatric Press, Washington, DC.

Evans, K., & Sullivan, J. M. (1995). *Treating addicted survivors of trauma.* New York: The Guilford Press.

Everly, G. S. (1995). An integrative two-factor model of post-traumatic stress. In G. S. Everly & J. M. Lating (Eds.), *Psychotraumotology: Key papers and core concepts in post-traumatic stress* (pp. 27–48). New York: Plenum Press.

Everly, G. S., & Lating, J. M. (Eds.). (1995). *Psychotraumatology: Key papers and core concepts in post-traumatic stress.* New York: Plenum Press.

Ewing. C. P. (1994, July). Judicial Notebook. *APA Monitor.*

False Memory Syndrome Foundation Newsletter. (1998, May). Philadelphia, PA.

Femina, D., Yeager, C. A., & Lewis, D. O. (1990). Child abuse: Adolescent records vs. adult recall. *Child abuse & Neglect, 14,* 227–231.

Ferenczi, S. (1988). *The clinical diary of Sandor Ferenczi* (J. Dupont, Ed., M. Balint & N. Z. Jackson, Trans.). Cambridge, MA: Harvard University Press. (Original work published 1932).

Fiering, C., Taska, L., & Lewis, M. (1998). The role of shame and attribution style in children's and adolescents' adaptation to sexual abuse. *Child Maltreatment, 3*(2), 129–142.

Figley, C. R. (Ed.). (1985). *Trauma and its wake: The study and treatment of post-traumatic stress disorder.* New York: Brunner/Mazel.

Figley, C. R. (Ed.). (1986). *Trauma and its wake (Volume II): The study and treatment of post-traumatic stress disorder.* New York: Brunner/Mazel.

Figley, C. R. (Ed.). (1995). *Compassion fatigue: Coping with secondary traumatic stress disorder in those who treat the traumatized.* New York: Brunner/Mazel.

Fink, L. A., Bernstein, D., Handelsman, L., Foote, J., & Lovejoy, M. (1995). Initial reliability and validity of the Childhood Trauma Interview: A new multidimensional measure of childhood interpersonal trauma. *American Journal of Psychiatry, 152,* 1329–1335.

Finkelhor, D. (1979). *Sexually victimized children.* New York: Free Press.

Finkelhor, D. (1990). Early and long-term effects of child sexual abuse: An update. *Professional Psychology: Research and Practice, 21* (5), 325–330.

Finkelhor, D. (1994). Current information on the scope and nature of child sexual abuse. *The Future of Children, 4*(2), 31–53.

Finkelhor, D. & Browne, A. (1985). The traumatic impact of child sexual abuse: A conceptualization. *Journal of Orthopsychiatry, 55,* 530–541.

Fish, V. (1998). The delayed memory controversy in an epidemiological framework. *Child Maltreatment, 3*(3), 204–223.

Fitzpatrick, F. L. (1997, March 21). *Synopsis of presentation for March 21, 1997.* Presented at Harvard Medical School Department of Continuing Education and Massachusetts Mental Health Center, Psychological Trauma Conference, Boston, MA.

Fivush, R. (1991). The social construction of personal narratives. *Merrill-Palmer Quarterly, 37,* 59–82.

Fivush, R. (1996). Young children's event recall: Are memories constructed through discourse? In K. Pezdek & W. P. Banks (Eds.), *The recovered memory/false memory debate* (pp. 151–168). New York: Academic Press.

Fivush, R., & Hammond, N. (1990). Autobiographical memory across the preschool years: Toward reconceptualizing childhood amnesia. In R. Fivush & J. A. Hudson (Eds.), *Knowing and remembering in young children* (pp. 223–248). Cambridge, England: Cambridge University Press.

Flannery, R. B. (1992). *Post-traumatic stress disorder: The victim's guide to healing and recovery.* New York: Crossroad.

Foa, E. B., Rothbaum, B. O., & Molnar, C. (1995). Cognitive-behavioral treatment of post-traumatic stress disorder. In M. J. Friedman, D.S. Charney, & A. Y. Deutch (Eds.), *Neurobiological and clinical consequences of stress: From normal adaptation to post-traumatic stress disorder* (pp. 483–494). New York: Raven Press.

Foa, E. B., Rothbaum, B. O., Riggs, D. S., & Murdock, T. B. (1991). Treatment of posttraumatic stress disorder in rape victims: A comparison between cognitive-behavioral procedures and counseling. *Journal of Counseling and Clinical Psychology, 59, 715–723.*

Follette, V. M., & Naugle, A. E. (1995). Discussion of Beutler and Davison: Psychology's failure to educate. In S. C. Hayes, V. M. Follette, R. M. Dawes, & K. E. Grady, (Eds.), (1995). *Scientific standards of practice: Issues and recommendations.* Reno, NV: Context Press.

Forensic corner: Record keeping in cases of suspected sexual abuse. (1998, Spring). *NJ Advisor: The American Professional Society on the Abuse of Children-New Jersey Newsletter, 3*(1), 5.

Forward, S., & Buck, C. (1978). *Betrayal of innocence: Incest and its devastation.* Los Angeles: J. P. Tarcher.

Fox, R. E. (1995). The rape of psychotherapy. *Professional Psychology: Research and Practice, 26*(2), 147–155.

Foy, D. W. (Ed.). (1992). *Treating PTSD: Cognitive-behavioral strategies.* New York: The Guilford Press.

Foy, D. W., Sipprelle, R. C., Rueger, D. B., & Carroll, E. M. (1984). Etiology of posttraumatic stress disorder in Vietnam veterans: Analysis of premilitary, military, and combat exposure influences. *Journal of Consulting and Clinical Psychology, 52, 79–87.*

Frankel, F. (1993). Adult reconstruction of childhood events in the multiple personality literature. *American Journal of Psychiatry, 150, 954–958.*

Fraser, S. (1987). *My father's house: A memoir of incest and of healing.* New York: Ticknor & Fields.

Frederickson, R. (1992). *Repressed memories: A journey to recovery from sexual abuse.* New York: Simon & Schuster.

Freud, S. (1959). The aetiology of hysteria. In J. Riviere (Trans.), *Sigmund Freud: Collected papers* (Vol. 1, pp. 183–219). New York: Basic. (Original work published 1896).

Freyd, J. J. (1993, August). Theoretical and personal perspectives on the delayed memory debate. Paper presented at the Center for Mental Health at Foote Hospital's continuing education conference: *Controversies Around Recovered Memories,* Ann Arbor, MI.

Freyd, J. J. (1994). Betrayal trauma: Traumatic amnesia as an adaptive response to childhood abuse. *Ethics and Behavior, 4, 307–329.*

Freyd, J. J. (1996). *Betrayal trauma: The logic of forgetting childhood abuse.* Cambridge, MA: Harvard University Press.

Freyd, P. (1991). How could this happen? Coping with a false accusation of incest and rape. *Issues in Child Abuse Accusations, 3, 154–165.*

Freyd, W. (1995, April 17). [Letter to WGBH-TV in Boston, MA].

Friedman, M. J. (1994). Biological and pharmacological aspects of the treatment of PTSD. In M. B. Williams & J. F. Sommer (Eds.), *Handbook of post-traumatic therapy* (pp. 495–509). Westport, CT: Greenwood Press.

Friedman, M. J. (1995). Biological approaches to the diagnosis and treatment of PTSD. In G. S. Everly & J. M. Lating (Eds.), *Psychotraumotology: Key papers and core concepts in post-traumatic stress* (pp.171–194). New York: Plenum Press.

Friedman, M. J., Charney, D. S., & Deutch, A. Y. (Eds.). (1995). *Neurobiological and clinical consequences of stress: From normal adaptation to PTSD*. Philadelphia: Lippincott-Raven.

Friedrich, W. N., Talley, N. J., Panser, L., Fett, S., & Zinsmeister, A. R. (1997). Concordance reports of childhood abuse by adults. *Childhood Maltreatment, 2*(2), 164–171.

Gabbard, G., & Wilkinson, S. (1994). *Management of countertransference with borderline patients*. Washington, DC: American Psychiatric Press, Inc.

Galatzer-Levy, R. M. (1997). Psychoanalysis, memory, and trauma. In P. S. Appelbaum, L. A. Uyehara, & M. R. Elin (Eds.), *Trauma and memory: Clinical and legal controversies* (pp. 138–157). New York: Oxford University Press.

Ganaway, G. K., (1989). Historical truth versus narrative truth: Clarifying the role of exogenous trauma in the etiology of MPD and its variants. *Dissociation, 2*, 205–220.

Gardner, M. (1993). Notes of a fringe-watcher. *Skeptical Inquirer, 17*, 270–275.

Gardner, R. A. (1991). *Sex abuse hysteria: Salem witch rituals revisited*. Cresskill, NJ: Creative Therapeutics.

Gardner, R. A. (1992). *True and false accusations of child abuse*. Cresskill, NJ: Creative Therapeutics.

Garfield, S. L. (1996). Some problems associated with "validated" forms of psychotherapy. *Clinical Psychology: Science and Practice, 3*, 218–229.

Gartner, R. B. (1997a). The controversy in context. In R. B. Gartner (Ed.), *Memories of sexual betrayal: Truth, fantasy, repression and dissociation* (pp. 13–28). Northvale, NJ: Jason Aronson Inc.

Gartner, R. B. (Ed.). (1997b). *Memories of sexual betrayal: Truth, fantasy, repression and dissociation*. Northvale, NJ: Jason Aronson Inc.

Geffner, R. (1998). Editor's note. *Journal of Child Sexual Abuse, 7*(1), 81–82.

Geiselman, R. E., Fisher, R. P., MacKinnon, D. P., & Holland, H. L. (1993). Eyewitness memory enhancement in the police interview: Cognitive retrieval mnemonics versus hypnosis. *Journal of Applied Psychology, 70*, 401–412.

Gelinas, D. J. (1983). The persistent negative effects of incest. *Psychiatry, 46*, 313–332.

Genova, P. (1993). A transference hazard in the therapy of the sexually abused. *Psychiatric Times, 10*(11).

Giannelli, P. C. (1995). The admissibility of hypnotic evidence in U.S. courts. *The International Journal of Clinical and Experimental Hypnosis, 43*(2), 212–233.

Gil, E. (1988). Treatment of adult survivors of childhood abuse. Walnut Creek: Launch Press.

Giller, E. (Ed.). (1990). *Biological assessment and treatment of posttraumatic stress disorder*. Washington, DC: American Psychiatric Press, Inc.

Gold, S. N., & Brown, L. S. (1997). Therapeutic responses to delayed recall: Beyond recovered memory. *Psychotherapy, 34*(2), 182–191.

Gold, S. N., Hughes, D., & Hohnecker, L. (1994). Degrees of repression of sexual abuse memories. *American Psychologist, 49*, 440–441.

Golding, J. M., Sanchez, R. P., & Sego, S. A. (1996). Do you believe in repressed memories? *Professional Psychology: Research and Practice, 27*, 429–437.

Goldstein, E., & Farmer, K. (Eds.). (1993). *True stories of false memories*. Boca Raton, FL: SIRS Publishing.

Golier, J. A., Yehuda, R., & Southwick, S. M. (1996). Memory and posttraumatic stress disorder. In P. S. Appelbaum, L. A. Uyehara, & M. R. Elin (Eds.), *Trauma and memory: Clinical and legal controversies* (pp. 225–242). New York: Oxford University Press.

Goodman, G. S., & Bottoms, B. L. (Eds.). (1993). *Child victims, Child witnesses: Understanding and improving testimony.* New York: The Guilford Press.

Goodman, G. S., Bottoms, B. L., Qin, J., & Shaver, P. R. (1993, December). *Repressed memories and allegations of ritual and religion-related child abuse.* Paper presented at Clark Conference on Memories for Trauma, Worcester, MA.

Goodman, G. S., Quas, J. A., Batterman-Faunce, J. M., Riddlesberger, M. M., & Kuhn, J. (1996). Predictors of accurate and inaccurate memories of traumatic events experienced in childhood. In K. Pezdek & W. P. Banks (Eds.), *The recovered memory/false memory debate* (pp. 3–18). New York: Academic Press.

Goodman, G. S., Rudy, L., Bottoms, B., & Aman, C. (1990). Children's concerns and memory: Issues of ecological validity in the study of children's eyewitness testimony. In R. Fivush & J. A. Hudson (Eds.), *Knowing and remembering in young children* (pp. 249–284). Cambridge, England: Cambridge University Press.

Gordon, M., & Alexander, P. C. (1993). Introduction. *Journal of Interpersonal Violence, 8*(3), 307–311.

Grand, S. (1995). Incest and the intersubjective politics of knowing history. In J. L. Alpert (Ed.), *Sexual abuse recalled: Treating trauma in the era of the recovered memory debate* (pp.235–256). Northvale, NJ: Jason Aronson Inc.

Grassian, S., & Holtzen, D. (1996). Sexual abuse by a parish priest: I. Memory of the abuse.

Gravitz, M. A. (1994). Memory reconstruction by hypnosis as a therapeutic technique. *Psychotherapy, 31*(4), 687–691.

Green, A. H. (1983). Dimensions of psychological trauma in abused children. *Journal of the American Academy of Child Psychiatry, 17,* 92–103.

Green, B. L. (1993). Identifying survivors at risk: Trauma and stressors across events. In J. Wilson & B. Raphael (Eds.), *International handbook of traumatic stress syndromes* (pp. 135–144). New York: Plenum Press.

Green, B. L. (1996). Psychometric review of Trauma History Questionnaire (Self-Report). In B. H. Stamm (Ed.), *Measurement of stress, trauma, and adaptation* (pp. 366–369). Lutherville, MD: Sidran Press.

Greenberg, S. A., & Shuman, D. W. (1997). Irreconcilable conflict between therapeutic and forensic roles. *Professional Psychology: Research and Practice, 28,* 50–57.

Gregory, T. (1997, November 10). $10 million award in psychiatry suit new blot on therapy. *The Chicago Tribune.*

Griffin, M. G., Nishith, P., Resick, P. A., & Yehuda, R. (1997). Integrating objective indicators of treatment outcome in posttraumatic stress disorder. In R. Yehuda & A. C. McFarlane (Eds.), *Annals of the New York Academy of Sciences, 821* (pp. 388–409). New York: New York Academy of Sciences.

Grinfeld, M. J. (1995, October). Psychiatrist stung by huge damage award in repressed memory case. *Psychiatric Times, 12*(10), pp. 1, 22.

Grinfeld, M. J. (1997, December). Criminal charges filed in recovered memory case: Psychiatrists liable for millions in civil suits. *Psychiatric Times, 14*(12), pp. 1,3,5.

Grunberg, F., & Ney, T. (1997). Professional guidelines on clinical practice for recovered memory: A comparative analysis. In J. D. Read & D. S. Lindsay (Eds.), *Recollections of trauma: Scientific evidence and clinical practice* (pp. 541–556). New York: Plenum Press.

Gudjonsson, G. H. (1984). A new scale of interrogative suggestibility. *Personality and Individual Differences, 5,* 303–314.

Gudjonsson, G. H. (1992). *The psychology of interrogations, confessions, and testimony.* Chichester, England: John Wiley & Sons.

Gutheil, T. G. (1995). Taking issue. *Psychiatric Services, 46*(6), 537.

Gutheil, T. G., & Simon, R. I. (1997). Clinically based risk management principles for recovered memory cases. *Psychiatric Services, 48*(11), 1403–1407.

Haaken, J. (1994). *The recovered memory debate as psychodrama: A psychoanalytic feminist perspective.* Unpubished manuscript.

Haaken, J., & Schlaps, A. (1991). Incest resolution therapy and the objectification of sexual abuse. *Psychotherapy, 28,* 3947.

Hammond, D. C. (Ed.). (1990). *Handbook of hypnotic suggestions and metaphors.* Des Plains, IL: American Society of Clinical Hypnosis Press.

Hammond, D. C. (1995, August/September). Clinical hypnosis and memory: Guidelines for clinicians. *The International Society for the Study of Dissociation News, 13,* 1,9.

Hammond, D. C., Garver, R. B., Mutter, C. B., Crasilneck, H. B., Frischolz, E., Gravitz, M. A., Hibler, N. S., Olson, J., Scheflin, A., Spiegel, H., & Wester, W. (1994). *Clinical hypnosis and memory: Guidelines for clinicians and for forensic hypnosis.* Des Plaines, IL: American Society for Clinical Hypnosis Press.

Harber, K. D., & Pennebaker, J. W. (1992). Overcoming traumatic memories. In S. Christianson (Ed.), *The handbook of emotion and memory: Research and theory* (pp. 359–387). Hillsdale, NJ: Erlbaum.

Harris, M. (1998). *Trauma recovery and empowerment: A clinician's guide for working with women in groups.* New York: The Free Press.

Harvey, M. R. (1994, March). Principles of practice with remembering adults. In *The nature of traumatic memory: A symposium concerning recovered memory of childhood abuse,* Cambridge, MA.

Harvey, M. R. (1996). An ecological view of psychological trauma and trauma recovery. *Journal of Traumatic Stress, 9,* 3–23.

Harvey, M. R., & Herman, J. L. (1994). Amnesia, partial amnesia, and delayed recall among adult survivors of childhood trauma. *Consciousness and Cognition, 3,* 295–306.

Harvey, M. R., & Herman, J. L. (1996). Amnesia, partial amnesia, and delayed recall among adult survivors of childhod trauma. In K. Pezdek & W. P. Banks (Eds.), *The recovered memory/false memory debate* (pp. 29–40). New York: Academic Press.

Harvey, M. R., & Herman, J. L. (1997). Continuous memory, amnesia, and delayed recall of childhood trauma: A clinical typology. In P. S. Appelbaum, L. A. Uyehara, & M. R. Elin (Eds.), *Trauma and memory: Clinical and legal controversies* (pp. 261–271). New York: Oxford University Press.

Haugaard, J. J. (1996). *A guide for including information on child abuse and neglect in the undergraduate curriculum* [Brochure]. Washington, DC: American Psychological Association.

Hauser-Hines, S. (1997). A retrospective tale of psychotherapy: An incest dream. *Psychotherapy, 32*(1), 33–37.

Hayes, S. C. (1995). What do we want from standards of psychological practice? In Hayes, S. C., Follette, V. M., Dawes, R. M., & Grady, K. E. *Scientific standards of practice: Issues and recommendations* (pp. 49–66). Reno, NV: Context Press.

Hayes, S. C., Follette, V. M., Dawes, R. M., & Grady, K. E. (Eds.). (1995). *Scientific standards of practice: Issues and recommendations.* Reno, NV: Context Press.

Hedges, L. E., Hilton, R., Hilton, V. W., & Caudill, O. B. (1997). *Therapists at risk: Perils of the intimacy of the therapeutic relationship.* Northvale, NJ: Jason Aronson Inc.

Hegeman, E. (1995). Transferential issues in the psychoanalytic treatment of incest survivors. In J. L. Alpert (Ed.), *Sexual abuse recalled: Treating trauma in the era of the recovered memory debate* (pp.185–214). Northvale, NJ: Jason Aronson Inc.

Herman, J. L. (1981). *Father-daughter incest.* Cambridge, MA: Harvard University Press.

Herman, J. L. (1992a). Complex PTSD: A syndrome in survivors of prolonged and repeated trauma. *Journal of Traumatic Stress, 3,* 377–391.

Herman, J. L. (1992b). *Trauma and recovery: The aftermath of violence-from domestic to political terror.* New York: Basic Books.

Herman, J. L. (1994). Presuming to know the truth. *Nieman Reports, 48,* 43–45.

Herman, J. L. & Harvey, M. R. (1997). Adult memories of childhood trauma: A naturalistic study. *Journal of Traumatic Stress, 10*(4), 557–571.

Herman, J. L., & Hirschman, L. (1977). *Father-daughter incest. Signs: Journal of Women in Culture and Society, 2,* 735–756.

Herman, J. L., Perry, J. C., & van der Kolk, B. A. (1989). Childhood trauma in borderline personality disorder. *American Journal of Psychiatry, 146,* 490–495.

Herman, J. L. & Schatzow, E. (1987). Recovery and verification of memories of childhood sexual trauma. *Psychoanalytic Psychology, 4,* 1–14.

Herman, J. L., & van der Kolk, B. (1987). Traumatic antecedents of borderline personality disorder. In B. van der Kolk (Ed.), *Psychological Trauma.* Washington, DC: American Psychiatric Press, Inc.

Hewitt, S. A. (1994). Preverbal sexual abuse: What two children report in later years. *Child Abuse & Neglect, 18*(10), 821–826.

Hilgard, E. R. (1986). *Divided consciousness: Multiple controls in human thought and action.* New York: Wiley.

Hill, C., & Alexander, P. (1993). Process research in the treatment of adult victims of childhood sexual abuse. *Journal of Interpersonal Violence, 8,* 415–427.

Hilton, V. W. (1997). The therapist's response to accusation: How to avoid complaints and suits. In L. E. Hedges, R. Hilton, V. W. Hilton, & O. B. Caudill, *Therapists at risk: Perils of the intimacy of the therapeutic relationship* (pp. 99–108). Northvale, NJ: Jason Aronson Inc.

Hinnefeld, B., & Newman, R. (1997). Analysis of the Truth and Responsibility in Mental Health Practices Act and similar proposals. *Professional Psychology: Research and Practice, 28*(6), 537–543.

Holmes, D. S. (1990). The evidence for repression: An examination of sixty years of research. In J. L. Singer (Ed.), *Repression and dissociation: Implications for personality theory, psychopathology, and health* (pp. 85–102). Chicago: University of Chicago Press.

Holmes, D. S. (1994, June). Is there evidence for repression? Doubtful. *Harvard Mental Health Letter, 10*(12), 4–6.

Horn, M. (1993). Memories lost and found. *U.S. News & World Report,* November 29.

Horowitz, M. J. (1976). *Stress response syndromes.* Northvale, NJ: Jason Aronson Inc.

Horowitz, M. J. (1986). *Stress response syndromes* (2nd Ed.). Northvale, NJ: Jason Aronson Inc.

Horton, J. M., Jr., (1993). Post-traumatic stress disorder and mild head trauma.: Follow-up of a case study. *Perceptual and Motor Skills, 76,* 243–246.

Hotelling, K. (1995, August). *Ethical issues in the recovery of sexual abuse memories.* Paper presented at the 103rd Annual Meeting of the American Psychological Association, New York City.

Howe, M. L., & Courage, M. L. (1993). On resolving the enigma of infantile amnesia. *Psychological Bulletin, 113,* 305–326.

Hyman, I. E., Husband, T. H., & Billings, F. J. (1995). False memories of childhood experiences. *Applied Cognitive Psychology, 9,* 181–197.

Hyman, I. E. & Loftus, E. F. (1997). Some people recover memories of childhood trauma that never really happened. In P. S. Appelbaum, L. A. Uyehara, & M. R. Elin (Eds.), *Trauma and memory: Clinical and legal controversies* (pp. 3–24). New York: Oxford University Press.

International Society for the Study of Dissociation. (1994). *Guidelines for treating dissociative identity disorder (multiple personality disorder) in adults* (1994). Skokie, IL: Author.

International Society for the Study of Dissociation. (1997). *Guidelines for treating dissociative identity disorder (multiple personality disorder) in adults* (1997). Glenview, IL: Author.

International Society for Traumatic Stress Studies. (1998). Childhood trauma remembered: A report on the current scientific knowledge base and its applications [Brochure]. Northbrook, IL: Author.

Jacobson, A., & Herald, C. (1990). The relevance of childhood sexual abuse to adult psychiatric inpatient care. *Hospital and Community Psychiatry, 41*(2), 154–158.

Jacobson, A., & Richardson, B. (1987). Assault experiences of 100 psychiatric inpatients: Evidence of the need for routine inquiry. *American Journal of Psychiatry, 144*(7), 908–912.

Janet, P. (1889). *L'automatisme psychologique*. Paris: Alcan.

Janet, P. (1907). *The major symptoms of hysteria*. New York: Macmillan.

Janet, P. (1977). *The mental state of hystericals* (C. R. Corson, Trans.; D. N. Robinson, Ed.). Washington, DC: University Publications of America.

Jeffery, J. (1997). Reflections on a false memory of childhood sexual abuse. In C. Prozan (Ed.), *Construction and reconstruction of memory: Dilemmas of childhood sexual abuse* (pp. 151–166). Northvale, NJ: Jason Aronson Inc.

Jehu, D. (1988). *Beyond sexual abuse: Therapy with women who were childhood victims*. New York: John Wiley & Sons.

Josephson, G. S., & Fong-Beyette, M. L. (1987). Factors assisting female clients' disclosure of incest during counseling. *Journal of Counseling and Development, 65*, 475–478.

Kaminer, W. (1993). *I'm dysfuntional, you're dysfunctional: The recovery movement and other self-help fashions*. New York: Vintage Books.

Kardiner, A. (1941). The traumatic neuroses of war [Monograph]. *Psychosomatic Medicine*, Washington, DC: National Research Council..

Keane, T. M., Fairbank, J. A., Caddell, J. M., Zimmering, R. T., Taylor, K. L., & Mora, C. A. (1989). Clinical evaluation of a measure to assess combat exposure. *Psychological Assessment: A Journal of Consulting and Clinical Psychology, 1*, 53–55.

Kempe, C. H., Silverman, F. N., Steele, B. F., Droegemueller, W., & Silver, H. K. (1962). The battered child syndrome. *Journal of the American Medical Association, 181*, 17–24.

Kendall-Tackett, K. A., Williams, L. M., & Finkelhor, D. (1993). Impact of sexual abuse on children: A review and synthesis of recent empirical studies. *Psychological Bulletin, 113*, 164–180.

Kepner, J. I. (1995). *Healing tasks: Psychotherapy with adult survivors of childhood abuse*. San Francisco: Jossey-Bass.

Kihlstrom, J. (1994). One hundred years of hysteria. In S. J. Lynn & J. W. Rhue (Eds.), *Dissociation: Clinical and theoretical perspectives* (pp. 365–394). New York: The Guilford Press.

Kingsbury, S. J. (1992). Strategic psychotherapy for trauma: Hypnosis and trauma in context. *Journal of Traumatic Stress, 5*(1), 85–95.

Kinsey, A. C., Pomeroy, W. B., Martin, C. E., & Gebhard, P. H. (1953). *Sexual behavior in the human female*. Philadelphia: Saunders.

Kirschner, S., Kirschner, D. A., & Rappaport, R. L. (1993). *Working with adult incest survivors: The healing journey*. New York: Brunner/Mazel.

Klein, R. M., & Doane, B. K. (1994). *Psychological concepts and dissociative disorders*. Hillsdale, NJ: Erlbaum

Kluft, R. P. (1984a). Aspects of treatment of multiple personality disorder. *Psychiatric Annals, 14*, 51–55.

Kluft, R. P. (1984b). Treatment of multiple personality disorder: A study of 33 cases. *Psychiatric Clinics of North America, 7*, 9–29.

Kluft, R. P. (Ed.) (1985). *Childhood antecedents of multiple personality.* Washington, DC: American Psychiatric Press, Inc.

Kluft, R. P. (1987). First-rank symptoms as a diagnostic clue to multiple personality disorder. *American Journal of Psychiatry, 144,* 293–298.

Kluft, R. P. (Ed.). (1990). *Incest-related syndromes of adult psychopathology.* Washington, DC: American Psychiatric Press, Inc.

Kluft, R. P. (1993). The initial stages of psychotherapy in the treatment of multiple personality disorder patients. *Dissociation, 6*(2/3), 145–161.

Kluft, R. P. (1994). Treatment trajectories in multiple personality disorder. *Dissociation, 7,* 63–76.

Kluft, R. P. (1995). The confirmation and disconfirmation of memories of abuse in DID patients: A naturalistic clinical study. *Dissociation, 8*(4), 253–258.

Kluft, R. P. (1996). Treating the traumatic memories of patients with dissociative identity disorder. *American Journal of Psychiatry, 153*(7), 103–110.

Kluft, R. P. (1997). The argument for the reality of delayed recall of trauma. In P. S. Appelbaum, L. A. Uyehara, & M. R. Elin (Eds.), *Trauma and memory: Clinical and legal controversies* (pp. 25–60). New York: Oxford University Press.

Kluft, R. P., & Fine, C. G. (Eds.). (1993). *Clinical perspectives on multiple personality disorder.* Washington, DC: American Psychiatric Press, Inc.

Knapp, S. J., & VandeCreek, L. (1996). Risk management fro psychologists: Treating patients who recover lost memories of childhood abuse. *Professional Psychology: Research and Practice, 27*(5), 452–459.

Knapp, S. J. & VandeCreek, L. (1997). *Treating patients with memories of abuse: Legal risk management.* Washington, DC: American Psychological Association Press.

Knight, C. (1997). Therapists' affective reactions to working with adult survivors of child sexual abuse: An exploratory study. *Journal of Child Sexual Abuse, 6*(2), 17–41.

Knight, J. (1997). Neuropsychological assessment in posttraumatic stress disorder. In J. P. Wilson & T. M. Keane (Eds.), *Assessing psychological trauma and PTSD* (pp.448–492). New York: Guilford.

Kolb, L. (1987). Neuropsychological hypothesis explaining posttraumatic stress disorder. *American Journal of Psychiatry, 144,* 989–995.

Koraleski, S. F., & Larson, L. M. (1997). A partial test of the transtheoretical model in therapy with adult survivors of childhood sexual abuse. *Journal of Counseling Psychology, 44*(3), 302–306.

Koss, M. P., & Gidycz, C. A. (1985). Sexual experience survey: Reliability and validity. *Journal of Consulting and Clinical Psychology, 53,* 422–423.

Koss, M. P., Tromp, S., & Tharan, M. (1995). Traumatic memories: Empirical foundations, forensic and clinical implications. *Clinical Psychology: Science and Practice, 2,* 111–132.

Koutstaal, W., & Schacter, D. L. (1997a). Inaccuracy and inaccessibility in memory retrieval: Contributions from cognitive psychology and neuropsychology. In P. S. Appelbaum, L. A. Uyehara, & M. R. Elin (Eds.), *Trauma and memory: Clinical and legal controversies* (pp.93–137). New York: Oxford University Press.

Koutstaal, W., & Schacter, D. L. (1997b). Intentional forgetting and voluntary thought suppression: Two potential methods for coping with childhood trauma. In L. J. Dickson, M. B. Riba, & J. M. Oldham (Series Eds.) & D. Spiegel (Vol. Ed.), *Section II of American Psychiatric Press review of psychiatry: Volume 16. Repressed memories* (pp. II-79–122). Washington, DC: American Psychiatric Press.

Kovacs, A. A. (1995). We have met the enemy and he is us! *The Independent Practitioner, 15,* 135–137.

Krinsley, K. E., Gallagher, J. G., Weathers, F. W., Kaloupek, D. G., & Vielhauer, M. (1997). *Reliability and validity of the Evaluation of Lifetime Stressors questionnaire.* Unpublished manuscript.

Kristiansen, C. M., Felton, K. A., Hovdestad, W. E., & Allard, C. B. (1995). *The Ottawa survivor's story: A summary of the findings.* Unpublished manuscript.

Kroll, J. (1993). *PTSD/borderlines in therapy: Finding the balance.* New York: W. W. Norton & Company.

Krystal, H. (1995). Trauma and aging: A thirty-year follow-up. In Caruth, C. (Ed.), *Trauma: Explorations in memory* (pp. 76–99). Baltimore, MD: The Johns Hopkins University Press.

Lating, J. M., & Everly, G. S. (1995). Psychological assessments of PTSD. In J. P. Wilson & T. M. Keane (Eds.), *Assessing psychological trauma and PTSD* (pp.103–128). New York: Guilford.

Lating, J. M., Zeichner, A., & Keane, T. (1995). Psychological assessments of PTSD. In G. S. Everly & J. M. Lating (Eds.), *Psychotraumotology: Key papers and core concepts in post-traumatic stress* (pp. 27–48). New York: Plenum Press.

Laub, D. (1995).Truth and testimony: The process and the struggle. In C. Caruth, (Ed.), *Trauma: Explorations in memory* (pp. 61–75). Baltimore, MD: The Johns Hopkins University Press.

Laub, D., & Auerhahn, N. C. (1993). Knowing and not knowing massive psychic trauma: Forms of traumatic memory. *International Journal of Psycho-Analysis, 74,* 287–301.

Laurence, C. (1997, November 7). Mother is awarded $10.6m in 'recovered memory' damages. *The London Telegraph.*

Lebowitz, L., Harvey, M. R., & Herman, J. L. (1993). A stage-by-dimension model of recovery from sexual trauma. *Journal of Interpersonal Violence, 8,* 378–391.

LeDoux, J. E. (1992). Emotion as memory: Anatomical systems underlying indelible neural traces. In S. Christianson (Ed.), *The handbook of emotion and memory: Research and theory* (pp. 269–288). Hillsdale, NJ: Erlbaum.

LeDoux, J. E. (1994). Emotion, memory, and the brain. *Scientific American, 270,* 50–57.

Leeds, A. M., & Korn, D. L. (1998, July). *Clinical applications of EMDR in the treatment of adult survivors of childhood abuse and neglect.* Paper presented at the annual meeting of the EMDR International Association, Baltimore, MD.

Leifer, M., Cairns, N. U., Connors, M. E., Lawrence, M. M., Gruenhut, P., Womack, A., Evans, H. L., & Downing, D. L. (1995). Illinois School of Professional Psychology predoctoral minor in sexual abuse. *Professional Psychology: Research and Practice, 26*(3), 252–256.

Levine, H. (1997). Psychoanalysis, reconstruction, and the recovery of memory. In P. S. Appelbaum, L. A. Uyehara, & M. R. Elin (Eds.), *Trauma and memory: Clinical and legal controversies* (pp. 293–315). New York: Oxford University Press.

Lief, H. I., & Fetkewicz, J. (1995). Retractors of false memories: The evolution of pseudo-memories. *Journal of Psychiatry and Law, 3,* 411–433.

Lindberg, F. H., & Distad, L. J. (1985). Post-traumatic stress disorders in women who experienced childhood incest. *Child Abuse and Neglect, 9,* 329–334.

Lindemann, E. (1944). Symptomatology and management of acute grief. *American Journal of Psychiatry, 101,* 141–148.

Lindsay, D. S. (1996). Contextualizing and clarifying criticisms of memory work in psychotherapy. In K. Pezdek & W. P. Banks (Eds.), *The recovered memory/false memory debate* (pp. 267–278). New York: Academic Press.

Lindsay, D. S. (1997). Increasing sensitivity. In J. D. Read & D. S. Lindsay (Eds.), *Recollections of trauma: Scientific evidence and clinical practice* (pp. 1–24). New York: Plenum Press.

Lindsay, D. S. (1998). Depolarizing views on recovered memory experiences. In S. J. Lynn & K. M. McConkey (Eds.), *Truth in memory.* New York: Guilford.

Lindsay, D. S., & Briere, J. (1997). The controversy regarding recovered memories of childhood sexual abuse: Pitfalls, bridges, and future directions. *Journal of Interpersonal Violence, 12*(5), 631–647.

Lindsay, D. S., & Read, J. D. (1994). Incest resolution psychotherapy and memories of childhood sexual abuse. *Applied Cognitive Psychology, 8,* 281–338.

Lindsay, D. S., & Read, J. D. (1995). "Memory work" and recovered memories of childhood sexual abuse: Scientific evidence and public, professional, and personal issues. *Psychology, Public Policy, and Law, 1*(4), 846–908.

Linehan, M. (1993). *Cognitive-behavioral treatment of borderline personality disorder.* New York: The Guilford Press.

Liotti, G. (1992). Disorganized/disoriented attachment in the etiology of the dissociative disorders. *Dissociation, 5*(4), 196–204.

Lipovsky, J. & Kilpatrick, D. (1992). The child sexual abuse victim as an adult. In W. O'Donahue & J. Geer (Eds.), *The Sexual Abuse of Children: Clinical Issues, 2,* 430–476.

Lister, E. D. (1982). Forced silence: A neglected dimension of trauma. *American Journal of Psychiatry, 139*(7), 872–876.

Littauer, F. (1990). *The promise of restoration: Breaking the bands of emotional bondage.* San Bernardino, CA: Here's Life Publishers.

Littauer, F., & Littauer, F. (1990). *Freeing your mind from memories that bind: How to heal hurts from the past.* San Bernadino, CA: Here's Life Publishers.

Litz, B. T., & Keane, T. M. (1989). Information processing in anxiety disorders: Application to the understanding of post-traumatic stress disorder. *Clinical Psychology Review, 9,* 243–257.

Loewenstein, R. J. (1991). Rational psychopharmacology in the treatment of multiple personality disorder. *The Psychiatric Clinics of North America, 14*(3), 721–740.

Loewenstein, R. J. (1993). Posttraumatic and dissociative aspects of transferences and countertransferencein the treatment of multiple personality disorder. In R. P. Kluft & C. G. Fine (Eds.), *Clinical perspectives on multiple personality disorder* (pp. 51–86). Washington, DC: American Psychiatric Press, Inc.

Loftus, E. F. (1992). Psi Chi/Frederick Howell Lewis Distinguished Lecture. Presented at the 100th Annual Meeting of the American Psychological Association, Washington, DC

Loftus, E. F. (1993). The reality of repressed memories. *American Psychologist, 48,* 518–537.

Loftus, E. F., & Coan, D. (1994). The construction of childhood memories. In D. Peters (Ed.), *The child witness in context: Cognitive, social and legal perspectives.* New York: Kluwer.

Loftus, E. F., Garry, M., & Feldman, J. (1994). Forgetting sexual trauma: What does it mean when 38% forget? *Journal of Consulting and Clinical Psychology, 62,* 1177–1181.

Loftus, E. F., & Ketcham, K. (1994). *The myth of repressed memory: False memories and allegations of sexual abuse.* New York: St. Martin's Press.

Loftus, E. F., & Pickrell, J. E. (1995). The formation of false memories. *Psychiatric Annals, 25,* 720–725.

Loftus, E. F., Polonsky, S., & Fullilove, M. T. (1994). Memories of childhood sexual abuse: Remembering and repressing. *Psychology of Women Quarterly, 18,* 67–84.

Loo, C. M. (1993). An integrative-sequential treatment model for posttraumatic stress disorder: A case of the Japanese American internment and redress. *Clinical Psychology Review, 13,* 89–117.

London, R. (1994). Therapeutic treatment of patients with repressed memories. *The Independent Practitioner,* 64–67.

Lundberg-Love, P. K., Marmion, S., Ford, K., Geffner, R., & Peacock, L. (1992). The long-term consequences of childhood incestuous victimization upon adult women's psychological symptomatology. *Journal of Child Sexual Abuse, 1,* 81–102.

Lynn, S. J., & McConkey, K. M. (1998). *Truth in memory.* New York: Guilford.

Lynn, S. J., & Rhue, J. (Eds.). (1994). *Dissociation: Clinical and theoretical perspectives.* New York: The Guilford Press.

Lynn, S. J., Myers, B., & Malinoski, P. (1996). Hypnosis, pseudomemories, and clinical guidelines: A sociocognitive perspective. In J. D. Read & D. S. Lindsay (Eds.), *Recollections of trauma: Scientific evidence and clinical practice* (pp. 305–336). New York: Plenum Press.

MacCarthy, B. (1988). Are incest victims hated? *Psychoanalytic Psychotherapy, 3* (2), 113–120.

Maltz, W. (1991). *The sexual healing journey: A guide for survivors of sexual abuse.* New York: HarperCollins.

Main, M. (1996). Introduction to the special section on attachment and psychopathology: 2. Overview of the field of attachment. *Journal of Consulting and Clinical Psychology, 64*(2), 237–243.

Marcus, B. F. (1989). Incest and the borderline syndrome: The mediating role of identity. *Psychoanalytic Psychology, 6,* 199–215.

Marmar, C. R., Foy, D., Kagan, B., & Pynoos, R. S. (1994). An integrated approach for treating posttraumatic stress. In R. Pynoos (Ed.), *Posttraumatic stress disorder: A clinical review* (pp. 99–132). Lutherville, MD: The Sidran Press.

Marmar, C. R., Weiss, D. S., Metzler, T. J., & Delucchi, K. (1996). Characteristics of emergency services personnel related to peritraumatic dissociation during critical incident exposure. *American Journal of Psychiatry, 153,* 94–102.

Marmar, C. R., Weiss, D. S., Schlenger, W. E., et al. (1994). Peritraumatic dissociation and post-traumatic stress in male Vietnam theater veterans. *American Journal of Psychiatry, 151,* 902–907.

Marshall, R. P. (1995). A general model for the treatment of post-traumatic stress disorder in war veterans. *Psychotherapy, 32,* 389–396.

Masson, J. M. (1984). *The assault on truth: Freud's suppression of the seduction theory.* New York: Farrar, Straus & Giroux.

Masters, C., & Dalenberg, C. (1996, June). *Symptom patterns of patients with recovered and continuous memories of child sexual abuse.* Poster session presented at the NATO Advanced Scientific Institute on Recollections of Trauma, Port de Bourgenay, France.

McCann, I. L., & Colletti, J. (1994). The dance of empathy: A hermeneutic formulation of countertransference, empathy, and understanding in the treatment of individuals who have experienced early childhood trauma. In J. Wilson & J. Lindy (Eds.), *Countertransference in the treatment of PTSD* (pp. 87–121). New York: Guilford.

McCann, I. L., & Pearlman, L. A. (1990a). *Psychological trauma and the adult survivor: Theory, therapy, and transformation.* New York: Brunner/Mazel.

McCann, I. L., & Pearlman, L. A. (1990b). Vicarious traumatization: A framework for understanding the psychological effects of working with victims. *Journal of Traumatic Stress, 3*(1), 131–149.

McCann, I. L., Pearlman, L. A., Sakheim, D. C., & Abrahamson, D. J. (1988). Trauma and victimization: A model of psychological adaptation. *The Counseling Psychologist, 16,* 531–594.

McConkey, K. M. (1997). Memory, repression, and abuse: Recovered memory and confident reporting of the personal past. In L. J. Dickson, M. B. Riba, & J. M. Oldham (Series Eds.) & D. Spiegel (Vol. Ed.), *Section II of American Psychiatric Press review of psychiatry: Volume 16. Repressed memories* (pp. II-55–78). Washington, DC: American Psychiatric Press.

McGaugh, J. L. (1989). Psychoneuroendicrinology of stress: A psychological perspective. In R. B. Brush & L. Levine (Eds.), *Psychoendocrinology* (pp. 305–339). New York: Academic Press.

McGaugh, J. (1992). Affect, neuromodulatory systems, and memory storage. In S. Christianson (Ed.), *The handbook of emotion and memory: Research and theory* (pp. 245–268). Hillsdale, NJ: Erlbaum.

McHugh, P. R. (1992, Autumn). Psychiatric misadventures. *The American Scholar, 61*, 497–510.

Mehren, E. (1993, December 7). Ex-priest gets 18 year term for sex abuse at five parishes. *Los Angeles Times* p. A-1 & A-31.

Meichenbaum, D. (1994). *A clinical handbook/practical therapist manual for assessing and treating adults with post-traumatic stress disorder (PTSD)*. Waterloo, Ontario, Canada: Institute Press.

Meiselman, K. C. (1978). *Incest: A psychological study of causes and effects with treatment recommendations*. San Francisco: Jossey-Bass.

Meiselman, K. C. (1990). *Resolving the trauma of incest: Reintegration therapy with survivors*. San Francisco: Jossey-Bass.

Melchert, T. P. (1996). Childhood memory and a history of different forms of abuse. *Professional Psychology: Research and Practice, 27*, 438–446.

Melchert, T. P., & Parker, R. L. (1997). Different forms of childhood abuse and memory. *Child Abuse and Neglect, 21*(2), 125–135.

Mellody, P. (with Miller, A. W., & Miller, J. K.). (1989). Facing codependence: What it is, where it comes from, how it sabotages our lives. San Francisco: Harper & Row.

Melton, G. B. (1994, Summer/Fall). Doing justice and doing good: Conflicts for mental health professionals. *The Future of Children, 4*, 102–118.

Merskey, H. (1993). The manufacture of personalities: the production of multiple personality disorder. *British Journal of Psychiatry, 160*, 327–340.

Merwin, M. R., & Smith-Kurtz, B. (1988). Healing of the whole person. In F. M. Ochberg (Ed.), *Post-traumatic therapy and victims of violence* (pp. 57–82). New York: Brunner/Mazel.

Metcalfe, J., & Jacobs, W. J. (Spring, 1996). A "hot-system/cool-system" view of memory under stress. *PTSD Research Quarterly*. White River Junction, VT: The National Center for PTSD.

Miller, A. (1981). *Prisoners of childhood: The drama of the gifted child and the search for the true self*. New York: Basic Books.

Miller, A. (1984). *Thou shalt not be aware: Society's betrayal of the child*. New York: Farrar, Straus, Giroux.

Mollica, R., Caspi-Yavin, Y., Bollini, P., Truong, T., Tor, S., & Lavelle, J. (1992). The Harvard Trauma Questionnaire: Validating a cross-cultural instrument for measuring torture, trauma, posttraumatic stress disorder in Indochinese refugees. *Journal of Nervous and Mental Disease, 180*, 111–116.

Mollica, R., Caspi-Yavin, Lavelle, J., Tor, S., Yang, T., Chan, S., Pham, T., Ryan, A., & de Marneffe, D. (1995). *Manual for the Harvard Trauma Questionnaire*. Brighton, MA: Indochinese Psychiatry Clinic.

Mulhern, S. (1994). Satanism, ritual abuse, and multiple personality disorder: A sociohistorical perspective. *International Journal of Clinical and Experimental Hypnosis, 42*, 265–288.

Mrazek, P. B., & Kempe, C. H. (Eds.). (1981). *Sexually abused children and their families*. New York: Pergamon.

Nagy, T. F. (1994, July/August). Repressed memories: Guidelines and directions. *The National Psychologist, 3*(4), 8–9.

Nash, M. R. (1994). Memory distortion and sexual trauma: The problem of false negatives and false positives. *International Journal of Clinical and Experimental Hypnosis, 42*(4), 346–362.

Nathan, P. (1998). Practice guidelines: Not yet ideal. *American Psychologist, 53*(3), 290–299.

National Association of Social Work National Council on the Practice of Clinical Social Work (1996). *Evaluation and treatment of adults with the possibility of recovered memories of childhood sexual abuse.* Washington, DC: Author.

National Institute of Mental Health, Division of Biometry and Applied Sciences, Antisocial and Violent Behavior Branch. (1990). *Research Workshop on Treatment of Adult Victims of Childhood Sexual Abuse,* Washington, DC.

Nelson, K. (1993). The psychological and social origins of autobiographical memory. *Psychological Science, 4,* 7–14.

Nemiah, J. C. (1985). Dissociative disorders. In H. I. Kaplan & B. J. Sadock (Eds.), *Comprehensive textbook of psychiatry* (4th ed.) (pp. 104–116). Baltimore, MD: Williams & Wilkins.

Neumann, D. S., Houskamp, B. M., Pollock, V. E., & Briere, J. (1996). The long-term sequelae of childhood sexual abuse in women: A meta-analytic review. *Child Maltreatment, 1,* 6–17.

New Zealand Psychological Society (1995). *Memory of traumatic childhood events.* New Zealand: Author.

Newman, E., Kaloupek, D. G., & Keane, T. M. (1996). Assessment of posttraumatic stress disorder in clinical and research settings. In B. A. van der Kolk, A. C. McFarlane, & L. Weisaeth (Eds.), *Traumatic stress: The effects of overwhelming experience on mind, body, and society* (pp. 242–278). New York: The Guilford Press.

Norris, F. (1992). Epidemiology of trauma: Frequency and impact of different potentially traumatic events on different demographic groups. *Journal of Consulting and Clinical Psychology, 60,* 409–418.

Norris, F., & Perilla, J. (1996). Reliability, validity, and cross-language stability of the Revised Civilian Mississippi Scale for PTSD. *Journal of Traumatic Stress, 9,* 285–298.

Norris, F. H., & Riad, J. K. (1997). Standardized self-report measures of civilian trauma and posttraumatic stress disorder. In J. P. Wilson & T. M. Keane (Eds.), *Assessing psychological trauma and PTSD* (pp.7–42). New York: Guilford.

Noyes, R., & Keltti, R. (1977). Depersonalization in response to life-threatening danger. *Comprehensive Psychiatry, 18,* 375–384.

Ochberg, F. M. (Ed.). (1988). *Post-traumatic therapy and victims of violence.* New York: Brunner/Mazel.

Ochberg, F. M. (1993). Posttraumatic therapy. In Wilson, J. P., & Raphael, B. (Eds.), *International handbook of traumatic stress syndromes* (pp. 773–784). New York: Plenum.

Ochberg, F. M. (1996). The counting method for ameliorating traumatic memories. *Journal of Traumatic Stress, 9*(4), 873–880.

Ofshe, R., & Singer, M. T. (1994). Recovered-memory therapy and robust repression: Influence of pseudomemories. *International Journal of Clinical and Experimental Hypnosis, 42,* 391–410.

Ofshe, R., & Watters, E. (March/April, 1993). Making monsters. *Society,* 4–16.

Ofshe, R., & Watters, E. (1994). *Making monsters: False memories, psychotherapy, and hysteria.* New York: Charles Scribner's Sons.

Ogata, S. N., Silk, K. R., Goodrich, S., Lofr, N. E., Westen, D., & Hill, E. M. (1990). Childhood sexual and physical abuse in adult patients with borderline personality disorder. *American Journal of Psychiatry, 147,* 1008–1013.

Olio, K. (1989). Memory retrieval in the treatment of adult survivors of sexual abuse. *Transactional Analysis Journal, 19*(2), 93–100.

Ornstein, P. (1995). Children's long-term retention of salient personal experiences. *Journal of Traumatic Stress, 8*(4), 581–606.

Ornstein, P., Ceci, S. J., & Loftus, E. F. (1996a). Adult recollections of childhood abuse: Cognitive and developmental perspectives. In J. Alpert, L. Brown, S. Ceci, C. Courtois, E. Loftus, & P. Ornstein. (Eds.), *Working group on investigation of memories of childhood abuse* (pp. 150–197). Washington, DC: American Psychological Association.

Ornstein, P., Ceci, S. J., & Loftus, E. F. (1996b). More on the repressed memory debate: A rejoinder to Alpert, Brown, and Courtois. In J. Alpert, L. Brown, S. Ceci, C. Courtois, E. Loftus, & P. Ornstein. (Eds.), *Working group on investigation of memories of childhood abuse* (pp. 221–240). Washington, DC: American Psychological Association.

Ornstein, P., Ceci, S. J., & Loftus, E. F. (1996c). Reply to the Alpert, Brown, and Courtois document: The science of of memory and the practice of psychotherapy. In J. Alpert, L. Brown, S. Ceci, C. Courtois, E. Loftus, & P. Ornstein. (Eds.), *Working group on investigation of memories of childhood abuse* (pp.106–131). Washington, DC: American Psychological Association.

Ornstein, P., Larus, D. M., & Clubb, P. A. (1991). Understanding children's testimony: Implications of research on the development of memory. In R. Vasta (Ed.), *Annals of Child Development, 8,* 145–176. London: Jessica Kingsley Publishers.

Orr, S. P., & Kaloupek, D. G. (1997). Psychophysiological assessment of posttraumatic stress disorder. In J. P. Wilson & T. M. Keane (Eds.), *Assessing psychological trauma and PTSD* (pp. 69–97). New York: Guilford.

Palm, K. M., & Gibson, P. (1998). Recovered memories of childhood sexual abuse: Clinicians' practices and beliefs. *Professional Psychology: Research and Practice, 29*(3), 257–261.

Parson, E. R. (1984). The reparation of the self: Clinical and theoretical dimensions in the treatment of vietnam combat veterans. *Journal of Contemporary Psychotherapy, 14*(1), 4–56.

Payne, A. B. (1995, August). *Training and supervision issues regarding trauma and recovery of memories.* Paper presented at the 103rd Annual Meeting of the American Psychological Association, New York City.

Pearlman, L. A. (1996). Psychometric review of TSI Belief Scale, Revison-L. In B. H. Stamm (Ed.), *Measurement of stress, trauma, and adaptation* (pp. 412–417). Lutherville, MD: The Sidran Press.

Pearlman, L. A., & McCann, I. L. (1994). Integrating structured and unstructured approaches to taking a trauma history. In M. B. Williams & J. F. Sommer (Eds.), *Handbook of post-traumatic therapy* (pp. 38–47). Westport, CT: Greenwood Press.

Pearlman, L. A., & Saakvitne, K. W. (1995). *Trauma and the therapist: Countertransference and vicarious traumatization in psychotherapy with incest survivors.* New York: W. W. Norton & Company.

Pelcovitz, D., van der Kolk, B., Roth, S., Mandel, F. S., Kaplan, S., & Resick, P. A. (1997). Development of a criteria set and a structured interview for disorders of extreme stress (SIDES). *Journal of Traumatic Stress, 10,* 3–17.

Pennebaker, J. W. (1989). Confession, inhibition, and disease. *Advances in Experiemental Social Psychology, 22,* 211–244.

Pennebaker, J. W. (1993). Putting stress into words: Health, linguistic, and therapeutic implications. *Behavioral Research and Therapy, 31*(6), 539–548.

Pennebaker, J. W., Kiecolt-Glaser, J. K., & Glaser, R. (1988). Disclosure of traumas and immune function: Health implications for psychotherapy. *Journal of Consulting and Clinical Psychology, 56*(2), 239–245.

Pennebaker, J. W., & Susman, J. R. (1988). Disclosure of traumas and psychosomatic processes. *Social Science and Medicine, 26,* 327–332.

Perry, B. D. (1993a). Neurodevelopment and the neurophysiology of trauma I: Conceptual considerations for clinical work with maltreated children. *The Advisor, 6*(1), 14–18.

Perry, B. D. (1993b). Neurodevelopment and the neurophysiology of trauma II: Clinical work along the alarm-fear-terror continuum. *The Advisor, 6*(2), 14–20.

Perry, B. D. (1994). Neurobiological sequelae of childhood trauma: PTSD in children. In M. M. Murburg (Ed.), *Catecholamine function in posttraumatic stress disorder* (pp. 233–256). Washington, DC: American Psychiatric Press.

Perry, N. W., & Wrightsman, L. S. (1991). *The child witness: Legal issues and dilemmas.* Newbury Park, CA: Sage.

Peters, J. J. (1976). Children who are victims of sexual assault and the psychology of offenders. *American Journal of Psychotherapy, 30,* 398–421.

Pezdek, K. (1994). The illusion of illusory memory. *Applied Cognitive Psychology, 8,* 339–350.

Pezdek, K., & Banks, W. P. (1996). *The recovered memory/false memory debate.* New York: Academic Press.

Piers, C. (1996). A return to the source: Rereading Freud in the midst of contemporary trauma theory. *Psychotherapy, 33,* 539–548.

Pillemer, D. B., & White, S. H. (1989). Childhood events recalled by children and adults. In H. W. Reese (Ed.), *Advances in child development and behavior* (Vol. 21, pp.297–340). San Diego, CA: Academic Press.

Pitman, R., & Orr, S. P. (in press). Psychophysiology of emotional memory networks in post-traumatic stress disorder. *Proceedings of the Fifth Conference on the Neurobiology of Learning and Memory.* Irvine, CA: Oxford University Press.

Polusny, M. M., & Follette, V. M. (1995). Long-term effects of child sexual abuse: Theory and review of the empirical literature. *Applied and Preventive Psychology: Current Scientific Perspectives, 4*(3), 143–166.

Polusny, M. M., & Follette, V. M. (1996). Remembering childhood sexual abuse: A national survey of psychologists' clinical practices, beliefs, and personal experiences. *Professional Psychology: Research and Practice, 27*(1), 41–52.

Poole, D., Lindsay, S., Memon, A., & Bull, R. (1995). Psychotherapy and the recovered memories of childhood abuse: U. S. and British practitioners' opinions, practices, and experiences. *Journal of Clinical and Consulting Psychology, 63*(3), 426–438.

Pope, H. G., & Hudson, J. I. (1995a). Can individuals "repress" memories of childhood abuse? An examination of the evidence. *Psychiatric Annals, 25,* 715–719.

Pope, H. G., & Hudson, J. I. (1995b). Can memories of childhood sexual abuse be repressed? *Psychological Medicine, 25,* 121–126.

Pope, K. S. (1996). Memory, abuse, and science: Questioning claims about the false memory syndrome epidemic. *American Psychologist, 51,* 957–974.

Pope, K. S., & Brown, L. (1996). *Recovered memories of abuse: Assessment, therapy, forensics.* Washington, DC: American Psychological Association Press.

Pope, K. S., & Feldman-Summers, S. (1992). National survey of psychologists' sexual and physical abuse history and their evaluation of training and competence in these areas. *Professional Psychology: Research and Practice, 23,* 474–479.

Pope, K. S., & Vasquez, M. J. T. (1998). *Ethics in psychotherapy and counseling: A practical guide* (2nd Ed.). San Francisco: Jassey-Bass.

Poston, C., & Lison, K. (1989). *Reclaiming our lives: Hope for adult survivors of incest.* New York: Little, Brown.

Pribor, E. F., & Dinwiddie, S. H. (1992). Psychiatric correlates of incest in childhood. *American Journal of Psychiatry, 149,* 52–56.

Price, M. (1994). Incest and the idealized self: Adaptations to childhood sexual abuse. *American Journal of Psychoanalysis, 54,* 21–36.

Putnam, F. W. (1985a). Dissociation as a response to extreme trauma. In Kluft, R. P. (Ed.), *Childhood antecedents of multiple personality.* Washington, DC: American Psychiatric Association Press, Inc.

Putnam, F. W. (1985b). Pieces of the mind: Recognizing the psychological effects of abuse. *Justice for Children, 1,* 6–7.

Putnam, F. W. (1989a). *Diagnosis and treatment of multiple personality disorder.* New York: Guilford.

Putnam, F. W. (1989b). Pierre Janet and modern views of dissociation. *Journal of Traumatic Stress, 2*(4), 413–429.

Putnam, F. W. (1993a). Dissociative disorders in children: Behavioral profiles and problems. *Child Abuse and Neglect., 17,* 39–45.

Putnam, F. W. (1993b). Dissociative phenomena. In D. Spiegel (Ed.), *Dissociative disorders: A clinical review* (pp. 1–16). Lutherville, MD: The Sidran Press.

Putnam, F. W. (1997). *Dissociation in children and adolescents: A developmental perspective.* New York: Guilford.

Putnam, F. W., Guroff, J. J., Silberman, E. K., Barban, L., & Post, R. M. (1986). The clinical phenomenology of multiple personality: Review of 100 recent cases. *Journal of Clinical Psychiatry, 47*(6), 285–293.

Pynoos, R. S. (Ed.). (1994). *Posttraumatic stress disorder: A clinical review.* Lutherville, MD: The Sidran Press.

Pynoos, R. S., & Eth, S. (1985). Developmental perspective on psychic trauma in childhood. In C. R. Figley (Ed.), *Trauma and its wake: The study and treatment of posttraumatic stress disorder* (pp. 36–52). New York: Brunner/Mazel.

Pynoos, R. S., & Nader, K. (1989). Children's memory and proximity to violence. *Journal of the American Academy of Child and Adolescent Psychiatry, 28,* 236–241.

Pynoos, R. S., Steinberg, A. M., & Aronson, L. (1997). Traumatic experiences: The early organization of memory in school-age children and adolescents. In P. S. Appelbaum, L. A. Uyehara, & M. R. Elin (Eds.), *Trauma and memory: Clinical and legal controversies* (pp. 272–292). New York: Oxford University Press.

Pynoos, R. S., Steinberg, A. M., & Goenjian, A. (1996). Traumatic stress in childhood and adolescence: Recent developments and current controversies. In B. A. van der Kolk & A. C. McFarlane (Eds.), *Traumatic stress: The effects of overwhelming experience on mind, body, and society* (pp. 331–358). New York: The Guilford Press.

Quintana, S. M. (1993). Toward an expanded and updated conceptualization of termination: Implications for short-term, individual psychotherapy. *Professional Psychology: Research and Practice, 24,* 426–432.

Rainer, J. P. (Ed.). (1996). Psychotherapy Outcomes [Special issue]. *Psychotherapy, 33*(2).

Rauch, S., van der Kolk, B. A., Fisler, R., Alpert, N. M., Orr, S. P., Savage, C. R., Fischman, A. J., Jenike, M. A., & Pitman, R. K. (1996). A symptom provocation study of posttraumatic stress disorder using positron emission tomography and script-driven imagery. *Archives of General Psychiatry, 53,* 380–387.

Rausch, K., & Knutson, J. F. (1991). The self-report of personal punitive childhood experiences and those of siblings. *Child Abuse and Neglect, 15,* 29–36.

Read, J. (1997). Child abuse and psychosis: A literature review and implications for professional practice. *Professional Psychology: Research and Practice, 28,* 448–456.

Read, J. D., & Lindsay, D. S. (Eds.). (1997). *Recollections of trauma: Scientific evidence and clinical practice.* New York: Plenum Press.

Renshaw, D. (1982). *Incest: Understanding and treatment.* Boston: Little, Brown.

Resick, P. A., & Schnicke, M. K. (1992). Cognitive processing therapy for sexual assault victims. *Journal of Consulting and Clinical Psychology, 60*(5), 748–756.

Resnick, H. S. (1996). Psychometric review of Trauma Assessment for Adults (TAA). In B. H. Stamm (Ed.), *Measurement of stress, trauma, and adaptation* (pp. 362–364). Lutherville, MD: The Sidran Press.

Reviere, S. L. (1996). *Memory of childhood trauma: A clinician's guide to the literature.* New York: The Guilford Press.

Rieker, P., & Carmen, E. (1986). The victim-to-patient process: The disconfirmation and transformation of abuse. *American Journal of Orthopsychiatry, 56,* 360–370.

Roediger, H. L. (1980). Memory metaphors in cognitive psychology. *Memory and Cognition, 8,* 231–246.

Rogers, M. (1995). Factors influencing recall of childhood sexual abuse. *Journal of Traumatic Stress, 8,* 691–715.

Ross, C. A. (1987). Inpatient treatment of multiple personality disorder. *Canadian Journal of Psychiatry, 32*, 779–781.

Ross, C. A. (1989). *Multiple personality disorder: Diagnosis, clinical features, and treatment.* New York: John Wiley & Sons.

Ross, C. A. (1995). *Satanic ritual abuse: Principles of treatment.* Toronto, ON: University of Toronto Press.

Ross, C. A. (1997). *Dissociative identity disorder: Diagnosis, clinical features, and treatment of multiple personality.* New York: Wiley.

Ross, C. A., Anderson, G., Fleisher, W. P., & Norton, G. R. (1992). Dissociative experiences among psychiatric inpatients. *General Hospital Psychiatry, 14*, 350–354.

Ross, C. A., Heber, S., Norton, G. R., & Anderson, G. (1989). Somatic symptoms in multiple personality disorder. *Psychosomatics, 30*(2), 154–160.

Ross, C. A., Joshi, S., & Currie, R. (1990). Dissociative experiences in the general population. *American Journal of Psychiatry, 147*,(11), 1547–1552.

Ross, C. A., Miller, S. D., Bjornson, P., Reagor, P., Fraser, G., & Anderson G. (1991). Abuse histories in 102 cases of multiple personality disorder. *Canadian Journal of Psychiatry, 36*, 97–101.

Ross, C. A., Norton, G. R., & Wozney, K. (1989). Multiple personality disorder: An analysis of 236 cases. *Canadian Journal of Psychiatry, 34*(5), 413–418.

Roth, S., & Batson, R. (1997). *Naming the shadows: A new approach to individual and group psychotherapy for adult survivors of childhood incest.* New York: The Free Press.

Roth S., & Friedman, M. J. (1998). Childhood trauma remembered: A report on the current scientific knowledge base and its applications. *Journal of Child Sexual Abuse, 7*(1), 83–110.

Rovee-Collier, C. (1993). What infants remember. *Current Directions in Psychological Science, 2*, 130–135.

Rovee-Collier, C. (1997). Dissociations in infant memory: Rethinking the development of implicit and explicit memory. *Psychological Review, 104*, 467–498.

Rowan, A. B., & Foy, D. W. (1993). Post-traumatic stress disorder in child sexual abuse survivors: A literature review. *Journal of Traumatic Stress, 6*, 3–20.

Royal Australian and New Zealand College of Psychiatrists (1996). *Guidelines for psychiatrists dealing with repressed traumatic memories.* (Clinical Memorandum No. 17).

Royal College of Psychiatrists' Working Group on Reported Recovered Memories of Child Sexual Abuse (1997). Recommendations for good practice and implications for training, continuing professional development and research. *Psychiatric Bulletin, 21*, 663–665.

Rubin, L. J. (1996). Childhood sexual abuse: False accusations of "false memory"? *Professional Psychology: Research and Practice, 27*, 447–451.

Rush, F. (1977). The Freudian cover-up. *Chrysalis*, 31–45.

Rush, F. (1980). *The best kept secret: Sexual abuse of children.* Englewood Cliffs, NJ: Prentice Hall.

Russell, D. E. H. (1983). The incidence and prevalence of intrafamilial and extrafamilial sexual abuse of female children. *Child Abuse and Neglect, 7*, 133–146.

Russell, D. E. H. (1984). *Sage Library of Social Research: Volume 155. Sexual exploitation: Rape, child sexual abuse, and workplace harassment.* Beverly Hills: Sage.

Russell, D. E. H. (1986). *The secret trauma: Incest in the lives of girls and women.* New York: Basic Books.

Saakvitne, K. W., & Pearlman, L. A. (1996). *Transforming the pain: A workbook on vicarious traumatization.* New York: W. W. Norton & Company.

Salter, A. C. (1995). *Transforming trauma: A guide to understanding and treating adult survivors of child sexual abuse.* Newbury Park, CA: Sage.

Saunders, B. E., & Williams, L. M. (Eds.). (1996). Treatment outcome research [Special seection]. *Child Maltreatment, 1*(4), 293–352.

Sauzier, M. C. (1997). Memories of trauma in the treatment of children. In P. S. Appelbaum, L. A. Uyehara, & M. R. Elin (Eds.), *Trauma and memory: Clinical and legal controversies* (pp. 378–393). New York: Oxford University Press.

Saxe, G. N., van der Kolk, B. A., Berkowitz, R., Chinman, G., Hall, K., Lieberg, G., & Schwartz, J. (1993). Dissociative disorders in psychiatric inpatients. *American Journal of Psychiatry, 150,* 1037–1042.

Schacter, D. L. (1996). *Searching for memory: The brain, the mind, and the past.* New York: Basic Books.

Scharff, J. S., & Scharff, D. (1994). *Object relations therapy of physical and sexual trauma.* Northvale, NJ: Jason Aronson Inc.

Scheflin, A. W. (1998). Risk management in treating child sexual abuse victims and adult survivors. *Journal of Child Sexual Abuse, 7*(1), 111–121.

Scheflin, A. W., & Brown, D. (Summer 1996). Repressed memory or dissociative amnesia: What the science says. *The Journal of Psychiatry and Law,* 143–188.

Scheflin, A. W., & Shapiro, J. L. (1989). *Trance on Trial.* New York: Guilford.

Schooler, J. W. (1994). Seeking the core: The issues and evidence surrounding recovered accounts of sexual trauma. *Consciousness and Cognition, 3,* 452–469.

Schooler, J. W. (1996). Seeking the core: The issues and evidence surrounding recovered accounts of sexual trauma. In K. Pezdek & W. P. Banks (Eds.), *The recovered memory/false memory debate* (pp. 279–296). New York: Academic Press.

Schooler, J. W., Ambadar, Z., & Bendiksen, M. (1997). A cognitive corroborative case study approach for investigating discovered memories of sexual abuse. In J. D. Read & D. S. Lindsay (Eds.), *Recollections of trauma: Scientific evidence and clinical practice* (pp. 379–387). New York: Plenum Press.

Schooler, J. W., Bendiksen, M., & Ambadar, Z. (1997). Taking the middle line: Can we accomodate both fabricated and recovered memories of sexual abuse? In M. A. Conway (Ed.), *Recovered memories and false memories* (pp.251–292). London: Oxford University Press.

Schwartz, H. L. (1994). From dissociation to negotiation: A relational psychoanalytic perspective on multiple personality disorder. *Psychoanalytic Psychology, 11*(2), 189–231.

Schwartz, M. F., & Cohn, L. (Eds.). (1996). *Sexual abuse and eating disorders.* New York: Brunner/Mazel.

Schwarz, R. (1996). Separating fact from fiction in the "false memory" question. In L.Vandecreek, S. Knapp, & T. L. Jackson (Eds.), *Innovations in clinical practice: Volume 15. A source book* (pp. 13–30). Sarasota, FL: Professional Resource Press.

Scurfield, R. M. (1985). Post-trauma stress assessment and treatment: Overview and formulations. In C. R. Figley (Ed.), *Trauma and its wake: The study and treatment of post-traumatic stress disorder* (pp. 219–256). New York: Brunner/Mazel.

Sedlak, A., & Broadhurst, D. (1996). *Executive Summary of the Third National Incidence Study of Child Abuse and Neglect.* Washington, DC: U.S. Department of Health and Human Services.

Seligman, S. (1997). Discussion: Clinical technique and the political surround: The case of sexual abuse. In C. Prozan (Ed.), *Construction and reconstruction of memory: Dilemmas of childhood sexual abuse* (pp. 207–222). Northvale, NJ: Jason Aronson, Inc.

Selye, H. (1976). *Stress in health and disease.* Boston: Butterworth.

Sgroi, S. M. (1982). *Handbook of clinical intervention in child sexual abuse.* Lexington, MA: Lexington Books.

Sgroi, S. M. (1988). *Vulnerable populations: Evaluation and treatment of sexually abused children and adult survivors* (Vol. 1). Lexington, MA: Lexington Books.

Sgroi, S. M. (1989). *Vulnerable populations: Sexual abuse treatment for children, adult survivors, offenders, and persons with mental retardation* (Vol. 2). Lexington, MA: Lexington Books.

Shalev, A. Y. (1996). Discussion: Treatment of prolonged posttraumatic stress disorder—learning from experience. *Journal of Traumatic Stress, 10*(3), 415–422.

Shalev, A. Y., Bonne, O., & Eth, S. (1996). Treatment of posttraumatic stress disorder: A review. *Psychosomatic Medicine, 58,* 165–182.

Shapiro, F. (1988). Efficacy of eye movement desensitization procedure in the treatment of traumatic memories. *Journal of Traumatic Stress, 2*(2), 199–223.

Shapiro, F. (1995). *Eye movement desensitization and reprocessing: Basic principles, protocols, and procedures.* New York: Guilford.

Shapiro, S. (1995). Impact of validation of recovered memories on patient's treatment. In J. L. Alpert (Ed.), *Sexual abuse recalled: Treating trauma in the era of the recovered memory debate* (pp.311–336). Northvale, NJ: Jason Aronson Inc.

Shepard, M. F., & Campbell, J. A. (1992). The Abusive Behavior Inventory; A measure of psychological and physical abuse. *Journal of Interpersonal Violence, 7,* 291–305.

Sherman, J. J. (1998) Effects of psychotherapeutic treatments for PTSD: A meta-analysis of controlled clinical trials. *Journal of Traumatic Stress, 11*(3), 413–435.

Shobe, K. S., & Kihlstrom, J. F. (1997). Is traumatic memory special? *Current Directions in Psychological Science, 6,* 70–74.

Siegel, D. J. (1995). Memory, trauma, and psychotherapy: A cognitive science view. *Journal of Psychotherapy Practice and Research, 4,* 93–122.

Silverman, A. B., Reinherz, H. Z., & Giaconia, R. M. (1996). The long-term sequelae of child and adolescent abuse: A longitudinal community study. *Child Abuse and Neglect, 20,* 709–723.

Simonds, S. L. (1994). *Bridging the silence: Nonverbal modalities in the treatment of adult survivors of childhood sexual abuse.* New York: W.W. Norton Company.

Sinason, V. (1991). Interpretations that feel horrible to make and a theoretical unicorn. *Journal of Child Psychotherapy, 17*(1), 11–24.

Slavin, J. H. (1997). Memory, dissociation, and agency in sexual abuse. In R. B. Gartner (Ed.), *Memories of sexual betrayal: Truth, fantasy, repression and dissociation* (pp. 221–236). Northvale, NJ: Jason Aronson Inc.

Solomon, S. D., Gerrity, E. T., & Muff, A. M. (1992). Efficacy of treatment for posttraumatic stress disorder: An empirical review. *Journal of the American Medical Association, 268,* 633–638.

Southwick, S. M., Krystal, J. H., Johnson, D. R., & Charney, D. (1995). Neurobiology of PTSD. In J. P. Wilson & T. M. Keane (Eds.), *Assessing psychological trauma and PTSD* (pp.69–97). New York: Guilford.

Spanos, N. P. (1994). Multiple identity enactments and multiple personality disorders: A sociocognitive perspective. *Psychological Bulletin, 116,* 143–165.

Spanos, N. P. (1996). *Multiple identities and false memories: A sociocognitive perspective.* Washington, DC: American Psychological Association Press.

Spence, D. P. (1994). Narrative and putative child abuse. *The International Journal of Clinical Hypnosis, 42*(4), 289–303.

Spiegel, D. (1984). Multiple personality as a post-traumatic stress disorder. *Psychiatric Clinics of North America, 7,* 101–110.

Spiegel, D. (1986a). Dissociating damage. *American Journal of Clinical Hypnosis, 29,* 123–131.

Spiegel, D. (1986b). Dissociation, double binds, and posttraumatic stress in multiple personality disorder. In B. G. Braun (Ed.), *Treatment of multiple personality disorder.* Washington, DC: American Psychiatric Press, Inc.

Spiegel, D. (1988). Commentary: The treatment accorded those who treat patients with multiple personality disorder. *The Journal of Nervous and Mental Disease, 176*(1), 535–536.

Spiegel, D. (1993). Hypnosis in the treatment of posttraumatic stress disorder. In J. W. Rhue, S. J. Lynn, & I. Kirsch (Eds.), *Handbook of clinical hypnosis* (pp. 493–508). Washington, DC: American Psychological Association Press.

Spiegel, D. (Ed.). (1994a). *Dissociation: Culture, mind, and body.* Washington, DC: American Psychiatric Press, Inc.

Spiegel, D. (1994b, November). *Out of sight, but not out of mind: Dissociation in acute and post-traumatic stress disorders.* Keynote address delivered at the meeting of the International Society of Traumatic Stress Studies, Chicago.

Spiegel, D. (Ed.). (1997). *Section II of American Psychiatric Press review of psychiatry, Volume 16: Repressed memories.* Washington, DC: American Psychiatric Press.

Spiegel, D., & Cardena, E. (1991). Disintegrated experience: The dissociative disorders revisited. *Journal of Abnormal Psychology, 100,* 366–378.

Spiegel, H., & Spiegel, D. (1978). *Trance and treatment: Clinical uses of hypnosis.* New York: Basic Books.

Spira, J. L. (Ed.). (1996). *Treating dissociative identity disorder.* San Francisco: Jossey-Bass.

Stamm, B. H. (1996). *Measurement of stress, trauma, and adaptation.* Lutherville, MD: The Sidran Press.

Stanton, M. (1994, May 7–9). Bearing witness: A man's recovery of his sexual abuse as a child. *Providence Journal,* Part 1: A-1, A-18; Part 2: A-1, A-8; Part 3: A-1, A-6.

Stanton, M. (1997). U-turn on memory lane: Press coverage of recovered memories. *Columbia Journalism Review, 36* (2), 44–46.

Stein, M. B., Hanna, C., Koverola, C., Torchia, M., & McClarty, B. (1997). Structural brain changes in PTSD: Does trauma alter neuroanatomy? *Annals of the New York Academy of Sciences, 821,* 76–82.

Steinberg, M.. (1994). *Interviewer's guide to the Structured Clinical Interview fpr DSM-IV Dissociative Disorders-Revised (SCID-D-R).* Washington, DC: American Psychiatric Press, Inc.

Steinberg, M. (1995). *Handbook for the assessment of dissociation: A clinical guide.* Washington, DC: American Psychiatric Press, Inc.

Stewart, S. H. (1996). Alcohol abuse in individuals exposed to trauma: A critical review. *Psychological Bulletin, 120*(1), 83–112.

Straker, G., & Waks, B. (1997). Limit setting in regard to self-damaging acts: The patient's perspective. *Psychotherapy, 34*(2), 192–200.

Strick, F. L., & Wilcoxon, S. A. (1991). A comparison of dissociative experiences in adult female outpatients with and without histories of early incestuous abuse. *Dissociation, 4*(4), 193–199.

Stricker, G., & Trierweiler, S. J. (1995). The local clinical scientist: A bridge between science and practice. *American Psychologist, 50,* 995–1002.

Sugar, M. (1992). Toddler's traumatic memories. *Infant Mental Health Journal, 13,* 245–251.

Summit, R. (1983). The child sexual abuse accommodation syndrome. *Child Abuse and Neglect, 7,* 177–193.

Swett, C., & Halpert, M. (1993). Reported history of physical and sexual abuse in relation to dissociation and other symptomatology in women psychiatric inpatients. *Journal of Interpersonal Violence, 8*(4), 545–555.

Symonds, M. (1980). The 'second injury' to victims [Special Issue]. *Evaluation and Change,* 36–38.

Tavris, C. (1993, January 16). Beware the incest-survivor machine. *The New York Times Book Review,* pp. 1–5.

Tayloe, D. R. (1995). The validity of repressed memories and the accuracy of their recall through hypnosis: A case study from the courtroom. *American Journal of Clinical Hypnosis, 37*(3), 25–31.

Tedeschi, R. G., & Calhoun, L. G. (1996). The posttraumatic growth inventory: Measuring the positive legacy of trauma. *Journal of Traumatic Stress, 9*(3), 455–471.

Terr, L. (1979). Children of Chowchilla: A study of psychic trauma. *Psychoanalytic Study of the Child, 34,* 552–623.

Terr, L. (1981). Psychic trauma in children: Observations following the Chowchilla school-bus kidnapping. *American Journal of Psychiatry, 138,* 14–19.

Terr, L. (1983a). Chowchilla revisited: The effects of psychic trauma four years after a school bus kidnapping. *American Journal of Psychiatry, 140,* 1543–1550.

Terr, L. (1983b). Life attitudes, dreams, and psychic trauma in a group of "normal" children. *Journal of the American Academy of Child and Adolescent Psychiatry, 22,* 221–230.

Terr, L. (1988). What happens to early memories of trauma? A study of twenty children under age five at the time of documented traumatic events. *American Journal of Child and Adolescent Psychiatry, 27,* 96–104.

Terr, L. (1990). *Too scared to cry: Psychic trauma in childhood.* New York: Harper & Row.

Terr, L. (1991). Childhood traumas: An outline and overview. *American Journal of Psychiatry, 148,* 10–20.

Terr, L. (1994). *Unchained memories: True stories of traumatic memories, lost and found.* New York: Basic Books.

Terr, L. (1996). True memories of childhood trauma: Flaws, absences, and returns. In K. Pezdek & W. P. Banks *The recovered memory/false memory debate* (pp. 69–80). New York: Academic Press.

Tessler, M., & Nelson, K. (1996). Making memories: The influence of joint encoding on later recall by young children. In K. Pezdek & W. P. Banks (Eds.), *The recovered memory/false memory debate* (pp. 101–120). New York: Academic Press.

Toglia, M. P. (1997). Repressed memories: The way we were? *Consciousness and Cognition, 4,* 111–115.

Trickett, P., & Putnam, F. W. (1993). Impact of child sexual abuse on females: Toward a developmental, psychobiological integration. *Psychological Science, 4*(2), 81–87.

Tromp, S., Koss, M. P., Figueredo, A. J., & Tharan, M. (1995). Are rape memories different? A comparison of rape, other unpleasant, and pleasant memories among employed women. *Journal of Traumatic Stress, 8*(4), 607–627.

Turkus, J. (1995). Crisis intervention. In C. Classen (Vol. Ed.) & I. D. Yalom (Series Ed.)., *Treating women molested in childhood: A volume in the Jossey-Bass library of current clinical technique* (pp. 35–62). San Francisco: Jossey-Bass.

Turkus, J., & Courtois, C. A. (1996, Summer). Stage-oriented treatment of trauma survivors. *Centering. Newsletter of The CENTER: Post-traumatic & Dissociative Disorders Program, 1,* 1–3.

Underwager, R., & Wakefiled, H. (1990). *The real world of child interrogations.* Springfield, IL: Thomas.

Urquiza, A. J., Wyatt, G. E., & Goodlin-Jones, B. I. (1997). Clinical interviewing with trauma victims: Managing interviewer risk. *Journal of Interpersonal Violence, 12*(5), 759–772.

Uyehara, L. A. (1997). Diagnosis, pathogenesis, and memories of childhood abuse. In P. S. Appelbaum, L. A. Uyehara, & M. R. Elin (Eds.), *Trauma and memory: Clinical and legal controversies* (pp. 394–424). New York: Oxford University Press.

Vaillant, G. E. (1990). Repression in college men followed for half a century. In J. L. Singer (Ed.), *Repression and dissociation: Implications for personality theory, psychopathology, and health* (pp. 259–274). Chicago: University of Chicago Press.

van der Hart, O., Brown, P., & van der Kolk, V. A. (1989). Pierre Janet's treatment of post-traumatic stress. *Journal of Traumatic Stress, 2,* 379–395.

van der Hart, O., Steele, K., Boon, S., Brown, P. (1993). The treatment of traumatic memories: Synthesis, realization, and integration. *Dissociation, 6*(2/3), 162–180.

van der Kolk, B. (Ed.). (1984). *Post-traumatic stress disorder: Psychological and biological sequelae.* Washington, DC: American Psychiatric Press, Inc.

van der Kolk, B. A. (1987). *Psychological trauma.* Washington, DC: American Psychiatric Press, Inc.

van der Kolk, B. A. (1988). The trauma spectrum: The interaction of biological and social events in the genesis of the trauma response. *Journal of Traumatic Stress, 1,* 273–290.

van der Kolk, B. A. (1996). The body keeps the score: Approaches to the psychobiology of posttraumatic stress disorder. In B. A. van der Kolk, A. C. McFarlane, & L. Weisaeth (Eds.), *Traumatic stress: The effects of overwhelming experience on mind, body, and society* (pp. 214–241). New York: The Guilford Press.

van der Kolk, B. A. (1997). Traumatic memories. In P. S. Appelbaum, L. A. Uyehara, & M. R. Elin (Eds.), *Trauma and memory: Clinical and legal controversies* (pp. 243–260). New York: Oxford University Press.

van der Kolk, B. A., & Fisler, R. (1995). Dissociation and the fragmentary nature of traumatic memories: Overview and exploratory study. *Journal of Traumatic Stress, 8,* 505–525.

van der Kolk, B. A., & Kadish, B. (1987). Amnesia, dissociation, and the return of the repressed. In B. A. van der Kolk (Ed.), *Psychological trauma* (pp. 173–190). Washington, DC: American Psychiatric Press, Inc.

van der Kolk, B. A., McFarlane, A. C., & van der Hart, O. (1996). A general approach to treatment of posttraumatic stress disorder. In B. A. van der Kolk, A. C. McFarlane, & L. Weisaeth (Eds.), *Traumatic stress: The effects of overwhelming experience on mind, body, and society.* New York: The Guilford Press.

van der Kolk, B. A., McFarlane, A. C., & Weisaeth, L. (Eds.). (1996). *Traumatic stress: The effects of overwhelming experience on mind, body, and society.* New York: The Guilford Press.

van der Kolk, B. A., & Saporta, J. (1993). Biological response to psychic trauma. In Wilson, J. P., & Raphael, B. (Eds.), *International handbook of traumatic stress syndromes* (pp. 25–34). New York: Plenum Press.

van der Kolk, B. A., Perry, J. C., & Herman, J. L. (1991). Childhood origins of self-destructive behavior. *American Journal of Psychiatry, 148*(12), 1665–1671.

van der Kolk, B. A., & van der Hart, O. (1991). The intrusive past: The flexibility of memory and the engraving of trauma. *American Imago, 48,* 425–454.

van der Kolk, B. A., & van der Hart, O. (1995). The intrusive past: The flexibility of memory and the engraving of trauma. In Caruth, C. (Ed.), *Trauma: Explorations in memory* (pp. 158–182). Baltimore, MD: The Johns Hopkins University Press.

VandenBos, G. R. (Ed.). (1996). Outcome assessment of psychotherapy [Special Issue]. *American Psychologist, 51*(10).

Vrana, S., & Lauterbach, D. (1994). Prevalence of traumatic events and post-traumatic psychological symptoms in a nonclinical sample of college students. *Journal of Traumatic Stress, 7,* 289–302.

Wagenaar, W. A., & Groeneweg, J. (1990). The memory of concentration camp survivors. *Applied Cognitive Psychology, 4,* 77–87.

Waites, E. A. (1993). *Trauma and survival: Post-traumatic and dissociative disorders in women.* New York: W. W. Norton & Company.

Waites, E. A. (1997). *Memory quest: Trauma and the search for personal history.* New York: W. W. Norton & Company.

Wakefield, H., & Underwager, R. (1992). Recovered memories of alleged sexual abuse: Lawsuits against parents. *Behavioral Sciences and the Law, 10,* 483–507.

Walker, L. E. (1979). *The battered woman.* New York: Harper and Row.

Walker, L. E. (1984). *The battered woman syndrome.* New York: Springer.

Wang, S., Wilson, J. P., & Mason, J. W. (1996). Stages of decompensation in combat-related posttraumatic stress disorder: A new conceptual model. *Integrative Physiological and Behavioral Science, 31,* 237–253.

Webb, L. P., & Leehan, J. (1996). *Group treatment for adult survivors of abuse: A manual for practitioners.* Thousand Oaks, CA: Sage Publications.

Weinberg, K. (1955). *Incest behavior.* New York: Citadel Press.

Weiss, D. S. & Marmar, C. R. (1993). Teaching time-limited dynamic psychotherapy for post-traumatic stress disorder and pathological grief. *Psychotherapy, 30*(4), 587–591.

Weiss, D. W., Marmar, C. R., Metzler, T. J., & Ronfeldt, H. (1995). Predicting symptomatic distress in emergency services personnel. *Journal of Clinical and Counseling Psychology, 63,* 361–368.

Wells, M., Glickhauf-Hughes, C., & Beaudoin, P. (1995). An ego/object relations approach to treating childhood sexual abuse survivors. *Psychotherapy, 32,* 416–429.

West, L. (1967). Dissociative reactions. In A. M. Freedman & H. I. Kaplan (Eds.), *Comprehensive textbook of psychiatry* (pp. 885–898). Baltimore, MD: Williams & Wilkin.

Westerlund, E. (1992). *Women's sexuality after childhood incest.* New York: W. W. Norton & Company.

Whitfield, C. L. (1987). *Healing the child within: Discovery and recovery for adult children of dysfunctional families.* Deerfield Beach, FL: Health Communications.

Whitfield, C. L. (1995). *Memory and abuse: Remembering and healing the effects of trauma.* Deerfield Beach, FL: Health Communications.

Wickramasekera, I. (1994). Somatic to psychological symptoms and information transfer from implicit to explicit memory: A controlled case study with predictions from the high risk model of threat perception. *Dissociation, 7,* 153–166.

Widom, C. S. (1997). Accuracy of adult recollections of early childhood abuse. In J. D. Read & D. S. Lindsay (Eds.), *Recollections of trauma: Scientific evidence and clinical practice* (pp. 49–70). New York: Plenum Press.

Widom, C. S., & Morris, S. (1997). Accuracy of adult recollections of childhood vicimization. Part II. Childhood sexual abuse. *Psychological Assessment, 9,* 34–46.

Widom, C. S., & Shepard, R. L. (1996). Accuracy of adult recollections of childhood victimization. Part I. Childhood physical abuse. *Psychological Assessment, 8,* 4, 412–421.

Wigren, J. (1994). Narrative completion in the treatment of trauma. *Psychotherapy, 31*(3), 415–423.

Williams, L. M. (1994a). Recall of childhood trauma: A prospective study of women's memories of child sexual abuse. *Journal of Consulting and Clinical Psychology, 62,* 1167–1176.

Williams, L. M. (1994b). What does it mean to forget child sexual abuse? A reply to Loftus, Garry, and Feldman (1994), *Journal of Consulting and Clinical Psychology, 62,* 1182–1186.

Williams, L. M. (1995). Recovered memories of abuse in women with documented child sexual victimization histories. *Journal of Traumatic Stress, 8,* 649–673.

Williams, L. M., & Banyard, V. L. (1997a). Gender and recall of child sexual abuse: A prospective study. In J. D. Read & D. S. Lindsay (Eds.), *Recollections of trauma: Scientific evidence and clinical practice* (pp. 371–378). New York: Plenum Press.

Williams, L. M., & Banyard, V. L. (1997b). Perspectives on adult memories of childhood sexual abuse: A research review. In L. J. Dickson, M. B. Riba, & J. M. Oldham (Series Eds.) & D. Spiegel (Vol. Ed.), *Section II of American Psychiatric Press review of psychiatry: Volume 16. Repressed memories* (pp. II-123–152). Washington, DC: American Psychiatric Press, Inc.

Williams, M. B., & Sommer, J. F. (Eds.), (1994). *Handbook of post-traumatic therapy.* Westport, CT: Greenwood Press.

Wilsnack, S. C., Vogeltanz, N. D., Klassen, A. D., & Harris, T. R. (1997). Childhood sexual abuse and women's substance abuse: National survey findings. *Journal of Studies on Alcohol, 58,* 264–271.

Wilson, J. P. (1989). *Trauma transformation and healing: An integrative approach to theory, research, and post-traumatic therapy.* New York: Brunner/Mazel.

Wilson, J. P., & Keane, T. M. (Eds.). (1997). Assesssing psychological trauma and PTSD. New York: The Guilford press.

Wilson, J. P., & Lindy, J. (Eds.) (1994). *Countertransference in the treatment of PTSD*. New York: Guilford.

Wilson, J., & Raphael, B. (Eds.). (1993). *International handbook of traumatic stress syndromes*. New York: Plenum Press.

Yapko, M. D. (1994a). Suggestibility and repressed memories of abuse: A survey of psychotherapists' beliefs. *American Journal of Clinical Hypnosis, 36*(3), 163–171.

Yapko, M. D. (1994b). *Suggestions of abuse: True and false memories of childhood sexual trauma*. New York: Simon & Schuster.

Yates, J. L., & Nasby, W. (1993). Dissociation, affect, and network models of memory: An integrative proposal. *Journal of Traumatic Stress, 6*, 305–326.

Yehuda, R. & Harvey, P. (1996). Relevance of neuroendecrine alterations in PTSD to memory-related impairments of trauma survivors. In J. D. Read & D. S. Lindsay (Eds.), *Recollections of trauma: Scientific evidence and clinical practice* (pp. 199–220). New York: Plenum Press.

Yehuda, R., & McFarlane, A. C. (1995). Conflict between current knowledge about posttraumatic stress disorder and its original conceptual basis. *American Journal of Psychiatry, 152*, 1705–1713.

Yehuda, R., & McFarlane, A. C. (1997a). Introduction. In R. Yehuda & A. C. McFarlane (Eds.), *Annals of the New York Academy of Sciences, 821* (pp. xi–xv). New York, New York: Academy of Sciences.

Yehuda, R., & McFarlane, A. C. (Eds.). (1997b). Psychobiology of posttraumatic stress disorder. *Annals of the New York Academy of Sciences, 821*, New York, New York: Academy of Sciences.

Yehuda, R., McFarlane, A. C., Pittman, R., Orr, S., Lasko, N., Shalev, A., & Peri, T. (1994b, November). *Biological basis of traumatic memory regulation in PTSD, Part II*. Scientific session presented at the annual meeting of the International Society for Traumatic Stress Studies, Chicago, IL.

Yuille, J. C. & Tollestrup, P. A. (1992). A model of diverse effects of emotion on eywitness memory. In S. Christianson (Ed.), *The handbook of emotion and memory: Research and theory* (pp. 201–213). Hillsdale, NJ: Erlbaum.

Yule, W., & Williams, R. M. (1990). Post-traumatic stress reactions in children. *Journal of Traumatic Stress, 3*, 279–295.

INDEX

abandonment, 120, 121, 216, 266, 268
    transference and, 301–2
Abrahamson, D. J., 148, 150
abreaction, 13, 20, 177, 184, 229, 233,
    303
abuse:
    alien abduction, 17, 38
    child, *see* child abuse; child sexual
        abuse
    emotional, 11, 133, 136, 229
    past life, 17, 38, 227
    physical, 7, 8, 11, 23, 32, 57, 102,
        133–37, 170, 226
    religiously-based, 228
abuse/trauma:
    in consensus model, 193–94, 315
    continuous/relatively continuous
        memory of, disclosure at initia-
        tion of treatment, 319–21
    continuous/relatively continuous
        memory of, no disclosure at out-
        set of treatment, 321–23
    countertransference reactions to,
        302–14
    decision model and, 315–18
    disclosure of, 222–23, 225–28

discontinuous memory or partial
    amnesia of, 323–25
new memories (delayed/recovered)
    of, while in current therapy,
    329–31
new memories (delayed/recovered)
    of, while in past therapy, 327–29
new memories (delayed/recovered)
    of, while not in therapy and
    without therapeutic interven-
    tion, 325–26
no memory of, but passionate belief
    in its occurrence and past
    involvement in suggestive self-
    help and alternative healing
    activities, 332–33
no memory of, but the individual
    suspects or believes it occurred,
    331
no memory of, but with third-party
    information/corroboration that it
    occurred, 334–35
non-disclosure of, 222, 228–31
transference reactions and, 298–303
accessibility, of therapist, 162–63
accidents, 10, 32, 57, 74, 102

accountability, 147, 148
Ackman, D., 123
acting-out, 123, 302, 305
acute catastrophic stress reaction, treat-
    ment of, 183
acute stress disorder (ASD), 78, 241
addictions, 195, 196, 197, 226
    see also alcoholism, alcohol abuse;
        drug abuse; substance abuse
adjunctive (collateral) treatment,
    170–72, 224
adult child, 15, 301
adults abused as children, xv, 6, 12, 182
    statutes of limitations and, 22
Aetiology of Hysteria, The (Freud), 4
affect and impulses, alterations in regu-
    lation of, 88
affect recognition, 191
"Age of Denial, The," 6, 304–5
"Age of the Backlash," 23, 307
"Age of Validation, The," 8, 305–6, 345
Ainsworth, M.D.S., 300
Al-Anon, 15
Albach, F., 80
Alcoholics Anonymous (AA), 15
alcoholism, alcohol abuse, 94, 195, 247
    parental, 15, 17, 26, 250
Aldridge-Morris, R., 254
Alexander, P. C., 21, 71, 149, 300
alien abduction abuse, 17, 38
Allard, C. B., 132
Allen, C. V., 14
Alpert, Judith L., 21, 53n, 99, 113, 153,
    213, 240, 292, 342
Alzheimer's disease, 94
Aman, C., 96
Ambadar, Z., 99, 101, 141, 142
American Humane Association, 23
American Medical Association (AMA),
Council on Scientific Affairs of, 51–52
    "Memories of Childhood Abuse,"
        51–52
American Psychiatric Association (APA),
    6, 9, 13, 32, 50–51, 65, 74, 78, 108,
    123, 147, 231, 252–56
    "Statement on Memories of Sexual
        Abuse, The," 50–51, 160–61, 270
American Psychological Association
    (APA), 8, 18, 29, 53–56, 69, 99,
    125, 147, 158, 161, 240, 319, 343,
    344
    Board of Directors of, 53–54

Working Group on Investigation of
    Memories of Childhood, 53–56
    final report, 54–56
    interim report, 53–54
American Society of Clinical Hypnosis
    (ASCH), 56–58, 280, 285, 286,
    294
    "Clinical Hypnosis and Memory,"
        56–58
amnesia, 4, 10, 35, 57, 81, 94, 102, 104,
    107, 112–14, 117–18, 120
    dissociative, 13, 42–43, 47, 72, 84, 86,
        112, 254
    infantile or childhood, 40, 94, 95,
        101, 109, 124, 135, 227
    partial or selective, 47, 93, 111, 126,
        130, 131, 136, 138
    predictors for, 142–44
    psychogenic, 11, 84, 120–21, 123
    studies documenting, 127–42
    use of term, 47
amygdala, 83, 92
Anderson, C., 21, 300
Anderson, G., 6, 11, 86
Andrews, B., 134, 140, 145, 347
anger:
    of patient, 171, 266, 302
    of therapist, 163, 305, 312–13
Annals of the New York Academy of
    Sciences, 245
Ann Arbor conference (1993), 25–26
anxiety, 4, 149, 190, 219
    chronic, 123
    countertransference and, 308–9
    treatment of, 172, 198
APA, see American Psychiatric
    Association; American
    Psychological Association
Applebaum, P. S., 148, 152, 172, 213,
    249
"Are Incest Victims Hated?"
    (MacCarthy), 313
"Are traumatic memories special?"
    (Shobe and Kihlstrom), 100
Armstrong, H., 62
Armstrong, J., 119
Armstrong, L., 6, 8, 14, 17, 23, 304, 305,
    307, 345
Aronson, L., 34, 98
art therapy, 36, 37
ASCH, see American Society of Clinical
    Hypnosis

assault, 78
    sexual, 10, 14, 17, 74
assertiveness, 192
assessment, xviii, 169, 190, 219–57, 369–70
    as baseline and process, 221–34
    in clinical scenarios, 318–39
    collateral, 170, 247–51
    in consensus model, 157, 190
    during crises, 231–34
    decision model and, 315–17
    disclosure of abuse/trauma in, 222–23, 225–28
    efficacy of, 147
    initial, 169–70, 221–25
    non-disclosure of abuse/trauma in, 222, 228–31
    ongoing, 170, 221
    summary of, 257
    see also diagnosis; trauma assessment
attachment, 196, 222
    ambivalent, 194
    transference and, 300
attachment abuse, 229
attack/aggression theme, countertransference and, 305, 312–13
attention, alterations in, 88
attorneys, therapists' use of, 167
attraction/approach theme, countertransference and, 305, 306–7, 311–12
Auerhahn, N. C., 81, 114, 205, 207, 319, 345
Australian Psychological Society, xix, 355–57
    "Guidelines Relating to Recovered Memories," 355–37
authority, authority figures:
    mistrust of vs. compliance toward, 159, 162, 190
    patient's questioning of, 156, 190
    protection of, 222
    therapist as, 190, 269–70
autobiographical memory, 94, 106, 107, 114, 268
Automatisme Psychologique, L' (P. Janet), 5
autonomic arousal, 84, 180, 181, 193, 198, 226, 231–32, 303
autonomy, 152–53, 156, 159, 170
avoidance, 94, 122, 180, 190–91, 274, 303
    countertransference and, 305, 308–11
    relational, 123
    sexual, 123

see also numbing/avoidance phase
Axis I disorders, 87, 177, 183, 237, 252, 254, 257, 283
Axis II disorders, 87, 177, 183, 237, 252, 254, 257, 283
Axis III disorders, 252

backup therapists, 164
Baker, T., 109
Banks, W. P., xv, 45, 47, 48, 68–69
Banyard, V. L., 70, 96, 97, 134–35, 142, 143, 144, 343
Barach, P. M., 300
Barban, L., 6, 121
Barden, R. C., 29
Barnes, M., 211
Barnier, A. J., 13
Barrett, M. J., 293
Bass, Ellen, 14, 15, 36, 38, 184
Batson, R., 21, 71, 80, 81, 86, 87, 149, 178, 182, 198, 205, 231, 244, 323
"Battered Child Syndrome, The" (Kempe, Silverman, Steele, Droegemueller, & Silver), 8
Batterman-Faunce, J. M., 121
Beattie, M., 15
Beauchamp, T. L., 153
Beaudoin, P., 21
Beckett, K., 26
behavioral memory, 94–95, 106, 108, 110, 111, 136
behavioral self-monitoring, 193
behavioral treatments, 181
Beitchman, J. H., 80, 122, 123
Belicki, K., 131
Belluck, P., 2, 253
Bendiksen, M., 99, 101, 141, 142
beneficence, 154, 155
Benward, J., 9
Berah, E. F., 205
bereavement, see grief
Berliner, L., xv, 258, 289
Bernstein, E. M., 256
Best Kept Secret, The (F. Rush), 6–7, 12
betrayal, 180
    in child sexual abuse, 119–22, 299
    countertransference and, 309–11
Betrayal Trauma (J. Freyd), 26, 120–21
billing, 167–68
Billings, F. J., 101
Binder, R. L., 125
biological assessment, 244, 245
bipolar depression, 169
bipolar disorder, 147

Bjornson, P., 11
Blake, D. D., 244
blaming, 28
    of children, 9, 118–19, 122, 233
    of patient, 165
    self-, 194, 228
Blank, A. S., 253
Blehar, M. C., 300
Blizard, R., 21, 194
Bloom, S. L., 178
Blume, E. Sue, 14, 15
Boakes, J., 360
body therapy, 37, 38
Bonne, O., 150
Boon, S., 85
borderline personality disorder (BPD),
    20, 78, 87, 174, 219, 283, 308
    treatment of, 149, 182, 188
Bottoms, B. L., 23, 96, 228
Boucock, A., 131
boundaries, 192, 198
    professional, maintenance of, 156,
        161–63, 264–65
    violation of, 161
Bowlby, John, 300
Bowman, E. S., 11
Bowman, M. L., 242
Brabin, P. J., 205
Bradshaw, John, 15
Brady, K. T., 252
Braff, D. L., 230
brain, 91, 101
    development of, 40
    hippocampus of, 83, 92, 104
    injury and damage to, 94
    PTSD and, 82–84
    storage and, 92
Brainin-Rodriguez, J. E., 223
Brandon, S., 360
Braun, B. G., 12
Bremner, J. D., 34, 98, 103, 104, 105
Brenneis, C. B., 157, 192, 206, 229, 268,
    346
Breuer, Josef, 3, 4, 13, 78, 84
Brewer, W. F., 105–6, 134, 137
Brewin, C. R., 134, 137
Briere, J., xv, 12, 20, 21, 36, 45–49, 86,
    87, 99, 123, 132, 145, 153, 178,
    180, 182, 185, 198, 207–8, 210,
    220, 221, 234, 240, 242, 258, 263,
    298, 302, 303, 324, 327, 329, 348
British Association of Counseling
    (BAC), xix, 363–64

British False Memory Society Report,
    58
British Journal of Psychiatry, 360
British Psychological Society, 319
    Report of the Working Party of,
        58–61
Broadhurst, D., 23
Broca's area, 83
Bronheim, Ben, 308
Brown, D., xv, 6, 12, 21, 27, 36–37, 38,
    41, 42, 45, 52, 56, 69, 90, 91, 93,
    99, 105, 106, 108n, 110, 111n, 113,
    114, 125, 126, 129n, 130, 131,
    143–44, 151, 153, 177, 178, 182,
    188, 204, 205, 211, 212, 213, 249,
    268, 270, 274, 280, 283–84,
    286–87, 318, 319, 324, 333, 347
Brown, L. S., xv, 53n, 69, 76, 99, 148,
    151, 153, 154, 155, 157, 159,
    263–64, 271, 275, 278–79, 283,
    327, 329, 333, 345
Brown, P., 5, 13, 85
Browne, A., 120, 123
Brownmiller, Susan, 9
Bruck, M., 23, 24, 40, 93, 96, 98, 101
Bruhn, A., 21, 194
Buck, C., 9, 14
Bull, R., 347
Burgess, A. W., 9, 12, 109, 136, 137
burnout, of therapists, 163
business relationship, confidentiality
    and, 167–68
Butler, K., xv, 48
Butler, L. S., 44, 99, 103, 110, 113
Butler, R. W., 230
Butler, S., 8, 9, 12, 14
bystander role, 162, 163, 168, 197, 300

Cahill, L., 82
Calof, David, 45, 269–70, 276
Cameron, C., 149
Campbell, J., 229
Campbell, J. A., 348
Canadian Psychiatric Association (CPA),
    61–64
    "Adult Recovered Memories of
    Childhood Sexual Abuse" 61–64
Cardeña, E., 84, 85
caretaking:
    by child, 301
    in therapy, 192, 199–200, 265
Carlson, E. B., 119, 121, 122, 123, 153,
    220, 242, 248, 249 328–29,
    332–33, 335, 339

Carlson, K., 348
Carmen, E., 220
Caruth, C., 76, 81, 345
catecholamines, 83
Caudill, O. Brandt, 148, 263, 267, 279
Ceci, Stephen J., 23, 24, 40, 53n, 69, 70, 91, 93, 96, 98, 99, 101
Chambless, D. L., 147, 150
Chapman, J. R., 9
Charcot, Jean-Martin, 3, 78, 84, 90
Charney, D. S., 82, 105
Cheit, Ross E., 71, 142, 335
Chew, J., 211
child abuse, xv, 8–11, 52, 78, 304
    emotional, 11, 133, 136
    neglect, 135
    ongoing, reporting of, 173
    physical, 7, 8, 11, 23, 133–37, 170
    prevention of, 23
    see also child sexual abuse
Child Abuse Prevention and Treatment Act (CAPTA; Mondale Act), 23
child development:
    memory and, 23, 40, 59, 94–97, 101, 106, 108
    sexual abuse and, 118–19
childhood (infantile) amnesia, 40, 94, 95, 101, 109, 124, 135, 227
children:
    backlash against, 46
    blaming of, 9, 118–19, 122, 233
    dissociation in, 34, 86, 117, 121, 122
    "events of impact" and, 98
    PTSD in, 106, 108, 110, 120
    suggestibility in, 23–24, 40, 93, 94
    traumatic memory in, 72, 73, 106, 108–12
    as witnesses, 23–24
Childress, J. F., 153
child sexual abuse, 182
    characteristics and dynamics of, xvii, 33, 117–24
    class and ethnic distribution of, 7–8
    controversy about memories of, see recovered/false memory controversy
    correlates of, 123–24
    decision not to explore, 166
    defined, 118
    disclosure of, 118–19
    false accusations of, 24–29, 43
    Ferenczi's views on, 5
    Freud's views on, 1, 4–7

in Kinsey's study, 7
lack of symptoms of, 122–23, 124
mechanisms for remembering or forgetting of, 142–44
memory and, 117–46
non-traumatic, 119
prevalence of, 7, 227
Rush's view of, 6–7
symptoms of, 123–24, 144–45, 166
traumagenic dynamics and, 120–23
underrecognition of, 52, 53
see also specific topics
child sexual abuse, review of scientific literature of recollections of, 124–42
    clinical samples in, 126, 127, 130–31
    nonclinical samples in, 126, 127, 131–32
    other studies in, 128–29, 138–42
    prospective case reports in, 137–38
    prospective studies in, 126, 128, 134–37
    random samples in, 126, 127–28, 132–34
child welfare, 7
Christianson, S. A., 81, 89–90, 97, 98, 101
Chu, J. A., xv, 11, 13, 16, 20–21, 35, 85, 86, 91, 103–4, 105, 121, 145–46, 157, 161, 163, 166, 177, 178, 182, 184, 192, 194, 196, 201, 202, 203, 256, 266, 301, 306, 348
Clinician-Administered PTSD Scale (CAPS), 244
Clubb, P. A., 92
Coan, D., 101
codependency, 15
cognitive-behavioral treatments, 181, 182, 183, 193–94, 198, 315
cognitive psychologists, 6
cognitive scientists, 22–25, 41
    defense attorneys' use of, 22, 23–24
Cohen, B. M., 211
Cohen, J. A., 348
Cohn, L., 216
Cole, P., 118, 119, 123
collaborative and empowering principle, 179
collateral assessments, 170, 247–51
collateral (adjunctive) treatment, 170–72, 224
Colletti, J., 161
combat trauma, see war trauma

communication:
  in adjunctive treatment, 171
  in patient-therapist relationship, 171
compassion fatigue, *see* vicarious trauma-
    tization
competence, of therapist, 263–64
complex posttraumatic stress disorder,
    see disorder of extreme stress, not
    otherwise specified
compulsions, 195, 196, 226, 268
concentration camp experiences, 10, 32,
    74
conditioned fear response, 92
confidentiality, 28, 166–68, 370–71
  business relationship and, 167–68
  limits of, 166–67, 173
confusion, countertransference and, 309
"Confusion of tongues between parents
    and the child" (Ferenczi), 5
connection, 192
consciousness, 5, 11, 86, 92
  altered state of, 3–4, 32, 88, 232
consensus model of posttrauma treat-
    ment (PTT), xviii, 157, 176–218,
    264, 320–21, 325
  abuse/trauma discussion in, 193–94,
    315
  approaches to traumatic memory in,
    207–12
  development of interpersonal rela-
    tionships and a support system in,
    200–201
  early phase of, 188–202, 315
  as growth cycle, 184–85
  hierarchy of issues, goals, and inter-
    ventions in, 186–88
  initial tasks and goals of treatment
    in, 191
  late phase of, 188, 215–17
  memory retrieval in, 212–13
  middle phase of, 188, 202–15, 315
  origins of, 183
  personal functioning in, 199–200
  preparation for treatment phase in,
    213–15
  pretreatment issues in, 188–89
  rationale for work with traumatic
    memories in, 204–6
  safety issues in, 190, 191, 193–97,
    201
  self-care in, 191, 197–98, 201
  self functions in, 191, 198
  as sequenced or phase-oriented,
    xviii, 6, 176, 177, 182–217

summary of, 217–18
  titration and modulation in, 180,
    185–86
  treatment frame in, 189–91
consent:
  empowered, 159, 190
  informed, 158–60, 190, 262, 269–70,
    376
consistency, of therapist, 163–64
consumers, demands of, 147
Conte, J., 36, 132
conversion, 6, 11, 84
Conway, M. A., 99
Coons, P. M., 11, 85
Cordes-Green, S., 211
Cormier, J. F., 254
Cornell, W. F., 180, 185, 210
Correy, B., 131
corroboration, patient's search for,
    291–92
Corwin, D. L., 109, 137, 141
countertransference, xviii–xix, 20, 21,
    163, 174, 192, 235–36, 296–98,
    302–14
  attack/aggression and, 305, 312–13
  attraction/approach and, 305, 306–7,
    311–12
  avoidance and, 305, 308–11
  balance in, 313–14
  in clinical scenarios, 318–39
  errors of, 168, 174, 304–13
  in historical perspective, 304–7
  risk management and, 268–69, 277
Courage, M. L., 96
Courage to Heal, The (Bass & Davis), 14,
    15, 36, 38
Courage to Heal Workbook, The (Davis),
    14
Courtois, Christine A. (author), 6, 7, 9,
    12, 17, 20, 21, 36, 45, 48, 68, 81,
    86, 91, 99, 118, 119, 122, 125, 148,
    151, 153, 156, 162, 164, 178, 182,
    184, 185, 191, 194, 198, 200–201,
    202, 205, 207, 210, 211, 220, 222,
    226, 229, 230, 243, 244, 249, 258,
    261, 268, 278, 279, 280, 289, 299,
    306, 319, 320, 323, 329, 342, 348
Cox, T. C., 211
Crasilneck, H. B., 295n
Crews, F., 6
crises, assessment during, 231–34
Criterion A, PTSD diagnosis, 241, 253
Criterion B, PTSD diagnosis, 253
Cuddy, M., 131

cults, 2, 11, 12, 17, 38, 39, 182, 227, 228, 233, 308
cultural issues, 238
Currie, R., 86

daCosta, G., 123
Dale, Peter, 220
Dalenberg, Constance J., 139–40, 153, 162, 223, 307n, 308, 312, 314, 315, 318, 327, 328–29, 332–33, 335, 339, 348
Danieli, Y., 20, 306
Davies, J. M., 21, 33, 162, 192, 207, 211, 298, 300, 302, 303
Davis, Laura, 14, 15, 36, 38, 184
Davis, M., 82
Dawes, R. M., 130, 150, 261
day care abuse, 11
DDIS (Dissociative Disorders Interview Schedule), 244, 256
DDNOS, see dissociative disorder not otherwise specified
death:
    threat of, 120
    see also homicidality; murder; suicide, suicidal behavior
decision-tree model, 155, 176, 297, 315–18
declarative memory, see explicit memory
decompensation and recompensation cycles of, 186–88
defense mechanisms, see specific defense mechanisms
defensiveness, of therapist, 311
delayed/recovered memory, 275
    of abuse/other trauma while in current therapy, 329–31
    of abuse/other trauma while not in therapy and without therapeutic intervention, 325–26
    in crisis assessments, 231, 232, 233
    reenactment dynamics and, 169
    supportive neutrality stance and, 162
    while in past therapy, 327–29
    treatment of, 147, 152–53, 192
    see also recovered/false memory controversy; recovered memories
Dell, P. F., 254
denial, 33, 104, 107, 121, 194, 221, 274, 302
    countertransference and, 309
Densen-Gerber, J., 9

dental hygiene, poor, 197–98
dependence, 299
    patient, 162–63, 192, 199, 201, 202, 269, 277, 283, 301
depersonalization, 11, 84, 86, 231
depression, 94, 113, 122, 147, 187, 219, 232, 283
    bipolar, 169
    treatment of, 149, 172, 193, 198
derealization, 11, 84, 123, 231
DESNOS, see disorder of extreme stress, not otherwise specified
detachment, 34, 85, 123
Deutch, A. Y., 82
dexamethasone suppression test (DST), 245
De Zulueta, F., 300
diagnosis, 250–57
    childhood abuse and trauma and, 219
    in crises, 233, 234
    multiple, 246
    prior, 169, 223
    self-, 169
Diagnostic and Statistical Manual (DSM), 6, 112, 244, 250, 252–55
Diagnostic and Statistical Manual, Third Edition (DSM-III), 9–10, 11, 32, 244
Diagnostic and Statistical Manual, Fourth Edition (DSM-IV), 74–75, 76, 79, 80, 86, 123, 140, 150, 241, 244, 252, 254
DID, see dissociative identity disorder
Dill, D. L., 11, 35, 85, 86, 121
Dinwiddie, S. H., 11
disasters, 10, 32, 57, 74, 85, 102
disbelief, countertransference and, 313
disempowerment, of therapist, 311
disorder of extreme stress, not otherwise specified (DESNOS; complex posttraumatic stress disorder), 80, 86–88, 254
    cycles of decompensation and recompensation in, 186–88
    structured interview for, 244
    symptoms of, 87, 88, 229
    treatment of, 177, 178, 182, 183, 186–88, 191, 201–2
dissociation, dissociative disorders, xvii, 6, 10–14, 78, 84–86, 94, 104, 112–13, 180, 219, 221, 226, 254
    during assessment, 227, 232, 233, 237
    in children, 34, 86, 117, 121, 122

in children vs. adults, 34
continuum of, 85
defined, 33–34, 85
false memory perspective on, 41, 42–43
Janet's view of, 4, 5, 6, 11, 84
normal, 85
peritraumatic, 33, 34, 85
prevalence of, 85–86
structured interview for, 244
symptoms of, 12, 34, 85, 170, 176, 315
transference and, 302, 303
traumatic stress perspective on, 32–35
types of, 11, 86
Dissociation, 14
dissociative amnesia, 13, 42–43, 47, 72, 84, 86, 112, 254
dissociative disorder not otherwise specified (DDNOS), 11, 86, 123
Dissociative Disorders Interview Schedule (DDIS), 244, 256
Dissociative Experiences Scale (DES), 256
dissociative fugue, 86
dissociative identity disorder (DID), 86, 123, 140, 169, 182, 284, 303
in crisis assessment, 232, 233
diagnosis of, 253–56
treatment of, 149, 287
Distad, L. J., 9
Doane, B. K., 84
Dobson, R., 29
Dolan, Y. M., 21
domestic violence, xv, 8–9, 11, 14, 17, 33, 78, 173, 222
Donaldson, M. A., 9, 211
doubt, countertransference and, 313
dreams:
distressing, 80, 84
interpretation of, 38, 192, 229
Droegemueller, W., 8
drug abuse, 195, 247
drugs, 170, 172, 197, 198
in consensus model, 177, 181, 182, 183, 194, 197
memory retrieval and, 29, 39
Duggal, S., 137, 141
Dunlop, A., 131

early memory, *see* implicit memory
eating disorders, 61, 147, 170, 195

education of patient, 180, 190, 193, 274, 315
ego resources, 177, 191, 201, 229
Elin, M. R., 76, 98, 106, 109, 119
Ellason, J. W., 149, 230
Ellenberger, H. F., 11
Ellenson, G. S., 230
Elliott, D. M., 86, 102, 123, 132, 145, 298, 302, 303, 324
EMDR, *see* eye movement desensitization and reprocessing
emotional abuse, 11, 133, 136, 229
emotions, 226
action vs., 191
healing of, 180
vehement, 3
empathy, 161–62, 163, 171, 179
empowered consent, 159, 190
empowerment, as focus of therapy, 154, 155–56, 159, 170, 192, 278–79
encoding, memory:
child sexual abuse and, 121, 122
in normal memory, 91, 92, 100, 101
in traumatic memory, 33, 34, 72, 97, 100, 102, 103, 104, 110, 113
endogenous opioids, 83
Engel, B., 14
Engelberg, E., 81, 89–90, 101
Enns, C. Z., 68, 156, 229, 293
episodic memory, *see* explicit memory
Eth, S., 10, 106, 150
ethics complaints, 28–29, 45, 152
ethnicity, 7–8, 238
Evans, K., 216, 246, 247
"events of impact," 97–98
Everaerd, W., 80
Everly, G. S., 82, 245
Ewing, C. P., 28, 172
exercise, 194, 197
expectations, patient, 228, 277
explicit memory (episodic, declarative, and late memory), 92, 95, 103, 104
eye movement desensitization and reprocessing (EMDR), 159, 262, 270, 288
eyewitness suggestibility, 42

false memories, false memory syndrome, xiii–xv, xvii, 24–28, 38–39, 94, 101
coining of term, 62–63
countertransference and, 313

defined, 26
hypnosis and, 13, 43, 57, 224–25,
    285–88
legislative initiatives and, xiii,
    172–73
litigation and, xiii, xiv, 2
media reports on, 26–27
memory discussed or recovered in
previous or current therapy recanted as,
    338–39
memory (usually recovered) of
    improbable, obviously false, or
    seemingly false, 335–37
risk management and, 152, 282–84,
    288–89
suggestibility and, 224–25, 269,
    282–84
VOCAL and, 24, 25
see also recovered/false memory con-
    troversy
false memory defense, xiii, 2
false memory perspective, 124, 258
extreme, 42–43, 45, 48
moderate, 41–42, 48
overview of, 38–43
False Memory Syndrome Foundation
    (FMSF), 24–28, 42, 62–64
Scientific Advisory Board of, 42–43,
    53
False Memory Syndrome Foundation
    Newsletter, 2
family, family issues:
collateral interviews with, 248,
    249–50
disruptions of, 24–27, 37–38, 39
dysfunctional, 15, 16, 17, 119, 222,
    227, 249; see also domestic vio-
    lence
risk management and, 268, 292–93
treatment issues and, 172–73, 268
see also domestic violence; fathers;
    mothers
fantasy, 94, 96, 224, 230, 268–69, 275
fantasy (oedipal) theory, 4–5, 6, 304
Farmer, K., 289
fathers, 4
sexually abusive, 25, 26, 172
fear, 180, 216, 228, 241
child sexual abuse and, 119, 120, 122
countertransference and, 308–9, 211
Feldman, J., 100, 135
Feldman-Summers, S., 347
Felton, K. A., 132
Femina, D., 136, 137

feminism, 6–9, 14
Ferenczi, Sandor, 5, 11
Fetkewicz, J., 199–200, 289, 339
Fett, S., 136
fidelity, 154
Fiering, C., 122
Figley, C. R., 12, 75, 78, 175, 177, 192
Figueredo, A. J., 89
financial resources, 223, 224
Fine, C. G., 21, 182
Finkelhor, D., 8, 9, 120, 122, 123, 343
Fish, V., 343
Fisler, R., 81, 82, 103, 104, 131, 137
Fitzpatrick, F. L., 71, 324, 335
Fivush, R., 96, 121
flashbacks, 35, 80, 83, 115, 123, 192,
    231, 279, 303, 312
Fleisher, W. P., 86
Foa, E. B., 149, 205
Follette, V. M., xvi, xix, 80, 123, 149,
    347
Fong-Beyette, M. L., 162, 222, 223
forced silence, 76, 220
Ford, K., 149
forensic cases, 237, 239, 266, 267
forensic hypnosis, 56, 58, 174
forensic psychologists, 22
forgetting, 33, 34, 59, 72, 81, 99, 112–15
dissociation compared with, 85
intentional, 80, 113
motivated, 44, 80, 94, 113, 122, 180
normal, 113
see also amnesia; dissociation, disso-
    ciative disorders; repression
forms:
informed consent, 158–59, 376
model, 369–76
Forward, S., 9, 14
Fox, R. E., 48
Foy, D. W., 80, 177, 180–82, 183n
fragmented identity, 84
Frankel, F., 41
Fraser, G., 11
Fraser, S., 14
Frawley, M. G., 21, 162, 192, 207, 211,
    298, 300, 302, 303
Frederickson, R., 37
Freud, Sigmund, 1, 11, 13, 78, 84, 117,
    304
hysteria as viewed by, 3–7
Frey, L. M., 91
Freyd, Jennifer, J., 25–26, 47, 81, 90, 96,
    112, 113, 118–27, 289
Freyd, Pamela, 25–26, 39

Freyd, Peter, 25–26
Friedman, M. J., 82, 84*n*, 105, 113, 115, 245
Friedrich, W. N., 136, 137
Friends of FMS, 29
Frischolz, E., 295*n*
Fromm, E., 12, 182
fugue states, 11, 84, 86, 115, 232
Fullilove, M. T., 247
Furby, L., 119

Galatzer-Levy, R. M., 206, 268
Ganaway, G. K., 42, 47, 206
Ganzel, B., 91
Gardner, M., 39
Gardner, R. A., 9, 41
Garfield, S. L., 148
Garry, M., 100, 135
Gartner, R. B., 5, 6, 21, 213
Garver, R. B., 295n
Gates, M., 9
Gebhard, P. H., 7
Geffner, R., 149
Gelinas, D. J., 9, 36, 220, 321
gender issues, 238
Genova, P., 300–301
Gerrity, E. T., 150
Giaconia, R. M., 123
Giannelli, P. C., 174
Gibson, P., 347
Gil, E., 12, 191
Giller, E., 82, 245
Glaser, D., 360
Glaser, R., 205
Glickhauf-Hughes, C., 21
glucocorticoids, 83
Goenjian, A., 34
Gold, S. N., 113, 125, 139, 154, 278–79, 319, 323, 327, 329, 333
Goldstein, E., 289
Goldstone, R. L., 125
Golier, J. A., 103, 105
Goodlin-Jones, B. I., 235–36
Goodman, G. S., 23, 96, 121, 228
Gordon, M., 149
Gotlib, I. H., 134
Gottlieb, M., 229
Grand, Sue, 81, 289, 310–11, 314, 323
Grassian, S., 109, 141, 144–45
Gravitz, M. A., 295n
Great Britain, 140
Green, A. H., 10
Green, B. L., 123
Green, R., 360

Greenberg, S. A., 266
grief, 10, 180, 216, 266, 301
Griffin, M. G., 82, 245
Grinfeld, M. J., 2, 253
Groth, A. N., 9
grounding, 191, 198
groups, self-help, 15–16, 19, 28, 283, 289–90
group therapy, 36, 149, 170, 200–201
Grunberg, F., 50, 258–60, 267
Gudjonsson, G. H., 224, 283
guided imagery, 36, 37, 38
guilt, 122, 228, 233, 301
Guroff, J. J., 6, 121
Gutheil, T. G., 261, 262, 263, 266, 267–68, 291
gynecological damage, 170

Haaken, J., 16, 17, 19, 20, 27, 41, 42, 47, 201
hallucinations, 232
Halpert, M., 86
Hammond, D. Corydon, xv, 56–57, 108*n*, 111*n*, 159, 224, 280, 285–86, 294, 295*n*
Hammond, N., 96
Hanna, C., 79
Harber, K. D., 205
Harris, M., 201
Harris, T. R., 246
Harter, S., 149
Hartman, C. R., 109
Harvey, M. R., 36, 113, 124, 125, 138–39, 148, 149, 182, 206, 207, 290–91, 319
Harvey, P., 82
Hauser-Hines, S., 289
Haverkamp, B. E., 153
Hayes, S. C., 151
head injury, 170
health-care delivery system, 147
Heber, S., 6
Hedges, L. E., 148, 152
Hegeman, E., 269
helplessness, 241
    child sexual abuse and, 118, 120
    countertransference and, 309–11
Hembrooke, H., 24
Herald, C., 220, 222
Herman, J. L., 1, 3, 9, 12, 20, 21, 36, 76, 86, 87, 113, 118, 121, 122, 124, 125, 130, 132, 138–39, 148, 149, 155, 177, 178, 182, 184, 196, 207, 211, 217, 319

Hewitt, S. A., 106
Hibler, N. S., 295n
Hilgard, E. R., 6
Hilton, R., 148
Hilton, V. W., 148, 165
Hinnefeld, B., 29, 173
hippocampus, 83, 92, 104
Hirschman, L., 9
HIV testing, 322
Hohnecker, L., 113
holistic health techniques, 180
Holmes, D. S., 39, 41, 112
Holmstrom, L. L., 9
Holtzen, D., 109, 141, 144–45
homicidality, 195, 232
Hood, J., 123
hormones, PTSD and, 83
Horn, M., 141
Horowitz, Mardi J., 10, 12, 79, 80, 103,
    182, 185, 191, 208
Horton, J. M., Jr., 245–46
hospitalization, 170, 171–72, 197
hostility, of therapist, 312–13
Houskamp, B. M., 123
Hovdestad, W. E., 132
"How Could This Happen?" (P. Freyd),
    25
Howe, M. L., 96
Hudson, J. I., 124, 126, 130, 132, 135
Huffman, M. L., 96
Hughes, D., 113
Husband, T. H., 101
Hyman, I. E., 101
hypermnesia, 4, 10, 32, 80, 81, 104, 107,
    115, 120
hypnosis, 42, 269
    false memories and, 13, 43, 57,
        224–25, 285–88
    forensic, 56, 58, 174
    forms for use with, 158–59
    hysteria and, 3, 5
    memory retrieval and, 12–13, 39, 41,
        52, 56, 57–58, 62, 64, 270, 285–88
    risk management and, 285–88
    in treatment, 36, 37, 224–25, 270,
        285–88
hysteria, 3–8, 11, 32, 78, 283

identity, 11, 26, 86
    formation of, 191
    fragmented, 84
    unstable, 191
identity disorder, dissociative, see disso-
    ciative identity disorder

ignorance, countertransference and, 312
illness, physical, 221
implicit memory (nondeclarative and
    early memory), 92, 95, 103, 104,
    111, 268
impulsivity, 152, 173
incest, xiv, 7, 9, 17, 33, 46, 182
    characteristics and dynamics of, xvii,
        117–24
    class and ethnic distribution of, 7–8
    correlates of, 123–24
    countertransference responses to,
        304–5, 307
    duration of, 118
    Freud's views on, 4–6
    transference reactions and, 302
    traumagenic dynamics and, 120–23
Incest History Questionnaire, 243–44
independence, transference and, 299,
    300–301
"index of suspicion," 321
individuality principle, 179–80
inexperience, countertransference and,
    312
infantile (childhood) amnesia, 40, 94,
    95, 101, 109, 124, 135, 227
information-gathering, 247–50
information-processing, 79–80
informed consent, 158–60, 190, 262,
    269–70, 376
informed refusal, 190
injury, 94, 118, 120, 122, 170
inner child, 15–16
insurance companies, insurance, 147,
    167, 191, 200, 220, 373–75
interactive theory of traumatic stress
    reactions, 76, 77, 78, 144
International Society for the Study of
    Dissociation (formerly the
    International Society for the
    Study of Multiple Personality and
    Dissociation), 14, 68
    "Guidelines for the Treatment of
    Dissociative Identity Disorder,"
    68
International Society for Traumatic
    Stress Studies, (formerly the
    Society for Traumatic Stress
    Studies), 14, 66–68, 150
    "Memories of Childhood Trauma,"
    66–68
interviews:
    collateral, 248, 249–50
    customized, 242

intake, 221–25
    structured, 243–44
intimacy, 192
    negative, 180
    transference and, 299, 300
intolerance, of therapist, 312–13
"intrusion error," 312
intrusive/reexperiencing phase, 79, 80,
    193, 278
intrusive memories, 35, 89, 115, 226
irritation, of therapist, 312–13
Issues in Child Abuse Accusations, 25

Jacobs, W. J., 105
Jacobson, A., 55, 220, 222
Janet, Pierre, 3–6, 11, 78, 84, 89, 90–91,
    104, 117
    sequenced posttrauma treatment
        model and, 183–84
Jeffery, J., 289
Jehu, D., 12, 71, 149, 186, 193, 198
Johnson, D. R., 82
Josephson, G. S., 162, 222, 223
Joshi, S., 86
Journal of Traumatic Stress, 14
justice, 154

Kadish, B., 141
Kagan, B., 180–82, 183n
Kaloupek, D. G., 245
Kaminer, W., 179
Kaplan, S., 88n
Kardiner, A., 10, 78
Keane, T. M., 208, 242, 245
Keene, T., 252
Keltti, R., 85
Kempe, Henry, 8
Kendall-Tackett, K. A., 122, 123–24
Kepner J. I., 21, 149, 182, 184–85, 277
Ketcham, K., 42, 112
kidnapping, 32, 74
Kiecolt-Glaser, J. K., 205
Kihlstrom, J. F., 5, 26, 99, 100
Kilpatrick, D., 123
Kinsey, A. C., 7
Kirschner, D. A., 21
Kirschner, S., 21
Klassen, A. D., 246
Klein, R. M., 84
Kluft, R. P., 6, 11, 12, 20, 21, 140–41,
    149, 178, 182, 185–86, 189, 190,
    201, 207, 230, 252, 254, 284–85,
    287, 308, 318

Knapp, S. J., xv, 148, 151, 152, 153, 157,
    173, 231, 252, 265–66, 280
Knight, J., 245, 246, 306
"Knowing and Not Knowing Massive
    Psychic Trauma" (Laub and
    Auerhahn), 114–15
knowledge, of therapist, 263–64
Kolb, L., 82
Koraleski, S. F., 149
Korean War, 9, 304
Korn, D. L., 278
Korsakoff's disease, 94
Koss, M. P., 89, 97
Koutstaal, W., 113
Kovacs, A. A., 148
Koverola, C., 79
Kristiansen, C. M., 131
Kroll, J., 20, 21, 87, 182
Krystal, J. H., 82, 98, 345
Kuhn, J., 121

Larson, L. M., 149
Larus, D. M., 92
late memory, *see* explicit memory
Lating, J. M., 245, 252
Laub, D., 81, 114, 205, 207, 319, 345
"lawsuit therapy," 308
lay literature, 14–16, 19, 25, 38, 148,
    155, 289–90
lay therapies, 14, 16–17, 169, 171
learning deficits and disabilities, 170,
    226
Lebowitz, L., 149, 182
LeDoux, J. E., 98, 101, 105
Leeds, A. M., 278
Leehan, J., 211
legislative initiatives, xiii–xiv, 21–22, 23,
    28, 29, 172–73
Leifer, M., 348
Levine, H., 206, 268, 269
Lewis, D. O., 136
Lewis, M., 122
licensing board complaints, 28, 45, 152
Lief, H. I., 199–200, 289, 339
life enhancement, 183, 188, 215–17
Lindberg, F. H., 9
Lindemann, E., 10
Lindsay, D. Stephen, xv, 45–49, 59, 91,
    99, 101, 130, 153, 220, 258, 259n,
    342
Lindsay, S., 347
Lindy, J., 21, 161, 192, 306, 348

Linehan, M., 71, 87, 149, 182, 188–89, 193, 196, 198, 200–201
Liotti, G., 300
Lipovsky, J., 123
Lison, K., 14
Lister, E. D., 76
litigation, 39, 172–74, 225
  children as witnesses in, 23–24
  countertransference and, 308
  false memory defense and, xiii, 2
  against parents, xiv
  by parents, 22, 28–29, 172
  risk management and, 152–53, 266–67, 288, 292–93
  standard of care and, 151
  against therapists, xiii, 2, 22, 28–29, 45, 48, 172–73
Litz, B. T., 208
Loewenstein, R. J., 244, 256, 303, 306
Loftus, Elizabeth F., 53n, 24, 40, 42, 43, 53n, 91, 93, 96, 99, 100, 101, 112, 130, 135, 220, 247
London, R., 293
Loo, C. M., 182
loss:
  crisis and, 231, 232
  transference and, 300, 301, 302
loyalty, 194, 228
  divided, 268
Lundberg-Love, P. K., 149
Lynn, S. J., 56, 84, 283–86

McCann, I. L., 12, 21, 75, 161, 174, 182, 193, 198, 235–36, 244, 299, 306
MacCarthy, B., 313
McClarty, B., 79
McConkey, K. M., xv, 13, 93, 99, 100
McFarlane, A. C., 6, 21, 36, 79, 82, 83n, 105, 245
McGaugh, J., 82, 98, 101, 105
McGuire, Alec, 363–64
McHugh, Paul R., 47, 249, 291
McNiel, D. E., 125
magnification, 227–28
Main, M., 300
Major Symptoms of Hysteria, The (Janet), 5
malingering, 230
Malinoski, P., 56, 283
Maltz, W., 216
managed care companies, 147–48
management, 191
  self-, 177, 191, 197, 198, 201, 277

see also risk management
Mandel, F. S., 87, 88n
Mannarino, A. P., 348
Marmar, C. R., 34, 85, 180–82, 183n, 348
Marmion, S., 149
Marshall, R. P., 182
Martin, C. E., 7
Mason, J. W., 178, 187n
Masson, J. M., 4, 5, 6
Matthews, J., 91
meanings, systems of, alterations in, 88
media influence, 17–18, 26–27, 48, 132, 155, 254, 283
medical problems, 221, 226
medication, see drugs
Mehren, E., 141
Meichenbaum, D., 182, 193, 198, 260–61
Meiselman, K. C., 9, 12, 21
Melchert, T. P., 133, 134
Mellody, P., 15
Melton, G. B., 266
Memon, A., 347
memory:
  accuracy of, 93–94, 96, 125–26
  alterations in, 34, 85
  autobiographical, 94, 106, 107, 114, 268
  behavioral, 94–95, 106, 108, 110, 111, 136
  child development and, 23, 40, 59, 94–97, 101, 106, 108
  child sexual abuse and, 117–46
  continuum of, 46, 48, 117–18, 125, 226
  in determination of therapeutic approach, 264
  encoding of, see encoding, memory
  explicit (episodic; declarative; late), 92, 95, 103, 104
  false, see false memories, false memory syndrome; false memory perspective; recovered/false memory controversy
  hysteria and, 3–4
  implicit (nondeclarative; early), 92, 95, 103, 104, 111, 268
  integration of, xviii, 4, 5, 35–36
  intrusive, 35, 89, 115, 226
  J. Freyd's research on, 26
  malleability of, 93, 275
  normal event, see normal event memory

recovered, *see* delayed/recovered memory; recovered/false memory controversy; recovered memories
    retrieval of, *see* retrieval, memory
    storage of, 33, 34, 72, 91, 92, 100
    trauma and, 72–117; see also traumatic memory
    verbal (narrative), *see* verbal (narrative) memory
Memory, Trauma, Treatment, and the Law (Brown et al.), 188
"memory recovery therapy," 177
memory researchers, 124, 142, 258
    on normal vs. traumatic memory, 99–101
memory trace, 92, 104
memory war, xv
"Mental Health Consumer Protection Act, The" ("The Consumer Fraud Protection Act;" "The Truth and Responsibility in Mental Health Practices Act"), 29, 172–73
Mental State of Hystericals, The (Janet), 5
Mersky, H., 254
Merwin, M. R., 197
Metcalfe, J., 105
midbrain, 92
military experiments, 11, 12
Miller, Alice, 14
Miller, S. D., 11, 35
Millon Clinical Multi-axial Inventory-III (MCMI-III), 224, 239
Milstein, V., 11, 85
minimization, 194
Minnesota Multiphasic Personality Instrument (MMPI), 239
Minnesota Multiphasic Personality Inventory-2 (MMPI-2), 224, 239
minorities, 7
misinformation effect, 93
Molnar, C., 205
Mondale Act (Child Abuse Prevention and Treatment Act; CAPTA), 23
mood disorders, 231
mood regulation, 191, 194, 198
Moore, M. K., 149
Morris, S., 135
mothers, 25, 26
motivated forgetting, 44, 80, 94, 113, 122, 180
Mrazek, P. B., 9
Mueser, K. T., 230

Mulhern, S., 228
multiple personality disorder (MPD), 6, 11, 12, 14, 28, 42, 182
murder, 7, 39, 102
Murdock, T. B., 149
Mutter, C. B., 295n
mutuality, 192
Myers, B., 56, 283
Myth of Repressed Memory, The (Loftus and Ketcham), 112

Nader, K., 106, 108
Nagy, T. F., 68, 280
naiveté, countertransference and, 312
narrative, 115, 274, 275, 278
    memory vs., 93
narrative memory, *see* verbal (narrative) memory
Nasby, W., 33–34, 85, 113
Nash, M. R., 69, 70, 343
Nathan, P., 148
National Association of Social Work (NASW), 64–66
National Council on the Practice of Clinical Social Work, 64–66
    "Evaluation and Treatment of Adults with the Possibility of Recovered Memories of Childhood Sexual Abuse," 64–66
National Institute of Mental Health, 149
Naugle, A. E., xvi, xix
Neimeyer, R. A., 149
Nelson, K., 96, 121
Nemiah, J. C., 85
neocortex, 92
neodissociation theory, 6
Neumann, D. S., 123
neuropsychological assessment, 244–247
Newman, E., 245, 248
Newman, R., 29, 173
New Zealand Psychological Society, xix, 68, 364–68
    "Memory of Traumatic Childhood Events," 364–68
Ney, T., 50, 258–260, 267
nightmares, 80, 84
Nishith, P., 82
nondeclarative memory *see* implicit memory
nonmaleficence, 154
norepinephrine (NE), 83
normal event memory, xvii, 3, 70–97

accuracy of, 93–94, 96
clarity and detail of, 58
principles of, 90–94
traumatic memory compared with, 34, 57, 72–73, 98–106
normalization principle, 179
normal stress response, treatment of, 183
Norris, F. H., 242
North Atlantic Treaty Organization (NATO) Advanced Studies Institute on "Recollections of Trauma," 49
Norton, G. R., 6, 86
Noyes, R., 85
numbing, 33, 34, 123, 193, 226, 231, 278, 303
numbing/avoidance phase, 79, 80

object constancy, 191
objectivity, 148, 154, 162, 223
object relations, 191–92, 268–69, 300
obsessive-compulsive disorder, 170
Ochberg, F. M., 12, 177, 179–80
oedipal theory, 4–5, 6, 304
Office Mental Status Examination for Complex Dissociative Symptoms and Multiple Personality Disorder, 244
Ofshe, R., 42, 43, 112
Ogata, S. N., 20
Olafson, E., 137, 141
Olio, K. A., 180, 185, 207, 210
Olson, J., 295n
omnipotence, 302
open-ended questions, 222–23, 226, 273, 278
Ornstein, Peter, A., 40, 53n, 91, 92, 97, 99, 100, 101
Orr, S. P., 82, 245
overbelief, countertransference and, 311–12
overcompensation, countertransference and, 311–312
overinvolvement, of therapist, 163, 265–66, 312

Palm, K. M., 347
panic disorder, 147, 193, 232
Panser, L., 136
paranoia, 230, 283, 309
parent-child bond, disruptions of, 87
parents:
    alcoholism of, 15, 17, 26, 250
    blaming by, 28

litigation against, xiv
litigation by, 22, 28–29, 172
VOCAL and, 24, 25
see also fathers; mothers
Parker, R. L., 133, 134
Parson, E. R., 12, 177, 178, 182
past life abuse, 17, 38, 227
patients:
    dependence of, 162–63, 192, 199, 201, 202, 269, 277, 283, 301
    education of, 180, 190, 193, 274, 315
    engagement in treatment process and responsibility for progress of, 156, 159, 165–66, 190
    expectations of, 228, 277
    philosophical foundations and, 152–157
    in relationship, 172–74, 192, 200–201, 202, 215–17, 231, 300
    responsibility of, 165–66, 192, 197, 265, 266
    rights of, 371
    safety issues and, 168–169, 190, 191, 193–97, 201, 226
    search for corroboration by, 291–292
    self-care of, 191, 197–98, 201
    treatment frame and, see treatment frame
payment, 167–68, 372–75
Payne, A. B., 348
Peacock, L., 149
Pearlman, Laurie Anne, 12, 21, 75, 76, 162, 163, 174, 182, 192, 193, 198, 202, 211, 235–36, 244, 265, 299, 306, 307n, 348
pedophilia, 11
peer review, 262, 285
Pelcovitz, D., 87, 88n, 244
Pennebaker, J. W., 71, 205
perception:
    alterations in, 34, 85, 86, 88, 303
    self-, 88, 299–300
Perry, B. D., 34, 98, 106, 109
Perry, J. C., 20, 196
Perry, N. W., 23
personal functioning, 199–200
personality disorders, 283
    borderline, see borderline personality disorder
    multiple (MPD), 6, 11, 12, 14, 28, 42, 182
personality measures, 224
personal resources, 223–24
Peters, J. J., 9

Pezdek, K., xv, 45, 47, 48, 68–69
pharmacotherapy, *see* drugs
philosophical foundations, 152–57, 159
phobias, 123
phone trees, 197
physical abuse, 32, 57, 102, 226
  of children, 7, 8, 11, 23, 133–37, 170
physical damage, *see* injury
Pickrell, J. E., 101
Pillemer, D. B., 94
Pitman, R., 82
Pollock, V. E., 123
Polonsky, S., 247
Polusny, M. M., 80, 123, 347
Pomeroy, W. B., 7
Poole, D., 347
Pope, H. G., 124, 126, 130, 132, 135
Pope, K. S., xv, 28, 45, 69, 151, 153, 155,
  157, 159, 263–64, 271, 342, 347
pornography, child, 11, 12
Porter, Father, 131, 141, 144
Post, R. M., 6, 121
Poston, C., 14
posttraumatic stress disorder (PTSD),
  9–10, 11, 13, 32, 34–37, 74, 78–84,
  94, 105, 219
  assessment and, 219, 227, 229, 237,
    239, 241, 242, 244–48, 250, 252
  in children, 106, 108, 110, 120
  without comorbidity (simple), 177,
    178, 183
  and DD, 186, 227, 237, 244, 247,
    248, 250, 257
  defined, 76
  delayed onset of, 122–23, 237
  diagnosis of, 252–57
  emerging data on the psychobiology
    and psychophysiology of, 73,
    81–84
  physiology of, 81–82, 84
  prediction of development of, 85
  psychosis and, 230
  substance abuse and, 247
  symptoms of, 155, 178, 193, 197, 198,
    227, 229, 245
  treatment of, 149, 172, 177, 178,
    180–83, 186–88, 191, 193, 198,
    201–2
posttraumatic stress reactions and symptoms, 107, 231–32, 264
  continuum of, 73, 78–81
  defined, 75–76
  measures of, 240–41
  as physioneurosis, 78

variety of strategies used with,
  278–79
posttrauma treatment (PTT):
  characteristics of, 178–82
  decision model and, 315–18
  goals and change mechanisms of,
    181–82
  models of, 182; *see also* consensus
    model of posttrauma treatment
powerlessness, in child sexual abuse,
  118, 121
preschoolers, as witnesses, 23
present context (overview of
  recovered/false memory controversy), 31–71
  current status of scientific and clini-
    cal issues in, 68–71
  factors contributing to the con-
    tentiousness of the debate in,
    45–48
  false memory perspective in, 38–43
  finding common ground in, 48–49
  findings and recommendations of
  professional association task forces and
    working groups in, 49–68
  summary of, 71
  traumatic stress perspective in,
    32–38
  traumatic stress rebuttal and counter-
    critique in, 43–44
pretreatment issues, 188–89
Pribor, E. F., 11
*Principles of Medical Ethics with
  Annotations Especially Applicable to
  Psychiatry, The,* 51, 52
Prins, B., 82
Prisoners of Childhood (Miller), 14
professional organizations, 48, 173,
  353–69
  development of, 13–14
  findings and recommendations of
    task forces and working groups of,
    49–68, 355–68
  Grunberg-Ney review and compara-
    tive analysis of, 258–60
  legal consultations as benefit of, 167
  record keeping guidelines of, 279
  see also specific organizations
professional roles, boundaries, and limitations, 156, 161–63, 264–68
prostitution, child, 11
psychoanalytic theory, 4–7, 37, 113
psychobiology of PTSD, 81–83
psychodynamic approaches, 180–83

psychogenic amnesia, 11, 84, 120–21, 123
psychogenic fugue, 11
Psychological Assessment Inventory (PAI), 239
psychological testing, 239–41
psychophysiological assessment, 244–45
psychosexual maturation, 178, 198
psychosis, 230
psychosomatic reactions, 226
psychotherapy:
    bills in state legislature and, xii–xiv, 29
    challenging of, 28, 190
    dilemmas of, 345–47
    general principles and guidelines for, xvi–xix; *see also* assessment; consensus model of posttrauma treatment; diagnosis; risk management; standard of care
    philosophical foundations and, 153–57
    rift between researchers and, 46–47
    suggestive, xiii, xiv, xvi, 2, 22, 24, 25, 26, 28, 29, 38, 41, 42, 43, 58, 60, 152, 154, 156–157, 220, 223–36, 274, 282–85
    in ten common clinical scenarios, 318–39
    as trigger for delayed abuse recall, 132–33
    see also treatment models, treatment; *specific topics*
Putnam, F. W., 6, 11, 12, 20, 34, 35, 84, 86, 99, 106, 110, 118, 119, 121, 123, 182, 254, 256
Pynoos, R. S., 10, 34, 76, 98, 106, 108, 109, 119, 144, 180–182, 183*n*

Quas, J. A., 121
questions:
    open-ended, 222–23, 226, 273, 278
    patient reactions to, 226–27, 235
Quin, J., 228
Quintana, S. M., 216–17

Rainer, J. P., 147
Ramona, Gary A., 29
Ramona v. Isabella, 28–29, 172, 249
Rankin, A. B., 211
rape, 10, 32, 74, 78, 225, 227, 304
Rappaport, R. L., 21
Rauch, R. S., 82, 104

Read, J. D., xv, 47, 49, 59, 91, 130, 230, 252, 259*n*, 342
Reagor, P., 11
record-keeping, 279–82
recovered/false memory controversy, xiii–xix, 17, 341–47
    caretaking in, 199–200
    key issues in, 31, 124; *see also* child sexual abuse, review of scientific literature of recollections of
    overview of, *see* present context
    in sociohistorical perspective, *see* sociohistorical perspective
recovered memories, 21, 102, 107, 274
    countertransference and vicarious traumatization reactions to, 307–14
    process of, 22
    spontaneous, 152
    transference and, 296, 301, 303–4
    variety of clinical approaches to, 276–78
    see also delayed/recovered memory
Recovered Memory/False Memory Debate, The (Pezdek and Banks), 45
recovered memory therapy (RMT), 26, 29, 38, 43, 201
    coining of term, 62–63
recovery, 154
recovery movement, 14–17
"red flag" issues, 294, 295
reenactment dynamics, 162, 168, 169, 192, 194–97, 226, 229
reexperiencing phenomena, 13, 79, 80, 84, 193, 278
    see also flashbacks; reenactment dynamics
refusal, informed, 190
regression, 16, 177, 192, 199, 202, 312
regressive techniques, avoiding, 284
rehearsal, false memories and, 94
Reinherz, H. Z., 123
rejection, transference and, 301–2
relationships:
    alterations in, 88
    dual, avoiding, 156, 161, 265–68
    instability of, 152
    patient in, 172–74, 192, 200–201, 202, 215–17, 231, 300
    therapist-patient, 152–72, 191–92, 200, 264–68
relaxation-based interventions, 194, 198
reliability, of therapist, 163–64

religiously-based abuse, 228
Renshaw, D., 304–5, 306, 308
Repressed Memories (Frederickson),
     36–37
repressed memory syndrome, defined,
     37
repression, 4, 6, 13, 15, 44, 72, 112, 113,
     121
   defined, 33
   dissociation compared with, 33
   use of term, 47
rescuer role, 162–63, 168, 190, 197, 265,
     284, 300
   countertransference and, 311–12
rescuer syndrome, secondary, 306
Resick, P. A.,. 82, 88*n*
responsibility:
   for abuse, 229–300, 301
   of patient, 165–66, 192, 197, 265, 266
   of therapists, 265
retention, in traumatic memory, 97, 100,
     103
retrieval, memory:
   in consensus model, 212–13
   hypnosis and, 12–13, 39, 41, 52, 56,
     57–58, 62, 64, 270, 285–88
   informed consent and, 159
   in normal memory, 91, 92, 101
   philosophical foundations and, 154
   risk management and, 152
   sodium amytal and, 29, 245
   in traumatic memory, 33, 34, 72, 100,
     103, 110
revenge, 230, 266
Reviere, S. L., 73–74, 99, 206, 214, 298,
     330
Rhue, J., 84
Riad, J. K., 242
Richardson, B., 55
Riddlesberger, M. M., 121
Rieker, P., 220
Riggs, D. S., 149
right hemisphere, 83
"rights and responsibilities" statement,
     160–61
risk management, xviii, 152–53, 172–74,
     258–95
   ascertaining what the patient
     remembers in, 278
   determination of therapeutic
     approach in, 264
   for EMDR, 288
   fairly conservative practices in,
     262–63

false memories and, 152, 282–84,
     288–89
hypnosis and, 285–88
informed consent and, 158–59, 262,
     269–70
knowledge and competence in,
     263–64
litigation and, 152–53, 266–67, 288,
     292–93
memory malleability and, 275
neutral perspective and, 271, 273–74
overly endorsing vs. overly defensive
     stance in, 261
patient's search for corroboration
     and, 291–92
record-keeping in, 279–82
"red flag" issues and, 294, 295
regressive techniques avoided in,
     284
self-help books and groups and,
     289–90
suggestibility and, 274, 282–85
summary of, 294
transference, countertransference,
     and self-care in, 268–69
traumatic memory and, 290–91
treatment frame and, 160, 264–68
treatment plan and, 271, 272–73
variety of clinical approaches to
     recovered memories and, 276–78
variety of strategies used with post-
     traumatic symptoms and memo
     ries in, 278–79
risk-taking, 195, 196, 229
RMT, *see* recovered memory therapy
Roediger, H. L, 91
Ross, C. A., 6, 11, 12, 21, 35, 86, 149,
     169, 182, 230, 244, 252, 254, 256
Roth, S., 21, 71, 80, 81, 86, 87, 88*n*, 113,
     115, 149, 178, 182, 198, 205, 231,
     244, 323
Rothbaum, B. O., 149, 205
Rovee-Collier, C., 95, 106
Rowan, A. B., 80
Royal Australian and New Zealand
     College of Psychiatrists, The, xix,
     358–59
"Guidelines for Psychiatrists Dealing
     with Repressed Traumatic
     Memories," 358–59
Royal College of Psychiatrists, The, xix,
     360–62
"Reported Recovered Memories of
     Child Sexual Abuse," 360–362

Rubin, L. J., 249
Rudy, L., 96
Runtz, M., 123
Rush, Florence, 4, 6–7, 9
Russell, D.E.H., 8, 9

sadism, 11, 12
safety issues, 168–69, 171, 226, 299
    in consensus model, 190, 191,
        193–97, 201
    treatment model and, 177, 181
Salter, A. C., 21
Saporta, J., 82
satanic cults, 2, 11, 12, 17, 38, 39, 182,
        228, 308
Saunders, B. E., 147
Sauzier, M. C., 275
Saxe, G. N., 85, 86
Schacter, D. L., 91, 92, 113
Schatzow, E., 130, 132, 211
Scheflin, Alan W., xv, 52, 56n, 108n,
        111n, 129n, 131, 148, 159, 174,
        225, 267, 288, 295n
schizoaffective disorder, 169
schizophrenia, 169, 230
Schlaps, A., 16, 17, 19, 20, 41, 42, 47,
        201
Schooler, J. W., 69, 99, 101, 141, 142,
        143, 145
Schwartz, M. F., 216
Schwarz, R., 227–28
Scientific and Professional Advisory
        Board, False Memory Syndrome
        Foundation, 25
scientific understanding, critics of, 148
Scurfield, R. M., 226
secondary traumatic stress, see vicarious
        traumatization
second opinions, 224
secrecy, 220, 250
    in child sexual abuse, 118, 120, 121
Secret Survivors (Blume), 15
Sedlak, A., 23
seduction theory, 4–7, 304
self, development of sense of, 177, 191,
        215–17
self-blame, 194, 228
self-care:
    of patient, 191, 197–98, 201
    of therapist, 269
self-concept, 181
self-depreciation, 194
self-determination, of patient, 156, 159
self-diagnosis, 169

self-esteem, 191, 199, 299
self functions, 191, 198
self-help groups, 15–16, 19, 28, 283,
        289–90
self-help literature, 14–16, 19, 38, 148,
        289–90
self-image, negative, 122
self-interest, of therapist, 154
self-management, 177, 191, 197, 198,
        201, 277
self-mutilation, 163, 168, 169, 195
self-perception:
    alterations in, 88
    transference and, 299–300
self-protection, of therapist, 309–11
self-punishment, 196
self-soothing, 191, 196
Self-Trauma Model, 207
Seligman, S., 345
Selye, H., 78
serotonin, 83
sexual assault, 10, 14, 17, 74
sexual behavior, 195
    Kinsey study of, 7
sexual dysfunction, 123
Sgroi, S. M., 9, 12, 118, 182
Shalev, A. Y., 82, 150, 178, 202
shame, 122, 142, 190, 194, 221, 222, 228,
        299
    countertransference and, 309–11
Shapiro, F., 149, 159, 248
Shapiro, J. L., 52, 159, 174, 225, 288
Shapiro, S., 292, 318
Shaver, P. R., 228
Shepard, R. L., 135
Sherman, J. J., 150, 178
Shlaes, J., 119
Shobe, K. S., 99, 100
Shuman, D. W., 266
Siegel, D. J., 90, 91, 102, 105, 205–6
Silberman, E. K., 6, 121
silence, 33, 222
    forced, 76, 220
Silver, H. K., 8
Silverman, A. B., 123
Silverman, F. N., 8
Simon, R. I., 261, 262, 263, 266, 267–68
Simonds, S. L., 211
Sinason, V., 309
Singer, M. T., 43
skepticism, countertransference and,
        313
Slavin, Jonathan, 345
sleep EEG, 245

sleeper effect, 122
sleep problems, 84, 197
    nightmares, 80, 84
Smith, E., 96
Smith-Kurtz, B., 197
social classes, 7–8
Society for Traumatic Stress Studies
    (now the International Society),
    14
sociohistorical perspective, xvii, 1–30
    contemporary events and initiatives
        in recovered/false memory contro-
        versy, 8–22
    development of the countermove-
        ment (emergence of the memory
        controversy) in, 23–30
    Freud, Janet, and the study of hyste-
        ria in, 3–8
    summary of, 30
sodium amytal, 29, 245
sodium lactate infusion, 245
Solomon, S. D., 150, 178
somatization, 10, 88, 195
somatoform disorders, 6, 136
Sommer, J. F., Jr., 84n, 177
source misattribution, 93
Southwick, S. M., 82, 98, 103, 105
Spanos, N. P., 42, 254
Spence, D. P., 206
Spiegel, D., 3, 4, 44, 84, 85, 89, 99, 103,
    110, 113, 224, 299, 311, 343
Spiegel, H., 224, 295n
splitting, 302
Sprock, J., 230
Sroufe, A., 137, 141
Stamm, B. H., 175, 192
standard of care, xvii–xviii
    defined, 151
    evolution of, 151–52
standard of practice, xvii–xviii, 147–75
    critics of, 148
    defined, 150–51
    empirical substantiation and, 147–48
    evolution of, 151–52
    informed consent as, 158–60
    patient in relationship and, 172–74
    philosophical foundations of, 152–57,
        159
    principles, 158–75
    summary of, 175
    transference, countertransference,
        and vicarious traumatization and,
        174–75
    see also treatment frame

Stanton, M., 27, 141
startle response, 84, 123
statutes of limitation, 22
Steele, B. F., 8
Steele, K., 85
Stein, M. B., 79
Steinberg, A. M., 34, 98
Steinberg, M., 244
Stewart, S. H., 246, 247
stigmatization, in child sexual abuse,
    118–19, 121–22
storage, memory, 33, 34, 72
    in normal memory, 91, 92, 100
Straker, G., 195
stress management, 197
Stress Response Syndromes (Horowitz), 79
Strick, F. L., 11
Stricker, G., 148
Structured Clinical Interview for DSM-
    IV Dissociative Disorders (SCID-
    D), 244, 256
Structured Interview for Disorders of
    Extreme Stress (SIDES), 244
structured interviews, 243–44
subcortical system, 92
substance abuse, 147, 152, 170, 172,
    195, 222, 226, 229, 231, 232
    assessment of, 246–47
Substitute Resolution 504, A-9e, 51
Sugar, M., 108
suggestibility, 230
    in adjunctive treatments, 171
    in children, 23–24, 40, 93, 94
    eyewitness, 42
    hospitalization and, 172
    measurement of, 224
    memory malleability and, 93
    risk management and, 274, 282–85
    in therapy, xiii, xiv, xvi, 2, 22, 24, 25,
        26, 28, 29, 38, 41, 42, 43, 58, 60,
        152, 154, 156–57, 220, 223–26,
        274, 282–85
suicide, suicidal behavior, 102, 123, 163,
    168, 169, 187, 188, 195, 226, 229,
    274, 302, 313
    in crises, 232, 233
    safety planning and, 196–97
Sullivan, J. M., 216, 246, 247
Summit, R., 119, 289
supportive neutrality, as therapist's
    stance, 161–62, 191, 271, 273–74
support network, 197, 224, 234, 267
    development of, 200–201
suppression, 72, 80, 94, 113, 220, 228, 309

survivors' support group, 169
Susman, J. R., 71
Swett, C., 86
Symonds, M., 76
Symptom Checklist-90—Revised (SCL-90-R), 239
symptoms:
    as coping mechanism, 178
    in determination of therapeutic
approach, 264
    stabilization of, xviii, 154, 155, 171, 177, 178, 183, 191, 197–98, 315
    underreporting vs. overreporting of, 237–38
    see also specific disorders

Talley, N. J., 136
Taska, L., 122
Tavris, C., 16
Tayloe, D. R., 141
television, 15, 17
Terr, L., 10, 34, 36, 106, 108n, 109, 110, 121, 122, 137, 141
Tessler, M., 96, 121
Tharan, M., 89, 97
Thelen, M. H., 254
therapeutic alliance, development of, 170, 190, 192, 200, 201
therapeutic relationship, 152–72, 264–68
    development of, 191–92, 200
    see also treatment frame
therapists:
    accessibility of, 162–63
    anger of, 163, 305, 312–13
    as authority figure, 190, 269–70
    backup, 164
    burnout of, 163
    confidentiality issues and, 28, 166–68, 173, 370–71
    defensiveness of, 311
    disempowerment of, 311
    empathy of, 161–62, 163, 171, 179
    errors of, 22, 168, 174, 304–13
    fairly conservative practices of, 262–63
    hostility of, 312–13
    intolerance of, 312–13
    irritation of, 312–13
    knowledge and competence of, 263–64
    litigation against, xiii, 2, 22, 28–29, 45, 48, 172–73

overly endorsing vs. overly defensive
    stance of, 261
    reliability and consistency of, 163–64
    responsibility of, 265
    risk management of, 152–53, 158–59, 160, 172–74, 258–95
    roles, boundaries, and limitations of, 156, 161–63, 264–68
    safety of, 168
    self-interest of, 154
    as substitute parent, 15, 269, 284, 300, 301
    supportive neutrality of, 161–62, 191, 271, 273–74
    treatment frame and, *see* treatment frame
therapy:
    art, 36, 37
    body, 37, 38
    group, 36, 149, 170, 200–201
    "lawsuit," 308
    lay, 14, 16–17, 169, 171
    recovered memory (RMT), 26, 29, 38, 43, 62–63, 201
    see also psychotherapy; treatment models, treatment
third parties, therapist obligation to, 2, 28–29, 172–73, 293
Thought Field Therapy (TFT), 262, 270
threats, 274
    in child sexual abuse, 118, 120, 121
    of violence, 266
Toglia, M. P., 99
tolerance, 191
Tollestrup, P. A., 97, 98
Torchia, M., 79
torture, 7, 32, 74, 78, 102
transference, xviii–xix, 20, 21, 163, 174, 192, 296–304
    Davies-Frawley on complications to analysis of, 302, 303
    Elliott-Briere on manifestations of, 302
    McCann-Pearlman schema and, 299
    recovered memories and, 296, 301, 303–4
    risk management and, 268–69, 277
    "traumatic," 299
"transference fields," 303
trauma, traumatization, xvii, 6
    of child sexual abuse, 4, 9

chronic, 182
in consensus model, 193–94, 202–15,
    315
deconditioning, mourning, resolution
    and integration of, 202–15
defined, 32–33, 73–78
forgetting of, 112–15; *see also* amne-
    sia; dissociation, dissociative dis-
    orders; repression
general, 182
hysteria and, 3–7
of incest, 9
measures of, 241–43
memory and, 72–117; *see also* trau-
    matic memory
social context of, 76, 78
treatment of, 147, 155
war, see war trauma
see also abuse/trauma
Trauma: Explorations in Memory, (C.
    Caruth), 81
trauma assessment, 234–57
collateral, 247–50
diagnosis in, 250–57
generic psychological testing and
    trauma-specific measures in,
    239–41
measures of traumatic events and
experiences in, 241–43
process of, 234–39
psychophysiological, biological, and
neurological, 244–46
structured interviews in, 243–44
for substance abuse, 246–47
trauma researchers, 142
on normal vs. traumatic memory,
    101–6
traumatic memory, xvii, 12, 97–116
accuracy of, 108, 111
in adults, 72
in adults, conclusions drawn from
    studies of, 107–8
approaches to, 207–12
in children, 72, 73, 106, 108–12
defined, 89
Janet's views on, 4, 5, 89
mastery and resolution of, 290–91
modification and integration of, 183
normal event memory compared
    with, 34, 57, 72–73, 98–106
rationale for work with, 204–6
reproductive qualities of, 91
summary of, 116

ten common clinical scenarios
    involving, 297, 318–39
treatment of, xviii, 176, 177, 181,
    183, 204–12, 278–79, 290–91
variety of strategies used with,
    278–79
traumatic stress position, xiii, xiv–xv
extreme, 36–37, 45, 48
moderate, 36, 48
overview of, 32–38
rebuttal and counter-critique from,
    43–44
traumatic stress reactions:
defined, 75
Wilson's interactive theory of, 76, 77,
    78
treatment frame, 160–72, 264–68
adjunctive or collateral treatment
    including hospitalization and
    medication in, 170–72
assessment in, 169–70
establishment and reinforcement of,
    189–91
other therapist-patient relationship
    issues in, 164–65
patient engagement and responsibili-
    ties in, 165–66, 265
professional privilege and the limits
    of confidentiality in, 166–68
professional roles, boundaries, and
    limitations in, 161–63, 264–68
"rights and responsibilities" state-
    ment and, 160–61
safety issues in, 168–69
therapist reliability and consistency
    in, 163–64
treatment models, treatment:
in clinical scenarios, 318–39
collateral, 170–72, 224
decision-tree approach to, 155, 176,
    297, 315–18
ending of, 165, 168, 216–17, 223,
    266, 267–68
"first generation," 11–13, 18–21
generic vs. trauma-oriented, 155
of Janet, 5–6
posttraumatic, 35–36
"second generation," 12, 21
splits in, 171
"third generation," 12, 21
traumatic stress perspective on,
    35–38
see also standard of care; therapy

treatment plans, 51, 155, 170, 224, 271
    for safety, 196–97
treatment trajectories, 178, 185
"treatment traps," 163, 174, 284,
    296–97, 301, 306
Trickett, P., 106
Trierweiler, S. J., 148
Tromp, S., 89, 97
trust, 170, 171, 192, 221, 299
truth, historical vs. narrative, 275
Turkus, Joan, 191, 193, 306
Type I childhood trauma, 110
Type II childhood trauma, 110, 121

unconscious, 11, 80, 300, 302
Underwager, Ralph, 25, 42
Urquiza, A. J., 235–36
Uyehara, L. A., 275, 291–92

vacations, 375
Vaillant, G. E., 33
VandeCreek, L., xv, 148, 151, 152, 153,
    157, 173, 231, 252, 265–66, 280
VandenBos, G. R., 147
van der Hart, O., 5, 6, 85, 89, 90, 104,
    105, 204, 205
van der Kolk, B. A., 5, 6, 12, 20, 21, 36,
    81, 82, 83n, 87, 88n, 89, 90, 102–5,
    131, 137, 141, 149–52, 177, 178,
    190, 196, 198, 202–3, 204, 210,
    215, 226
vehement emotions, 3
verbal (narrative) memory, 94, 95, 96,
    108–11, 115, 136–37
vicarious traumatization (VT; secondary
    traumatic stress; compassion
    fatigue), xviii, 21, 174–75, 235–36,
    296, 306
    balance in, 313–14
    recovered memory issues and,
        307–14
victimizer role, 162, 163, 168, 300
victim role, 162, 163, 168, 300
Vietnam War, 9, 177, 304
violence:
    in child sexual abuse, 118, 121, 122
    domestic, xv, 8–9, 11, 14, 17, 33, 78,
        173, 222
    interpersonal, 152, 157, 168, 195,
        222, 226, 315
    sexual, 9, 173; see also rape
VOCAL (Victims of Child Abuse Laws),
    24, 25

Vogeltanz, N. D., 246
VT, see vicarious traumatization

Waites, E. A., 21, 203–4, 207, 213, 268,
    298
Wakefield, Hollida, 25, 42
Waks, B., 195
Walker, L. E., 8, 9
Wall, S., 300
Wang, S., 178, 182, 184, 186–87, 202,
    217
war trauma, 9–11, 14, 32, 57, 74, 78, 102,
    304
    dissociation and, 85
    treatment of, 13, 177, 182
Waters, E., 300
Watters, E., 42, 43, 112
Watts, D. L., 12
Webb, L. P., 211
Weber, M., 82
Weinberg, K., 305
Weisaeth, L., 21, 36, 83n
Weiss, D. S., 34, 348
Wells, M., 21, 191, 198, 201, 229
West, L., 33, 85
Wester, W., 295n
Westerlund, E., 216
White, S. H., 94
Whitfield, C. L., 15, 48, 249, 250, 251n,
    292
"whole person" philosophy, 155–56
Widom, C. S., 135–36, 137
Wigren, J., 204
Wilcoxon, S. A., 11
Williams, L. M., 47, 70, 96, 97, 122,
    134–35, 137, 138, 142, 143, 144,
    147, 289, 319, 343
Williams, M. B., 84n, 177
Williams, R. M., 10
Wilsnack, S. C., 246
Wilson, J., 76, 77, 78n, 144, 177
Wilson, J. P., 12, 21, 161, 178, 192, 242,
    306, 348
withdrawal, of therapist, 312–13
women:
    backlash against, 46
    overmedication in, 198
    violence against, 8–9, 46; see also
        domestic violence; rape; sexual
        assault
Women's Liberation Movement, 8
World War I, 7, 9, 11, 177, 304
World War II, 9, 11, 177, 304

Wosney, K., 6
"wounded child," 15, 284
Wrightsman, L. S., 23
writing/journaling exercises, 36, 37, 38
Wyatt, G. E., 235–36

Yapko, M. D., 41, 42, 91, 347
Yates, J. L., 33–34, 85, 113
Yeager, C. A., 136

Yehuda, R., 79, 82, 103, 105, 245
Yuille, J. C., 97, 98
Yule, W., 10

Zeichner, A., 252
Zinmeister, A. R., 136
Zoltek-Jick, R., 148, 152, 172, 249
Zucker, K. J., 123